An Introduction to
MONEY & BANKING
Second Edition

An Introduction to
MONEY & BANKING
Second Edition

COLIN D. CAMPBELL
Dartmouth College

ROSEMARY G. CAMPBELL

The Dryden Press
Hinsdale, Illinois

Photo Credits

Chapter

Copyright © 1975 by The Dryden Press,
A Division of Holt, Rinehart and Winston
All rights reserved
Library of Congress Catalog Card Number: 74–31533

ISBN: 0–03–089410–7

Printed in the United States of America

5 6 7 8 032 9 8 7 6 5 4 3 2 1

Preface

In writing the second edition of *An Introduction to Money and Banking*, the authors have again attempted to provide college students with an introductory text that fully reflects recent developments in the field of money and banking. During the past fifteen years, new facts about the historical behavior of money have been discovered; the history of monetary policy during the Great Depression has been reinterpreted; the factors affecting the supply of money have been more systematically analyzed; there has been a debate over the appropriate targets and indicators of Federal Reserve policy; new theories have been developed to explain the way changes in the quantity of money affect income and prices; monetary policy has been viewed as a more powerful type of control than it was previously thought to be; the effect of monetary policy on prices has been differentiated from its effect on real output; the growing use of the dollar as a type of international money has had important effects on our balance of payments; and inflation has emerged as a major economic problem.

The authors believe that the study of money and banking at the undergraduate level ought to include a considerable amount of material on financial institutions. The text includes descriptions of the operations of commercial banks, financial intermediaries, the Federal Reserve System, the U.S. government securities market, and the foreign exchange market. Throughout the text, they have also used historical examples and experiences in foreign countries to illustrate the principles discussed. The authors' purpose here is to give the student a background for understanding current economic problems and for pursuing further studies in business administration or economics involving extensive theoretical analysis.

The text is designed for a one-semester college course. The major topics covered are the nature of money, commercial banking, central banking, monetary theory, monetary policy, inflation, and the international monetary system. The text was written both for students majoring in economics and business administration and for non-majors who wish to take courses in economics beyond the usual introductory course in the principles.

The length of the text is short enough to allow for supplementary reading. The authors recommend that each student be asked to prepare a written paper that involves subscribing to, reading and clipping the financial articles in a major newspaper for a period of 4 to 6 weeks, placing them in a notebook and commenting on them briefly. Appropriate news articles to be included are those about commercial banking,

Federal Reserve policy, Treasury debt management, the balance of payments and gold, financial intermediaries, and the money market. This project helps keep the subject matter in the course up-to-date and helps students develop an interest in the subject that may be maintained after the course is completed.

The second edition is a substantial revision of the first edition. Considerable historical material has been added. The statistical data in the charts and tables have been brought up-to-date through December 1973. Since the publication of the first edition, there have been several important legislative changes affecting banking and the monetary system—the Federal government's wage and price control program from 1971 to 1974, the floating of exchange rates in 1973, the adoption of a new system of reserve requirements for member banks in 1972, changes in interest rate ceilings on savings and time deposits, the removal in 1974 of the interest equalization tax on purchases of foreign securities and of the controls on foreign investment, the ending of sales of gold by the United States Treasury to foreign governments in 1971, the passage of the Bank Secrecy Act of 1970, and the rise in interest rates on U.S. savings bonds in 1973. These changes are included in the new edition.

The authors are particularly indebted to Professor Milton Friedman and Dr. Anna J. Schwartz, who have done so much to stimulate research and new ideas in the field of money and banking, and to Professors Benjamin J. Klebaner of City College of the City University of New York and David E. Lindsey of Macalester College, both of whom read the entire manuscript of the first edition. Others who have aided the authors with suggestions are their colleagues, Professors William A. Carter, Steven W. Dobson, and Michael A. Mazur; Dr. Adrian W. Throop of the Federal Reserve Bank of Dallas and Dr. Homer Jones, former Senior Vice President of the Federal Reserve Bank of St. Louis; Professor John W. Bay of the University of Maine at Portland; Professor Erwin A. Blackstone of Cornell University; Professor Peter A. Frost of the University of Washington; Professor Frank G. Steindl of Oklahoma State University; Mr. Fred A. White, President of Dartmouth National Bank of Hanover; Mr. Stephen C. Francis of Fisher, Francis, Trees, and Watts; and Mr. Robert A. Gunst, Assistant Vice President of the First National Bank of Chicago. In addition, the authors owe much to their own teachers in college and graduate school and to their colleagues and students. Mrs. Campbell was Instructor of Economics at Iowa State University, Ames, Iowa, from 1948 to 1951. Finally, Professor Campbell has benefited greatly from his associations with the Research Department of the Board of Governors of the Federal

Reserve System from 1954 through 1956, and from his membership on the Board of Directors of the Dartmouth National Bank of Hanover since 1961 and the Student Loan Marketing Association (Sallie Mae) in Washington, D.C. since 1973.

Hanover, New Hampshire
January 1975

Colin D. Campbell
Rosemary G. Campbell

Contents

Chapter 1
Introduction

*Three fundamental subjects underlie and motivate the study of money
and banking. The first is the examination of the workings of the banking
and financial institutions that provide the economic system with
money. The second is the evaluation of their effectiveness. And the third
is the search for ways in which those institutions might be improved.*

Money and banking are so closely related that they must be studied
together. Although this book is concerned primarily with money, one
of its objectives will be to describe the institutional arrangements for
providing the money used in carrying on economic activities. The major
institutions that supply money to the economic system are the commercial banks, the Federal Reserve banks, and the United States Treasury.
Other institutions that are involved are the Federal Deposit Insurance
Corporation, the Office of the Comptroller of the Currency, the International Monetary Fund, and the savings banks and other financial institutions that are similar to commercial banks in many ways. The monetary
system consists of a complicated network of these different institutions.

Commercial banks provide the economy with checking accounts,
the major medium of exchange in use today. The Federal Reserve banks
issue Federal Reserve notes, the principal type of paper money in circulation. To understand how the economy is supplied with these types of
money, the operations of both the commercial banks and the Federal
Reserve banks must be studied. The United States Treasury issues coins,
the only important type of money not issued by banks.

MONEY SUPPLY

There are several ways to define money and therefore several ways to
measure the supply of money statistically. Table 1.1 shows the growth
of the money supply from 1959 to 1973 according to two measures—
Money Supply I and *Money Supply II*.

The statistical series on Money Supply I has only two major com-

Table 1.1
Money Supply of the United States,
1959—1973, seasonally adjusted (in billions of dollars)

December	CURRENCY OUTSIDE BANKS[a]	DEMAND DEPOSITS[b]	MONEY SUPPLY I (1) + (2)	TIME DEPOSITS IN COMMERCIAL BANKS[c]	MONEY SUPPLY II (3) + (4)
	(1)	(2)	(3)	(4)	(5)
1959	$28.9	$113.7	$142.6	$ 67.4	$210.0
1960	28.9	112.8	141.7	72.9	214.6
1961	29.6	116.5	146.0	82.7	228.7
1962	30.6	117.6	148.1	97.8	245.9
1963	32.5	121.1	153.6	112.2	265.8
1964	34.2	126.3	160.5	126.6	287.1
1965	36.3	131.7	168.0	146.8	314.8
1966	38.3	133.4	171.7	158.3	330.0
1967	40.4	146.5	186.9	162.7	349.7
1968	43.4	158.1	201.5	180.9	382.4
1969	46.1	162.5	208.6	183.5	392.1
1970	49.1	172.2	221.2	203.9	425.2
1971	52.6	182.6	235.2	237.9	473.0
1972	56.9	198.7	255.7	269.9	525.5
1973	61.6	208.8	270.4	300.3	570.7

Recession—May 1960 to Feb. 1961

Slowdown—Jan. 1967 to May 1967

Recession—Nov. 1969 to Nov. 1970

[a] Excludes currency in commercial banks, the Federal Reserve banks, and the United States Treasury.
[b] Excludes interbank deposits and the amount of checking accounts held by the United States Treasury. It is also adjusted to take account of the estimated amount of checks in process of collection. It includes foreign-owned deposits at the Federal Reserve banks.
[c] After 1967, large certificates of deposit are excluded from time deposits.
Source: *Federal Reserve Bulletin*, various issues, p. A17; December 1970, pp. 895–898; and February 1974, pp. 81–95.

ponents: *currency* (coins and paper money) outside banks, and *demand deposits* (checking accounts). Currency in commercial banks is excluded because it is used as partial backing for demand and time deposits. The quantity of demand deposits is over three times as large as the quantity of currency. These deposits are held in approximately fourteen thousand commercial banks and are owned by persons, business firms, and state and local government units.

Money Supply II includes the components of Money Supply I and the total amount of *time and savings deposits* in commercial banks, except for certificates of deposit in denominations of $100,000 or more, which are a special type of time deposit. Time and savings deposits include passbook deposits as well as various types of time deposits which have different lengths of maturity and terms for withdrawal. The major characteristics of these time and savings deposits are that they pay interest and that legally the owner may be required to notify the bank in advance before withdrawing cash. Economists call these deposits *liquid assets* or *near money*. Like currency and demand deposits, their nominal value is certain. One hundred dollars placed in a time deposit is always worth $100 (although time deposits grow with interest accumulation and demand deposits do not).

Some economists believe that Money Supply II does not include enough kinds of liquid assets. Excluded are savings deposits in mutual savings banks and capital shares in savings and loan associations, both of which have a fixed nominal value and are similar to time and savings deposits in commercial banks. In addition, both U.S. savings bonds and short-term marketable U.S. government securities have characteristics that make them similar to money. The broadest measure of money now published by the Federal Reserve System, *Money Supply III,* includes *deposits of mutual savings banks* and *savings and loan shares.* In December 1973, the total amount of Money Supply III was $893.2 billion, compared to $570.7 billion for Money Supply II, and $270.4 billion for Money Supply I.

No matter which definition is used, the total quantity of money in the economy is large. In 1973, Money Supply I was equal to 21 percent of the gross national product (GNP)—which is the total amount of goods and services produced during the year; Money Supply II was equal to 44 percent of GNP; and Money Supply III was equal to 69 percent of GNP.

The real value of money is its purchasing power or command over goods and services, and varies inversely with changes in prices. Changes in the real value of all the outstanding money can be measured by changes in the ratio of the total money stock (M) to a price index (P): M/P.

GROWTH OF THE MONEY SUPPLY IN THE UNITED STATES

Reliable data on Money Supply II go back to 1867, over one hundred years ago. At that time Money Supply II amounted to only $1.3 billion— of which a little less than half was currency and the rest was deposits of different types. Some increase has occurred almost every year, although the amount of the yearly increases has varied considerably.

From December 1962 through 1973, the expansion in the money stock was particularly rapid. Money Supply I increased 80 percent over this period. During the same period Money Supply II increased even more rapidly.

In recent decades, growth of the money stock has been a result of Federal Reserve policy. But even before the Federal Reserve System was set up, the money stock tended to grow.

CYCLICAL VARIATIONS OF THE MONEY SUPPLY

Table 1.1 shows that periods in which the money supply declined, or increased very little, have been followed by periods of economic recession. In 1960, 1966, and 1969, when the growth in Money Supply I declined or slowed up, business activity soon declined. For the past one hundred years, the rate of change in the money stock has varied cyclically, rising and falling in the same way that business activity has risen and fallen. The upward and downward movements in the rate of change in the money stock have preceded the movements in business activity. Soon after the rate of change in the money stock started to decline, business activity turned downward. And soon after the money stock series started upward, business activity reversed itself.

One of the challenging questions in the study of money and banking is whether this statistical relationship between the rate of increase in the money supply and the business cycle can be accounted for. Although movements of the money stock are interrelated with changes in the total output of the economy, there may also be a *causal* relationship between changes in the money supply and changes in the level of business activity. Whether the causal link runs from the rate of change in the money stock to the business cycle or in the reverse direction is an important issue in monetary economics. While there is evidence that the connection has gone in both directions, some economists argue that the former influence is the dominant one.

VOLUME OF CREDIT

Variations in the quantity of credit may have effects on economic activity that are just as important as changes in the money supply. A government booklet which was published originally in 1939 by the Board of Governors of the Federal Reserve System, and which has gone through five editions, states that the Federal Reserve System's function is "to foster a flow of credit and money that will facilitate orderly economic growth, a stable dollar, and long-run balance to our international payments."[1]

Credit is created when people borrow money. The borrower from a commercial bank signs a promissory note, promising to pay back to the bank the amount of money he has borrowed, together with interest. For this note, he usually receives an addition to the balance in his checking deposit, which he then spends. People borrow money from mutual savings banks, savings and loan associations, personal finance associations, and insurance companies as well as from commercial banks.

Economists are interested in the quantity of the various types of loans outstanding and how they vary. The principal types of credit include business loans, mortgage loans, consumer loans, financial loans, and personal loans. Table 1.2 illustrates the way the total quantity of

Table 1.2
Automobile Credit Outstanding, 1959–1973
(in billions of dollars)

END OF	AMOUNT	
1959	$16.4	
1960	17.7 ⎱	
1961	17.1 ⎰	Recession—May 1960 to Feb. 1961
1962	19.4	
1963	22.3	
1964	24.9	
1965	28.4	
1966	30.0	
1967	29.8 }	Slowdown—Jan. 1967 to May 1967
1968	32.9	
1969	35.5 ⎱	
1970	35.2 ⎰	Recession—Nov. 1969 to Nov. 1970
1971	38.7	
1972	44.1	
1973	51.1	

Source: *Federal Reserve Bulletin*, various issues, p. A54.

automobile credit, which is a type of consumer credit issued by commercial banks, sales finance companies, and other financial institutions, varied from 1959 to 1973. Although this is just one of the major types of credit, the way in which it has varied is typical of the other types too.

Since most persons purchase automobiles with borrowed funds, the volume of automobile credit is large. Automobile loans are installment loans that are paid off in equal, monthly installments over a period up to three years. At the same time that new automobile loans are being made, outstanding automobile loans are being paid off. An increase in the total amount of automobile credit indicates that the quantity of new loans has been larger than the amount paid off.

The variations in the quantity of automobile credit outstanding reflect conditions in the economy. During the recessions of 1960–1961 and 1969–1970, and during the slowdown of 1967, the volume of automobile credit declined. During the long period of expansion from 1961 to 1969, the quantity of automobile credit doubled. This borrowing probably contributed to the prosperity of this period.

Table 1.3
Bank Rates on Short-term Business Loans,
Annual Average, 1959–1973 [a]

YEAR	RATE	
1959	5.0%	
1960	5.2 ⎫	
1961	5.0 ⎬	Recession—May 1960 to Feb. 1961
1962	5.0	
1963	5.0	
1964	5.0	
1965	5.1	
1966	6.0	
1967	6.0 ⎬	Slowdown—Jan. 1967 to May 1967
1968	6.7	
1969	8.2 ⎫	
1970	8.5 ⎬	Recession—Nov. 1969 to Nov. 1970
1971	6.3	
1972	5.8	
1973	8.3	

[a] Beginning in February 1967, this series was revised to expand the coverage from 66 banks in 19 cities to 126 banks in 35 cities.
Source: *Economic Report of the President, February 1974* (Washington, D.C.: U.S. Government Printing Office, 1974), p. 317.

INTEREST RATES

Interest rates are a measure of the price of borrowed funds. If a person borrows $1,000 for one year and agrees to pay $70 interest at the end of the year, the rate of interest would be 7 percent a year. Table 1.3 shows the trend of the rate of interest for short-term business loans from 1959 to 1973. An example of a typical short-term business loan would be one to a merchant for the purchase of inventory. Variations in the cost of borrowing, like trends in the quantity of money and the volume of credit, reflect conditions in the economy. When business activity declined in 1960–1961, 1967, and 1969–1970, interest rates on short-term business loans, as well as on other types of loans, either stopped rising or sooner or later fell.

Movements in interest rates are believed to have significant effects on economic activity. Changes in interest rates are an important part of the mechanism through which monetary policy affects the output of the economy and the level of prices. How the Federal Reserve System influences movements in interest rates, and how such efforts are interrelated with changes in the quantity of money, are important questions in the study of money and banking.

THE DEVELOPMENT OF OUR MONETARY SYSTEM

Before the United States Constitution was adopted, several of the states minted coins and issued paper money. The Constitution denied those powers to the states and gave the federal government the right to coin money and to regulate its value (in terms of gold and silver). Curiously, it is not clear whether the Constitution gives the federal government the right to issue paper money. (A clause in the original draft giving the federal government the right to issue "bills of credit" was struck out before the final draft).[2]

Before the Civil War, most of the paper currency in use was issued by state-chartered commercial banks. The states could charter banks that issued paper money even though the states themselves could not issue it. These privately owned banks also accepted deposits, and by the end of the Civil War, the total quantity of demand and savings deposits created by them was only slightly smaller than the total amount of currency.

The federal government first issued paper currency during the Civil War. Though the constitutionality of the "greenbacks" was initially a matter of dispute, in 1870 and 1874 the Supreme Court clarified the issue in several decisions and decided that the federal government had the right to issue paper money and make it legal tender.

During the Civil War, the federal government also established the National Banking System in which national banks (private banks chartered by the federal government) were authorized to issue paper money called national bank notes. From 1865 to 1914, when the Federal Reserve System was established, the principal types of paper money in use were these national bank notes, the Civil War "greenbacks," and silver certificates that were backed by silver bullion and were issued by the Treasury. However, during the latter half of the nineteenth century, bank deposits became an increasingly important type of money, and gradually the total amount of deposits became much larger than the total amount of the various types of paper money.

The establishment of the Federal Reserve banks in 1914 created a system of central banking. The Federal Reserve Act authorized the Federal Reserve banks to issue Federal Reserve notes, which are now the only important type of paper money in circulation. The Federal Reserve System's principal function is to regulate the lending and deposit-creating activities of the commercial banks. These activities of the commercial banks are believed to have significant effects on the level of economic output and of prices. How the Federal Reserve System can most effectively use its powers to regulate the commercial banks so as to achieve broad economic objectives, such as economic prosperity and stable prices, is one of the more difficult questions in the study of Federal Reserve policy.

The money of the United States not only serves as money within the country, but has become part of the money used by foreign countries for international trade. Other familiar types of international money are gold and the British pound. A new type of international money—called *special drawing rights* (SDRs)—was created by the International Monetary Fund in 1970. International money is held by persons engaging in international trade and by governments to settle temporary differences between their expenditures in international trade and their receipts. The study of money and banking includes the international as well as the domestic monetary system.

SUMMARY

Three subjects are interrelated in the study of money and banking: money, credit, and interest rates. We are interested in how money, credit, and interest rates vary over the business cycle and in their historical trends, the way in which the Federal Reserve System attempts to control them, and their impact on prices, unemployment, economic growth, and the balance of international payments.

NOTES

1. Board of Governors of the Federal Reserve System, *The Federal Reserve System: Purposes and Functions,* 5th ed. (Washington, D.C., 1967), p. 1.
2. For an interesting account of the monetary provisions in the Constitution, see Bray Hammond, *Banks and Politics in America from the Revolution to the Civil War* (Princeton: Princeton University Press, 1957), chapter 4.

QUESTION

1.1. Know the meaning and significance of the following terms and concepts: monetary system, money supply, real value of money, credit, interest rates.

"Malikanua, if you had it to do over again, would you still pay my father thirty-five chickens, four cows, and seventeen goats for me?"

Drawing by Whitney Darrow, Jr.; © 1971 The New Yorker Magazine, Inc.

Chapter 2
Functions of Money

Money is used as a unit of account, medium of exchange, and store of value. The varied functions of money are important because whatever is used as money is money.

Conceptually, there are two distinct types of money. First, there is the *money unit of account*. It is used to measure the value of things—just as ounces and pounds are used to measure weight, and inches and feet to measure size. Though the unit of account is abstract, it is useful for computation and record keeping. Second, there are *coins, paper money,* and *demand deposits* which serve as a medium of exchange and store of value. People use these types of money to purchase the goods and services they want. They may also wish to accumulate them because their nominal value is constant. Some other assets such as savings and time deposits and U.S. savings bonds are similar to currency and demand deposits as stores of value, even though they are not part of the medium of exchange. Their redemption values also do not vary at all.

MONEY UNIT OF ACCOUNT

Each country has its own unit of account. The money unit of account in the United States is the dollar. In Germany it is the deutsche mark. In Mexico it is the peso.

Having a widely accepted unit of account is extremely useful. It is, of course, the basis of accounting. By having prices of everything in dollars and cents, persons can immediately and without effort compare values. If one item is priced at $10 and another at $5, a person knows immediately the relative cost of each item—the first costs twice as much as the second.

The unit of account sometimes is different from the medium of exchange. In China during the long period of rapid inflation from 1937 to 1949, many merchants kept their accounts in U.S. dollars but used Chinese currency to make transactions.[1] Prices were calculated by applying the daily exchange rate between the yen and the dollar to a price in U.S. dollars on their books. This resulted in two prices for everything, one in terms of the dollar unit of account and the other in terms of the yen circulating medium. A separate unit of account is useful when inflation is so rapid that the prices of goods and services would depend on when they were purchased: in such circumstances, since business transactions take place at different times, purchase prices would no longer provide an accurate comparison of the value of different things.

In colonial America, the money in circulation included the Spanish peso or dollar even though the unit of account was the British pound. Officially the unit of account of the United States was changed to the dollar in 1792. The first Coinage Act passed by Congress provided for the coinage of gold eagles, half eagles, and quarter eagles (worth $10.00, $5.00, and $2.50 respectively), and silver dollars, half dollars, quarters, dimes, half dimes, copper cents, and half cents. The decimal system was an improvement over the British unit of account in which there were 12 pence in a shilling and 20 shillings in a pound. Despite the greater convenience of the new system, customary ways of accounting were so persistent that the dollar was not universally used as a unit of account until after the Civil War.[2] Before that time, prices were frequently quoted in dollars and ninepence, dollars and shillings, dollars and levies, or dollars and bits. Both a levy and a bit were worth 12½ cents.

In recent years, most countries that had nondecimal units of account have changed to a decimal system. The cost of converting to a decimal system is high: Australia reported it to be nearly $100 million. Great Britain itself converted its currency to a decimal system in 1971. The argument for a decimal system is that computations are simpler. Compare addition in dollars with addition in the old British unit of account. Adding $1.60 and $2.40 is easy—the sum is $4.00. Before the conversion to a decimal system, adding 1 pound, 6 shillings, and 3 pence to 2 pounds, 13 shillings, and 9 pence was more difficult—the sum was 4 pounds.

MONETARY REFORMS AND THE UNIT OF ACCOUNT

After World War II, many countries enacted monetary reforms and exchanged old bank notes and deposits for new ones with a substantially reduced monetary value.[3] In the South Korean monetary reform of 1953, for example, the conversion ratio was 100 to 1. One hundred old *won* were exchanged for one new *hwan*. The principal objectives of the South Korean reform were to slow down the rate of inflation and to reduce all prices to more reasonable levels. As in some other monetary reforms, a portion of the money supply was removed from circulation and put in "blocked accounts." Persons retained their blocked holdings, but could not use them to purchase goods and services.

In a monetary reform in the Soviet Union in 1960, all circulating ruble bills were called in and replaced by new ruble bills at a ratio of 10 to 1. Prices of goods sold in the state stores were also reduced to one-tenth their former level. The *New York Times* reported that the new price of a Volga automobile was 4,500 rubles. Before the reform, the price of the same vehicle would have been 45,000 rubles.[4] The purpose of this reform was primarily to simplify the unit of account and perhaps also to confiscate the gains of black-market operators. In the decade prior to 1960, the Soviets had little inflation, and stabilization was not a problem.

MONEY MEDIUM OF EXCHANGE

The money medium of exchange in the United States consists primarily of currency and demand deposits, Money Supply I. The usefulness of a medium of exchange in a country increases with the development of trade and specialization. If family units are self-sufficient, there is little trade and little need for coins, paper money, or deposits in banks. In colonial America, when most families were engaged in farming, there was much less need for money than there is today. Work has become increasingly specialized; most persons are now employees, who receive their wages in money and use the money received to purchase whatever goods and services they consume. If an economy is specialized and people trade to obtain most of their needs, the use of money is almost essential. Except for occasional transactions, barter is rare because of its extreme inefficiency. It takes too much time and effort to find persons who both have what you want and want what you have to trade. The advantage of money as a medium of exchange is that it provides the owner with *generalized* purchasing power. It gives the owner freedom over the type and quantities of goods he buys, the time and place of his purchases, and the parties with whom he chooses to deal.

Even in primitive societies, a medium of exchange is used if agriculture is specialized. In the Quiche Indian communities of Guatemala, some farmers grow corn, others cabbage, others onions, and others grow still different crops. On market day, usually once a week, the farmers bring their produce to market. Each farmer sells for money what he produces and then uses the money he has received to purchase what he wants. There is almost no barter. Although modern money has replaced the cacao beans used as money by the Mayas, the technology of these Indian communities has changed little since the arrival of the Spanish in the New World.[5]

A possible alternative to the use of money or barter is a system of rationing. With rationing, persons are paid in ration coupons rather than money. The ration coupons distributed to each person entitle him to certain quantities of specific items, and retail stores sell goods for ration coupons. In a complex modern society with a great variety of goods, it would be difficult to create a complete system of rationing with no use of money. Ration coupons would have to be distributed for every possible item produced. In the systems of rationing that existed in most countries during World War II, in order to purchase rationed items people had to pay both the governmentally controlled price in money and the necessary number of ration coupons. During the first five-year plan in the Soviet Union, from 1928 through 1932, the distribution of goods was handled partly by a system of rationing. At the time of the Russian revolution, there was some discussion of whether to discard the use of money completely. Socialist theorists, including Marx, had visualized a communist society without money. The Soviets never entirely did away with the use of money, and in 1935, rationing as a primary method of distributing goods was discarded.[6] The advantage of monetary exchange over rationing is that it gives people greater choice. Some persons prefer a different group of commodities than those allocated to them in the form of ration coupons. Because money is generalized purchasing power, exchange with the use of money is more convenient than trading with the use of ration coupons.

Furthermore, the use of money probably simplified economic planning in the Soviet Union. Some method of equating the demand and supply of each commodity is necessary. With rationing, the total quantity of ration coupons handed out for each item has to be roughly equal to the supply of that item. But this equalization can be accomplished just as well when people are paid wages and permitted to spend as they wish the money wages they receive. The quantity of each good demanded by the public varies with its price. Through appropriate control over the price of each consumer good and service, Soviet planners have been able to equate the demand for each commodity with the supply available.[7] Although the idea of discarding the use of a medium of exchange still appeals to some radical reformers, money is used in the Soviet Union and most other communist countries in the same way that it is used in noncommunist countries. In economies that have developed highly specialized types of production, the use of money as a medium of exchange has many advantages over barter or systems of rationing.

When inflation is rapid, the holding of money becomes very costly because the real value of money falls as prices rise. The more rapid the rate of inflation, the more costly it is in real terms to hold money. But holding money so as to facilitate the making of transactions is still much to be preferred over barter, and people continue to hold money despite inflation. In Chile, for example, the average annual rate of inflation from 1931 to 1955 was 20 percent. At this rate of inflation, the cost of holding $100 throughout the year would be $20. Chileans have had inflation so long that they expect this. Even though they know that the money they are holding is depreciating, they still use it. Under inflationary conditions, people try to hold less money in real terms, but this just means that the money in use circulates faster. The public cannot hold less money by spending it. It moves from one person to another, and someone is always holding it.

It is sometimes claimed that if money is depreciating in value because of inflation, people will lose faith in it and money will no longer be acceptable. Actually, it is not a matter of faith. The experience in Chile and several other countries shows that people may be fully aware that money is depreciating in value and still prefer the use of money to barter exchange. It is a question of relative advantages. At some very high rate of inflation, it may be preferable to barter rather than to use money, but the rate of inflation that is necessary to induce people to discard the use of money is not often reached.

In some countries, the preference of the public for barter over the use of money has resulted primarily from price controls and rationing that have been in existence for a long time, rather than from the rapid rate of the inflation. This was the situation in Germany from 1946 to 1948, just after World War II. It was difficult to do business solely in the rationed markets where prices were controlled. Between the time that prices were initially fixed in 1936 and the postwar year of 1947, the quantity of money had increased approximately 10 times. There was an oversupply of money compared to goods valued at their fixed 1936 prices. As a result the usefulness of money was limited, business firms often found it necessary to exchange commodities for commodities in order to get the materials they needed to stay in business, and there was considerable barter between city people and country people.[8]

A common error is to attribute the collapse of a monetary system during rapid inflation to the inconvenience of having to use bales of paper bills. Stories are told about merchants having to carry paper money in baskets or wheelbarrows. Such situations, however, are quite rare. As inflation progresses, most governments simply issue paper notes in larger denominations, and the possible inconvenience of having to use large quantities of bills of small denominations does not arise.

The development of credit cards and the usefulness of electronic computers in transferring funds has led to speculation over the development of a moneyless economy. The use of credit cards could conceivably make the use of both currency and checks on demand deposits unnecessary. Actually, in recent years the use of coins and paper money has increased relative to the use of checking accounts. This is because automation has had significant effects on merchandising through the development of vending machines. Also, although the use of electronic computers for transferring funds will reduce the use of checks, it is the deposit behind the check, and not the check, that constitutes money. When a person uses his credit card, his deposit at the bank must soon be reduced by the amount of the transaction. People hold money as a medium of exchange to bridge the gap between the receipt of payments for their own services and the purchase of goods and services they wish to consume. As long as persons and business firms do not wish to spend their entire receipts the moment they receive them, there will never be a moneyless economy.

In countries in which most trade is carried on with money, there are often some examples of barter and payment in kind. Such exchanges in kind are sometimes arranged in order to minimize taxes or to avoid criminal prosecution (in case of illegal bribes). A store that gives employees a discount on goods purchased or a school that gives teachers' children free tuition is giving employees a wage supplement in kind that is usually not included in taxable income. These wage supplements in kind may sometimes be arranged to reward particularly capable employees, in order to get around customary salary schedules that apply to most employees in an organization. Gifts in kind that are in payment for a favor generally are tax-free and sometimes provide a way of paying for a service or good not ordinarily obtainable in the marketplace.

DEMAND DEPOSITS AS A
MEDIUM OF EXCHANGE

Over the years, the most important type of money used in exchange in the United States has become demand deposits, which now make up approximately 80 percent of Money Supply I. The use of demand deposits as money is a vast bookkeeping system. More than fourteen thousand commercial banks keep the books. If you have a demand deposit of $100, this is recorded on the books of your bank, and if you write a check for $10 and give it to Mr. Smith, your bank reduces by $10 the amount of your deposit, and Mr. Smith's bank increases his deposit by $10. The use of demand deposits as money is safer than the use of currency. Currency has to be stored, and it can be stolen. Also, checks are a relatively safe method of making payments by mail because they are valueless until endorsed; they are convenient because they can be written for the exact amount of the payment and they provide a record of expenditures. Checks on demand deposits are especially convenient as a method of payment for large transactions.

In Great Britain until 1960, the use of checks was somewhat limited by a curious law that made it illegal for employers to pay their employees by check. Instead, payment had to be made in coin and currency. This law was included in the Truck Act of 1831 and was designed to prevent types of payment that might require workers to cash their checks and trade at a company store.[9]

Fifty years ago, economists defined money solely in terms of coins and specie. Even as late as 1930, when John Maynard Keynes, the leading economist of his day, included demand deposits as money in his *Treatise on Money*, H. Parker Willis, an older professor at Columbia University, was critical.[10] Demand deposits are now considered to be money because they are, in fact, used to buy goods and services. Economists have a functional conception of money: whatever is used as money is money. The public's use of demand deposits as money is not based on authorization by the federal government. Instead, demand deposits became money through common usage. Even today, legal tender—the kind of money in which debts are legally payable—does not include demand deposits. In practice, this is unimportant because demand deposits may be immediately converted into types of money that are legal tender.

Although demand deposits are now the predominant medium of exchange in the United States, they are still not as acceptable as currency because the person accepting a check usually does not know for sure that the deposit behind it is large enough to cover it. Because of this uncertainty, it is surprising that checks are, in fact, as readily accepted as they are. The way in which our legal system protects those who accept checks has facilitated their use. It is a criminal offense for a person to pay for goods by check knowing that there is nothing behind the check and intending not to pay for the goods. As a criminal offense, the cost of prosecution is borne by the government rather than by the person who has been defrauded. For conviction, it is necessary to prove that fraud was intended. This is usually not too difficult to do. If, upon appropriate notice by the merchant, the purchaser does not attempt to make good the payment, evidence of intent to defraud is usually considered to exist. In countries that do not have laws of this type, the use of checks and checking accounts is limited.

A check may be made more acceptable by having it certified. When a check is certified, an officer of the bank has acknowledged that the check is adequately backed, and the bank actually transfers the amount of the certified check from the account of the person involved to an account for certified checks. Some businesses, such as interstate trucking companies, do not wish to become involved in delays or problems of check collection, and will accept checks only if they are certified. Certified checks are also useful for international transactions.

MONEY AS A STORE OF VALUE

As a store of value, the dollar medium of exchange cannot be sharply separated from time and savings accounts, U.S. savings bonds, and short-term marketable U.S. government securities. These latter assets are like the medium of exchange because they have nominal values that are fixed or vary only slightly, and they are liquid because they may be converted into other types of assets quickly and at little cost.

As shown in Table 2.1, the total volume of private liquid asset holdings (the medium of exchange plus other liquid assets) in the United States at the end of 1973 amounted to over $1 trillion. *Time deposits* in commercial banks and in the thrift institutions—mutual savings banks and savings and loan associations—are the most important type of liquid asset. One hundred dollars placed in a time deposit is worth $100, plus interest, whenever the owner wishes to convert it. It can never be worth less than $100 in nominal terms, although its real value declines as prices rise. Although some types of time deposits cannot be converted to cash until they reach their maturity date, or after a waiting period, the owner of a savings deposit can almost always convert it into cash immediately by presenting his passbook at the bank.

Table 2.1
Private Liquid Asset Holdings, Nonfinancial
Investors, December 1973
(in billions of dollars)

TYPE	AMOUNT
Currency and demand deposits	$ 245.9
Time deposits in commercial banks	294.6
Time deposits in nonbank thrift institutions	347.0
U.S. savings bonds	60.9
U.S. government securities maturing within one year	52.4
Negotiable certificates of deposit	57.2
Commercial paper	22.8
Total liquid assets	$1,080.9

Source: *Economic Report of the President, February 1974* (Washington, D.C.: U.S. Government Printing Office, 1974), p. 314.

U.S. savings bonds, another type of liquid asset, also have an assured value so that there is never the possibility of a loss in nominal terms. Series E savings bonds, which appreciate between the date of purchase and the date of maturity, have a redemption schedule showing the exact cash value of the bond for each six-month interval after the date of purchase. Series H savings bonds, which pay the owner interest every six months, may be redeemed for their purchase price at any time after a short, initial waiting period.

Another type of liquid asset is short-term marketable U.S. government securities that mature within a year. This type of liquid asset includes government securities that had a maturity of one year or less at the time they were initially sold by the United States Treasury, and also those issues that originally had a longer maturity but have come to within one year of their maturity date. The nominal value of short-term marketable securities is not fixed, but varies so little that they are considered to be near money. Their prices vary with changes in prevailing market interest rates, but, because of the closeness to their maturity date, the variations in their prices are small. Drawing a sharp line between those securities that have less than one year to maturity and those that have just slightly more than one year to maturity has little justification except that the line must be drawn somewhere. Longer-term marketable securities vary too widely in price to be classified as liquid assets.

The other important liquid assets are *negotiable certificates of deposit* and *commercial paper.* Negotiable certificates of deposit (called CDs) are a type of time deposit with a minimum denomination of $100,000. Although they cannot be turned in for cash until their maturity date, because they are negotiable they can be sold. If interest rates have risen since the time they were issued, they have to be sold at a discount. However, they are still considered liquid since the amount of the discount will be small because of their short maturity. Commercial paper is a type of short-term security issued by business corporations, which has approximately the same liquidity as short-term marketable U.S. government securities. Life insurance policies are sometimes classified as liquid assets, even though they are not included in Table 2.1. Many of these policies have fixed cash values, depending on the length of time held. Insurance companies will cash them immediately. When cashed, the insurance that a person has received terminates. Just how important the cash value is to most owners of insurance policies is debatable.

Other forms of wealth—such as corporation stocks and bonds, municipal bonds, longer-term marketable U.S. government securities, and physical assets such as homes, farms, and nonresidential real estate—are important stores of value, but they are not liquid. Corporation stock, if listed on one of the national exchanges, or if important enough to be traded frequently over the counter, can be sold quickly, but the price is uncertain. A person does not know what his holdings of stock will be worth at some time in the future when he might have need for money. Longer-term marketable bonds—federal, municipal, or corporate—are also uncertain as to price. Bonds of solvent firms eventually have a maturity date when they are worth their par value. But if the owner wishes to sell them prior to their maturity dates, he must take whatever he can get in the market. Houses and farms are very illiquid types of assets. It usually takes time to find a buyer, the cost of the transaction through a real estate agent is high, and the price is uncertain.

Interest-earning liquid assets usually do not yield the high rates of return that are typically received by investors in stocks, bonds, or real estate. Nevertheless, a certain amount of liquidity is so useful that people are willing to forgo a higher return in order to hold part of their wealth in money and liquid assets. Such assets provide protection in case of certain emergencies, such as loss of job, sickness, or an automobile accident. The rapid growth of savings deposits in commercial banks, mutual savings banks, and savings and loan associations shows that people want to hold considerable amounts of liquid assets. Individuals have accumulated assets of this type to protect themselves and at the same time to earn a small rate of return.

Liquidity is also important to persons in business and their firms. Managing a business is unavoidably risky and having a sizable stock of money or liquid assets is necessary in order to meet contingencies that regularly occur such as unexpected increases in costs, unpaid bills, or disappointing sales. It is advantageous for a business firm to own liquid assets rather than money because liquid assets earn interest. The balance sheets of large corporations show that they typically have large amounts of liquid assets relative to their total assets. These balance sheets also show that the bulk of their liquid assets consists of short-term marketable securities or certificates of deposit. For example, in the balance sheet of Eastman Kodak ending December 28, 1973, their holdings of currency and demand deposits amounted to $151 million, and short-term marketable securities to $885 million. Together these were more than 24 percent of the corporation's total assets.

During rapid inflation, the medium of exchange does not serve well as a store of value because it does not keep its real value. Other assets then become preferable as stores of value. If interest rates on interest-earning liquid assets are high enough, persons will increase the amount of them that they hold relative to their holdings of the medium of exchange. In countries where interest-earning liquid assets are not available, in periods of rapid inflation persons and business firms typically hold foreign currencies rather than their own money or they hoard stable, readily salable commodities as stores of value. As reserves, commodities are not perfectly liquid or very reliable; but when inflation is rapid, they are still better than holding money. Even after persons discard money as a store of value during rapid inflation, they usually still use money as a medium of exchange in order to avoid the inconvenience of barter.

MEASURING THE STOCK OF MONEY

If money were used solely as a medium of exchange, there would be little difficulty in measuring it statistically. The narrow measure—Money Supply I—would be adequate. But money is a store of value as well as a medium of exchange. The broader statistical definition of money, Money Supply II, includes time and savings deposits which are normally not part of the medium of exchange. A person usually cannot purchase goods and services with a savings deposit. The broader measures of the money stock are based on the conception of money as a store of value.

Money Supply II is the only available measure of the money supply providing a continuous series that goes back historically to the Civil War. Before the establishment of the Federal Reserve System in 1914, commercial banks did not distinguish sharply between time deposits and demand deposits. Both might earn interest. A sharp distinction was created only when the Federal Reserve System established different reserve requirements for the two types of deposits. Because of the long period for which data are available, Money Supply II has been a useful series for studies of the cyclical and secular movements of the money supply. A separate statistical series is available since 1914 for Money Supply I. The chief justification for using it as a measure of the money supply is that it is the medium of exchange.

Some economists prefer broader measures of the money supply, such as Money Supply III, because they believe that such concepts more accurately measure the influence of liquidity on the economy. In defining Money Supply II, there is little justification for including time and savings deposits in commercial banks while excluding savings deposits in mutual savings banks and savings and loan associations. Money Supply II still has the advantage of being a measure that is relatively easily regulated by the Federal Reserve System. The instruments of control that the Federal Reserve System uses have little effect on the volume of savings deposits in mutual savings banks and savings and loan associations, or on the quantity of various types of liquid U.S. government securities. Operationally, using the total quantity of liquid assets as a measure of the money stock would be less useful than using Money Supply I or II.

An additional advantage of using Money Supply II over other measures is that since 1962 the relationship between the gross national product and Money Supply II has been more stable than that between the GNP and the other measures of the money supply.[11] The gross national product divided by the quantity of money is called the *income velocity* of money, and there is a different estimate of velocity for each of the different measures of the money supply. Since 1962, the velocity of Money Supply II has been stable while the velocity of Money Supply I has increased. Whether the velocity of Money Supply II will stay at a relatively constant level is not certain, but there is no obvious reason why it should change sharply. As a guide to government policy, the use of Money Supply II appears to have the advantage of not requiring an allowance for an uncertain secular trend in velocity.

MONEY AS A STANDARD OF DEFERRED PAYMENT

The use of money as a standard of deferred payment is sometimes included as a fourth function of money. This function is derived from the use of money both as a unit of account and as a medium of exchange. Debts are almost always stated in terms of the unit of account and paid off with the money medium of exchange. A corporate bond, for example, is a promise by a corporation to make periodic interest payments to the owner and to redeem the bond at par on its maturity date. Both the interest payments and the repayment of capital are to be made in the form of money. This use of money is similar to the use of money for the purchase of goods and services except that it applies to the payment of debt.

Under inflationary conditions, money is sometimes discarded as a standard of deferred payment. If a creditor expects inflation but is uncertain about how much inflation to expect, he may protect himself by requiring that the debtor pay off his debt in the money of a country that has a more stable money, in gold, or even in commodities. It is not necessary, however, that the money medium of exchange be discarded as a standard of deferred payment when prices are rising rapidly. By using escalator clauses linking debt to a price index, the lender of money may use money and still protect himself.

MOTIVES FOR HOLDING MONEY

Another way of viewing the functions of money is in terms of the motives that people have for holding it. The famous British economist John Maynard Keynes had a three-fold classification—*transactions, precautionary,* and *speculative* motives. The same dollar held may serve all three of these purposes. Yet the differences are sufficiently distinct to warrant separate treatment.

The transactions motive results in the use of money as a medium of exchange. People need money to handle ordinary transactions and are seriously inconvenienced if they do not have money available. The amount of money needed for transactions depends in part on the volume of the purchases made. In addition, the frequency—whether weekly, monthly, or quarterly—of income received makes a difference. The more frequent the payments, the smaller the average cash balance that must be on hand to finance transactions. Regularity of payments is also important. The more certainly that one can count on receipts and payments, the less money one needs to hold.

The precautionary motive for holding money is related to the use of money as a store of value. Money gives people a type of protection, as insurance does, against some risks. People need the kind of protection that money provides if they become ill, have an accident, or lose their job. Business firms also have many needs for liquidity, among them unexpected increases in costs, lower sales, and unusual opportunities for expansion or profit. The amount of money held as a precaution will depend on the likelihood of needs for it developing. That likelihood depends significantly on the stability of the economy.

Money is also held because it provides people with the liquidity needed to shift readily to other assets. This is referred to as the speculative motive for holding money because it involves outguessing the movements in the prices of securities or goods. If a person expects the prices of goods to fall, he may build up his money balances so as to take advantage of the lower prices in the future. If people expect interest rates to rise (and bond prices to fall), they will tend to build up their money balances so as to be in a position to purchase bonds when bond prices reach bottom. On the other hand, if they expect interest rates to fall (and bond prices to rise), the speculative demand for money will be relatively small.

DEFINING MONEY

Because it has various functions, money is difficult to define in a simple way. Different economists have emphasized different functions. A widely used definition of money is that it is "anything which is widely accepted in payment for goods, or in discharge of other kinds of business obligation." [12] This definition is based primarily on the conception of money as a medium of exchange. Another definition emphasizes primarily the accounting function: "Money is that commodity in which prices are expressed."[13] Some economists have conceived of money more broadly as any highly liquid asset with a relatively fixed nominal value. From this point of view, it is is said that "money is property with which the owner can pay off a definite amount of debt with certainty and without delay."[14] Though the emphasis has changed over the years, there is still a difference of opinion concerning the relative importance of the functions of money as a medium of exchange, as a unit of account, and as a store of value. The store-of-value function may be so important that broader definitions of money, such as Money Supply II and III, may be particularly significant.

SUMMARY

The efficient operation of a complicated economic system requires the use of a money unit of account for business accounting, the existence of a medium of exchange for making payments, and the availability of types of monetary assets which provide people and business firms with liquidity.

The reason for the different statistical measures and definitions of money is that money has a wide variety of functions.

NOTES

1. Colin D. Campbell and Gordon C. Tullock, "Hyperinflation in China, 1937–49," *Journal of Political Economy* 62 (June 1954), pp. 236–245.

2. Horace White, *Money and Banking* (Boston: Ginn and Company, 1896), p. 15.

3. There were twenty-four monetary reforms in Europe from 1944 to 1952. See John G. Gurley, "Excess Liquidity and European Monetary Reforms, 1944 to 1952," *American Economic Review* 43 (March 1953), pp. 76–100.

4. Osgood Caruthers, "Russians Queue Up at Banks to Trade Old Rubles for New," *New York Times,* 3 January 1961, p. 9.

5. Thomas Gann, *Glories of the Maya* (New York: Charles Scribner's Sons, 1939), p. 98; and Sol Tax, *Penny Capitalism, A Guatemalan*

Indian Economy (Washington, D.C.: U.S. Government Printing Office, 1953).

6. Leonard E. Hubbard, *Soviet Money and Finance* (London: Macmillan, 1936), pp. 118–121.

7. In the USSR some prices have been set below the equilibrium price, possibly in order to avoid inventory surpluses and the resulting storage costs. See Colin D. Campbell and Rosemary G. Campbell, "Soviet Price Reductions for Consumer Goods, 1948–1954," *American Economic Review* 45 (September 1955), p. 622.

8. Horst Mendershausen, "Prices, Money, and the Distribution of Goods in Postwar Germany," *American Economic Review* 39 (June 1949), pp. 646–672.

9. George W. Hilton, *The Truck System* (Cambridge, England: W. Heffer and Sons, 1960), pp. 150–152; and "Wages by Cheque?" *Economist,* 14 June 1958, Banking Supplement, pp. 15–16.

10. *New York Times,* 22 March 1931, Section IV, p. 10.

11. Milton Friedman, "How Much Monetary Growth?" *Morgan Guaranty Survey,* February 1973, pp. 5–10.

12. Dennis H. Robertson, *Money,* rev. ed. (New York: Pitman, 1948), p. 2.

13. See Charles R. Whittlesey, *Principles and Practices of Money and Banking,* rev. ed. (New York: Macmillan, 1954) p. 2.

14. Albert G. Hart and Peter B. Kenen, *Money, Debt and Economic Activity,* 3d ed. (Englewood Cliffs, N.J.: Prentice-Hall, 1961), p. 4.

QUESTIONS

2.1. Compare (a) the money unit of account and the medium of exchange, and (b) the medium of exchange and money as a store of value.

2.2. How would a monetary reform affect the money unit of account, and why might this be desirable?

2.3. Explain the advantages of using money as a medium of exchange over barter or the use of ration coupons.

2.4. Will people stop using money as a medium of exchange if they expect prices to rise rapidly? Explain.

2.5. Will the use of electronic computers to transfer funds lead to the development of a moneyless economy?

2.6. Why do merchants in the United States readily accept checks on demand deposits?

2.7. Why are savings deposits almost as useful as money as a store of value?

2.8. Why do persons and business firms desire to hold not only stocks and bonds but also some money or various types of liquid assets?

2.9. How would you expect a rapid rate of inflation to affect the use of liquid assets as a store of value?

2.10. Is Money Supply II a good statistical measure of the total amount of assets that serve as a monetary store of value? Explain.

2.11. Compare the transactions, precautionary, and speculative motives for holding money.

2.12. How would you define money?

2.13. Know the meaning and significance of the following terms and concepts: unit of account, medium of exchange, monetary reform, barter, rationing, legal tender, illiquid and liquid assets.

Chapter 3
Currency

For many types of transactions, people still customarily use currency rather than checks written on checking accounts. In recent years the growth of currency in circulation has been slightly more rapid than the growth of demand deposits. Historically, the use of currency has declined in importance relative to deposits.

There are two basic types of currency—*coins* and *paper money*. The Constitution gives the United States Treasury the sole right to issue coins and prohibits the states from issuing them. The first United States mint was established in Philadelphia in 1793, and the Bureau of the Mint has been supplying the country with coins ever since. During the first half of the nineteenth century, a substantial volume of foreign coins circulated alongside the domestically produced coins, and certain types of foreign coins were not deprived of their legal status as money until 1857.

The authority to issue Federal Reserve notes, the principal type of paper money now in use, was granted by the Federal Reserve Act of 1913, the same act that established the Federal Reserve banks. Federal Reserve notes are liabilities of those banks. In most countries, paper money is now issued by their central banks. Since the establishment of the Federal Reserve System, most types of paper money that were formerly used— gold certificates, national bank notes, and silver certificates—have, one after the other, been added to the list of currencies in process of retirement. United States notes are the only type of paper money other than Federal Reserve notes still circulating.

People obtain additional Federal Reserve notes and coins by cashing deposits at commercial banks. These banks always have currency on hand as part of their cash in vault. When commercial banks need additional coins or Federal Reserve notes, they order them from the Federal Reserve banks, paying for them from their checking accounts at those banks.

TOKEN COINS

In 1973, the amount of dollar coins and fractional coins in circulation—
half-dollars, quarters, dimes, nickels, and pennies—amounted to $7.8
billion. The volume of coins in use was much smaller than the volume of
paper money. Most of the coins were *token coins*. They are called token
because their metal content is worth less than their nominal value. It is
a surprising fact that an essential requirement of a good system of coinage is that token coins rather than full-bodied ones be used. If full-bodied, a sharp rise in the price of the metal in the coins may cause them to
be worth more as metal than their nominal value. When this occurs, coins
are hoarded and disappear from circulation, they are melted down or
exported, the public is inconvenienced by a shortage of coins, and new
types of coins must be produced.

A rise in the price of silver in the 1960s made it necessary for the
United States to replace its silver coinage with token coins containing
no silver. In September 1963, the price of silver in the open market rose
to $1.29 an ounce, the market value of the silver backing silver certificates
that were then still in use and the silver content of standard silver dollars.
From 1963 to 1967 the Treasury had to sell silver to prevent the price of
silver from rising above $1.29. This was done to discourage people from
hoarding silver coins before Congress authorized a new coinage and to
give the mints time to manufacture enough new coins. The Coinage
Act of 1965 authorized the mints to produce new dimes and quarters
made of copper and nickel to replace the old silver coins and to reduce
the silver content of 50-cent pieces from 90 percent to 40 percent. The
Coinage Act of 1970 authorized the mints to produce silverless half-dollars and dollars. In other countries also, when the price of silver has risen
sharply, recoinage has been necessary. In 1903–1906, a sharp rise in the
price of silver forced Japan, the Philippine Islands, the British Colony of
the Straits Settlements (now the Federation of Malaya), and Mexico to
change the content or the weight of their coins.[1]

The bulk of the dollar coins currently in circulation consists of standard silver dollars that contain three-quarters of an ounce of silver. At
prices of silver above $1.29 an ounce, silver dollars are worth more as
silver than as money. After the Treasury decontrolled the price of silver
in 1967, the price rose to over $2.50 an ounce and has varied from $1.30
to $6.70 an ounce since then. Because no silver dollars have been minted
since 1935, these coins have also become valuable as collectors' items.
In 1974 the price of a roll of twenty standard silver dollars, as quoted by
coin dealers, was approximately $100. People began hoarding silver dol-
lars in 1961—six years before the Treasury gave up holding the price of
silver down to $1.29—because they believed that eventually the Treasury

could no longer prevent the price of silver from rising. Because of their large size, one of the uses of silver dollars had been in gambling casinos. When the price of silver was expected to rise, the casinos had to shift to coins manufactured by private mints. Even though the old dimes and quarters had a lower proportion of silver than silver dollars, they became worth more as silver than as coins when the price of silver rose above $1.38 an ounce, and they have gradually disappeared from circulation.

Recent difficulties with coins are not our first with this type of money. Prior to 1853 the system of coinage was a cause of continuous complaint. The weight, thickness, and metallic content of coins were considered important, and some coins had special edges that made it more difficult to shave off tiny amounts. The United States had originally attempted to create a coinage system in which the coins were full-bod-ied.[2] It was widely believed at that time that to issue or circulate coins with a metallic content worth less than their nominal value was to de-fraud the public. The advantages of token coins over full-bodied ones were not recognized. Most of the early full-bodied coins produced by the United States mint were exported, and coins in circulation consisted of a confusing variety of lightweight foreign coins. Small coins were sometimes in such short supply that postage stamps had to be used for change. In 1853, Congress authorized the mint to produce token coins. Though it was a simple change, it is considered an important develop-ment in the history of money in the United States. Token coins are not only more satisfactory as a circulating medium than full-bodied ones, but they also create a source of income for the Treasury. They are worth more than their cost. The profit made on coinage is called *seigniorage,* a term derived from *seigneur* (the French word for lord) and the practice of medieval lords of manors of issuing coins.

The rise in prices—including the price of silver—during the inflation-ary period of the Civil War also created a shortage of coins. The value of the silver in coins rose above their nominal value, causing them to be hoarded and withdrawn from circulation. Congress could have prevented the hoarding of silver coins by reducing their silver content, but it did not do so. To remedy the situation, the Treasury issued paper money in fractional denominations. After the war, the decline in prices eventually caused the value of the silver in the coins to fall below the nominal value and, to everyone's surprise, coins which had not been seen in circula-tion for years returned to use.

In 1973, sharply rising copper prices caused hoarding and dwindling supplies of pennies. The metal value of pennies is greater than their face value when the price of copper rises above $1.51 per pound. After reach-ing a record $1.52 per pound in early 1974, later in the year the prices of copper dropped sharply. During the penny shortage the Treasury Department set a maximum penalty of $10,000 and five years in prison for melting or exporting them.* The director of the mint also offered an Exceptional Public Service Certificate to persons cashing in $25 worth of pennies at a bank. Although over thirty million pennies a day were produced by the mints, speculation that they might be worth more as metal doubled the demand for them. Efforts by the Treasury to get Congress to pass a new law permitting the substitution of aluminum for copper in pennies—with potential savings estimated at $40 million a year—were unsuccessful. During the World War II shortage of copper, pennies were made of zinc-coated steel. In the fall of 1974, Congress authorized the secretary of the Treasury to lower the copper content of pennies.

GRESHAM'S LAW

The usual statement of Gresham's Law, "bad money drives out good," is neither clear nor precise. A better statement is the following: *"Money that has value in a nonmonetary use (including use as money in another country) will tend to move, if it is free to do so, to the use (monetary or nonmonetary) in which its value is the higher."* [4] The principle of basing a system of coinage on token coins so as to assure that they will not be used as metal is based on this law. The importation into the United States of lightweight foreign coins prior to 1853 is an example of the operation of this law. They were imported because their value as a circulating medium was higher in the United States than in the issuing country.

Gresham's Law also explains why the bimetallic standard established in the United States by the American Coinage Act of 1792 did not work. The dollar was made equivalent both to 371.25 grains of fine silver and to 24.75 grains of fine gold, a mint ratio of 15 to 1. Over time, changes in the supply of and demand for the two metals inevitably caused the ratio between the world market prices of these two metals to be different from the established mint ratio. This made the exportation of either silver or gold from the bimetallic country a profitable undertaking, and the bimetallic country sooner or later found itself with only one metal. With a bimetallic standard and a fixed official ratio, one of the two metals will necessarily be more valuable in a monetary use than the other whenever the price ratio in the world market differs from the official domestic price ratio. From 1792 to 1834, for example, the market ratio between

---

* Attempts to prohibit exportation of coins to foreign countries where their value as coins or metal may be higher have usually failed. For instance, late in 1905 the Philippine government made it a criminal offense with fairly severe penalties to export silver coins (or bullion obtained by melting coins down). Nevertheless, because of the sharp rise in the price of silver, considerable amounts were smuggled to China (see note 3 to this chapter).

silver and gold was approximately 15½ to 1. Since the official ratio in the United States was 15 to 1, silver was overvalued. Under these conditions, relatively little gold would be brought to the mint; it was shipped to foreign countries where its price was higher—in foreign countries it was possible to get 15½ ounces of silver, rather than 15 ounces, for 1 ounce of gold. During this period the United States was actually on a silver standard. In 1834, the official mint ratio was changed to 16 to 1. The market ratio was still nearer 15½ to 1. The official ratio now overvalued gold and created a de facto gold standard. When the official ratio overvalued gold, its value in monetary use exceeded its value in nonmonetary uses. The opposite was true for silver money, which tended to disappear from circulation under these circumstances.

PRESSURE FOR SILVER
COINAGE, 1873–1900

Coinage became a major political issue in the last three decades of the nineteenth century. The Coinage Act of 1873 demonetized silver by replacing the bimetallic standard with the gold standard. The act did not provide for the minting of any standard silver dollars containing a dollar's worth of silver, but only for the minting of "trade dollars" whose silver content was similar to that of half dollars, quarters, and dimes. Thus silver was to be used for token coins but not as a standard of value. Originally, silver producers did not object because they were not interested in selling to the mint when prices were higher in the free market than at the mint. Shortly thereafter, however, increased supplies of silver from domestic and foreign mines—and the decreased demand when many countries shifted to the gold standard—drove the market price of silver down, and the attitude of the silver producers changed.

Only small amounts of silver were needed for the minting of token coins, and people began to agitate for free and unlimited coinage of silver. The passage of the Coinage Act of 1873 was attributed to a conspiracy and labeled the "Crime of '73." With the help of such slogans, logrolling by Western legislators, and popular support for measures that might reverse the long decline in prices, Congress passed several silver purchase bills. Under the Bland-Allison Act of 1878, $2 million of silver had to be purchased each month at the market price. Not all of the large amount acquired was coined. It was also held in vaults and used as backing for silver certificates.

Under the Sherman Silver Purchase Act of 1890, the United States Treasury had to purchase monthly a specified number of ounces of silver rather than $2 million worth. This initially provided a large increase in revenues for silver producers, but prior to the 1893 repeal of that Act, the price of silver fell and the monthly value of purchases returned to approximately its pre-1890 level. To pay for the silver, Congress authorized the Treasury to issue a new type of currency redeemable in either gold or silver. These "Treasury notes of 1890" were later retired and replaced with silver certificates.

In the bitter presidential campaign of 1896, William Jennings Bryan advocated free (unlimited) coinage of silver. He was defeated by William McKinley, who ran on a platform favoring a gold standard. Improved economic conditions just before the turn of the century decreased the popular appeal of government purchases of silver. Also, gold discoveries and the increased output of gold set the stage for passage of the Gold Standard Act in 1900.

COIN SHORTAGE OF THE 1960s AND 1970s

Beginning in 1959, there were frequent shortages of coins in the United States.[5] Merchants were unable to get the quantity of coins they wanted from banks. At first pennies and nickels were scarce, but by 1962 other coins were also in short supply. Shortages were particularly acute around Christmas. Merchants who were unable to obtain the quantity of coins they needed from banks were willing to buy them from coin dealers at a premium of up to 8 percent.

The sharp increase in the demand for coins in the 1960s was unexpected. Between 1941 and 1959, the ratio of the dollar value of coins in circulation to the GNP had fallen 17 percent. The Bureau of the Mint expected the decline in the relative importance of coins to continue. Shortages resulted when inventories were depleted and the mints were unable to increase the supply of coins as fast as demand increased.

From the beginning of 1960 to the end of 1973, the value of coins in circulation increased from $2,304 million to $7,759 million—an increase of 237 percent. During the same period, the dollar value of paper currency in circulation increased from $30,287 million to $64,738 million—only a 114 percent increase—and the GNP showed an increase of 166 percent. The principal reason for this remarkable increase in the volume of coins in circulation is Gresham's Law—the rise in the price of silver caused speculation in coins and took large amounts of them out of use. Coin collecting and hoarding became more popular. Money was melted and used as a metal. In addition, the demand for coins may also have been increased somewhat by the development of techniques of automatic distribution: vending machines, telephone booths, do-it-yourself laundries, parking meters, change makers, and coin-operated amusement devices. Toll highways, school lunch programs, and sales taxes have also increased the use of coins.

One solution to the coin shortage was to increase the output. The mints were operated on a three-shift schedule. Congress authorized the construction of a new mint that was completed in Philadelphia in 1969. To prevent the hoarding of coins, the production of silverless coins was provided for. To thwart collectors, the secretary of the Treasury was authorized not to change the mintage date on coins each year.

HISTORY OF THE EARLY USE OF COINS AND PAPER MONEY

Paper money was adopted much later in history than were coins.[6] The use of coins is believed to have developed independently in both China and the ancient Aegean country of Lydia in the seventh century B.C. In approximately 500 B.C., a Persian king, Darius, revolutionized the economy of his empire by adopting the use of coins as a substitute for barter. Archaeologists have found evidence of this use of coinage among the well preserved rock carvings and inscriptions in the buildings that Darius started at Persepolis in what is now the modern country of Iran.[7]

Paper money was first used in China, where printing with movable blocks was invented in about 50 B.C., and paper was first manufactured in approximately 100 A.D. The use of paper money developed in China during the eighth century from the practice of circulating receipts either for valuables deposited for a fee in a special shop for safekeeping, or for taxes paid in kind and held in a provincial capital rather than sending them physically to the central capital. Visitors to China in the twelfth and thirteenth centuries were impressed by the use of paper money. Marco Polo described the use of paper money in China in a short chapter in his book.[8] He regarded "the coinage of this paper money" as a novel way of doing what the alchemists had tried. Counterfeiting paper money in China was a capital offense, and the government of the Great Khan readily exchanged the notes for gold and silver. By 1500 the governments of China had given up the issuance of paper money because of difficulties with oversupply and inflation, but private banks continued to issue such money.

In Europe in the Middle Ages, there were important developments in banking and credit in the large trading centers of Florence, Venice, Genoa, Constantinople, and Bruges. However, they did not use paper money, even though banks transferred money with the use of letters of exchange, and extended credit in the form of delayed payments. It is believed that paper currency was first used in Europe in the seventeenth century along with the development of early commercial banks in Sweden and Great Britain. The French colonists in Canada in 1685 used playing cards carrying official seals and signatures to alleviate a critical shortage of hand-to-hand money. The American colonists had difficulties because of counterfeiting and oversupply with their many issues of early paper currency. In 1781 the printing of Continental currency that was used to finance the Revolutionary War was stopped, and for the next eighty years, the United States government did not issue any paper money. Instead, the paper money in use during this period was issued by private banks.

UNITED STATES NOTES

Although the bulk of the $64.7 billion in paper money in circulation in the United States in December 1973 consisted of Federal Reserve notes, $321 million was in the form of U.S. notes. Initially U.S. notes were issued by the Treasury during the Civil War, and were popularly known as "greenbacks." The maximum total amount outstanding is now limited by law to $347 million and has not varied substantially since 1878. Until the printing of $2 bills was discontinued in 1966, many U.S. notes were $2 bills.

The issuance by the Treasury of U.S. notes not redeemable in specie is an example of the financing of government operations by means of the printing press.* Between the outbreak of the Civil War in 1861 and its end in 1865, only 21 percent of the federal government's expenditures were financed by taxes. The rest was financed either by money creation or by borrowing. When the war ended in 1865, so many U.S. notes had been issued that they constituted almost half the total amount of currency in circulation. In the North, both the total money stock and prices rose approximately 2.3 times from 1861 to 1865.

In the Confederacy, tax revenues were even less adequate than in the North, and large quantities of paper money were issued as a method of government finance. From January 1861 to January 1864, the amount of money issued by the Confederacy increased almost 12 times, and prices rose 28 times.[10] In February 1864, the Confederate Congress enacted a currency reform, exchanging the old currency for a smaller amount of new currency and eliminating about one-third of the total amount in

---

* Money creation was also necessary to finance World Wars I and II, but in the twentieth century deposits had become the principal type of money and no special issues of paper money were necessary. (See note 9 to this chapter.)

circulation. They still had to continue to finance the war mostly by money creation, and the reform had little effect on prices. From January 1861 to April 1865, prices in the South rose over 92 times. After the war, the Confederate issues were worthless and disappeared from circulation.

During the late 1860s and the 1870s, there was considerable political controversy over whether the volume of greenbacks was excessive and whether they were legal tender. When the Treasury originally issued them, U.S. notes were not redeemable in gold by either the Treasury or the banks. After the Civil War, most persons considered redeemability of these notes an important goal and regarded the contraction of their volume as necessary to achieve this. In 1866 Congress authorized the retirement of $10 million in greenbacks per month for six months and thereafter $4 million per month. Westerners, farmers, and others burdened by the falling price level soon opposed this currency contraction. By 1868, when Congress suspended the retirement of greenbacks, the volume had been reduced to $356 million from its wartime peak of $449 million. In later years, during periods of crisis, secretaries of the Treasury temporarily reissued greenbacks, claiming that they were a reserve that could be drawn on. Controversies raged on both this and the question of whether it was legal for Congress to decree that creditors must accept greenbacks in payment for debts contracted before the greenbacks were issued and even after they were issued. There resulted numerous court decisions, new laws, and proposed laws. Even though the output of goods in the United States rose rapidly from the Civil War to 1897, the price decline during most of this period affected people unevenly and caused some unrest.

The period in which U.S. notes were unredeemable lasted until 1879, when the Specie Resumption Act of 1875 authorized the Treasury to redeem these notes in gold. The 1875 Act also provided that the Treasury reduce greenbacks in circulation by $4 every time there was a $5 increase in national bank notes, but this was ended three years later about the time a new political group called the Greenback Party polled 10 percent of the votes and won fourteen seats in Congress. When U.S. notes were made redeemable in gold, the United States was said to have shifted from a paper standard to a gold standard. Under the paper standard, the price of an ounce of gold in terms of greenbacks varied. Because gold was used as foreign exchange to purchase goods from other countries, this meant that the price of foreign exchange also varied. During this period exchange rates were uncontrolled and flexible. After 1879 the price of an ounce of gold was fixed at $20.67 and the Treasury stood ready to convert U.S. notes or other types of currency into gold at that price, ending the period of flexible exchange rates.

CURRENCY IN CIRCULATION

Table 3.1 shows that the total amount of *currency in circulation* consists of the total amount outstanding, less that held by the Treasury and by the Federal Reserve banks. No gold or gold certificates are in circulation. *Treasury currency outstanding* includes dollar coins, fractional coins, U.S. notes, and several types of paper money that are in process of retirement. *Treasury cash* includes the amount of the various types of currency held in the Treasury, excluding the gold held as security against gold certificates. It includes the Federal Reserve notes and Treasury currency held by the Treasury, as well as the gold bullion on which no gold certificates have been issued. Table 3.1 is important because it includes all the types of money controlled by the Treasury, although it also includes Federal Reserve notes that are controlled by the Federal Reserve banks. As will be explained in later chapters, four very significant monetary variables included in this table are the total amount of gold bullion, Treasury currency outstanding, Treasury cash, and currency in circulation.

GOLD BULLION

Table 3.1 shows that currency outstanding, but not in circulation, includes $11,567 million of gold bullion. In 1933, two executive orders by the President and the Secretary of the Treasury required all persons,

Table 3.1
**Kinds of United States Currency Outstanding
and in Circulation, December 31, 1973
(in millions of dollars)**

KIND OF CURRENCY	TOTAL OUTSTANDING	TREASURY CASH	HELD BY FEDERAL RESERVE BANKS	CURRENCY IN CIRCULATION [a]
Gold	$11,567	$107	—	—
Gold certificates	(11,460)	—	$11,460	—
Federal Reserve notes	68,161	134	3,897	$64,130
Treasury currency[b]	8,716	77	271	8 368
Total	$88,443 [c]	$317	$15,628	$72,497

[a] Outside Treasury and Federal Reserve banks. Includes any paper currency outside the United States and currency and coins held by banks.
[b] Dollars, fractional coins, U.S. notes, and Treasury currency in process of retirement including Federal Reserve bank notes, silver certificates, and national bank notes.
[c] The total excludes gold certificates because they are secured by gold.
Columns do not add to total because of rounding.
Source: *Federal Reserve Bulletin*, February 1974, p. A15.

including banks, to sell their holdings of both gold bullion and gold certificates that were backed by gold bullion to the Federal Reserve banks or the Treasury at the legal price then prevailing of $20.67 an ounce. Rare coins were excepted. The price of gold was then raised to $35 an ounce. It was illegal for individuals in the United States to own gold from 1933 to 1974. In 1974, one of the first acts of President Ford was to sign a bill allowing American citizens to buy and sell gold starting in 1975. The United States government had long opposed the removal of the ban on private ownership of gold because it was thought that it would encourage speculation in the gold markets and harm the international monetary system. Because of the accelerating inflation in 1973 and 1974, there was pressure on Congress to end the ban so that Americans could purchase gold as a hedge against inflation.

The gold bullion owned by the United States Treasury is stored at Fort Knox, Kentucky. From 1934 to 1971, it was valued at the official price established by Congress of $35 a fine ounce. In December 1971, following a crisis in the international foreign exchange market, President Nixon announced that he would recommend to Congress that the official price of gold be raised to $38 a fine ounce, and Congress took this action in 1972. After another international monetary crisis in February 1973, there was a further increase—to $42.22 an ounce—in the official price of gold. Each time the price of gold was raised by Congress, the value of the stock of gold bullion owned by the Treasury as well as the dollar value of the gold certificate account in the Federal Reserve banks was increased.

Gold bullion is an important type of international money. Although the United States Treasury adopted a policy in the fall of 1971 of terminating entirely all purchases and sales of gold, throughout the world gold may be used by countries to settle their accounts with other countries if the value of their imports should exceed the value of their exports. The dollar, the pound, and SDRs (special drawing rights) are also used as international money. In recent years, the growing importance of the dollar combined with the IMF policy of pricing gold officially at a level far below the free market price, has reduced the importance of gold. At the end of 1972, the total amount of gold held as international money was valued at 35.8 billion SDRs (approximately $43 billion) and comprised approximately 25 percent of the total amount of international money in the noncommunist world.[11] A small portion of the Treasury's gold bullion on which no gold certificates have been issued is shown in column 3 of Table 3.1 under "Treasury cash." This gold used to be held as Treasury cash so as to be readily available for international transactions.

From 1961 to 1968 the major trading countries of the world operated a "gold pool" in London for the purpose of keeping the free market price of gold at $35—equal to the official United States price at that time. This attempt to control the free-market price of gold had to be given up in 1968 and is an illustration of the difficulties that may be encountered when governments attempt to keep prices of commodities from rising. The ceiling price of $35 an ounce turned out to be below the equilibrium price. As illustrated by the supply (S) and demand (D) graph in Figure 3.1, at $35 an ounce the supply of gold from private sources was less than the demand. To prevent a rise in the price, the participating governments had to sell from their stocks an amount of gold equal to the amount of the shortage (X). Without this increase in supply from government stocks, demand would have been greater than supply, and the price would have been bid above $35 by those buyers who were willing to pay more for it but were unable to get it at $35 an ounce. In the six months preceding the dissolution of the gold pool, the United States had to sell over $2.5 billion in gold as its share in the pool (60 percent). Rather than deplete their stocks of gold completely, the partners decided to dissolve the pool.

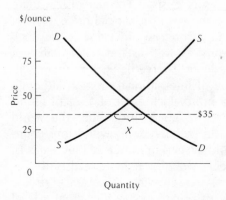

Figure 3.1   Gold

Since 1968, there has been a two-price system for gold—a fixed official price, and a fluctuating free-market price. In the United States, private mining companies that produce gold and manufacturers that use gold as a raw material are permitted to sell and buy gold at free-market prices. The official price of gold is used for official transactions between countries. When the gold pool was dissolved in 1968, the Treasury announced that it would continue to sell gold only to foreign governments for international reserve purposes. Then, in August 1971, the

United States government discontinued all purchases and sales of gold.

Soon after the dissolution of the gold pool, the free-market price of gold rose to over $40 a fine ounce. When the gold pool was established, it had been feared that if the free-market price rose far above the official price, there might be a massive attempt by foreign owners of dollars to convert their dollars into gold at the official price of $35 an ounce. In 1969, however, the price of gold moved downward—much to the surprise of speculators who had purchased gold expecting the price to rise. This caused a reversal in the gold policy of the major trading countries. In place of their previous efforts to prevent the price of gold from rising, they took measures to keep the free-market price of gold from falling below $35 an ounce. The International Monetary Fund agreed to purchase gold from South Africa when the price fell to $35 or lower, or when South Africa had a deficit in its balance of payments. In 1970, $640 million worth of gold was purchased from South Africa. In 1971, the free-market price of gold rose to over $40 a fine ounce, and after the international monetary crises in the fall of 1971 it began a spectacular ascent, climbing to over $175 an ounce in April 1974. The IMF agreement with South Africa was terminated in 1973.

Historically, the use of gold bullion as money was part of the international gold standard that functioned to keep the international payments of countries in balance. From 1834 until recent decades, the United States operated on a gold standard, except during and following the Civil War—from 1861 to 1879—when the United States was on an inconvertible paper standard under which the dollar was not convertible into a fixed quantity of gold. Under the gold standard, the quantity of gold bullion in the United States significantly determined the quantity of reserves of the banks, and, as will be explained in later chapters, this set a limit to the expansion of the money supply. After the Federal Reserve System was established in 1914, the monetary authorities themselves began to control bank reserves through open-market operations and have usually offset the effects on bank reserves of international gold flows.

GOLD CERTIFICATES

Gold certificates were historically a type of paper money backed by gold bullion owned by the Treasury. Currently they are obligations of the Treasury that are owned by the Federal Reserve banks, and they are no more than accounting entries on the books of the Treasury and the Reserve banks. Table 3.1 shows that at the end of 1973, they amounted to $11,460 million.

Until March 1968, gold certificates were required as legal reserves of the Federal Reserve banks. When the Federal Reserve banks were established in 1914, gold backing was required for both their deposits and their notes. At that time, the gold standard existed among the major countries of the world, and the reserves of the commercial banking systems in different countries as well as the reserves of their central banks were expected to vary with the inflow and outflow of gold. In 1934, the gold reserve requirements were 40 percent for Federal Reserve notes and 35 percent for deposit liabilities. In 1945 both of these were reduced to 25 percent, in 1965 the reserve requirement for deposits was dropped, and in 1968 it was dropped for Federal Reserve notes.

The elimination of reserve requirements for Federal Reserve notes in 1968 was unavoidable. In the previous two decades, the amount of currency in use by the public increased on the average about 3.4 percent a year. Such a rate of growth could not be continued if Federal Reserve notes—the principal type of currency—had to be based on a fixed or diminishing amount of gold certificates. The Treasury's stock of gold on which these certificates are based had declined from over $24 billion in 1949 to less than $11 billion in 1968.

CURRENCY IN PROCESS OF RETIREMENT

Silver certificates, national bank notes, and Federal Reserve bank notes (the latter are different from Federal Reserve notes), though in process of retirement, have each had an interesting history. They illustrate the various ways in which the federal government has arranged for the creation of paper money.

Silver Certificates

Prior to 1961, silver certificates were important, and there was no intention of removing them from circulation. They had been issued by the Treasury in $1, $2, $5, and $10 denominations, and each dollar in silver certificates was backed by three-quarters of an ounce of silver bullion stored at West Point.

The Treasury had used the large amounts of silver acquired under the silver purchase acts of the late 1800s primarily for backing silver certificates and also for the manufacture of silver coins. Silver bullion in excess of those needs was "free silver." In the 1930s there was again pressure to increase silver purchases to help the silver mining industry and to counteract deflationary pressures. Legislation passed in 1934 required the United States Treasury to purchase both domestic and foreign silver in order to support the price of silver. Silver certificates were issued to pay for much of this silver. The Treasury continued to purchase newly mined domestic silver from 1942 up to the 1960s, when the rise in the price of silver made purchases unnecessary.

In 1961, the Treasury and the Federal Reserve banks started to withdraw from circulation silver certificates in $5 and $10 denominations and to replace them with Federal Reserve notes. In June 1963, legislation was passed by Congress enabling the Federal Reserve banks to issue $1 bills, and they began issuing them by the end of the year. With this change, the entire supply of silver certificates could be replaced by Federal Reserve notes. These measures were taken to expand the stock of free silver so as to assure an adequate supply for the manufacture of silver coins. In the early 1960s, the Treasury had been forced to sell a large portion of its stock of free silver to prevent the price of silver from rising.

In 1965, people began to hoard silver certificates and to redeem them for silver. Their disappearance from circulation was another example of Gresham's Law. They were considered more valuable in obtaining silver from the mint than in circulation. People wanted to hold silver because they anticipated that eventually the Treasury's stock of silver would be depleted and the Treasury would be unable to keep the price of silver from rising above $1.29 an ounce. Between 1965 and 1968, silver certificates could be sold in the free market at a premium. In 1967, the Treasury discontinued its policy of holding the price of silver at $1.29 and announced that they would discontinue converting silver certificates into silver bullion in July 1968. The rise in the price of silver above $1.29 brought about the end of the use of silver certificates as money. The metal for which they could be redeemed was worth more than their face value. The total quantity of silver certificates in circulation had declined from over $2,370 million in 1961 to $269 million in July 1968. Since July 1968, silver certificates have been included with those types of currency in process of retirement.

National Bank Notes

National bank notes were initially authorized by the Currency Act of 1863, the provisions of which were clarified and strengthened by the National Bank Act of 1864. These notes were an important type of currency prior to the establishment of the Federal Reserve banks in 1914. No national bank notes have been issued since 1935. Approximately $20 million are still "in circulation," although in fact most of them have probably been lost or are in collections.

The acts of 1863 and 1864 created a Currency Bureau, run by the comptroller of the currency, that granted charters for national banks and printed notes for these banks to issue. In 1865, Congress enacted a tax of 10 percent on all state bank notes issued after July 1, 1866. The objective was to drive out of business the large number of banks continuing to operate under state charters or force them to attempt to qualify for national charters. In response to this tax, most state banks applied for national charters, and the circulation of state bank notes declined sharply. State bank notes had not been satisfactory. The large number of different kinds of notes was confusing, and counterfeiting was common. Banks and many merchants had to subscribe to weekly publications which described and sometimes pictured the approximately ten thousand types of genuine bank notes that were circulating, plus numerous fraudulent ones. In addition, notes from country banks sometimes would be refused in payment or would be accepted only at a discount. In Boston in the early 1800s, the Suffolk Bank System experimented with new institutional arrangements for exchanging notes and clearing payments. This was done partly because of the complexity of determining the worth of notes and also because Boston banks were usually paid with their own notes or had them presented for specie payment, while the issues of country banks, in accordance with Gresham's Law, circulated widely as the medium of exchange.[12]

To assure their safety, national bank notes had to be backed by Treasury bonds deposited with the Office of the Comptroller of the Currency. The amount of notes a bank might issue was limited to 90 percent of the bonds deposited and to no more than the amount of paid-in capital of the bank. In addition, the total volume of national bank notes could not exceed $300 million and was originally to be apportioned to states on the basis of population and business indicators. The notes were not legal tender; but since they could be used to pay federal taxes at par, they were the equivalent of legal tender.

The national bank notes were a far better type of paper currency than the state bank notes. The printing of the notes by the United States Treasury reduced the risk of counterfeiting. Each national bank was obligated to redeem the notes of any other national bank at par. The main shortcoming of national bank notes compared to Federal Reserve notes was that they were not issued by a central bank, and thus their supply could not be expanded rapidly when there were financial panics. Between the time when state bank notes were retired and the time when the Federal Reserve banks were established, national bank notes were the only bank notes issued and together with Civil War greenbacks and silver certificates issued by the Treasury constituted the paper currency in circulation.

Notes issued by private commercial banks, such as the national bank notes and state bank notes, are similar to demand deposits. Both their notes and their deposits were liabilities of these banks. A bank making a loan could give the borrower either its own bank notes or a deposit in return for the borrower's promissory note. The borrower could purchase whatever he desired either by spending the notes he had received or by writing a check on his new demand deposit. When the 10 percent tax was placed on state bank notes, it was expected that state banks would no longer be profitable. Most banks became national banks, and by 1868 there were only 247 state banks compared to 1,640 national ones. Within the following decade, state banks discovered that they could operate profitably even though they could issue only deposits. By 1887, the number of state banks exceeded the number of national banks.

Federal Reserve Bank Notes

The Federal Reserve Act provided for the issuance of two varieties of bank notes—*Federal Reserve bank notes* and *Federal Reserve notes*. Over the years, the Federal Reserve notes have become the predominant type of paper money in use; Federal Reserve bank notes are primarily an historical curiosity. Although Federal Reserve bank notes are in process of retirement and authority for their issuance was terminated in 1945, there are still $57 million in circulation.

The original purpose of the Federal Reserve bank notes was to replace national bank notes. It was expected that the Federal Reserve banks would purchase from the national banks the bonds backing their national bank notes and would, in turn, issue Federal Reserve bank notes on the security of the bonds. The national banks were to notify the Treasury of their willingness to sell the bonds, but none did, and the plan miscarried. The Federal Reserve bank notes in circulation were later issued on three occasions, in 1918, 1933, and 1942–1943, when crises required a rapid expansion of currency in circulation.

DEMAND FOR CURRENCY

During much of the history of the United States, the use of currency has declined relative to the use of deposits. Currency made up 45 percent of Money Supply II in 1867 but only 8 percent in 1929. Growing industrialization and urbanization—conditions conducive to the use of checks on deposits—are probably the principal reasons for the decline in the amount of currency in use relative to demand and time deposits.

In the 1930s and early 1940s, the downward trend in the ratio of currency to deposits reversed itself. At the end of the war in 1945, currency made up 20 percent of Money Supply II. After 1945 the importance of currency relative to Money Supply II declined again, but since 1960 there has been a surprising rise in the amount of currency in use relative to Money Supply I.

The amount of currency in circulation varies for different days of the week, days of the month, and seasons. As shown in Figure 3.2, large increases occur before Christmas and other holidays when additional currency is used for shopping and travel. After the holidays, the amount in circulation decreases when it is redeposited in commercial banks, which in turn send it to the Federal Reserve banks.

The demand for currency also varies cyclically. The annual percentage increases in currency are large in periods of business expansion when retail sales are growing, and small in periods of recession when retail sales are slack.[13] The aggregate volume of currency responds automatically to changes in the public's desire for it, because demand deposits are convertible into currency at any time.

In addition to the regular seasonal and cyclical movements, unusual events may affect the demand for currency. During the Great Depression the holding of currency increased because many persons feared bank failures. During World War II, when workers and servicemen moved frequently, they found currency more useful than checks on demand deposits because currency is more readily accepted by strangers. In addition, the armed forces' policy during World War II of paying persons

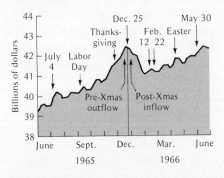

Figure 3.2   Currency in Circulation

Source: Board of Governors of the Federal Reserve System, *The Federal Reserve System: Purposes and Functions,* 5th ed. (Washington, D.C., 1967), p. 181.

in cash rather than by check increased the use of currency. (During World War II the total number of persons in the armed forces reached over eleven million and was about one-fifth the size of the civilian labor force.)

A significant aspect of the demand for currency is that changes in the ratio of currency to demand deposits can affect the total quantity of money. At the end of 1973, for example, Money Supply I consisted of $61.6 billion in currency and $208.8 billion in demand deposits, a ratio of 30 percent. If this ratio increases, the total supply of money may decrease, and if it decreases, the total may increase. The way in which such effects occur will be considered in later chapters.

DENOMINATIONS OF CURRENCY

The denominations of the currency in circulation also reflect the demands of the public. When persons or business firms obtain currency at their banks, they may specify the denominations of the currency that they desire. If they wish $5 bills, the teller gives them bills of this denomination, or if they wish $100 bills, they will receive them. The Bureau of Printing and Engraving adjusts its production of the different denominations to the inventory levels of each.

Table 3.2 shows the dollar value in each denomination of currency outstanding. The surprising fact is the large amount in $100 bills. They amount to approximately one-fourth of the total amount of currency. Bills of this size are not frequently used for transactions and are seldom seen. Some of these large bills may be held in the vaults of banks or hoarded by individuals. In addition, some of them are used for transactions where no record of payment is desired. Accumulations of wealth on which taxes are not paid or from illegal activities may be concealed in this way. For most other accumulations of wealth—the ownership of deposits, corporation stock, or real estate—there is a record of the acquisition and ownership of the property. During World War II the circulation of $500 and $1,000 bills increased sharply, probably because they were used to evade wartime rationing and price and production controls. When controls were discontinued after the war, the volume of the large denomination bills in circulation declined.

In 1973, currency per person in the United States amounted to approximately $345, and currency per household to over $1,000. These surprisingly large amounts are probably related to the volume of large-denomination bills in circulation. The figures also suggest that a few persons hold currency not merely for transactions but to accumulate wealth in a way that is easy to conceal. The typical family undoubtedly

Table 3.2
**United States Currency: Denominations
in Circulation, December 1973**

TYPE	AMOUNT IN MILLIONS
Coins	$ 7,759
Paper bills in denominations of: $ 1	$ 2,639
2	135
5	3,614
10	10,226
20	23,915
50	6,514
100	17,288
500	185
1,000	216
5,000	2
10,000	4
Total Currency	$72,497

Source: *Federal Reserve Bulletin*, February 1974, p. A15.

does not hold as much currency as these averages indicate, and probably only a small portion of the total is held by retail businesses.

In countries with inflation, the average denomination of currency outstanding tends to rise. As prices rise, people find larger denomination currency more convenient and obtain such denominations for their use from banks. Inflation in some foreign countries has caused their small denomination coins to become a nuisance.

Since 1945, Treasury Department regulations have required every financial institution in the United States to file a monthly report on large and unusual currency transactions. These reports were developed for the purpose of discovering large currency transactions resorted to by racketeers, dealers in narcotics, foreign agents, and others engaged in illegal activities or seeking to avoid taxes. Banks are also required to obtain satisfactory identification of customers making large or unusual currency transactions. Financial institutions are required to report cash transactions involving $2,500 or more of U.S. currency in denominations of $100 or higher; $10,000 in any denomination; or any amount in any denominations which in the judgment of the financial institution may be out of proportion to the usual conduct of the customer concerned. To protect the relationship between the bank and its customers, the Internal Revenue Service does not divulge to the customers of financial institutions the source of their information on currency transactions. In 1970, a new law, popularly known as the Bank Secrecy Act, greatly strengthened the enforcement of the Treasury's regulations requiring reports on currency transactions.[14] This law also requires that persons opening new accounts provide the financial institution with their social security number and that all businesses must provide their IRS employer-identification number. In addition, financial institutions must keep extensive records, usually on microfilm, of checks in excess of $100 deposited or drawn on the institution. These records of checking activity are useful to the federal government in the investigation of tax, regulatory, and criminal matters.

SUMMARY

A good system of coinage is one that provides token coins. Otherwise, coins may disappear from circulation, if the price of the metals used to make them rises.

Over the years, Federal Reserve notes have become the dominant type of paper money in circulation. Two types of paper money that were once important, but that are no longer seen in circulation and are in process of retirement, are national bank notes and silver certificates.

The role of gold in the U.S. monetary system has steadily declined. From 1933 to 1974, it was illegal to circulate gold as money in the United States. In 1968, the legally required gold certificate backing for Federal Reserve notes was dropped. In 1971, the United States Treasury terminated all purchases and sales of gold.

People typically use currency for certain types of purchases, checks on demand deposits for other transactions, and savings deposits as a liquid asset. Unless there is a change in customary payment practices, one would expect the growth of currency, demand deposits, and savings deposits to be rather similar.

NOTES

1. Edwin W. Kemmerer, "The Recent Rise in the Price of Silver and Some of Its Monetary Consequences," *Quarterly Journal of Economics* 26 (February 1912), pp. 215–274.
2. Charles R. Whittlesey, *Principles and Practices of Money and Banking,* rev. ed. (New York: Macmillan, 1954), pp. 200–205.
3. Kemmerer, "Recent Rise in the Price of Silver," pp. 244–246.
4. Whittlesey, *Principles and Practices,* p. 195.

5.   Joseph J. Spengler, "Coin Shortage: Modern and Premodern," *National Banking Review,* 3 (December 1965), pp. 201–216.

6.   Gordon Tullock, "Paper Money—A Cycle in Cathay," *Economic History Review* 9 (April 1957), pp. 393–407; and Fred Reinfeld, *The Story of Paper Money* (New York: Sterling, 1957).

7.   Richard N. Frye, *Iran* (New York: Holt, Rinehart, and Winston, 1953), p. 37.

8.   *The Travels of Marco Polo,* Book 2, chapter 18.

9.   See Milton Friedman, "Price, Income, and Monetary Changes in Three Wartime Periods," *American Economic Review, Papers and Proceedings* 42 (May 1952), pp. 612–625; reprinted in *The Optimum Quantity of Money and Other Essays* (Chicago: Aldine, 1969), pp. 157–170.

10.   Eugene M. Lerner, "Inflation in the Confederacy, 1861–65," in Milton Friedman, ed. *Studies in the Quantity Theory of Money* (Chicago: University of Chicago Press, 1956), pp. 163–175.

11.   International Monetary Fund, *1973 Annual Report* (Washington, D.C., July 1973), p. 35. In 1973, the price of one SDR was raised to approximately $1.20 at the same time that the official U.S. price of gold was raised from $38.00 an ounce to $42.22.

12.   See Ross M. Robertson, *History of the American Economy,* 3d ed. (New York: Harcourt Brace Jovanovich, 1973), pp. 178–180.

13.   See Phillip Cagan, *Determinants and Effects of Changes in the Stock of Money, 1875–1960* (New York: Columbia University Press, 1965), chapter 4; and Norman N. Bowsher, *Currency and Demand Deposits* (Federal Reserve Bank of St. Louis, Reprint Series Number 11, March 1965), p. 4.

14.   See *Federal Reserve Bulletin,* December 1970, pp. 929–939; and U.S. Department of the Treasury, *Annual Report of the Secretary of the Treasury on the State of Finances for the Fiscal Year Ended June 30, 1973* (Washington, D.C.: U.S. Government Printing Office, 1973), pp. 327–335.

QUESTIONS

3.1.   What was the reason for the Coinage Act of 1965 authorizing silverless dimes and quarters?

3.2.   Why is it advantageous for coins to be token coins rather than full-bodied coins?

3.3.   State Gresham's Law. Give some examples of its application.

3.4.   What was the nature of the bimetallic standard that existed in the

United States from 1792 to 1873? Why was it replaced by the gold standard?

3.5.   What was the reason for the coin shortage of the 1960s?

3.6.   Explain briefly the history of U.S. notes, national bank notes, and silver certificates.

3.7.   What is the difference between the total amount of currency outstanding and in circulation?

3.8.   What is the difference between the total amount of currency outstanding and Treasury currency outstanding?

3.9.   Explain the declining importance of gold bullion in our monetary system.

3.10. Why was the "gold pool," which was established in 1961 to keep the price of gold at $35 an ounce, dissolved in 1968?

3.11. Explain the changes in the role of gold certificates as a type of money in the United States.

3.12. Explain the seasonal, cyclical, and long-run changes in the amount of currency demanded by the public.

3.13. What are the uses of large-denomination currency, and what are the reasons for the government regulations requiring banks to report transactions of large-denomination currency?

3.14. Explain why a shortage of pennies developed in 1974.

3.15. Know the meaning and significance of the following terms and concepts: full-bodied coins, token coins, silver certificates, national bank notes, state bank notes, Gresham's Law, bimetallic standard, currency outstanding, currency in circulation.

THE UNITED STATES OF AMERICA

B FOR VALUE RECEIVED PROMISES TO PAY TO THE BEARER THE SUM OF

ONE THOUSAND DOLLARS   24 590

ON THE DUE DATE, AND TO PAY INTEREST ON THE PRINCIPAL SUM FROM THE DATE HEREOF, AT THE RATE SPECIFIED HEREON. THIS NOTE AND INTEREST COUPONS ARE PAYABLE AT THE DEPARTMENT OF THE TREASURY, WASHINGTON, D. C., OR AT ANY FEDERAL RESERVE BANK OR BRANCH. THIS NOTE IS ONE OF A SERIES OF NOTES, AUTHORIZED BY THE SECOND LIBERTY BOND ACT, AS AMENDED, ISSUED PURSUANT TO THE DEPARTMENT OF THE TREASURY CIRCULAR REFERRED TO HEREON, AND IS NOT SUBJECT TO CALL FOR REDEMPTION PRIOR TO MATURITY. THE INCOME DERIVED FROM THIS NOTE IS SUBJECT TO ALL TAXES IMPOSED UNDER THE INTERNAL REVENUE CODE OF 1954. THIS NOTE IS SUBJECT TO ESTATE, INHERITANCE, GIFT OR OTHER EXCISE TAXES, WHETHER FEDERAL OR STATE, BUT IS EXEMPT FROM ALL TAXATION NOW OR HEREAFTER IMPOSED ON THE PRINCIPAL OR INTEREST HEREOF BY ANY STATE, OR ANY OF THE POSSESSIONS OF THE UNITED STATES, OR BY ANY LOCAL TAXING AUTHORITY. THIS NOTE IS ACCEPTABLE TO SECURE DEPOSITS OF PUBLIC MONEYS. IT IS NOT ACCEPTABLE IN PAYMENT OF TAXES.

WASHINGTON, D. C., NOVEMBER 6, 1974.

SECRETARY OF THE TREASURY

7⅞%
TREASURY
NOTE
SERIES
D-1979
DATED
NOVEMBER 6, 1974
DUE
MAY 15, 1979
CUSIP 912827 DY5
INTEREST PAYABLE
MAY 15 AND
NOVEMBER 15
CIRCULAR No. 12-74

THE UNITED STATES OF AMERICA	THE UNITED STATES OF AMERICA
WILL PAY TO BEARER ON AT THE DEPARTMENT OF THE TREASURY, WASHINGTON, OR AT A DESIGNATED AGENCY, **NOV. 15, 1978** INTEREST THEN DUE ON **$39.38** $1,000 Treasury Note, Series D-1979 24 590 — 8	WILL PAY TO BEARER ON AT THE DEPARTMENT OF THE TREASURY, WASHINGTON, OR AT A DESIGNATED AGENCY, **MAY 15, 1979** INTEREST THEN DUE ON **$39.38** $1,000 Treasury Note, Series D-1979 24 590 — 9
WILL PAY TO BEARER ON AT THE DEPARTMENT OF THE TREASURY, WASHINGTON, OR AT A DESIGNATED AGENCY, **NOV. 15, 1977** INTEREST THEN DUE ON **$39.38** $1,000 Treasury Note, Series D-1979 24 590 — 6	WILL PAY TO BEARER ON AT THE DEPARTMENT OF THE TREASURY, WASHINGTON, OR AT A DESIGNATED AGENCY, **MAY 15, 1978** INTEREST THEN DUE ON **$39.38** $1,000 Treasury Note, Series D-1979 24 590 — 7
WILL PAY TO BEARER ON AT THE DEPARTMENT OF THE TREASURY, WASHINGTON, OR AT A DESIGNATED AGENCY, **NOV. 15, 1976** INTEREST THEN DUE ON **$39.38** $1,000 Treasury Note, Series D-1979 24 590 — 4	WILL PAY TO BEARER ON AT THE DEPARTMENT OF THE TREASURY, WASHINGTON, OR AT A DESIGNATED AGENCY, **MAY 15, 1977** INTEREST THEN DUE ON **$39.38** $1,000 Treasury Note, Series D-1979 24 590 — 5
WILL PAY TO BEARER ON AT THE DEPARTMENT OF THE TREASURY, WASHINGTON, OR AT A DESIGNATED AGENCY, **NOV. 15, 1975** INTEREST THEN DUE ON **$39.38** $1,000 Treasury Note, Series D-1979 24 590 — 2	WILL PAY TO BEARER ON AT THE DEPARTMENT OF THE TREASURY, WASHINGTON, OR AT A DESIGNATED AGENCY, **MAY 15, 1976** INTEREST THEN DUE ON **$39.38** $1,000 Treasury Note, Series D-1979 24 590 — 3
	WILL PAY TO BEARER ON AT THE DEPARTMENT OF THE TREASURY, WASHINGTON, OR AT A DESIGNATED AGENCY, **MAY 15, 1975** INTEREST THEN DUE ON **$41.30** $1,000 Treasury Note, Series D-1979 24 590 — 1

THE UNITED STATES OF AMERICA

Chapter 4
United States
Government Securities

The many different kinds of federal government securities and the market in which they are purchased and sold play an important role in our monetary system. It is through this market that the Federal Reserve System operates to control the volume of money and credit.

The national debt of the United States—amounting in January 1974 to $468 billion—consists of a variety of different kinds of government securities. The market for these government securities is very active. Though this market is not as well known as the stock market, Wall Street's daily dollar volume of transactions in government securities is approximately three times the volume of transactions on the New York Stock Exchange. Commercial banks and other financial institutions invest heavily in these securities. The open-market operations of the Federal Reserve banks—the system's most important instrument of control—consist of purchases or sales of federal securities.

KINDS OF FEDERAL SECURITIES

There are several different categories of federal securities. The principal types are Treasury bills, notes and bonds, savings bonds, and special issues. The amount outstanding of each of the major categories as of January 1974 is shown in Table 4.1.[1]

The total debt is divided into marketable and nonmarketable issues. Most people are familiar with U.S. savings bonds, a type of nonmarketable security, but few are acquainted with the various types of marketable securities—Treasury bills, notes, and bonds—even though there was a flurry of consumer interest in these securities in 1969–1970 and in 1973–1974 when their yields rose above interest rates paid on savings deposits. Marketable securities are typically purchased by banks, insurance com-

Table 4.1
United States Government Debt,
by Type of Security, End of January 1974
(in billions of dollars)

Treasury bills	$107.8	
Treasury notes	124.6	
Treasury bonds	37.7	
Total marketable debt		$270.1
Convertible bonds	2.3	
U.S. savings bonds and other nonmarketable issues[a]	87.7	
Special issues	106.2	
Non-interest-bearing debt[b]	1.9	
Total nonmarketable debt		198.1
Total gross debt		$468.2

[a] Includes depository bonds, retirement plan bonds, foreign currency series, foreign series, and Rural Electrification Administration bonds.
[b] Includes primarily matured debt on which interest has ceased and two types of currency—U.S. notes and silver certificates.
Source: *Federal Reserve Bulletin*, February 1974, p. A42.

panies, large corporations, pension funds, and foreign holders of dollars, including foreign central banks. The round lot for transactions in them is usually considered to be $1 million, and transactions of over $20 million are not unusual.

Marketable U.S. government securities can be bought and sold at any time after they are issued by the Treasury. Their prices fluctuate, just as do the prices of corporation stock in the stock market. The market is well organized and consists of about twenty-four dealers. Dealers may be a department of a large commercial bank, a department of a brokerage firm, or a separate firm that specializes in this business. Most large purchases and sales are done through the dealers, although direct transactions are possible. If a commercial bank wishes to make a purchase, it usually contacts a dealer by phone, and the dealer quotes the prices at which he is willing to sell securities of different types.

The various issues of marketable securities outstanding on January 31, 1974 are shown in Table 4.2. There were forty-one different issues of bills, thirty-nine issues of notes, and twenty-one issues of bonds. Bills are required by statute to mature within a year or less from the time they are issued. Bonds have no prescribed maturity but usually have been issued with original maturities of over five years and, prior to 1971, had a legal limit of 4¼ percent on their coupon rate of interest. In 1971, Congress authorized the Treasury to issue up to $10 billion in bonds without reference to this limitation. This was done to enable the Treasury to sell bonds when market rates were above 4¼ percent. Treasury notes have no ceil-

Table 4.2
United States Government Marketable
Securities, January 31, 1974
(in millions of dollars)

ISSUE	AMOUNT	ISSUE AND COUPON RATE	AMOUNT	ISSUE AND COUPON RATE	AMOUNT
Treasury bills		Treasury notes		Treasury bonds	
Feb. 7, 1974	$4,303	Feb. 15, 1974 $7\frac{3}{4}$	$ 2,960	Feb. 15, 1974 $4\frac{1}{8}$	$2,466
Feb. 12	1,801	Apr. 1 $1\frac{1}{2}$	34	May 15 $4\frac{1}{4}$	2,848
Feb. 14	4,309	May 15 $7\frac{1}{4}$	4,334	Nov. 15 $3\frac{7}{8}$	1,214
Feb. 21	4,254	Aug. 15 $5\frac{5}{8}$	10,284	May 15, 1975–85 $4\frac{1}{4}$	1,202
Feb. 28	4,303	Sept. 30 6	2,060	June 15, 1978–83 $3\frac{1}{4}$	1,481
Mar. 7	4,320	Oct. 1 $1\frac{1}{2}$	42	Feb. 15, 1980 4	2,574
Mar. 12	1,790	Nov. 15 $5\frac{3}{4}$	5,442	Nov. 15 $3\frac{1}{2}$	1,896
Mar. 14	4,304	Dec. 31 $5\frac{7}{8}$	2,102	Aug. 15, 1981 7	807
Mar. 21	4,305	Feb. 15, 1975 $5\frac{3}{4}$	4,015	Feb. 15, 1982 $6\frac{3}{8}$	2,702
Mar. 28	4,327	Feb. 15 $5\frac{7}{8}$	1,222	Aug. 15, 1984 $6\frac{3}{8}$	2,353
Apr. 4	4,302	Apr. 1 $1\frac{1}{2}$	8	May 15, 1985 $3\frac{1}{4}$	952
Apr. 9	1,802	May 15 $5\frac{7}{8}$	1,776	Nov. 15, 1986 $6\frac{1}{8}$	1,216
Apr. 11	4,308	May 15 6	6,760	Aug. 15, 1987–92 $4\frac{1}{4}$	3,690
Apr. 18	4,304	Aug. 15 $5\frac{7}{8}$	7,679	Feb. 15, 1988–93 4	228
Apr. 19 [a]	3,009	Sept. 30 $8\frac{3}{8}$	2,042	May 15, 1989–94 $4\frac{1}{8}$	1,466
Apr. 25	4,307	Oct. 1 $1\frac{1}{2}$	30	Feb. 15, 1990 $3\frac{1}{2}$	3,964
May 2	4,308	Nov. 15 7	3,115	Feb. 15, 1993 $6\frac{3}{4}$	627
May 7	1,800	Dec. 31 7	1,731	Aug. 15 $7\frac{1}{2}$	1,364
May 9	1,801	Feb. 15, 1976 $6\frac{1}{4}$	3,739	Feb. 15, 1995 3	839
May 16	1,801	Feb. 15 $5\frac{7}{8}$	4,945	May 15, 1993–98 7	692
May 23	1,800	Apr. 1 $1\frac{1}{2}$	27	Nov. 15, 1998 $3\frac{1}{2}$	3,102
May 30	1,798	May 15 $5\frac{3}{4}$	2,802		
June 4	1,801	May 15 $6\frac{1}{2}$	2,697		
June 6	1,801	Aug. 15 $7\frac{1}{2}$	4,194		
June 13	1,801	Aug. 15 $6\frac{1}{2}$	3,883		
June 20	1,799	Oct. 1 $1\frac{1}{2}$	11		
June 21 [a]	2,000	Nov. 15 $6\frac{1}{4}$	4,325		
June 27	1,802	Feb. 15, 1977 8	5,163		
July 2	1,802	Apr. 1 $1\frac{1}{2}$	5		
July 5	1,803	Aug. 15 $7\frac{3}{4}$	4,918		
July 11	1,809	Oct. 1 $1\frac{1}{2}$	17		
July 18	1,811	Feb. 15, 1978 $6\frac{1}{4}$	8,389		
July 25	1,798	Apr. 1 $1\frac{1}{2}$	15		
July 30	1,804	Oct. 1 $1\frac{1}{2}$	2		
Aug. 1	1,803	Nov. 15 6	8,207		
Aug. 27	1,805	Aug. 15, 1979 $6\frac{1}{4}$	4,559		
Sept. 24	1,802	Nov. 15 $6\frac{5}{8}$	1,604		
Oct. 22	1,802	Nov. 15 7	2,244		
Nov. 19	1,801	May 15, 1980 $6\frac{7}{8}$	7,265		
Dec. 17	1,803				
Jan. 14, 1975	1,802				

[a] Tax-anticipation series.
Note: Direct public issues only. Based on Daily Statement of United States Treasury.
Source: *Federal Reserve Bulletin,* February 1974, p. A45.

ing on their coupon rates, and, prior to 1967, the maturity of notes at time of issue was always between one and five years. Since 1967 the Treasury has sold notes with a maturity at time of issue of seven years.

TREASURY BILLS

In January 1974 the total amount of bills outstanding was $108 billion. In recent years, Treasury budget deficits have typically been financed by expanding the total volume of Treasury bills.

The Treasury always sells new issues of bills by auction. At the auction, the Treasury invites both noncompetitive and competitive tenders. Noncompetitive tenders for up to $200,000 from any one bidder are accepted in full at the average price of accepted competitive bids. Competitive tenders are made in multiples of $10,000, and the prices bid are stated on the basis of 100 and to the third decimal place (for example, 97.836). Since February 1970 bills have not been sold in denominations of less than $10,000. Upon expiration of the time set for placing bids, all tenders received are opened, the bids are arranged in descending order of price offered, and the details communicated by wire to the office of the secretary of the Treasury. The total amount of bills auctioned each week is usually the same as the amount maturing although there is occasionally a difference of $100 or $200 million. After the amount of the noncompetitive tenders is deducted from the total to be awarded, the Treasury awards bids in full, starting with the highest price until obtaining the approximate amount of funds desired. At the auction on April 8, 1974, $2.5 billion of ninety-one-day bills were sold. The total amount of noncompetitive bids was $536 million, and the price was 97.814. For competitive bids, the high bid was 97.836 and the low bid was 97.809. The low bidders received only 27 percent of the amount that they bid for. The successful bidders each paid the price they bid. After the allotments are determined, the secretary of the Treasury announces to the public the results of the auction, and the bills are dated and issued on Thursday of that week. Payments may be made either in cash or in Treasury bills maturing on that date.

On the face of a bill there is no rate of interest mentioned—just the issue date, the date payable, and the maturity value. Bills are sold for less than their face value and the return that a purchaser of a bill receives is in the form of the difference between the price he pays for the bill and the price for which he sells it—or, if he holds it until it matures, its maturity value.

A purchaser of a ninety-one-day $1,000,000 bill at the price of $978,140 would receive $21,860 interest if he held the bill until it matured.

On an annual basis, this is a rate of 8.648 percent and is equivalent to a yield of 8.96 percent. The formula for the bill rate is

$$r = \frac{100 - P}{100} \cdot \frac{360}{d} \tag{4.1}$$

where r = bill discount rate in decimal form, P = price paid per \$100, and d = days to maturity. Thus

$$r = \frac{100 - 97.814}{100} \cdot \frac{360}{91} = 0.08648$$

The formula for the coupon issue yield equivalent is

$$i = \frac{100 - P}{P} \cdot \frac{365}{d} \tag{4.2}$$

where i = the coupon issue yield equivalent in decimal form. Thus

$$i = \frac{100 - 97.814}{97.814} \cdot \frac{365}{91} = 0.08960$$

The formula for the coupon issue yield equivalent (formula 4.2) is based on a 365-day year and takes into account that the investor earns his return not on the face value, but on the price paid. This calculation is accurate only for bill maturities of less than 182 days. For longer maturities, a more complex formula is needed in order to include the value of reinvesting a hypothetical coupon payment.

Though the most common type is the ninety-one-day or three-month bill, there are also six-month bills, one-year bills, and tax-anticipation bills. The three-month and six-month bills are sold on Monday of each week at the Federal Reserve banks, and the one-year bills are sold monthly. Tax-anticipation bills range in maturity up to nine months. They mature one week following the tax payment date. When used for taxes, they are in effect redeemed for par one week early.

NOTES AND BONDS

The other marketable U.S. government securities—*notes* and *bonds*—have usually been sold by exchange or subscription. A recent change has been the use of auctioning for sales of some of the Treasury notes and bonds.

In an exchange (also called a refunding), the Treasury usually offers persons owning the maturing securities a choice of two or more new issues. Listed in Table 4.3 are the maturing issues and the new issues taken in a refunding that occurred on February 15, 1969. Owners of the maturing securities must notify the Treasury of the type and quantity of new issues they want, and they have the right to take cash if they wish. The total amount of cash taken in a refunding is called *attrition*.

Table 4.3
Government Securities Refunding,
February 1969

MATURING ISSUES	AMOUNT (IN BILLIONS)	NEW ISSUES TAKEN IN EXCHANGE	AMOUNT (IN BILLIONS)
Feb. 15, 1969, Note $5^5/_8\%$	$10.7	May 15, 1970, $6^3/_8\%$ [a]	$ 8.8
Feb. 15, 1969, Bond 4%	3.7	Feb. 15, 1976, Note $6^1/_4\%$ [b]	3.7
		Attrition	1.9
Total	$14.4	Total	$14.4

[a] Sold at discount to yield 6.42 percent.
[b] Sold at discount to yield 6.29 percent.

The sale of a new issue by subscription or auction may be used to finance a budget deficit or to make up for the attrition on a refunding. In a subscription sale, the Treasury announces the coupon rate of interest and other features of the issue, and by a certain date investors subscribe for the amount they want at par value. The total amount that investors offer to buy is usually much larger than the Treasury wishes to sell. The Treasury then gives the subscribers a percentage of the amount they offered to buy. The percentage allocated is just sufficient to cover the entire amount that the Treasury desired to raise. Auction sales of notes and bonds are analogous to the way of handling sales of Treasury bills. Commercial banks in which the Treasury has deposits are usually permitted to purchase newly issued government securities by crediting the Treasury's account on the bank's books.

DEALERS' QUOTATIONS

Table 4.4 shows the dealers' quotations for United States Treasury bonds taken from the *Wall Street Journal* for the close of the market on June 6, 1974. This list is prepared daily by the Federal Reserve Bank of New York by averaging the quotations from five major dealers at 3:30 P.M. It is

Table 4.4
Over-the-Counter Quotations for United
States Treasury Bonds, June 6, 1974 [a]

ISSUE AND COUPON RATE			BID	ASKED	BID CHANGE	YIELD
$3^7/_8$s,	1974	Nov.	98.0	98.8	+0.1	8.07
4s,	**1980**	**Feb.**	**82.0**	**82.16**	**+0.2**	**7.88**
$3^1/_2$s,	1980	Nov.	78.0	79.0	—	7.77
7s,	1981	Aug.	95.14	96.14	+0.2	7.65
$6^3/_8$s,	1982	Feb.	92.2	93.2	+0.2	7.58
$3^1/_4$s,	1978–83	Jun.	72.24	73.24	+0.6	7.27
$6^3/_8$s,	1984	Aug.	91.30	92.30	+0.4	7.37
$3^1/_4$s,	1985	May	72.12	73.12	+0.4	6.73
$4^1/_4$s,	1975–85	May	75.28	76.28	+0.4	7.37
$6^1/_8$s,	1986	Nov.	89.22	90.22	+0.2	7.27
$3^1/_2$s,	1990	Feb.	72.8	73.8	+0.6	6.18
$4^1/_4$s,	1987–92	Aug.	72.26	73.26	+0.10	6.77
4s,	1988–93	Feb.	72.12	73.12	+0.4	6.48
$6^3/_4$s,	1993	Feb.	87.2	88.2	+0.6	7.99
$7^1/_2$s,	1988–93	Aug.	94.28	95.12	+0.10	7.98
$4^1/_8$s,	1989–94	May	72.14	73.14	+0.6	6.52
$8^1/_2$s,	1994–99	May	103.24	104.8	+0.8	8.10
3s,	1995	Feb.	72.8	73.8	+0.6	5.11
7s,	1993–98	May	89.14	90.14	+0.4	7.89
$3^1/_2$s,	1998	Nov.	72.8	73.8	+0.6	5.50

[a] Decimals in Bid, Asked, and Bid Change columns represent 32nds (101.1 means 101 1/32).
Source: *Wall Street Journal,* 7 June 1974, p. 21. Reproduced by permission.

published regularly in the financial section of major newspapers. These quotations change each day and show the prices at which dealers were willing to buy and sell these securities.

Consider in detail the quotation for one issue of bonds: the 4s of February 1980. The first of several offerings of these bonds was sold on January 23, 1959, and over the years the Treasury issued $2,574 million of them. The owners are entitled to cash equal to the face value of their bonds on February 15, 1980, the date of maturity. Some bonds listed in Table 4.4, such as the 3¼s of June 1978–1983, have a call date as well as a maturity date. If the Treasury wishes, it may pay off the owners of this bond as early as its call date—June 15, 1978—or on any interest payment date thereafter, up until its maturity on June 15, 1983. The coupon rate of the 4s of February 1980 is 4 percent. These are sold in denominations of $500, $1,000, $5,000, $10,000, $100,000, and $1,000,000. On a $1,000,000 bond, the interest paid would be $40,000 a year. Bonds are sold in both registered and coupon form. Interest is paid every six months. Attached to a $1,000,000 coupon bond would be coupons for $20,000 each. Each coupon is equivalent to a check payable by the Treasury to the owner and may be deposited by the owner in his checking account. On registered bonds, the Treasury pays the interest semiannually by check to the owner, and there are no coupons attached to the bond.

Under "Bid" is the price that dealers were paying for this bond at the close of business on June 6, 1974. Instead of quoting the price of this bond in dollars and cents, the bid price is stated as a percentage of the bond's face value, with the number to the right of the decimal point indicating the fractional amount expressed in thirty-seconds. (Though unusual, it is customary business practice to express fractional amounts of the prices of Treasury notes and bonds in thirty-seconds of a dollar.) Table 4.4 shows that government bond dealers were willing to pay 82 percent of the face value of these particular bonds—or $820,000 for a $1,000,000 bond. The bond is said to be selling at a discount, a price less than its maturity value. When the market price of a bond is higher than its maturity value, it is said to be selling at a premium.

The "Asked" price is that at which dealers would be willing to sell the bond. It is slightly higher than the bid price and amounted to $82^{16}\!/_{32}$ percent or $825,000 for a $1,000,000 bond. Dealers purchase securities for their own inventory and may hold them a short time before they sell them. The difference between the bid and the asked is called the *spread*. In this example, the spread amounted to $5,000 on the purchase and sale of a $1,000,000 bond, and is a source of income for the dealers.

The "Bid Change" shows the change from the bid price for the same issue on the previous day. The price of this bond had risen $^2\!/_{32}$ or $620 on a $1,000,000 bond. Dealers take losses on their inventory when prices of government securities fall. A successful dealer must manage his inventory in such a way that gains are larger than losses.

The "Yield" is the yield to maturity on the bond if purchased at the price shown and held until it matures. At a price of $825,000, the purchaser would receive in addition to the annual interest of $40,000 a capital gain equal to $175,000. For the remaining five years and 254 days until maturity, the prorated annual capital gain is approximately 18 percent of the total capital gain, or $30,695. Because the bond will rise from its present value to its par value at maturity, the average value of this investment over the remaining five years and eight months is the average of the asked price and the maturity value. A very rough estimate of the yield to maturity may be made with the formula

$$i = \frac{A + C}{(P + M)/2} \tag{4.3}$$

where i = yield, A = interest payment per year, C = prorated annual capital gain or loss, P = asked price, and M = maturity value. Thus

$$i = \frac{40,000 + 30,695}{(825,000 + 1,000,000)/2} = 7.75\%$$

The estimated yield of 7.75 percent is slightly different from the 7.88 percent quoted in the newspaper column.

VARIATIONS IN YIELDS

A decline below par in the price of the 4s of February 1980 caused the yield on purchases of these bonds to rise. If the price of this bond had risen above par, its yield would have fallen. In 1959 when the first issue of the 4s of February 1980 was sold, the prevailing market rate of interest for a twenty-one-year government security was approximately equal to its coupon rate of 4 percent. New issues are sold by the Treasury either at par or very close to par, and the coupon rate on the bond must be high enough to attract buyers. In 1974 when this bond had over five years to go, prevailing market rates of interest for a five-year government security were almost 8 percent. The decline in the price of this bond raised its yield so that it was competitive with all other securities, including the new issues that were being offered with higher coupon rates. If its price had not fallen, no well informed investor would have been willing to buy it.

Falling bond prices may create problems for financial institutions that purchased these securities when the price was high.* If they sell them before the maturity date, they must incur a loss. This type of risk is called *interest risk* because it results from rising interest rates. It is different from *credit risk,* which is the risk of default. U.S. government bonds lack credit risk.

Bonds with *short* maturities have little interest risk, and differ significantly in this respect from those with long maturities. This is because prices of short-term issues do not decline much when market interest rates rise while the prices of the longer term issues do. Yields on both

---

*Federal tax law has the opposite effect. It encourages banks to sell securities at a loss when prices are low. For securities other than bills, losses on security sales in any taxable year (net of all gains taken) may be deducted from income in their entirety. The Tax Reform Act of 1969 no longer permits banks to claim the discount earned on coupon securities as a long-term capital gain. All bank earnings from bonds are taxed as ordinary income. Prior to 1969, banks had the additional advantage of being taxed at preferential capital gains rates on long-term gains. (See note 2 to this chapter.)

short-term and long-term securities tend to rise and fall together, although not in exactly the same proportion. When yields are calculated, the capital gain that a person earns when he buys a bond below par is prorated annually. To earn a similar annual capital gain, the price of a long-term bond that matures in the distant future must fall much further than the price of a short-term bond.

DETERMINANTS OF THE BID PRICE

To obtain a better understanding of the relationship between the present value, the maturity value, and the yield to maturity of a bond, note, or bill, it is helpful to consider several formulas for the *present value* (sometimes called the *bid price* or *price*) of such a security. Formula 4.3 showed how to estimate the yield to maturity, assuming that the present value is known. The formulas below show how to estimate the present value of a security if the yield or expected rate of interest is known.

Formula 4.4 shows how to estimate the present value of a security maturing in one year:

$$P = \frac{M}{1 + i} \tag{4.4}$$

where P = present value; M = maturity value; and i = expected interest rate, stated decimally. The amount a person would pay now for the promise of a certain sum of money a year from now (maturity value) depends on the expected rate of interest. If he expects an annual yield to maturity of 8 percent, he would pay $92.59 now for a security worth $100.00 a year from now:

$$P = \frac{\$100}{1.08} = \$92.59$$

The higher the yield expected on investments, the larger the gap between the present value and the maturity value. If the yield on alternative investments were 9 percent, the security would currently be worth $91.74.

If the security were a promise to pay a certain amount of money two years from now (assuming no interest payments), the formula is

$$P = \frac{M}{(1 + i)^2} \tag{4.5}$$

Allowing for a yield of 8 percent, a buyer would pay $85.76 now for a security worth $100 two years from now. The two-year security would be worth less than the one-year so as to provide the owner with the same rate of return over a longer period of time.

$$P = \frac{\$100}{1.166} = \$85.76.$$

The formula for a security to be held n years, assuming no change in the yield and no interest payments, is

$$P = \frac{M}{(1 + i)^n} \tag{4.6}$$

Most Treasury securities not only have a maturity value, but pay the owner fixed amounts of interest at intervals. The price would reflect the value of the interest payments as well as the maturity value. The formula for the price of such a security maturing in n years, paying interest once a year, would be

$$P = \frac{A}{1 + i} + \frac{A}{(1 + i)^2} + \frac{A}{(1 + i)^3} + \cdots + \frac{A}{(1 + i)^n} + \frac{M}{(1 + i)^n} \tag{4.7}$$

where $A =$ annual interest payment. If the expected yield were 8 percent, the maturity three years, the annual interest payment $6, and the maturity value $100, the price would be

$$P = \frac{\$6}{1.08} + \frac{\$6}{1.166} + \frac{\$6}{1.260} + \frac{\$100}{1.260}$$

$$= \$5.56 + \$5.15 + \$4.76 + \$79.37 = \$94.84$$

This formula shows that the higher the yield, the smaller the bid price. When yields are high, it takes a smaller investment to achieve a given flow of income in the future than when yields are low. Also, the smaller the annual interest payments, the smaller the bid price of the bond. If the annual interest payments in the above example were only $5, the bid price of the bond would be only $92.26. More complicated formulas are required when interest is paid more frequently than once a year and when the bid price is computed on dates other than coupon payment dates.

NONMARKETABLE DEBT

U. S. savings bonds were designed for individual investors rather than financial institutions. They cannot be sold or transferred by the owner, but they may be redeemed for cash before the maturity date. Sales and redemptions of savings bonds are handled for the Treasury by commercial banks, business corporations operating payroll savings plans, and some mutual savings banks, savings and loan associations, credit unions, and post offices. Because of the ease with which these bonds may be cashed and because of the certainty of their redemption value, they are included in the statistical measures of the total stock of liquid assets.

Two kinds of savings bonds—Series E and H—are currently offered for sale. Beginning in late 1973, both types have yielded 6 percent if held to maturity. The rate of return on savings bonds not held until maturity varies according to the length of time held. Interest rates on savings bonds held to maturity were raised from 2.9 percent to 3.0 percent in 1952, to 3.25 percent in 1957, to 3.75 percent in 1959, to 4.15 percent in 1966, to 5.0 percent in 1969, and to 5.5 percent in 1970.

Series E are *appreciation* bonds. The smallest denomination is purchased for $18.75 and may be cashed for $25 at the time of maturity five years later. The difference between the price paid and the maturity value represents the accumulated interest received by the owner. The largest denomination Series E bond currently has a maturity value of $1,000. Series E bonds may be redeemed at any time beginning two months after their issue date. The redemption value of the bond and the rate of return received depend on the length of time the bond is held.

Series H are *current income* bonds and are currently sold in three denominations—$500, $1,000, and $5,000. Interest is paid by check semiannually. The interest payments are graduated, and the owner receives an average of 6 percent only if the bond is held until maturity ten years from its issue date. Series H bonds are redeemable at par at a Federal Reserve bank or at the United States Treasury in Washington, D.C., six months after the date of issue. A person may currently purchase no more than $10,000 (face value) of Series E bonds annually and the same amount of Series H bonds, excluding exchanges of previously purchased Series E bonds. Series E bonds are automatically extended beyond their maturity date for a ten-year period, and all E bonds now outstanding—regardless of age—are still earning interest.

Nonmarketable securities issued by the Treasury to foreign governments and monetary authorities—the foreign series and foreign currency series—increased sharply from $3.8 billion in 1969 to $26.0 billion in

1973. The denomination of the foreign series is in dollars, and that of the foreign currency series is in the currency of the country making the purchase. The sale of foreign series securities was related to large deficits in the balance of payments of the United States and the accumulation of dollar balances by foreign governments. Through the sale of these non-marketable securities, dollar balances of foreign governments were reduced.

The convertible bonds (Investment Series B, dated April 1, 1975–1980, bearing a coupon rate of 2¾ percent) are not marketable and also cannot be redeemed for cash. They can, however, be converted by their owners into 1½ percent marketable notes maturing within five years. Since 1951–1952, when these bonds were issued in exchange for outstanding marketable bonds, the amount outstanding has declined sharply as the investors who acquired them have converted them into the 1½ percent notes.

Special issues are sold only to federal agencies and trust funds and cannot be held by the public. The principal agencies that have accumulated special issues are the Federal Old Age and Survivors Insurance Trust Fund, the Unemployment Trust Fund, the Civil Service Retirement Fund, the Railroad Retirement Account, and the National Service Life Insurance Fund. These agencies and trust funds are legally required to invest their funds solely in U.S. government securities. Although they may purchase marketable issues, approximately 80 percent of their holdings consist of special issues. The federal agencies or trust funds may redeem special issues whenever they need cash. In some cases the coupon rate on special issues is related to the average interest rate that the Treasury pays on its outstanding interest-bearing debt, and in others it is regulated by legislation.

When the total amount of special issues increases, it means that the tax receipts of some federal agencies have exceeded their expenditures and that they have invested the excess tax receipts in special issues. Through the purchase of special issues, these tax revenues are made available to finance the expenditures of other departments of the government. An increase in the volume of special issues shows that funds have been transferred from one department to another within the federal government. In contrast, when the total volume of all types of federal securities outstanding increases, it indicates that federal expenditures have exceeded federal receipts and additional securities had to be sold to the public. Since World War II, the value of special issues outstanding has quadrupled.

OWNERSHIP OF THE NATIONAL DEBT

The important groups that own federal securities are individuals, commercial banks, foreign central banks and other foreign accounts in the United States, industrial corporations, the pensions and other funds of state and local governments, insurance companies, and savings institutions. In Table 4.5, the amount owned by each of these groups at the end of 1973 is compared with the amount owned ten years earlier.

In 1973, individuals held almost 30 percent of the total federal debt held by the public. Over three-fourths of their securities consisted of savings bonds.

Commercial banks are another large ownership group. Their holdings at the end of 1973 amounted to 23 percent of the publicly held federal debt. Commercial banks are one of the principal buyers of maturities of from one to five years. They also own a substantial amount of short-term securities maturing within a year. During and immediately following World War II, the Treasury classified securities maturing in ten years and over as "bank-restricted," and commercial banks were not permitted to purchase them. The total amount of government securities owned by commercial banks usually declines during periods of pros-

Table 4.5
Ownership of U.S. Government Securities,
December 1963 and December 1973
(par value in billions of dollars)

TYPE OF HOLDER	END OF DECEMBER 1963	END OF DECEMBER 1973
Individuals	$66.9	$77.2
Commercial banks	64.1	60.3
Nonfinancial corporations	20.7	10.9
State and local governments	20.8	29.2
Insurance companies	11.0	5.7
Mutual savings banks	5.8	2.0
Foreign and international	16.0	55.6
Other investors[a]	13.2	20.8
Debt held by the public	$218.5	$261.7
U.S. government agencies and trust funds	58.0	129.6
Federal Reserve banks	33.6	78.5
Total gross debt	$310.1	$469.8

[a] Includes savings and loan associations, dealers and brokers, corporate pension funds, and nonprofit institutions.
Source: *Federal Reserve Bulletin,* February 1964, p. 206, and March 1974, p. A42.

perity and rises during periods of recession. In periods of prosperity, banks typically get funds to lend by selling or cashing at maturity some of their U.S. government securities. In business recessions, when the demand for loans is slack, banks build up their portfolios of government securities. At the end of 1973, a year of heavy demand for loans, commercial banks held $7 billion less in government securities than they did a year earlier.

In recent years, foreign and international accounts in the United States have become the third largest ownership group, holding in 1973 only $5 billion less than the amount owned by United States commercial banks. Foreign central banks and other foreign and international institutions hold part of their dollar balances in U.S. government securities rather than in demand or time deposits. In the postwar period, the favorable balances of payments of foreign countries have caused their dollar balances to increase steadily, and in the period of international monetary turmoil from 1971 to early 1973, their holdings of U.S. government securities approximately tripled. In 1973, the amount held by the foreign and international accounts began to fall. In recent years, special types of nonmarketable securities have been issued for these foreign holders.

The amount of federal securities owned by industrial (nonfinancial) corporations typically varies between $10 billion and $20 billion, and has declined in recent years because of increasing competition with CDs (certificates of deposit in commercial banks) and commercial paper. Large industrial and utility companies need to hold substantial liquid assets for contingencies and large anticipated outlays. Funds accumulated to pay taxes are usually held in the form of federal securities maturing around tax payment dates. As much as possible, they prefer to hold liquid assets that earn interest rather than demand deposits. They own mainly short-term issues and intermediate issues maturing in from one to five years.

Investments in federal securities by state and local governments have increased gradually since World War II. Retirement systems for public school teachers and other public employees have grown, and a portion of these funds are invested in federal securities, usually maturing in over ten years. Some state and local governments invest their idle balances— accumulated between the tax payment date and the time when funds are needed—in federal securities maturing within one year, as a substitute for holding deposits. Also, funds obtained from the sale of state and local government bonds or turnpike bonds are usually invested in federal securities between the time the funds are collected and the time they are spent.

Holdings of government securities by mutual savings banks, life insurance companies, and fire, casualty and marine insurance companies have declined in most years since 1945. These financial institutions invested heavily in those securities during World War II. Since then, they have reduced their holdings of government securities in order to accommodate the demand for mortgage loans.

Other investors include savings and loan associations, dealers and brokers, corporate pension funds, and nonprofit institutions. The rapidly growing savings and loan associations have invested in significant amounts of government securities for liquidity purposes. The holdings of U.S. government securities by other miscellaneous investors are about the same in 1973 as they were in 1965.

YIELD CURVES

Interest yields for different federal securities vary, but reflect differences in maturity rather than in credit risks. For other types of securities, yields also vary because they are not equally safe. The way interest yields vary with the maturity of a bond (the term structure of interest rates) may be illustrated by the yield curves shown in Figure 4.1 for August 31, 1970 and April 30, 1974. These yield curves were obtained by charting the closing yield on those two dates for issues with maturities up to ten years.

The yield curve for August 31, 1970 rises up to a maturity of six years, and then gradually declines. Rising yield curves are typical of periods of economic slack. August 1970 was during the recession of 1969–1970. In recessions, when interest rates are low, the usual expectation is that eventually interest rates are going to rise. Borrowers who expect higher interest rates in the future try to borrow now on long-term contracts. This drives long-term rates up. Lenders, on the other hand, tend to prefer shorter terms if they believe interest rates may be higher later on. This drives short-term rates down. The combination of upward pressure from borrowers on long-term rates and downward pressure from lenders on short-term rates caused the August 1970 yield curve to rise up to a maturity of six years. The gradual decline in the yield curve for maturities from six to ten years was probably the result of the fact that interest rates in 1970 were relatively high for a period of recession. At that time, people apparently expected that after the recovery following the recession, interest rates would level off or decline slightly. The shape of the yield curve is determined both by the expected long-term trend of interest rates and expected cyclical movements. If interest rates were widely judged to be rising secularly, the yield curve would tend to be positive. On the other hand, if people expected a secular decline in rates, the yield curve would be negative for the longer maturities, as it was in August 1970. It is believed by some economists that there is a basic tendency for yield curves to be upward-sloping to compensate for the illiquidity of long-term securities and the greater interest risk.

The downward-sloping yield curve for April 30, 1974 is typical of periods of prosperity when interest rates are high. Relatively high interest rates usually lead to expectations that they will fall later on. If borrowers believe rates may be lower later on, they tend to borrow for short terms, which drives short-term rates up. Lenders, on the other hand, try to put their funds out at long term, reducing long-term rates.

There are two principal theories explaining the relationship between short-term and long-term interest rates—the *expectations* theory and the theory of *market segmentation*.[3] According to the expectations theory, long-term interest rates are an average of the consecutive expected short-term interest rates over the long period. This is illustrated by the equation

$$(1 + R_n)^n = (1 + r_1) (1 + r_2) (1 + r_3) \cdots (1 + r_n) \tag{4.8}$$

where

R_n = interest rate on a long-term security

n = number of years to maturity of the long-term security

$r_1, r_2, \ldots, r_n$ = expected interest rates on one-year securities from the first to the final year of the long-term security

Taking the nth root of both sides of the equation, one plus the interest rate on an n-year security is equal to the geometric average of one plus the individual single-period interest rates that are expected to prevail during the period of n years. This is because investors can choose securities with maturities of different length. If the final value of the longer-term security were less than the final value of investing in a series of short-term securities, investors would bid up the price of the short-term securities until they yielded no more than the longer-term security. According to this theory, a downward-sloping yield curve implies that investors are anticipating a fall in interest rates in the future. If long-term rates are lower than present short-term rates, short-term rates are expected to fall sometime in the next few years. A rising yield curve implies anticipations of a rise in interest rates in the future. Also, according to this theory, one would expect short-term interest rates to fluctuate more

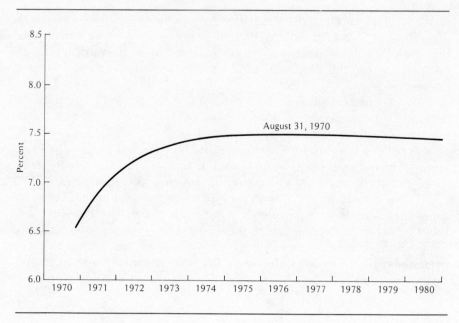

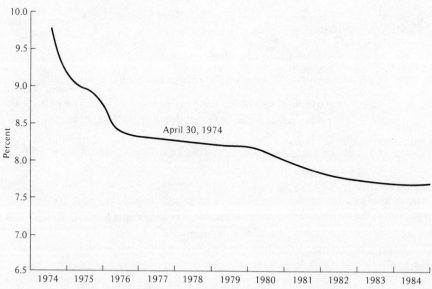

Note: The smooth curve is fitted by eye. Market yields on coupon issues due in less than three months are excluded.

Figure 4.1   Yields of Treasury Securities, August 31, 1970, and April 30, 1974 (based on closing bid quotations).

Source: Treasury Bulletin, September 1970, p. 75, and May 1974, p. 78.

widely than long-term rates because a change in any short-term rate has only a small effect on the sum of short-term rates on which the long-term rate is based.

According to the theory of market segmentation, differences in interest rates are the result of different conditions of supply and demand in the markets for securities with different maturities. It is claimed that the prevalence of the upward-sloping yield curve is the result of hedging against risks. Some investors and financial institutions prefer short-term securities because their prices do not fluctuate widely when interest rates vary; investors invest in them even though the rate of return may be less than on long-term securities. The lower interest rates on short-term than on long-term securities is referred to as a *liquidity premium*. According to this theory, the downward-sloping yield curve that typically occurs during the late part of a business expansion is the result of the need for commercial banks to liquidate more of their short-term government securities in the face of pressure exerted by the Federal Reserve System and of continued demands for loans. Such sales cause the substantial increases in yields on these securities.

INTEREST YIELDS, 1950–1973

Figure 4.2 shows the trend of interest rates for three classes of U.S. government securities from 1950 to 1973. The rate for three-month bills shows the movement of short-term rates; the rates on three- to five-year notes and bonds show the movement of intermediate rates, and the rates on long-term bonds show the movement of long-term interest rates.

Interest rates have risen as the economy has prospered. The demand for credit appears to have increased faster than the supply. In recent years, expectations of inflation have added to the upward trend of interest rates. When inflation is expected, lenders seek higher rates of interest so as to earn a real rate of return, and borrowers are willing to pay higher rates of interest because they anticipate earning a higher rate of return because of the expected inflation.

SUMMARY

The principal kind of nonmarketable United States government security —savings bonds—is an important type of liquid asset.

The different ways in which the United States Treasury may sell marketable securities are by auction, exchange, and subscription.

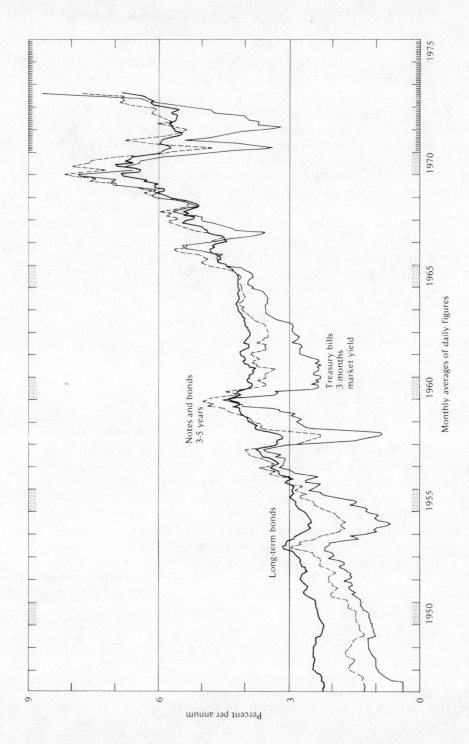

Figure 4.2 Yields on U. S. Government Securities, 1950–1973

Source: Board of Governors of the Federal Reserve System, *Historical Chart Book, 1973,* p. 25.

The yields on marketable United States government securities fall when their prices rise and rise when their prices fall. The movements of these yields reflect changing conditions in the economy, and they also have an impact on other types of lending and securities markets.

Yield curves show the variations in the yields of United States government securities that have maturities of different length. When the yields on issues with long maturities are less than those with short maturities, this may indicate that traders are expecting interest rates to fall in the future. On the other hand, when yields on longer-term issues are higher than those on shorter-term issues, it may indicate expectations of rising interest rates.

NOTES

1. For a detailed description of the kinds of U.S. government securities, see *Handbook of Securities of the United States Government and Federal Agencies,* 25th ed. (New York: First Boston Corp., 1972); and G. Walter Woodworth, *The Money Market and Monetary Management,* 2d ed. (New York: Harper and Row, 1972), chapter 5.
2. Robert H. Parks, "Income and Tax Aspects of Commercial Bank Portfolio Operations in Treasury Securities," *National Tax Journal* 11 (March 1958), pp. 21–34.
3. Eli Shapiro, Ezra Solomon, and William L. White, *Money and Banking,* 5th ed. (New York: Holt, Rinehart, and Winston, 1968), pp. 334–341.

QUESTIONS

4.1. Explain the difference between marketable and nonmarketable U.S. government securities.
4.2. What are the different characteristics of United States Treasury bills, notes, and bonds?
4.3. Explain and compare the different techniques that the United States Treasury uses to market government securities.
4.4. Calculate the bill rate for a bill with ninety-one days to maturity and a price of 98.827. Calculate the coupon-issue yield equivalent for the same bill.

4.5.   If a bond, priced at $94.27, has a coupon rate of interest of 4⅛ percent and has exactly four years to its maturity date, what would be the approximate yield to maturity?

4.6.   Explain why prices of bonds may fall below their maturity value and sell at a discount. At times, why may they sell at a premium?

4.7.   Why are U.S. savings bonds considered to be liquid assets?

4.8.   What are some of the different types of investors in U.S. government securities?

4.9.   What is a yield curve? Explain why yield curves may slope downward in periods of prosperity and high interest rates generally. Why may they slope upward in periods of recession?

4.10.   What are the reasons for the upward trend of interest yields on U.S. government securities since World War II?

4.11.   Why do interest yields on U.S. government securities tend to rise in periods of prosperity and fall in periods of recession?

4.12.   Know the meaning and significance of the following terms and concepts: national debt, marketable and nonmarketable securities, bill auction, debt refunding, bill rate, yield to maturity, yield curve, interest risk, credit risk.

FOUNDED A.D. MDCCXCV.

Chapter 5
The Commercial
Banking System

Commercial banks are organized in many different ways. Some
commercial banks are national banks, and others are state banks;
some are members of the Federal Reserve System, but a majority are
not; some banks have branches, but most do not. In recent years,
holding companies owning banks have grown in importance.
Government regulations have significantly influenced the number
and organization of commercial banks.

In early 1974, there were 14,172 commercial banks in the United
States. Each of those banks had received a charter authorizing it to do
business as a corporation and to engage in banking. Commercial banks
hold demand deposits upon which customers write checks. They may
also accept savings deposits, operate a trust department, rent out safe
deposit boxes, deal in U.S. government securities or foreign exchange,
sell travelers' checks, issue credit cards, record stock transfers, and offer
computer services.

The number of commercial banks today is less than half the number
just after World War I. In 1921, there were 29,788 banks in the United
States. By 1929 the number had declined to 24,026, as many small banks
in declining agricultural areas went out of business. During the Great
Depression, one-third of the banks ceased operations, and by 1934 there
were only 15,484. Following World War II the banking population continued to decline primarily because of mergers. Table 5.1 shows that
from 1947 to 1962 the number of banks declined from 14,181 to 13,427.
From 1962 to 1973 there have been periods in which there have been
significant increases in the number of banks because of a more liberal
government policy toward the granting of new charters. In 1973 the
number of banks was approximately the same as in 1947.

The percentage distribution of banks by size of their deposits is
shown in Table 5.2. In 1973, the largest commercial banking company,

Table 5.1
The Number of Commercial Banks and Bank
Branches Located in the United States,
Selected Years, 1934–1973

END OF YEAR	NUMBER OF BANKS	NUMBER OF BANK BRANCHES
1934	15,484	3,007
1941	14,278	3,564
1947	14,181	4,161
1951	14,089	5,153
1962	13,427	12,345
1963	13,569	13,498
1964	13,761	14,601
1965	13,804	15,756
1966	13,770	16,908
1967	13,721	17,928
1968	13,679	19,013
1969	13,662	20,208
1970	13,688	21,643
1971	13,784	23,104
1972	13,928	24,622
1973	14,172	26,454

Source: *Federal Reserve Bulletin,* February 1974, p. A98.

the BankAmerica Corporation in California, had total deposits of $41 billion.[1] Forty-eight banking companies in the United States each have total deposits over $2 billion. Most banks, however, are small. In 1972, the median size was close to $10 million in deposits.

NATIONAL BANKS AND STATE BANKS

A national bank is a bank that obtained its charter to do business from the comptroller of the currency in the United States Treasury Department. All other commercial banks are state banks and obtained their charters from their state governments. At the end of 1973, there were 4,661 national banks. Although this was only 32 percent of the total number of banks, they held almost 60 percent of the total deposits in commercial banks. The term *national* is included in the name of many banks and indicates their chartering authority.

Table 5.2
Size Distribution of Insured Commercial
Banks, Member Banks, and Insured
Nonmember Banks, 1972

NUMBER OF BANKS	INSURED COMMERCIAL BANKS	MEMBER BANKS	INSURED NONMEMBER BANKS
	13,733	5,706	8,027
Total Deposits (in millions)	**Percentage in Class**		
Less than $2	5%	2%	7%
$2–$5	19	10	26
$5–$10	24	20	27
$10–$25	30	34	27
$25–$50	12	16	8
$50–$100	5	9	3
$100–$500	4	7	2
$500 and over	1	2	0
Total	100%	100%	100%

Source: Federal Deposit Insurance Corporation, *Annual Report 1972* (Washington, D.C., 1973), p. 231.

The first modern bank in the United States was the Bank of North America established in Philadelphia on December 31, 1781. After the American Revolution, banking developed quite rapidly. In 1800 there were twenty-nine banks in the United States, and twenty years later the number exceeded three hundred. These earliest banks were chartered by special acts of state legislatures. Before the existence of these state-chartered banks, there were colonial loan offices or private associations that made loans—usually with land as collateral—and issued paper money. They were not incorporated, were usually designed to finance specific needs, lasted only for the duration of their loans, and did not have deposits on which customers wrote checks.[2]

In the late 1830s, both Michigan and New York passed "free banking acts" establishing general incorporation of banks and making it unnecessary for state legislatures to approve each charter application. These laws made it relatively easy to establish a bank. About half of the states adopted similar laws by 1860. Along with those changes came increased regulation by state banking commissions. Bank examinations were made on a regular basis, rather than only at times of difficulty. Several states required a specified amount of specie reserves (gold and silver) behind the notes issued by a bank, but others required only bonds and certain types of securities. As time went on, banks began holding deposits in large urban banks as part of their reserves. Only two states required reserves against deposit liabilities before 1863.

National charters for banks were provided for in the Currency Act of 1863, as amended by the National Bank Act of 1864. The granting of charters of incorporation by the federal government is unusual. Most corporations have charters granted by state governments. The original intention of the Civil War banking acts was to set up a single system of national banks coordinated by the federal government. These banks would issue a uniform currency, strengthen the market for federal securities, and be of assistance to the federal government in managing the relatively large national debt that had been created during the Civil War.

The regulations governing the chartering of national banks allow much room for judgment on the part of the comptroller of the currency. From 1864 to 1875 many applications for national bank charters were not approved.[3] After the Specie Resumption Act of 1875, the policy changed and banks that met certain standards were said to be "entitled" to a charter. A period of "free banking" existed from then until 1925. In the 1920s the comptrollers became more restrictive because of the bank failures connected with depressed agricultural conditions. After the wave of bank failures in the 1930s, it was widely believed that state bank chartering should be curtailed. In the end, states retained their privilege of chartering banks, but after the Federal Deposit Insurance Corporation was set up in 1934, federal authorities achieved some control over most state banks by being able to withhold deposit insurance if the banks did not meet certain standards. For many years after the Great Depression, comptrollers of the currency exercised extreme caution in granting national bank charters. During the administration of James J. Saxon from 1961 to 1966, this policy was changed. Table 5.3 shows that in the four years starting in 1962, 512 newly organized banks received national charters—compared to only 307 in the previous sixteen years. Since 1970 there has been a slight increase in the number of newly chartered national banks, and since 1969 the number of newly chartered state banks has increased significantly.

Existing banks oppose the organization of competing banks, and have often succeeded in preventing the granting of new charters. Federal authorities do not want to charter a bank that will eventually fail because of inadequate resources or incompetent management. Failure of a bank is costly and inconvenient for the public, subjects the regulatory agency to criticism, and may be destabilizing for the banking system and the economy. The chances of failing are greater for a new bank than for an established one, and there is always a possibility that a new bank may harm an established one. However, avoiding the risk of chartering new banks that may fail must be balanced against the gain in competition and

Table 5.3
Number of New Commercial Banks,
by Chartering Authority, 1946–1972

YEAR	NATIONAL	STATE	TOTAL
1946	21	124	145
1947	19	93	112
1948	14	64	78
1949	12	55	67
1950	6	61	67
1951	9	51	60
1952	15	52	67
1953	12	52	64
1954	18	54	72
1955	28	87	115
1956	29	90	119
1957	20	64	84
1958	18	74	92
1959	23	92	115
1960	32	93	125
1961	26	82	108
1962	63	116	179
1963	163	137	300
1964	200	135	335
1965	88	111	199
1966	25	98	123
1967	18	91	109
1968	15	75	90
1969	16	119	135
1970	40	145	185
1971	37	166	203
1972	55	218	273

Source: Federal Deposit Insurance Corporation, *Annual Report,* various issues, Tables 101 and 102.

the increase in banking facilities. In recent years the growth in the number of banks chartered and of bank branches has increased competition among banks. This has been regarded as a cause of some of the changes favoring bank customers, such as the expansion and greater convenience of banking hours and the reduction in service charges. Professor Alhadeff, an authority on the banking system, is critical of the rejection of charter applications on the basis of the usual attempts to forecast the need in the community for another bank. He believes that such efforts are unreliable and result in inefficiency and reduced competition.[4]

Historically, one of the major requirements of a national bank was its minimum capital investment. To qualify for a charter, a national bank has to sell a minimum amount of stock and, in addition, has to have a surplus of 20 percent of its outstanding capital stock. For banks in communities with a population of less than 6,000, the minimum amount of capital stock is $50,000; for those in towns with between 6,000 and 50,000 people, it is $100,000; and for larger communities, it is $200,000. Today these requirements are relatively small and of little practical significance. The capital requirement of most state banks is even smaller than that for national banks.

The combination of national and state chartered banks is frequently referred to as a "dual system" of banking. Although national banks enjoy more prestige and some other advantages, the higher capital requirements, higher reserve requirements, and stricter regulation of national banks have encouraged many banks to operate under state charters.

MEMBER AND NONMEMBER BANKS

A member bank is a commercial bank that has applied and been accepted for membership in the Federal Reserve System. By law, all national banks must be members. State banks may join the system if they desire to do so and if they meet the qualifications. At the end of 1973, only 12 percent of approximately 9,300 state banks were member banks. The state banks not belonging to the system were generally small. At the end of 1973, member banks accounted for only 41 percent of the number of insured commercial banks, but they held 79 percent of the total deposits.

Table 5.2 shows the distribution by size of the 5,706 member banks in 1972. Though the median size bank had between $10 million and $25 million in deposits, 9 percent had deposits of over $100 million and 12 percent had deposits of less than $5 million. The median size of nonmember insured banks was between $5 million and $10 million in deposits.

Both the national banks and the state banks that belong to the Federal Reserve System must meet the reserve requirements established. The System requires all member banks to hold a certain percentage of their deposits either as vault cash or as deposits at the Federal Reserve banks. A small fine is assessed against deficient reserves, and banks are not allowed to negotiate new loans or pay dividends until the deficiency is corrected. A bank with prolonged or recurrent deficiencies is in danger of losing Federal Reserve membership. State banks that are not members of the Federal Reserve System are also required to hold some reserves behind deposits, but these requirements vary from state to state and are usually less restrictive than those for the member banks.

While member banks have several privileges that nonmember banks do not have, nonmember banks can arrange to use the Federal Reserve's check-clearing facilities. The checks of all banks using these facilities have numbers in the upper right corner identifying the Federal Reserve district, its branch, the city or state, and the bank itself—information needed for routing. All banks using the Federal Reserve's check-clearing facilities must remit at par. This means that they cannot deduct an exchange charge (usually one-tenth of one percent) on checks written on themselves but presented for collection by the Federal Reserve banks. About one percent of the commercial banks do not remit at par. Checks on nonpar banks are usually cleared through correspondent banks.

REGULATION OF BANKS

The Office of the Comptroller of the Currency uses the surprise call as one of its major types of regulation. At least two times every year, on unannounced dates, the comptroller of the currency requires each national bank to report a complete balance sheet of its accounts. There are also regular calls at the end of June and December. The balance sheet for the call date must be published in a local newspaper. In order to be prepared for calls, a bank must keep its accounts at all times in accordance with legal regulations.

The various governmental units concerned with bank examinations have divided among themselves the responsibility for making examinations, so as to avoid duplication. The comptroller of the currency provides for the periodic examination of national banks. The Federal Reserve System examines state banks that are members of the System. The Federal Deposit Insurance Corporation examines state banks that are insured by them but are not member banks. State bank examiners are responsible only for examining the small number of state banks that are not insured by the FDIC but may also examine any other state banks.

The examination of a bank by one of the regulatory agencies occurs at least once a year. The reports of each examining agency are available to the others. Bank examiners check the assets of the bank and their collateral. If a loan is past due and the prospects of being paid off appear to be doubtful, the examiners require the bank to remove the loan from its reported assets. Bank examiners also evaluate whether the bank is being properly managed and look for any possible indications of fraud. After the examiners have completed an examination, they prepare a formal report that is sent to the bank's directors. The directors are responsible for complying with the recommendations made.

During the administration of Comptroller Saxon in the early 1960s, extensive changes were made that removed administrative restrictions on the activities of commercial banks.[5] Few types of businesses have been subject to such extensive government regulation as have commercial banks. Much of the regulation is based on statutes legislated a generation or more ago. Among the recent changes are new rules making it possible for national banks to use preferred stock, capital debentures, and unsecured promissory notes (commercial paper) as methods of financing. Banks have also been allowed to issue stock options to the management and to organize employee stock purchase plans. They are now permitted to engage in the business of underwriting securities issued by state and local governments. The types of securities that banks are allowed to hold have been broadened. As a result of efforts by the comptroller, legislation was passed transferring authority over the trust powers of national banks from the Federal Reserve to the comptroller. These powers have been liberalized to allow banks to develop various types of collective investment funds. A more liberal approach is now taken toward the terms and variety of loans made by national banks. The limits on lending to any one borrower have been increased from 10 percent of capital stock and surplus to 10 percent of capital stock, surplus, and undivided profit. Banks are now allowed to engage in the business of providing computer and payroll services. They have also been permitted to offer savings accounts to business corporations.

Almost all of these innovations were achieved by changing the administrative rules and regulations of the comptroller of the currency. In only a few cases was it necessary to have new legislation passed by Congress. These changes reflected a general movement among the commercial banks to break through the complicated mass of restrictive controls that prevented them from developing new methods of finance suitable for a growing, more complicated economy.

Historically, much of the restrictive banking regulation had been supported by banks themselves and their trade associations. These regulations not only kept banks from competing among themselves, but prevented them from competing with the nonbank intermediaries that had grown very rapidly from 1945 to 1960—the savings and loan associations, mutual savings banks, credit unions, life insurance companies, and pension funds. The new changes were welcomed by the more aggressive bankers. They were opposed by those who feared competition and by federal and state authorities who resisted efforts to curtail their activities.

   In general, the effects of government regulation of commercial banking have been somewhat limited because of the development and growth
of other financial institutions. However, the restrictions on new bank
charters and branches, the maximum limits set on interest paid on deposits, the regulations on certain types of assets and liabilities, and the
federal law limiting the value of the bank building that can be constructed
to a percentage of the bank's equity, have probably lessened competition. A study made in 1965 estimated that if free entry were permitted,
2,200 banks would have entered the industry.[6]

THE FEDERAL DEPOSIT INSURANCE
CORPORATION

The Federal Deposit Insurance Corporation was established in 1934 following the failure of a very large number of banks during the Great
Depression. The establishment of deposit insurance is usually considered
to be the most significant banking legislation since the creation of the
Federal Reserve System. Initially, it did not have the support of the new
administration of President Franklin D. Roosevelt and was bitterly opposed by some important interests.[7]
   A system of compulsory deposit insurance had been established by
the Safety Fund Act in the state of New York as early as 1829. It required
banks, as their charters came up for renewal, to join a contributory fund
in order to protect both depositors and the holders of notes which at
that time were issued by commercial banks. Although this fund helped
in the repayment of bank creditors in the depression of the late 1830s,
it had to be assisted by the state. Five other states set up state-operated
bank insurance systems between 1829 and 1858. After the banking difficulties in the Panic of 1907, eight states set up such plans. Most insurance
systems provided for bank examinations in order not to penalize well-
managed banks. All of these early insurance programs either failed or
ceased operating after a few years.
   Banks that are members of the Federal Reserve System are required
to belong to the FDIC. Although the bulk of the nonmember banks have
also joined, at the end of 1972 there were still 152 state banks that were
not insured—either because they did not choose to belong or because
they could not meet the minimum standards required.
   Today the FDIC insures the deposit of each individual or firm in each
bank up to $40,000. The premium for coverage is one-twelfth of one
percent of total deposits, and is paid by the bank. One criticism of this
insurance is that, even though it insures each deposit only up to $40,000,

the premium charged is based on the total amount of the bank's deposits. Because of the ceiling on coverage, not all of the deposits of banks are insured.

Table 5.4 shows that since World War II only a few banks have been suspended each year. In the early years of the FDIC, the number suspended was much larger. The closed banks have usually been small. In 1967, for example, the four insured banks that failed had either engaged in fraud or were reported to have managerial weaknesses. The total deposits of those four banks averaged only $2.7 million. More than 98 percent of their depositors were reimbursed in full. In most cases, when the FDIC authorities take over, they arrange for a merger with another bank. This results in a minimum of inconvenience for both the depositors and the borrowers. The FDIC has aimed to avoid shutting down banks in order to assure that normal banking service can continue in the community.

In the last ten years several very large banks have failed—the Public Bank of Detroit in 1966, the United States National Bank of San Diego in 1973, and the Franklin National Bank of New York in 1974. The latter bank had been the twentieth largest bank in the United States, but had had large losses on loans and foreign exchange. In all cases the FDIC arranged for an immediate merger with another bank. The European-American Bank and Trust company—owned by six large European banks, but chartered by the state of New York—won the bid to take over the Franklin National.

The FDIC does more than protect depositors against possible losses. The psychological effect of insuring deposits diminishes the prospect of having runs on banks. Prior to the establishment of the FDIC, if people feared that a bank might fail, they withdrew their deposits. Because banks typically have only a small amount of cash reserve behind their deposits, such runs caused them extreme difficulty. In the century prior to the establishment of the FDIC, runs on banks contributed to the financial panics that accompanied most recessions. The removal of this incentive to withdraw deposits is an important contribution to financial stability.

BRANCH BANKING

In most foreign countries there are only a few banks, each with numerous branches. In the United States, the most common type of bank is the *unit bank,* a bank without branches. At the end of 1972, 68 percent of the total number of commercial banks were of this type.

Table 5.1 shows the rapid increase in the number of bank branches in the United States since World War II. In 1947 there were only 4,161

Table 5.4
Number of Banks Closed Because
of Financial Difficulties, 1934–1972

YEAR	INSURED BY FDIC	NONINSURED	TOTAL NUMBER CLOSED
1934	9	52	61
1935	26	6	32
1936	69	3	72
1937	76	7	83
1938	73	7	80
1939	60	12	72
1940	43	5	48
1941	14	2	16
1942	20	3	23
1943	5	0	5
1944	2	0	2
1945	1	0	1
1946	1	1	2
1947	5	1	6
1948	3	0	3
1949	5	4	9
1950	4	1	5
1951	2	3	5
1952	3	1	4
1953	4	1	5
1954	2	2	4
1955	5	0	5
1956	2	1	3
1957	2	1	3
1958	4	5	9
1959	3	0	3
1960	1	1	2
1961	5	4	9
1962	1	2	3
1963	2	0	2
1964	7	1	8
1965	5	4	9
1966	7	1	8
1967	4	0	4
1968	3	0	3
1969	9	0	9
1970	7	1	8
1971	6	0	6
1972	1	2	3

Source: Federal Deposit Insurance Corporation, *Annual Report, 1972* (Washington, D.C., 1973), p. 277.

branch offices. By 1973, the number of branches had risen to over 26,000. Since 1960, the number of banks having branches has almost doubled.

The regulations of some states do not allow banks to have branches. In other states, branches must be within the city or county in which the bank is located. Supervisory officials must approve both the formation of new branches and mergers with other banks. Restrictions on branch banking are gradually breaking down, and in 1972 a presidential commission on the regulation of financial institutions, known as the Hunt Commission, recommended that state laws be changed to allow branching on a statewide basis.[8]

From 1869 to 1911, rulings by the Comptroller of the Currency severely restricted the development of branch banking even though, before the Civil War, branch banking had developed in the Middle West and in the South.[9] The legislation setting up the National Banking System neither forbade nor allowed national banks to have branches, and the 1865 law which taxed state bank notes 10 percent (so as to induce state banks to become national banks) had mentioned circumstances under which state banks with branches could become national banks. Even so, before 1918 the comptrollers of the currency did not permit any national banks to have branches. After World War I, continuous efforts were made to liberalize those laws, and in 1927 the McFadden Act permitted national banks to open branches within the limits of the city, town, or village if state laws did not forbid them. During the 1930s and 1940s, few permits to open up branches were granted because of the Great Depression and World War II. It was not until after World War II that branch banking expanded rapidly.

The resistance to branch banking is due partly to the reluctance of bankers and bank owners in rural areas to give up control of their banks. Many small communities appear to prefer local control of their banking institutions. There is a question about which type of bank, the branch bank or the unit bank, can best serve the needs of rural communities and suburbs. Unit banks can obtain many of the services that branches have by maintaining a correspondent relationship with larger banks. Although large-scale operations may increase the efficiency of banking, decentralization may have the opposite effect. Several studies have concluded that the economies of scale in banking are relatively small and are less than the diseconomies of branch banking.[10] On the other hand, one important statistical study concluded that large banks with branches are, on the average, more profitable than large unit banks of comparable size.[11] This study found that average costs per $100 of loans and investments for unit banks declined as bank size increased up to $2 million in deposits, were fairly constant from a size of $2 million deposits to $50 million, and declined again for banks above that size.[12]

Since 1965, there has been a rapid expansion of foreign branches of United States banks.[13] The Board of Governors of the Federal Reserve System must approve applications made by member banks to establish branches in foreign countries. These foreign branches are not included in the number of bank branches in Table 5.1. In 1972, 107 United States banks had 627 foreign branches. By late 1973, their assets amounted to $121 billion—over 15 percent of the total U.S. assets of all commercial banks. United States banks have expanded their overseas operations in order to serve better the expanding multinational corporations. Also, measures taken by the federal government to reduce the United States balance of payments deficit, such as the Interest Equalization Tax of 1963 and the Voluntary Foreign Credit Restraint programs had, until they were ended in 1974, the effect of stimulating the growth of foreign sources of financing.

In recent years, the number of foreign banks with operations in the United States has expanded rapidly.[14] They must operate under state charters since the directors of national banks must be United States citizens. By 1972, there were about 150 foreign banks with offices, agencies, or branches in this country, and their assets in the United States reached $13 billion. Many of these foreign banks have only a representative office which develops business to be handled by the parent bank. To make loans in the United States, these banks must establish either an *agency* which accepts only foreign-owned deposits, or a *branch* which can accept both foreign and domestic-owned deposits. Nine states allow no foreign-bank operations of any kind, and very few allow extensive operations. The laws of the State of New York allow foreign banks to accept both domestic and foreign-owned deposits and to make the same types of loans that domestic banks make. Since 1973, Illinois has allowed full-service branches of foreign banks in downtown Chicago if reciprocity is granted. The FDIC does not offer insurance for depositors in foreign branches. Some foreign banks have branches or agencies in more than one state, making an interstate set-up possible that is not allowed for domestic banks. In 1974, the Federal Reserve Board was studying proposals for curbing interstate foreign banking. These foreign banks can engage in investment banking as well as commercial banking, while the Glass-Steagall Act prevents domestic banks from engaging in investment banking. Both in the United States and in Europe, some of the major banks in the world have combined to establish branches or agencies. These are known as *multibanks* and have the advantage of pooling the expertise of bankers familiar with conditions in different countries.

BANK MERGERS

From 1952 through 1972, there have been between 100 and 200 consol-idations, mergers, or absorptions a year. In most cases, small banks are combined with large ones. In 1972, 112 banks which together had re-sources of $3 billion were absorbed by 100 banks which together had assets of $30 billion. A bank wishing to expand its operations often finds it easier to get permission to absorb a small bank than to set up a new branch. Mergers reduce the number of banks and eliminate the compe-tition between the branch and the parent bank.

The Bank Merger Act of 1960 makes federal bank regulatory agen-cies responsible for the approval of mergers—the comptroller of the currency for national banks that plan to absorb another bank, the Board of Governors of the Federal Reserve System for state member banks, and the FDIC for insured nonmember banks. The Bank Merger Act of 1966 forbids mergers that substantially lessen competition unless some other advantages outweigh this and make a merger desirable.[15] In addition, the Justice Department has used antitrust legislation to prevent several bank mergers that would have seriously threatened competition. In the im-portant Philadelphia National Bank case of 1963, the United States Su-preme Court approved of action taken by the Department of Justice to prevent a merger of the Philadelphia National Bank and the Girard Trust Corn Exchange Bank, even though the merger had been approved by the comptroller of the currency.[16] If the Justice Department intervenes, it must start proceedings within thirty days after the agency's final approval, and the merger must be suspended until litigation resolves the issue. Some proposed mergers have been aborted by this type of action.

BANK HOLDING COMPANIES

Bank holding companies—either separate corporations, or banks that own a sufficient amount of the stock in one or more banks to have a controlling interest—are a means of linking together the management of a group of banks or of a group of enterprises engaged in businesses related to banking. Historically they were set up to obtain some of the advantages of branch banking, and had the unique advantage of making it possible to control a group of banks in more than one state. In 1960, Western Bancorporation, one of the earliest large bank holding com-panies of this type, controlled banks in California, Oregon, Washington, Nevada, Arizona, Idaho, New Mexico, Utah, Colorado, Wyoming, and Montana.[17]

Because some bank holding companies are very large and may concentrate economic power, there has been pressure to bring them under government control. Federal legislation, starting with the Banking Act of 1933, has also aimed at a basic separation of bank (and bank-related) activities from other business activities. Because of the unclear legal status of bank holding companies that existed for many years, and the opposition of some banking interests, bank holding companies did not expand rapidly until the mid-1960s. The Bank Holding Company Act of 1956 provided for registration of companies holding 25 percent or more of the stock of two or more banks, barred new bank acquisitions across state lines, and set up regulations over the acquisition of additional voting stock in banks. It also prohibited registered holding companies from engaging in non-bank-related activities, and several banking corporations were required to separate their banking and nonbanking activities. After 1956, one-bank holding companies that were excluded from regulation increased rapidly in number. In 1970, new legislation extended government regulation to one-bank holding companies—usually those owning 25 percent or more of the stock of a bank.[18] The Federal Reserve Board was given authority to administer the 1970 regulations and to determine when undue control exists and when exceptions should be allowed. The bill aimed especially to prevent banks from requiring special tie-in deals in order to obtain bank loans.

Table 5.5 shows that the number of registered holding companies increased sharply in 1972 after one-bank holding companies were required to register. In 1965 there were estimated to be approximately 400 one-bank holding companies, most of which controlled small banks. Between then and the end of 1968, the number of one-bank holding companies almost doubled.[19] Many large banks have established holding companies to get around interest rate ceilings on savings and time deposits. Federal regulations do not prevent holding companies from raising funds by selling commercial paper at rates above those set by the Federal Reserve's Regulation Q on savings and time deposits. As a result, when market interest rates rose above the ceilings set by Regulation Q, some of the large bank holding companies were able to replace funds lost from time and savings deposits with funds raised through the sale of commercial paper. In the early 1970s, another major objective of bank holding companies was to diversify into bank-related activities such as leasing, factoring, and investment or advisory services. The organization of bank holding companies has enabled banks to extend their operations outside the usual state boundaries. Table 5.5 shows that in 1972 over 60 percent of the deposits in commercial banks in the United States were in banks owned by holding companies.

Table 5.5
Number of Registered Bank Holding
Companies, Banks and Branches
Controlled, and Total Deposits,
Selected Years, 1957–1972

END OF YEAR	NUMBER OF REGISTERED HOLDING COMPANIES	BANKS HELD	TOTAL BRANCHES	TOTAL DEPOSITS OF BANKS HELD (IN BILLIONS)	TOTAL DEPOSITS OF BANKS HELD AS PERCENT OF TOTAL U.S. COMMERCIAL BANK DEPOSITS
1957	50	417	851	$ 15.1	7.5%
1963	52	454	1,278	22.5	8.2
1968	80	629	2,262	57.6	13.2
1970	121	895	3,260	78.1	16.2
1972	1,607	2,720	13,441	379.4	61.5

Source: *Federal Reserve Bulletin*, October 1958, p. 1,224; June 1964, p. 783; August 1969, p. A96; August 1971, p. A98; and June 1973, p. A102.

CORRESPONDENT BANKING

Not as close a relationship exists between correspondent banks as between branch banks, but the correspondent bank relationship does lead to a certain amount of group cooperation. Through their correspondent relationship, banks in an informal way have arranged themselves into a network of cooperating units. A small bank establishes a correspondent relationship by keeping deposits in a larger bank. Larger banks may establish a similar relationship by keeping deposits with each other. In January 1974 there was $31.6 billion in interbank demand deposits and $6.4 billion in interbank time deposits.

Large banks compete to hold the interbank deposits of smaller banks because they provide the larger banks with funds to invest. State banks that are not members of the Federal Reserve System typically are required to deposit some funds in a larger bank as reserves. In return for the deposit, the smaller bank receives from the larger bank advice, information, borrowed funds in time of need, help on international transactions, and the provision of some infrequently needed services that it would not pay the smaller bank to offer. Correspondent banks may lend to each other and cooperate on making loans to customers.

ASSOCIATED BANKS

Banks may be associated with each other by having one or more common directors. Independent banks linked in this way are sometimes called chain banks and are most common in states that prohibit branch banking and where holding companies are not widely used to operate banks.[20] A study of the sixty-four national banks chartered in 1962 found that over half had some connection with another bank.[21] This relationship was in the form of a common director or owner. Generally the associated bank will supply the new bank with services and funds more automatically and at less cost than would a correspondent bank. The new national banks chartered in 1962 that were associated with other banks had advantages in their earliest years over those that were completely independent. Since 1935, the Clayton Act has prohibited interlocking directorates between member banks of the Federal Reserve System located in the same or neighboring cities or towns. It was feared that such interlocks diminished competition. In the early 1970s, some states extended the prohibition of interlocking directorates in the same locality to all insured commercial banks, mutual savings banks, and savings and loan associations.

THE RESPONSIBILITIES OF BANK DIRECTORS AND OFFICERS

The stockholders of a bank elect the bank's directors. The number of votes of each stockholder depends on the number of shares of stock owned. The chairman of the board of directors is elected by the directors. The directors usually meet at least once a month to pass on certain routine matters, to set charges, to hear and discuss reports, to approve changes in officer personnel, and to discuss problems and policies with the officers of the bank. Directors of national banks must be stockholders of the bank, and their legal responsibilities are usually greater than those of directors of other corporations.[22] Directors are subject to severe penalties for falsifying records or accepting fees from customers.

The president, and in some important banks the chairman of the board and the vice-chairman, are usually the top management of the organization. They conduct the affairs of the bank and hire and supervise the employees. Other important officers are the vice-presidents in charge of the various banking activities, the trust officers, and the cashier and other officers in charge of bank operations.

SUMMARY

Although over the years competition may have been reduced by the decline in the number of commercial banks and by barriers to entering the field of banking, the rapid growth of other financial institutions outside commercial banking has increased competition.

Most banks have some connection with other banks through a correspondent relationship, branching, or a common owner or holding company. In recent years, bank holding companies and foreign branches of United States banks have expanded rapidly.

Supervision and examination of banks by the Federal Reserve System, the Office of the Comptroller of the Currency, and state banking commissions have probably made banks more stable institutions than they were in the past.

The nature of modern commercial banking has evolved over the years and continues to change because of new regulations, new demands, opportunities for profit, tax advantages, and the development of specialized markets in which certain assets can be traded. In the past decade banks have entered several new bank-related fields—among them the credit-card and computer services fields.

NOTES

1. "The Fifty Largest Banking Companies," *Fortune* 90 (July 1974), pp. 114–115.
2. Bray Hammond, *Banks and Politics in America* (Princeton: Princeton University Press, 1957), chapters 1 and 6.
3. Ross M. Robertson, "The Comptroller and Bank Supervision: A Historical Appraisal," *National Banking Review* 4 (March 1967), pp. 247–261.
4. David A. Alhadeff, "A Reconsideration of Restrictions on Bank Entry," *Quarterly Journal of Economics* 76 (May 1962), pp. 246–263.
5. "Years of Reform: A Prelude to Progress," in U. S. Comptroller of the Currency, *101st Annual Report, 1963* (Washington, D.C., 1964), pp. 1–32.
6. Sam Peltzman, "Bank Entry Regulation: Its Impact and Purpose," *National Banking Review* 3 (December 1965), p. 174.
7. Carter H. Golembe, "The Deposit Insurance Legislation of 1933," *Political Science Quarterly* 75 (June 1960), pp. 181–200.
8. *Report of the President's Commission on Financial Structure and Regulation* (Washington, D.C.: U.S. Government Printing Office, December 1971), pp. 61–62.
9. Ross M. Robertson, *The Comptroller and Bank Supervision* (Wash-

ington, D.C.: Office of the Comptroller of the Currency, 1968), p. 101.

10.   Paul M. Horvitz, "Economies of Scale in Banking," in Commission on Money and Credit, *Private Financial Institutions* (Englewood Cliffs, N.J.: Prentice-Hall, 1963), pp. 1–54; George J. Benston, "Economies of Scale and Marginal Costs in Banking Operations," in Kalman J. Cohen and Frederick S. Hammer, eds., *Analytical Methods in Banking* (Homewood, Ill.: Richard D. Irwin, 1966), pp. 545–574, and "Branch Banking and Economies of Scale," *Journal of Finance* 20 (May 1965), pp. 312–331; and Frederick W. Bell and Neil B. Murphy, *Economies of Scale in Commercial Banking* (Boston: Federal Reserve Bank of Boston, 1967), pp. 20–21.

11.   David A. Alhadeff, *Monopoly and Competition in Banking* (Berkeley: University of California Press, 1954), p. 192.

12.   *Ibid.*, pp. 77–87. For a review of research on the economies of scale, see Robert C. Holland, "Research into Banking Structure and Competition," *Federal Reserve Bulletin* 50 (November 1964), pp. 1383–1399.

13.   Board of Governors of the Federal Reserve System, *59th Annual Report, 1972* (Washington, D.C.: U.S. Government Printing Office, 1973), p. 213.

14.   See Federal Reserve Bank of San Francisco, "Foreign Banks," *Business and Financial Letter,* December 14, 1973.

15.   William A. Carter, "Bank Mergers: The New Law and Renewed Litigation," *Antitrust Bulletin* 12 (Spring 1967), pp. 109–126.

16.   Irwin M. Stelzer, *Selected Antitrust Cases,* 3d ed. (Homewood, Ill.: Richard D. Irwin, 1966), pp. 130–153; and Administrator of National Banks, United States Treasury, "Part One: Merger Policy: The Philadelphia Case," in *Studies in Banking Competition and the Banking Structure* (Washington, D.C., 1966), pp. 3–96.

17.   Gerald C. Fischer, *Bank Holding Companies* (New York: Columbia University Press, 1961).

18.   *Federal Reserve Bulletin,* January 1971, pp. 29–33.

19.   See Carter H. Golembe, "One-Bank Holding Companies," in Herbert V. Prochnow, ed., *The One-Bank Holding Company* (Chicago: Rand McNally, 1969), pp. 66–81.

20.   Jerome C. Darnell, "Determinants of Chain Banking," *National Banking Review* 4 (June 1967), pp. 459–468.

21.   David C. Motter, "Bank Formation and the Public Interest," *National Banking Review* 2 (March 1965), p. 317.

22.   U. S. Comptroller of the Currency, *Duties and Liabilities of Directors of National Banks,* rev. ed. (Washington, D.C., 1968).

QUESTIONS

5.1. What are the differences between a national and a state bank? Between a member and a nonmember bank?

5.2. What are the arguments for and against "free banking"?

5.3. What are the functions of the comptroller of the currency?

5.4. How does the Federal Deposit Insurance Corporation promote economic stability?

5.5. Describe bank examinations as a method of governmental regulation of banks.

5.6. Describe the history of the regulations preventing bank branches in the United States.

5.7. What are the objectives of bank holding companies?

5.8. Describe some of the ways in which unit banks may achieve some of the advantages of branch banking.

5.9. Know the meaning and significance of the following terms and concepts: commercial bank, national bank, state bank, correspondent bank, deposit insurance, bank examination, bank holding company.

Chapter 6
The Cash
Assets and Investments
of Commercial Banks

The principal financial activities that commercial banks engage in may be illustrated by examining each of the items on the balance sheet of a commercial bank. Their assets include various types of cash and investments.

The balance sheet as of April 24, 1974, of the Dartmouth National Bank, located in Hanover, New Hampshire, is shown in Table 6.1. Although banks differ somewhat from one another, the balance sheet of this bank is typical of small and medium-sized banks. On the date when the balance sheet was prepared, the cash in vault and the securities (valued at their purchase prices) were counted, the amount of the loans was calculated, and a value was determined for each of the other types of assets, liabilities, reserve for bad debt losses, and capital accounts. The assets are the property that the bank owns; the liabilities are its debts; and the capital accounts show the amount originally invested by the owners, modified by retained profits and losses thereafter. The assets must equal the liabilities plus the reserve for bad debt losses and the capital accounts. Each transaction affecting a bank's operations results in two balancing entries: for example, in increasing one asset and decreasing another asset, or in increasing an asset and simultaneously increasing a liability. The fundamental technique that is involved is called double-entry bookkeeping.

The first item listed on the balance sheet consists of three types of cash assets: cash in vault, balances with other banks (including its Federal Reserve bank), and cash items in process of collection.

Table 6.1
Report of the Condition of the Dartmouth
National Bank of Hanover, April 24, 1974 [a]

Assets

Cash, balances at other banks, and checks in process of collection	$ 2,029,233.31
U.S. Treasury securities	1,513,421.88
Obligations of states and political subdivisions	3,183,252.97
Other securities	41,000.00
Loans	8,855,647.22
Federal funds sold	1,000,000.00
Furniture, fixtures, and miscellaneous	291,399.21
Total assets	$16,913,954.59

Liabilities

Demand deposits of individuals, partnerships, and corporations	$11,315,010.53
Time and savings deposits of individuals, partnerships, and corporations	1,091,760.73
Deposits of United States government	472,406.49
Deposits of states and political subdivisions	640,436.01
Certified and officers' checks, etc.	116,374.12
Other liabilities	309,314.37
Total liabilities	$13,945,302.25

Reserve for bad debt losses on loans

(set up pursuant to IRS rulings)	$ 142,260.26

Capital accounts

Common stock—total par value	$ 200,000.00
Surplus	1,000,000.00
Undivided profits	1,538,392.08
Reserve for contingencies and other capital reserves	88,000.00
Total capital accounts	$ 2,826,392.08
Total liabilities, reserves, and capital accounts	$16,913,954.59

[a] Published in response to a call made by the comptroller of the currency.

CASH IN VAULT

Cash in vault consists of the coins and paper money in the bank's vault or cash drawers. A bank must always have coins and paper money on hand because its demand and time deposits are legally payable in cash. Each day some of the customers can be expected to request cash. A bank must have all of the various denominations of coins and paper money on hand so that it can provide its customers with the kind as well as the quantity of cash they want.

Because, on a daily basis, the cash deposited by customers approximately balances the cash withdrawn, a bank can operate with a relatively small amount of cash in vault compared to its deposits. Excessive amounts of cash on hand are avoided because of the relative ease with which cash can be stolen and because it earns no interest income. Since 1960, banks that are members of the Federal Reserve System have been allowed to count vault cash as part of their legal reserves. This has encouraged banks to hold larger amounts of it.

To illustrate the way in which the movements of cash affect a bank, we use the T-account technique. On one side of the "T" are assets, and on the other side liabilities and capital accounts. If $1,000 in currency were deposited in the bank, the balance sheet would be affected as shown in T-account 6.1:

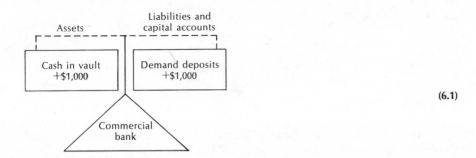

(6.1)

The cash in vault would be increased by $1,000, and the depositor would receive in return an increase in his deposit of $1,000.

A withdrawal of $1,000 in currency would affect the balance sheet as follows:

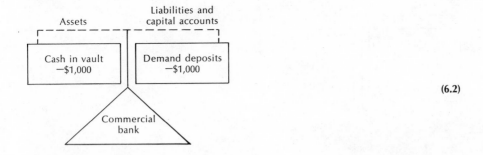

(6.2)

The bank would give the depositor $1,000 from its cash in vault, and the depositor would pay for it by a reduction in his demand deposit of the same amount. Note that the term "deposit" is misleading. The deposit is just a bookkeeping record. The cash received when a person deposits currency is an asset of the bank, and the deposit is merely a recorded obligation of the bank.

If the outflow of cash is more than the inflow, a bank may replenish its stock of currency and coins by ordering an additional amount from the Federal Reserve bank. The balance sheet changes would be as shown in T-account 6.3 when $1,000 in cash had been obtained from the Federal Reserve:

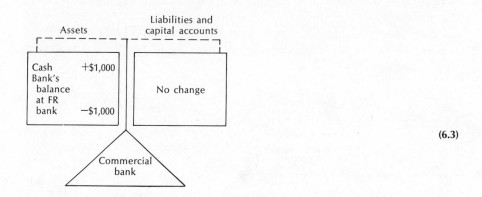

(6.3)

The bank would now hold more cash, but its deposit at the Federal Reserve bank would be less. Commercial banks have deposits in a Reserve bank that are basically the same as the kind of deposits persons have in commercial banks. When $1,000 in cash is deposited in the Federal Reserve bank, the commercial bank's balance at the Reserve bank is increased and its cash in vault decreased as shown in T-account 6.4:

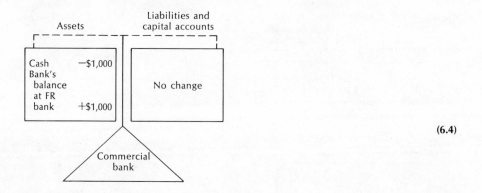

(6.4)

BALANCES AT OTHER BANKS

The item "balances at other banks" listed on the balance sheet of the Dartmouth National Bank includes both its reserve deposit at the Federal

Reserve Bank of Boston and its demand deposits at several large commercial banks. Because its reserve deposit earns no interest, a member bank typically holds in this account no more than is required, plus a small additional amount to meet check-clearing needs. Its demand deposits at the large commercial banks establish a correspondent relationship with those urban banks. Although members of the Federal Reserve System are not permitted to count these interbank deposits in other commercial banks as legal reserves, nonmember banks can usually use them for this purpose. Reserve requirements for nonmembers are established by the governments of the states in which they are located rather than by the Federal Reserve System.

Balances at the Federal Reserve Bank

The deposit at the Federal Reserve Bank of Boston is used for check clearing and collection in addition to being the major portion of the bank's legally required reserves. Except for checks requiring special attention (those on foreign banks and those on banks not on the par list), the Dartmouth National Bank sends to the Federal Reserve Bank of Boston all of the checks it receives that are written on other banks. On the way to the Federal Reserve Bank of Boston, these checks go through the computer services division of the First National Bank of Boston where the Dartmouth National Bank's deposit bookkeeping is done. Banks without computers and related machines find it less costly to contract out their deposit bookkeeping than to do it themselves. Suppose a check for $1,000 written on the National Shawmut Bank in Boston were received by the Dartmouth National Bank from one of its depositors. As soon as the check had been processed by the computer services division of the First National Bank of Boston, the impact on the balance sheet of the Dartmouth National Bank would be as shown in T-account 6.5:

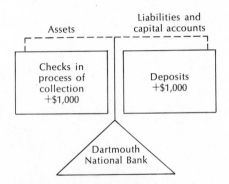

(6.5)

The deposit of the person depositing the check would be increased by $1,000. While the check was still en route to the Federal Reserve Bank of Boston, checks in process of collection would be increased. After the check had been processed by the Federal Reserve Bank of Boston, the balance sheet would be changed as follows:

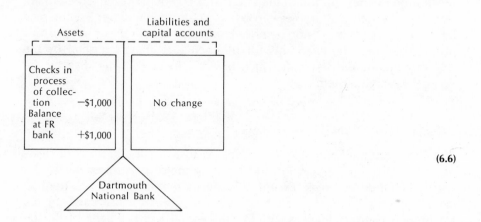

(6.6)

The Dartmouth National Bank's balance in the Federal Reserve Bank of Boston would be increased, and the amount of checks in process of collection would decline. The Federal Reserve Bank of Boston would also decrease the balance of the National Shawmut Bank by $1,000 and would, in effect, collect this amount for the Dartmouth National Bank.

At the same time that the Dartmouth National Bank is receiving checks written on other banks, other banks are receiving checks written on the Dartmouth National Bank. These checks are also sent to the Federal Reserve Bank of Boston. When another bank sends a check for $1,000 written on the Dartmouth National Bank back for collection through the Federal Reserve bank, the following changes occur on the balance sheet:

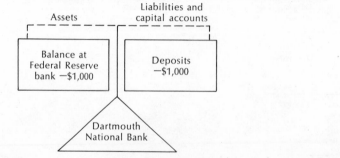

(6.7)

The Federal Reserve Bank of Boston decreases the Dartmouth National Bank's deposit there, and there is also a reduction in the deposit of the customer of the Dartmouth National Bank who wrote the check.

The daily balance of the Dartmouth National Bank at the Federal Reserve Bank of Boston increases if the total value of checks on other banks that it deposits there is greater than the value of checks on itself that other banks send to the Federal Reserve for collection. Its balance at the Federal Reserve Bank of Boston decreases if its clearing balance is unfavorable. Such changes in the size of its balance at the Federal Reserve are important because this deposit is the principal part of its legal reserve, and changes in reserves determine whether a bank expands or contracts its loans and investments. A bank will immediately invest or lend the amount of its balance at the Reserve bank in excess of its needs so as to earn additional interest. If its balance at the Reserve bank is not sufficient to meet its reserve requirements and its check clearing needs, a bank must obtain a larger balance, possibly by selling securities or letting loans run off.

Balances at Correspondent Banks

The Dartmouth National Bank's deposits in large commercial banks are located in Boston and New York. The Dartmouth National Bank's use of its correspondent balances as checking accounts is limited to the collection of special checks not handled by the Reserve banks. However, the principal purpose of the correspondent relationship is to achieve some of the advantages of branch banking while at the same time maintaining local ownership and control. The large city banks provide the Dartmouth National Bank with advice on investments and legal matters and the credit ratings of business borrowers. They also may assist in finding officer personnel, and they may invite the Dartmouth National Bank to participate in large loans that they have arranged. The size of a bank's deposit in a correspondent bank is determined informally, but if a rural bank relies heavily on its correspondent city bank for assistance, one would expect its deposit in the urban bank to be relatively large.

CHECKS IN PROCESS OF COLLECTION

The volume of checks written on other banks that have been received by the Dartmouth National Bank and are still en route to the Federal Reserve bank are counted as assets because they represent claims to funds. The dollar amount of those checks is included in the balance sheet under "checks in process of collection." Between the time the checks are received by the Dartmouth National Bank and processed by the bookkeeping division of the large commercial bank in Boston, the amount of the checks in process of collection is balanced on the liability side of the balance sheet by the same amount in a transit account included in "other liabilities."

BANK INVESTMENTS

The investments of banks consist of the various types of securities owned by the bank. Banks purchase securities from dealers who are in the business of buying and selling them. Such transactions are impersonal. The dealers are middlemen. There is seldom a direct relationship between the bank as lender and the borrower who has issued the securities. Investing in securities may be done very promptly. Although at times yields may be unattractive, a wide variety of securities is always immediately available for purchase.

In recent years, bank investments in securities have declined sharply as a percentage of their total assets. Twenty-five years ago, it was not uncommon for a bank to have over two-thirds of its earning assets in various types of securities.

The major types of bank investments are U.S. government securities, municipal bonds, commercial paper, Federal funds sold, and corporate bonds. Even though the money rate of return received varies, each type of investment has its particular advantages. The way in which the total assets are distributed among the various types is one of the fundamental aspects of bank management.

U.S. Government Securities

Commercial banks invest in large amounts of marketable U.S. government securities. Most of these are direct obligations of the Treasury, although in recent years securities of federally sponsored agencies, such as the Federal National Mortgage Association, Federal Home Loan Banks, and Federal Land Banks, have grown in importance. Since World War II, the relative importance of U.S. government securities in the portfolios of banks has declined. Table 6.2 shows that the total dollar amount of those securities owned by all commercial banks was smaller in 1973 than in 1948—in sharp contrast with the rapid expansion of their loans and their other securities, which consist primarily of municipal bonds.

Despite the decline in the relative importance of U.S. government securities in bank portfolios, in 1972 commercial banks obtained over 11

Table 6.2
Loans and Investments, Commercial Banks,
Selected Years, 1948–1973,
seasonally adjusted
(in billions of dollars)

END OF YEAR	LOANS	U.S. GOVERNMENT SECURITIES	OTHER SECURITIES	TOTAL LOANS AND INVESTMENTS
1948	$ 41.5	$62.3	$ 9.2	$113.0
1953	66.2	62.2	14.7	143.1
1958	95.6	65.1	20.5	181.2
1963	149.6	61.7	35.0	246.2
1968	258.2	60.7	71.3	390.2
1969	279.1	51.5	71.1	401.7
1970	291.7	57.9	85.9	435.5
1971	320.3	60.1	104.4	484.8
1972	377.8	61.9	116.7	556.4
1973	447.3	52.8	130.2	630.3

Source: *Federal Reserve Bulletin,* July 1974, p. A15.

percent of their gross income from interest on securities issued by the Treasury and by United States government agencies (see Table 6.3). The balance sheet of the Dartmouth National Bank shows that it held 9 percent of its total assets in investments of this type.

Table 6.3
Sources of Revenue, Insured Commercial
Banks, 1972

Interest and discounts on loans	63.7%
Income from Federal funds sold and securities held under repurchase agreements	2.6
Interest on U.S. Treasury securities	8.4
Interest on obligations of states, etc.	8.7
Interest on securities of U.S. government agencies	2.8
Interest and dividends on other securities	0.8
Service charges on deposits	3.1
Trust department	3.4
Other service charges, commissions, and fees	2.7
Other revenue	3.8
Total operating revenue	100.0%

Source: Federal Deposit Insurance Corporation, *Annual Report, 1972* (Washington, D.C., 1973), p. 262.

A principal reason for investing in U.S. government securities is their marketability. Although yields on tax-exempt municipals have been higher than the after-tax yields on U.S. government securities, most municipals have the disadvantage of not being readily marketable. Most states and units of local government issue such small amounts of bonds that their securities are not traded often and their prices are not well established in an organized market. If a bank wishes to sell a municipal bond, the price quoted may be low partly because of the "thinness" of the market.

A second reason why banks invest in U.S. government securities is the availability of types of securities with intermediate or short maturities. Municipals are typically long-term. Banks invest primarily in U.S. government securities maturing in five years or less. Their intermediate-term U.S. government securities are not as risky as long-term municipals because prices of intermediate-term issues do not fall as much as long-term issues when market interest rates rise. Also, some commercial banks invest in short-term federal government securities, usually Treasury bills, as "working reserves." When they need to reduce earning assets because of a loss of deposits, they may sell some of their short-term U.S. government securities. Or this may be a useful source of funds to lend to important customers on short notice. The cash assets of banks—cash in vault, balances at the Federal Reserve bank, and balances at correspondent banks—are usually of little use in time of need. Reserve assets cannot be reduced very much when deposits decline, and correspondent balances are small and are expected to be retained at their customary level. Banks prefer to hold working reserves rather than excess legal reserves because working reserves earn interest income, and balances at the Federal Reserve and cash do not. Treasury bills are useful as working reserves because they can usually be sold immediately without incurring a loss. Because of their very short maturity, their prices do not vary much when market interest rates fluctuate.

A third reason why banks invest in U.S. government securities is that when their prices fall, banks can realize tax losses by switching from the issues in their portfolios to other similiar issues. Because of their marketability, this is easier to do with U.S. government securities than with most other investments. A realized tax loss is the difference between the price paid for the bond and the price at which it was sold. The tax advantage of such losses was reduced by new legislation in 1969, but such losses may still be deducted from net income in calculating the bank's federal income tax liability. These losses will be offset later because there will be larger gains from the new securities purchased than there would have been on those that were sold. When these gains are realized, the tax liability of the bank will be larger, but in the meantime the bank has had the use of the funds that would have had to be paid in taxes. This amounts to an interest-free loan from the federal government.

A fourth important reason why banks invest in U.S. government securities is that the deposits of the federal government and of many state governments must be backed by U.S. government securities. If a bank has large deposits of either the federal government or the state in which it is located, the amount of U.S. government securities that it must hold may be substantial. U.S. government securities are also used as collateral when borrowing from a Federal Reserve bank, and a bank may hold some U.S. government securities as a safeguard for this purpose.

Municipal Bonds

The "obligations of states and political subdivisions," commonly called municipals, consist of the bonds issued by states, cities, counties, towns, school districts, and turnpike authorities. There are over 91,000 separate units of state and local government that have used bond issues to finance a variety of projects, among them the construction of schools and other public buildings, water facilities, sewage plants, bridges, tollroads, airports, subways, and low-cost public housing. These units of government finance about two-thirds of their capital expenditures through the sale of municipal bonds. The other third comes from current revenue and state and federal grants.[1]

At the end of 1972 there was over $176 billion in municipal bonds outstanding, and commercial banks held about 52 percent of them. In 1972, there were new issues of $24 billion of these bonds. The capital market for municipal securities is second in size only to the market for U.S. government securities. The market for new issues, known as the *primary market,* is handled by investment banks, which buy the issues from the state or local government units and undertake to resell them to investors for a profit. The market for outstanding issues is known as the *secondary* or *trading market.* This market consists of several hundred dealers, which are mostly banks and a small number of brokers.

Municipal bonds are typically issued in $5,000 denominations. Most of them have coupons attached for semiannual interest payments. Interest on municipal bonds has the special advantage of being exempt from federal income taxes. Banks are subject to the corporation income tax which taxes net income in excess of $25,000 at the rate of 48 percent. At this rate, a tax-exempt yield of 5 percent on a municipal bond would be the equivalent of a taxable yield of 9.6 percent on U.S. government or corporate bonds. In recent years, the rate of return on municipal bonds has been more attractive than on other bonds when the tax exemption is taken into account. In 1973, the average tax-exempt yield on high-grade municipals was 5.2 percent, while the taxable yield averaged 7.4 percent on high quality corporate bonds and 6.3 percent on long-term U.S. government bonds.

In 1973, state and local government debt made up 14 percent of the total loans and investments of all commercial banks, compared to 5 percent in 1947. The increase was largest in medium-sized and larger banks. The balance sheet of the Dartmouth National Bank in April 1974 shows almost one-fifth of its assets in municipals. A major reason why commercial banks have expanded their holdings of municipals more rapidly than their holdings of U.S. government bonds is because of the higher rate of return. Also, while the supply of long-term U.S. government bonds has steadily diminished as a result of the Treasury's policy of issuing mostly short-term and intermediate-term securities, the supply of municipal bonds has expanded rapidly. In the 1960s, when interest rates on savings and time deposits rose sharply, there was a need for banks to invest their rapidly expanding funds from savings and time deposits in investments that yielded relatively high rates of return.

Not all municipals held by banks are long-term. As much as one-tenth of those held by large commercial banks have been *tax warrants*. These are notes and bills maturing within one year. They provide local governments with the funds they need before the dates when taxes are paid.

Banks tend to hold municipal bonds with the four highest ratings—Standard and Poor's listings of AAA, AA, A, and BBB, or Moody's of Aaa, Aa, A, and Baa. Municipal bond ratings are important guides to bond selection. Bonds with the highest rating have the least risk as measured by the diversity of industry and stability of employment in the community and by the debt load that has been incurred. Legal opinions are now commonly printed on the back of municipal bonds (for older issues, the legal opinions are attached) concerning the legality of the method of financing, the amount issued, the purpose, and the terms of the contract. These legal opinions are useful because of the diversity of state and local restrictions.

Some municipals can be retired by the issuer before maturity if the issuer wishes to do so. The call option would be used if interest rates became relatively low. Banks dislike this call feature because they would then have to relend at those lower rates the amount paid off.

Since the 1930s, very few units of state and local government have had difficulty in paying interest charges and principal on their indebtedness. However, two examples of bond issues that have had difficulty are the West Virginia Turnpike and Chicago's Calumet Skyway bonds (each involving over $100 million). Municipals that are backed by the full power to tax of the locality issuing them are called *general obligation bonds*. *Revenue bonds* are repaid solely from the earnings of the project financed —for instance, from the fees charged by a tollroad or a water company. From the point of view of the credit base, general obligation bonds have less risk than revenue bonds. However, the terms of revenue bonds usually limit the additional debt that can be assumed by the issuer, while the holder of a general obligation bond is given no such assurance. Probably the highest grade tax-exempt municipal bonds are those issued by local housing agencies, but backed by federal resources through the Public Housing Administration, a federal agency. These bonds are called *New Housing Authority Bonds*, or PHAs.

Commercial Paper

Commercial paper is a type of security issued by business and financial corporations needing short-term financing. It is unsecured, and only companies having a high credit standing can obtain funds in this way. In the late 1960s there were approximately 400 business and financial companies that issued commercial paper. To avoid the registration requirements of the Securities and Exchange Commission, most issues mature in less than nine months. The period of borrowing is usually between three and six months, but may be for only three days. The most common denomination is $1 million, but the range is from $25,000 to $5 million.[2] On the balance sheet of the Dartmouth National Bank, commercial paper would be included under "other securities." This type of investment has been widely held by banks, even though banks have been less active in this field in recent years.

Commercial paper is in the form of a discounted promissory note. The borrowing corporation promises to pay the holder of the commercial paper a stated sum of money, for example $100,000, on a certain date. Commercial paper is sold for less than its maturity value, and the rate of interest depends on the size of the discount. Figure 6.1 shows that the yields on commercial paper have typically been approximately one-half of one percent above the Treasury bill rate. The principal reason why some banks invest in commercial paper is its relatively high rate of return. Moreover, commercial paper can be purchased so as to mature on dates when the owner expects a need for cash.

Table 6.4 shows the rapid increase in the volume of commercial paper outstanding from 1964 to 1973—from approximately $8 billion to well over $40 billion. Commercial paper is not a new type of financing and had been a major borrowing instrument immediately following World

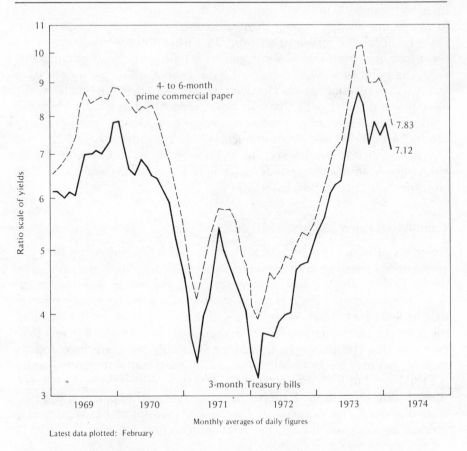

Figure 6.1   **Rates on Commercial Paper and
3-Month Treasury Bills, 1969–1974**

Source: Federal Reserve Bank of St. Louis, *Monetary Trends,* 20 March 1974.

War I. The volume of commercial paper has grown rapidly because some borrowers have been able to obtain funds at lower rates through this market than by borrowing from commercial banks, and lenders have received a higher rate of return from owning commercial paper than from U.S. Treasury bills or certificates of deposit in commercial banks. In 1973, the total amount of commercial paper outstanding was equal to approximately 9 percent of total bank loans.

Commercial paper is sold either through dealers or directly to buyers. At the end of 1973, 68 percent (in terms of value) of commercial paper

Table 6.4
Commercial and Finance Company Paper
Outstanding, 1964–1973
(in millions of dollars)

END OF YEAR	AMOUNT
1964	$ 8,361
1965	9,300
1966	13,645
1967	17,085
1968	21,173
1969	32,600
1970	33,071
1971	32,126
1972	34,721
1973	41,073

Source: *Federal Reserve Bulletin,* various issues, p. A37, and February 1974, p. A31.

outstanding was *direct paper.* This was sold directly to buyers by the issuer, with a bank or sales organization acting only as an agent for the sale. Sales finance companies and bank holding companies are the principal issuers of direct paper. The largest sales finance companies depend on this source for about a quarter of their needed funds. An advantage of direct paper is that the exact maturity date desired may be agreed upon by the borrower and the lender.

Dealer paper is purchased mainly by a small number of dealers for resale to customers at a slightly higher price. Since the dealer takes some risk by holding the paper for a while, and since he recommends it to his customers, he attempts to assess the credit standing of the issuer carefully. He may require the company to have a line of credit with a commercial bank equal to the amount of the issues.

Although commercial paper is issued primarily by manufacturers, utilities, and some finance companies, in 1969–1970 bank holding companies began to issue commercial paper of their own as a method of obtaining funds at rates of interest above those allowed on bank time deposits by the Federal Reserve's Regulation Q. Bank holding companies were induced to sell commercial paper for this purpose only when market rates of interest were above the ceiling rates permitted on their time deposits. This inducement was curtailed sharply in 1970 and 1973 when the Federal Reserve System changed Regulation Q by eliminating ceiling rates on large certificates of deposit. After this change, banks could attract funds by offering higher rates of interest on CDs rather than by selling commercial paper.

Because commercial paper is unsecured, it has some risk, but rigorous credit standards must be met before it is given a high credit rating by the National Credit Office (Dun and Bradstreet). Issues with "desirable" through "prime" ratings are considered relatively safe. Purchasers of commercial paper are occasionally reminded of the risks involved—as they were when the Penn Central started bankruptcy proceedings in mid-1970 with $100 million in commercial paper outstanding, representing large potential losses.[3]

Not only have industrial corporations borrowed through this market, but at times they have owned as much as 60 percent of the commercial paper outstanding. Commercial paper competes with certificates of deposit and Treasury bills as a way for corporations to hold short-term funds. When Regulation Q ceilings on interest rates caused CDs to become unattractive relative to commercial paper, corporations with funds to invest shifted to the commercial paper market.

Corporate Bonds

Commercial banks invest in only limited amounts of corporate bonds. Municipal bonds, federal securities, and commercial paper either offer more attractive rates of return or are more liquid. On the Dartmouth National Bank's balance sheet, corporate bonds would be included under "other securities."

Corporate bonds have the same basic characteristics as U.S. Treasury bonds or municipal bonds. The principal difference is that they are issued by private business corporations rather than by government. They have definite maturity dates and fixed interest payments, and the yield to maturity varies with changes in their prices. The initial maturity is usually from ten to thirty years. They are an important source of corporate finance, especially for utilities. For bonds of well established corporations, risk of default is slight. Corporate bonds that are called *debentures* are general obligations of the issuing company and those secured by specific physical assets are called *mortgage bonds.*

Commercial banks are not allowed to invest in most types of corporation stocks. Banks that are members of the Federal Reserve System are required to purchase a limited amount of stock of the Federal Reserve banks. They may also purchase the stock of certain corporations that the federal government is attempting to promote, such as the Student Loan Marketing Association and the housing corporations under the Housing Act of 1968.

Federal Funds Sold

The lending of Federal funds (deposits in Federal Reserve banks) has been one of the important developments in banking since the 1950s.[4] On the balance sheet of a bank, Federal funds sold is the amount of those deposits lent by one commercial bank to another commercial bank or to a dealer in those funds. Table 6.5 shows that the volume of Federal funds sold by commercial banks increased from $2.1 billion in 1965 to $27.7 billion in mid-1973. Table 6.6 shows that during this period the Federal funds rate fluctuated from less than 4 percent to almost 10 percent.

Table 6.5
Federal Funds Sold, All Commercial
Banks, 1965–1973

END OF YEAR	AMOUNT (IN MILLIONS)
1965	$ 2,103
1966	2,544
1967	4,057
1968	6,747
1969	9,928
1970	16,241
1971	19,954
1972	26,662
1973 (June)	27,652

Source: *Federal Reserve Bulletin,* various issues, pp. A22 and A24.

Table 6.6
Federal Funds Rate and New York
Discount Rate, 1964–1973

DECEMBER	FEDERAL FUNDS RATE	NEW YORK DISCOUNT RATE
1964	3.85%	4.0%
1965	4.32	4.5
1966	5.40	4.5
1967	4.51	4.5
1968	6.02	5.5
1969	8.97	6.0
1970	4.90	5.5
1971	4.14	4.5
1972	5.33	4.5
1973	9.95	7.5

Source: *Federal Reserve Bulletin,* various issues, pp. A8, A9, A33, and A35.

The way in which the Dartmouth National Bank lends such funds is typical of many other banks too. The amount that it had sold on April 24, 1974 was $1 million. It attempts to hold no more deposits in the Federal Reserve bank than are required as reserves, and, by a standing arrangement with the First National Bank of Boston, it lends to them any excess reserve balances that it has. Federal funds are usually lent for a period of one day so that the amount sold may, if necessary, be varied daily. The minimum unit is $100,000. Larger banks also may buy and sell these funds among themselves through Federal funds dealers.

When the Dartmouth National Bank sells $100,000 in Federal funds, the effect on its balance sheet is a reduction in its balance at the Federal Reserve bank and an increase in Federal funds sold:

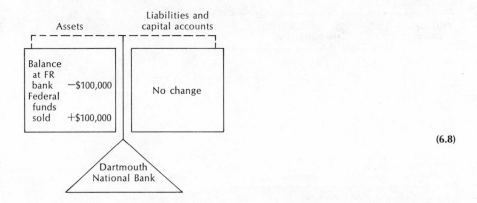

(6.8)

And the effect on the balance sheet of the First National Bank of Boston is to increase its balance at the Federal Reserve bank and its liability, Federal funds purchased:

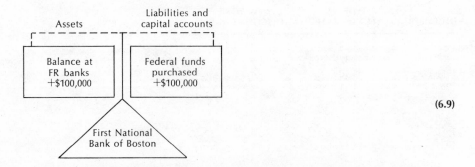

(6.9)

The Dartmouth National Bank gives the First National Bank of Boston a check for $100,000 on the Federal Reserve bank (this may be done by telephone). When this check is received by the Federal Reserve bank, the deposit of the Dartmouth National Bank is reduced and the deposit of the First National Bank of Boston increased. To the First National Bank of Boston, Federal funds purchased is a type of borrowing used to acquire more funds to work with.

The Dartmouth National Bank and many other banks use Federal funds sold as their primary holding of liquid assets or their working reserves. They must hold some type of liquid asset even though its yield may be at times much lower than yields obtainable on other assets. If a bank has on hand an adequate amount of Federal funds sold, a decline in deposits and the resulting loss of legal reserves may be replenished immediately by reducing the amount of Federal funds sold. By providing for liquidity in this way, no unpleasant repercussions on lending activities are necessary, and there need be no forced sales of long-term securities at a loss. Since Federal funds are sold for one day at a time, they are available promptly to replace lost reserves. Banks also must have funds available at all times to accommodate credit-worthy borrowers who are also important depositors. If a bank is unable to accommodate such borrowers, it runs the risk of losing their deposits. Whether a small bank uses Federal funds sold or Treasury bills as working reserves depends primarily on the relative rates of return. Federal funds sold have a shorter maturity than Treasury bills and are probably more convenient.

Table 6.6 shows that in 1964–1965 the Federal funds rate was below the discount rate charged by the Federal Reserve banks on their loans to member banks. Since then, the Federal funds rate has been above the discount rate, except in 1970–1971. Formerly, the principal reason for borrowing Federal funds was to replenish reserves to meet requirements. At that time the Federal funds rate did not rise above the discount rate because, if it did, a bank would choose to borrow from the Federal Reserve banks rather than in the Federal funds market. Since 1966 the reasons for borrowing Federal funds have changed. Large banks borrow to obtain additional funds to lend. Rates on Federal funds have risen above the discount rate because banks purchasing funds have been able to lend them at even higher rates, and there are limitations to the amount they can borrow from the Federal Reserve banks.

BUILDING, FURNITURE, AND FIXTURES

The assets of a bank include its building and its furniture and equipment in addition to its loans and investments and its cash. These assets are not a source of money income, but the use of them by the bank provides real income. The estimated value of these assets is based on such factors as their original cost and depreciation. The balance sheet of the Dartmouth National Bank shows that its total real assets are valued at less than $300,000. This is because it rents the building it occupies and owns no real estate.

SUMMARY

A small amount of cash in vault is always needed to meet a bank's obligation to pay deposits in cash. A bank that is a member of the Federal Reserve System is legally required to hold a certain amount of cash plus balances in its Federal Reserve bank. Though not required by law, small balances in other commercial banks are used for clearing special types of checks and for establishing correspondent relationships.

Because liquid assets such as Treasury bills or Federal funds sold earn interest, banks prefer to invest in them rather than to hold larger amounts of cash in vault and balances in other banks than are needed. Many banks invest in Treasury bills or Federal funds sold, despite lower rates of return than those available on other possible investments, because of their liquidity. Investments of this type give a bank flexibility in obtaining funds to cover losses of deposits or to accommodate important borrowers.

Banks desire to invest in U.S. government securities with intermediate-term or long-term maturities because of their marketability, and because banks must hold U.S. government securities as backing for U.S. Treasury deposits.

Municipal bonds are attractive investments to many banks because the interest received from them is tax-exempt, and municipal bonds usually have relatively high rates of return.

NOTES

1. For a discussion of municipal bonds, see Frank P. Smeal, "Municipal Bonds in the Bank's Portfolio," in William H. Baughn and Charls E. Walker, eds., *The Bankers' Handbook* (Homewood, Ill.: Dow-Jones–Irwin, 1966), pp. 646–667.
2. For a discussion of recent developments in the commercial paper market, see Robert Johnston, "Rebirth of Commercial Paper," Federal Reserve Bank of San Francisco, *Monthly Review*, July 1968, pp. 137–142. See also G. Walter Woodworth. *The Money Market*

and *Monetary Management,* 2d ed. (New York: Harper & Row, 1972), chapter 6; and Richard T. Selden, *Trends and Cycles in the Commercial Paper Market* (New York: National Bureau of Economic Research, Occasional Paper 85, 1963).

3. "Commercial-Paper Investors to Reinforce Scrutiny of Issuers Due to Penn Central," *Wall Street Journal,* 23 June 1970, p. 23.

4. Parker B. Willis, *The Federal Funds Market,* 4th ed. (Boston: Federal Reserve Bank of Boston, 1970); and G. Walter Woodworth, *The Money Market and Monetary Management,* 2d ed. (New York: Harper & Row, 1972), chapter 4.

QUESTIONS

6.1. How would the receipt of $100 in currency from a depositor affect the balance sheet of a commercial bank?

6.2. If a commercial bank orders $1,000 in currency from its Federal Reserve bank, how would the commercial bank's balance sheet be affected?

6.3. What uses do balances at a Federal Reserve bank have?

6.4. Explain why commercial banks have balances with correspondent banks.

6.5. How are bank investments different from bank loans?

6.6. Compare U.S. government securities with municipal bonds as types of bank investments. What are their advantages and disadvantages?

6.7. Describe commercial paper as a type of investment.

6.8. Why may the amount of commercial paper outstanding increase rapidly when interest rates are very high?

6.9. Why is the amount of corporate bonds owned by commercial banks relatively small?

6.10. Summarize some of the objectives that a bank takes into consideration when managing its portfolio of investments.

6.11. What are Federal funds?

6.12. Explain why some banks desire to sell Federal funds and other banks desire to purchase them.

6.13. Why is it important for a commercial bank to have some investments in highly liquid assets such as U.S. Treasury bills or Federal funds sold?

6.14. Know the meaning and significance of the following terms and concepts: balance sheet, assets, liabilities, capital accounts, cash in vault, checks in process of collection, Federal funds sold and purchased, municipal bonds, commercial paper, working reserves, marketability, balance at the Federal Reserve banks.

"Now, just what is it that has driven you into our clutches?"

Chapter 7
Commercial
Bank Loans

Commercial banks make loans to business enterprises primarily for the purpose of purchasing plant, equipment, and inventory goods, and to individuals for the purpose of purchasing housing and consumer durables. An expansion in these types of spending may have an especially stimulating effect on the economy.

Most bank loans consist of *promissory notes*. A promissory note is an unconditional promise in writing, made by one person, business firm, or unit of government (*the maker*), to another (*the payee or bearer*), to pay a specific amount of money, at a fixed or determinable future date, or upon demand. The note must be signed by the one promising to pay. It may also include the signatures of cosigners who agree to pay if the maker fails to do so. The note may provide for repayment in installments, on a single date, or on demand. If on demand, either the borrower or the lender is free to end the contract at any time. Most loans are *time loans,* and the borrower cannot be required to pay back the amount he has borrowed until the payment date of the loan. If a borrower fails to meet the terms of his note, the bank may start legal proceedings to recover the amount due.

In Britain and some other countries, bank loans may be in the form of overdrafts on checking accounts. The banks charges interest on the negative balance in the borrower's account. In the United States, this method of making loans was quite rare until the recent development of check loans and credit cards. Banks here have traditionally preferred written evidence of the loan.

Many bank loans are backed by *collateral*—real estate, corporation stock, savings deposits, life insurance policies, or automobiles and other consumer durables purchased on the installment plan. In case the borrower defaults, the bank has the right to take the collateral and sell it to recoup the amount owed to the bank. The use of collateral reduces the risk and enables banks to lend at lower interest rates than would otherwise be possible. If a loan is backed by collateral, it is said to be *secured*.

As shown in Table 7.1, bank loans are classified in the following six categories: commercial and industrial loans, agricultural loans, loans for purchasing and carrying securities, loans to financial institutions, real estate loans, and others (mainly installment loans to purchase consumer goods and personal loans to individuals). This classification is based on the use of the funds, not on the type of collateral. A business loan secured by real estate, for example, is a commercial and industrial loan, not a real estate loan; and a personal loan secured by stock certificates is classified as "other" rather than as a loan for carrying securities. All types of bank loans have increased rapidly in the post–World War II period. Table 7.1 shows that in December 1947 the total amount of bank loans was only $38 billion but by June 1973 had increased to approximately $430 billion.

Some loans are called *discounts* because of the way interest is charged. On a regular 7 percent loan of $100 for one year, the borrower receives $100, and pays back $107 at the end of the year. On a 7 percent discount, he would receive $93 and pay back $100. In the latter case, the borrower is paying an interest rate slightly higher than the stated discount rate of 7 percent.

Borrowers are charged interest rates that reflect the amount of risk involved. Small businesses have a higher rate of failure than large businesses and are usually charged more. And small loans usually have higher interest rates because of the higher administrative costs per dollar lent. Since the markets for most types of loans are quite competitive, a similar rate of interest usually prevails for a given level of risk and administrative cost.

The lowest rate charged for the least risky commercial and industrial loans is known as the *prime rate*.[1] The announcement of the prime rate is an example of "price leadership" and reflects control over interest rates rather than perfectly competitive conditions. Rates of interest in very competitive financial markets fluctuate considerably more than the prime rate does. Although this rate was changed only nineteen times between 1934 and 1966, since then changes have become much more frequent. When the prime rate is changed by one of the major banks in the country, this event is given wide publicity in the press; and other major banks then follow. Many banks in smaller communities adjust their own interest charges on commercial and industrial loans to changes in the prime rate. *Credit rationing* is often related to the use of the prime rate. If the prime rate is lower than would be justified by competitive conditions, the demand for bank credit by qualified borrowers would exceed the supply. Banks must then ration the available supply of loanable funds, and bor-

Table 7.1
Selected Assets and Liabilities of All Commercial Banks, December 31, 1947 and June 30, 1973 (in millions of dollars)

ASSETS	12/31/47	6/30/73
Cash in vault	$ 2,216	$ 7,669
Cash balances		
At Federal Reserve banks	$17,796	$ 25,143
At other commercial banks [a]	10,216	29,842
Total	$28,012	$ 54,985
Securities		
U. S. Treasury	$69,221	$ 57,877
State and local government	5,276	91,312
Other	3,729	29,787
Total	$78,226	$178,976
Federal funds sold	—	$ 27,652
Loans		
Commercial and industrial	$18,167	$150,390
Agricultural	1,660	15,985
For carrying securities	2,050	12,118
To financial institutions	115	37,538
Real estate	9,393	108,199
Others	6,670	105,436
Total	$38,057	$429,666

LIABILITIES	12/31/47	6/30/73
Demand deposits		
General	$ 84,987	$207,625
U. S. Government	1,343	10,434
State and local government	6,799	18,166
Interbank	12,792	31,047
Certified, officer checks, etc.	2,581	11,162
Total	$108,502	$278,434
Time deposits		
General	$ 34,383	$303,727
Interbank	240	5,590
State and local government	866	40,734
U. S. government and postal savings	111	730
Total	$ 35,600	$350,781
Borrowings	$ 65	$ 49,299
Capital accounts	$ 10,059	$ 55,740

[a] Excludes reciprocal balances.
Source: *Federal Reserve Bulletin*, February 1974, pp. A18, A22, and A23.
Note: This is not a balance sheet. It does not include total assets and total liabilities.

rowers are not able to obtain all of the funds they would like to have at the prime rate. In 1971, the prime rate set by some of the large banks became more flexible and was changed weekly according to a formula. The prime rate is no longer the same for all of the large banks. In 1971, President Nixon appointed a Committee on Interest and Dividends as part of the federal government's program of wage and price controls. During 1973, a period of rising interest rates, this committee attempted to persuade banks not to raise interest rates—particularly the prime rate—on bank loans.

Normally, a national bank cannot legally lend to any one borrower more than 10 percent of its capital stock, surplus, and undivided profit. As computed from the balance sheet in Table 6.1, the maximum loan that the Dartmouth National Bank was permitted to make to one person was less than $300,000. The purpose of this limitation is to assure diversity among the loans of the bank, thus reducing the risk of loss by a borrower's default. Bank loans are a major source of credit to local borrowers who are typically also important depositors.

COMMERCIAL AND INDUSTRIAL LOANS

The most important type of loan made by banks is to commercial enterprises and industries. In 1973, such loans amounted to over $150 billion —approximately 35 percent of the total. Most commercial and industrial loans are for the purchase of inventory goods and are for less than a year. Some of them, however, are *term loans* for as long as ten years. These latter are often used to finance purchases of machinery and are usually paid off in installments.

When feasible, commercial and industrial loans are secured by the firm's accounts receivable, by the inventory, equipment, or machinery purchased, or by the firm's plant. Many of these loans, however, are unsecured because it is inconvenient to require collateral. Whether or not they are secured, all of these loans must be supported by accounting records summarizing the financial condition of the borrower—the balance sheet and the income statement, certified by a public accountant. By examining those documents and by keeping in contact with the operations of the borrower, the bank officers can estimate the chances that the loan will be paid off when due, and they can attempt to determine whether it is advisable to continue the loan if an extension is requested. Government bank examiners also review those accounting statements. If there is some doubt whether the loan will be paid off when due, the examiners require the bank to remove the loan from the assets recorded on its balance sheet.

Some businesses that borrow often and have a good credit record are able to arrange a *line of credit* over a specified period of time. The line of credit is usually not used at all times, but an unsecured loan up to a specified amount is understood to be available for seasonal and special needs. For the customer, this reduces the time required in obtaining a loan, and, for the bank, the need to make recurring credit investigations. The terms of such loans may require a deposit balance equal to a certain percentage of the loan.

The federal government's Small Business Administration has several types of programs to promote the granting of commercial loans to small businesses. Although these programs are not extensive, they enable some enterprises to obtain loans that they probably could not obtain otherwise. The Small Business Administration works with banks in making such loans and usually guarantees a substantial portion of the loan.

In the 1930s the volume of commercial and industrial loans dropped sharply, and it was commonly believed that this was because large corporations had become able to supply themselves from retained profits with almost all of the funds they needed. The rapid expansion in commercial and industrial loans during the past twenty-five years indicates that the decline in the demand for loans in the 1930s was due to the depression and was not the result of their being replaced by retained profits as a source of funds, even though this idea persists.[2]

Making short-term commercial loans used to be considered the primary function of commercial banks, and historically it is from this type of loan that commercial banks got their name. According to the *commercial loan theory* of bank liquidity, only short-term self-liquidating loans to business firms were appropriate for banks. These loans are considered to be *self-liquidating* because the merchant or manufacturer acquires the funds to repay the loan with interest when he sells his inventory or his output. From the point of view of the bank, short-term loans have the advantage that due dates can be staggered so that funds are constantly coming in. Nevertheless, to assure liquidity, most banks in recent years have relied more on the shiftability of assets—usually Treasury bills or Federal funds sold—than on the cash inflow from commercial loans.[3] The basic principle of the commercial loan theory of banking—that restricting bank loans to short-term commercial loans would assure the stability of the entire banking system in times of financial crisis—is today not generally accepted.[4] Instead it is believed that deposit insurance or the existence of a central bank is required if financial panics are to be avoided. Commercial and industrial loans have, over the years, declined in relative importance as commercial banks have expanded into other types of lending and investing.

AGRICULTURAL LOANS

Agricultural loans now account for a smaller proportion of total loans than in previous periods. As shown in Table 7.1, in mid-1973 they comprised less than 4 percent of total bank loans.

For banks in farming areas, agricultural loans are important. Farmers need financing both for recurring seasonal expenses and for long-term investments in machinery and land. Farming now involves more expensive machinery, larger units of land, and the use of chemical fertilizers, sprays, hybrid seeds, and prepared foods, vitamins, and antibiotics for livestock. These agricultural costs often require financing. Not all agricultural financing, however, is obtained from local banks. Purchases of new equipment are often financed by the seller. And when they can, farmers borrow at subsidized rates from federal credit agencies, such as the Federal Land Banks and the Banks for Cooperatives.

LOANS FOR PURCHASING AND
CARRYING SECURITIES

Persons may borrow from banks to finance purchases of corporation stock and other securities. In 1973, loans totaling approximately $12 billion—3 percent of total bank loans—were of this type.

A large amount of stock market speculation, financed by bank credit, in the late 1920s caused widespread financial difficulties when stock prices fell sharply in 1929. In 1934, the Federal Reserve's Board of Governors was given the power to use selective credit controls over loans of this type. Their Regulation U applies to lending by commercial banks on stocks listed on the national stock exchange, and the board has the power to set minimum margin requirements ranging from 25 percent to 100 percent. In 1973, the margin requirement for stock was 65 percent—meaning that the maximum amount of the loan was 35 percent of the market value of the stock. In 1974 the margin requirement was lowered to 50 percent.

The Federal Reserve's margin requirements apply to loans from lenders other than commercial banks and to loans which are for the purchase of stocks but which are secured by land or other physical assets. Margin requirements do not apply to loans which are secured by stocks but which are to be used for purposes other than stock purchases—for example, a loan for home improvements using common stock as collateral. In practice, it may be difficult for a bank to know whether money borrowed is being used for purchasing stock or for financing some other need. A person in need of funds might use securities as collateral in order to avoid selling the stock so as to be able to profit by expected capital gains, to avoid capital gains taxes, to avoid brokerage commissions, to retain voting rights on the stock, or to be able to borrow at a lower rate of interest.

LOANS TO FINANCIAL INSTITUTIONS

In 1973, 9 percent of bank loans went to other financial institutions, such as correspondent banks, finance and consumer credit companies, and brokers and dealers. Finance companies obtain a large proportion of their funds from bank loans, although large finance companies have also obtained a substantial part of their funds from the sale of commercial paper.

Both brokers financing stock purchases for customers and dealers in government securities obtain a large proportion of their funds from bank loans. These may be call loans that can be terminated by either the bank or the borrower without a waiting period. Since the mid-1930s, banks have made broker's loans only to brokers who are also depositors. The Board of Governors of the Federal Reserve System can set limits on security loans of member banks and suspend privileges to banks not observing them. Brokers and dealers typically change the amount of their loans and substitute one stock for another as collateral when their needs and sales change. They have what is called an *accordion-type loan*.

REAL ESTATE LOANS

In 1973, real estate loans amounted to over $100 billion—about 25 percent of total loans. In 1947, total real estate loans amounted to only $9 billion. These mortgages finance the purchase, construction, and remodeling of both housing and commercial and industrial facilities. About 80 percent of mortgage credit is provided by financial institutions, including banks. The rest is obtained from individuals or United States credit agencies. As a source of real estate credit, commercial banks are less important than savings and loan associations, but more important than life insurance companies.[5]

Although the installment feature of most modern real estate loans was quite rare before the 1930s, most mortgages today are repaid in this way. The average maturity of real estate loans is close to twenty-five years, but it may vary between ten and thirty years. During the life of an installment mortgage the monthly payments are constant, and the mortgage is gradually paid off. In 1973, a down payment of 25 percent, or $7,500, would usually be required on a $30,000 house, the amount lent would amount to $22,500, and the rate of interest charged was typically 8½ percent. For a twenty-five-year mortgage of this size, the monthly payment of principal plus interest would be $181.18. The first monthly payments consist mostly of interest charges, but as time passes, the portion paying off principal gradually increases. The borrower must also pay for fire insurance up to the value of the mortgage.

It is an advantage to banks to have some funds invested over a long period without the need to renegotiate as frequently as for commercial or consumer loans. Mortgages are also fairly safe loans because they are secured. Requiring the owner to have some equity in the house makes the collateral adequate in most circumstances if the value of the property should go down. The amount of the average first mortgage made in 1973 was over 70 percent of the value of the home.[6]

About 40 percent of residential mortgages are underwritten by either the Federal Housing Administration or the Veterans Administration. Banks negotiate such mortgages, although officials of the FHA or VA participate by inspecting the property. FHA-insured mortgages require a smaller down payment than is needed for conventional bank mortgages. In case of default, the ownership of the property is shifted to the FHA, and the bank is reimbursed with U.S. government securities. VA-guaranteed mortgages require no down payment, and in case of default the bank is paid in cash for any loss. These programs were designed to aid veterans and other persons in need, and to stimulate housing construction by facilitating the supply of housing credit.[7] Financial institutions support such programs because they reduce the risk to themselves.

In recent years, the FHA and VA programs have been criticized by students of urban problems.[8] The programs have applied almost solely to new houses built in the suburbs and almost never to the rehabilitation of existing houses in the cities. As a result, they have subsidized the movement of the middle class out of the central cities. The poor who have had to live in the older cities have not been able to get subsidized mortgages of this type. The movement of people out of the city has indirectly aided poor urban families by increasing the supply of housing in the cities available for them.

Widely fluctuating interest rates may have a disrupting effect on the mortgage market. If interest rates fall, persons who borrowed at the higher rates have timed their borrowing badly. If they rise, the banks who lent the money at the lower rates find themselves holding unattractive earning assets. The sharp rise in market interest rates during the accelerated inflation in the late 1960s and early 1970s caused difficulties for banks with large amounts of older mortgages carrying 4 to 6 percent interest rates. The rate of interest that banks have had to pay to acquire time deposits exceeds the interest rates earned on many of their older mortgages. To attempt to meet this problem of the effect of fluctuating rates of inflation on interest rates, it has been suggested that mortgages ought to be made with flexible interest rates that vary with the rate of inflation. If the rate of inflation rose one percent, for example, the rate of interest on mortgages would be raised one percent. Escalated interest rates of this type would tend to eliminate both the gain that borrowers at low mortgage rates might have made and the loss that financial institutions might have incurred.

Some states have ceiling limits on interest rates for mortgages. When market rates of interest rise above the legal ceiling, banks tend to shift to other types of loans and investments, and the supply of funds for mortgages dries up.[9] FHA-insured and VA-guaranteed mortgages also have ceiling rates, and new mortgages of this type tend to decline sharply when market rates rise above the ceilings. The ceiling rates on federally underwritten mortgages have become more flexible in recent years in order to prevent mortgage money from drying up at a time when better yields are available on other loans and investments. They were raised sharply in 1969–1970 from 6¾ percent to 8½ percent and in 1973–1974 from 7 percent to 8½ percent—both in periods of rising market interest rates.

CONSUMER AND PERSONAL LOANS

Commercial banks make many consumer and personal loans. These are included under "other" loans in Table 7.1. From 1947 to 1973, they increased in importance—from 18 percent to almost a quarter of total loans. Most of them are made to persons to finance purchases of consumer durable goods such as automobiles and TV sets.

At the end of 1973, over 80 percent of the total amount of consumer credit outstanding was classed as *installment credit*. The rest consisted of single-payment loans, charge accounts, and service credit (doctors' bills and so forth). Commercial banks held 47 percent of the total amount of consumer installment credit outstanding (see Table 7.2). Table 7.3 shows that almost half of the consumer installment credit of commercial banks consisted of loans for the financing of automobiles.

Table 7.2
Total Consumer Installment Credit Held
by Different Types of Financial Institutions,
December 1973

Commercial banks	47%
Finance companies	25
Retail outlets	12
Credit unions	13
Other	3
Total	100%

Source: *Federal Reserve Bulletin,* February
1974, p. A54.

Table 7.3
Types of Consumer Installment Credit Held
by Commercial Banks, December 1973

Automobile paper, purchased or negotiated	45%
Personal loans	21
Other consumer goods paper	28
Repair and modernization loans	6
Total	100%

Source: *Federal Reserve Bulletin,* February 1974, p.
A55.

In 1974, the terms of a typical loan for $2,000 for a new automobile
with at least one-third equity were as follows:

Amount borrowed	$2,000.00
Life insurance on borrower	20.84
Interest	202.04
Total amount owed bank	$2,222.88
Monthly payment for 24 months	$92.62

In order to qualify for these terms, the price of the new car would have
to be $3,000 or higher, giving the owner an equity in the car of at least
one-third. Many borrowers are able to pay for most of the equity portion of the cost of a new car by trading in their old car. The terms of this
loan require the borrower to pay back the loan with interest in twenty-
four monthly payments of $92.62 each. In addition to the amount bor-
rowed, the monthly payments include interest amounting to about $202
plus life insurance on the borrower over twenty-four months costing
over $20.

The coverage of the life insurance policy is equal to the unpaid portion of the loan on the automobile and declines as the loan is paid off. If the borrower dies, his estate benefits by acquiring complete title to the automobile, debt-free, and the bank gets immediate payment of the unpaid balance of the loan. The bank does not have to get involved in the probate of wills and avoids delays in receiving payment.

If the borrower fails to meet his installment payments, the bank has the right to take or *repossess* the car. Then the bank attempts to obtain the unpaid portion of the loan by selling the car.

Because of the installment feature of automobile loans, the rate of interest that the borrower pays is not obvious. The important rate of interest is that based on the unpaid balance. A simple way of calculating this measure of the cost of borrowing is shown in the following formula:

$$i = \frac{2mA}{P(n+1)} \tag{7.1}$$

where i = interest rate on the unpaid balance, m = number of payments a year, A = interest in dollars, P = principal, and n = number of payments needed to discharge the debt. Applying this formula to the terms of the installment loan shown above, the rate of interest on the unpaid balance is 9.6 percent a year:

$$i = \frac{2 \times 12 \times 202.04}{2020.84 \,(24+1)} = 9.6\%$$

This is a rough estimate and is slightly above the rate of 9.3 percent on a loan with these terms given in the interest rate tables used by loan officers. For loans on automobiles in which the equity is less than one-third, the rate of interest charged is typically almost two percentage points higher.

In order to protect consumers, Congress passed the Truth in Lending Act which became effective July 1, 1969.[10] The job of writing the new regulation, known as Regulation Z, was assigned to the Board of Governors of the Federal Reserve System. The regulation applies not just to banks, but also to savings and loan associations, department stores, credit card issuers, credit unions, automobile dealers, consumer finance companies, residential mortgage brokers, craftsmen such as plumbers and electricians, doctors, dentists, hospitals, and any other persons who extend consumer credit. Enforcement is to be shared by nine different federal agencies including the Federal Reserve System. The purposes of the regulation are to make customers aware of the cost of credit and to enable them to compare the terms available from various credit sources.

The borrower must be told both the finance charges and the annual percentage rate. The finance charges include all of the various costs required by the creditor—interest plus such costs as premiums for credit life insurance. The computations are more complex than in the above formula; creditors are not expected to make the calculations themselves, but to obtain from the Board of Governors of the Federal Reserve System sets of tables that may be used to determine the annual percentage rate for each transaction. Regulation Z covers both installment credit and open-end credit such as revolving charge accounts and credit cards. It does not set minimum or maximum rates. A creditor who violates the law may face criminal penalties or suit by the customer for twice the amount of the finance charge, court costs, and a reasonable attorney's fee.

Installment loans have relatively high rates of interest because of the bookkeeping involved in recording the payments and the time required in making this type of loan. There are also some losses on these loans. For example, if a car taken as collateral is in bad condition, the collateral may not be worth the unpaid balance of the loan. Or if a borrower moves to another part of the country and stops making payments before paying off the loan, collecting the balance due may be difficult and not worth the cost.

In the loan market for financing automobiles, banks compete among themselves as well as with automobile dealers who do their own financing. Each lender cannot charge more than he does without losing customers, and he does not lower his charges because other types of loans and investments would be more profitable for him if he did. The rates charged do not vary much, although they are different for old and new cars (cars, not customers, are differentiated as to credit risk). The automobile manufacturers attempt to keep the interest costs as attractive as possible so that they can sell more cars.

Installment loans have been popular with consumers.[11] Historically, there has been a shift from the purchase of services outside the home and the employment of household servants to the provision of similar services by consumers themselves using highly technical equipment. Consumers have replaced laundry services with washers and dryers, taxi and bus services with automobiles, entertainment services with TV sets, meals at restaurants with prepared foods kept in freezers, and household servants with dishwashers and electric floor polishers. Most people have difficulty saving the amount of money needed for the purchase of expensive durable goods. By borrowing the total and repaying it in monthly installments, they avoid the need to accumulate funds before making the purchase, and they obtain the machine's use while they would otherwise still be saving to buy it. The development of this type of finance occurred in the 1920s and coincided with the mass production of automobiles. A mass market for automobiles based on the use of installment loans was a necessary counterpart of mass production based on assembly-line techniques and scientific management.

Banks also make *personal loans*. These loans sometimes have collateral or cosigners, but may also be accepted simply on the signature of the borrower. In recent years, commercial banks have promoted a new type of personal loan called *check loans*. The borrower is given special checks for this purpose. When he writes one of these checks, he is in effect borrowing from the bank. The rate charged on such loans has been typically 1 percent or 1½ percent a month on the outstanding balance plus 25 cents for each check drawn. The maximum limit to the amount that can be borrowed is usually $4,800 or less depending upon the borrower's income, and is determined at the time the borrower is given the account. The borrower usually repays the amount borrowed on the installment plan. The principal advantage of this method of extending credit is that it is speedy and impersonal. The borrower has credit available at all times up to the maximum limit of the account.

Many banks now also offer holders of credit cards (Master Charge and BankAmericard are the two principal ones) credit up to $300. If the amount charged is paid within twenty-five days after the monthly billing, such charges are not treated like bank loans and no interest is charged. Holders of these cards do not have to pay immediately for the amount charged, however, and may elect to pay, on the installment plan, for items purchased with the card. In some states, even federal income taxes may be paid in this way. The rate of interest on such loans has been 1½ percent a month on the unpaid balance. Such loans are typically paid off in installments up to ten months.

Personal loans to finance the education of college students are being encouraged by the federal government. The Higher Education Act of 1965 set up a guaranteed student loan program in which commercial banks have participated. No repayment of such loans need be made during college years. The maximum rate of interest is 7 percent. Approximately four million students have borrowed to finance their education since the program began. In 1972, approximately 62 percent of the total amount of these loans was made by commercial banks. There are over five million of these loans outstanding.

CYCLICAL VARIATIONS IN LOANS AND INVESTMENTS

Cyclical variations in the total amount of loans and investments of banks from 1951 to 1963 are shown in Figure 7.1. The series shown are the annual rates of change of commercial bank loans and investments, as well as of member bank reserves. In order to reduce the effects of random fluctuations, three-month moving averages of each of the series are plotted. The bars represent annual rates of change of seasonally adjusted data for the periods indicated. During this period, there were three recessions, shown by the shaded areas.

The top series in Figure 7.1 shows that in the middle of the 1953–1954 and 1957–1958 recessions and at the start of the 1960–1961 downturn, member bank reserves were increased markedly. As will be explained in Chapter 9, when banks acquire larger total reserves, they may increase the total amount of their loans and investments, and when they lose total reserves, they must usually decrease the total amount of those assets. The bottom series in Figure 7.1 shows that the immediate impact of the increases in reserves in each of those recessions was on investments rather than on loans. The middle series in Figure 7.1 shows that

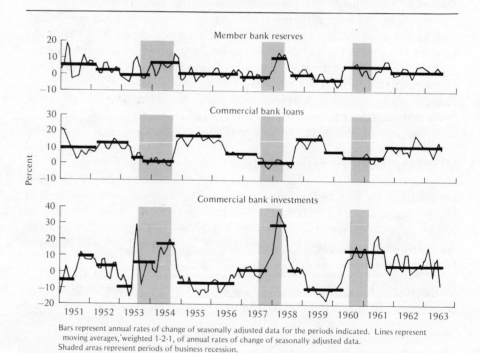

Bars represent annual rates of change of seasonally adjusted data for the periods indicated. Lines represent moving averages, weighted 1-2-1, of annual rates of change of seasonally adjusted data.
Shaded areas represent periods of business recession.

Figure 7.1 Member Bank Reserves and Commercial Bank Loans and Investments, 1951–1963 (annual rates of change)

Source: Federal Reserve Bank of St. Louis, *Review*, October 1963, p. 4.

loans did not respond quickly to increases in reserves. Loans expanded slowly for the entire period of each contraction and for the first few months of each recovery, probably because of the weak demand for loans. Several months after the trough of each cycle, however, the expansion in loans rose sharply. At this stage of the cycle, the improvement in business conditions would be expected to increase the demand for loans.

The top series in Figure 7.1 shows that shortly after the recovery was under way in both the 1954–1957 and 1958–1960 periods of expansion, the rate of increase in reserves was sharply reduced. The combination of the slower rate of increase in reserves and the increased demand for loans made it necessary for banks to liquidate investments to provide funds for loans. Then, as the expansion progressed, the rate of increase in loans slowed up ahead of the peak of the cycle. In the long business expansion from 1961 to 1969, the rate of increase in reserves was not reduced sharply shortly after the recovery started, and banks did not have to liquidate investments to get funds to make loans. There was a simultaneous expansion in loans and investments. This may have been one of the reasons for the unusual length of this expansion.

ALLOCATING CREDIT RESOURCES EFFICIENTLY

The supply of loanable funds is a scarce resource, which bankers in their everyday activities allocate among various possible uses. Credit is wasted if bankers make loans to business firms that fail to use the funds productively and are unable to pay back the amount borrowed with interest. Fortunately, most loans do not turn out to be bad ones. But in order to achieve the best allocation of credit, bankers must lend funds to borrowers who can successfully pay the highest rates of return. Society is usually believed to benefit if scarce supplies of loanable funds are used in ways that yield, for example, 8 percent rather than 7 percent. To pay the higher rate of interest, the funds borrowed would have to be used to finance investments in plant, equipment, homes, and inventories that yielded a return at least as high as the rate of interest.

Private ownership of banks provides an inducement for bankers to lend money successfully and in ways in which the rate of return is highest. Owners of banks receive higher rates of return on their common stock if banks successfully lend funds in ways in which the rate of return is the highest possible. In countries in which banks are publicly owned, other forms of incentives must be used, and other ways of evaluating the efficiency of the management and of rationing scarce funds must be employed. In some of these countries, bankers have been criticized for making loans on a "political rather than on an economic basis." The objective of allocating scarce resources efficiently is the same in both socialist and capitalist countries. Both types of economies need some system of avoiding waste and of allocating credit resources to their most productive uses.

SUMMARY

Bank loans are relatively secure because they are typically either backed by collateral or made to well established firms that provide the bank with current accounting statements certified by a public accountant.

Commercial banks make loans to individuals as well as to business firms. Consumers borrow for the purpose of purchasing homes, automobiles, and other consumer durables, and for personal needs.

The calculation of the rate of interest on installment loans is more complicated than on other types of loans, because the amount of the unpaid balance keeps changing.

When banks acquire additional funds, they initially expand their investments, but then they gradually shift from investments to a larger volume of loans.

A basic economic function of banks is to allocate a limited supply of credit among competing uses. Bank credit is allocated efficiently if banks lend to the firms and individuals who can use the funds most productively.

NOTES

1. For a description of the nature of the prime rate, see Murray E. Polakoff and Morris Budin, *The Prime Rate* (Chicago: Association of Reserve City Bankers, 1973).
2. John Kenneth Galbraith, *The New Industrial State,* 2d ed. (Boston: Houghton Mifflin, 1971), chapter 4.
3. G. Walter Woodworth, "Theories of Cyclical Liquidity Management of Commercial Banks," *National Banking Review* 4 (June 1967), pp. 377–395.
4. For a historical analysis of the commercial loan theory of banking (also known as the *real bills doctrine*), see Lloyd W. Mints, *A History of Banking Theory* (Chicago: University of Chicago Press, 1945).

5. For a detailed survey of the market for real estate loans, see Saul B. Klaman, *The Postwar Residential Mortgage Market* (Princeton: Princeton University Press, 1961).

6. *Federal Reserve Bulletin,* February 1974, p. 35. In addition, some homes have smaller second mortgages that have legal claim to payment after the first mortgage has been satisfied.

7. George Break, *The Economic Impact of Federal Loan Insurance* (Washington, D.C.: National Planning Association, 1961); and Robert J. Saulnier, Harold G. Halcrow, and Neil H. Jacoby, *Federal Lending and Loan Insurance* (Princeton: Princeton University Press, 1958).

8. Edward C. Banfield, *The Unheavenly City* (Boston: Little, Brown, 1970), pp. 15–16.

9. Clifton B. Luttrell, "Interest Rate Controls—Perspective, Purpose, and Problems," Federal Reserve Bank of St. Louis, *Review* 50 (September 1968), pp. 6–14 (published also as Reprint Series No. 32).

10. "Truth in Lending," *Federal Reserve Bulletin* 55 (February 1969), pp. 98–103.

11. For an analysis of the historical background of the growth of consumer credit, see Board of Governors of the Federal Reserve System, *Consumer Instalment Credit,* Part 1, Vol. 1, *Growth and Import* (Washington, D.C.: U. S. Government Printing Office, 1957), chapter 2.

QUESTIONS

7.1. What is a promissory note? How are promissory notes used in banking?

7.2. What is the collateral of a loan? Why may a bank require collateral?

7.3. What is the purpose of bank laws restricting the amount lent to any one borrower?

7.4. Explain the principal characteristics of each of the following types of loans: commercial loans, real estate loans, consumer loans, personal loans, agricultural loans, loans for purchasing and carrying securities, and loans to financial institutions.

7.5. What are installment loans? What advantages do they have to borrowers as well as to banks?

7.6. What are some of the methods used by commercial banks to reduce the risk of making loans?

7.7.   Why may laws setting ceiling rates of interest on mortgages cause sharp variations in the supply of mortgage credit?

7.8.   What is the commercial loan theory of banking?

7.9.   Describe the federal government's programs to induce banks to negotiate mortgages.

7.10. What are the purposes and principal features of the Truth in Lending Act?

7.11. Calculate the rate of interest on an installment loan of $3,500.00 if the total interest charged is $454.96 and there are twenty-four monthly payments of $164.79.

7.12. Why is the rate of interest charged on personal loans relatively high compared to that on other types of bank loans?

7.13. How do total bank loans and total bank investments vary during the expansion and contraction phases of the business cycle?

7.14. Explain the social role of banks in allocating loanable funds.

7.15. Know the meaning and significance of the following terms and concepts: commercial loan, promissory note, collateral, prime rate, line of credit, margin requirement, installment loan, consumer loan, credit rationing, overdraft, unsecured and secured loans, commercial loan theory of bank liquidity.

4-00-351-55 (R7/73)

CONTINENTAL BANK

CONTINENTAL ILLINOIS NATIONAL BANK AND TRUST COMPANY OF CHICAGO

231 SOUTH LA SALLE STREET, CHICAGO, ILLINOIS 60693

SAVINGS **NON-NEGOTIABLE** TIME CERTIFICATE OF DEPOSIT

SCD 0516910-2

CHICAGO _____

TERM

PAYABLE TO

THERE HAS BEEN DEPOSITED IN THIS BANK THE SUM OF $

SPECIMEN

OR REGISTERED ASSIGNS ON _____

_____ DOLLARS

WITH INTEREST COMPOUNDED CONTINUOUSLY FROM THE DATE HEREOF ONLY TO MATURITY AT THE RATE OF _____ % PER ANNUM

UPON SURRENDER OF THIS CERTIFICATE PROPERLY ENDORSED

REMIT INTEREST ☐ SEMIANNUALLY
☐ MONTHLY ☐ ANNUALLY
☐ QUARTERLY ☐ AT MATURITY

CREDIT ACCOUNT

AUTHORIZED SIGNATURE

IBM R88998

Chapter 8.
The Liabilities Side of the Balance Sheet

*The liabilities side of the balance sheet of a commercial bank lists
primarily the various types of deposits. The asset side of the balance
sheet showed the ways that banks use their funds; the liabilities
side shows their sources of funds.*

Commercial banks have two principal classes of liabilities: *demand
deposits* and *savings and time deposits*.

DEMAND DEPOSITS

Demand deposits are checking accounts. An owner of a demand deposit
is entitled to write checks on his deposit and use them to pay for his
purchases. He is also entitled to withdraw, on demand, currency up to
the amount of his demand deposit. On April 24, 1974, the Dartmouth
National Bank had $11.3 million in demand deposits of individuals, part-
nerships, and corporations.

   If a bank is a member of the Federal Reserve System, behind its
demand deposits it must keep a certain amount of reserves consisting of
cash in vault or balances with its Federal Reserve bank. The rest of the
funds obtained from deposits are lent or invested. Because deposits
provide a bank with funds to lend and invest, there is advertising and
active competition for them. Banks attract depositors primarily by giving
them real services—the safety and convenience of making payments by
writing checks and of withdrawing cash on demand. In the 1920s banks
typically paid interest on the demand deposits of their larger depositors,
but in 1933 Regulation Q made it illegal for banks to attract demand
deposits in this way. In 1973, Congress passed an unusual law that permits banks located in Massachusetts and New Hampshire to allow persons
to write checks called *negotiable orders of withdrawal* (NOWs) against
interest-bearing savings accounts. This is equivalent to permitting banks

in those two states to pay interest on checking accounts and to compete for deposits in this way. An important way in which banks have competed for business deposits is by granting loans more readily to their depositors than to those who do not have a deposit at the bank. A business that has no deposit in the bank may have more difficulty obtaining a loan and may have to pay a higher rate of interest. Banks also compete for deposits by advertising, having impressive banking offices, and offering additional services such as faster check-processing.[1]

Keeping the records for each check transaction and maintaining exact accounts are costly operations. In recent years, most banks have installed more complicated, mechanized types of bookkeeping. Because of the cost of bookkeeping, many banks charge some type of service fees. Service fees for writing checks usually vary with the size of the deposit. Depending on the amount of his deposit, a depositor receives a credit against the total fees incurred. Some banks have no service fees on each check written; but they may require a minimum balance (often $100) and charge the depositor a fee (today often $3) if his balance falls below this minimum amount during the month.

In 1973, business enterprises owned over 60 percent of the total amount of demand deposits (see Table 8.1). Only 33 percent was owned by individuals. Over two-thirds of all families now have a checking account.

Table 8.1
Demand Deposits Owned by Individuals, Partnerships, and Corporations at All Commercial Banks, September 1973

	DEPOSITS (IN BILLIONS)	PERCENTAGE OF TOTAL
Financial business	$ 18.8	8.9%
Nonfinancial business	108.3	51.5
Consumer	69.1	32.9
Foreign	2.1	1.0
All other	11.9	5.7
Total	$210.2	100.0%

Source: *Federal Reserve Bulletin*, February 1974, p. A30.

SAVINGS AND TIME DEPOSITS

The total amount of savings and time deposits in commercial banks increased over five times during the past fifteen years and has become larger than total demand deposits. This rapid expansion has been primarily the result of changes in the Federal Reserve System's Regulation Q.

From 1936 to 1957, the highest rate of interest that commercial banks were permitted to pay on passbook deposits was only 2½ percent. In 1957, the maximum rate for most types of savings and time deposits was raised to 3 percent, and between 1962 and 1973 there were further important increases. In 1970, ceilings were suspended for large certificates of deposit with maturities of thirty to eighty-nine days, and in 1973, maximum rates of interest on all certificates of deposit in denominations of $100,000 or over were suspended. These changes are shown in Table 13.4 in Chapter 13. They enabled commercial banks to compete more effectively with savings and loan associations and mutual savings banks.

In 1969, 85 percent of time and savings deposits were owned by individuals and 15 percent by business firms. The amount of time deposits owned by corporations is still relatively small, even though the growth in the ownership of time deposits by business firms was an important new development during the 1960s. Business corporations typically invest in certificates of deposit in denominations of $100,000 or more.

The principal types of savings and time deposits are savings or passbook deposits, notice savings deposits and savings certificates, open account time deposits, certificates of deposit, and the new NOW savings accounts.

Savings Deposits

Approximately 40 percent of the total amount of savings and time deposits in insured commercial banks consist of this type of deposit. There are two types—passbook deposits and statement savings deposits—and in 1973 the maximum interest rate allowed was 5 percent. When funds are deposited or withdrawn from a passbook account, the passbook must be presented and the transaction recorded. Passbook deposits are the most popular type of savings deposit, although statement savings deposits have grown in importance in recent years. Persons may deposit and withdraw funds from a statement savings deposit at the bank or by mail, and the bank sends a record of the amount of the savings deposit plus interest earned monthly to the depositor. Even though banks are legally entitled to require a notice for a period of time before funds can be withdrawn from a savings deposit, this option is seldom used, and depositors generally assume that they can withdraw their funds immediately. Savings deposits may be held only by individuals and certain nonprofit organizations.

Notice Savings Deposits and Savings Certificates

Notice savings deposits are similar to passbook or statement savings deposits except that a ninety-day notice before withdrawal is required.

Table 8.2
Types of Time and Savings Deposits,
Insured Commercial Banks, July 31, 1973

TYPE OF DEPOSIT		AMOUNT (IN MILLIONS)	PERCENTAGE OF TOTAL
Savings		$123,034	40.3%
Time deposits in denominations of less than $100,000, with original maturity of:			
Less than 1 year	$43,154		
1 up to 2½ years	49,068		
2½ years to 4 years	9,425		
4 years and over	3,964		
Total		105,611	34.6
Time deposits in denominations of $100,000 or more			
Negotiable CDs	$50,618		
Nonnegotiable CDs and open account	19,191		
Total		69,809	22.9
Christmas savings and other special funds		6,584	2.2
Total		$305,038	100.0%

Source: *Federal Reserve Bulletin,* October 1973, p. 730.

Since 1973, the maximum interest rate allowed on these deposits has been 5½ percent. In Table 8.2, the amount of notice savings deposits and savings certificates is included in "time deposits in denominations of less than $100,000."

The owner of a savings certificate is given a receipt showing the amount deposited, the interest rate, the maturity date, and other terms of the contract. Certificates are issued in denominations varying between $1,000 and $100,000 and are sold only to individuals, nonprofit organizations, and fiduciaries. In 1973, the maximum interest rates allowable on savings certificates were 5½ percent on maturities from ninety days to one year, 6 percent on maturities from one year to two and a half years, and 6½ percent on longer maturities. In addition, a ceiling rate of 7¼ percent was permitted on certificates with a maturity as long as four years and a minimum denomination of $1,000. The minimum maturity of savings certificates is usually three months. Savings certificates may be redeemed before maturity by notifying the bank ninety days in advance and agreeing to take a 25 percent cut in the interest rate.

Open Account Time Deposits

The unique feature of open account time deposits is that the amount in the account may be added to after the deposit is opened. They cannot be cashed before the set date of maturity. This type of deposit has been popular with business firms, although the number of banks offering deposits of this type is small. The maximum rate of interest payable on these deposits depends on their maturity and amount. Christmas savings funds owned by small savers are a type of open account deposit. In Table 8.2, all of the classifications except savings deposits include open account time deposits.

Certificates of Deposit

Table 8.3 shows that the volume of large negotiable certificates of deposit (popularly known as CDs) grew very rapidly from 1961 to 1973. These large negotiable CDs have denominations of $100,000 or more and are owned primarily by business firms with sizable amounts of funds to invest for short periods of time, charitable organizations, governmental institutions, and foreign banks. The suspension of interest rate ceilings on large certificates of deposit in 1970 and 1973 was intended to discourage the shifting of deposits from United States banks to Eurodollar banks in foreign countries where there are no interest rate ceilings.

CDs are in the form of a certificate, and both negotiable and nonnegotiable types are available. The depositor determines the date of issue of the certificate and its maturity date. At maturity they are redeemed by the issuing bank. The unit of nonnegotiable certificates may be smaller than $100,000.

Commercial banks first began to issue large negotiable CDs in significant volume in the 1960s. A dealer-operated secondary market for them was established in 1961. Since then, owners in need of cash have been able to sell negotiable CDs to dealers or other investors before maturity. Since the early 1960s the number of banks issuing large negotiable CDs has increased rapidly.

For business firms with funds to invest, certificates of deposit compete with commercial paper and Treasury bills. The amount of CDs outstanding used to decline when market rates of interest on U.S. Treasury bills and commercial paper rose above the maximum rates of interest that were formerly set on CDs. The quantity of CDs declined in the last half of 1966, in the second quarter of 1968, and in 1969. In each of those periods, rates of interest on competing types of securities were close to or above the maximum rate of interest allowed on CDs.

Table 8.3
Large Negotiable Certificates of Deposits
at Commercial Banks, 1961–1973
(seasonally adjusted)

DECEMBER	AMOUNT (IN BILLIONS)
1961	$ 3.3
1962	6.1
1963	9.5
1964	13.2
1965	16.7
1966	15.7
1967	21.0
1968	24.0
1969	11.2
1970	25.3
1971	33.0
1972	43.4
1973	62.8

Source: *Federal Reserve Bulletin,* various issues, pp. A16 and A17. Data prior to 1967 were provided by the Federal Reserve Bank of St. Louis.

NOW Accounts

The important characteristic of this newest type of savings account is that persons may write checks on them. They have been permitted, in Massachusetts and New Hampshire only, since 1974. Banks that are members of the Federal Reserve System may issue them only to individuals and nonprofit associations. The maximum rate of interest allowed is 5 percent, and the number of checks processed against an individual NOW account may not exceed 150 per year.[2] Authority to issue NOW accounts was given to commercial banks so as to enable them to compete with mutual savings banks, which were the first type of financial institution to offer them. Granting this authority to commercial banks in Massachusetts and New Hampshire may put the banks in neighboring states at a competitive disadvantage. The rules of the Federal Reserve System permit member banks in Massachusetts and New Hampshire to offer NOW accounts only to residents or persons who work in the state and to their current customers. Also, the advertising of NOW accounts by those banks is to be directed only toward state residents.

DEPOSITS OF THE UNITED STATES GOVERNMENT

The United States government has deposits called *tax and loan accounts* in most commercial banks. Federal income taxes and social security taxes withheld by local business firms are deposited directly into these accounts in the local commercial banks. When these taxes are paid, the bank reduces the deposit of the taxpayer and increases the deposit of the United States government. When a bank sells U.S. savings bonds, the payments for those bonds are credited to the Treasury's deposit.

The United States Treasury does not spend money directly from its tax and loan accounts but first transfers the funds to its deposits in the Federal Reserve banks. These transfers are made several times each week. The scheduled withdrawals from commercial banks are announced in advance. The Treasury tries to manage its tax and loan accounts so as to avoid sudden or unexpectedly large withdrawals.

DEPOSITS OF STATES AND POLITICAL SUBDIVISIONS

Local units of government usually have deposits in their local banks; some banks, particularly those located in state capitals, hold the deposits of the government of the state. The Town of Hanover has its checking deposit in the Dartmouth National Bank.

OTHER DEPOSITS

The deposits behind certified and cashier's checks are shown separately on a bank's balance sheet under "other deposits." When a bank certifies a check, the amount of the check is taken from the deposit of the person whose check is certified and put in a separate account behind the check. When a bank writes a cashier's check to pay for its own expenditures, a deposit equal to the cashier's check is created.

OTHER LIABILITIES

By far the largest component of "other liabilities" of the Dartmouth National Bank is its *transit account*. The deposit accounting and record-keeping of the Dartmouth National Bank is done at the machine-record division of a large bank in Boston. During the time in which the checks drawn on other banks received for deposit by the Dartmouth National Bank are en route to Boston and have not yet been credited to the accounts of the depositors, the total amount of those checks is included in the transit account in "other liabilities." In banks that handle their own bookkeeping for checking accounts, the "other liabilities" item on the balance sheet would be relatively small because it would not include a transit account. "Other liabilities" also include unearned interest on installment loans and accumulated wages and taxes that have not yet been paid.

BORROWING

In the 1960s the total amount and variety of bank borrowing increased sharply. There are three principal types: borrowing by member banks from the Federal Reserve banks, borrowing of Federal funds from other member banks, and borrowing of Eurodollars. These three types of borrowing have been done primarily by larger banks.

Borrowing from the Federal Reserve banks has been available to member banks ever since the Federal Reserve System was established. The purpose of such borrowing is to cover a short-term deficiency of reserves.

As was shown in Table 6.5, the borrowing of Federal funds from other member banks increased sharply after 1965. These funds are usually borrowed for only one day, but the loan may be continuously renewed. The purpose of borrowing Federal funds may be either to acquire additional funds to lend or to cover a reserve deficiency.

In the 1960s there was a rapid expansion in Eurodollar borrowing from foreign banks and from branches of United States banks in foreign countries. This type of borrowing also existed in the 1920s. Only the largest United States banks borrow in this way because most transactions are in amounts over ten million dollars. When depositors shift their deposits in banks in the United States to foreign banks or to overseas branches of United States banks to take advantage of higher interest rates there, the United States banks may, if they wish, get these funds back by borrowing from their branches.

Until recently, an advantage of Eurodollar borrowing was that no reserve requirements were necessary. A shift from deposit liabilities to borrowing reduced a bank's required reserves. In 1969, Regulation M was revised, and banks are now required to hold reserves behind borrowings from foreign banks. The required reserve ratio is 3 percent for borrowings amounting to 4 percent or less of total deposits subject to reserve requirements. For additional amounts of these borrowed funds a reserve of 10 percent is required. A 10 percent additional reserve ratio is required for borrowing in excess of the bank's average level of Euro-dollar borrowing in May 1969.

CAPITAL NOTES AND BONDS

A few large commercial banks have recently raised funds by issuing *notes* or *bonds*.[3] Industrial corporations have customarily sold bonds as well as stock as a method of financing their activities, but financing of this type has been very rare among banks. In December 1962, Comptroller of the Currency James J. Saxon ruled that debentures that are subordinate to the claims of depositors could be used to raise funds. All national banks and a number of state banks are permitted to borrow in this way up to 100 percent of capital stock plus 50 percent of surplus.

In a further development in 1974, some of the large bank holding companies attracted considerable attention by issuing floating-rate notes. Because these notes were issued by bank holding companies rather than by banks, they could legally carry interest rates above those permitted on time and savings deposits. Citicorp in New York sold $650 million of floating-rate notes yielding an initial interest rate of 9.7 percent. These notes were sold for Citicorp by a group of investment banking companies in the same way that such companies normally handle the sale of new issues of stocks and bonds for corporations needing to raise funds. The rate on floating-rate notes is to be adjusted semiannually and will be at 1 percent above the coupon equivalent of the average of the weekly rates for three-month Treasury bills during a twenty-one-day period shortly preceding the period for which the rate is to be determined. The notes were issued in denominations of $1,000; they mature in 1989; and after an initial period of approximately two years they are repayable semi-annually at the option of the owner at their principal amount.

The development of sources of funds other than deposits has been an important change in banking. These sources include various types of borrowing as well as the issuance of capital notes and bonds. A significant aspect of the growth of these new sources of funds is that they provide an alternative way of supplying the liquidity needs of a bank. The principal way in which most banks have traditionally assured that they have funds to cover deposit withdrawals, or to lend to important customers, has been to hold short-term securities. With the development of these new sources of funds, banks may meet a loss of funds by borrowing

Federal funds, and large banks with foreign branches may obtain funds by borrowing from the Eurodollar market rather than by selling liquid assets.[4]

RESERVE FOR BAD DEBT LOSSES

The amount of a bank's reserve for bad debt losses is based on tax considerations. A bank is permitted to deduct from its annual net income a certain amount for reserve for bad loans. This reduces its federal income tax liability. The amount that is allowed for this purpose depends on the volume of bad loans that the bank has experienced in the past.

When the reserve for bad debt losses is increased, undivided profits are reduced. The purpose of setting up such a reserve is to show that in the future some of the assets of the bank may not be worth their face value even though the exact amount of the loss is unknown. Reserve items on the liabilities side of the balance sheet should be distinguished sharply from the reserve assets of a bank, consisting of its cash in vault and balance at the Federal Reserve bank. Like surplus and undivided profits, the reserve items on the liabilities side do not represent funds that may be spent.

CAPITAL ACCOUNTS

There are four principal types of capital accounts: capital stock, surplus, undivided profits, and reserve for contingencies and other capital reserves. The value of the common stock of a bank as listed on its balance sheet is the total amount of shares of stock outstanding, valued at par. The Dartmouth National Bank has 20,000 shares of stock outstanding, valued at $10 per share: its capital stock is listed at $200,000. Like other corporations, banks sell stock when they are initially chartered in order to raise part of the funds needed for operation. After a bank is in operation, it may sell additional shares of stock or declare dividends payable in stock, adding to the total par value of the shares outstanding. Bank stockholders receive the dividends declared by the bank, and they have voting rights enabling them to have a voice in running the bank.

Surplus is a portion of the undivided profits that has been allocated to surplus by a vote of the bank's directors. When the directors decide to increase surplus, undivided profits are reduced by an identical amount. The amount allocated to surplus is considered to be somewhat more permanently a part of the capital accounts than the undivided profits. Since 1935, national banks have been required to accumulate a surplus equal to the total value of their capital stock. Before this requirement was made, if a bank failed, each stockholder was personally liable for an amount equal to the par value of the stock he held in the bank, an arrangement called double liability.

Undivided profits is the balancing item in the balance sheet. It measures the excess in the total value of the assets over the value of all the liabilities plus other capital accounts. The total amount of the undivided profits is whatever that excess happens to be. It varies each time the balance sheet is prepared.

The difference between the balance sheet items called surplus and undivided profits is a minor one. Together, they measure how much the total assets of the bank exceed its total liabilities, capital stock, and the various specific types of reserves listed on the liabilities side of the balance sheet.

The sum total of the capital stock, surplus, undivided profits, and reserve for contingencies and other capital reserves is significant to the owners of the bank. It measures the *book value* of the shares of stock outstanding—which is related to how much an owner might be willing to sell the shares for and how much others might pay for them—as compared with the *par value* at which the value of the capital stock is listed on the balance sheet. The book value of a share of stock of the Dartmouth National Bank was just under $150 when the balance sheet in Chapter 6 was prepared. If this sum increases, it means that the assets of the bank are larger relative to its liabilities, and the claims of the owners of the bank are increased. The prices of the stocks of the larger banks are quoted in major newspapers, and there is a market price for the stock. The stock of small banks is not often traded, and the price must be negotiated between the buyer and seller.

The total value of the capital accounts of a bank is expanded by retaining profits. When a bank makes profits, its gross income during the year exceeds its gross expenditures. The receipts of a bank consist primarily of interest from its loans and investments, plus service fees. The expenses consist primarily of the wages of its employees, interest on time deposits, and other costs of operating the bank. A bank may either pay out the profits it has earned in dividends to the stockholders, or it may retain them. If the bank retains profits, undivided profits increase, because banks usually use retained profits to increase their loans and investments. The bank's assets would be increased relative to its liabilities, and the value of its capital accounts would be larger.

Bank examiners typically require banks to keep the amount of their total capital accounts equal to approximately one-tenth of the value of their deposits. This is called the *10 percent rule*. If a bank's deposits are increasing, profits must be retained in order to maintain this ratio. An alternative way to maintain the desired capital-deposit ratio would be to sell additional stock, but this is seldom done. The capital-deposit ratio is usually smaller than 10 percent for larger banks. However, the appropriate capital-deposit ratio for a bank varies with the condition of the bank and is affected by the quality of a bank's assets and the proportion of its assets in loans. Historically, the capital-deposit ratio of banks has declined. For all commercial banks, it was 23 percent in 1900, 22 percent in 1910, 14 percent in 1920, 17 percent in 1930, 12 percent in 1940, and has averaged less than 10 percent since World War II.

The 10 percent rule is intended to protect depositors because capital accounts act as a buffer to absorb bad loans. If a loan is considered bad by examiners, the bank must remove it from its recorded assets even though it may eventually be paid off. When a bank has to write off a bad loan for $1,000, undivided profits are also reduced as shown in T-account 8.1:

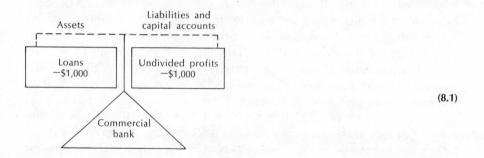

(8.1)

The write-off of bad loans is balanced by a reduction in undivided profits. The value of the owners' interests in the bank is reduced. As long as the amount of a bank's undivided profits is sufficiently large so that bad loans may be taken out of it, the public's deposits are protected by being fully backed by assets.

The reserve for contingencies and other capital reserves, the fourth category under capital accounts in the Dartmouth National Bank's balance sheet in Table 6.1, are reserves for expected losses on securities or reserves to supplement future obligations of employee pension programs.

A common error is to conceive of surplus, undivided profits, or the reserve for contingencies and other capital reserves as funds that can be used to meet expenditures. Only assets such as cash or earning assets that can be sold for cash can be used to cover the expenditures of the bank or to pay its debts. The capital accounts are intangible and are the way in which the balance sheet shows the amount of the claims of the bank's owners on the assets of the bank.

BANK FAILURES

A bank fails because of bad loans or the decline in the value of the securities it owns. Either of these contingencies may cut into its capital accounts. When the value of its capital accounts is below zero, the bank's liabilities are larger than its assets. It is then said to be insolvent, and it is required by the examiners to cease operating.

The most dramatic period of bank failures in the United States occurred from 1930 through 1933 when more than 9,000 banks suspended operations. The major reason for these failures was the decline in the market value of their bonds rather than bad loans. Currently, bonds are listed on the balance sheet at their purchase price, so that a decline in the market prices of bonds does not cause a reduction in the bank's assets and its capital accounts. During the 1930s, accounting practices were different. Bonds for which continuous price quotations were available had to be valued at market price. As a result, when bond prices fell during the Great Depression, the listed value of the bonds that banks had in their portfolios declined, reducing the value of their capital accounts.

Today when bond prices fall, undivided profits are reduced only if the bank is forced to sell its bonds at a loss. T-account 8.2 shows the effect on the balance sheet of a commercial bank of a $200 loss:

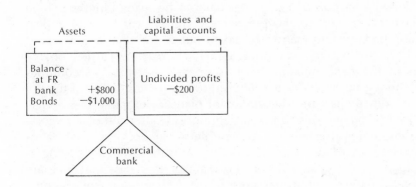

(8.2)

The bank's balance at the Federal Reserve bank would be increased by $800, the sale price of the bond. The purchaser of the bond would pay for it by a check written on his bank. The bank receiving the payment for it would deposit this check in its Federal Reserve bank, thus increasing its deposit there by $800. Since the bond had been listed on the balance sheet as worth $1,000, the difference of $200 would have to come out of undivided profits. Banks normally are able to avoid losses of this type by holding liquid securities such as U.S. Treasury bills, commercial paper, or Federal funds sold. Liquid securities can be disposed of without incurring large losses. Only if a bank is caught short of liquid assets and has to sell long-term securities would it be forced to incur a loss of this type.

Banks experienced similar difficulties in the Great Depression when some of their loans went bad and had to be written off. Particularly in the early part of the depression, loans of low quality that had been made during the prosperous 1920s turned out to be bad.

The failure of banks causes losses to both stockholders and depositors. Total losses to both stockholders and depositors in the Great Depression have been estimated to amount to $2.5 billion. The most serious problem caused by bank failures is the resulting decline in the total money supply. The decline in Money Supply II of more than 35 percent from 1929 to 1933 contributed to the length and severity of the depression.

BAD LOAN POLICIES OF FOREIGN BANKS

Compared to government policies regarding bad loans in many other countries, those of the United States bank examiners are relatively tough. In the United States, a loan does not have to be many months behind in its repayments, nor do the prospects of repayment have to appear particularly bad, for the loan to be taken out of the recorded assets of the bank. In some other countries, bad loans may be carried on the accounts of the bank indefinitely. This practice is typical in countries where there is a considerable amount of government direction of the use of bank credit. As part of a development plan, for example, banks may be required to grant loans to certain enterprises; after the plan is completed, those enterprises are not always able to pay back the principal of the loan. Funds may have been allocated to firms that are unable to operate efficiently. Their costs may be too high, or the price that they are able to get for their output may be too low. The government planning authority may control not only the allocation of bank credit, but the price at which the goods produced are sold and the wages and other costs that must be paid. If the output consists of electric power, railway or bus transportation, or other widely consumed services, the government may be induced for political reasons to subsidize consumers by keeping the price below cost. Under such conditions, enterprises cannot be expected to operate at a profit or to pay back the principal of bank loans with interest, and it would be unreasonable for bank examiners to require the banks to write off such loans.

The carrying of worthless notes on the books of such banks does not cause difficulties in their normal operations. In those countries, the public usually has no reason to fear that banks would ever fail. The banks may even be owned by the government. If a loss of public confidence in them starts a run on banks, it is usually not a serious problem. As long as a bank can obtain more paper money from a central bank, it can convert deposits into currency. Although the accumulation of bad loans by banks need not cause banks to fail, there may, of course, be real economic costs to the economy. If a bank makes bad loans, it has probably wasted the credit resources of the country.

COMMERCIAL BANKS AS FINANCIAL INTERMEDIARIES

Commercial banks are financial intermediaries between depositors and borrowers. These two groups are frequently not able to deal directly with each other on terms acceptable to each. The terms on which banks accept many of their deposits—repayment on demand—are different than the terms on which most of their loans are made—repayment on time. Depositors want to be able to transfer money by check and to get cash whenever needed. But a merchant, manufacturer, or other borrower wants time to accumulate funds to repay his loan. His repayment schedule would not fit the demands of most depositors. As intermediaries, banks have been able to lend funds on different terms than they accept them. In a general way, commercial banks can be compared to other types of middlemen. A wholesaler of goods also buys on different terms than he sells. He buys in bulk from the manufacturer and sells in quantities that retailers desire. Banks have been successful as intermediaries because there are many borrowers and many depositors who like the terms on which commercial banks lend and accept funds.

SUMMARY

Commercial banks provide people and business firms with the principal type of money that is used for making payments—demand deposits.

The variety and volume of time and savings deposits in commercial banks have grown rapidly in recent years. Rates of interest paid on these deposits have been raised, and banks have become more aggressive in developing sources of funds.

Bank examiners require banks to have capital accounts that are considered sufficiently large to cover a substantial volume of losses from bad loans. Their objective is to assure that all of the bank's deposits are fully backed by assets.

NOTES

1. George J. Benston, "Interest Payments on Demand Deposits and Bank Investment Behavior," *Journal of Political Economy* 72 (October 1964), pp. 431–449.
2. *Federal Reserve Bulletin,* December 1973, pp. 921–923.
3. Paul S. Nadler, *Time Deposits and Debentures: The New Sources of Bank Funds* (New York University Graduate School of Business Administration, Bulletin No. 30, 1964).
4. See James L. Pierce, "Commercial Bank Liquidity," *Federal Reserve Bulletin,* August 1966, pp. 1093–1101.

QUESTIONS

8.1. What is back of demand deposits?
8.2. What are some of the different ways that banks compete for demand deposits?
8.3. Explain the rapid growth of time and savings deposits in commercial banks during the past decade.
8.4. Why have ceiling rates of interest on CDs been suspended?
8.5. What is a NOW account?
8.6. Explain the principal characteristics of savings or passbook deposits, notice savings deposits, savings certificates, open account time deposits, and certificates of deposit.
8.7. What are the different types of borrowings of commercial banks?
8.8. What is the difference between a bank's surplus and its undivided profits?
8.9. Explain the way in which a bank's undivided profits may be increased. How might they be decreased?
8.10. Why do bank examiners urge banks to have capital accounts equal in total to approximately 10 percent of their deposits?

8.11. If a bank needs funds to purchase a new accounting machine, can it use its undivided profits? Explain.

8.12. Explain the ways in which banks become insolvent and fail.

8.13. Know the meaning and significance of the following terms and concepts: demand deposit, savings deposit, capital stock, surplus, undivided profits, certificates of deposit (CDs), tax and loan account, interbank deposits, savings certificate, time deposit, reserve for bad loans, 10-percent rule for capital accounts, insolvent bank, capital notes, floating-rate notes.

Chapter 9
The Creation
of Deposits

The way in which commercial banks create deposits is one of the most important processes in the monetary system. The possibility of deposit creation usually depends on an expansion in bank reserves or on a reduction in the reserve ratios required by banks—conditions that may be controlled by the Federal Reserve System.

To understand the way banks create deposits, it is important to distinguish between the individual bank and the banking system consisting of thousands of individual banks. From the point of view of the individual bank, an obvious way in which deposits may be created is by the deposit of currency in the bank. But deposits are also destroyed when currency is withdrawn from a bank—and deposits of currency tend to be offset by withdrawals of currency. Most deposits are actually not created in this way. To the individual banker, deposits are also created by the deposit of a check written on another bank. Most of his deposits appear to be created in this way. But from the point of view of the banking system, the deposit of a check on another bank merely transfers deposits from one bank to another. For the system as a whole, total deposits are unchanged.

The principal process by which the banking system creates deposits occurs when a bank makes a loan or buys a security. When making a loan, a bank usually increases the borrower's checking account by the amount of the loan. Even though the bank making the loan can expect to lose the deposit when the borrower writes a check on it, another bank receiving that check will experience an increase in deposits. The total amount of deposits in the banking system is increased when banks expand their total loans and investments. But this type of deposit creation can occur only when banks are in a position to expand their total loans and investments.

UPPER LIMIT TO DEPOSIT CREATION

There is an upper limit to the amount of deposits that each bank can create by expanding its loans and investments. This limit is determined by the level of reserves required of the bank.

The total reserves that member banks are required by law to hold either as cash in vault or as deposits at the Federal Reserve bank are called *required reserves*. Reserves held beyond those legally needed are called *excess reserves*. In the simplified balance sheet shown in T-account 9.1, the commercial bank has one type of liability—demand deposits—and three types of assets—reserves, U.S. government securities, and loans. Assume that the required reserve ratio is 20 percent, a ratio somewhat higher than those that actually exist. Under these circumstances, commercial bank A would have no excess reserves, and it cannot expand its earning assets beyond $80,000 or its deposits beyond $100,000. In exchange for additional loans, the bank would have to give borrowers deposits, and the increase in the bank's demand deposits above $100,000 would lower the bank's reserve ratio below the 20 percent legal minimum. Moreover, if the bank used funds from its reserves either to buy additional securities or to make more loans, the drop in reserves below $20,000 would also cause the bank's reserve ratio to be less than the legal minimum. Only if the commercial bank acquired larger reserves than $20,000, or if its minimum reserve ratio were lowered below 20 percent, could it expand its earning assets above $80,000 and create additional deposits. The Federal Reserve System regulates both the reserve ratios and the total reserves of its member banks.

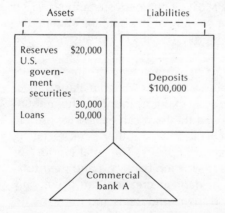

(9.1)

INCREASING RESERVES

Banks as a whole obtain additional reserves in the form of deposits at the Federal Reserve banks primarily through open market purchases by the Federal Reserve banks of U.S. government securities. There are other ways of increasing reserves (these are included in the bank reserve equation explained in Chapter 12), but open-market operations are by far the most important. Federal Reserve banks invest in U.S. government securities and have demand deposit liabilities much as commercial banks do. Their deposits belong mostly to commercial banks. Partly for this reason, Federal Reserve banks are often called bankers' banks. These deposits at the Reserve banks are the principal type of reserves of commercial banks.

The way in which an open-market purchase of $1,000 would affect the balance sheets of both the Federal Reserve banks and the particular commercial bank initially affected by the open-market purchase is shown in T-account 9.2:

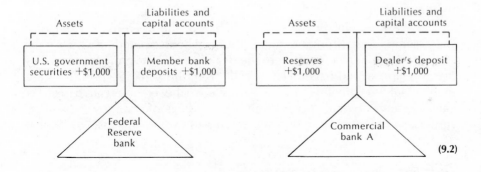

(9.2)

The holdings of U.S. government securities by the Federal Reserve banks increase by $1,000 because of the purchase. The Federal Reserve banks pay for government securities by a check written on themselves. A fundamental characteristic of the Federal Reserve banks is that they can purchase government securities in this way, and the end result of such purchases is the creation of additional reserves for the commercial banking system. Assuming that the securities were purchased from a dealer that was not a commercial bank, the dealer's deposit in commercial bank A increases by $1,000 when he deposits the check he received in payment for them. Commercial bank A's balance at the Federal Reserve bank (its reserves) increases when it deposits the check that it received from the dealer. The simplified balance sheet of commercial bank A would now be as shown in T-account 9.3:

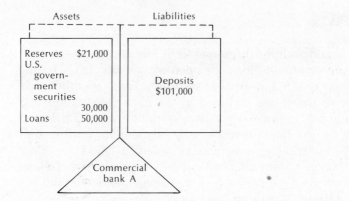

(9.3)

With total reserves of $21,000, commercial bank A is now in a position to expand its loans and create deposits. Its required reserves—its deposits multiplied by its required reserve ratio—amount to $20,200. It has excess reserves of $800, which is the difference between its total reserves and its required reserves.

In the example shown in T-account 9.3, the open-market purchase was assumed to be from a nonbank dealer who deposited his check in his bank. If a commercial bank were the dealer in U.S. government securities, the purchase would have been directly from the bank itself. In that case, there would be no increase in deposits in the commercial bank. The bank's reserves would increase, and its holdings of U.S. government securities would decrease. Its excess reserves would increase by $1,000.

MULTIPLE EXPANSION OF BANK LOANS AND DEPOSITS

When total reserves are increased through open-market purchases, the expansion in the loans and investments of banks and the amount of deposits created will be larger than the increase in reserves. This process is known as the *multiple expansion* of bank loans and deposits. A decrease in total reserves would result in a *multiple contraction* of bank loans and deposits.

A fundamental paradox in the way banks operate is that even though an individual bank cannot expand its loans by any more than its excess reserves, the banking system as a whole can. When an individual bank acquires excess reserves of $800, as shown in T-account 9.3, it may expand its loans or securities by $800 but no more. This can be seen by following through the impact on a bank's balance sheet of an increase in bank loans.

In most cases, the bank gives the borrower a deposit when it makes a loan, as shown in T-account 9.4:

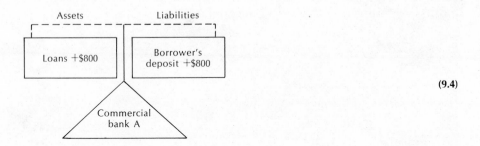

(9.4)

The borrower will then write a check on this deposit to make the purchase he had planned to make, and the person who receives the check will probably deposit it in another bank. When the borrower's check is cleared, commercial bank A loses reserves equal to $800, and the deposit of the borrower, which had been increased by $800, is reduced by the same amount. The end result is shown in T-account 9.5. If commercial bank A expanded its loans by more than its excess reserves, its reserves would fall below the legal minimum. With total deposits of $101,000, it must hold $20,200 in reserves. This limit to the individual bank's ability to expand its loans is the result of the high probability that the borrower's check will be deposited in some other bank.

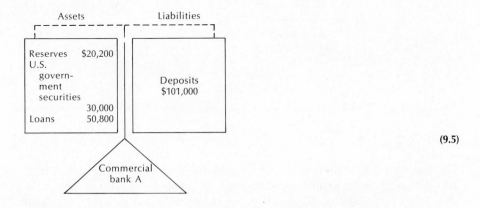

(9.5)

Despite the fact that the individual bank cannot safely expand its loans by more than its excess reserves, all banks together can. This is because there are important effects on other banks when the person who borrows from one commercial bank spends the money lent him. The check he writes will probably be deposited in another commercial bank—for instance, commercial bank B. This will initially increase commercial bank B's deposits and reserves, as shown in T-account 9.6:

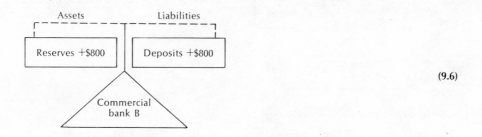

(9.6)

When the person receiving the check for $800 deposits it in commercial bank B, his deposit is increased by $800; and when commercial bank B deposits the check in its Federal Reserve bank, its reserve balance there is increased by the same amount.

Commercial bank B now has excess reserves of $640, and it can be expected to expand its loans and deposits by this amount, as shown in T-account 9.7:

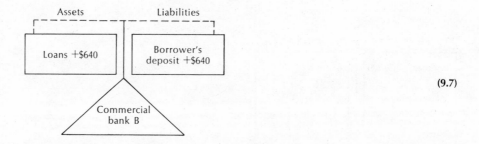

(9.7)

The borrower, however, will soon spend the $640 lent him. The result of this is to reduce the reserves and deposits of commercial bank B by $640—if the check he writes for $640 is deposited in another bank. The end result for commercial bank B of the chain of events involving the balance sheets in T-accounts 9.6 and 9.7 is shown in T-account 9.8:

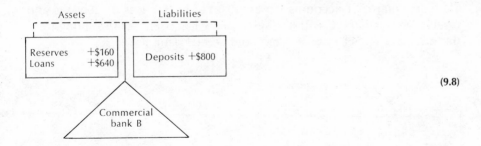

(9.8)

Again, when the borrower uses his deposit, the check that he gives to someone else will probably be deposited in a third commercial bank—let us call it commercial bank C—as shown in T-account 9.9:

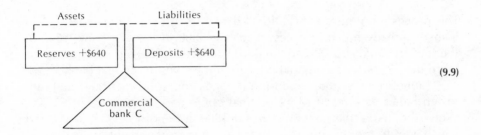

(9.9)

When commercial bank C deposits the check in its Federal Reserve bank, its reserves there will be increased. The Federal Reserve banks will then transfer $640 from commercial bank B to commercial bank C. Now bank C has $512 in excess reserves, and when it lends the $512, the initial impact is shown in T-account 9.10:

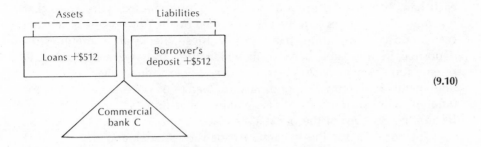

(9.10)

When the borrower pays out the check for $512 to a supplier who has an account in a fourth bank, bank C loses $512 in both reserves and deposits.

The sum total of T-accounts 9.9 and 9.10 after this loss of deposits and reserves leaves bank C with the situation in T-account 9.11 resulting from the original deposit of $640 from commercial bank B:

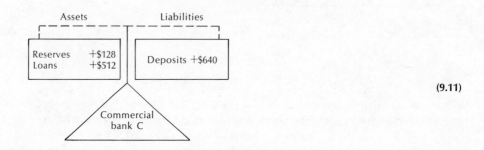

(9.11)

This process continues as additional banks are affected. The expansion in loans is already much in excess of $800—$800 in the first bank, $640 in the second bank, and $512 in the third bank. Also, deposits have increased more than $1,000 (the original increase in reserves in the first bank).

Table 9.1 shows the expansion in loans and deposits occurring in up to ten banks as a result of an original open-market purchase of $1,000. When the first bank makes a loan for $800, a deposit of $800 is created which goes to the second bank. Each bank keeps 20 percent of the deposit it receives as reserves and lends the rest. As the process continues, the amount of the deposit received by each bank and the amount each bank can lend gets smaller. The original $1,000 of additional reserves becomes distributed among all of the banks affected.

The example in Table 9.1 is simplified in order to illustrate the process involved. It assumes that the initial effect of an open-market purchase is solely on one bank. This is possible, but not necessary. It assumes that each bank was loaned up and immediately uses the excess reserves that it acquired. It assumes that the check written by the borrower was, in each case, deposited in another bank. In fact, these checks are sometimes redeposited in the same bank from which the funds were borrowed. A reserve requirement of 20 percent is used, even though legal reserve requirements are below this and vary for banks of different size and for different types of deposits. It also assumes that no other transactions affecting the reserves of the banks take place.

The formula for the maximum expansion of demand deposits that may result from an increase in reserves is

$$\Delta D = \frac{\Delta H}{r}$$

(9.1)

Table 9.1
Illustration of the Maximum Expansion of
Bank Loans and Deposits Resulting from
an Open Market Purchase of $1,000 [a]

BANK	DEPOSITED IN CHECKING ACCOUNTS	LENT	RETAINED AS RESERVES
First	$1,000.00	$ 800.00	$ 200.00
Second	800.00	640.00	160.00
Third	640.00	512.00	128.00
Fourth	512.00	409.60	102.40
Fifth	409.60	327.70	81.90
Sixth	327.70	262.20	65.50
Seventh	262.20	209.80	52.40
Eighth	209.80	167.80	42.00
Ninth	167.80	134.20	33.60
Tenth	134.20	107.40	26.80
Total for 10 banks	$4,463.30	$3,570.70	$ 892.60
Additional banks	536.70	429.30	107.40
Total, all banks	$5,000.00	$4,000.00	$1,000.00

[a] Assuming reserve requirements equal to 20 percent of demand deposits.

where Δ = increased or decreased dollar amount, D = demand deposits, H = reserves (also called the monetary base or high-powered money), and r = reserve requirement. Thus,

$$\$5,000 = \frac{\$1,000}{.20}$$

Assuming an increase in reserves of $1,000 and a legal reserve requirement of 20 percent, the maximum expansion of demand deposits would be $5,000. The maximum expansion of loans and investments is equal to the expansion of deposits less the expansion in reserves, or $4,000.

LEAKAGES

The actual expansion in demand deposits that occurs is considerably below the maximum possible because of several types of *leakage*. Leakages occur because there are several uses for the increased reserve deposits at the Federal Reserve banks that result from open-market purchases. Leakages will occur if there is an increase in currency held outside banks, in excess reserves of commercial banks, or in savings and time deposits.

Currency Drains

An expansion of bank loans and deposits tends to lead to an increase in the amount of currency outside banks. When banks make loans, some people prefer to take cash rather than an increase in their deposits, and others take some of each. When there is a multiple expansion of loans and deposits, some people who receive checks from those who have borrowed from the banks will cash them rather than deposit them. If businesses borrow for payroll purposes, cash withdrawals will take place when their employees cash their checks. The withdrawal of currency from commercial banks has the significant effect of directly reducing the reserves of the banking system and consequently the amount of expansion in loans and deposits that can be created by the banking system.

Table 9.2 shows the way in which both currency outside banks and demand deposits increased from 1964 to 1973. As the total money supply expands, both currency and demand deposits usually increase in approximately the same proportion, because the percentage of total transactions paid for by currency and the percentage paid for by checks on demand deposits are based on customary ways of making payments that do not change much. From 1964 to 1973, the currency-to-deposit ratio, shown in column 3 of Table 9.2, rose from 27.1 percent to 29.5 percent. This was unusual and was the result of a particularly large drain of currency. During much of the history of the United States, the currency-to-deposit ratio has fallen because the increase in deposits has been somewhat more rapid than the increase in currency. The recent rise in the currency-to-deposit ratio has been attributed primarily to the increase in the proportion of the total population consisting of young persons who tend to use currency rather than checks on demand deposits as a medium of exchange.

Because the customary ratio of the public's holdings of currency to their demand deposits is large, currency drains significantly reduce the ability of the banking system to create deposits. The expansion formula, taking into consideration the probable expansion of currency in circulation, is

$$\Delta D = \frac{\Delta H}{(r + c)} \tag{9.2}$$

The additional variable c is the customary ratio of currency to demand deposits that the public wishes to hold. If this ratio were 25 percent, it would mean that people wish to hold twenty-five cents in currency for each dollar held in checking accounts. If ΔH were $1,000, the currency-deposit ratio 25 percent, and the banks' legal reserve requirement 20

Table 9.2
The Ratios of Currency, Time Deposits and
Excess Reserves to Demand Deposits,
1964–1973

December	CURRENCY OUTSIDE BANKS (IN BILLIONS)	DEMAND DEPOSITS (IN BILLIONS)	RATIO OF CURRENCY TO DEMAND DEPOSITS	TIME DEPOSITS INCLUDING LARGE CDs (IN BILLIONS)	RATIO OF TIME DEPOSITS TO DEMAND DEPOSITS	EXCESS RESERVES (IN BILLIONS)	RATIO OF EXCESS RESERVES TO DEMAND DEPOSITS
	(1)	(2)	(3)	(4)	(5)	(6)	(7)
1964	$34.2	$126.3	27.1%	$126.6	100.2%	$0.411	0.325%
1965	36.3	131.7	27.6	146.8	111.5	0.452	0.343
1966	38.3	133.4	28.7	158.3	118.7	0.392	0.294
1967	40.4	146.5	27.6	183.1	125.0	0.345	0.235
1968	43.4	158.1	27.5	204.2	129.2	0.455	0.288
1969	46.1	162.5	28.4	194.4	119.6	0.257	0.158
1970	49.1	172.2	28.5	229.2	133.1	0.272	0.158
1971	52.6	182.6	28.8	270.9	148.4	0.165	0.090
1972	56.9	198.7	28.6	313.3	157.7	0.219	0.110
1973	61.6	208.8	29.5	363.1	173.9	0.262	0.125

Source: *Federal Reserve Bulletin,* March 1968, p. A6; December 1970, pp. 896–898; and February 1974, pp. 81–95, A6, and A16.

percent, the estimated expansion of demand deposits would be $2,222:

$$\$2,222 = \frac{\$1,000}{(.20 + .25)}$$

Note that, of the original increase in bank reserves of $1,000, only $444—20 percent of the increase in demand deposits of $2,222—remains as bank reserves. The amount drained into currency held by the public is $555—25 percent of the increase in demand deposits.

Holdings of Excess Reserves

Another type of drain that may cause the creation of demand deposits to be less than the maximum possible is an expansion of excess reserves. Banks hold small balances of excess reserves to cover possible shortages of required reserves, and this total amount may increase with an expansion of total demand deposits. If working balances of excess reserves were increased as bank deposits expand, there would result a loss of reserves available for the expansion of bank deposits. If a bank should decide to hold a larger quantity of excess reserves, the amount of loans that it would make as a result of receiving additional reserves would be smaller and the expansion of deposits would also be less. Using the symbol i to refer to the percentage of their demand deposits that banks customarily hold as excess reserves, the formula for the expansion of demand deposits is

$$\Delta D = \frac{\Delta H}{(r + c + i)} \tag{9.3}$$

If the banks' usual ratio of excess reserves to demand deposits were 2 percent, the expansion in total demand deposits would be reduced to $2,128:

$$\$2,128 = \frac{\$1,000}{(.20 + .25 + .02)}$$

From 1951 to 1969, total excess reserves actually declined despite the growth of demand deposits. Excess reserves of all member banks averaged $760 million in 1951, compared to about $260 million in December 1969. Since 1969, the level of excess reserves has been relatively constant, although the ratio of excess reserves to demand deposits has continued to fall.

A major reason for the downward trend of excess reserves was probably the rise in the rates of return on all types of loans and investments of commercial banks. Higher interest rates on their loans and investments would induce banks to reduce their holdings of excess reserves. Another reason why banks are holding less excess reserves is the growth of the Federal funds market. This market permits banks with excess reserves to lend them on a day-to-day basis to other banks. Banks are willing to hold smaller balances of excess reserves because of the availability of additional reserves through the Federal funds market. The growth in the size of banks may also have contributed to the smaller holdings of excess reserves. Larger banks generally hold a smaller proportion of excess reserves to total reserves than do smaller banks. Banks, on the average, have expanded in size because the establishment of new banks has been limited and the Federal Reserve System has provided the base for a growing commercial banking system.

In 1968 the Federal Reserve System adopted new procedures for calculating reserve requirements that enable banks to cut down on their excess reserve holdings. Each bank now uses average deposits two weeks earlier to calculate required reserves for the week. To calculate the bank's actual reserves, it uses cash in vault held two weeks earlier, together with average balances at the Federal Reserve bank for the current week. In addition, the new regulations permit banks to carry forward to the next reserve week excesses or deficiencies averaging up to two percent of required reserves. These regulations made it easier for banks to predict the amount of required reserves needed and to avoid shortages of reserves. After the regulations became effective in September 1968, average excess reserves of all member banks dropped from typical levels of about $400 million to $250 million or less.

The Need for Reserves for Time Deposits

Commercial banks create time deposits as well as demand deposits. Table 9.2 shows that from 1964 to 1973 the growth of time deposits (including all interest-bearing deposits) was especially large. In the expansion process, some people prefer additional time deposits rather than additional demand deposits because of the interest paid on them. The almost certain increase in time deposits causes another drain of reserves that reduces the possible expansion of demand deposits. Because banks must hold reserves behind the additional time deposits, they will have less reserves to support demand deposits. Let r' be the reserve requirement for time deposits and t be the percentage of their demand deposits that the public customarily holds in savings and time deposits. The formula for the expansion of demand deposits would be as follows:

$$\Delta D = \frac{\Delta H}{[r + c + i + (r')(t)]} \tag{9.4}$$

If the reserve requirement for time deposits were 4 percent and the ratio of time deposits to demand deposits were 100 percent, the estimated total expansion in demand deposits would be $1,961:

$$\$1,961 = \frac{\$1,000}{[.20 + .25 + .02 + (.04)(1.00)]}$$

Although the expansion of demand deposits is smaller if people shift from demand deposits to time deposits, the increase in total deposits—demand plus time—and the increase in total bank loans and investments will be larger. If the public shifts from time deposits to demand deposits, the opposite may occur—a contraction in total deposits and bank credit. In January 1974, legal reserve requirements were 3 percent for all savings deposits as well as for other time deposits up to a total of $5 million, and 5 percent for time deposits over $5 million. Because reserve requirements for savings and time deposits are lower than for demand deposits, when the public shifts from demand deposits to time deposits, excess reserves are created which the banks may lend, and a multiple expansion of loans and deposits may result. The formula showing the multiple expansion of demand deposits illustrates the way in which a shift from demand to time deposits increases total deposits. In Equation 9.4, when the monetary base increased by $1,000, demand deposits increased by $1,961, and one of the assumptions was that time deposits increased by the same amount, making a total increase in deposits of $3,922. If the ratio of time deposits to demand deposits were 200 percent instead of 100 percent, demand deposits would increase by $1,818 and time deposits by twice this—a total increase in deposits of $5,454.

VARIATIONS IN RESERVE REQUIREMENTS

If the reserve requirements behind either demand or time deposits are raised, the possible expansion of demand deposits is reduced; and if these requirements are lowered, the expansion can be larger. The Board of Governors of the Federal Reserve System has the authority to change, within limits, these requirements. Moreover, because there are different reserve requirements for banks of different size, shifts by the public in deposits from one category of bank to another affect the average values of r and r' for the entire banking system. For demand deposits there are now five categories of bank size: $2 million or less, over $2 million to $10 million, over $10 million to $100 million, over $100 million to $400 million, and over $400 million. As shown in Table 13.2 (Chapter 13), the reserve requirements in effect in January 1974 were graduated from 8 percent for net demand deposits of $2 million or less to 18 percent for net demand deposits over $400 million. There are also different reserve requirements for time deposits below and above $5 million. Thus, the values of r and r' in Equation 9.4 may change either because of changes in reserve requirements set by the Federal Reserve authorities or because of changes in the preferences of the public. If people shift their deposits to large banks which have high reserve requirements from small banks that have lower reserve requirements, the average values of r and r' for the entire banking system rise. Or if they shift deposits to banks with lower legal reserve requirements, the average values of r and r' fall. For example, if the average value of r in Equation 9.4 fell from 20 percent to 19 percent, the expansion in demand deposits would be raised to $2,000. Or if the average value of r' fell from 4 percent to 3.5 percent, the expansion in demand deposits would be raised to $1,980.

THE MONEY MULTIPLIER

In Equation 9.4, the expansion of demand deposits (ΔD) was $1,961. The increase in currency outside banks—which is added to demand deposits to calculate Money Supply I—is equal to $490 (25 percent of the expansion of demand deposits). The expansion of Money Supply I would be $2,451. The ratio $\Delta M_I / \Delta H$ is called the *money multiplier* or the *expansion ratio,* and in this example it is equal to 2.45. The expansion of M_{II} based on the example used for Equation 9.4 for demand deposits would be $4,412. An increase of time deposits equal to $1,961 would be added to the increase in currency and demand deposits. The money multiplier for M_{II} would be 4.41.

The symbol H in the numerator of Equation 9.4 includes currency outside banks in addition to bank reserves and is more accurately called the *monetary base* or *high-powered* money rather than bank reserves. The monetary base consists of the total amount of those types of money that can be used as bank reserves. A portion of the monetary base could be used as bank reserves but is not. The formula for the monetary base is

$$H = C + R \tag{9.5}$$

where C is *currency outside of banks* and R is *bank reserves.* Bank reserves include both cash in the vaults of commercial banks and their balances at the Federal Reserve banks. Thus, the monetary base is also equal to the sum of *currency in circulation* (outside the Federal Reserve banks and the United States Treasury) and the total reserve deposits of member banks at the Federal Reserve banks. The monetary base may be measured in either of those two ways, depending on whether cash in the vaults of banks is counted as reserves or currency.

The formula for the expansion of Money Supply I is

$$\Delta M_\mathrm{I} = \frac{\Delta H(1 + c)}{[r + c + i + (r')(t)]} \qquad (9.6)$$

This formula is based on Equation 9.4.

$$\text{Since } \Delta M_\mathrm{I} = \Delta D + \Delta C$$
$$\text{and } \Delta C = c(\Delta D),$$
$$\Delta M_\mathrm{I} = \Delta D + c(\Delta D) = \Delta D(1 + c).$$

ΔM_I is thus equal to the formula for the increase in demand deposits times $(1 + c)$.

The formula for the expansion of Money Supply II is

$$\Delta M_\mathrm{II} = \frac{\Delta H(1 + c + t)}{[r + c + i + (r')(t)]} \qquad (9.7)$$

$$\text{Since } \Delta M_\mathrm{II} = \Delta D + \Delta C + \Delta TD$$
$$\text{and } \Delta C = c(\Delta D)$$
$$\text{and } \Delta TD = t(\Delta D),$$
$$M_\mathrm{II} = \Delta D + c(\Delta D) + t(\Delta D) = \Delta D(1 + c + t).$$

ΔM_II is thus equal to the formula for the increase in demand deposits times $(1 + c + t)$.

In recent years the money multiplier in the United States for Money Supply I has been between 2 and 3.5.[1] The money multiplier for Money Supply II is somewhat larger, because the reserve requirements for time deposits are lower than for demand deposits, and in 1974 it was over 5. The time it takes for an increase in the monetary base to work through the multiple expansion process is very short. A study by Professor Horwich of the expansion process concluded that the response to changes in the monetary base usually occurred within a month and often much quicker.[2]

The money multiplier in the United States is higher today than in most periods in the past. In December 1973, the public's ratio of currency to Money Supply II was 11 percent, compared to 45 percent in 1867, 32 percent in 1875, and 19 percent in 1900. As people hold proportionately less in currency, the possibilities of expansion are greater. Also, lower bank reserve requirements and smaller holdings of excess reserves would tend to cause the money multiplier to be larger. Estimates by Cagan show a decline in the ratio of bank reserves to deposits from almost 40 percent in 1875 to 19 percent in 1955.[3] The larger the money multiplier, the smaller the increase in the monetary base needed to achieve a given increase in the money supply.

The symbol for the money multiplier is m, and the formula for the M_I money multiplier is derived as follows:

$$\text{Since } \Delta M_I = \frac{\Delta H(1 + c)}{[r + c + i + (r')(t)]}$$

$$m = \frac{\Delta M_I}{\Delta H} = \frac{(1 + c)}{[r + c + i + (r')(t)]} \tag{9.8}$$

The money multiplier for M_{II} would be slightly different from that for M_I, as shown in Equation 9.9:

$$m = \frac{\Delta M_{II}}{\Delta H} = \frac{(1 + c + t)}{[r + c + i + (r')(t)]} \tag{9.9}$$

The formula for the *total* supply of money (M_I or M_{II}) in terms of the two basic variables, the monetary base and the money multiplier, is

$$M = H \cdot m \tag{9.10}$$

Equations 9.6 and 9.7 may be used to calculate the increase in the money supply resulting from an increase in the monetary base, assuming no change in any of the variables affecting the money multiplier. However, if the money multiplier changes, calculations of the expansion in the money supply are more complicated than shown in those equations. Because of the interrelationships between the monetary base and the money multiplier, the equation for a change in the total money supply in terms of the monetary base and the money multiplier is

$$\Delta M = H\Delta m + m\Delta H + \Delta m\Delta H \tag{9.11}$$

To estimate a change in the money supply resulting from simultaneous changes in both the base and the multiplier, it is necessary to determine the change in both the monetary base and the money multiplier and then to determine the change in the money supply using Equation 9.11.

Figure 9.1 shows that there has been a relatively close relationship

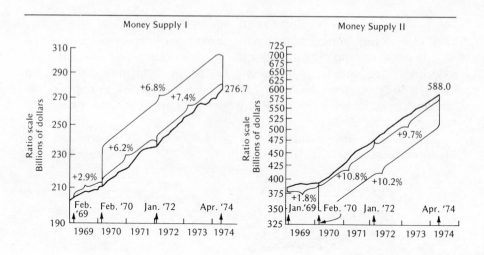

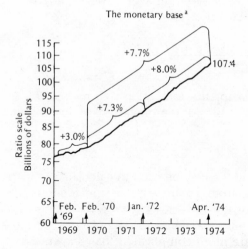

The monetary base [a]

[a] Uses of the monetary base are member bank
reserves and currency held by the public and
nonmember banks. Adjustments are made for
reserve requirement changes and shifts in
deposits among classes of banks. Data are
computed by the Federal Reserve Bank of
St. Louis.

Percentages are annual rates of change for
periods indicated.
Latest data plotted: April

**Figure 9.1   The Money Supply and the Mon-
etary Base, 1969–1974**

Source: Federal Reserve Bank of St. Louis, *Monetary Trends,* 15 May 1974.

from 1969 to 1974 between the rate of change in the monetary base and the rate of change in both Money Supply I and II. In 1969, when the rate of increase in the monetary base was relatively small, the rate of expansion in both Money Supply I and II was also small. From 1970 to 1974, the rate of expansion of Money Supply I was slightly less than that of the monetary base, and the rate of expansion of Money Supply II was slightly more rapid than that of the monetary base. Figure 9.2 shows the close long-run relationship between the monetary base and Money Supply I from 1952 to 1974.

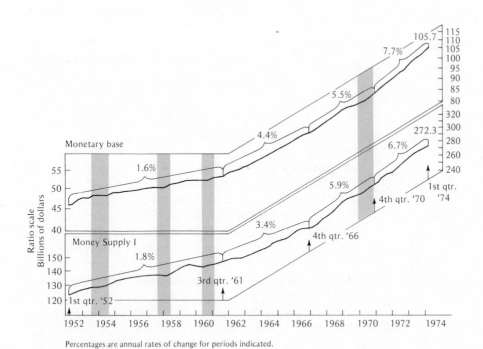

Percentages are annual rates of change for periods indicated.
Shaded areas represent periods of business recession.
Latest data plotted: 1st quarter 1974

Figure 9.2 The Monetary Base and Money Supply I, 1952–1974 (seasonally adjusted)

Source: Darryl R. Francis, "How and Why Fiscal Actions Matter to a Monetarist," in Federal Reserve Bank of St. Louis, *Review*, May 1974, pp. 2–7.

HISTORICAL VARIATIONS IN
EXCESS RESERVES

A problem that is frequently raised concerning the effectiveness of monetary policy is whether commercial banks will hold additional reserves as excess reserves rather than use them to expand loans and deposits. If additional reserves lead to an accumulation of excess reserves, monetary policy would not be an effective way of stimulating recovery.

To avoid reserve deficiencies banks almost always must hold some excess reserves. This is partly because their deposits, for which reserves must be held, change as funds continuously move from one bank to another. The inflow and outflow of deposits seldom balance either for a day or for a week, and the fluctuations in their reserve balances are unpredictable. The amount of excess reserves held relative to required reserves varies among banks. Large banks typically manage their reserve balances more carefully than smaller banks.

Even though banks hold some excess reserves, they probably try to hold as little as practicable because excess balances at the Federal Reserve banks are nonearning assets. In managing reserve balances, bankers must keep in mind two conflicting objectives—avoiding shortages, and avoiding loss of earnings by leaving funds uninvested. If a bank has more excess reserves than it desires, it can reduce its excess reserves to the desired level by expanding loans, buying securities, or reducing its indebtedness to other banks from which it has borrowed funds. Conversely, if a bank wishes to replenish its excess reserves, it may sell securities, reduce loans, or borrow funds.

Because of large excess reserves in the 1930s, the accumulation of excess reserves used to be considered a possible obstacle to the control of the supply of bank credit and money by the Federal Reserve. It was thought that if the Federal Reserve took measures to increase bank reserves, this might not have any effect on the total amount of bank loans and investments or total bank deposits, because banks might simply accumulate excess reserves. In recent decades this possibility has not been a problem. Figure 9.3 shows the volume of excess reserves that member banks held, and the increase in their total reserves from 1951 to 1963. Banks did not add to excess reserves despite the substantial increase in total reserves. (In this figure, total reserves are adjusted for changes in reserve requirements.) Instead, as banks have acquired additional reserves, they have expanded their loans and investments. The resulting expansion in their deposits has caused their required reserves to increase as rapidly as the increase in total reserves. Since 1963, required reserves have continued to increase in proportion to total reserves, and there have been no significant accumulations of excess reserves.

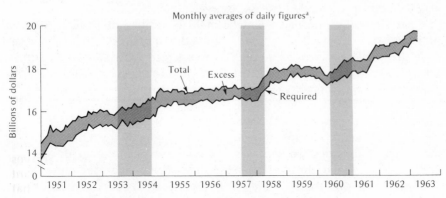

Monthly averages of daily figures[a]

Figure 9.3 Total, Required, and Excess Reserves of Member Banks, Monthly averages of daily figures[a]

Source: Federal Reserve Bank of St. Louis, *Review*, April 1963, p. 12.

In contrast to the experience since World War II, the excess reserves of banks increased sharply in the 1930s. During the first two years of the Great Depression, excess reserves were at the low levels that had prevailed in the 1920s. Starting at $60 million in December 1931, excess reserves rose to $526 million in one year. They continued to rise sharply from 1933 to 1935, fell in 1936 and 1937, and then rose to $6,646 million in December 1940.

The increase in total bank reserves from 1933 to 1940 was caused primarily by the large inflow of gold. When the United States Treasury purchases gold, member bank reserves increase. The inflow of gold was the result of the increase from $20.67 per ounce to $35 in 1934 in the price paid for gold by the Treasury, and the inflow of capital resulting from the unsettled political conditions in Europe.

There are two widely different views as to why the banks did not use the additional reserves that they acquired as a result of the gold inflow. One view, which was expressed in some Federal Reserve publications, is that there was little demand for loans, and the supply of securities available was limited. According to this view, the large volume of excess reserves constituted an unneeded stock of funds during a period of heavy unemployment. The volume of excess reserves was expected to fluctuate with changes in loan activity and gold inflows, changes over which the banks had little control. When the Federal Reserve System raised the legal reserve requirements for member banks in 1936 and 1937, its intention was to mop up unneeded excess reserves.

An alternative point of view is held by critics of Federal Reserve policy from 1933 to 1940, particularly Friedman and Schwartz.[4] They believe that banks held large amounts of excess reserves at this time because they wanted them. In their opinion, the structure of assets that banks hold depends on the available rates of return on various bank assets and on other conditions affecting bank operations. The critics believe that if reserves had increased above the quantity that banks desired, those reserves would have been exchanged for other assets. Probably the most important reason why banks desired very large excess reserves in the 1930s was that they had just been through an extremely severe financial crisis. From 1929 to 1933, one-third of the banks in the United States had ceased operations. Banks may have wanted the kind of liquidity that would protect them from failure. With large amounts of excess reserves, banks were well protected against withdrawals of deposits or forced sales of securities at a loss. Another reason banks might have desired to hold large amounts of idle reserves in the 1930s is that interest rates were very low. Interest rates on three-month Treasury bills were one quarter of one percent on the average in 1934 and reached extraordinarily low levels in 1940. The accumulation of excess reserves may have been related to the speculative motive for holding money. Interest yields on corporate Aaa bonds fell from 4.00 percent in 1934 to 2.84 percent in 1940. Because of the rise in bond prices, banks may have been unwilling to invest in them, because they expected that eventually their prices would fall.

A comparison of the Canadian and United States experience during the 1930s supports the view that banks in the United States desired to hold large amounts of excess reserves because of the runs and bank failures during the Great Depression.[5] The excess reserve ratios of Canadian banks did not increase as they did in the United States, even though the decline in interest rates and the severity of the depression were similar in both countries. The major difference between the two countries appears to be that during the Great Depression the Canadian banking system experienced no bank failures and no significant runs on banks.

Moreover, banks in the United States responded to the increase in reserve requirements in 1936 and 1937 by trying to maintain their excess reserves by selling securities—a further indication that banks *wanted* to hold their large excess reserves. When reserve requirements were raised at that time, yields on government securities rose, and the rate of growth in the money supply at first slowed down and then declined. In November 1941, when reserve requirements were again raised, there was no noticeable impact on the money market or the rate of growth of the money supply. By this time, the attitudes of bankers were probably changing because of the war.

SUMMARY

There is a fundamental paradox in the deposit creation process. In the banking system as a whole, deposits expand as a result of an increase in reserves. In an individual bank, reserves increase when deposits expand.

In the banking system, the total amount of deposits in banks will expand by several times the amount that the monetary base is increased.

Several types of leakages—increased demands for currency by the public, the desire of banks to hold larger amounts of excess reserves, and larger amounts of reserves needed for increased time deposits—reduce the amount of the expansion in demand deposits that occurs when the monetary base is increased.

Although in the 1930s banks accumulated large amounts of excess reserves, since World War II the portion of reserves held as excess reserves of banks has not expanded when the Federal Reserve has expanded the total supply of bank reserves.

NOTES

1. An analysis of some of these estimates is in David I. Fand, "Some Implications of Money Supply Analysis," *American Economic Review, Papers and Proceedings* 57 (May 1967), p. 385. See also Robert E. Weintraub, *Introduction to Monetary Economics* (New York: Ronald Press, 1970), chapter 10.
2. George Horwich "Elements of Timing and Response in the Balance Sheet of Banking, 1953–1955," *Journal of Finance* 12 (May 1957), pp. 238–255.
3. Phillip Cagan, *Determinants and Effects of Changes in the Stock of Money, 1875–1960* (New York: Columbia University Press, 1965), pp. 366–367.
4. Milton Friedman and Anna J. Schwartz, *A Monetary History of the United States, 1867–1960* (Princeton: Princeton University Press, 1963), chapter 9.
5. George R. Morrison, *Liquidity Preferences of Commercial Banks* (Chicago: University of Chicago Press, 1966), chapter 5.

QUESTIONS

9.1. Define the terms *required reserves* and *excess reserves*.

9.2. Give an example of a bank's balance sheet showing that the bank has reached the upper limit and cannot create additional deposits by making loans.

9.3. If an individual bank has excess reserves of $500, explain why it cannot normally expand its loans by more than $500.

9.4. If the reserves of the banking system are increased by $1,000, explain how the result may be an expansion in bank loans and investments and in bank deposits of several times the increase in bank reserves.

9.5. What are the two components of the monetary base, and why are they included in the monetary base?

9.6. Explain the meaning of the following equation and each of the symbols in it:

$$\Delta D = \frac{\Delta H}{[r + c + i + (r')(t)]}$$

9.7. Explain how currency drains, the holding of larger excess reserves by member banks, and the growth of time and savings deposits in member banks reduce the expansion ratio between the monetary base and the money supply.

9.8. Explain why an expansion of demand deposits tends to cause currency drains, increased holdings of excess reserves by member banks, and the growth of time and savings deposits in member banks.

9.9. What are some of the factors affecting the overall ratios of reserves to demand deposits and reserves to time deposits in the banking system?

9.10. What is the money multiplier, and what are the principal factors determining the size of the money multiplier?

9.11. Discuss the reasons for the downward trend in the total amount of excess reserves in the banking system in recent decades.

9.12. Give the alternative explanations for the expansion of the total amount of excess reserves in the banking system in the 1930s.

9.13. Know the meaning and significance of the following terms and concepts: excess reserves, required reserves, creation of deposits, multiple expansion process, leakages, money multiplier.

Chapter 10
Financial
Intermediaries

The financial system includes, in addition to commercial banks,
important types of institutions such as savings and loan associations,
mutual savings banks, life insurance companies, and many others.
These institutions have grown rapidly since World War II.

Financial intermediaries are middle-men between savers and borrowers. They generally lend funds on different terms than they accept
them. Commercial banks are themselves financial intermediaries. However, in this chapter we are concerned with the other important financial
intermediaries such as mutual savings banks, savings and loan associations,
credit unions, insurance companies, pension funds, finance companies,
investment companies, and government credit organizations.[1]

The most important intermediaries are those that create savings deposits—the depositary intermediaries. Mutual savings banks, for example,
give people savings deposits in return for funds that they use to acquire
long-term mortgages. They create liquid debt of their own to obtain
funds with which to buy the illiquid debt of others.

Financial intermediaries attempt to offer persons rates of return and
types of assets that are as attractive as possible. Although an individual
might invest directly in mortgages or securities, investment through an
intermediary has many advantages: highly qualified managers, opportunity for greater diversification, large-scale operation, and most of all, a
basically different type of asset with greater liquidity.

The way commercial banks create deposits was described in Chapter
9. In this chapter, we are concerned with the way depositary intermediaries create savings deposits. We are also interested in the characteristics of different types of nonbank intermediaries and the possible impact
of their activities on the stability of the economy.

Table 10.1 shows the comparative size of the major financial intermediaries, including commercial banks, and their rapid growth from

Table 10.1
Total Assets of Financial Intermediaries
at Year-End (in billions of dollars)

FINANCIAL INTERMEDIARY	1945	1955	1965	1973
Commercial banks	$160.3	$210.7	$377.3	$806.4
Life insurance companies	44.8	90.4	158.9	252.1
Savings and loan associations	8.7	37.7	129.6	272.4
Mutual savings banks	17.0	31.3	58.2	106.6
Finance companies	4.3	18.3	44.8	88.3
Investment companies	1.3	7.8	35.2	46.5
Credit unions	0.4	2.7	10.6	28.6
Private pension funds	2.8	18.3	73.6	131.5
State and local pension funds	2.6	10.8	33.2	80.2
Total	$242.2	$428.0	$921.4	$1,812.6

Source: United States League of Savings Associations, '74 Savings and Loan Fact Book (Chicago, 1974), p. 53.

1945 to 1973. In recent years, they have held approximately half of the total national wealth.[2] In 1800 they held less than 10 percent of the national wealth, and by 1900 still only 14 percent. From 1956 to 1965, assets of pension funds, credit unions, investment companies, and savings and loan associations increased, on the average, more than 10 percent a year, while assets of finance companies, insurance companies, mutual savings banks, and commercial banks increased from 5 to 10 percent annually.

MUTUAL SAVINGS BANKS

In November 1973, the approximately 500 mutual savings banks in the United States had a total of $95.3 billion in deposits, as shown in Table 10.2. All were chartered under state law, and almost all are located in New England, New York, and New Jersey. Most were organized many years ago, and the motivation for establishing them was social and charitable. They were designed to encourage thrift and to provide a safe place for the savings of the general public. Their lending has been cautious, and losses from bad loans have been small. Before the days of social security, they provided one of the major ways in which persons of all income levels could make provision for their retirement.[3] Mutual savings banks have no stockholders, but instead a large number of self-perpetuating incorporators—usually prominent persons in the community. The incorporators select the trustees, and the trustees select the officers. Profits either are paid out to the depositors in interest or are retained. In recent years, because of ceilings set on their interest rates by the FDIC, some mutual savings banks have accumulated large amounts of undivided profits. Although they are mutual institutions, federal government regulations do not permit them to pay out their profits to the depositors in the form of higher interest rates.

Although the Banking Act of 1933 granted mutual savings banks the right to apply for Federal Reserve membership, very few have joined. About one-tenth of them belong to the Federal Home Loan Bank System. Two-thirds of them belong to the Federal Deposit Insurance Corporation.

In 1973, most mutual savings banks paid a rate of interest on their passbook deposits of 5¼ percent, the maximum allowed by the FDIC. Mutual savings banks usually cash savings deposits immediately upon presentation of a depositor's passbook, although legally they may require a notice of thirty to ninety days, depending on state laws. They also offer *savings certificates,* and in 1973 the FDIC raised the maximum rates of interest allowed to 5¾ percent on savings certificates with a maturity from ninety days to one year, 6½ percent for certificates maturing in from one year to two and a half years, and 6¾ percent for longer maturities. Although historically mutual savings banks have not offered checking account service, they are currently moving into this type of banking. In Massachusetts and New Hampshire, they have been authorized to offer persons interest-earning savings deposits on which checks may be written—called NOW accounts. In New York City, mutual savings banks in 1974 introduced a non-interest-earning account, called the *payment account,* providing a checking service to their customers.

Table 10.2 shows that mutual savings banks have invested over two-thirds of their assets in mortgages. They intermediate between persons who want savings deposits and persons who want to borrow to purchase homes, and they create savings deposits as rapidly as people wish them. They also invest in some corporate and U.S. government bonds, and state laws usually allow them to invest in a limited amount of corporation stock. Prior to 1951, mutual savings banks were tax-exempt and had no incentive to purchase tax-exempt state and local government securities. They still invest in very few municipals even though the Revenue Act of 1951 imposed the corporation income tax on the bulk of their retained earnings.

No set proportion of cash assets is prescribed for mutual savings banks. They have been able to operate successfully with very small ratios of cash assets to deposits, because their deposits have been relatively stable compared to those of other types of banks. Table 10.2 shows that in late 1973 their cash-to-deposit ratio was less than 2 percent. During the Great Depression, they did not experience the runs that occurred on commercial banks, and there were almost no failures.[4] Some states

Table 10.2
Assets, Liabilities, and Net Worth of Mutual
Savings Banks, November 30, 1973

ASSETS	AMOUNT (IN BILLIONS)	PERCENT	LIABILITIES AND NET WORTH	AMOUNT (IN BILLIONS)	PERCENT
Cash assets	$ 1.5	1.4%	Deposits	$ 95.3	89.9%
Financial assets:			Other liabilities	3.2	3.0
Mortgages	72.8	68.7	General reserve		
Other loans	4.9	4.2	accounts	7.5	7.1
Securities:					
U. S. Government	2.9	2.7			
State and local	0.9	0.8			
Corporate and other	21.2	20.0			
Other assets	2.3	2.2			
Total	$106.00	100.0%		$106.0	100.0%

Source: *Federal Reserve Bulletin*, February 1974, p. A37.

have set limits on the size of an individual deposit, but in recent years most of these restrictions have been removed.

Although the total assets of mutual savings banks have increased to approximately five times their value of twenty-five years ago, the national income has increased proportionately. Over the years, one would expect the volume of savings deposits to increase, because people tend to save a portion of their income each year. The deposits of mutual savings banks, however, have not increased as fast as the accounts in savings and loan associations. The savings and loan associations are located in the more rapidly expanding regions of the country, and they were earlier in offering low down-payments and long repayment periods for mortgages.

SAVINGS AND LOAN ASSOCIATIONS

At the end of 1973, there were 5,244 savings and loan associations in the United States; the number has declined significantly in recent years because of mergers.[5] These associations operate under either state or federal charters. All federally-chartered S&Ls must belong to the Federal Home Loan Bank System established by the federal government; and state-chartered S&Ls, and mutual savings banks and life insurance companies, may also belong if they qualify. The total assets of S&Ls have grown rapidly since World War II—from less than $9 billion in 1945 to thirty times that in 1973 (see Table 10.3). Savings and loan associations invest in a higher proportion of mortgages and fewer corporate securities than mutual savings banks. In 1968, federal legislation empowered them to finance mobile homes, and nonmortgage loans are becoming a more important part of their total assets. Although their cash plus their securities amount to approximately 9.5 percent of their savings accounts outstanding, most of this consists of U.S. government securities, and only a small percentage is cash.

Savings and loan associations deal with the same types of savers and borrowers as mutual savings banks. Historically, they were conceived of as creating *shares* rather than savings deposits. These shares were not liabilities, and the owner was not legally entitled to demand cash. In practice, any amount could be added to or withdrawn from a passbook account at any time. Until the 1960s, the passbook account was the major savings instrument issued by savings and loan associations. In the latter half of the 1960s, they began to issue a wide assortment of accounts, and by 1972 almost half of their accounts consisted of savings certificates and other types of special savings deposits. Although most savings and loan associations are mutuals, a few are owned by stockholders, and the stock of some of these is traded on the stock exchanges.

Since 1966, the board of the Federal Home Loan Bank has set ceiling rates of interest for member savings and loan associations after consulting with the other regulatory agencies. In 1970 and in 1973, when the Federal Reserve System raised the ceiling rates for member banks and the Federal Deposit Insurance Corporation raised them for insured nonmember banks and mutual savings banks, the board of the Federal Home Loan Bank raised them for savings and loan associations. The ceiling rate on their passbook deposits was set at 5¼ percent in 1973, and

Table 10.3
Assets, Liabilities, and Net Worth of Savings and Loan Associations, November 30, 1973

ASSETS	AMOUNT (IN BILLIONS)	PERCENT	LIABILITIES AND NET WORTH	AMOUNT (IN BILLIONS)	PERCENT
Cash and investment securities	$ 21.4	7.9%	Savings capital	$224.9	82.6%
Mortgages	231.3	84.9	Reserves and undivided profit	17.4	6.4
Other	19.6	7.2	Borrowed money	16.4	6.0
			Loans in process	5.0	1.8
			Other	8.6	3.2
Total	$272.3	100.0%	Total	$272.3	100.0%

Source: *Federal Reserve Bulletin*, February 1974, p. A38.

the maximum rates payable on their savings certificates with a minimum balance of $1,000 were 5¾ percent for ninety-day certificates and 6½ percent for one-year certificates. With a minimum balance of $5,000, the ceiling rate set was 6½ percent for two-year certificates and 6¾ percent for certificates maturing in thirty months.

Members of the Federal Home Loan Bank System are subject to "liquidity" requirements set at from 4 to 8 percent of the amount of their savings accounts, as determined by the Federal Home Loan Bank Board. These reserves may be held either in cash, in deposits with a Federal Home Loan Bank, or in U.S. government securities and certain obligations of federal agencies and state and local governments. In recent years, these minimum reserve requirements have been raised in periods of tightness and lowered when credit conditions were easy. In August 1971, the minimum percentage was set at 7 percent. During the 1930s, many savings and loan associations failed, and recently, in 1966, some of them ran into financial difficulties during a "financial crunch" in which interest rates rose sharply.[6] Since 1963, there has been a growing number of mergers of savings and loan associations. They have their own Federal Savings and Loan Insurance Corporation, and shareholders are insured up to $40,000 per account.

POSTAL SAVINGS SYSTEM

In 1911, the federal government set up a savings institution associated with the postal service. This system operated until 1967. Originally only $500 could be deposited in an account, but later this was raised to $2,500. Two percent interest was paid. Until 1935, these postal savings deposits could be exchanged for postal savings bonds.

The Postal Savings System offered more convenient hours than most banks, could be more easily used by people who moved frequently, and appealed to European immigrants who were accustomed to government-run banks. Britain, France, and Germany are among the countries which have had savings bank facilities run by the postal service. During the Great Depression from 1929 to 1933, many people transferred their savings from commercial banks to the Postal Savings System.

A reserve of 5 percent of postal savings deposits was required to be held with the United States Treasury. The remainder of their assets was to be held partly in interest-earning savings accounts in national or state banks and partly in U.S. government bonds. The Postal Savings System reached its peak in 1947 when it held savings deposits totaling $3 billion for four million depositors. Even after all interest ceased to accrue on those deposits in 1967, $38 million was still unclaimed.

CREDIT UNIONS

Although there are over 23,000 credit unions in the United States, most of them are small. In late 1973 their total assets amounted to approximately $29 billion. Credit unions are typically sponsored by an occupational, union, religious, or other group. Usually only members who have purchased at least one share in the credit union can borrow. The shareholders receive a rate of interest comparable to that paid by other saving institutions. Loans are for short periods, are repaid in installments, and are usually for the purchase of consumer durables, home improvements, or personal needs. Credit unions generally have small overhead costs. Often the employer, company, school, or government department provides them with rent-free space, and the managers receive no wages or fees—possible competitive advantages. Since they are organized mainly to serve members with a particular affiliation, the market they reach is somewhat limited and to some extent the profitability of their lending is reduced. Their risks are lessened, however, by their close contact with borrowers.

Credit unions have grown rapidly during the past twenty-five years. At the end of 1973, they lent 13 percent of all installment credit outstanding.

LIFE INSURANCE COMPANIES

There are over 1,800 life insurance companies in the United States.[7] At the end of 1973, thirty-six of them had over $1 billion each in assets.[8] Table 10.4 shows that in 1973, the total assets of all life insurance companies amounted to approximately $250 billion.

These companies appear to be very different from savings institutions because of the insurance feature. In fact, they are quite similar even though they are insurance intermediaries rather than depositary intermediaries. Their premiums are a source of funds like deposits. The owner of an insurance policy is not only insured, but he also owns a potentially liquid asset with a fixed nominal value. Most life insurance policies have a specified cash value and can be converted into cash immediately. In the early years of a policy, the cash value is not large because of the cost of the immediate insurance protection that is provided. As the policy becomes older, it becomes worth close to the amount paid in plus interest.

Insurance companies are important intermediaries between persons who want life insurance on the one hand and corporate and individual borrowers on the other. In 1973, life insurance companies had 47 per-

Table 10.4
Life Insurance Company Assets,
November 30, 1973

ASSET		AMOUNT (IN BILLIONS)	PERCENT
Government securities		$ 11.5	4.6%
United States	$ 4.5		
State and local	3.4		
Foreign	3.5		
Business securities		118.0	47.0
Bonds	91.8		
Stocks	26.2		
Mortgages		80.2	32.0
Real estate		7.8	3.1
Policy loans		19.9	7.9
Other assets		13.6	5.4
Total assets		$251.1	100.0%

Source: *Federal Reserve Bulletin*, February 1974, p. A37.

cent of their assets in corporate securities (mostly bonds), as compared to the mutual savings banks with 20 percent and the savings and loan associations with less than 7 percent. Most states limit the amount of corporation stock that life insurance companies can hold—in some cases to 5 percent of assets. Because some insurance companies are very large, their investments in corporate securities are negotiated directly rather than purchased in the regular securities markets. In 1973, insurance companies held 32 percent of their assets in mortgages. Their mortgages are not so closely confined to one locality as are those of most banks.

Life insurance companies hold a negligible amount of cash and in late 1973 had only 1.8 percent of their assets in U. S. government securities. Because their disbursements are to some extent predictable, and because premium payments and mortgage payments flow in continuously, they have less need for asset liquidity than most other financial institutions.

PENSION FUNDS

Many employers, units of government, and unions operate pension funds for their members. These pension funds collect savings regularly from wage-earners or their employers, invest the funds received (mainly in corporation stock), and give the wage-earners a contract guaranteeing a regular monthly income upon retirement. The Social Security Administration's Old-age and Survivors Insurance System is by far the largest pension program in the United States, but it is usually not considered to be a financial intermediary. It is currently on a pay-as-you-go basis and its trust fund is very small compared to its obligations. Most states and cities have pension funds for their employees similar to private pension funds.

Table 10.5 shows the growth in the assets of private and state and local government pension plans. These plans have been popular because of the increasing emphasis on provision for old age. There are tax incentives encouraging *employer* contributions to these plans. Employees are not taxed on that part of their current earnings that is contributed directly to a pension fund by their employer.

Many pension systems have earned attractive rates of return because of their investments in corporate stocks during the period of prosperity since World War II. By investing in equities, the managers of these funds hope to be able to adjust benefits to keep up with rising prices.

INVESTMENT COMPANIES

Mutual funds (open-end investment companies) and other types of investment companies sell their own stock for the purpose of obtaining funds to buy the stock of a diversified group of corporations. The amount of stock sold by an open-end mutual fund is unlimited, and more can be sold at any time. As more stock is sold, the mutual fund can expand its holdings of corporation stock. If the shareowner of an open-end mutual fund wishes to sell his shares, he sells them back to the company

Table 10.5
Assets of Retirement Funds, 1945–1973
(in billions of dollars)

END OF YEAR	PRIVATE PENSION FUNDS	STATE AND LOCAL GOVERNMENT FUNDS
1945	$ 2.8	$ 2.6
1955	18.3	10.8
1960	38.2	19.6
1965	73.6	33.2
1970	110.8	57.7
1973	131.5	80.2

Source: United States League of Savings Associations, '74 *Savings and Loan Fact Book* (Chicago, 1974), p. 53.

at a price that depends on the net asset value per share of the company's portfolio at that time. In 1973 shares in over 800 mutual funds were registered for sale in the United States.

There are also closed-end investment companies. The amount of their stock outstanding is restricted usually to the amount originally sold, although it may later be expanded. The stock is not redeemable by the company but is bought and sold on the national stock exchanges or over the counter. In 1973, there were approximately eighty closed-end companies with total assets of almost $7 billion.

Investment companies offer to savers the economies of large-scale buying, diversification, and professional management. The equity claims created by a mutual fund are not necessarily more liquid than the assets the company holds. The managers of these companies hope to be able to offer savers an asset that keeps up with inflation. The value of a share is not fixed in nominal terms and can increase as prices rise.

Investment companies are incorporated under state laws and have officers and directors much as do other corporations. They are subject to both state and federal regulation. The Security Act of 1933 requires that they give full and accurate information to prospective buyers. The companies vary in size, age, and nature.

In 1973 the total assets of mutual funds were almost ten times those of closed-end investment companies. In 1945, there were only seventy-three funds belonging to the Investment Company Institute, and they had total assets of $1 billion. By 1973, assets of its 410 members had reached $60 billion.[9] In addition, there were many small companies not belonging to this trade association. Since 1968, mutual funds have had large redemptions relative to sales, and in 1972 redemptions exceeded sales. In 1969, 1970, and 1973 there were declines in the total value of assets of mutual funds because of redemptions and partly because of a reduction in the upward trend in stock prices.

FIRE AND CASUALTY INSURANCE COMPANIES

In 1971, the total assets of fire and casualty insurance companies amounted to $67 billion. They obtain some funds from premiums but have also obtained significant amounts—over 40 percent of total assets—from equity capital, either by the sale of their own stock or by retaining earnings. Their cash assets are large because of the uncertainty as to when they will have to reimburse policy-holders for losses. Because of their relatively low liability-to-assets ratio, they can invest in substantial amounts of corporation stock and profit from high earnings rates on these investments. They also invest in federal, municipal, and corporation bonds. Policies of these companies have no cash value and are not liquid assets.

FINANCE COMPANIES

Finance companies make relatively small installment loans in the form of personal loans to individuals and consumer loans for purchases of automobiles, TV sets, and other types of consumer durables. At the end of 1973, they held over $37 billion in consumer credit. This was over 25 percent of all installment credit outstanding—second only to the proportion held by commercial banks.

They differ from many financial intermediaries in that they do not obtain most of their funds directly from small savers. They borrow from commercial banks or raise funds through the sale of their own stock. Some finance companies lend directly to persons. Others lend to retailers, such as automobile dealers, by purchasing installment contracts that the retailers have negotiated with buyers. Forty-five percent of the amount of the credit they hold is in the form of personal loans, and 32 percent is in the form of automobile paper.

FEDERAL FINANCIAL INTERMEDIARIES

A number of federally sponsored and regulated agencies sell their own securities to obtain funds to lend to cooperatives and savings institutions, and to purchase mortgages and certain types of loans originally arranged by other institutions. The objective of these agencies is not primarily to make profits, but to promote or subsidize existing private institutions. Among them are the three principal agricultural credit agencies supervised by the Farm Credit Administration—the Banks for Cooperatives, the Federal Intermediate Credit Banks, and the Federal Land Banks—and agencies that supply housing credit—the Federal Home Loan Banks and the Federal National Mortgage Association. The federal government originally held a portion of the stock of these agencies, but eventual ownership by their borrowers was an objective. Most have completed this shift and no longer have subsidies from the government in the form of interest-free capital.[10] All the federal farm credit agencies have a competitive advantage in not being subject to state usury laws, and the Federal Land Banks pay no federal income taxes.[11]

Table 10.6
Total Amount of Securities Outstanding,
Government-Sponsored Credit Agencies,
December 31, 1973

ISSUE	AMOUNT (IN MILLIONS)
Banks for Cooperatives, debentures	$ 2,670
Federal Intermediate Credit Banks, debentures	6,861
Federal Land Banks, bonds	9,838
Federal National Mortgage Association, debentures and notes	23,001
Federal Home Loan Banks, bonds and notes	15,362
Total	$57,732

Source: *Federal Reserve Bulletin,* February 1974, p. A38.

Table 10.6 shows that in December 1973 there were outstanding $58 billion in securities issued by the five principal federal credit agencies. This amount has increased sharply in recent years. Their securities are traded in the U.S. government securities market and are regarded as having little more risk than U. S. Treasury securities. These agencies are subject to restrictions on the value of their issues outstanding (some number times the value of their capital plus surplus) and to certain other government regulations. Their issues, however, are not obligations of the federal government.

National banks may invest in these securities without regard to statutory limits generally applied to investment securities, and these issues may be used as security for their tax and loan accounts. Banks have invested in large amounts of them because they yield slightly more than U. S. Treasury securities. The issues held by commercial banks are usually short-term or intermediate-term.

The twelve *Banks for Cooperatives* and the Central Bank for Cooperatives were set up under the Farm Credit Act of 1933. They lend to farmers' cooperatives on commodities to be marketed; on buildings and equipment needed in storing, handling, or marketing commodities; and for short-term operating needs.[12]

The twelve *Federal Intermediate Credit Banks* were authorized by the Agricultural Credit Act of 1923. They are owned in part by the Production Credit Associations. They lend to these associations and provide a secondary market for agricultural and livestock loans.[13] Most of the securities issued by both the Banks for Cooperatives and the Federal Intermediate Credit Banks mature within one year.

The twelve *Federal Land Banks* were established by the Federal Farm Loan Act of 1916. They make first mortgages on farm properties through approximately 800 Federal Land Bank Associations. Their bonds outstanding have various maturities, with some as long as fifteen years.

The largest federal credit agency is the *Federal National Mortgage Association* (FNMA—popularly known as Fannie May). It dates back to 1938, but it was rechartered under the Housing Act of 1954. Formerly it was supervised by the U. S. Department of Housing and Urban Development, part of its stock was held by the Treasury, and it was included in the federal budget. In 1968 it was reorganized and shifted to private ownership; but it is still subject to government supervision, and the Treasury continues to control the timing and amount of its issues. It sells its own securities to obtain funds to buy FHA-insured and VA-guaranteed mortgages from private financial institutions. Formerly, it also assisted in financing special housing programs and in liquidating and managing mortgages obtained from other agencies.[14] During the 1968 reorganization, a new agency, the Government National Mortgage Association, which is government-owned, took over some of its previous functions. In 1969 Fannie May's holdings of mortgages increased nearly $4 billion. The purpose was to dampen the effect of the tight money policy in that year on the mortgage market. A similar increase in 1970 was intended to stimulate housing construction. Approximately one-tenth of its outstanding issues were short-term discount notes, similar to commercial paper, with a maturity range of 30 to 270 days as arranged. Its debentures have various maturities from one to twenty-five years.

The twelve *Federal Home Loan Banks* were authorized by the Federal Home Loan Bank Act in 1932 and are supervised by the Federal Home Loan Bank Board. They have been privately owned since 1951. Almost all of the larger savings and loan associations hold stock in those banks. The Federal Home Loan Banks issue obligations (mainly short-term and intermediate-term) to obtain the funds they lend to the savings and loan associations.[15] During a period of tight money in 1969, they increased their lending to savings and loan associations substantially for the purpose of preventing an excessive decline in the mortgage market.

In 1972, the federal government authorized the creation of the *Student Loan Marketing Association* ("Sallie Mae"). Its purpose is to stimulate the granting of guaranteed student loans by providing additional sources of funds for banks and educational institutions making these loans. Its operations are expected to be similar to those of FNMA. Its stock is sold only to educational institutions and banks.

ROTATING CREDIT ASSOCIATIONS

Foreign countries have types of financial intermediaries not found in the United States. A curious type in the Far East is the small, rotating credit association.[16] It is believed that they originated centuries ago in China. In a rotating credit association, a group of relatives or friends—often fewer than a dozen individuals—agrees to put in an equal amount each month and to assign, in advance, the monthly "kitty" to one of the members. The amounts involved are usually small, but they provide funds for weddings, home improvements, small business expenditures, clothing, or educational expenses. The arrangement ends as soon as each member has received the kitty once. Deposit schedules for these associations do not include any explicit mention of interest. The first member to receive the kitty, in effect, receives a loan and the payments that he makes are the installment payments on the loan. The last member to receive the kitty is a depositor who receives back more than the total amount he deposited. Those receiving the kitty in between the first and the last have a combination of installment loan and interest-earning series of deposits.

One reason for the prevalence of rotating credit associations (called *kyes*) in South Korea in the early 1960s was the unattractive interest rate on savings deposits allowed at banks. At that time, the legal interest rate at banks was below the rate of inflation, and savings deposits in banks yielded a negative real rate of return. Estimates of interest rates in kyes in South Korea indicate that they were much higher than the rate paid by banks. In a survey made in South Korea in 1959, approximately half the families were lending and borrowing through rotating credit associations.

CREATION OF LIQUID ASSETS BY DEPOSITARY INTERMEDIARIES

Mutual savings banks create savings deposits and savings and loan associations create shares—both types of liquid assets. Suppose a person shifts $1,000 from his checking account in a commercial bank to a savings deposit in a mutual savings bank. The initial impact on the balance sheets of the savings bank, the commercial bank, and the public is as shown on the left-hand side of Figure 10.1. The person's savings deposit in the savings bank would be increased by $1,000. The savings bank would then deposit the check received in its account in a commercial bank, where

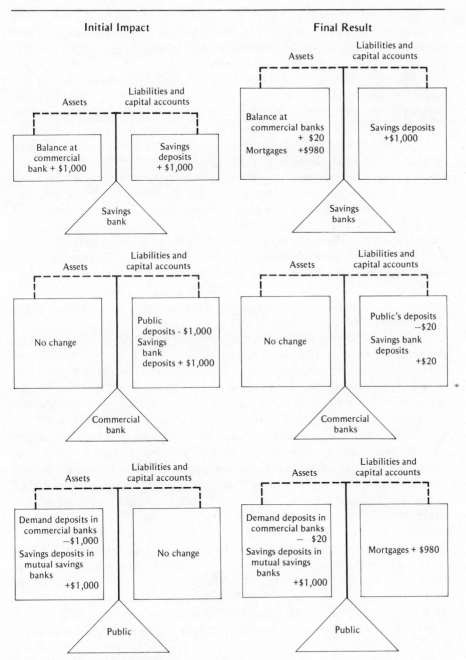

Figure 10.1 Shifting Deposits from a Commercial Bank to a Savings Bank

savings banks typically hold their reserves. From the point of view of the commercial banks the decline in the deposits of the public has been offset by an increase in the deposits of savings banks. The public has less demand deposits and more savings deposits.

Although the savings bank will hold a small amount of reserves behind the new savings deposit, the bulk of the increase in its reserve deposit at the commercial bank will be lent. Assuming that the savings bank has a reserve ratio of 2 percent, it will keep $20 behind the new deposit and expand its loans and investments by $980. When the savings bank makes a loan (usually a mortgage) of $980, the mortgages of the savings bank will increase by $980, and its balance at a commercial bank will decrease by the same amount. In return for the promissory note received from the borrower, the savings bank must give to the borrower a check for $980 written on its deposit at a commercial bank. When the person receiving the $980 check from the borrower deposits it in a commercial bank, his deposit will be increased by $980 and the savings bank deposit will be reduced by $980. The final result is an increase in savings bank deposits in commercial banks of only $20 and a decrease in public deposits of only $20, as shown in the commercial bank's balance sheet on the right-hand side of Figure 10.1.

When savings banks or savings and loan associations create savings deposits, there is a difference between what the public intended and the actual effects. The public intended to reduce its demand deposits by an amount equal to the increase in its savings deposits. In fact, its demand deposits declined by only $20, its savings deposits increased by the amount intended, and its mortgage indebtedness increased by $980.

In this example, when the mutual savings banks received additional reserves of $1,000, savings deposits expanded by the same amount. The increase in savings deposits is just equal to the initial increase in reserves, and the expansion ratio is one. The expansion ratio for savings banks could theoretically be very large with a reserve requirement of only 2 percent; but it is no larger than one, because the person who receives the funds from the borrower from the savings bank will probably deposit them in a commercial bank rather than redeposit them in a savings bank. As a result, the mutual savings banks retain only a very small amount of the initial increase in their reserves. The amount that they lose is equal to the amount that they lend. If the reserve ratio is 2 percent, the amount of reserves lost will be 98 percent of the original increase in reserves. The reserves lost when the savings bank makes a loan is a type of leakage. In the savings banking system, the leakage is so large that there is little, if any, multiple expansion of deposits of the type that occurs in the commercial banking system.

ECONOMIC SIGNIFICANCE OF FINANCIAL INTERMEDIARIES

The Federal Reserve System does not have the power to control other financial institutions in the same way it controls member banks even though it may influence them indirectly by affecting interest rates and the expansion of commercial bank deposits. Although the deposits and the total amount of the loans and investments of commercial banks may be controlled quite precisely, the Federal Reserve has little control over the activities of the financial intermediaries.

The expansion of financial intermediaries would be important if it affected the velocity of money. The velocity of Money Supply II, Y/M_{II}, for example, is the ratio of the amount of income received by people, Y, to the amount of Money Supply II they hold. It represents the number of times money circulates. The main factors affecting the velocity of money will be discussed in later chapters. An increase in savings deposits in mutual savings banks and savings and loan associations would be expected to increase the velocity of money, and a decrease would have the opposite effect. If, for example, savings deposits in mutual savings banks and savings and loan associations increased sharply, there would be less need for people to hold money and they would probably not want to hold as much money relative to their income—thus increasing the velocity of M_{II}. This could offset the effect of the Federal Reserve's control over the quantity of Money Supply II, because spending depends on both the velocity and the quantity of money. Attempts to restrain the economy during inflation might be unsuccessful, if at the same time intermediaries expanded rapidly.[17] The Federal Reserve might attempt to take increases in velocity into consideration in determining its own monetary policy, but this would not be easy to do effectively.

Even though one would exepct the volume of savings deposits in mutual savings banks and savings and loan associations to have some effect on the velocity of money, the extent to which variations in the volume of these savings deposits have actually affected velocity is not yet well understood. The growth of the savings deposits in mutual savings banks and savings and loan associations has usually varied in much the same way as the growth of savings and time deposits at commercial banks. Nevertheless, under some circumstances the growth of the financial intermediaries might differ sharply from the growth of commercial banks and this could create difficulties for the Federal Reserve System in its attempts to control the economy through monetary policy.

Another significant aspect of the activities of all types of financial intermediaries combined is their role in expanding the supply of credit.

They facilitate the expansion of total private credit—mortgages, consumer loans, corporation stocks and bonds, and other types of credit. Table 10.7 shows the annual growth of public and private credit from 1970 to 1972. During the long period of prosperity since World War II, the growth in all types of credit has been substantial, and financial intermediaries have been the principal source of much of this expansion. Wide variations in the annual growth of total credit could have a destabilizing effect on the level of economic activity. To those economists who stress the importance of changes in the volume of credit, what is important is that this growth be steady, being neither so rapid that it contributes to inflation nor so sluggish that it causes a recession.

In the 1960s and 1970s, there was particular concern over the problem of *disintermediation,* the contraction in the lending activities and deposits of the financial intermediaries. In 1966, 1969, and 1974, interest rates on Treasury bills, commercial paper, and Eurodollar deposits in foreign banks rose above the maximum rates allowed on savings deposits. It was feared that this rise in rates might cause large withdrawals of deposits from those thrift institutions and a sharp contraction in the types of credit typically financed by them. There was particular concern over the effects on the mortgage market and thus on the housing industry. Although in 1966 and 1969 large withdrawals generally did not occur, the growth in savings deposits dropped sharply for a short time and caused conditions that are usually referred to as a credit crunch. In 1969,

Table 10.7
Types of Net Private and Public Debt
Outstanding, 1970–1972 (in billions of dollars)

TYPE OF DEBT	1970	1971	1972
Corporate	$ 793.5	$ 858.6	$ 952.3
Farm	58.7	63.2	67.8
Mortgages	320.9	352.6	397.8
Commercial and financial	69.1	76.9	91.5
Consumer	127.2	138.4	157.6
Total private	$1,369.4	$1,489.6	$1,667.0
Federal government	$ 301.1	$ 325.9	$ 341.2
Federal financial agency	38.8	39.8	42.6
State and local government	144.8	163.0	176.5
Total public	$ 484.7	$ 528.7	$ 560.3
Total	$1,854.1	$2,018.3	$2,227.3

Source: *Economic Report of the President, February 1974* (Washington, D.C.: U.S. Government Printing Office, 1974), p. 323.

both the Federal Home Loan Banking System and the Federal National Mortgage Association took expansionary measures to counteract the effects of disintermediation on the supply of mortgage loans.

In recent years there has also been growing concern about the stability of the thrift institutions.[18] The accelerated inflation that started in 1965 has been the fundamental cause of the difficulties. Because their assets (primarily home mortgages) are long-term, while their deposits are in practice due on demand, a sharp rise in interest rates would create a crisis for them even if there were no government ceilings on the rates of interest they may pay on deposits. The mortgages in their portfolios were mostly issued before inflation was expected and before current market interest rates had risen to peak levels. Because the income from those mortgages is fixed, the thrift institutions would probably not be able to pay high enough rates on their deposits to compete with the other forms of saving that were paying the higher rates; as a consequence, they run the risk of losing deposits. Because these institutions typically hold only small amounts of liquid assets, many of them are not well prepared for a loss of deposits. In 1966, the Board of Governors of the Federal Reserve System granted temporary authority to the Federal Reserve banks to lend money to *nonmember* depositary intermediaries as a precautionary move.[19] With such borrowing facilities available, financial intermediaries in difficulty would be able to replace a loss of deposits with funds from the Federal Reserve banks and to avoid the necessity of liquidating assets under unfavorable conditions. Without such aid, financial intermediaries would have to liquidate some of their mortgages and investments when their deposits declined. At the time when their deposits were being withdrawn because of higher interest rates on other types of investments, the market prices of their mortgages and securities would also be low. If the coupon rate of interest on their securities and the rates on their mortgages were below current market rates, these assets could not be sold except at a discount. Taking losses would lower the value of their capital accounts, and these intermediaries would be insolvent as soon as their deposits exceeded the value of their remaining assets.

SUMMARY

Federal government regulations permit depositary financial intermediaries, such as mutual savings banks and savings and loan associations, to pay a higher rate of interest on time and savings deposits than do commercial banks.

There is no direct federal government control over the expansion of most financial intermediaries. The total amount of savings deposits in mutual savings banks and savings and loan associations expands when individuals deposit money in them.

The time and savings deposits in mutual savings banks and savings and loan associations are liquid assets that have most of the characteristics of such deposits in commercial banks.

Sharp variations in total time and savings deposits in mutual savings banks and savings and loan associations could have a destabilizing effect on the economy by causing excessive fluctuations in the supply of mortgage credit.

NOTES

1. Edward S. Shaw, "Financial Intermediaries," in *International Encyclopedia of the Social Sciences,* Vol. 5 (New York: Macmillan, 1968), pp. 432–438.

2. Raymond W. Goldsmith, *Financial Institutions* (New York: Random House, 1968), pp. 4–10, 43.

3. For an analysis of the modern role of mutual savings banks see George J. Benston, "Savings Banking and the Public Interest," *Journal of Money, Credit, and Banking* 4 (February 1972), pp. 133–226.

4. Alan Teck, *Mutual Savings Banks and Savings and Loan Associations: Aspects of Growth* (New York: Columbia University Press, 1968), pp. 118–119.

5. United States League of Savings Associations, *'74 Savings and Loan Fact Book* (Chicago, 1974), p. 61.

6. Irwin Friend, *Study of the Savings and Loan Industry* (Washington, D.C.: Superintendent of Documents and Federal Home Loan Bank Board, 1970).

7. Institute of Life Insurance, *Life Insurance Fact Book, 1973* (New York, 1973), p. 89.

8. "The Fifty Largest Life Insurance Companies," *Fortune* 90 (July 1974), p. 116.

9. Arthur Wiesenberger Services, *Investment Companies, Mutual Funds and Other Types,* 1973 ed. (New York: Wiesenberger Services, 1973), pp. 5, 12, 19; and *Federal Reserve Bulletin,* February 1974,, p. A47.

10. D. Gale Johnson, "Agricultural Credit, Capital, and Credit Policy

in the United States," in Commission on Money and Credit, *Federal Credit Programs* (Englewood Cliffs, N.J.: Prentice-Hall, 1963), p. 386.

11. John A. Prestbo, "The Ever-Growing Farm Credit System," *Wall Street Journal,* 3 November 1970, p. 10.

12. D. Gale Johnson, "The Credit Programs Supervised by the Farm Credit Administration," in Commission on Money and Credit, *Federal Credit Agencies* (Englewood Cliffs, N.J.: Prentice-Hall, 1963), p. 266.

13. Ibid., p. 260.

14. Jack M. Guttentag, "The Federal National Mortgage Association," in *Federal Credit Agencies,* pp. 67–158.

15. Ernest Bloch, "The Federal Home Loan Bank System," in *Federal Credit Agencies,* pp. 159–257.

16. Colin D. Campbell and Chang Shick Ahn, "Kyes and Mujins—Financial Intermediaries in South Korea," *Economic Development and Cultural Change* 11 (October 1962), pp. 55–68; Clifford Geertz, "The Rotating Credit Association: A 'Middle Rung' in Development," *Economic Development and Cultural Change* 10 (April 1962), pp. 241–263.

17. For a discussion of some of the questions involved, see Jack M. Guttentag and Robert Lindsay, "The Uniqueness of Commercial Banks," *Journal of Political Economy* 76 (September–October 1968), pp. 992–993; Joseph Aschheim, "Commercial Bank Uniqueness," *Journal of Political Economy* 78 (March–April 1970), pp. 353–355; John M. Culbertson, *Macroeconomic Theory and Stabilization Policy* (New York: McGraw-Hill, 1968), pp. 196–199 and 350–365; and David E. W. Laidler, "The Definition of Money," *Journal of Money, Credit, and Banking* 1 (August 1969), pp. 508–525.

18. Milton Friedman, "Using Escalators to Help Fight Inflation," *Fortune* 90 (July 1974), pp. 94–97 and 174–176.

19. Board of Governors of the Federal Reserve System, *Annual Report, 1966* (Washington, D.C., 1967), p. 10.

QUESTIONS

10.1. Explain why a mutual savings bank is a depositary intermediary.

10.2. What are the differences between mutual savings banks and savings and loan associations?

10.3.   Compare the kinds of assets in which mutual savings banks, savings and loan associations, and life insurance companies typically invest.

10.4.   Describe the following types of financial institutions: credit unions, pension funds, investment companies, fire and casualty insurance companies, and sales finance companies.

10.5.   Describe the following federal credit agencies: Banks for Cooperatives, Federal Home Loan Banks, Federal Intermediate Credit Banks, Federal Land Banks, and the Federal National Mortgage Association.

10.6.   Explain the way in which the mutual savings banks create savings deposits.

10.7.   Even though people may decide to hold smaller amounts of demand deposits and larger amounts in deposits in mutual savings banks or savings and loan associations, actually the amount of demand deposits they hold will remain approximately the same while their deposits in mutual savings banks and savings and loan associations will increase as intended. Explain.

10.8.   What is meant by disintermediation? What are some of the causes of disintermediation and some of the resulting problems?

10.9.   Why are some persons concerned about the growing importance of financial intermediaries other than commercial banks?

10.10.   Explain why a continuation of high rates of inflation may threaten the future of thrift institutions.

10.11.   Know the meaning and significance of the following terms and concepts: financial intermediary, depositary intermediary, mutual savings bank, savings and loan association, mutual fund, federal credit agency, disintermediation.

Chapter 11
The Federal Reserve System

The Federal Reserve System is similar to central banks in other countries, even though its organization is more complicated. The central policy-making unit of the Federal Reserve System is the board of governors in Washington, D.C. The operating units are the twelve Federal Reserve banks located in major cities throughout the United States.

The Federal Reserve System has not been in existence as long as most of the other major central banking systems in the world. The Bank of England was founded in 1694, the Bank of France in 1800, and the Bank of Japan in 1882. The Federal Reserve Act establishing the Federal Reserve System was passed by Congress in 1913. The System includes a Board of Governors located in Washington, D.C., twelve Federal Reserve banks with twenty-four branches located in important cities scattered across the United States, and approximately six thousand commercial banks that are members of the system.

PANIC OF 1907

Steps that eventually led to the creation of the Federal Reserve System were taken following the panic of 1907. The financial difficulties in that year had started in England. Because of disturbances in the London money market, the British had taken steps that resulted in an outflow of gold from the United States. This loss of gold reserves forced banks to contract their loans and deposits, and there was a recession that was severe even though it lasted only eleven months. Output and employment fell sharply. During this recession, several large trust companies in New York that had been operating with lower reserves and less supervision than national banks had to be assisted financially by joint action among the trust companies and by increased government deposits. There were runs on banks, and there was a scramble by smaller banks in rural areas to get more currency from their correspondent banks in large cities. The situation got so bad that the governors of several states suspended the obligation of the banks to convert deposits into currency or specie, and savings banks typically required notice of withdrawal. Because depositors could not get currency from the banks, for several months currency was traded at a premium and merchants and employers were seriously inconvenienced.

As a result of the panic, in 1908 Congress passed the Aldrich-Vreeland Act which provided for the appointment of a National Monetary Commission to study possible long-run reforms leading toward the establishment of a central bank. The commission, consisting of nine senators and nine representatives, held hearings and arranged for a large number of special studies of domestic and foreign banking. So extensive were these studies that their publication required twenty-three volumes.

ANTECEDENTS OF THE FEDERAL RESERVE SYSTEM

In the early history of the United States, both the First Bank of the United States, from 1791 to 1811, and the Second Bank of the United States, from 1816 to 1836, had performed some central banking functions. In each case, the bank's twenty-year charter was not renewed because of political opposition. Both had been owned partially by the federal government and partially by private individuals. Both had branches in important cities and performed commercial banking functions—they accepted deposits and made loans to individuals and business firms. Both handled federal government deposits (although government funds were withdrawn from the Second Bank of the United States by President Andrew Jackson three years before its charter ended). Because of their large size, both of these banks were able to regulate the lending and note issuing of the numerous state banks. This power was similar to the control that the Federal Reserve banks have over the expansion of bank credit and deposits by the member banks. If either the First or the Second Bank of the United States wished to restrain the state banks, it could reduce the specie reserves of the state banks and force them to contract by presenting some of their outstanding notes to them for redemption. To create easy monetary conditions, the Banks of the United States would either hold on to outstanding notes of state banks or hand them out to their own customers. The reserves of the state banks could also be reduced by cutting down on the lending activities of the Banks of the

United States, because the loans would usually be paid off with checks written on a state bank. On the other hand, if the Banks of the United States expanded their loans, the reserves of the state banks were usually increased.

At the time of the Civil War, the idea of a central bank was still politically unpopular. However, there was enough support for an improved system of currency to allow passage of the Currency Act of 1863 and the National Bank Act of 1864. These acts set up a system of national banks and established a relationship between the federal government and the banks that had not existed since the charter of the Second Bank of the United States had run out in 1836. The acts created the position of the comptroller of the currency who was authorized to grant charters to national banks and to regulate them. The acts also provided for the printing of uniform national bank notes, set capital requirements for the national banks, limited the amount of their notes, and established higher reserve ratios for national banks in certain large cities (designated as "redemption cities") than for other banks.[1]

In the years just prior to the establishment of the Federal Reserve System, the Treasury intervened regularly in the money market and in effect was engaging in central banking activities. Secretary of the Treasury Leslie M. Shaw, who was appointed in 1902, was an explicit advocate of using Treasury powers to control the money market. In periods of tightness when bank reserves were low relative to their deposits, the Treasury would ease conditions by increasing government deposits in the banks, purchasing government bonds, or inducing the national banks to expand the quantity of national bank notes in circulation. Secretary Shaw intervened in the market both to moderate contractions and to even out seasonal fluctuations. Although there was a small contraction in 1902, he claimed that his actions prevented a panic.

FOUNDING OF THE FEDERAL RESERVE SYSTEM

In 1913 President Woodrow Wilson, in spite of the considerable opposition to a central bank that still prevailed, pressed for legislation that resulted in the establishment of the Federal Reserve System. The type of control conceived of by the founders was different than the type relied on at the present time. The federal government, bankers, businesses, and consumers were expected to work together to achieve the objectives of the program. Their aim was to replace laissez faire by a type of cooperative system. Later the conception developed of the central government as a manager of the economy, and this idea dominates today.[2]

Initially the Federal Reserve System was meant to aid and supervise banks in order that periodic financial panics such as the one that occurred in 1907 could be avoided. It was regarded more as a banking institution than as a monetary one. The United States was then on the gold standard, and it was assumed that gold would continue to regulate the quantity of money. What was desired was a central bank that could provide discounting facilities and an elastic supply of currency.

The Federal Reserve System also was meant to provide banking services for the United States Treasury. The Treasury keeps its active deposits in the Federal Reserve banks; it also needs convenient locations for the redemption and issuing of securities, for handling foreign exchange, and for storing U. S. currency.

The original Federal Reserve Act lacked a detailed blueprint of the role of the twelve Federal Reserve banks as compared to that of the Federal Reserve Board in Washington (called the Board of Governors after the Banking Act of 1935). From 1914 to 1922 officials of the twelve Reserve banks held meetings to determine policy for the whole system, and they tended to make the decisions. Several factors—popular opposition to central control; the isolation of Washington, D.C., from important financial markets; and the leadership qualities of Benjamin Strong, the executive officer of the New York Federal Reserve Bank—helped the banks to hold a dominant role in the system in those early years.[3] Mr. Strong had been president of the Bankers Trust Company of New York City and was a prominent member of the financial community. There was continuous conflict between the Federal Reserve Board in Washington and the twelve Federal Reserve banks until the 1930s when the Board eventually achieved control over most decisions.

INDEPENDENCE OF THE FEDERAL RESERVE SYSTEM

According to law, the Federal Reserve System is an *independent agency* of the federal government. There are many independent agencies including, among others, the Federal Trade Commission and the Securities and Exchange Commission. As an independent agency, the Federal Reserve System is not under the direction of the executive branch of the federal government. Because of its close working relationship with the Treasury Department, one might expect a line of command from the Secretary of the Treasury to the board of governors. In fact, there is no such chain of command, and it is still widely considered that executive interference in the operations of the Federal Reserve System is improper. On several occasions, Congressman Wright Patman, long a member of the Banking and Currency Committee of the House of Representatives and its chairman since 1963, has initiated congressional hearings into this matter.[4]

The Federal Reserve System is legally an agent of Congress. As such it submits its annual report to Congress and regularly publishes several other reports requested by them. Members of Congress typically have attempted to guard their authority over the Federal Reserve System against encroachment by the executive branch and have reminded newly appointed officials of the system that they were agents of Congress rather than of the executive.[5]

One of the reasons for limiting the influence of the Treasury over the Federal Reserve System is to prevent political manipulation of the monetary system. Actually the Secretary of the Treasury and the comptroller of the currency were, for two decades, ex officio members of the board of governors, but the Banking Act of 1935 ended this arrangement. And Congress has, over the years, set some limits on the amount of debt sold by the Treasury directly to the Federal Reserve. This type of control actually has little effect because the Federal Reserve can invest in securities that the Treasury has first sold to others.

Another means of avoiding political control was to have an independent budget. No budgetary appropriations from Congress are necessary since the Federal Reserve banks are supported primarily by interest on their investments in U. S. government securities. The board is supported in turn by the Federal Reserve banks. To avoid political control and abrupt changes in policies, the terms in office of members of the board of governors are long and do not coincide with the terms of the president.

Despite the legal basis for the independence of the Federal Reserve System, its monetary policy ought to reinforce other federal governmental policies aimed at preventing inflation and promoting full employment. In fact, there are regular weekly meetings of the chairman of the Federal Reserve Board, the Secretary of the Treasury, and the chairman of the Council of Economic Advisors at which these officials discuss overall economic conditions and the appropriate economic policies of the federal government.

Central banks in other countries have the same problem of relating their policies to the overall economic policies of the government. The trend for the Federal Reserve System to participate in stabilization policy as an equal partner rather than as an independent player is typical of the way other central banks also have developed.

Although some persons regard the independence of the Federal Reserve System highly, others are just as critical whenever a discrepancy is observed between the economic goals of the executive and the Federal

Reserve System's policies. In December 1965, the board of governors approved a rise in the discount rate despite the disapproval of President Johnson and his economic advisors. The Joint Economic Committee immediately arranged for hearings at which Federal Reserve officials and several economists were asked to appear.[6] Professor J. Kenneth Galbraith told the committee, "Men who prefer shadow to substance still speak of the independence of the Federal Reserve System. It hasn't existed for years." Professor Seymour Harris stated, "I have never had much sympathy with the theory of independence . . . . The government certainly should not move in one direction and the monetary authority in another."

The significance of the Federal Reserve System's independence from the executive branch of the government ought not to be exaggerated.[7] The independent agencies appear to behave in much the same way as other departments and their branches. It is usually not in the interests of the officials involved, or of their organizations, to be in open conflict with top officials in the executive branch of the government, and they act accordingly. A Bank of England official, when questioned about the Bank of England's independence from the British treasury's influence, is said to have replied, "We value our independence highly and would not think of doing anything to show it."

BOARD OF GOVERNORS

On the board of governors of the Federal Reserve System are seven salaried, full-time members appointed by the president of the United States with the approval of the Senate. The governors cannot be connected with a bank during their fourteen-year term of office. To provide for geographical representation, no two can come from the same Federal Reserve district. Each appointee may serve only one full term and cannot be reappointed for another. One term expires every two years, and unexpired terms are filled for the years left to run. Members of the board of governors are the only politically appointed officials in the Federal Reserve System. They in turn choose three of the directors, including the chairman, of each of the Federal Reserve banks and must approve the selection of the president of each bank. The ability of a president of the United States to influence the board by appointing persons of his choice is limited because of the long term of appointment of members of the board and, barring resignations or deaths, the possibility of only two appointments in each four-year presidential term of office. For many years, the background of most appointees to the board was in banking and finance. In recent years, several members of the board have been professional economists.

The board of governors has a chairman and vice-chairman. They are appointed by the president of the United States, and each holds office for a period of four years. From 1951 to 1970, the chairman of the board was William McChesney Martin. He served on the board for part of one unexpired term and one full fourteen-year term. He received appointments as chairman from Presidents Truman, Eisenhower, Kennedy, and Johnson. In January 1970, President Nixon appointed Arthur F. Burns to the board of governors as its chairman.

The governing members of most of the independent agencies such as the Interstate Commerce Commission and the Federal Trade Commission must include members of both political parties. There is no requirement of this type for governors of the Federal Reserve System. During 1969, the first year after President Nixon was elected, all seven members of the board of governors were members of the Democratic party. Political bias of the board of governors could be important. Tight monetary policies are politically less popular than easy monetary policies, and board members might be reluctant to pursue the former if it meant possible defeat of their party.

The offices of the board of governors are located in Washington, D.C. The top members of the staff are economists, lawyers, examiners, and administrators. Included are departments engaged in research on domestic and international financial trends—information needed by the board in assessing the prevailing economic and credit conditions. These departments publish the results of their research and up-to-date statistics on money and credit in the monthly *Federal Reserve Bulletin*.

The board of governors is a central policy-making organization; the operations of the system are performed by the Federal Reserve banks. Since the board was given few specific objectives in the Federal Reserve Act, it has broad powers in formulating and carrying out its chosen objectives.

Only one of the three principal instruments used to carry out monetary policy—changes in legal reserve requirements of member banks—is the sole responsibility of the board of governors. Responsibility for the other two is shared. Policies concerning open-market operations—the most important of the three—are determined by the Federal Open Market Committee, on which both members of the board and presidents of the Federal Reserve banks sit. Changes in the discount rate are initiated by the individual Federal Reserve banks but must be approved by the board. Two other less important instruments are the responsibility of the board rather than the Federal Reserve banks: controls over interest rates on savings deposits in member banks, and controls over margin requirements on loans made by banks, brokers and dealers, and others to purchase securities. Since September 1966, the board of governors has been directed to consult with the Federal Deposit Insurance Corporation and the Board of the Federal Home Loan Banks in setting ceiling interest rates on savings deposits. Joint regulation of margin requirements by the Securities and Exchange Commission and the board of governors was provided by the Securities and Exchange Act of 1934. Brokers on the exchanges can borrow only from banks complying with all federal laws pertaining to the securities business.

FEDERAL OPEN MARKET COMMITTEE

The Federal Open Market Committee (FOMC) meets every four weeks in Washington and is the principal policy-making unit of the system. Members of the board of governors make up a majority of the committee. It consists of twelve members: the seven governors of the Federal Reserve Board and presidents of five of the twelve Federal Reserve banks. The chairman of the board of governors is chairman of the committee. The president of the Federal Reserve Bank of New York is always a member of the committee. The other four positions on the committee are rotated among the remaining presidents of the Federal Reserve banks. In practice, all twelve presidents attend committee meetings and take part in the discussion, although seven of them are nonvoting members.

The FOMC was formally established in 1935, although a committee to coordinate open-market purchases had been set up by the Federal Reserve banks in the early 1920s. As its name indicates, the FOMC is specifically responsible for determining policy with respect to the purchase and sale of U. S. government securities. At its meetings, conditions in the economy are discussed and a decision must be made concerning the appropriate monetary policy in view of the economic situation. Staff economists of the board of governors and the Federal Reserve banks are called on to provide information. The policies determined by the FOMC are issued as directives to the manager of the System Open Market Account, a vice-president of the Federal Reserve Bank of New York.

The actual purchase and sale of securities is performed by the Federal Reserve Bank of New York. The purchases and sales are made through private U. S. government securities dealers, most of whom have their offices in New York. The securities and currency transactions made by the Federal Reserve Bank of New York are apportioned among all the Federal Reserve banks according to each bank's share of total Federal Reserve bank assets.

FEDERAL ADVISORY COUNCIL

The Federal Advisory Council was established by the Federal Reserve Act to provide communication between the banking industry and the Federal Reserve System. The council consists of twelve members, one selected annually by each of the Federal Reserve banks. Members usually are prominent bankers from the district. The council meets four times a year with members of the board of governors and confers on banking policy and the conditions of the economy. They also carry back information to the banks in their areas. There is no obligation on the part of the board of governors to execute any recommendations of the council. Since this council has no power to act or set policy, it receives little public attention, and its usefulness and effectiveness are questioned by some.

FEDERAL RESERVE BANKS

The Federal Reserve Act authorized the division of the United States into twelve districts, each with a Federal Reserve bank. The boundaries of those districts and the location of the twelve Federal Reserve banks and their branches are shown in Figure 11.1

The Federal Reserve banks are the operating units of the system. Each of the twelve banks performs routine services for its region. Each issues and supplies Federal Reserve notes, clears checks on commercial banks, processes Treasury checks, stores coins, handles government debt issues, and examines and supervises the state-chartered member banks in its area. Five Federal Reserve bank presidents are on the important Federal Open Market Committee.

Each Federal Reserve bank is a federally chartered corporation with stockholders, directors, and a president. The stockholders of a Federal Reserve bank are the member banks in its district, and they select six of its nine directors. At present, a member bank purchases an amount of stock in its district Federal Reserve bank equal to 3 percent of its capital stock and surplus, although legally it may be asked to purchase twice this amount. As the common stock and surplus of a commercial bank grow, it must purchase more Federal Reserve bank stock to keep the percentage at 3 percent. Dividends paid on the stock are limited to 6 percent.

There are three types of directors of Federal Reserve banks—Class A, Class B, and Class C—and there are three of each type. Terms of all directors are for three years. One director of each type is elected (or appointed) each year.

June 23, 1965

Legend
——— Boundaries of Federal Reserve districts   ——— Boundaries of Federal Reserve branch territories
⊛ Board of Governors of the Federal Reserve System
○ Federal Reserve bank cities   • Federal Reserve branch cities

**Figure 11.1   The Federal Reserve System:
Boundaries of Federal Reserve Districts and
Their Branch Territories**

Source: Board of Governors of the Federal Reserve System, *The Federal Reserve System,
Purposes and Functions* (Washington, D.C., 1967), p. 16.

Class A directors are elected by the member banks. They may be
and usually are bankers, and it was the intention of the founders of the
Federal Reserve System that they should represent the lenders of money.
The member banks are divided into small, medium, and large banks, and
each group selects one Class A director.

Class B directors are also elected by the member banks. They may not
be bankers. They are usually prominent persons in business, commerce,
or agriculture and are expected to represent the borrowers of money. The
three groups of member banks, classified according to size, each select
one Class B director.

The three Class C directors are appointed by the board of governors.
It was the intention of the founders of the Federal Reserve System that
the Class C directors should represent the public, and they must not be
officers of any bank. The board of governors also selects the chairman and
the deputy chairman of the board of directors of each Federal Reserve
bank. These are always Class C directors. Although originally the chairman

was the chief executive officer of the bank, this was changed by the Banking Act of 1935.[8] The directors of each Federal Reserve bank select the managing officials of the bank—the president, vice-president, and others. The appointments of the officers are for five years and must be approved by the board of governors.

Some bankers are on the board of directors of each Federal Reserve bank, but the majority of members are not bankers. Congressman Wright Patman has for many years felt that the influence of banking interests on the operations of the Federal Reserve System was too great. He has been critical of the Federal Advisory Council and of the representation of banking interests on the boards of directors of the Federal Reserve banks. The interests of banking institutions are frequently reflected in Federal Reserve policy. As with most of the regulatory agencies of the federal government, a certain amount of regulation has been combined with serving the interests of those regulated.

The Federal Reserve banks are semi-public corporations. Though they are privately owned, the profits earned by the owners are limited, and the owners share control of the selection of the officials of the bank with the board of governors. The purpose of the Federal Reserve banks is not to maximize profit, but to implement monetary policy and supervise the member banks. Each bank must submit its budget to the board of governors for approval.

The twelve Federal Reserve banks report their financial accounts weekly to the board of governors, and this information is summarized and published in newspapers each Friday. The Federal Reserve banks and their branches are examined at least once a year by examiners from the board of governors. The Interdistrict Settlement Fund in Washington, D.C., maintained by the Federal Reserve banks, settles claims between these banks. Most Federal Reserve banks have their own monthly bulletin containing articles on current economic problems, and some of these bulletins circulate widely. Each bank, to some extent, guards its individuality and independence.

The Federal Reserve banks vary in size. Ten of them have branches, which are located in twenty-four important cities. Each branch is controlled by a small board, the majority of members of which is chosen by the district Federal Reserve bank and the rest by the board of governors. Branches are closely regulated by the district bank.

MEMBER BANKS

All national banks are required by law to be members of the Federal Reserve System, and some state banks have voluntarily applied for admission and have been accepted. State banks belonging to the system do so because they desire the resulting privileges and prestige. Member banks must forego some opportunity to invest because they must set aside more reserves than is required of most nonmember banks. Historically, interest rates on their savings deposits have been subjected to greater regulation than those of other banks; more extensive and frequent reports and examinations are sometimes required; they cannot make exchange charges on checks on themselves presented for payment by other banks (they must remit at par); they can hold only certain types of assets; and there are special regulations concerning capital, mergers, branches, holding companies, and officers. The Federal Reserve System is restrained from making the conditions of membership too severe lest member banks withdraw and obtain state charters. Member banks have the privilege of withdrawing after six months' notice, or sooner if this time period is waived by the Federal Reserve banks. In recent years, several national banks have given up their membership by withdrawing from the national banking system and obtaining state charters.

Member banks can obtain loans, currency, information, and advice from their Federal Reserve bank. They can use check-clearing facilities and transfer funds over the Federal Reserve's leased teletype wires. Member banks elect six of the nine directors of the Federal Reserve bank. Some of the privileges of Federal Reserve membership can be obtained by nonmember banks by qualifying as a "clearing bank" at the district Federal Reserve bank.

The privileges and prestige of membership have not been worth the costs and disadvantages to many state banks. From the beginning, Federal Reserve authorities had hoped to enlist the state banks, but they were not successful. During World War I there was an increase in such membership because of changes in government regulations that made membership more attractive and because of the increased need to borrow from Federal Reserve banks. Many state banks still choose not to belong, and they are supported in their independence by some of the large city banks that like the correspondent arrangement of holding state bank reserves as interbank deposits. In 1972, the President's Commission on Financial Structure and Regulation recommended the enactment of federal legislation requiring all state banks to become members of the Federal Reserve System, and in 1973 this action was recommended by the chairman of the Board of Governors of the Federal Reserve System.[9]

SUMMARY

The Federal Reserve System is responsible for the formation and administration of monetary policy.

The organization of the Federal Reserve System was designed to maintain representation from borrowers, lenders, and the public within different geographical regions. It has retained a high degree of participation by those its policies affect.

The Federal Reserve System is an independent agency and is not subject to supervision by the executive branch of the federal government. Although its monetary policies might conflict with other governmental economic programs, such conflicts have been rare.

NOTES

1. See Ross M. Robertson, *History of the American Economy,* 3d ed. (New York: Harcourt Brace Jovanovich, 1973), pp. 402–411.
2. Herbert Stein, *The Fiscal Revolution in America* (Chicago: University of Chicago Press, 1969), pp. 12–16.
3. For an account of the early history of the Federal Reserve System, see Lester V. Chandler, *Benjamin Strong, Central Banker* (Washington, D.C.: The Brookings Institution, 1958), pp. 40–48.
4. See, for example, U.S., Congress, Joint Economic Committee, Subcommittee on Economic Stablization, *Conflicting Official Views on Monetary Policy: April 1956, Hearing,* 84th Cong., 2nd sess., 1956, pp. 2–3.
5. See, for example, U.S., Congress, Senate, Committee on Banking and Currency, Subcommittee on the Nomination of Charles Noah Shepardson, *Hearing, February 25, 1955,* 84th Cong., 1st sess., 1955, pp. 2–3.
6. U.S., Congress, Joint Economic Committee, *Recent Federal Reserve Action and Economic Policy Coordination, Hearings, Parts 1 and 2, December 13–16, 1965,* 89th Cong., 1st sess., 1966.
7. James M. Buchanan, "Easy Budgets and Tight Money," *Lloyds Bank Review* (April 1962), pp. 17–30, reprinted in Richard A. Ward, ed., *Monetary Theory and Policy* (Scranton, Pa.: International Textbook Co., 1966) pp. 164–177.
8. For an analysis of the administrative organization of the Federal Reserve System, see George L. Bach, *Federal Reserve Policy-Making* (New York: Alfred A. Knopf, 1950), p. 25.

9. *Report of the President's Commission on Financial Structure and Regulation* (Washington, D.C.: U.S. Government Printing Office, December 1971), pp. 65, 87, 91, and 93; and Arthur F. Burns, "The Structure of Reserve Requirements," *Federal Reserve Bulletin* (May 1973), pp. 339–343.

QUESTIONS

11.1. Describe some of the attempts to establish a central bank in the United States prior to the Federal Reserve System.

11.2. What are the characteristics of the Federal Reserve System as an "independent agency"?

11.3. Give the arguments for and against the "independence" of the Federal Reserve System.

11.4. What are the different functions of the board of governors of the Federal Reserve System, the Federal Open Market Committee, and the Federal Reserve banks?

11.5. Which unit of the Federal Reserve System controls open market operations, changes in the discount rate, changes in reserve requirements, margin requirements, and maximum rates of interest allowed on savings and time deposits?

11.6. In what ways does the organization of the Federal Reserve System provide for some political control by the executive branch of the government?

11.7. In what way does the organization of the Federal Reserve System make possible the influence of bankers, borrowers, the public, and different geographical areas of the country?

11.8. Why do some commercial banks prefer not to be member banks?

11.9. Know the meaning and significance of the following terms and concepts: board of governors of the Federal Reserve System, member bank, Federal Open Market Committee, independent agency, Federal Reserve district, semi-public corporation.

Chapter 12
Central Banking

Historically, the principal function of central banks was to prevent bank panics even though it is no longer their predominant objective. Modern central banking is concerned with the formation of policies that affect the factors in the bank reserve equation and thus influence the monetary base.

The principal types of assets and liabilities of the twelve Federal Reserve banks combined, as of December 31, 1973, are shown in Table 12.1. Although each Federal Reserve bank is a separate corporation and keeps its own accounts, in this table the individual accounts of the twelve Federal Reserve banks are added together.

Table 12.1
Balance Sheet,
Twelve Federal Reserve Banks Combined,
December 31, 1973 (in millions of dollars)

ASSETS		LIABILITIES AND CAPITAL ACCOUNTS	
Gold certificate account and cash	$ 11,731	Federal Reserve notes	$ 64,262
Special drawing rights certificate account	400	Deposits: Member bank	27,060
U.S. government securities and federal agency obligations	80,495	U.S. treasurer	2,542
Loans	1,258	Foreign and other	1,884
Acceptances	68	Deferred availability cash items	4,855
Cash items in process of collection	8,168	Other liabilities and accrued dividends	981
Bank premises and other assets	1,152	Capital accounts	1,688
Total assets	$103,272	Total	$103,272

Source: *Federal Reserve Bulletin*, February 1974, p. A12.

PRINCIPAL ASSETS OF THE
FEDERAL RESERVE BANKS

The first of the seven categories of assets in the balance sheet of the Federal Reserve banks is the *gold certificate account* and *cash*. Gold certificates are a type of paper money that must be backed fully by gold bullion, valued at the official price of gold—currently $42.22 an ounce. The amount of gold certificates declines when the Treasury sells gold and increases when the Treasury buys gold. Also, in 1971 and 1973, when the official price of gold was raised by Congress, the amount of gold certificates outstanding was increased. The federal government took gold certificates out of public circulation in 1934. Since then they have been owned only by the Federal Reserve banks. When the Treasury increases the amount of gold certificates, they are issued to the Federal Reserve banks in exchange for Treasury deposits at the Federal Reserve banks. The gold certificate account is a record of the gold certificates owned by the Federal Reserve banks. Transactions involving gold certificates are carried out through book entries rather than through the issuance of paper certificates.

In 1968, the legal requirement that the Federal Reserve banks hold an amount in their gold certificate account equal to 25 percent of their outstanding Federal Reserve notes was discontinued. Before 1965, this 25 percent reserve requirement had applied not only to oustanding Federal Reserve notes, but also to the deposit liabilities of the Federal Reserve banks; up until 1946, the required reserve ratios for both notes and deposits were larger than 25 percent. Until they were discontinued, these requirements set an upper limit to the expansion of the notes and deposits of the Federal Reserve banks.

The amount of *cash* (listed in the balance sheet with the gold certificate account) usually amounts to approximately $300 million and consists of coins and a very small quantity of U.S. notes. Both coins and U.S. notes are issued by the Treasury. The Federal Reserve banks acquire coins when new coins, manufactured by the U.S. mints, are deposited in them. Commercial banks also may deposit any coins in excess of their needs. The Federal Reserve banks must have an adequate supply of all of the different kinds of coins on hand in order to meet requests for coins from the commercial banks. New coins go from the U.S. mints to the public by way of the Federal Reserve and the commercial banks.

The *special drawing rights certificate account* is based on the special drawing rights that have, since January 1970, been acquired by the United States Treasury. SDRs are issued by the International Monetary Fund—an institution founded in 1944 to faciliate world trade—and are an alternative to gold, dollars, or pounds as a type of international money. They are accounts in the IMF that the governments of countries may use to obtain the currency of other countries. A unique aspect of SDRs is that they are not a type of money based on a balance sheet, and they are neither assets nor liabilities of the IMF. When SDRs are traded between the governments of two countries, the IMF simply records the transfer.

When the United States Treasury obtains an allocation of SDRs from the IMF, it may issue SDR certificates to the Federal Reserve banks in exchange for a special Treasury deposit at the Federal Reserve banks. SDR certificates can be owned only by the Federal Reserve banks, and the amount issued by the Treasury cannot exceed the amount of SDRs that the Treasury owns. Since 1970, the amount of SDR certificates issued by the Treasury has been considerably less than the amount of their SDRs.[1] The SDR certificate account is a record of the SDR certificates owned by the Federal Reserve banks and is similar to the gold certificate account. Transactions between the Federal Reserve banks and the United States Treasury are carried out through book entries, rather than the issuance of paper SDR certificates.

The types of *U.S. government securities and federal agency obligations* owned by the Federal Reserve banks are the same as those owned by commercial banks and other financial institutions. They are their principal earning asset. The interest income received from them is much more than they need to cover their expenses and the dividend paid to stockholders, and since 1947 the bulk of their profits has been returned to the Treasury. Open market operations—the Federal Reserve System's principal instrument of control—consist of varying the total amount of these securities. The purpose of such operations is to achieve the broad objectives of monetary policy rather than to maximize profits or provide for bank liquidity.

Federal Reserve banks make *loans* to member banks rather than to businesses or persons. One of the explicit purposes of the original Federal Reserve Act was to provide member banks with facilities for borrowing. Loans were formerly listed on the balance sheet as "discounts and advances." In recent years, borrowing by member banks has almost always consisted of advances—loans in the form of promissory notes signed by member bank officials and backed by collateral in the form of U.S. government securities. Discounts consist of commercial loans, owned by the member banks, which are sold to the Federal Reserve banks at a discount for a given period of time. At the end of the duration of the discount, the commercial loan is returned to the member bank.

The rate of interest charged for loans to member banks is known as the discount rate, and raising or lowering this rate is one of the Federal Reserve banks' three major instruments of control. Borrowing is normally only for very short periods—seldom more than fourteen days. All member banks must calculate reserve requirements weekly. If a bank finds itself with less than its required amount of reserves (cash in vault plus deposits in its Federal Reserve bank), it can usually borrow to make up the difference. Instead of borrowing from the Reserve bank in order to acquire needed reserves, a bank might sell some of its securities or borrow reserve funds from another member bank.

The Federal Reserve banks usually own a small amount of *bankers' acceptances*. These are short-term investments and are competitive with short-term U.S. government securities and commercial paper.[2] Bankers' acceptances are bills of exchange that are payable at a future date and are used primarily in international trade. They are readily marketable because they have been marked as "accepted" by the bank on which they are drawn. They are sold at a discount. In order to stimulate the use of acceptances in international trade, the Federal Reserve banks purchase bankers' acceptances at prevailing interest rates in any quantity in which they are offered.[3] A commercial bank can replenish its reserves by selling bankers' acceptances to the Reserve banks.

Cash items in process of collection consists of those checks that have been received and are in the process of being sent for collection to other Federal Reserve banks. When a Federal Reserve bank receives a check written on a bank in another Federal Reserve district, the check is sent to the appropriate Federal Reserve bank for collection. During the time a check is in process of collection, it is counted as an uncollected cash item.

Other assets consists of the premises of the Federal Reserve banks, holdings of foreign currencies in the form of bank balances in foreign central banks, and certain operating assets such as accrued interest, other accounts receivable, and the premium on securities. Foreign currencies are held for the purpose of controlling exchange rates between the dollar and other currencies.

PRINCIPAL LIABILITIES AND CAPITAL ACCOUNTS OF THE FEDERAL RESERVE BANKS

The combined balance sheet of the twelve Federal Reserve banks shown in Table 12.1 lists seven principal categories of liabilities and capital accounts. The first and most important of these is the *Federal Reserve notes* —the total amount of this type of paper money that has been issued to the commercial banks and the public. When outstanding, these notes are liabilities of the Federal Reserve banks. Each of the Federal Reserve banks has a large amount of brand-new notes in its own vaults ready for issue when requested by the member banks. However, until issued, these notes are not liabilities and have no economic significance.

Member bank deposits are the checking accounts of the member banks at the Reserve banks and are the major portion of their legal reserves. Each member bank deposits in its account at its Federal Reserve bank the checks it receives on other banks. The account of the depositing bank is credited, and the account of the bank on which the check was written is debited. Also, member banks may withdraw currency from their deposit accounts if they need additional coins or paper money, and they may deposit excess currency in their accounts. Variations in the total amount of these reserve balances are significant because they affect the activity of the member banks.

The *treasurer's deposit* is the checking account of the *United States* Treasury. Although the Treasury usually deposits tax payments first in commercial banks, these are transferred to the Federal Reserve banks several times each week. All of the checks that the Treasury writes to pay for its expenditures are written on its deposits at the Reserve banks.

Foreign deposits are checking accounts of foreign governments or their central banks. Central banks of different countries typically have deposits in one another for international settlement purposes. *Other deposits* consists of nonmember bank deposits used for check clearing, officers' and certified checks, deposits of international organizations, a special account of the secretary of the treasury, and deposits of various federal corporations such as the National Railroad Passenger Corporation (AMTRAK) and the Communications Satellite Corporation (COMSAT). There are no deposits of business firms, individuals, or state and local governments in the Federal Reserve banks.

Deferred availability cash items is a liability account that results from the practice of not immediately crediting to a bank's account the amount of the checks deposited that are written on distant banks. Credit for checks that must be sent to other Federal Reserve banks for collection may be delayed up to two days. There is a time schedule based on the distance to the other bank. The purpose of crediting checks in this way is to reduce fluctuations in member bank deposits resulting from changes in the volume of cash items in process of collection. *Float* is the difference between cash items in process of collection (on the asset side) and deferred availability cash items. It represents the amount credited to the accounts of member banks that has actually not yet been collected. Variations in float may have important short-run effects on bank reserves.

The *other liabilities and accrued dividends* item is an estimate of the operating obligation of the banks which have been incurred but not yet paid at the time of the preparation of the balance sheet.

The *capital accounts* includes capital paid in (capital stock), surplus, and other capital accounts. The stock of the Federal Reserve banks is owned by the member banks and pays a maximum dividend of 6 percent. Each member bank currently subscribes to an amount of stock equal to 3 percent of its own capital stock (at par value) and surplus. The total amount of the stock of the Reserve banks gradually expands as the member banks increase their own capital stock and surplus.

Since 1964, surplus has been maintained at an amount equal to the capital paid in. The Federal Reserve banks do not have the inducement to increase the size of their capital accounts that profit-maximizing enterprises have. If the Reserve banks were dissolved, the law provides that the surplus be paid to the U.S. government rather than to the owners—the member banks. As their capital stock expands, the Federal Reserve banks increase the amount of their surplus by retaining some of their net earnings. If they were to operate at a loss in any year, and nevertheless paid their regular dividend, their surplus would be reduced. The third type of capital account—other capital accounts—is an estimate of the unallocated net earnings for the year to the date of the preparation of the balance sheet.

HISTORICAL FUNCTION OF CENTRAL BANKS

With a central bank, a banking system ought to be able to terminate runs on commercial banks quite promptly. The way this may be done was first clearly described many years ago by a British economist, Walter Badgehot, in his book entitled *Lombard Street*. Although the possibility of runs on banks in the United States or in most of the larger countries is now remote, unstable banking conditions may still develop in smaller countries. In 1965 runs were reported on the banks in Hong Kong as the result of a rumor that checks on one of the banks there had not been honored in the United States. In September 1970 there were runs on banks in Santiago, Chile, following the election of a Marxist president.

The historical function of a central bank is to make it possible for commercial banks to supply the public with all of the additional currency it wants at any time. Normally, banks operate satisfactorily even though they have little currency behind their deposits, because the daily currency inflow tends to equal the outflow. But throughout the nineteenth century the public periodically lost confidence in the solvency of banks. The outflow of currency would exceed the inflow; and since there was no central bank to supply commercial banks with additional currency, supplies of currency eventually ran out.

Runs start when the public fears that banks might fail. Usually this occurs after some banks have gone bankrupt. Prior to 1934 it was a serious matter to have a deposit in a bank that failed. Deposits were not insured by the federal government and were only rarely insured by states. Depositors had to wait until the bank had gone through bankruptcy before being paid off. The percentage of their deposits paid off depended on the value of the bank's assets.

Prior to 1914 the usual technique of handling panics was to suspend specie payments. This was usually done through a proclamation by the governor of the state. The banks remained open and continued to lend money, persons continued to write checks on demand deposits and to deposit checks received by them, but it was not possible to cash a check. The suspension of specie payments was a serious inconvenience not only to the public, but also to merchants who needed currency for their cash registers and to businessmen who needed currency for their payrolls. As soon as people regained faith in the banks and stopped mass attempts to convert deposits into currency, the panic was over.

The Federal Reserve System was explicitly designed to provide "an elastic currency." If a run starts, it provides a system in which the supply of currency can be expanded. The technique involves two essential elements. First, a central bank is a banker's bank and a "lender of last resort." When in need of reserves, member banks can borrow from a Federal Reserve bank. As shown in Figure 12.1, when a member bank borrows, it receives additional reserve deposits in return for its loan.

The second essential feature of a central bank such as the Federal Reserve System is that its deposits and notes—both liabilities—are interconvertible. A member bank in need of cash may convert the additional reserves it has borrowed into Federal Reserves notes, as shown in the T-accounts in Figure 12.2.

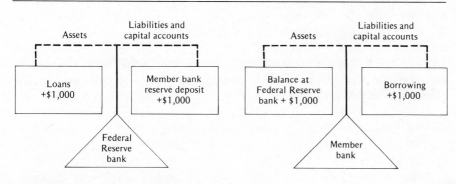

Figure 12.1   Borrowing from the Federal Reserve Banks

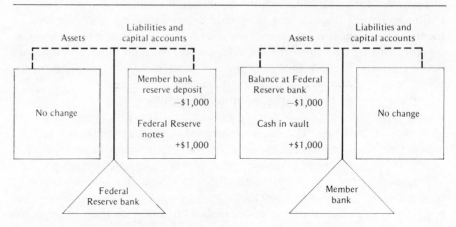

Figure 12.2 Exchanging Member Bank Reserve Deposits for Additional Cash in Vault

A fundamental characteristic of a central bank is that its notes are liabilities. While the supply of an asset can always be exhausted, liabilities are expansible. A basic need when there are runs on banks is that the supply of currency be increased. Because the Federal Reserve banks can provide commercial banks with a readily available source of additional cash in vault, the commercial banks are able to cash deposits as rapidly as the public wishes. Also, because member banks can borrow from the Federal Reserve banks, declines in their deposits may be offset by an increase in their borrowing. There need be no reduction in their total liabilities and total assets. This has a very desirable effect on the stability of the economy because any significant contraction in the total assets of commercial banks would tend to have a depressing effect on business activity.

Historically, there were several limitations to the process of expanding the quantity of Federal Reserve notes. Federal Reserve banks used to be required to hold reserves of gold certificates equal to 25 percent of their Federal Reserve notes outstanding; they were able to expand the amount of notes only if they had excess reserves. This restriction was discontinued in 1968. A second limitation was the requirement that the Federal Reserve banks have as collateral behind Federal Reserve notes an equivalent amount of assets consisting of gold certificates and *eligible paper*—certain types of short-term commercial loans. The collateral acceptable has been broadened several times and now includes U.S. government securities. At the present time, the issuing of Federal Reserve notes is not at all restrained by the collateral requirements. The amount of the assets owned by the Federal Reserve banks which is eligible as collateral exceeds by a substantial margin the amount of Federal Reserve notes outstanding.

Financial panics of the type that used to occur periodically have become very rare. Nevertheless, experience during the Great Depression in the United States shows that runs on banks and the problems related to runs may occur even when a country has a central bank that can itself issue notes and create deposits. The Federal Reserve's original technique of combating runs can be relied upon only if member banks increase their borrowing. In 1930–1933, borrowing was not increased sufficiently to maintain the volume of bank reserves. The runs reduced bank reserves and caused a contraction of loans and investments and deposits. An alternative technique that would have worked, even if the commercial banks did not increase borrowing, would have required the Federal Reserve System, on its own initiative, to keep total bank reserves from declining. The monetary authorities had the ability to create money quickly on their own authority through open-market purchases, but during most of the period from 1930 to 1933 they did not make sufficient open-market purchases. The result was a gradual economic breakdown that eventually ended in the banking holiday of 1933 in which every bank in the country was shut down by presidential proclamation.

The establishment of the Federal Deposit Insurance Corporation in 1934 reduced the likelihood of runs on banks. When deposits are insured, persons are much less anxious about the safety of their deposits if events cause them to anticipate possible bank failures.

ASSISTING THE TREASURY

In most countries, the central bank at times assists domestic Treasury operations. After the Federal Reserve System had been operating for only three years, the monetary authorities were faced with the problem of helping to finance the large Treasury deficits caused by World War I. During this war and for several years afterwards, Federal Reserve loans to commercial banks were expanded rapidly. This enabled the banks to purchase some of the bonds issued to finance the war. During World War II, the Federal Reserve System also expanded bank reserves in order to help finance the large budget deficits and to make the selling of government securities at low rates of interest possible. Both of these efforts by the Federal Reserve System to assist Treasury wartime financing resulted in a rapid expansion of the money supply and problems of inflation.

In recent years, the Federal Reserve has usually supported Treasury debt operations during periods of refundings. They maintain an "even-keel" policy designed to keep changes in monetary policy from interfering with Treasury debt operations. When Treasury securities are refunded, the Treasury announces the rate of interest on the new issues prior to the date of the exchange. The quantity that investors are willing to purchase at the rate set cannot be known in advance and may be more or less than desired. Because the owners of the maturing issues may desire cash instead of the new issues offered, the exchange may be only partially successful. A factor that affects attrition, or the amount taken in cash, is a change in monetary policy between the time when the terms of the exchange are announced and the time when the exchange is closed. Because the Treasury attempts to keep the coupon rates on its new issues as low as possible, a small rise in market interest rates could make the new issues unattractive relative to other available investments. To keep attrition relatively low, the Federal Reserve usually purchases securities in the open market so as to prevent interest rates from rising. If they have to purchase more securities than they believe is desirable from the point of view of their other objectives, they may attempt later to sell the excess amount purchased.

The Federal Reserve may also assist the Treasury during periods of deficit financing. When its expenditures are greater than its revenues, the Treasury must issue additional securities to finance the difference. Through open-market purchases, the Federal Reserve increases the reserves of the member banks so that the banks are provided with funds with which to purchase a portion of the new issues. This may enable the Treasury to sell the new debt at slightly lower interest rates than would otherwise be possible. Member banks own a significant percentage of the total national debt outstanding and are an important part of the total market for U.S. government securities.

If the Treasury could rely more on marketing techniques that did not require Federal Reserve assistance in their debt operations, the implementation of monetary policy would be simpler. With the auction technique used for Treasury bills, the Treasury always sells the amount it wishes because it is willing to accept the best price that it can get, and the Treasury need never be concerned about selling the quantity of bills it wishes to sell. One would expect that the even-keel policy used with debt operations would occasionally conflict with attempts by the Federal Reserve authorities to achieve their other targets. During the period of assisting the Treasury, monetary policy would have to depart from its usual target, and overcompensation would later be required to get back on the target. Such actions would either be destabilizing in the short run or result in missing the long-run target.

BANK RESERVE EQUATION

The most carefully watched item on the combined balance sheet of the twelve Federal Reserve banks is the deposits of the member banks. Changes in this item may signify a change in Federal Reserve policy. An increase in member bank reserve deposits may be a signal of an easier policy, and a decrease would indicate a tighter policy. Bank reserves consist of both these member bank balances at the Federal Reserve banks and cash in vault, although the balances at the Reserve banks are by far the more important of these two components.

The factors that may cause changes in the member bank balances at the Federal Reserve banks are listed in the bank reserve equation.[4] There are thirteen factors in the equation. Seven of them *supply* reserve funds. An increase in these items tends to increase member bank reserve deposits. The other six factors *absorb* reserve funds. If they increase, the effect is to decrease member bank reserve deposits.

The seven factors supplying member bank balances at the Reserve banks are:

U.S. government securities owned by the Federal Reserve banks;
loans of the Federal Reserve banks;
the float of the Federal Reserve banks;
other Federal Reserve assets;
the gold stock;
special drawing rights certificate account;
treasury currency outstanding.

The six factors absorbing member bank balances at the Reserve banks are:

currency in circulation;
Treasury cash holdings;
Treasury deposits in the Federal Reserve banks;
foreign government deposits in the Federal Reserve banks;
other deposits in the Federal Reserve banks;
other Federal Reserve liabilities and capital accounts.

In addition to changes in member bank reserve deposits, we are interested in changes in the monetary base—total member bank reserve deposits plus total currency in circulation (outside the Federal banks and the Treasury). The difference between the totals for factors supplying and absorbing reserves in the bank reserve equation is equal to member bank reserve deposits at the Federal Reserve banks. The other component of the monetary base, currency in circulation, is one of the factors in the bank reserve equation absorbing reserve funds. In equations 9.6 and 9.7 (see Chapter 9), the monetary base was the most important variable determining the expansion in the money supply. If the monetary base increases, the total money stock tends to increase; and if it decreases, the money stock tends to decrease.

Table 12.2 shows the bank reserve equation for December 31, 1973. The figures in this equation are derived from two sources: the balance sheet of the twelve Federal Reserve banks combined and the monetary accounts of the United States Treasury. Table 12.1 shows the balance sheet of the twelve Federal Reserve banks for December 31, 1973. The items in the monetary account of the Treasury for the same date are included in Table 3.1. The significant monetary accounts of the Treasury are (1) the gold stock, (2) Treasury currency outstanding, (3) currency in circulation, and (4) Treasury cash holdings.

FACTORS SUPPLYING RESERVE DEPOSITS

It is important to understand the way in which each of the factors in the bank reserve equation affects member bank reserve deposits. Consider first the seven factors supplying member bank reserve deposits. These are the items that if increased cause member bank reserves to increase.

1. Changes in the quantity of *U.S. government securities owned by the Federal Reserve banks* are the result of open-market operations. These operations are solely at the initiative of the Federal Reserve authorities and reflect the attempts to achieve their broad economic objectives. This is the most important item in the bank reserve equation because the Federal Reserve System may control total bank reserves through control of this item.

Open-market purchases increase the reserve deposits of the member banks, and sales decrease their reserve deposits. The way in which open market sales decrease member bank reserves is illustrated in the T-accounts shown in Figure 12.3. When the Federal Reserve banks sell $1,000 of securities to a nonbank dealer, the latter would pay for the securities with a check written on a member bank. The Federal Reserve bank, on receiving the check, would reduce the member bank's balance at the Federal Reserve bank. The check would then be sent to the member bank, which would reduce the deposit of the dealer. If securities are sold to a member bank that is also a dealer in government securities, the effect on the T-accounts would be slightly different. The member bank would acquire

**Table 12.2
The Bank Reserve Equation, Member Bank
Reserves, and the Monetary Base,
December 31, 1973**

	AMOUNT (IN MILLIONS)
Factors supplying reserve funds at the Federal Reserve banks	
Federal Reserve credit:	
U. S. government securities	$ 80,495
Loans and acceptances	1,326
Float	3,099 [b]
Other Federal Reserve assets	1,152
Gold stock	11,567
Special drawing rights certificate account	400
Treasury currency outstanding	8,716
Total	$106,755
Factors absorbing reserve funds at the Federal Reserve banks	
Currency in circulation	$ 72,497
Treasury cash holdings	317
Deposits with Reserve banks:	
Treasury	2,542
Foreign	251 [b]
Other	1,419 [b]
Other Federal Reserve liabilities and capital	2,669
Total	$ 79,695
Member bank reserves	
With Federal Reserve banks	$ 27,060 [a]
Currency and coin	6,781
Total	$ 33,841
The monetary base	
Member bank reserves with Federal Reserve banks	$ 27,060
Currency in circulation	72,497
Total	$ 99,557

In some cases, details do not add to totals because of rounding
[a] Equals the total amount of the factors supplying reserve funds less the total amount of the factors absorbing reserve funds at the Federal Reserve banks: $106,755 million − $79,695 million = $27,060 million.
[b] On December 31, 1973, the amount of float and the total of foreign and other deposits in the bank reserve equation was less than the amount of those items in the combined balance sheet in Table 12.1. This is because the estimates of those items in the combined balance sheet may be affected by local holidays which prevent some Reserve banks from remitting funds to other Reserve banks, whereas an adjustment in the bank reserve equation is made for this effect.
Source: *Federal Reserve Bulletin*, February 1974, pp. A4, A5, and A12.

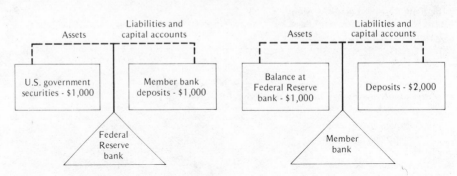

Figure 12.3　Open-Market Sales to a Non-bank Dealer

additional U.S. government securities, and there would be no change in its deposit liabilities. When the member bank pays for the securities, its balance at the Reserve bank would be decreased by the amount of the transaction.

2. Changes in *loans* occur when there are changes in the volume of borrowing by the member banks. Borrowing is always at their initiative. The Federal Reserve authorities typically lend to member banks that desire to make loans in order to meet their reserve requirements. The Federal Reserve banks may attempt to influence the volume of borrowing by changing the discount rate. An increase in member bank loans at the Federal Reserve banks causes a similar increase in their member bank deposits. In exchange for the loan from the Federal Reserve bank, the member bank receives an increase in its reserve deposit.

3. *Float* is the difference between cash items in process of collection and deferred availability cash items. It tends to be higher toward the end of each week when there is an increase in the volume of checks in process of collection, and reaches a peak near the beginning and middle of most months. These seasonal variations reflect the bill-paying patterns of individuals and businesses. In addition, anything that causes a delay in the transfer of checks, such as a snowstorm affecting air transport, causes float to increase. Float may change sharply from week to week and often has significant short-run effects on reserve funds that are difficult for the monetary authorities to control.

When, for example, the Federal Reserve Bank of Boston receives a check for $1,000 that is written on a member bank in the San Francisco district, its cash items in process of collection are increased by $1,000 and for a period of two days it may credit deferred availability cash items as shown in the T-accounts in Figure 12.4. Thus far, float has not been increased because float is the difference between cash items in process of collection and deferred availability cash items. At the end of two days, even though the Federal Reserve Bank of Boston will probably still have the cash item in process of collection of $1,000, it will have to credit the deposit of the member bank that deposited the check for $1,000. When this occurs, float increases and there is an increase in the total reserves of the banking system. The reserves of the member bank in the Boston district have been increased while the reserves of the member bank on the West Coast have not yet been reduced. When the check is collected, the deposit of the member bank on which the check was written and the gold certificate account of the Federal Reserve Bank of San Francisco would be reduced. At the same time, cash items in process of collection at the Federal Reserve Bank of Boston would be decreased and its gold certificate account increased. The records of these transfers of gold certificates are handled by the Interdistrict Settlement Fund. As shown by the changes in T-account (c) in Figure 12.4, both float and total bank reserves decline when the check is collected from the Federal Reserve Bank of San Francisco.

4. *Other Federal Reserve assets* include the bank premises, assets denominated in foreign currencies, and other assets not listed separately on the balance sheet. The purchase of these assets would tend to be balanced on the liabilities side of the balance sheet by an increase in member bank reserves.

5. Changes in the *gold stock* are controlled by the Treasury rather than by the Federal Reserve banks, and historically they were an important factor affecting bank reserves. Purchases of gold tended to increase member bank reserves, and sales tended to decrease them. When the Treasury—through the Exchange Stabilization Fund established by Congress in 1934—sold gold, the foreign central bank that was buying the gold would usually pay for it by writing a check on its deposit account in a member bank. As shown in the T-accounts in Figure 12.5(a), when the Treasury deposited the check it received at the Federal Reserve bank, the Treasury deposit would be increased and the deposit of the member bank on which the check was drawn would be reduced. The Reserve bank would then return the check to the member bank which would reduce the deposit of the foreign government.

Gold sales often involved a second step. Because the gold certificate account must be backed by gold bullion, the amount of this account would have to be reduced. When the Treasury reduced its gold certificate account at the Federal Reserve banks, its deposit there was also simultaneously reduced, as shown in the T-account in Figure 12.5(b). The *net* effect of gold sales on the balance sheet of the Federal Reserve banks was a reduction in both the gold certificate account and member bank de-

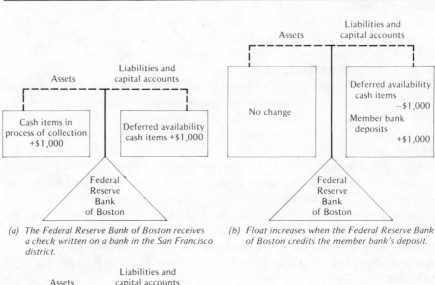

(a) The Federal Reserve Bank of Boston receives a check written on a bank in the San Francisco district.

(b) Float increases when the Federal Reserve Bank of Boston credits the member bank's deposit.

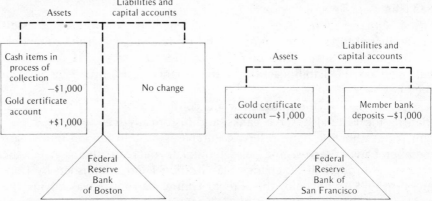

(c) The reduction of cash items in process of collection at the Federal Reserve Bank of Boston reduces float, and settlement between the two Federal Reserve banks is made through changes in their gold certificate accounts.

Figure 12.4   Changes in Federal Reserve Float

posits, and the amount of the Treasury's deposit at the Federal Reserve banks was unchanged.

6. The *special drawing rights certificate account* is based on the new SDRs issued by the International Monetary Fund.[5] The Treasury receives allocations of SDRs from the IMF and may also purchase and sell SDRs to the governments of other countries. The purpose of SDRs is to provide additional international reserves that may be used to facilitate international transactions. The government of a country would typically sell

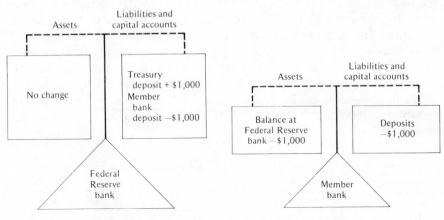

(a) *The United States Treasury receives payment for the gold.*

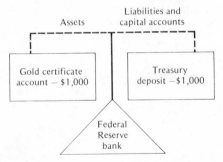

(b) *The Treasury reduces its gold certificate account.*

Figure 12.5   Treasury Sales of Gold

SDRs when importers needed foreign exchange to pay for an excess of imports over its exports. If, for example, importers in the United States needed pounds to cover a deficit, the first step would be for the Treasury's Exchange Stabilization Fund to sell SDRs for pounds. According to the procedures established by the IMF, these pounds would not be purchased from Great Britain, but from the government of another country with a surplus in its balance of payments, for example West Germany. When the Exchange Stabilization Fund had purchased pounds with SDRs, it would then sell the pounds it had received to a foreign exchange dealer. When the check received in payment for the pounds was deposited in the Federal Reserve bank, the special Treasury account would be increased and the member bank deposit on which the check was written would be decreased, as shown in the T-account in Figure 12.6(a). Because the Treasury has used some of its SDRs to obtain foreign currency, it may decide to reduce the SDR certificate account at the Reserve banks. If so, both the SDR certificate account and the special Treasury account at the Federal Reserve banks would be reduced, as shown in the T-account in Figure 12.6(b). The net effect of these two transactions on the balance of the Federal Reserve banks, as shown in the T-accounts in Figure 12.6 (a) and (b), is a reduction in both the SDR certificate account and in member bank deposits.

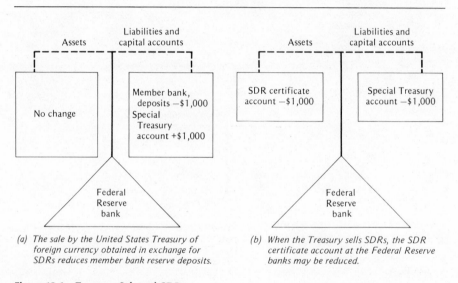

(a) The sale by the United States Treasury of foreign currency obtained in exchange for SDRs reduces member bank reserve deposits.

(b) When the Treasury sells SDRs, the SDR certificate account at the Federal Reserve banks may be reduced.

Figure 12.6   Treasury Sales of SDRs

If the governments of other countries need foreign exchange and use their SDRs to obtain it from the United States, the effect on the T-accounts would be the opposite of that illustrated in Figure 12.6. When the Exchange Stabilization Fund exchanges foreign currencies for SDRs, it must first obtain the foreign currencies from foreign exchange dealers in the United States. The dealer receiving payment from the Treasury would probably deposit the check received in a member bank. Member bank reserve deposits would be increased and the special Treasury account would be decreased. Also, when the Treasury's Exchange Stabilization Fund purchases these SDRs, the Treasury may decide to increase its SDR certificate account; if so, both the SDR certificate account on the asset side of the balance sheet of the Federal Reserve banks and the special Treasury account on the liability side would be increased. The net effect would be an increase in the SDR certificate account at the Reserve banks and an increase in member bank reserve deposits, and there would be no net change in the special Treasury account.

The United States Treasury may acquire SDRs through allocations from the International Monetary Fund as well as through purchases from foreign governments. Upon receiving additional SDRs, the Treasury may issue a larger quantity of SDR certificates. If it did, both the SDR certificate account at the Reserve banks and the special Treasury account would be increased. There would not be any effect on member bank reserve deposits until the additional funds in the special Treasury account were spent. If the Treasury did not issue additional SDR certificates when its holdings of SDRs were increased, there would be no effect on the balance sheet of the Federal Reserve banks and no effect on member bank reserve deposits. In December 1973, the Treasury had issued only $400 million in SDR certificates out of the $1,949 million of SDRs that it owned.

7. *Treasury currency outstanding* consists of coins and a small amount of U.S. notes and other notes in process of retirement. The volume of coins outstanding increases as a result of the production of new coins by the United States mints. The amount of U.S. notes outstanding has declined since they were originally issued during the Civil War.

When newly minted coins are deposited in the Federal Reserve banks, the cash of the Reserve banks and the deposits of the Treasury increase. When the Treasury spends these funds, the Treasury's deposits are decreased, and member bank reserve deposits are increased. The Treasury would have to spend part of the additional deposit to pay for the manufacture of the new coins. In addition, it earns a profit called seigniorage—the difference between the nominal value of the coins and their cost of production. This is a source of government revenue that will eventually be spent. The person receiving payment from the Treasury would deposit the check received in a member bank; when the member bank deposits the check in its Federal Reserve bank, the member bank's deposit there would be increased and the Treasury's deposit decreased, as shown in the T-account in Figure 12.7 (b).

FACTORS ABSORBING RESERVE DEPOSITS

An increase in any of the absorbing factors results in a decrease in member bank reserves.

1. *Currency in circulation* consists of both Federal Reserve notes and Treasury currency not owned by either the Treasury or the Federal Reserve banks. The public gets more currency by withdrawing it from its

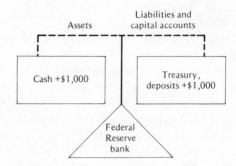

(a) The Treasury deposits newly minted coins in the Federal Reserve banks.

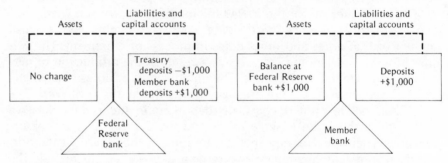

(b) When the Treasury spends the amount in its deposit, member bank reserve deposits increase.

Figure 12.7 An Increase in Treasury Currency Outstanding

demand deposits at commercial banks. The commercial banks then have to replenish their cash in vault by ordering additional currency from the Federal Reserve banks. When currency in circulation increases, member bank deposits at the Federal Reserve banks are decreased. As shown in Figure 12.8(c), in order to obtain additional cash in vault, the member bank's balance at the Federal Reserve bank will be decreased. If the increase in currency in circulation consists of Federal Reserve notes, the T-accounts in Figure 12.8(a) show that there will be an increase in the Federal Reserve bank's liability "Federal Reserve notes" and a decrease in the amount of its member bank deposits. On the other hand, if the increase in currency in circulation consists of coins, Figure 12.8(b) shows that there will be a reduction in the Federal Reserve bank's asset "cash" as well as a reduction in the amount of its member bank deposits.

If the entire increase in the amount of Federal Reserve notes and

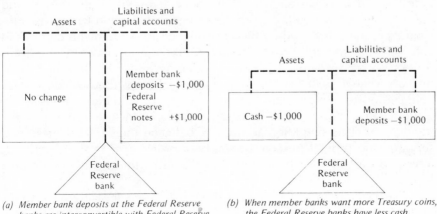

(a) *Member bank deposits at the Federal Reserve banks are interconvertible with Federal Reserve notes.*

(b) *When member banks want more Treasury coins, the Federal Reserve banks have less cash.*

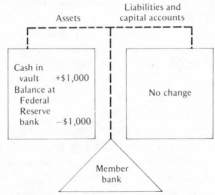

(c) *Member banks exchange deposits at the Federal Reserve banks for either Treasury coins or Federal Reserve notes.*

Figure 12.8 An Increase in the Amount of Currency Held by Member Banks

Treasury coins in circulation were retained by the member banks as cash in vault, total member bank reserves would be unaffected because cash in vault is counted as legal reserves. If, however, the additional cash in vault were withdrawn by the public, total member bank reserves would be reduced.

A decrease in currency in circulation would have the opposite effect of that shown in the T-accounts in Figure 12.8. When a member bank deposits currency in a Federal Reserve bank, its balance there will increase.

2. *Treasury cash holdings* include the amount of Federal Reserve notes and Treasury currency that the United States government holds and the quantity of gold bullion in the Exchange Stabilization Fund. The principal type of money used by the Treasury consists of demand deposits in commercial banks and Federal Reserve banks, but the Treasury also holds some cash for types of transactions requiring this type of money. Gold in the Exchange Stabilization Fund is *free gold*, not used as backing for gold certificates. Before the suspension in 1971 of gold transactions by the United States, the free gold was readily available for use in international transactions. This simplified accounting between the United States Treasury and the Federal Reserve banks, because changes in the amount of free gold did not affect the amount of gold certificates in the Reserve banks.

The T-accounts in Figure 12.9 show that if the Treasury were to increase its holdings of Federal Reserve notes or coins by withdrawing them from a Federal Reserve bank, or if it withdrew gold certificates from the account of the Reserve banks so as to increase the volume of gold bullion on which no certificates are issued, the deposits of the Treasury at the Federal Reserve banks would be reduced. None of the transactions shown in Figure 12.9 has directly affected member bank reserve deposits. However, if the Treasury replenished its deposits at the Federal Reserve banks by depositing tax revenues, member bank reserve deposits would be reduced. The effect on the T-accounts would be as shown in Figure 12.10. The Treasury would replenish its deposits at the Federal Reserve banks because of its policy of keeping these deposits at a constant level.

An increase in Treasury cash holdings could be acquired from the public, rather than from the Federal Reserve banks. However, if the Treasury acquired additional Federal Reserve notes or coins from the public, there would be a decrease in currency in circulation, which is one of the other factors absorbing member bank reserve deposits. The T-account analysis in Figure 12.10 explains the effect of an increase in Treasury cash holdings assuming no change in any of the other factors in the bank reserve equation.

3. The *U.S. Treasurer's deposit* consists of the amount of Treasury balances at the Federal Reserve banks. The Treasury attempts to keep this amount constant. In 1973, the target level was approximately $2.5 billion. Funds are transferred to this account from the commercial banks three times a week. The amount to be transferred is announced in advance in order to give adequate warning. The amount of this account in a Federal Reserve bank goes down as the Treasury writes checks on it and as the checks are deposited for collection in a commercial bank. It goes up as taxes are deposited directly in it or as funds are transferred from the commercial banks. If the Treasury officials could know exactly how much

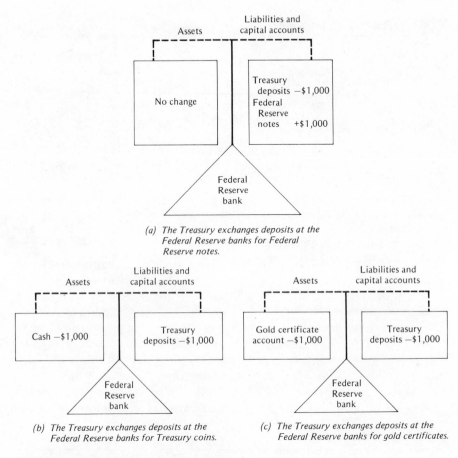

(a) The Treasury exchanges deposits at the Federal Reserve banks for Federal Reserve notes.

(b) The Treasury exchanges deposits at the Federal Reserve banks for Treasury coins.

(c) The Treasury exchanges deposits at the Federal Reserve banks for gold certificates.

Figure 12.9 An Increase in Treasury Cash Holdings

the federal government was spending each day and how quickly recipients would cash their checks, they could keep the balance constant by transferring from the commercial banks the exact amount needed. Because they are unable to make such accurate predictions, the amount of this deposit varies. If checks are cashed more quickly than expected, it will fall below the desired goal; or if checks are cashed slowly, it may rise above the target.

The T-accounts in Figure 12.11 show that when the Federal Reserve banks receive an addition to the Treasury's deposits, the reserve deposits of the member banks on which the checks were written are decreased.

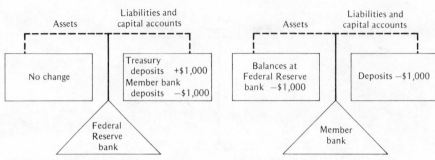

(a) The Treasury deposits a check on a member bank in its deposit at the Federal Reserve bank.

(b) When the check is returned to the member bank, the taxpayer's deposit is reduced.

Figure 12.10   Treasury Deposits at the Federal Reserve Banks Are Replenished

At the same time, the U.S. government deposits in the member banks are also reduced.

4. and 5. *Foreign* and *other deposits* are deposits of foreign central banks, nonmember banks, and numerous governmental institutions. Changes in these deposits have the same effect on member bank reserves as changes in Treasury deposits. These deposits are usually increased by the foreign governments or nonmember banks by depositing checks written on member banks. This absorbs member bank reserves. When checks are written on these deposits by the foreign governments or nonmember banks, the opposite occurs. The member banks receiving the checks de-

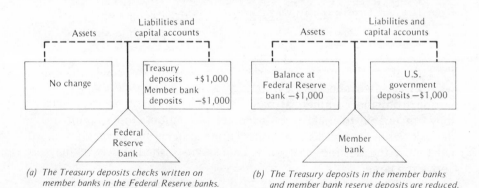

(a) The Treasury deposits checks written on member banks in the Federal Reserve banks.

(b) The Treasury deposits in the member banks and member bank reserve deposits are reduced.

Figure 12.11   An Increase in the U. S. Treasurer's Deposit at the Federal Reserve Banks

posit them in a Reserve bank, and member bank reserves are increased and the deposits of the foreign or the nonmember bank are reduced.

6. *Other Federal Reserve liabilities and capital accounts* includes all of the items on the liabilities side of the balance sheet that might affect member bank reserves, other than Federal Reserve notes and the various types of deposits. The bulk of this item consists of the capital accounts.

If the capital accounts were to increase, this would reduce member bank reserve deposits; if they should decrease, those deposits would increase. For example, when a dividend payment is made by a Federal Reserve bank, the dividend check received by a member bank would be deposited in its Federal Reserve bank. Member bank deposits would be increased and "other capital accounts" would be decreased. The opposite would occur when a member bank purchases additional FRB stock. The stock would be paid for by a check written on the member bank's deposit. Paid-in capital would be increased, and member bank deposits would be reduced.

CHANGES IN THE MONETARY BASE
FROM DECEMBER 31, 1972 TO
DECEMBER 31, 1973

The way in which the factors in the bank reserve equation change over time and affect the monetary base may be illustrated by comparing the sources of the monetary base on two different dates. Table 12.3 shows that from December 31, 1972 to December 31, 1973 the monetary base increased $7,394 million.

The holdings of U.S. government securities by the Federal Reserve banks were $9,265 million higher on December 31, 1973 than a year earlier. During the year, open-market purchases were considerably larger than open market sales, and the result was a substantial net increase. The amount of U.S. government securities acquired by the Federal Reserve banks was more than the $7,394 million increase in the monetary base and was the predominant factor affecting the change in the size of the base. Although several other factors supplying the monetary base increased, they were offset by a decrease in float of $875 million, a decrease in loans and acceptances held by the Federal Reserve banks of $761 million and a decrease of $108 million in other Federal Reserve assets. The value of the gold stock increased $1,157 million as a result of an increase in the official price of gold, and Treasury currency outstanding (additional coins) rose $403 million. There was no change in the SDR certificate account.

The bulk of the absorption of the monetary base was the result of

Table 12.3
Sources and Uses of the Monetary Base,
December 31, 1972 and December 31, 1973
(in millions of dollars)

SOURCES OF THE BASE	12/31/72	12/31/73
Federal Reserve credit		
U.S. government securities	$71,230	$80,495
Loans and acceptances	2,087	1,326
Float	3,974	3,099
Other Federal Reserve assets	1,260	1,152
Gold stock	10,410	11,567
Treasury currency outstanding	8,313	8,716
Special drawing rights certificate account	400	400
Treasury cash holdings	−345	−317
Deposits with Reserve banks:		
Treasury	−1,855	−2,542
Foreign	−325	−251
Other	−840	−1,419
Other Federal Reserve accounts	−2,143	−2,669
Total	$92,163	$99,557

USES OF THE BASE	12/31/72	12/31/73
Currency in circulation	$66,516	$72,497
Member bank balances at the Federal Reserve banks	25,647	27,060
Total	$92,163	$99,557

Details do not add to totals in some cases because of rounding.
Source: *Federal Reserve Bulletin*, February 1973, pp. A4–5 and A12, and February 1974, pp. A4–5 and A12.

an increase of $687 million in Treasury deposits and $579 million in "other deposits" at the Reserve banks, and an increase of $526 million in "other Federal Reserve accounts." Changes in these items are not easy to predict and cannot be controlled directly by the Federal Reserve banks. Both Treasury cash holdings and foreign deposits at the Reserve banks declined, tending to reduce the absorption of the monetary base.

The amount of open-market purchases is usually affected by the changes in the other factors in the reserve equation. For example, because loans and acceptances declined, the Federal Reserve banks bought a larger quantity of government securities. Otherwise the monetary base would not have increased as much as desired. The change in the monetary base is not left to chance but is the result of the objectives of the monetary authorities.

SUMMARY

By far the largest type of asset of the Federal Reserve banks is their holdings of U.S. government securities.

The two most important types of liabilities of the Federal Reserve banks are the total amount of Federal Reserve notes outstanding and the member bank reserve deposits.

A central bank protects commercial banks against runs by providing an elastic supply of currency and by making loans to commercial banks whenever needed.

The bank reserve equation lists all of the items both from the balance sheet of the twelve Federal Reserve banks combined and from the accounts of the United States Treasury that determine the amount of the reserve balances of the member banks at the Federal Reserve banks.

To control the monetary base, the Federal Reserve banks must buy and sell enough U.S. government securities to offset changes in factors in the bank reserve equation that may have an undesired effect on the monetary base.

NOTES

1.   For data on the amount of SDRs owned by the United States Treasury, see table entitled "U.S. Reserve Assets" (A75) in the monthly issues of the *Federal Reserve Bulletin*.
2.   For a description of the bankers' acceptance market, see G. Walter

Woodworth, *The Money Market and Monetary Management,* 2d ed. (New York: Harper and Row, 1972), chapter 7.

3. For an account of the early history of Federal Reserve policy toward the acceptance market, see Charles O. Hardy, *Credit Policies of the Federal Reserve System* (Washington, D.C.: The Brookings Institution, 1932), chapter 12.

4. See "The Bank Reserve Equation," in Board of Governors of the Federal Reserve System, *The Federal Reserve System: Purposes and Functions,* 5th ed. (Washington, D.C., 1967), chapter 12; and Federal Reserve Bank of Chicago, *Modern Money Mechanics* (Chicago, 1968).

5. "SDRs in Federal Reserve Operations and Statistics," *Federal Reserve Bulletin,* May 1970, pp. 421–424.

QUESTIONS

12.1. Describe each of the following assets of the Federal Reserve banks:
> Gold certificates
> Cash
> U. S. government securities
> Loans and acceptances
> Cash items in process of collection

12.2. Describe each of the following liabilities of the Federal Reserve banks:
> Federal Reserve notes
> Member bank deposits
> U. S. Treasurer's deposits
> Foreign and other deposits
> Deferred availability cash items

12.3. Explain the way in which a central bank helps commercial banks to meet the problems created by runs on the banks.

12.4. Compare the following alternative methods of preventing or solving the problem of runs on banks:
> Suspending specie payment
> Federal deposit insurance
> A central bank

12.5. Explain the reasons for the Federal Reserve's "even-keel" policy during periods of debt financing by the Treasury.

12.6. What is the purpose of the bank reserve equation?

12.7. Which of the factors in the bank reserve equation are from the monetary accounts of the United States Treasury, and which from the balance sheet of the Federal Reserve banks?

12.8. Explain the way in which an increase in each of the following factors in the bank reserve equation may increase member bank reserve deposits in the Federal Reserve banks:

> U. S. government securities owned by the Federal Reserve banks
> Loans of the Federal Reserve banks
> Float of the Federal Reserve banks
> The gold stock
> SDR certificate account
> Treasury currency outstanding

12.9. Explain the way an increase in each of the following factors in the bank reserve equation may decrease member bank reserve deposits at the Federal Reserve banks:

> Currency in circulation
> Treasury cash holdings
> Treasury deposits in the Federal Reserve banks
> Foreign government deposits in the Federal Reserve banks

12.10. Explain the way in which the Federal Reserve banks might offset the effect of a gold outflow on member bank reserve deposits in the Federal Reserve banks.

12.11. Explain the way in which the Federal Reserve banks might offset the effect of a decrease in currency in circulation on member bank reserve deposits at the Federal Reserve banks.

12.12. Know the meaning and significance of the following terms and concepts: Federal Reserve notes, float, bank panic, elastic currency, bank reserve equation, factors supplying member bank reserves, factors absorbing member bank reserves, Treasury currency outstanding, Treasury cash holdings, uses of the monetary base.

Chapter 13
The Federal Reserve
System's Instruments
of Control

*Open-market operations have become the most important instrument
of control of the Federal Reserve System. Purchases and sales of
U.S. government securities are made continuously and in a precise
way to achieve the objectives of monetary policy.*

Monetary policy is concerned both with the objectives of the Federal
Reserve System and the way in which it may pursue these objectives by
the use of its instruments of control. Each year the board of governors
discusses in its *Annual Report* its objectives of the previous year and the
measures it took to achieve them.[1] One of the most important of its
objectives has been to stabilize the economy against cyclical fluctuations.
When the economy needs stimulation, the Federal Reserve System attempts to create easier conditions in the money market. At other times,
it attempts to maintain prevailing conditions or to make conditions firmer.
In recent years, the Federal Reserve System has also attempted to reduce
the deficit in our balance of international payments, to promote economic growth, and to combat inflation. At times the monetary authorities take measures to meet unusual problems. In November 1967, when
the British devalued the pound from $2.80 to $2.40, the Federal Reserve
banks raised the discount rate for the purpose of assuring the orderly
functioning of financial markets. In mid-1970, they made large purchases
of government securities to avoid a financial panic after the failure of
the Penn Central Transportation Company.

   To achieve its objectives, the Federal Reserve has three principal
instruments of control: open-market operations, changes in the discount
rate, and changes in the reserve requirements of the member banks. It
also has several selective instruments of control: margin requirements

for loans to purchase corporation stock, ceilings on interest rates paid by banks on deposits, and eligibility requirements for discounting at the Federal Reserve banks. In the past, it had control over the terms of consumer installment and real estate credit. In some years, the Federal Reserve has used all three of its major instruments of control, although open-market operations is the only one that it uses continuously. The purpose of this chapter is to describe the way the Federal Reserve uses both its major and its selective instruments of control.

MAJOR INSTRUMENTS OF CONTROL

Open-Market Operations

In the original Federal Reserve Act, open-market operations were not conceived of as an instrument of control. The Federal Reserve banks were given the power to buy and sell certain types of securities for the purposes of promoting the use of acceptances in foreign trade and of enabling the banks to acquire sufficient earning assets to pay their expenses at times when there was little discounting. Most of the Reserve banks found it convenient to make their transactions in securities in the New York money market, and in the early 1920s an informal committee consisting of officials of the Federal Reserve banks began to coordinate those transactions. It was not long before purchases and sales were used to offset or prevent gold flows and sometimes to create additional reserves for the commercial banking system.

In the early 1920s, the Federal Reserve authorities seemed to use their instruments of control effectively. However, in the late 1920s, there was disagreement—particularly between the board of governors in Washington and the twelve banks—about how to deal with rising real estate prices and increased stock market speculation. The board was in favor of cutting off loans to member banks that were making financial loans on securities—in order to reduce speculative activity—and was opposed to raising the discount rate for this purpose. The board felt that raising the discount rate might be too hard on business and that European currency difficulties threatened our agricultural markets. Officials of the Federal Reserve Bank of New York, on the other hand, held that attempting to control the use of credit by inducing member banks not to make speculative loans was ineffective. In 1927 the Federal Reserve System actively purchased securities in the open market and reduced the discount rate—which seemed to make the problem of speculation worse. Efforts were then made in 1928 and through the summer of 1929 to tighten monetary policy for the purpose of combating rising prices on the stock market, and a serious stock market crash occurred soon afterward—in October 1929.

In the Great Depression, large-scale open-market purchases were not used until 1932. The money supply contracted sharply when commercial banks reduced their borrowing at the Federal Reserve banks, when persons withdrew funds from banks, and when foreigners purchased gold from us because they expected the United States would go off the gold standard and the price of gold in terms of dollars would rise. Again, there was disagreement among the monetary authorities as to the appropriate policy. By 1930, the Reserve Board in Washington had become dominant and was opposed to the more expansionist policies advocated by the officials of the Federal Reserve Bank of New York. Among the reasons for not using open-market purchases sooner were: (1) few people at that time realized that the situation was as serious as it was, or had a clear understanding of the actions a central bank ought to take in a period of recession and financial difficulties; (2) bankers opposed open-market purchases because they thought they would lower interest rates even further than they had already fallen; (3) it was thought that open-market purchases would not have a stimulating effect because they would cause banks to borrow less; (4) maintaining the quantity of money during a serious depression was not then regarded as an important objective of monetary policy; and (5) it was thought that more aggressive open-market purchases would stimulate a gold outflow.

The Banking Act of 1935 set up the Federal Open Market Committee (FOMC) in its present form, and it is now the most important policy-making unit in the Federal Reserve System. As this committee operates today, a directive is prepared at each meeting for the manager of the open-market account, who is a vice-president of the Federal Reserve Bank of New York.[2] The specific function of the Open-Market Committee is to review the available information on economic conditions and to decide upon the appropriate policy. The directive does not specify when and how much to buy or sell in the open market: these decisions are made by the manager of the open-market account. The terms of the directive have been very general.[3] Slight changes in its wording indicate a change either toward an easier or a tighter monetary policy. Starting in 1970, the directives began mentioning as an objective the control of the money supply, and the reports of the meetings gave evidence of more interest in monetary aggregates than formerly. In 1972, the FOMC adopted as a target the monetary aggregate "reserves against private deposits" (RPDs).

The manager of the open-market account has a staff that executes the transactions decided upon. All transactions are made with government securities dealer firms. Any dealer who demonstrates his readiness to make quotations and fulfill transactions may compete, provided the firm meets reasonable standards of credit-worthiness. As a semi-public institution, the Federal Reserve System must conduct its transactions in such a way that it gets as good a price as can be had. When the account manager decides to buy or sell, the usual procedure for outright transactions is first to brief the members of the trading staff. Then all traders begin simultaneously to telephone dealers to ask for bids or offerings. As the traders complete their contacts with the dealers, the bids or offers are assembled and the best bids or offers selected. The entire operation is usually completed in thirty minutes.

Some purchases of securities in the open market are under repurchase agreements with dealers. When this type of operation is used, the Federal Reserve Bank of New York acquires securities from a dealer under a contract which binds the dealer to repurchase the same securities at the same price on or before a stipulated final date. The length of the period for such agreements is usually fifteen days or less, although the contracts may be renewed. Any given repurchase agreement may be terminated virtually without notice at the option of either the Federal Reserve or the dealer, although the Federal Reserve has not found the need to use its option. The rate of interest is usually the same as the discount rate of the Federal Reserve Bank of New York, but it need not be the same and at times has been below the discount rate. If the account manager decides to purchase securities in this way, he contacts the dealers to find out which ones wish to sell and then allocates the total amount purchased among them. Repurchase agreements assist dealers in financing their inventories of securities by making it possible for them to sell some of their securities temporarily to the Federal Reserve banks. The weekly statement of the condition of the twelve Federal Reserve banks shows separately the amount of securities owned under those agreements. The amount purchased in this way is small compared to outright purchases, and at times they own no securities under these agreements.

From September 1953 to July 1958, the Federal Open Market Committee limited outright open-market operations to bills or other short-term securities maturing within one year. This was known as the "bills-only" policy. Supporters of the policy pointed out the advantages of minimum uncertainty as to which maturities would be affected by Federal Reserve operations. Open-market operations are still usually in short-term securities, but the policy of limiting operations to short-term securities was criticized as unnecessarily restrictive and was discarded in 1958. Critics argued that, at times, the monetary authorities ought to use open-market operations to purchase long-term securities in an attempt to lower long-term interest yields relative to short-term rates.[4]

In the early 1960s, the Treasury and the Federal Reserve System attempted to lower long-term interest rates and raise short-term interest rates. The policy was known as "operation twist" because the objective was to twist the yield curve. The purpose of lowering long-term rates was to stimulate the domestic economy, and the objective of raising short-term rates was to encourage foreign owners of dollars to keep them invested in short-term securities in the United States. The policy appeared to have little effect on raising short-term rates, and although long-term yields on U.S. government securities were lowered, there was little effect on mortgage rates and corporate bond yields—the real objectives of the program.

The Federal Reserve System is required by law to publish a weekly statement on the condition of the twelve Federal Reserve banks. Selected statistical data from this statement, entitled "Federal Reserve Report" or "Federal Reserve Statement," are published each Friday in major newspapers. By comparing successive weekly statements, it is possible to determine the kind of open-market operations that occurred during the week as well as other changes in the bank reserve equation that affect member bank reserves. The Reserve authorities do not include with the weekly statement an explanation of the changes in it

The bulk of the Federal Reserve's operations are *defensive.* They are designed not to bring about a change in monetary circumstances, but to prevent other factors from causing changes that are not desired. In the bank reserve equation discussed in Chapter 12, there are thirteen factors affecting the supply of reserve funds. The Federal Reserve authorities directly control only one of these factors—their holdings of U.S. government securities. They may also try to influence the volume of discounts and advances through variations in the discount rate, but the volume of discounting depends on the commercial banks and cannot be precisely controlled through changes in the discount rate. Through defensive open-market operations, however, the Federal Reserve authorities can offset the effect on reserves of the other factors in the reserve equation.

Prior to 1971, one of the most important objectives of those defensive operations was to offset the effect of outflows of gold. In 1957 the gold stock of the United States Treasury amounted to $22.9 billion. By January 1971 this had fallen to less than half this amount, to $10.7 billion. If this gold outflow had not been offset by open-market purchases it would have caused a decrease in bank reserves. From the beginning of the Federal Reserve System until 1971 when transactions by the Treasury in gold ceased, open-market operations were frequently used to offset the effect of both inflows and outflows of gold.

Another important objective of defensive operations is to offset the weekly variations in float and in the deposits of the Treasury. Both of these factors may change sharply from one week to the next. Such changes can have disturbing short-run effects on bank reserves, and although they are not easy to offset perfectly, the Federal Reserve authorities attempt to neutralize their effects through appropriate open-market operations.

Table 13.1 shows that the amount of U.S. government securities owned by the twelve Federal Reserve banks increased in almost every year between 1965 and 1973, and approximately doubled over this period. Part of this increase was necessary to offset the sharp decline in the gold stock. But—more important—part of it supplied the monetary base for an expanding money supply. Purchases and sales of U.S. government securities that are made for the purpose of promoting economic stability or of providing for economic growth are referred to as *dynamic* operations in order to distinguish them from defensive operations. A growing money supply may be provided either by open-market purchases or by lowering legal reserve ratios. In the 1950s the expansion in the money supply had been accomplished largely by lowering legal reserve ratios.

Since 1962 the Federal Reserve has bought and sold foreign currencies in addition to U.S. government securities. The objective of these transactions is to control exchange rates between the dollar and foreign currencies rather than the general objectives of monetary policy. By holding foreign currencies, the Federal Reserve is in a position to purchase dollars in the foreign exchange market whenever it believes such action is necessary in order to keep exchange rates between the dollar and other currencies at the desired level.

Table 13.1
The Total Amount of U. S. Government Securities Owned by the Twelve Federal Reserve Banks, 1965–1973

DECEMBER	AMOUNT (IN BILLIONS)
1965	$40.9
1966	43.8
1967	48.9
1968	52.5
1969	57.5
1970	62.1
1971	70.2
1972	69.9
1973	78.5

Source: Federal Reserve Bulletin, various issues, p. A.12.

Changes in the Discount Rate

Changes in the discount rate charged on their loans to the member banks was the principal instrument of control initially authorized in the Federal Reserve Act. Although currently discount rates are usually not changed more than once or twice a year, every fourteen days the board of directors of each Federal Reserve bank must either reestablish or change the existing rate. The action taken is immediately reported to the board of governors, which may either veto or approve the rate selected.

In the 1950s the Federal Reserve rehabilitated the use of the discount mechanism and established its current discount policy. A revision of the 1937 text of Regulation A, *Advances and Discounts by Federal Reserve Banks,* was made in 1955.[5] Except under special circumstances, member banks are expected to borrow only for short periods and for the purpose of adjusting their reserves. The Federal Reserve banks are expected to discourage continuous borrowing as well as borrowing for profit, and are to consider member bank applications for accommodation in the light of circumstances in each case. In practice it is not easy for them to refuse to lend to member banks desiring to borrow in order to meet their reserve requirements. At most, the discount officers might consult with persistent borrowers. The availability of borrowing is considered an important inducement to membership. Also, Federal Reserve officials would be reluctant to do anything that might reflect on the soundness of a member bank. Furthermore, during periods of active discounting, to screen discounts promptly in accordance with the Act would be a costly administrative task.

Figure 13.1 shows the changes in the discount rate at the Federal Reserve Bank of New York from 1950 to 1973. As shown in this figure, the Federal Reserve authorities have usually raised the discount rate in periods of expansion, when other short-term interest rates have risen, and lowered it in periods of contraction, when interest rates have fallen. They tend to keep the discount rate in line with other short-term rates. As a method of obtaining reserves to meet reserve requirements, member bank borrowing from the Federal Reserve banks competes with borrowing Federal funds or selling short-term U.S. government securities. Member banks tend to use the method which costs the least. If market rates rise much above the discount rate, the discount rate must be raised so as to prevent borrowing from becoming very profitable. In periods of economic decline, if market rates fall much below the discount rate, the discount rate must be lowered in order to avoid discouraging banks from borrowing.

In periods of recession, lower discount rates would be expected to

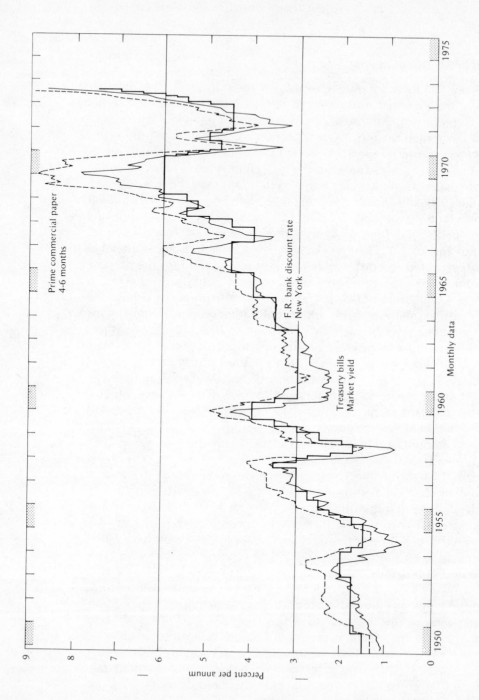

Figure 13.1 The Discount Rate, the Treasury Bill Rate, and the Prime Commercial Paper Rate, 1950–1973

Source: Board of Governors of the Federal Reserve System, *Historical Chart Book, 1973,* p. 27.

increase member bank borrowing and bank reserves and thus to counteract the downturn in business activity. In periods of expansion, higher
discount rates would be expected to reduce member bank borrowings
and thus tend to restrain the expansion. Actually, Figure 13.2 shows that,
despite countercyclical changes in the discount rate, from 1966 to 1974
member bank borrowings have risen in periods of expansion and fallen
in periods of contraction. This is because in periods of prosperity other
short-term rates have risen even more than the discount rate, and in
periods of recession they have fallen further than the discount rate. Figure 13.2 shows a close relationship between fluctuations in member bank

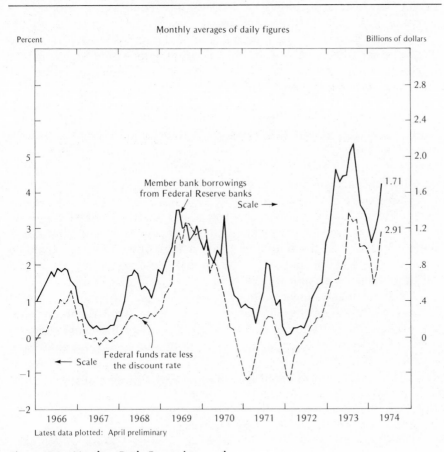

**Figure 13.2   Member Bank Borrowings and
Short-Term Interest Rate Differential**

Source: Jerry L. Jordan, "Interest Rates and Monetary Growth," in Federal Reserve Bank
of St. Louis, *Review,* January 1973, pp. 2–11.

borrowings and the differential between the Federal funds rate and the discount rate. When the Federal funds rate has been substantially higher than the discount rate, member bank borrowings have increased, and when the differential between the two rates has become smaller, member bank borrowings have decreased. One would expect member bank borrowings to be sensitive to the differential between the discount rate and the Federal funds rate, because discounting and borrowing Federal funds are alternative ways for a bank to obtain reserves.

Federal Reserve authorities believe that the cyclical variations in member bank borrowing ought to be evaluated in relation to their use of the other instruments of control. For example, they could offset the effect of an increase in discounting by selling securities in the open market. To offset a decline in borrowing, they could do the opposite—purchase U. S. government securities.

Countercyclical changes in the discount rate may have desirable psychological effects. A rise in the discount rate would signal to the public that monetary policy is becoming tighter. A lowering of the discount rate would have the opposite effect. If a rise in the discount rate causes business firms to become more cautious about their spending plans, this in itself would have the effect desired. However, if the discount rate is used in this way, it must not mislead the public. Unless the Federal Reserve authorities used the other instruments of control to achieve the results indicated by changes in the discount rate, relying on discount rate changes as a signal could be hazardous.

The way in which the Federal Reserve has used changes in the discount rate as an instrument of control has been criticized by many writers.[6] It has even been suggested that discounting by member banks might just as well be discontinued. Open-market operations have become so important that the power of the Federal Reserve authorities would not be diminished significantly if discounting were discontinued.

It has also been suggested that the discount rate ought to be changed continuously as other rates change in the money market.[7] When discount rate changes are infrequent, they tend to lag behind the cyclical movements of other short-term rates of interest and to cause member bank borrowing to increase in periods of prosperity and to decrease in recessions. The discount rate might be automatically adjusted to the bill rate each week. Canada has had a policy of this type since 1956. Their discount rate is set at one-fourth of one percent above the latest average tender rate for their ninety-one-day Treasury bills.

Discounting may be more significant as a method of providing liquidity for individual banks than as an instrument of control. If banks can provide for their liquidity by borrowing, they need not rely so heavily on investing in liquid assets such as Treasury bills, commercial paper, or

Federal funds sold. Even though borrowing is limited to fourteen days, it gives the bank time to accumulate funds by letting loans run off. Most discounting is done by the very large banks, and they appear to be relying more on discounting, as a method of providing for their liquidity needs, than on the methods used by smaller banks. A 1968 Federal Reserve study recommends more adequate discounting facilities as a method of assuring bank liquidity.[8] In recent decades, banks have become less liquid because of the sharp rise in the loan-to-deposit ratio of member banks from 17 percent in 1945 to 75 percent in January 1974.

Changes in Legal Reserve Requirements

In 1917, reserve requirements were set at 13, 10, and 7 percent for demand deposits at the different classes of banks, and 3 percent for all time deposits. These ratios were in effect for over fifteen years. In the original Federal Reserve Act, reserve requirements had been somewhat higher than this. Under the National Banking System that operated from the Civil War until 1914, required reserves were 25 percent for banks both in New York City (the central reserve city) and in redemption cities (later called reserve cities), and 15 percent for banks in all other cities (country banks). Reserve requirements were the same for both demand and time deposits.

Although there had been pressure to allow the monetary authorities to use changes in reserve requirements as an instrument of control, there were no changes allowed before 1933. In 1933, the Federal Reserve Board was given emergency authority, to be exercised only with the permission of the president, to vary reserve requirements to up to double the former percentages—so that requirements would range between 13 and 26 percent for demand deposits at central-reserve-city banks, between 10 and 20 percent at reserve-city banks, and between 7 and 14 percent at country banks; and between 3 and 6 percent for time deposits at all banks. The Banking Act of 1935 made this instrument of control permanent, and presidential approval was no longer required. The current legal ranges for reserve requirements are:

	Range
Net demand deposits	
Reserve-city banks	10–22 percent
Other banks	7–14 percent
Time deposits	3–10 percent

To calculate *net demand deposits,* a bank deducts from its total deposits both the amount of its balances at other commercial banks and the volume of the checks it has received in process of collection.

Although this instrument of control was created during a period of widespread unemployment, Congress was concerned about the possibility of inflation resulting from the rapid accumulation of excess reserves. When the official price of gold was raised from $20.67 to $35.00 per fine ounce in 1934, the value of the total gold stock owned by the United States Treasury automatically increased sharply, causing the excess reserves of commercial banks to rise sharply. An objective of the Banking Act of 1935 was to enable officials to reduce excess reserves by raising reserve requirements. Although usually the Federal Reserve authorities can reduce bank reserves by selling securities in the open market, at that time they did not own sufficient government securities to be able to eliminate the accumulation of excess reserves in this way. Starting in 1935, a large inflow of gold—as troubles in Europe caused people there to send their savings to safety—added further to the volume of excess reserves, and in 1936–1937 the Federal Reserve sharply raised member bank reserve requirements. This was followed by the depression of 1937–1938, and with it came a decline in bond prices and rise in interest yields. These events were attributed in part to the action taken by the Federal Reserve. In 1938 the Federal Reserve reversed its policy and reduced reserve requirements for the purpose of stimulating recovery.

Table 13.2
Reserve Requirements of Member Banks
(percent of deposits)

Effective date[a]	DECEMBER 31, 1949, THROUGH JULY 13, 1966			
	Net demand deposits			Time deposits (all classes of banks)
	Central-reserve-city banks	Reserve-city banks	Country banks	
In effect Dec. 31, 1949	22	18	12	5
1951 Jan. 11, 16	23	19	13	6
Jan. 25, Feb. 1	24	20	14	
1953 July 1, 9	22	19	13	
1954 June 16, 24	21			5
July 29, Aug. 1	20	18	12	
1958 Feb. 27, Mar. 1	19½	17½	11½	
Mar. 20, Apr. 1	19	17	11	
Apr. 17	18½			
Apr. 24	18	16½		
1960 Sept. 1	17½			
Nov. 24			12	
Dec. 1	16½			
1962 Oct. 25, Nov. 1				4

Table 13.2 *(continued)*

JULY 14, 1966, THROUGH NOVEMBER 8, 1972

| | Net demand deposits | | | | Time deposits (all classes of banks) | | |
| | Reserve-city banks | | Country banks | | | Other time deposits | |
Effective date[a]	Under $5 million	Over $5 million	Under $5 million	Over $5 million	Savings deposits	Under $5 million	Over $5 million
1966 July 14, 21	16½		12		4	4	5
Sept. 8, 15							6
1967 Mar. 2					3½	3½	
Mar. 16					3	3	
1968 Jan. 11, 18	16½	17	12	12½			
1969 Apr. 17	17	17½	12½	13			
1970 Oct. 1							5

BEGINNING NOVEMBER 9, 1972

| | Net demand deposits | | | | | Time deposits up to $5 million and savings deposits | Time deposits in excess of $5 million |
	Under $2 million	Over $2 million to $10 million	Over $10 million to $100 million	Over $100 million to $400 million	Over $400 million (Reserve-city)		
Nov. 9, 1972	8	10	12	16½ ; 13 [b]	17½	3	5
Nov. 16, 1972	8	10	12	13	17½	3	5
July 19, 1973	8	10½	12½	13½	18	3	5
In effect Jan. 31, 1974	8	10½	12½	13½	18	3	5

[a] When two dates are shown, the first applies to the change at central-reserve- or reserve-city banks and the second to the change at country banks.
[b] 16½ percent on the former designation of reserve-city banks and 13 percent on other member banks.
Source: *Federal Reserve Bulletin,* February 1971 and February 1974, p. A9.

Table 13.2 shows the changes in reserve requirements from 1949 to 1974. Although the bulk of bank reserves consists of deposits at the Federal Reserve banks, since 1960 banks have been permitted to count vault cash as reserves. In the original Federal Reserve Act, member banks were permitted to count half of their vault cash as reserves. Between 1917 and 1960, only deposits at the Reserve banks had qualified as reserves.

In 1966, smaller reserve requirements were established for the first $5 million of time deposits (excluding savings deposits) than for those in excess of this amount. In 1968, a similar size differential was extended to demand deposits. These were the first steps toward a policy of basing reserve requirements on the size of the bank, rather than on geographical location as provided for in the original Federal Reserve Act. In 1972, a restructuring of reserve requirements was adopted with the introduction of a five-fold classification of banks based on the amount of a bank's net demand deposits. Banks with net demand deposits over $400 million, the largest of the five classes, were designated as reserve-city banks. The original policy of basing reserve requirements on geographical location had the disadvantage of prescribing different reserve requirements for banks of the same size.

Starting in 1969, the reserve authorities extended reserve requirements to some of the new sources of funds that were being developed by banks. Banks in the United States were required to hold reserves behind certain of their deposits belonging to their foreign branches and behind their borrowings from foreign banks. This was done to discourage the use of those sources of funds. Although the Federal Reserve authorities were attempting to tighten up monetary policy in 1969, member banks had been able to expand loans quite rapidly with funds from those other sources. Later—in 1973—the reserve requirements on borrowings from foreign banks were cut from 20 percent to 8 percent in order to encourage such borrowing and reduce the deficit in the United States balance of payments.

In addition, in 1970 the Federal Reserve authorities extended reserve requirements to commerical paper issued by bank holding companies. Bank holding companies had issued commercial paper as a method of avoiding maximum interest rate regulations on time deposits. Market interest rates had risen so high relative to the ceilings on time deposits that banks were losing these deposits and wished to replace them with other sources of funds.

In mid-1973, the Federal Reserve introduced several changes in reserve requirements in order to restrain the expansion of new sources of commercial bank funds such as large CDs, commercial paper issued by bank holding companies, and finance bills (a special type of bankers' acceptance). It was feared that the growth of these sources of funds might slow up the expansion of savings deposits in thrift institutions and thus be harmful to housing construction. The monetary authorities adopted a new technique of placing a marginal reserve requirement of 3 percent on certain additional sources of funds. Reserve requirements were raised from 5 percent to 8 percent on any large CDs, commercial paper, or finance bills in excess of the amount held in mid-May 1973 or $10 million—whichever is the larger.

In 1974, additional changes in reserve requirements were made to encourage banks to lengthen the maturity of CDs. This was done to improve the liquidity of the banking system by reducing the volatility of CDs. Reserve requirements for CDs that mature in four months or longer were first lowered from 8 percent to 5 percent and then from 5 percent to 3 percent. The reserve requirements for CDs maturing in less than four months and in excess of $5 million were raised from 5 percent to 6 percent.

The Federal Reserve's policy of establishing different reserve requirements—whether based on geographical location, type of deposit, or size of bank—has frequently been criticized. Whenever the public shifts from demand deposits in smaller banks with lower legal reserve ratios to demand deposits in larger banks with higher legal reserve ratios, the quantity of deposits in the banking system is reduced because the expansion ratio is smaller in the banks with the higher reserve requirements. The same occurs when the public shifts from time deposits to demand deposits because of the higher reserve requirements for demand deposits. Also, there is a reduction in deposits if persons shift time deposits from banks with less than $5 million in time deposits to banks with time deposits over $5 million. The opposite—an expansion in total bank deposits—occurs whenever the public shifts deposits to banks with lower reserve ratios.

The capacity of the Federal Reserve authorities to control the money supply precisely has been diminished by the recent changes that they have made in the regulations for reserve requirements. By increasing the number of categories of deposits with different reserve requirements, the possibility of shifts in deposits affecting the money supply has been increased. From 1960 to 1966, there were only three categories of deposits with different reserve requirements: demand deposits in central-reserve- and reserve-city banks, demand deposits in country banks, and time deposits in all classes of banks. In 1973, there were five categories for banks with different amounts of demand deposits, two categories for banks with different amounts of time deposits, and several other categories— for foreign borrowings of United States banks, commercial paper issued by bank holding companies, funds raised by banks through the sale of finance bills, and increases in the aggregate of outstanding CDs of $100,000 or more over and above a specified base. Although the Federal Reserve authorities may attempt to offset the effect of shifts among deposits with different reserve requirements through appropriate open-market operations, the need to take such actions complicates the administration of monetary policy. There may be a lag in the time between such shifts and the time they become known to the monetary authorities. Shifts from deposits in nonmember banks, which are not required to hold reserves in the Federal Reserve banks, to member banks may also affect the quantity of deposits and make it more difficult to control the money supply precisely. In 1974, the Federal Reserve recommended to Congress that nonmember banks with over $2 million in demand deposits be subject to the same reserve requirements as member banks.

Variations in reserve requirements are one of the Federal Reserve's major instruments of control. In a period of recession, reserve requirements may be lowered so as to stimulate the economy, and in periods of prosperity, they may be raised so as to avoid inflation. The results of lowering reserve requirements are the same as open-market purchases. Open-market purchases increase member bank reserves, while lower reserve requirements permit member banks to hold a larger volume of deposits based on the same amount of reserves. Raising reserve requirements has the same impact as open-market sales. When reserve requirements are raised, the individual bank must increase its reserves by selling securities or reducing its loans.

If the required ratio for deposits were raised from 10 to 11 percent, for example, an indivdual bank might be affected as shown in the tables below. Bank A would meet the increase in its required reserves by reducing loans or by selling investments. These actions would affect other banks. Bank A's gain in reserves must cause a loss of reserves in some other bank. The securities sold by bank A would probably be paid for by a check written on another bank, or the loans that bank A collected

Bank A

	ORIGINAL HOLDINGS (10% RESERVE RATIO)	REVISED HOLDINGS (11% RESERVE RATIO)
Assets		
Required reserves	$ 50,000	$ 55,000
Loans and investments	450,000	445,000
Liabilities		
Deposits	$500,000	$500,000

might be paid for by a check on another bank. As shown below, if the entire impact were on bank B, it would lose both reserves and deposits equal to $5,000:

Bank B

	ORIGINAL HOLDINGS	HOLDINGS AFTER LOSS OF $5,000 IN DEPOSITS AND RESERVES
Assets		
Reserves	$ 55,000	$ 50,000
Loans and investments	445,000	445,000
Liabilities		
Deposits	$500,000	$495,000

Although bank B originally had 11 percent reserves, it is now short of having sufficient reserves. It must increase its reserves to 11 percent of $495,000—to $54,450—by contracting loans or selling securities. This would lead to a further contraction of deposits and of loans or investments in other banks.

The impact of these responses by individual banks on the entire banking system would be as follows if the banking system originally consisted of ten banks each with $500,000 in deposits:

All Member Banks

	ORIGINAL HOLDINGS (10% RESERVE RATIO)	REVISED HOLDINGS (11% RESERVE RATIO)
Assets		
Reserves	$ 500,000	$ 500,000
Loans and investments	4,500,000	4,045,454
Liabilities		
Deposits	$5,000,000	$4,545,454

There has been no change in total reserves. Even though each bank attempts to increase its reserves, collectively the banks cannot increase the total reserves of the system. In the process of attempting to increase their reserves, however, they reduce their loans and investments and this results in a reduction in bank deposits. Eventually, as deposits get smaller, their reserve ratios meet the new higher level. In this example, it has been assumed that there is no leakage. The decline in deposits shown is the maximum possible, given the quantity of bank reserves and their reserve ratios.

The principal reason why the Federal Reserve authorities do not often change required reserve ratios is because changing them is a clumsy instrument of control. Small changes in reserve requirements result in large changes in the volume of bank loans and deposits. The principal argument in favor of using this instrument of control is that it may affect directly every member bank in the country. In contrast, open-market operations initially affect only a few banks—although eventually the effects are scattered throughout the system. This instrument of control is sometimes used instead of open-market operations because of its greater psychological impact. The announcement of a change in reserve requirements is always widely publicized and indicates in a dramatic way a change in monetary policy.

Table 13.2 shows that between 1949 and 1973 most of the changes in reserve requirements were downward. Current legal reserve ratios are significantly lower than they were following World War II. The reductions in legal reserve ratios in 1953, 1954, and 1958 occurred during periods of business slack. During the economic slowdown in 1970, reserve requirements for time deposits in a commercial bank in excess of $5 million were lowered from 6 to 5 percent. In the 1950s, lowering legal reserve ratios was also one of the principal ways in which growth of the money supply was made possible. The monetary authorities have been reluctant to raise legal reserve requirements because a rise could embarrass certain banks that might not be sufficiently liquid to meet the higher reserve requirements easily. In addition, raising legal reserve requirements would worsen the competitive disadvantage of member banks relative to nonmember banks. In 1973, Federal Reserve officials stated that their operations were being hampered because the reserve requirements for nonmember banks were below those for member banks.[9] Even when raising reserve requirements would have been the best way to signal a restraining monetary policy, the Federal Reserve has felt that it was not able to use this instrument of control because it would threaten a further erosion of membership in the system. Despite these handicaps, in 1973 when the rate of inflation rose much more rapidly than had been anticipated, the Federal Reserve raised reserve requirements for banks holding net demand deposits over $2 million by one-half of one percent.

Many bankers believe that the growth of the money supply should be provided by lowering legal reserve ratios rather than by open-market operations. Lower reserve requirements would increase the percentage of their assets earning income and improve their competitive position relative to nonmember banks, mutual savings banks, and savings and loan associations. The relatively higher legal reserve ratios required by the Federal Reserve System for time deposits may have retarded the growth of member banks relative to other savings institutions. On the other hand, an argument for using open-market operations rather than lowering reserve requirements to provide for growth in the money supply is that it reduces the interest cost of the national debt payable to the public. The earnings of the Federal Reserve banks, over what they need to cover operating expenses, pay the fixed rate of dividend, and build up their surplus, are required by law to be paid to the Treasury. Increasing the money supply through open-market purchases means a larger portion of the national debt owned by the Federal Reserve banks, and a smaller amount of interest paid by the Treasury to the public.

Some foreign countries use changes in reserve requirements as an instrument of control because they do not have sufficiently developed financial markets for open-market operations.[10] Even in developed countries, changes in legal reserve requirements may be necessary if the central bank is in danger of depleting its portfolio of government securities by further open-market sales.

SELECTIVE CREDIT CONTROLS

The Federal Reserve System has several types of control that are usually considered to be much less important than its major instruments of control: regulation of margin requirements for purchases of stock, regulation of maximum interest rates on time deposits, and eligibility requirements for borrowing from the Federal Reserve banks. The objectives of these selective instruments of control are usually basically different from the objectives of the three general instruments of control. Selective instruments of control attempt to influence the allocation of credit. They are usually designed to cut back on the use of a particular type of credit without decreasing the total volume of credit.

Margin Requirements

Following the stock market boom in the 1920s, the crash in 1929, and the depressed economic conditions that resulted, the Securities and Exchange Act of 1934 empowered the board of governors to regulate lending for purchasing and carrying securities. Regulation U applies to credit from all banks, Regulation T to credit from brokers and dealers, and, since 1968, Regulation G to credit from all others. The margin requirements on credit from banks apply to purchases of all corporation stocks registered on the national exchanges, bonds convertible into listed stocks, and several hundred over-the-counter stocks.

The margin requirement sets, in percentage terms, the customer's margin required at time of purchase. The minimum margin that can be required by the Federal Reserve is 25 percent, and the maximum 100 percent, of the market value of the stocks purchased and pledged as collateral. With a margin of 80 percent, for example, an individual may borrow $200 on the purchase of $1,000 of stock. If the price of the stock falls after purchase, or if the Federal Reserve raises the required margin, the borrower does not have to reduce the amount he has borrowed so as to meet the requirements set by the Federal Reserve. Lenders, however, may set their own margin requirements and their own terms about paying up part of a loan if the value of the stock falls.

Table 13.3 shows the changes from 1955 to 1974 in the margins required when borrowing from banks. This percentage is the same as that required by brokers and dealers. The purpose of the Federal Reserve's margin requirements is to prevent the excessive use of credit in financing stock market speculation. Raising those requirements is intended to dampen the demand for securities by making it more difficult for persons to borrow. Variations in margin requirements probably have little effect on business activity generally.

Table 13.3
Margin Requirements for Credit Extended
by Banks, 1955–1974

	MARGIN REQUIREMENTS FOR:	
EFFECTIVE DATE	STOCKS	BONDS CONVERTIBLE INTO LISTED STOCK
April 23, 1955	70%	—
Jan. 16, 1958	50	—
Aug. 5, 1958	70	—
Oct. 16, 1958	90	—
July 28, 1960	70	—
July 10, 1962	50	—
Nov. 6, 1963	70	—
Mar. 11, 1968	70	50%
June 8, 1968	80	60
May 6, 1970	65	50
Dec. 6, 1971	55	50
Nov. 24, 1972	65	50
Jan. 3, 1974	50	50

Source: *Federal Reserve Bulletin* 60, February 1974, A10.

These regulations have had the effect of inducing borrowers to obtain their funds from financial institutions not covered by the law rather than from commercial banks. In 1968 the regulations were extended by Congress to credit granted by some others not originally covered by the law in order to eliminate this evasion. It is questionable whether these requirements actually act as a safeguard against the excessive use of financial credit, as intended by Congress. Instead, they may simply alter the sources of these funds.

Regulation of Interest Rates on Deposits

The Federal Reserve's Regulation Q prohibiting the payment of interest on demand deposits, and setting maximum rates of interest payable on time and savings deposits in commercial banks, was established in 1933. At first these controls were largely ineffective because banks could not then afford to pay interest on demand deposits, and the rates that they offered on time deposits were less than the maximum allowed. Instead, to obtain sufficient revenues, banks had to increase their service fees for writing checks.

Ceiling rates of interest on time deposits were initially supported by commercial bankers because they appeared to make it possible for them to obtain funds at a lower cost than they otherwise would have had to pay. The original explanation given for Regulation Q was that with unrestricted competition for deposits, banks would invest in excessively risky loans and investments. Risky loans would have been necessary to earn high enough rates of return to pay the higher interest rates on time deposits than those allowed. This is the usual argument for government price-fixing—that producers will engage in unethical or socially unwise activities unless they receive adequate protection. This is not a strong argument, because even with ceilings set on interest rates there would be an inducement for banks to maximize their profits by seeking loans and investments with the highest possible rates of return. After World War II, growing competition between commercial banks and the other major savings institutions—savings and loan associations and mutual savings banks—resulted in a change in attitude of many commercial bankers. They turned against Regulation Q because the maximum interest rates that they were allowed to pay were below those offered by these other thrift institutions. In the 1950s, the rate of growth of time deposits in commercial banks was far below that in savings and loan associations and mutual savings banks.

In recent years, the usefulness of interest rate ceilings has also been questioned because of their disruptive effect on certain credit markets. In 1971, the report of the President's Commission on Financial Structure and Regulation (the Hunt Commission) proposed the eventual elimination of interest rate ceilings on time deposits because of the danger of disintermediation in periods of high market rates of interest.[11] Ceiling rates on time deposits not only in commercial banks, but also in mutual savings banks and savings and loan associations, have had the undesirable effect of causing relatively wide fluctuations in the number of new housing units on which construction has been started. As shown in Figure 13.3, private housing starts have varied with the spread between interest rates on commercial paper and the Regulation Q ceiling rates. Many savers withdraw funds from savings accounts in banks if interest rates on competitive ways of saving are higher. When the commercial paper rate rose relative to the ceiling rates on savings deposits, the flow of funds into thrift institutions decreased, these institutions had less to invest in mortgages, and new housing starts declined; and when the commercial paper rate fell relative to rates on savings deposits, the result was a rise in new housing starts. In 1970 and 1973, the federal government increased the ceiling rates of interest allowed on time deposits in order to enable commercial banks and other thrift institutions to compete more effectively with the high yields available on market securities and to provide savers with a higher rate of return in periods of rapid inflation and rising interest rates.

The recent trend toward more liberal maximum interest rates allowed on savings and time deposits is shown in Table 13.4. The only change in

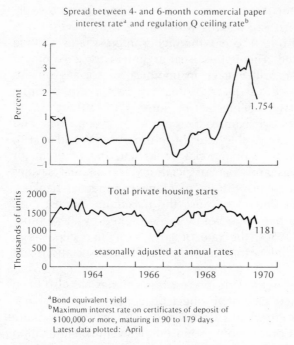

Figure 13.3 shows two graphs. The top graph is labeled "Spread between 4- and 6-month commercial paper interest rate[a] and regulation Q ceiling rate[b]" with a y-axis labeled "Percent" ranging from −1 to 4, and a data point marked 1.754. The bottom graph is labeled "Total private housing starts" with a y-axis labeled "Thousands of units" ranging from 0 to 2000, noting "seasonally adjusted at annual rates" and a data point marked 1181. The x-axis spans 1964 to 1970.

[a]Bond equivalent yield
[b]Maximum interest rate on certificates of deposit of
$100,000 or more, maturing in 90 to 179 days
Latest data plotted: April

**Figure 13.3 The Effect of Regulation Q on
Private Housing Starts**

Source: Federal Reserve Bank of St. Louis, *Review,* May
1970, p. 4.

these rates between 1936 and the early 1960s had occurred in 1957 when
rates were raised from a high of 2½ percent to 3 percent for certain types
of deposits. In the early 1960s, the relatively low maximum rates allowed
for very short maturities were raised and replaced by a uniform ceiling
of 4 percent for savings deposits and 5½ percent for time deposits. By
1973, interest rates had reached 5 percent for savings deposits and up to
7¼ percent for time deposits, and there was again more differentiation
of rates according to maturity. In 1970 and in 1973, interest ceilings were
suspended in two steps on all certificates of deposit of $100,000 or larger.
This was done to enable banks in the United States to compete for time
deposits with banks in Europe and other foreign countries which do not
have such ceilings. Also, according to Regulation Q, member banks cannot pay a higher rate than the laws of a state allow state banks to pay.
    In the 1960s, the Federal Reserve used Regulation Q in an attempt

Table 13.4
Maximum Interest Rates Payable on Time and Savings Deposits (percent per annum)

TYPE OF DEPOSIT	JULY 20, 1966	SEPT. 26, 1966	APR. 19, 1968	JAN. 21, 1970	JUNE 24, 1970	MAY 16, 1973	JULY 1, 1973	NOV. 1, 1973
Savings deposits	4	4	4	4½	4½	4½	5	5
Other time deposits:								
Multiple maturity:[a]								
30–89 days	4	4	4	4½	4½	4½	5	5
90 days–1 year	5	5	5	5	5	5	5½	5½
1 year–2 years	5	5	5	5½	5½	5½		
1 year–2½ years							6	6
2 years and over	5	5	5	5¾	5¾	5¾		
2½ years and over							6½	6½
4 years and over (minimum denomination of $1,000)							[b]	7¼
Single maturity:								
Less than $100,000:								
30–89 days	5½	5	5	5	5	5	5	5
90 days–1 year	5½	5	5	5	5	5	5½	5½
1 year–2 years	5½	5	5	5½	5½	5½		
1 year–2½ years							6	6
2 years and over	5½	5	5	5¾	5¾	5¾		
2½ years and over							6½	6½
4 years and over (minimum denomination of $1,000)							[b]	7¼
$100,000 and over:								
30–59 days	5½	5½	5½	6¼	[b]			[b]
60–89 days	5½	5½	5¾	6½	[b]			
90–179 days	5½	5½	6	6¾	6¾	[b]		
180 days–1 year	5½	5½	6¼	7	7	[b]		
1 year or more	5½	5½	6¼	7½	7½	[b]		

[a] Multiple-maturity time deposits include deposits that are automatically renewable at maturity without action by the depositor and deposits that are payable after written notice of withdrawal.
[b] Suspended.
Source: *Federal Reserve Bulletin*, February 1974, p. A10.

to combat inflation.[12] By keeping ceiling rates on time deposits low in a period of rising interest rates, the Federal Reserve attempted to cut down on the total volume of bank deposits—demand and time deposits—and to slow up the expansion of bank credit. When interest rates on time deposits become relatively low, the growth of time deposits tends to slow up. The decrease in time deposits could mean more demand deposits requiring larger reserves, and this would reduce total deposits and total bank credit. As an alternative to controlling total deposits and credit through Regulation Q, the Federal Reserve could probably have achieved the same results through open-market operations. The principal effect of controls on interest rates appears to have been to reroute the flow of credit rather than to limit its total amount. If measures are taken to reduce the rate of return on time deposits relative to other short-term rates, business firms with excess funds will withdraw their time deposits and put their funds in commercial paper or other short-term securities. This would reduce the amount of funds available to business firms through banks; but business firms in need of funds would still be able to obtain them by selling commercial paper.

Eligibility Requirements

The Federal Reserve's eligibility requirements refer to the *kind of backing* required for loans made to member banks. Though still an essential element in the procedures followed by the Federal Reserve banks, eligibility requirements serve little purpose at the present time. Originally, loans to member banks were in the form of rediscounted bills or promissory notes that had been used to finance commercial loans. In World War I, discounting was extended to loans backed by government securities, and in the early 1930s the requirements were further relaxed. The original justification for eligibility requirements was based on the real bills doctrine, the theory of central banking that developed in eighteenth-century England and that still predominated when the Federal Reserve Act was written. According to this theory, the Federal Reserve System would provide the banking system with the appropriate amount of bank reserves if borrowing by member banks from the Federal Reserve banks were limited to the rediscounting of real bills. Actually, the kind of collateral on which the Federal Reserve extends credit need not be connected with the ultimate use made of the credit. Today it is believed that the total amount of bank reserves must be regulated so as to avoid wide fluctuations in the money supply, and that permitting the volume of bank reserves to be determined by the willingness of banks to borrow from the Federal Reserve banks will not avoid destabilizing fluctuations in the money supply.[13]

Controls over Consumer and Real Estate Credit

During World War II, the board of governors was given the power to regulate minimum down payments and maximum maturities of credit lent for the purchase of automobiles and other consumer durables. Originally, the minimum down payment was set between 10 percent and 33⅓ percent, and the maximum maturity was eighteen months. Because of wartime controls curtailing the production of durable consumer goods, credit controls—aimed at reducing the demand for these items—were largely unnecessary. These controls ended in 1947, but they were restored in 1948–1949 and during the Korean War period of 1950–1952. In 1950–1952, the Federal Reserve extended its controls to cover down payments and maturities of loans for residential construction. Regulations required down payments of 10 to 50 percent, depending on the value of the home, and allowed maturities only up to twenty years in most cases. A principal problem in the administration of this type of control has been the extreme difficulty in avoiding evasion.[14]

The Federal Reserve System probably does not need any of the selective instruments of control for the purpose of influencing total output or prices. One of the criticisms of those controls is that they are sometimes looked upon as a substitute for the use of the major instruments of control when in fact they have very little overall impact. Their principal effect would appear to be on the allocation of resources. But even in this respect, it is usually not too difficult to reroute credit through alternative channels.

SUMMARY

Purchases of U.S. govermnent securities by the Federal Reserve banks have an expansionary effect on the monetary base, and sales have a restraining effect. Open-market policy is formulated by the Federal Open Market Committee and administered by the manager of the open-market account at the Federal Reserve Bank of New York.

Variations in the volume of member bank borrowing from the Federal Reserve banks depend on changes in the relative level of the discount rate as compared with the Federal funds rate. Member banks typically increase their borrowing from the Federal Reserve banks in periods of business expansion and decrease it during periods of business contraction.

The Federal Reserve authorities do not often use changes in the legal reserve requirements of member banks as an instrument of control, because the administration of open-market operations is simpler and the results are less severe.

The different reserve requirements that have been set for demand and time deposits in banks of different size reduce the effectiveness of the Federal Reserve authorities in administering monetary policy.

The most important selective instrument of control of the Federal Reserve System is its power to set ceiling rates of interest on savings and time deposits in commercial banks. Although those ceilings have been raised, higher market rates of interest have shifted funds into other channels and resulted in increasing criticism of those controls.

NOTES

1. See Board of Governors of the Federal Reserve System, *59th Annual Report, 1972,* pp. 42–47.
2. For a description of the technique of open-market operations, see Paul Meek, *Open Market Operations* (New York: Federal Reserve Bank of New York, 1973).
3. For examples of directives, see Board of Governors of the Federal Reserve System, *59th Annual Report, 1972,* pp. 106–114.
4. For the arguments for and against the bills-only policy, see Otto Eckstein and John Kareken, "A Background Memo on the Federal Reserve's 'Bills Only' Policy," in U.S. Congress, Joint Economic Committee, *Employment, Growth, and Price Levels: Hearings, July 24–30, 1959, Part 6A,* 86th Cong., 1st sess., 1959, pp. 1248–1249.
5. See *Federal Reserve Bulletin* 41 (January 1955), pp. 8–14.
6. Edward C. Simmons, "A Note on the Revival of Federal Reserve Discount Policy," *Journal of Finance* 11 (December 1956), pp. 413–421; Warren L. Smith, "The Discount Rate as a Credit-Control Weapon," *Journal of Political Economy* 66 (April 1958), pp. 171–177; Charles R. Whittlesey, "Credit Policy at the Discount Window," *Quarterly Journal of Economics* 73 (May 1959), pp. 207–216; and Milton Friedman, *A Program for Monetary Stability* (New York: Fordham University Press, 1960), chapter 2.
7. Joseph Aschheim, *Techniques of Monetary Control* (Baltimore: The Johns Hopkins Press, 1961), pp. 7–8.
8. "Reappraisal of the Federal Reserve Discount Mechanism," *Federal Reserve Bulletin* 54 (July 1968), pp. 545–551.
9. Arthur F. Burns, "The Structure of Reserve Requirements," *Federal Reserve Bulletin,* May 1973, pp. 339–343.

10. See Peter G. Fousek, *Foreign Central Banking: The Instruments of Monetary Policy* (New York: Federal Reserve Bank of New York, 1957), pp. 10–11; and J. Aschheim, *Techniques of Monetary Control*, p. 32.

11. *Report of the President's Commission on Financial Structure and Regulation* (Washington, D.C.: U.S. Government Printing Office, December 1971), pp. 23–27.

12. James Tobin, "Deposit Interest Ceilings as a Monetary Control," *Journal of Money, Credit, and Banking* 2 (February 1970), pp. 4–14; and Milton Friedman, "Controls of Interest Rates Paid by Banks," ibid., pp. 15–32.

13. Western economists have been surprised that the real bills doctrine was adhered to in the Soviet Union long after it was discarded in the West. See Raymond P. Powell, "Recent Developments in Soviet Monetary Policy," in Franklyn D. Holzman, ed., *Readings on the Soviet Economy* (Chicago: Rand McNally, (1962), Section VIII; see also book review by Zbigniew M. Fallenbuchl, *Journal of Economic Literature* (September 1974), pp. 927–928.

14. Board of Governors of the Federal Reserve System, *Consumer Instalment Credit*, Vol. I, Part I, *Growth and Import* (Washington, D.C.: Government Printing Office, 1957), pp. 310–315.

QUESTIONS

13.1. Describe the way in which the Federal Reserve banks purchase and sell government securities.

13.2. What is the objective of defensive open-market operations?

13.3. Under what conditions is the discount rate typically lowered? Under what conditions is it raised?

13.4. Explain why the total amount of discounting may increase in a period of inflation even though the discount rate is raised? Why may total discounting decline in a period of recession even though the discount rate is lowered?

13.5. What are the shortcomings of changes in the discount rate as an instrument of control?

13.6. Should discounting at the Federal Reserve banks be eliminated?

13.7. What are some of the recent changes in the reserve requirements of the member banks?

13.8. Explain the way in which a reduction in the legal reserve ratios of the member banks makes possible an expansion in their loans and investments and in their deposits, and explain the process by which this comes about.

13.9.   What are the advantages and disadvantages of changes in reserve requirements as an instrument of control?

13.10.   Explain the nature of margin requirements for borrowing for the purchase of corporation stock.

13.11.   The Federal Reserve's margin requirements for borrowing to purchase corporation stock have been criticized as ineffective. Why?

13.12.   What are the objectives of the Federal Reserve's controls over maximum rates of interest payable on time deposits?

13.13.   Explain the conditions in which ceiling interest rates on time deposits may cause wide fluctuations in new housing starts.

13.14.   It has been proposed that keeping the ceiling rates on time deposits low relative to other money market rates is an effective way to combat inflation. Explain.

13.15.   Know the meaning and significance of the following terms and concepts: easy monetary policy, tight monetary policy, open-market operations, selective instruments of control, bills-only policy, defensive operations, dynamic operations, discount rate, net demand deposits, legal ranges for reserve requirements, margin requirements, operation twist.

Chapter 14
Targets and Indicators of Monetary Policy

Whether the goals of price stability and full employment can be achieved more effectively by using the level of interest rates or by using the rate of increase in the money supply as an indicator of the thrust of the Federal Reserve System's actions is a major issue for monetary policy.

To conduct monetary policy, the Federal Reserve authorities need a target that will serve as a gauge to guide their open-market operations. They need a measure of monetary policy which they can watch and which will tell them whether the actions they have taken are expansionary, restraining, or neutral. During most of the post–World War II period, the principal target used by the Federal Reserve was the level of free reserves. The level of free reserves is the difference between the total excess reserves of the member banks and the total amount of their borrowing from the Federal Reserve banks. A negative level of free reserves is referred to as *net borrowed reserves*. When a more expansionary policy has been desired, the monetary authorities have taken the necessary actions to raise the level of free reserves, and when a more restraining policy was their objective, they have taken the actions necessary to lower the level of free reserves.

Alternative targets that have become more important in recent years are the rates of increase in one of the monetary aggregates, such as the monetary base, total member bank reserves, or reserves against private deposits (RPDs). The use of these new targets has been advocated because of dissatisfaction with the use of free reserves. The monetary base is more inclusive as a target than either total member bank reserves or RPDs. The monetary base includes currency in the hands of the public in addition to total member bank reserves, while RPDs include only total member bank reserves less those reserves required against government demand deposits and less net interbank deposits.

Free reserves and the monetary base as operational targets are compared in Figure 14.1. Whether the target used is the level of free reserves or the annual rate of increase in the monetary base, the basic goals are the same—control of the price level, the rate of unemployment, economic growth, and the balance of payments. These ultimate objectives cannot serve as targets, primarily because it takes at least six months for a change in monetary policy to have its main effect on the real national income, and still longer to affect prices. Also, real output and prices may be affected by fiscal policy and governmental wage and price ceilings, as well as by monetary policy.

The policy instruments themselves are also not useful as targets. Changes in the discount rate would be a poor target because the effect

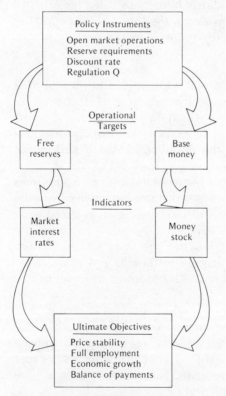

Figure 14.1   Two Methods of Implementing Monetary Policy

Source: Albert E. Burger, "The Implementation Problem of Monetary Policy," in Federal Reserve Bank of St. Louis, *Review,* March 1971, p. 23.

of such a change depends on the response of the member banks. The volume of open-market purchases or sales alone would be an unsatisfactory measure of monetary policy because of the numerous other factors in the bank reserve equation affecting bank reserves and the monetary base.

BEFORE THE TARGETS: INTEREST RATE CEILINGS

The use of operational targets by the Federal Reserve developed after 1951. From 1941 to 1951, the Federal Reserve's main objective was to establish ceiling interest rates for U.S. government securities rather than to stabilize the level of economic activity. The ending of the bond-support program in 1951, known as the Treasury–Federal Reserve Accord, constituted one of the major changes in monetary policy in the post-war period.

The World War II policy of preventing interest rates on government securities from rising had at least two objectives: to keep interest costs in the federal budget as low as possible, and to avoid speculation by investors that interest rates might rise during the war. It was feared that such speculation might cause investors to postpone purchases of bonds, as they had during World War I. In addition to these wartime budgetary considerations, after World War II low interest rates were desired as a method of stimulating the economy.

At the beginning of World War II, the Federal Reserve set the following interest rate ceilings on bills, certificates, and bonds:

TYPE OF SECURITY	CEILING RATE OF INTEREST
Bills, 90-day	$3/8\%$
Certificates, 1-year	$7/8$
Bonds, over 10 years	$2^1/_2$

Control of interest rates was designed to assist the United States Treasury in its debt operations. The ceilings were in effect a bond-support program because, in order to keep interest rates from *rising* above those rates, the authorities had to prevent bond prices from *falling*. Interest yields were kept from rising by purchasing government securities in the open market whenever prices fell below the support levels.

The bond-support program was continued for several years after the war because it was thought that ending it might cause a panic in the government securities market. In addition it was felt that investors who had purchased securities during the war should be protected against incurring losses. Also, it was feared that a decline in bond prices would reduce the liquidity of banks and other financial institutions. Actually, since 1938 commercial banks had been permitted to list their government securities at cost. Even though a decline in bond prices might have had a restraining effect on banks, it would not have had a serious impact on their solvency.

Figure 14.2 shows the trend of interest rates on U.S. government securities from 1941 to 1951. The efforts to keep yields from rising above the ceilings were successful for a fairly long period of time. Occasionally, yields fell below the ceiling levels, but very seldom did they rise above the ceilings. The ceiling rates on several of the shorter maturities were relaxed in 1947, but the ceiling rate on bonds was retained until 1951. The relatively effective price and wage controls during World War II probably contributed to the success of these efforts. If prices of goods had risen, interest rates would have tended to rise in order to discount the expected rate of inflation. An even larger volume of open-market purchases would have been necessary in order to keep interest rates at the ceiling levels.

After the Korean War, which began in late June 1950, the bond-support program contributed to a serious inflation. The war-induced business expansion tended to cause interest rates to rise and bond prices to fall. Under the bond-support program, to prevent interest rates from

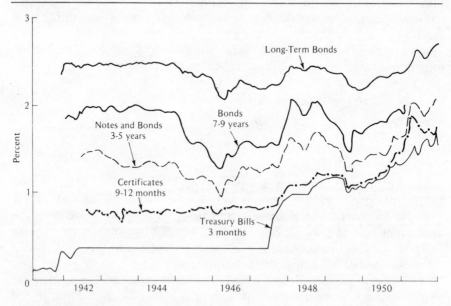

Figure 14.2   Yields on U. S. Government Securities, 1941–1951

Source: Board of Governors of the Federal Reserve System, *Historical Supplement to Federal Reserve Chart Book on Financial and Business Statistics*, September 1960, p. 39.

rising, the Federal Reserve had to accelerate its purchases of U.S. government securities, and this accelerated the expansion in bank reserves. During the first seven months of the war, member bank reserves were increased 12 percent by open-market purchases. This was followed by an increase of nearly 20 percent in bank loans and 8 percent in demand deposits. Wholesale prices rose 11 percent, and consumer prices rose 6 percent. The purpose of discontinuing the bond-support program was to enable the Federal Reserve to stop increasing bank reserves excessively.

TARGET I: THE LEVEL OF FREE RESERVES

Free reserves—the excess reserves of member banks *less* their borrowing from the Federal Reserve banks—were an especially important target from the Accord of 1951 until 1970, and they are still one of the targets used.[2] As part of the Accord, it was agreed that the Federal Reserve would again create conditions in which bank borrowing—one of the two components of free reserves—would be more important. From 1934 to 1941, member banks had borrowed very little from the Federal Reserve banks, because the discount rate was high relative to market rates, and the excess reserves of banks were very large. From 1941 to 1951, member bank borrowing had continued to be relatively unimportant because member banks were able to obtain needed reserves by selling U.S. government securities in a guaranteed market because of the bond-support program.

When using free reserves as a target, in order to achieve greater monetary ease the System would purchase a sufficient quantity of securities to raise the level of free reserves. On the other hand, when inflation occurred, the account manager would sell a sufficient quantity of securities to lower the level of free reserves. During periods in which the target was unchanged, he would take whatever actions were necessary to keep the level of free reserves relatively constant. Figure 14.3 shows the movements of the two components of free reserves—excess reserves and borrowings at Federal Reserve banks—from 1950 to 1973. The countercyclical changes in borrowings at Federal Reserve banks have been much more significant than the changes in excess reserves. Borrowings fell, causing free reserves to rise, during the recessions of 1953–1954, 1957–1958, 1960–1961, 1967, and 1969–1970.

Open-market purchases increase the level of free reserves temporarily by increasing excess reserves. Banks then typically use part of the excess reserves to pay off loans at the Federal Reserve banks. This keeps free reserves at the higher level. Open-market sales decrease the level of free reserves by decreasing excess reserves and by inducing banks to borrow more in order to meet their reserve requirements.

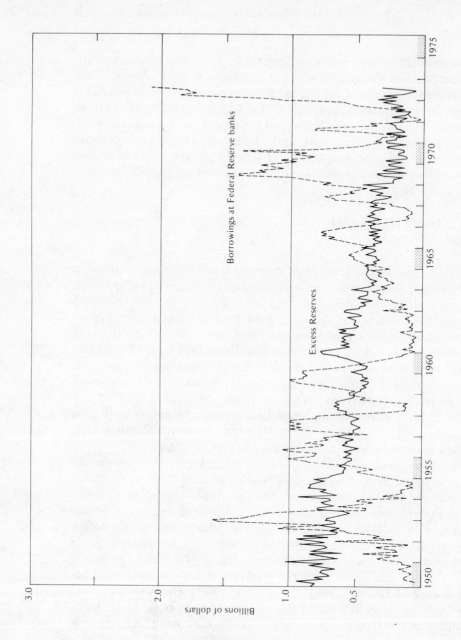

Figure 14.3   Excess Reserves and Borrowings of Member Banks, 1950–1973

Source: Board of Governors of the Federal Reserve System, *Historical Chart Book, 1973*, p. 6.

When free reserves are used as a target of monetary policy, the *indicator* used is the level of interest rates, and particularly short-term interest rates. When the level of free reserves is high, interest rates are expected to be low, and when free reserves are negative, interest rates are expected to be high. Changes in the level of free reserves by themselves do not have important effects on the national income, the price level, or other economic conditions that monetary policy seeks to control. Changes in free reserves are expected to affect the economy primarily through their effect on interest rates. As a result, the effectiveness of changes in the level of free reserves is measured by whether or not interest rates have moved in the direction desired. If interest rates rose, for example, when the level of free reserves was reduced, this would be taken as an indication that monetary policy had in fact become tighter.

The level of free reserves affects interest rates by affecting the *willingness* of member banks to expand loans and investments. When the level of free reserves is low or negative, banks are heavily in debt to the Reserve banks, and their excess reserves are low. This illiquidity causes banks to be less willing to expand loans and investments. Two reasons are given: (1) that member banks are reluctant to be heavily in debt to the central bank, and (2) that some pressure for repayment exists for reserves obtained through borrowing. The feeling against borrowing is the survival of a tradition that existed prior to 1914 when obtaining funds from a correspondent bank was regarded as a sign of weakness. There is also pressure for repayment of loans from the Federal Reserve bank, because these loans are limited to short periods of time. In addition, banks are less liquid when they are in debt because it is increasingly difficult to borrow more. When banks are less willing to expand loans and investments because they are illiquid, interest rates tend to be high. On the other hand, if bank debt to the Reserve banks is small, it is easy for banks to increase their borrowing and expand their loans and investments, and interest rates tend to be low. Table 14.1 shows that from 1964 to 1973, interest rates have generally risen when the level of free reserves has fallen.

Although the objective of changes in free reserves has been primarily to affect interest rates, such changes may also affect the rate of expansion in the money supply. The following diagram shows the possible chain of reactions between an increase in open-market purchases and the rate of expansion in the money supply. Open-market purchases may be used to raise free reserves; higher free reserves in turn may increase the willingness of banks to lend and invest; and if banks are more willing to lend and invest, there will be a more rapid rate of expansion in bank reserves, credit, and the money supply if the Federal Reserve System holds to a given target level of free reserves:

> An increase in open market purchases
>
> ↓
>
> Raises the level of free reserves
>
> ↓
>
> Increases willingness of banks to lend and invest
>
> ↓
>
> Increases the rate of expansion in bank reserves, credit, and the money supply

If banks are willing to expand credit more rapidly, they can do so. This is because some banks can always get the funds needed to expand loans and investments by borrowing from the Federal Reserve or by using part of their excess reserves. If, however, banks obtain funds to lend either by using excess reserves or by borrowing from the Federal Reserve banks, the actual level of free reserves would fall below the target level. To keep on the target, open-market purchases would have to be increased. As a result, the higher the level of free reserves, the more willing banks are to lend and invest, and the larger the increase in total reserves necessary

Table 14.1
Free Reserves, Interest Rates, and the
Annual Rate of Change of
Money Supply I, 1964–1973

YEAR	FREE RESERVES (DECEMBER) (in millions)	RATE ON 3-MONTH U. S. TREASURY BILLS (annual average)	YIELD ON CORPORATE BONDS—Aaa (ANNUAL AVERAGE) (percent per year)	ANNUAL RATE OF INCREASE OF MONEY SUPPLY I (4th quarter to 4th quarter)
1964	$ 168	3.5%	4.4%	4.0%
1965	— 2	4.0	4.5	4.3
1966	— 165	4.9	5.1	2.6
1967	107	4.3	5.5	6.4
1968	— 310	5.3	6.2	7.5
1969	— 829	6.7	7.0	4.2
1970	— 49	6.5	8.0	5.8
1971	58	4.3	7.4	6.6
1972	— 830	4.1	7.2	7.7
1973	— 1,036	7.0	7.4	6.1

Source: *Federal Reserve Bulletin,* various issues, pp. A6, A29, and A30; Federal Reserve Bank of St. Louis, *Rates of Change in Economic Data for Ten Industrial Countries,* various issues.

to keep on the target. On the other hand, when the target level of free reserves is lowered, banks are usually less willing to lend and invest, and the necessary expansion in bank reserves would be less.

The difficulty with using free reserves to control the money supply is that it is not the only factor affecting the willingness of banks to lend and invest. Other factors are the demand for loans, the rates of interest on available securities, and the relationship of market rates of interest to the discount rate. The willingness to borrow from the Reserve banks depends on whether the discount rate is above or below other important short-term interest rates. If borrowing becomes less attractive because the bill rate has fallen below the discount rate, banks might not be more willing to lend and invest even though free reserves are raised. Also, even if the level of free reserves were unchanged, because of changes in the demand for bank loans there could be changes in the willingness of banks to lend and invest—causing the expansion in the money supply to be different from that indicated by a constant level of free reserves.

Table 14.1 shows that from 1964 to 1973 the target level of free reserves was lowered each year except during the mini-recession in 1967 and the recession of 1970. The lower levels of free reserves might have caused banks to become less willing to expand loans and investments and thus might have caused a slower rate of expansion in the money supply, but it did not work out that way. When interest rates rose, the level of free reserves that banks desired to hold must have fallen. Even though the actual level of free reserves fell, the desired level was apparently falling even faster, and banks expanded their loans and investments at a more rapid rate. These divergent movements of free reserves and the rate of change in the money stock caused confusion concerning the nature of monetary policy. While some persons pointed to free reserves and interest rates and said that monetary policy was becoming tighter, others looked at the money stock and said that monetary policy was becoming more expansionary.

Cyclical Movements of Interest Rates

Figure 14.4 shows that interest yields on corporate Aaa bonds and 3-month Treasury bills fell during the recessions of 1953–1954, 1957–1958, 1960–1961, and 1969–1970, and during the slowdown of 1967. During periods of expansion, those interest yields usually rose. Other important interest rates have varied in approximately the same way. Short-term rates have fluctuated more widely than long-term rates. Because interest rates are used as an indicator of monetary policy, the lower interest rates in periods of recession and high rates in periods of prosperity may have been to some extent the result of Federal Reserve policy. In addi-

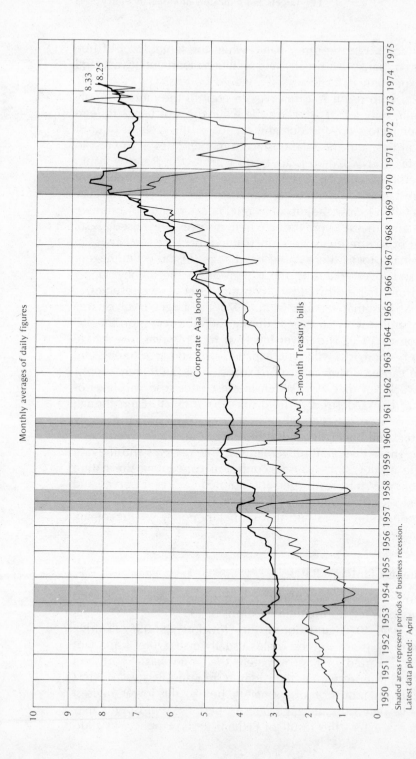

Monthly averages of daily figures

Corporate Aaa bonds

3-month Treasury bills

8.33
8.25

1950 1951 1952 1953 1954 1955 1956 1957 1958 1959 1960 1961 1962 1963 1964 1965 1966 1967 1968 1969 1970 1971 1972 1973 1974 1975

Shaded areas represent periods of business recession.
Latest data plotted: April

Figure 14.4 Selected Interest Rates, 1950–1974

Prepared by Federal Reserve Bank of St. Louis.

tion, cyclical movements in interest rates may occur automatically because of changes in demand. When business turns downward, firms cut down on their borrowing, and interest rates tend to fall. In periods of prosperity, business borrowing expands and interest rates rise.

Falling interest rates in periods of recession and rising rates in periods of expansion have desirable stabilizing effects on the economy. This is illustrated in Figure 14.5, which shows the conditions of demand and supply in the market for loanable funds.[3] The demand schedule for credit slopes downward, indicating that borrowers will borrow larger amounts per year as borrowing becomes less costly. Most borrowing is done by business firms for the purpose of investing in capital equipment designed to increase their productive capacity. A larger quantity of borrowing occurs at lower rates of interest, because more types of capital improvements become profitable when borrowing costs are lower.

The supply schedule for credit slopes upward, indicating that savers and financial institutions are willing to lend larger amounts the higher the rate of interest. A major way in which persons save for old age, emergencies, and future opportunities is by lending money to others on the condition that the money will be paid back to them at some future date. They tend to value future dollars less highly than present ones because of the uncertainty of collecting on promises in the future or the possibility that they may die before collecting them. An individual balances his present consumption and his saving so that the last dollar spent today has the same value to him that one more dollar saved for the future has. Persons discount the future value of the dollar to the present. If the interest rate were 4 percent, for example, a dollar to be delivered a year from now would not be worth today more than about 96 cents—$1/(1 + .04)$; similarly it would be worth less—$1/(1 + .04)^2$—two years from now. If interest rates go up, a person pays less for a dollar in the

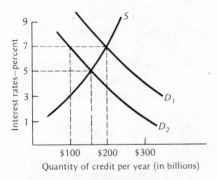

Figure 14.5 The Credit Market

future and this makes saving more attractive. Thus, at higher rates of interest, the amount of dollars he is willing to lend increases.

In Figure 14.5, if the demand schedule were D_1, the equilibrium rate of interest would be at 7 percent, where the supply of credit is equal to the demand. When the Federal Reserve authorities step up the increase in the monetary base, this usually causes the supply schedule for credit to shift to the right: with a given demand schedule, this would lower interest rates. A decrease in the monetary base would shift the supply schedule to the left.

In a period of declining business activity, the demand curve for loanable funds in Figure 14.5 would shift downward from D_1 to D_2. Because of the deterioration in business conditions, only $100 billion worth of loanable funds is now demanded at 7 percent, rather than $200 billion. Whereas previously 7 percent had been the equilibrium rate of interest—where demand is equal to supply—the supply of funds at that rate is now greater than the demand. This causes interest rates to fall because some banks are willing to lend at less than 7 percent rather than not lend at all. As interest rates fall, the quantity of credit demanded increases and the supply decreases. At 5 percent, the equilibrium quantity of loanable funds lent is now back near the original volume of $200 billion. In this example, although there has been no shift in the supply schedule because of a change in Federal Reserve policy, the automatic decline in interest rates would be an important stabilizing force in the economy. In a period of prosperity, if the demand for loanable funds increases, a rise in interest rates also tends to be stabilizing. As interest rates rise, the quantity of loanable funds demanded decreases.

INTEREST RATES AS AN INDICATOR

Despite the desirability of cyclical movements in interest rates, using interest rates as an indicator of monetary policy may be misleading. This is because a decline in interest rates may be caused either by a decrease in the demand for loanable funds or by an increase in the supply. Monetary policy is properly classified as easy only if the reduction in interest rates is the result of a Federal Reserve policy that increased the monetary base and thus the supply of bank credit. The Federal Reserve authorities, for example, were mistaken when they described their monetary policy during the Great Depression as easy because short-term interest rates had fallen sharply.[4] In fact, the supply of bank credit had declined and many banks were failing. In the Great Depression, interest rates fell because the effect of the reduction in the demand for credit was greater than that of the reduction in the supply, not because Federal Reserve policy was easy.

Attempting to control interest rates may also be destabilizing at cyclical peaks. Ideally, it would be desirable for interest rates to fall immediately following a peak. The monetary authorities may not know, however, that a peak has been reached until several months afterwards. In the meantime, to restrain a business expansion thought to be in progress, the monetary authorities would try to keep interest rates high. This would require reducing the supply of bank credit, thus adding to the forces contributing to the downturn.

If interest rates are used as an indicator, they ought to be adjusted for the probable discounting by borrowers and lenders of the expected rate of inflation. The high nominal rates of interest in the late 1960s and the 1970s undoubtedly reflected expectations of inflation. The failure to distinguish between nominal and real interest rates resulted in exaggerating the tightness of monetary policy. Figure 14.6 compares the market yield (nominal rate) on highest-grade seasonal corporate bonds from 1966 to 1974 with the yield adjusted for inflation. The adjusted yield (real rate) is equal to the market yield *less* the average annual rate of change in consumer prices over the three previous years. This adjustment is based on the assumption that the rate of inflation that persons anticipate is related to the rate of inflation experienced in recent years. From 1966 to 1970, the trend of the adjusted yield did not rise even though market yields rose sharply. In 1973, when market yields rose, the adjusted yield fell.

TARGET II: THE MONETARY BASE

When the monetary base is used as a target of monetary policy, the rate of change in the money supply is used as the indicator of the effectiveness of the changes in the monetary base. The reason for using the rate of change in the money stock as an indicator is the possibility that changes in the money supply have significant effects on aggregate demand. If the amount of money people have is greater than the amount that they want to hold, they are expected to spend the excess and cause the demand for goods and services to increase. Or if the amount of money people have is less than they want, they are expected to cut down their spending in their efforts to increase their holdings of money.

The monetary base is a useful target, because the monetary authorities control the most important source of the monetary base through their operations in the open market. The Federal Reserve authorities can

Latest data plotted: April

Figure 14.6 Yields on Highest-Grade Seasonal Corporate Bonds, 1966–1974

Prepared by Federal Reserve Bank of St. Louis.

use open-market operations to offset those factors in the bank reserve equation over which they have no direct control.

A change in the monetary base will result in a predictable change in the money supply only if the money multiplier remains constant. As was explained in Chapter 9, the principal factors affecting the money multiplier are the ratio of excess reserves to deposits that the banks desire to hold, the distribution of deposits between different kinds of accounts, and the amount of currency relative to demand deposits that the public desires to hold. The Federal Reserve authorities have little control over the expansion process. Although they have considerable control over r (the ratio of reserves to demand deposits) and r' (the reserve requirement for time deposits), they have almost no control over c (the ratio of currency to demand deposits) and i (the ratio of excess reserves to demand deposits), and quite limited control of t (the ratio of time deposits to demand deposits). Shifts in deposits among banks with different reserve requirements will affect the average legal reserve requirements for both demand and time deposits. The public's ratio of currency to demand deposits is determined by the desires of the public, and appears to vary closely with fluctuations in economic activity. The growth in time deposits depends ultimately on the desires of the public, although in recent years attempts have been made to control t by varying the maximum rates of interest payable on time deposits. The amount of excess reserves depends largely on the actions of the banks and appears to be sensitive to changes in interest rates, uncertainty, and the demand for bank credit. Because the monetary authorities do not completely understand and have little control of the factors underlying the money multiplier, their control of the money supply is much weaker than their control of the monetary base.

To control the money stock using the monetary base as a target, the monetary authorities have to predict the money multiplier. If they do not predict it correctly, the increase in the money supply resulting from an increase in the monetary base will be different than anticipated. They might then attempt to offset the error, but to do so would require time, and there would be a lag in obtaining the quantity of money or bank credit desired.

The simplest way to predict the currency-to-deposit ratio, the ratio of time to demand deposits, and the ratio of excess reserves to demand deposits, is to assume that they will continue at the same levels as in the past. Actually, as was shown in Table 9.2, these ratios have changed. New regulations for the calculation of reserve requirements adopted in 1968 have had significant effects on the ratio of excess reserves to demand deposits. Raising the maximum rates of interest allowed on time deposits has increased the ratio of time to demand deposits. In addition, movements of interest rates and cyclical movements in business activity may affect these ratios. Some economists have attempted to formulate more accurate forecasting techniques by assuming that these ratios have a predictable relationship with such factors as movements of interest rates, the level of income, and price expectations.[5] They have set up equations for the money multiplier that are more complicated than equations 9.8 and 9.9.

The money multiplier may be affected by factors not included in equations 9.8 and 9.9—Treasury deposits, interbank deposits, large CDs, and deposits in nonmember banks. Changes in each of those may cause changes in the money supply that are difficult to anticipate. Although member bank reserves are based on all deposits, Treasury and interbank deposits and CDs are not included in the statistical series on the money supply. If Treasury or interbank deposits increase, the money supply will decrease; and if Treasury or interbank deposits decrease, the money supply will increase. As a result, a shift in deposits between either the Treasury or the banks and the public causes a change in the money supply even though the monetary base and total deposits are unchanged. Furthermore, deposits in nonmember banks are included in the money supply, but the formulas for the multiple expansion process refer solely to member banks. Nonmember banks are not required to hold reserves at the Federal Reserve banks. Their reserves consist primarily of deposits in other commercial banks, and are not controlled by the Federal Reserve System. To control the total money supply, the Federal Reserve authorities have to allow for changes in the volume of nonmember bank deposits.

A problem that might arise if the Federal Reserve attempted to implement monetary policy by controlling the monetary base is that a change in the monetary base could itself affect the money multiplier through its effect on i (the ratio of excess reserves to demand deposits) and t (the ratio of time deposits to demand deposits). An increase in the monetary base might decrease interest rates—which in turn might increase the quantity of excess reserves that banks desire to hold. This would cause the money supply to rise by a smaller proportion than the monetary base. A decrease in interest rates might reduce t by making time deposits less attractive relative to demand deposits. Because of the lower reserve ratio for time deposits, a decline in t would tend to reduce Money Supply II but have the opposite effect on Money Supply I. The effects of changes in the monetary base on the multiplier could conceivably be large enough to make it impossible to control the money supply by manipulating the monetary base. Increases in the monetary base might be completely offset by decreases in the money multiplier. Despite these possibilities, there has usually been a close relationship between the monetary base and both Money Supply I and II. Table 14.2 shows the relationship between the monetary base and both Money Supply I and Money Supply II in 1972 and 1973. The changes in the money multiplier from month to month have been small. In general, when the base increases at a more rapid rate, the money supply also increases more rapidly.

The recent shift to the use of monetary aggregates as one of the

Table 14.2
The Monetary Base and the Money Supply,
1972 and 1973 (seasonally adjusted)

MONTH AND YEAR	MONETARY BASE (IN BILLIONS OF DOLLARS)	MONEY SUPPLY I	MONEY MULTIPLIER I	MONEY SUPPLY II (IN BILLIONS OF DOLLARS)	MONEY MULTIPLIER II
1972					
Jan.	$ 90.2	$235.5	2.61	$477.3	5.29
Feb.	90.6	238.2	2.63	482.9	5.33
Mar.	91.5	240.5	2.63	487.6	5.33
Apr.	92.2	242.0	2.62	490.6	5.32
May	92.6	242.8	2.62	494.1	5.34
June	93.0	244.2	2.63	498.4	5.36
July	93.3	246.6	2.64	503.7	5.40
Aug.	93.8	247.9	2.64	507.8	5.41
Sept.	94.1	249.5	2.65	511.9	5.44
Oct.	95.4	251.3	2.63	516.6	5.42
Nov.	96.3	252.6	2.62	520.1	5.40
Dec.	97.0	255.7	2.64	525.5	5.42
1973					
Jan.	97.9	256.7	2.62	529.6	5.41
Feb.	98.1	257.9	2.63	532.3	5.43
Mar.	99.1	258.1	2.60	534.6	5.39
Apr.	99.8	259.4	2.60	538.3	5.39
May	100.2	262.4	2.62	543.6	5.43
June	100.8	265.5	2.63	549.4	5.45
July	101.4	266.4	2.63	552.0	5.44
Aug.	101.4	266.2	2.63	554.9	5.47
Sept.	101.8	265.4	2.61	556.6	5.47
Oct.	102.7	266.5	2.59	561.6	5.47
Nov.	103.5	268.8	2.60	566.7	5.48
Dec.	104.3	270.4	2.59	570.7	5.47

Source: Federal Reserve Bank of St. Louis, *Monetary Trends,* 15 February 1973, p. 12, and 21 February 1974, p. 6; and *Federal Reserve Bulletin,* February 1974, p. 90.

targets of Federal Reserve policy is an important change. The use of free reserves as a target may have been one of the causes of the accelerated rate of inflation during the 1960s. When free reserves are used as a target, the actions of banks and business firms may have an important effect on the expansion in the supply of money and credit, and the rate of expansion may be excessive. This is because the growth in the supply of money and credit depends both on the level of free reserves and on how banks and business firms respond to the level of free reserves. The recent interest in monetary aggregates as targets may result in much firmer control by the Federal Reserve authorities of the rates of expansion in the supply of money and bank credit than when the level of free reserves was the principal target.

Other Monetary Aggregates as Targets

Instead of using the monetary base as a target, the monetary authorities might use total member bank reserves or reserves against private deposits (RPDs).[6] Starting in 1972, the Federal Reserve has emphasized the use of RPDs. The three monetary aggregates are so closely related that it probably makes little difference which aggregate is used. Figure 14.7 illustrates the relationship between the three monetary or reserve aggregates and the money stock. It shows that the control of RPDs is more difficult than control of the monetary base because the monetary authorities would have to predict accurately the quantity of currency in the hands of the public, government deposits, and interbank deposits. However, predicting the multiplier between RPDs and private demand deposits is easier than between the monetary base and the money supply. In either case, predicting the quantity of currency in the hands of the public, of government deposits, and of interbank deposits is necessary, and such predictions may turn out to be incorrect.

THE MONEY STOCK AS AN INDICATOR

An important issue in using the money stock as an indicator is to decide whether fixed or discretionary changes in the money stock would best achieve the objectives of monetary policy. Professor Friedman has suggested that the Federal Reserve authorities should follow a rule that the stock of money be increased at a fixed rate. Others have suggested that the rate of increase in the quantity of money be varied so as to counteract fluctuations in business activity. The difficulty with attempts to counteract the business cycle is that if serious errors are made in forecasting or in judging the time lags, the actions of the monetary authorities might accentuate the instability of the economy.

Relatively wide fluctuations in the rate of change in the money stock may have been one of the principal causes of depressions.[7] If so, eliminating fluctuations in the rate of change in the money stock would eliminate ups and downs in business activity. However, if business cycles are caused primarily by other factors such as changes in investment op-

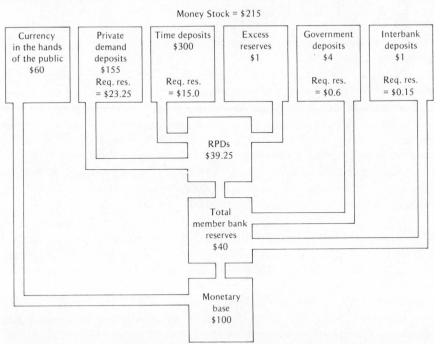

Money Stock = $215

| Currency in the hands of the public $60 | Private demand deposits $155 Req. res. = $23.25 | Time deposits $300 Req. res. = $15.0 | Excess reserves $1 | Government deposits $4 Req. res. = $0.6 | Interbank deposits $1 Req. res. = $0.15 |

RPDs $39.25

Total member bank reserves $40

Monetary base $100

ᵃThe illustration excludes consideration of nondeposit sources of funds and vault cash of nonmember banks. Reserve requirements are assumed to be 15 percent on private demand, government demand, and interbank deposits, and 5 percent on time deposits.

Figure 14.7 Illustrations of Uses of Reserve Aggregatesᵃ **(in billions of dollars)**

Source: Charlotte E. Ruebling, "RPDs and Other Reserve Operating Targets," in Federal Reserve Bank of St. Louis, *Review*, August 1972, p. 5.

portunities, cycles would continue even if the rate of increase in the money supply were kept stable.

A policy of increasing the money supply at a stable rate might also counteract economic instability caused by other factors than unstable monetary conditions. If the supply of money were increased at a steady rate, interest rates would vary primarily with changes in the demand for loanable funds, rising in periods of prosperity and falling in periods of recession. This would be stabilizing. In depressions, a fall in interest rates would counteract the downward movement of business activity; and in booms, a rise in interest rates would restrain excessive increases in spending. A steady increase in the money supply would also have a stabilizing psychological effect on expectations. Businessmen would know that even though business activity was declining, the quantity of money in the economy would increase steadily and might eventually counteract the downward trend. In a period of inflation, they would know that the quantity of money would not accelerate so as to contribute to the rise in prices.

Critics of the use of the money stock as a target for monetary policy usually emphasize the importance of interest rates and believe the monetary authorities should attempt to influence their movements.[8] They usually analyze changes in the level of economic activity in terms of theories in which interest rates play a crucial role. In the *interest rate–investment theory* of income determination, changes in interest rates may have significant effects on investment and thus on aggregate demand. A decline in interest rates would have a stimulating effect and a rise in interest rates a restraining effect. On the other hand, the supporters of the use of monetary aggregates analyze changes in the level of income in terms of the *quantity theory* of money, in which the stock of money plays a crucial role. In the latter approach, although changes in a broad range of interest rates have an important role in transmitting monetary impulses to the level of economic activity, interest rates are not used as indicators.

The use of the monetary base as a target of monetary policy has important effects on interest rates even though interest rates need not be used as an indicator. Although it was thought formerly that a more rapid rate of increase in the money supply would lower interest rates and a slower expansion would raise them, recent studies have concluded that the short-run effects on interest rates of changes in the rate of monetary expansion are different from the long-run effects.[9] When the Federal Reserve speeds up the increase in the monetary base, at first both the resulting increase in the supply of bank credit and the increase in the money supply cause interest rates to fall. This comes about because, with additional funds, banks and persons bid up the prices of securities and cause their yields to fall. Eventually, however, the expansionary effect of the increase in the money supply on the demand for loanable funds causes interest rates to rise. And if the increase in the money supply results in inflation, interest rates may rise further in order to discount the rate of inflation and to compensate for the increased taxes on a higher amount of nominal interest income. The rising interest rates during the 1960s, for example, appear to have been the result of an expansionary monetary policy, not a restraining policy. Because the short-run effects of changes in the money supply on interest rates are different from the long-run effects, it is hazardous to use interest rates as indicators of monetary policy.

SUMMARY

The ease or tightness of monetary policy may be measured either by the level of interest rates or by the rate of increase in the money supply.

The bond-support program adopted during World War II to keep interest rates from rising became a cause of inflation, because the Federal Reserve System had to purchase government securities in order to keep their prices from falling, and this resulted in excessively large increases in the monetary base.

It is desirable for interest rates to fall in periods of recession and rise in periods of expansion, because the demand for loans is stimulated by falling interest rates and restrained by rising interest rates.

Falling interest rates need not be a reliable measure of Federal Reserve policy, since interest rates may fall either because of expansionary actions by the Federal Reserve System or because of a decline in the demand for loans.

The Federal Reserve authorities do not have complete control over changes in the money supply, primarily because of the difficulties in predicting the money multiplier. The money multiplier depends primarily on changes in the demand of banks for reserves and of individuals for currency and time deposits.

NOTES

1. See Albert E. Burger, "The Implementation Problem of Monetary Policy," Federal Reserve Bank of St. Louis, *Review*, March 1971, pp. 20–30; Jack M. Guttentag, "The Strategy of Open Market Operations," *Quarterly Journal of Economics* 80 (February 1966), pp. 1–30; and Thomas R. Saving, "Monetary-Policy Targets and Indicators," *Journal of Political Economy* 75 (August 1967), Part 2, pp. 446–465.

2. For discussions of the use of free reserves as a target, see "The Significance and Limitations of Free Reserves," Federal Reserve Bank of New York, *Monthly Review* 30 (November 1958), p. 164; William G. Dewald, "Free Reserves, Total Reserves, and Monetary Control," *Journal of Political Economy* 71 (April 1963), pp. 141–153; A. James Meigs, *Free Reserves and the Money Supply* (Chicago: University of Chicago Press, 1962); and K. Brunner and A. H. Meltzer, *The Federal Reserve's Attachment to the Free Reserve Concept*, Subcommittee Print (U.S., Congress, House, Committee

on Banking and Currency, Subcommittee on Domestic Finance, 88th Cong., 2nd sess., 1964).

3. For a more detailed explanation of equilibrium conditions in the market for credit, see Edwin G. Dolan, *Basic Microeconomics, Principles and Reality* (Hinsdale, Ill.: Dryden Press, 1974), pp. 106–113.

4. Milton Friedman and Anna J. Schwartz, *A Monetary History of the United States, 1867–1960* (Princeton, N.J.: Princeton University Press, 1963), pp. 374–375.

5. John T. Boorman and Thomas M. Havrilesky, *Money Supply, Money Demand, and Macroeconomic Models* (Boston: Allyn and Bacon, 1972), pp. 28–35.

6. Charlotte E. Ruebling, "RPDs and Other Reserve Operating Targets," Federal Reserve Bank of St. Louis, *Review,* August 1972, pp. 2–7.

7. Milton Friedman and Anna J. Schwartz, *A Monetary History of the United States;* Phillip Cagan, *Determinants and Effects of Changes in the Stock of Money, 1875–1960* (New York: Columbia University Press, 1965); and Leonall C. Andersen and Keith M. Carlson, "Monetarist Model for Economic Stabilization," Federal Reserve Bank of St. Louis, *Review,* April 1970, pp. 7–25.

8. Walter W. Heller, "Is Monetary Policy Being Oversold?" in Milton Friedman and Walter W. Heller, *Monetary vs. Fiscal Policy* (New York: W. W. Norton & Company, 1969), pp. 20–21.

9. William E. Gibson, "Interest Rates and Monetary Policy," *Journal of Political Economy* 78 (May–June 1970), pp. 431–455.

QUESTIONS

14.1. Why can the ultimate objectives of monetary policy not serve as targets?

14.2. Explain why a Federal Reserve System policy of supporting the prices of U.S. government securities may be inflationary.

14.3. Explain the way in which the Federal Reserve authorities may raise or lower the level of free reserves.

14.4. Why do interest rates tend to be low when the level of free reserves is high, and high when the level of free reserves is low?

14.5. Explain why a decline in interest rates in a period of recession has a desirable effect on the market for loanable funds.

14.6. What are the disadvantages of using interest rates as an indicator of the ease or tightness of monetary policy?

14.7. Explain the way in which the Federal Reserve authorities may control the rate of increase in the money supply.

14.8. Should the Federal Reserve authorities attempt to increase the money supply at a fixed rate, or should they attempt to vary the rate of increase in the money supply so as to counteract business fluctuations?

14.9. Know the meaning and significance of the following terms and concepts: free reserves, net borrowed reserves, operational target, indicator of monetary policy, bond-support program, Treasury–Federal Reserve accord of 1951, willingness of banks to lend and invest, nominal interest rate, monetary aggregate, reserves against private deposits.

Chapter 15
The Behavior of Money

*The cyclical changes in the expanding volume of money suggest a
relationship between the money supply and business activity. Statistical
data for more than a hundred years show such a relationship.*

Since the establishment of the Federal Reserve System in 1914, changes
in the money supply have been the result both of the actions taken by the
Federal Reserve authorities and of general conditions in the economy.
The Federal Reserve authorities usually have not tried to control the
money stock precisely, although since 1970 they have given more attention to controlling it than formerly. Prior to 1914, there was no central
bank, and changes in the money supply were caused by gold discoveries
and international movements of gold, as well as by economic conditions.

MONEY SUPPLY II AND
BUSINESS CYCLES

Business cycles may be divided into four parts: the expansion phase, the
peak, the contraction phase, and the trough. At the peak, business activity
reaches a turning point between an expansion and a decline. The trough
is the lower turning point when economic activity starts upward after a
contraction.

Table 15.1 shows the dates of the troughs and peaks of the business
cycles in the United States from 1854 to 1970. The duration of the 27
expansion phases varied from 10 months to 105 months, and the average
length was 33 months. The shortest contraction lasted 7 months, and the
longest 65 months. The average duration of the 27 contraction phases
was 19 months. Starting in February 1961, the United States economy
experienced a longer period of unbroken expansion than at any time
since 1854. There was a slowdown in 1967 and then a recession in 1969–
1970.

Table 15.1
National Bureau of Economic Research:
Business Cycle Reference Dates and
Duration of Expansions and Contractions,
1854 to 1970

| BUSINESS CYCLE REFERENCE DATES | | DURATION IN MONTHS | |
Trough	Peak	Contraction (trough from previous peak)	Expansion (trough to peak)
December 1854	June 1857		30
December 1858	October 1860	18	22
June 1861	April 1865	8	46
December 1867	June 1869	32	18
December 1870	October 1873	18	34
March 1879	March 1882	65	36
May 1885	March 1887	38	22
April 1888	July 1890	13	27
May 1891	January 1893	10	20
June 1894	December 1895	17	18
June 1897	June 1899	18	24
December 1900	September 1902	18	21
August 1904	May 1907	23	33
June 1908	January 1910	13	19
January 1912	January 1913	24	12
December 1914	August 1918	23	44
March 1919	January 1920	7	10
July 1921	May 1923	18	22
July 1924	October 1926	14	27
November 1927	August 1929	13	21
March 1933	May 1937	43	50
June 1938	February 1945	13	80
October 1945	November 1948	8	37
October 1949	July 1953	11	45
August 1954	July 1957	13	35
April 1958	May 1960	9	25
February 1961	November 1969	9	105
November 1970		12	
Average, all cycles:			
27 cycles, 1854–1970		19	33
11 cycles, 1919–1970		15	42
5 cycles, 1945–1970		11	49
Average, peacetime cycles:			
22 cycles, 1854–1970		20	26
8 cycles, 1919–1970		16	28
3 cycles, 1945–1970		10	32

Source: U.S. Department of Commerce, *Business Conditions Digest* (March 1974), p. 116.

Cycles in the Total Amount of Money Supply II

The average reference-cycle patterns in Figure 15.1 show the way in which the *total* amount of Money Supply II has varied over the cycle. The average reference cycles for the *rate of change* in Money Supply II are shown in Figure 15.2. Each of the reference-cycle patterns is based on a group of cycles and shows the typical movements of the total money stock or of the rate of change in the money stock during them. The lower axis of each figure shows the months before and after the peak. The "reference-cycle relatives" on the vertical axis of Figure 15.1 measure the percentage above and below the average amount of the total money stock during the cycles. For both deep and mild depression cycles in these figures, two patterns are shown—a five-point pattern for the period 1867–1908 based on annual and semiannual data, and a nine-point pattern for the period 1908–1961 based on monthly data.

Each average reference-cycle pattern covers an entire cycle. The first point of the nine-point pattern shows the reference-cycle relative at the trough at the beginning of the cycle; the fifth point shows it at the peak; and the ninth point shows it at the trough at the end of the cycle. Both the upswing and downswing are divided into three equal periods, and there are three points showing the reference-cycle relative for these periods. The five-point reference cycles are similar, except that there is

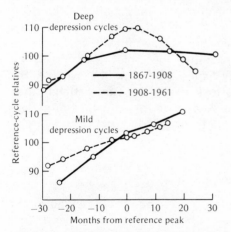

Figure 15.1 Money Supply II: Average Reference-Cycle Patterns for Mild and Deep Depression Cycles, 1867–1961

Source: Milton Friedman and Anna J. Schwartz, "Money and Business Cycles," *Review of Economics and Statistics* 45, Supplement (February 1963), p. 34.

Table 15.2
Deep Depression Cycles, 1867–1960

PERIOD	PERCENTAGE DECLINE IN MONEY SUPPLY II
1873–79	4.9%
1892–94	5.8
1907–08	3.7
1920–21	5.1
1929–33	35.2
1937–38	2.4

Source: Milton Friedman and Anna J. Schwartz, "Money and Business Cycles," *Review of Economics and Statistics* 45, Supplement (February 1963), p. 34.

just one reference-cycle relative for each of the phases. Deep and mild depression cycles are plotted separately. The six deep depression cycles are listed in Table 15.2. All others are mild depression cycles. The war cycles in 1914–1919 and 1938–1945 were not included in the estimated reference-cycle patterns shown in these figures.

Figure 15.1 shows that in the six deep depression cycles the *total amount* of Money Supply II has followed a regular cyclical pattern, rising during the expansion and falling during the contraction. Between the Civil War and 1960, in each of the six periods in which Money Supply II declined sharply, there was a major economic contraction. For the deep depression cycles from 1908 to 1961, at the initial trough the money stock was approximately 9 percent less than the average for the cycle. At the peak it was approximately 9 percent above the cycle's average. At the ending trough, it was approximately 5 percent below the average. For mild depression cycles, the money stock rises almost in a straight line, though there is some indication of a slower rate of growth from midexpansion to midcontraction. The total money stock does not vary cyclically in mild depression cycles.

Cycles in the Rate of Change in Money Supply II

The reference cycle patterns for the *rate of change* in Money Supply II in Figure 15.2 show a cyclical behavior in both mild and deep depression cycles. In mild depression cycles, changes in the total money stock shown in Figure 15.1 are so strongly influenced by its long-run upward movements that they do not show any cyclical pattern. The reference-cycle patterns in Figure 15.2 are constructed in the same way as those in Figure 15.1, except that the vertical axis measures the percentage deviation from the average rate of change in the money stock over the cycle. For

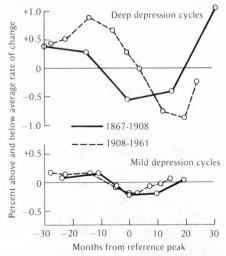

Figure 15.2   Rate of Change in Money Supply II: Average Reference-Cycle Patterns for Mild and Deep Depression Cycles, 1867–1961

Source: Milton Friedman and Anna J. Schwartz, "Money and Business Cycles," *Review of Economics and Statistics* 45, Supplement (February 1963), p. 36.

example, for the deep depression cycles from 1908 to 1961 shown by the nine-point pattern, at the initial trough the rate of change in the money stock was almost 0.5 percent above the average percentage change in the money stock during the cycle. At the final trough, it was about 0.2 percent below the average for the cycle.

The movements in the rate of change in Money Supply II are similar in both deep and mild depression cycles. Also, the peak rate of change occurs early in the expansion and the trough occurs early in the contraction. The cycles in the rate of change in Money Supply II conform to the trend of business with a long lead. In both of those respects, the cyclical movements of the rate of change in the money stock are different from the cyclical movements of the total money stock. In addition, the amplitude of the rate of change in the money stock is larger in deep depression cycles than in mild depression cycles. When a statistical series has a pattern that conforms to the business cycle, but turns downward prior to the peak in business activity and upward prior to the trough, it is called a *leading* series. Examples of other leading series are the National Bureau of Economic Research's index of stock prices and industrial material prices.

The rate of change in Money Supply II has led all of the specific peaks and troughs in all of the cycles from 1867 to 1961. The lead is a long one—for specific cycle dates, the average lead is eighteen months at the peak and twelve months at the trough. The lead is also variable—the standard deviation of the lead is seven months at peaks and six months at troughs.[1]

Determinants of the Money Supply

The cyclical fluctuations in Money Supply II are the result of fluctuations in its three principal determinants—the monetary base, the public's ratio of currency to deposits, and the banks' ratio of reserves to deposits.* A study by Professor Cagan of the eighteen cycles from 1877 to 1954 found that variations in the public's ratio of currency to deposits accounted on the average for half of the cyclical variability in the rate of increase in the money supply. Changes in the monetary base and the banks' ratio of reserves to deposits each accounted for about 25 percent of the variations. It is significant that the cyclical variations in the money supply have been caused primarily by changes in the public's ratio of currency to deposits and the banks' ratios of reserves to deposits, factors over which the Federal Reserve System has little control. Although in recent years the Federal Reserve System might have attempted to counteract the effect of these factors on the movements of the money supply by controlling the monetary base, it did not do so.

In the typical cycle, from midexpansion to midcontraction the currency-to-deposit ratio has increased and caused the rate of increase in Money Supply II to decrease. Just why this ratio varies in the way it does is not well understood. One possible theory is that it is the result of a shift in money holdings from businesses to consumers during periods of expansion. Since consumers typically have higher currency-to-deposit ratios than business firms, the aggregate currency-to-deposit ratio would rise. Such a shift would occur if businesses responded more aggressively than consumers to the improvement in business activity, and cut down on their money balances so as to increase their spending. This would cause their money balances to become relatively small and those of consumers relatively large.

Changes in the monetary base account for part of the cyclical variations in the money stock. The expansion of the monetary base has usually tended to get smaller as an expansion has progressed. Under the gold

---

* Note that these three determinants are similar to the factors in equation 9.7 for the multiple expansion of Money Supply II discussed in Chapter 9. In the study by Professor Cagan, demand deposits are combined with time deposits, and the ratio of bank reserves to deposits combined both required and excess reserves. See note 2 for this chapter.

standard, the rise in prices in periods of prosperity tended to reduce exports relative to imports, caused a gold outflow, and thus reduced the expansion of the monetary base. Since 1914 the movements of the monetary base have reflected both Federal Reserve policy and the tendency for the volume of loans by member banks at the Federal Reserve banks to conform with the cycle.

Fluctuations in the ratio of bank reserves to deposits have contributed to the cyclical variations in Money Supply II because this ratio has typically fallen when loan demand was strong and risen when loan demand has dropped. At first banks may reduce their excess reserves when business expands; but as the period of expansion continues, they are unwilling to reduce their excess reserves any further. This would tend to cut back on the expansion of the money supply. When a recession starts, bankers probably feel that their excess reserves have fallen too far, and they take the first opportunity they have to increase those excess reserves. This would tend to cut back on the expansion in the money supply during the early months of a recession.

GROWTH OF THE
MONEY STOCK

During the past hundred years, the money stock has almost always expanded from one year to the next, except during major depressions. Figure 15.3 shows the remarkable growth of Money Supply II from $1.3 billion in 1867 to over $200 billion in 1960. From 1914 to 1960, the growth of Money Supply I has closely paralleled the growth of Money Supply II.

From 1875 to 1955, Money Supply II grew at an average annual rate of nearly 6 percent. Over the long run, the principal factor accounting for the growth in the money stock has been the growth of the monetary base. The studies of Professor Cagan found that it accounted for nine-tenths of the long-run growth of the money stock. The remaining one-tenth was accounted for by declines in the public's ratio of currency to deposits and the banks' ratio of reserves to deposits.[3]

From 1950 to 1973, the average increase per year in Money Supply II was 5.8 percent. For Money Supply I, the annual rate of increase has averaged 3.7 percent. In the mid-1950s, the Federal Reserve's Chairman Martin said, "There is no firm yardstick, but we have looked on the normal growth of the country in terms of perhaps 2, 3, 4 percent, no fixed formula, and we have added to the money supply generally for that purpose. But we have to gauge things in terms of the demand and supply of credit and business activity."[4] A policy of increasing the money supply in line with the growth in real output tends to prevent deflation. If the money supply were not increased, prices would gradually decline as real

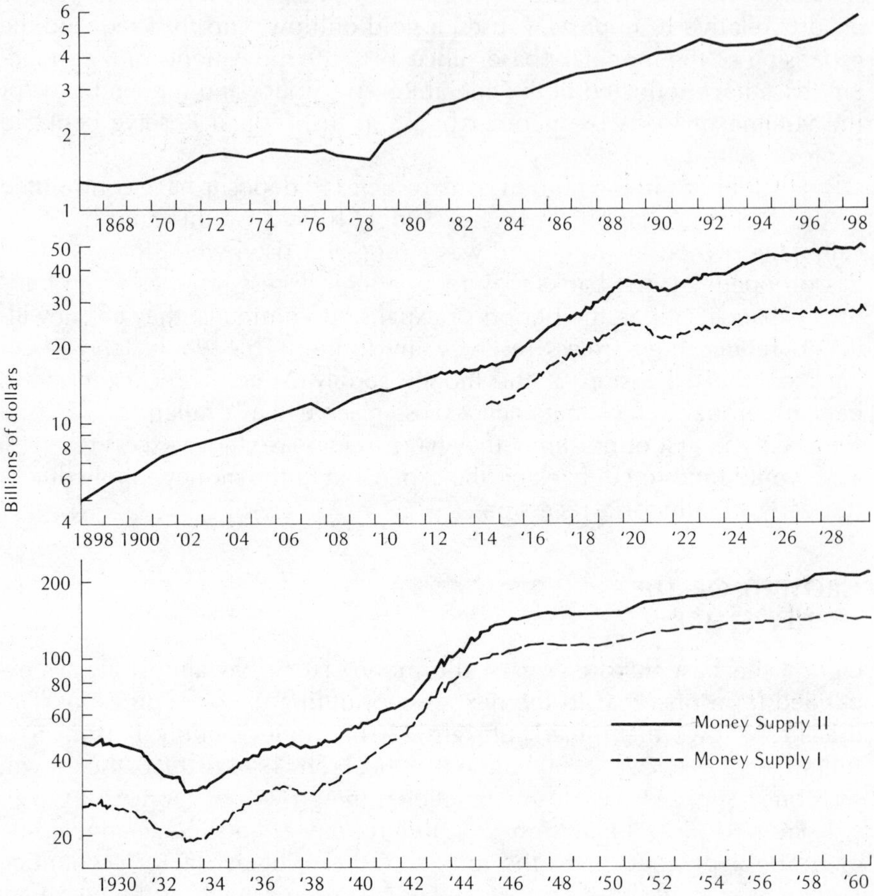

Billions of dollars

**Figure 15.3   Money   Supply   II,   1867–1960,
and Money Supply I, 1914–1960**

Source: Milton Friedman and Anna J. Schwartz, "Money and Business Cycles," *Review of Economics and Statistics* 45, Supplement (February 1963), p. 33.

output increased. The growth of the money stock has been made possible by actions of the Federal Reserve System—open-market purchases and the lowering of legal reserve ratios.

Even before the establishment of the Federal Reserve System, the money stock grew, but its growth was not directly the result of government policy. Up until World War I, the monetary base expanded largely as a result of the growth in the domestic supply of silver and gold. Professor Cagan estimated that from 1875 to 1914, changes in the gold stock accounted for about two-thirds of the annual changes in the monetary base. Following the creation of the Federal Reserve System, from 1915 to 1955, changes in the gold stock accounted for only 40 percent of those changes. Particularly during World Wars I and II, changes in Federal Reserve credit (primarily their government securities plus loans) accounted for the substantial increases in the monetary base.

When countries were on the gold standard, their money stock grew because of an increasing gold stock. An increase in the world's gold supply tended to be widely distributed among all countries even though the domestic supply of gold in the United States did not vary exactly with the changes in the world's gold stock. Under the gold standard, the money supply of each country was based primarily on bank reserves consisting of gold, and if a country's gold reserves increased, the money stock increased. Because the exchange rates among the gold standard countries were fixed, if the increase in the monetary base in one country lagged behind that in other countries its balance of payments was usually affected. Prices in the lagging country tended to be lower than those elsewhere, its exports increased relative to its imports, and a gold inflow followed.

MONEY AND INCOME, 1870–1961

The similar movements between 1870 and 1961 of the rate of change in the money supply and the rate of change in the total income of the economy, excluding intracyclical effects, are shown in Figure 15.4. When the rate of increase in the money supply rose, the rate of increase in income rose, and when the rate of increase in the money supply fell, income also fell. With few exceptions, the series have moved up and down together. The rate of change in Money Supply II is shown for the entire period, and in Money Supply I for the period since World War I. The rate of change in the total income of the economy is based on Kuznets' estimates of net national product and is called *nominal* income because it is measured in current prices.[5] To eliminate intracyclical effects, the rates of change are computed from average values covering an entire cyclical phase—expansion or contraction.

Statistical measures of the total income of an economy are estimates of *either* the total annual output of goods and services of the country, *or* the total annual income that was received to produce the output. Thus, the terms *output* and *income* are used interchangeably. There are three principal statistical measures of the total income of the economy: gross national product (GNP), net national product (NNP), and national income (NI). The term *national income* is commonly used to refer to any of those

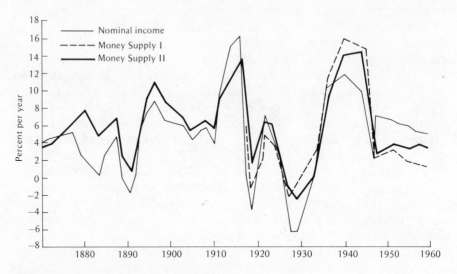

Figure 15.4   The Relationship between the Rate of Change in Nominal Income and the Money Stock, 1870–1961, Excluding Intra-cyclical Effects

Source: Milton Friedman, *Dollars and Deficits* (Englewood Cliffs, N.J.: Prentice-Hall, 1968), p. 128.

three measures. *Gross national product* is the sum of the amount of each final good and service produced multiplied by its price, and it may rise because of inflation as well as because of an increase in real output. It is the most inclusive of the three measures. GNP counts only final goods, eliminating the double counting that would occur if sales of intermediate goods, such as the cotton cloth sold to make shirts, were included. *Net national product* is equal to the GNP *less* the cost of depreciation—the manufacturing plants, machinery, housing, and other capital goods used up during the year. A large portion of the GNP includes the production of goods that are needed to replace items that have worn out during the year. National income excludes both the cost of capital depreciation and the total amount of indirect business taxes—sales, excise, and property taxes. In 1973, GNP was equal to $1,288.2 billion, NNP amounted to $1,178.6 billion, and NI was $1,054.2 billion.

The relationships between the rates of change in (1) both Money Supply I and II and (2) prices and real income (the two components of net national product in current prices), from 1870 to 1961, are shown in Figure 15.5. The correlation with the money supply is higher for the national income of the economy, as measured by net national product

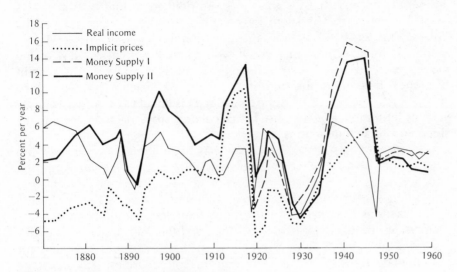

Figure 15.5   The Relationship between the Rate of Change in Prices and Real Income and the Rate of Change in the Money Stock, 1870–1961, Excluding Intracyclical Effects

Source: Milton Friedman, *Dollars and Deficits* (Englewood Cliffs, N.J.: Prentice-Hall, 1968), p. 129.

in current prices, than for either prices or output separately. Nevertheless, the rate of change in both prices and output has usually moved up and down with the rate of change in the money supply. As in Figure 15.4, intracyclical effects are excluded from the series.

VELOCITY OF MONEY

The relationship between the amount of money people have relative to either their income or their total transactions is known as the *velocity of money*. The concept of the velocity of money is based on the equation of exchange that was made famous by Irving Fisher many years ago: $MV = PT$. In this equation, M represents the quantity of money in the economy; V, the velocity of money per year; P, prices; and T, the quantity of everything bought and sold during the year.[6] The equation states that the quantity of money in an economy multiplied by the number of times per year it is spent is equal to the sum of the quantities of all of the items sold during the year multiplied by their prices. The equation is an identity because the variables in it are defined so that it must always be true. Money that is spent by certain persons must be received by others. The left-hand side of the equation refers to the spending of money. It looks at payments of all types from the point of view of the money used to make them. The right-hand side refers to the receipt of money. It refers to the sum of the quantity of each good and service sold per year multiplied by its price. Velocity is equal to PT/M. To estimate velocity arithmetically, it must be calculated from data on the money stock and total transactions.

In recent years, Fisher's equation has been altered significantly and is based on *income* rather than on transactions. In its income form, the equation is as follows: $MV = Py$. The right-hand side of the equation now refers to the national income or GNP rather than to the total value of transactions. The symbol y includes only those goods and services included in the national income or GNP, and P is their prices. It is different from the total value of transactions in that it excludes payments for intermediate transactions and for transfers of securities. An advantage of the equation of exchange in this form is that the statistics on GNP are better than those for total transactions. Also, the concepts of GNP and the national income are more meaningful than the concept of total transactions because they measure the total payments people have received for their contribution to production either from their own labor or from the property they own. The measure of velocity based on the new version of the equation of exchange, $MV = Py$, is referred to as *income velocity*. The measure of velocity based on the Fisher equation of exchange, $MV = PT$, is referred to as *transactions velocity*.

The equation of exchange is important because it shows the relationships between the quantity of money, the velocity of money, the level of prices, and real output. However, misuse of the equation is very common because persons are tempted to view the relationships between money and prices or real output as simultaneous. Too often, for example, persons attempt to explain price movements in a given year by variations in the money supply in that year. Empirical studies have found that price movements in any given year are determined by the trend of the rate of increase in the money supply several years previously.

Table 15.3 shows the striking decline in income velocity based on Money Supply II during the nineteenth century. The historical trend has been for people to hold more money relative to their incomes, causing the ratio of national income to the money supply to decline. For many years, there was sharp disagreement on the long-run trend of velocity.[7] Some economists believed that velocity would rise as the frequency and regularity of payments increased and financial institutions became more developed. It is now well established that the velocity of Money Supply

Table 15.3
Income Velocity in the United States,
Selected Years, 1799–1899

YEAR	RATIO OF NATIONAL INCOME TO TOTAL DEPOSITS AND CURRENCY
1799	24.2
1809	14.1
1819	10.1
1829	7.5
1839	5.8
1849	7.7
1859	6.0
1869	3.4
1879	2.8
1889	2.1
1899	1.8

Source: Clark Warburton, "The Secular Trend in Monetary Velocity," *Quarterly Journal of Economics* 63 (February 1949), p. 76; reprinted in Clark Warburton, *Depression, Inflation, and Monetary Policy* (Baltimore: Johns Hopkins Press, 1966), p. 200.

II declined almost continuously for about a century and a half, from 1799 to 1946. The estimates in Table 15.3 are for ten-year intervals, and for the earlier half of the nineteenth century they are unavoidably rough. There are many explanations of this decline in velocity. The shift from agriculture to manufacturing and the steadily increasing proportion of the nation's output passing through the market economy would cause people to hold larger amounts of money relative to their incomes. Also, the increasing proportion of the population working for wages probably contributed to this trend. The greater insecurity of employment for wage earners as compared to farmers would tend to raise the amount of money held by people as a reserve for bad times. Also, as will be explained in Chapter 16, several statistical studies have related the long-run trends of velocity to movements of interest rates and real income.

Figure 15.6 shows the trend of income velocity in the United States from 1869 to 1960 for both Money Supply I and II. Prior to 1946, the trend of income velocity was downward, although there were significant periods, such as from 1869 to 1881 and from 1932 to 1942, when the trend of velocity of Money Supply II moved upward. From 1946 to 1960, income velocity for both Money Supply I and II rose sharply. From 1914 to 1960, the overall trend of income velocity for Money Supply I is similar to the trend for Money Supply II. However, during the 1920s, the trend

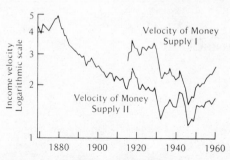

Figure 15.6   Income Velocity in the United States, 1869–1960

Source: Milton Friedman and Anna J. Schwartz, *A Monetary History of the United States, 1867–1960* (Princeton: Princeton University Press, 1963), chart 57, p. 640. (Copyright © 1963 by National Bureau of Economic Research; reprinted by permission of Princeton University Press.)

of the velocity of money based on Money Supply I did not move downward as did the trend of the velocity of Money Supply II, and during the 1930s the velocity of Money Supply I changed very little while the velocity of Money Supply II rose sharply.

In addition to these long-run trends, velocity typically rises during business expansions and falls during contractions, and peaks and troughs in velocity have often coincided with business cycle peaks and troughs. Velocity declined during the relatively serious depressions in 1920–1921, 1929–1932, and 1937–1938. In both World War I and World War II, income velocity rose initially, and then fell during the later war years. In several recent cycles, velocity has tended to decline somewhat before peaks and then to continue to decline during recessions. In the early stages of recovery, velocity has accelerated sharply, and then it has slowed down in the later stages of recovery.

Table 15.4 shows the trend of income velocity for both Money Supply I and Money Supply II from 1964 to 1973. These estimates of velocity are based on currently published data—the estimates of net national product made by the United States Department of Commerce and the data on currency and deposits published by the Federal Reserve System. Although the velocity of Money Supply I increased almost every year from 1964 to 1973, the velocity of Money Supply II was relatively constant. The principal causes of changes in velocity—changes in interest rates, the rate of inflation, and real income—appear to have had different effects on the velocity of Money Supply I than on the velocity of

Table 15.4
Income Velocity in the United States,
1964–1973

CALENDAR YEAR	NET NATIONAL PRODUCT (IN BILLIONS)	MONEY SUPPLY I (IN BILLIONS)	INCOME VELOCITY I (1) ÷ (2)	MONEY SUPPLY II[a] (IN BILLIONS)	INCOME VELOCITY II (1) ÷ (4)
	(1)	(2)	(3)	(4)	(5)
1964	$ 576.3	$157.2	3.67	$276.7	2.08
1965	625.1	163.8	3.82	301.4	2.07
1966	685.9	171.0	4.01	325.0	2.11
1967	725.0	181.6	3.99	335.5	2.16
1968	789.7	194.3	4.06	365.5	2.16
1969	848.7	206.5	4.11	389.9	2.18
1970	889.8	215.7	4.13	407.0	2.19
1971	961.6	230.7	4.17	454.9	2.11
1972	1,052.8	245.6	4.29	501.4	2.10
1973	1,178.6	263.6	4.47	549.2	2.15

[a] Starting in 1967, M_{II} excludes large certificates of deposit.
Source: *Federal Reserve Bulletin*, December 1970, pp. 897–898, and February 1974, p. 90; and *Economic Report of the President, February 1974* (Washington, D.C.: U.S. Government Printing Office, 1974), p. 265.

Money Supply II. The rise in interest rates during those years may explain the differences in the two series. When interest rates rise, demand deposits become unattractive to hold relative to time deposits. There would be an inducement for people to hold a smaller quantity of demand deposits and a larger quantity of time deposits relative to their incomes.

The belief that the historical changes in velocity shown in Tables 15.3 and 15.4 and in Figure 15.6 may be explained by changes in such factors as interest rates, rates of inflation, and levels of income is not accepted by everyone. There is the point of view that velocity is passive, that it changes in response to changes in its two components—the money stock and the national income. In terms of the equation of exchange, if velocity were passive, an increase in the money supply would probably be offset by a decrease in velocity, and prices and incomes would be unaffected. Also, if velocity were passive, even if the money stock were unchanged, velocity would rise sufficiently to accommodate an increase in prices or incomes. Recent studies of the statistical relationships between velocity and interest rates, the level of income, and rates of inflation do not support the concept of velocity as passive.[8] Nevertheless it is a possibility, and until recently it was not uncommon for economists to assume tacitly that velocity was passive. Over short periods of time velocity may change because of different movements in the money stock or income. But, given the time necessary for changes in income to adjust to changes in the money stock, most changes in velocity can be explained in other ways.

TURNOVER OF DEMAND DEPOSITS

Statistical data on the turnover of demand deposits may be compared with the recent trends of income velocity. The turnover of demand deposits is the total value of the checks written on demand deposits (debits to demand deposits) during the year, divided by the average quantity of demand deposits. It indicates the number of times per year that demand deposits change hands. Table 15.5 shows that, except for periods of business recession, there has been a fairly steady rise in the turnover of demand deposits from 1946 to 1973. The estimates for 1943 to 1964 are for banks in 343 Standard Metropolitan Statistical Areas and the series from 1964 to 1973 is for 232 SMSAs; New York City is excluded because there the large volume of financial transactions results in a much larger turnover than in the rest of the country. The volume of debits is similar to Fisher's concept of total transactions except that it excludes transactions by cash. Total debits reflect increases in both prices and real output. Prior to the development of national income statistics in the 1930s, data on total debits to demand deposits were widely used as a measure of the level of business activity.

SUMMARY

The rate of change in Money Supply II has tended to decline in advance of the downturn in business activity, and to rise in advance of the recovery during most business cycles.

The cyclical movements of Money Supply II are related to similar movements in the three principal determinants of Money Supply II: the monetary base, the public's ratio of currency to deposits, and the banks' ratio of reserves to deposits.

The equation of exchange is an identity showing the relationship between money, velocity, real output, and prices.

During recent years, the income velocity of Money Supply II has been relatively constant, while the income velocity of Money Supply I has risen.

Table 15.5
The Turnover of Demand Deposits in Large
Centers Excluding New York City,
1943–1964 and 1964–1973

	IN 343 CENTERS EXCLUDING NEW YORK CITY			IN 232 CENTERS EXCLUDING NEW YORK CITY	
Year	Debits to Demand Deposits (in billions)	Annual Rate of Turnover of Demand Deposits	December	Debits to Demand Deposits (in billions)	Turnover of Demand Deposits
				(seasonally adjusted annual rates)	
1943	$ 476.3	16.2	1964	$2,809.9	33.4
1944	521.1	15.8	1965	3,276.3	37.5
			1966	3,567.0	39.9
1945	541.7	14.7	1967	3,960.9	41.2
1946	610.3	15.4	1968	4,736.5	45.3
1947	705.3	16.7			
1948	784 3	18 0	1969	5,430.5	50.0
1949	760.1	17.3	1970	5,915.7	52.9
			1971	6,859.9	57.3
1950	870.8	18.7	1972	8,178.9	61.8
1951	998.2	20.0	1973	10,520.6	75.5
1952	1,045.0	20 0			
1953	1,126.3	20.8			
1954	1,148.4	21.0			
1955	1,276.7	22.3			
1956	1,384.8	23.7			
1957	1,468.3	25.1			
1958	1,481.0	24.9			
1959	1,655.6	26.7			
1960	1,735.9	28.2			
1961	1,832.3	29.0			
1962	2,020.6	31.3			
1963	2,198.7	33.1			
1964	2,404.9	35.2			

Source: Board of Governors of the Federal Reserve System, *Supplement to Banking and Monetary Statistics, Section 5, Bank Debits,* November 1966, pp. 6 and 12; and *Federal Reserve Bulletin,* July 1972, pp. 634–635, and February 1974, p. A14.

NOTES

1. Within one standard deviation of the average are approximately 68 percent of the examples observed.
2. Phillip Cagan, *Determinants and Effects of Changes in the Stock of Money, 1875–1960* (New York: Columbia University Press, 1965).

3. Ibid., p. 280.
4. U. S., Congress, Joint Economic Committee, Subcommittee on Economic Stabilization, *Monetary Policy: 1955–1956, December 10–11, 1956, Hearings,* 84th Cong., 2nd sess., 1956, p. 127.
5. Simon Kuznets, *National Product Since 1869* (New York: National Bureau of Economic Research, 1946).
6. Irving Fisher, *The Purchasing Power of Money,* 2d ed. (New York: Macmillan, 1926).
7. For a summary of the studies by economists of the velocity of money, see Richard T. Selden, "Monetary Velocity in the United States," in Milton Friedman, ed., *Studies in the Quantity Theory of Money* (Chicago: University of Chicago Press, 1956), pp. 179–257.
8. Richard T. Selden, "Cost-Push versus Demand-Pull Inflation, 1955–1957," *Journal of Political Economy* 67 (February 1959), p. 9.

QUESTIONS

15.1. Explain the difference between the cyclical movements of the total money supply and the rate of increase in the money supply.

15.2. Explain the reasons for the cyclical variations in the rate of increase in the money supply in terms of changes in total bank reserves, the public's ratio of currency to deposits, and the banks' ratio of reserves to deposits.

15.3. Explain the reasons for the growth of the money supply of the United States, both before and after the establishment of the Federal Reserve System.

15.4. Define each of the variables in the equation of exchange: $MV = PT$.

15.5. Explain why the equation of exchange is an identity.

15.6. What is the difference between Fisher's equation of exchange, $MV = PT$, and the equation $MV = Py$?

15.7. How has the velocity of money varied in the United States both during business cycles and over longer periods of time?

15.8. Discuss some of the different ways of measuring the velocity of money.

15.9. Know the meaning and significance of the following terms and concepts: business cycle, reference-cycle patterns, leading series, national income, equation of exchange, velocity of money, income velocity, transactions velocity, turnover of demand deposits, view of velocity as passive.

Chapter 16
The Demand for Money

The wealth accumulated by individuals includes money as well as stocks, bonds, and real estate. An individual's demand for money depends on his total wealth, the attractiveness of money compared to other types of wealth, and how much he desires the liquidity and other advantages of owning money.

The demand for money refers to the amount that people *want* to hold. In an economic system using money, people typically work for wages and are paid with money. They then spend it for the goods and services they desire. The demand for money refers to the quantity that people want to hold to bridge the period between the receipt of earnings and the spending of income. It is the amount a person or business firm typically wants to have in his bank account or in cash. The quantity desired depends on its usefulness. Holding money may be useful in various ways—convenience in making transactions, reliability when there are contingencies, and advantages in speculation. The conditions that affect how much money people want to hold may change. Under certain conditions, people will want to hold more of it; under other conditions, the amount people want to hold will be smaller.

There are several possible sources of confusion arising from the use of the term "demand for money." This demand is different from the demand for money income. People may demand a certain income from their employers. A person's salary requirement is this demand for money income, but not a demand for money. Moreover, the demand for loanable funds is frequently confused with the demand for money. In monetary theory, the demand for money does not mean the amount of money a person would like to borrow.

It is important to distinguish between the demand for money and the supply of money. In earlier chapters, we were concerned primarily with the supply of money. The way in which this supply has grown and varied in relation to fluctuations in business activity was described in Chapter 15. The amount of money people actually have may be different from the amount that they want to hold. The impact of changes in the money supply on prices, income, and interest rates depends on its relationship to the demand for money. The supply of money may vary with changes in income and interest rates, because such changes may affect variables in the money supply equation such as the currency-demand deposit ratio, the banks' ratio of excess reserves to demand deposits, and the public's ratio of time deposits to demand deposits. Under equilibrium conditions, the demand for and supply of money are equal, and the supply of money that is in existence and measurable would be equal to the demand for money.

MONEY AND OTHER TYPES OF WEALTH

In the theory of the demand for money, money is conceived of as a type of wealth.[1] People think of money as part of their wealth in everyday affairs. For estate-tax purposes, for example, a person's estate includes his money holdings as well as other property owned. From the point of view of the individual who owns wealth, all wealth may be divided into the following five classes: money, bonds, equities, physical capital, and human capital. In financial affairs, the different kinds of wealth are more complicated than this, and they are better classified in ways that are more detailed. Although oversimplified, the above classification is useful for the purpose of contrasting the characteristics of money and other types of wealth.

Money

Of the five types of wealth, money is the only one that has a fixed nominal value. A dollar's worth of any of the types of assets classified as money is always worth a dollar. This gives money assets their special characteristics of safety and liquidity. Included in money assets are holdings of currency and demand deposits; holdings of time deposits in commercial banks, mutual savings banks, and savings and loan associations; and holdings of U.S savings bonds. Even though the holding of currency and demand deposits usually does not provide the owner with a source of money income, having money on hand is convenient for making transactions and provides security against certain contingencies. The holding of currency and demand deposits provides income in kind rather than money income, just as home ownership provides income in kind. Savings and time deposits and U.S. savings bonds are types of money assets that yield an interest income.

Bonds

An essential characteristic of a bond is that the nominal amount of its interest payments does not vary. If a $1,000 bond has a coupon rate of 6 percent, the owner receives a fixed interest payment of $60 a year during the life of the bond. Though interest payments on bonds do not vary, their prices do. As was explained in Chapter 4, prices of bonds fall when market interest rates rise, and they rise when interest rates fall. The return a person receives from owning bonds includes both the amount of the interest payment and any gain or loss realized when the bond matures or is sold. Because of the fluctuations in bond prices, bonds may not be a reliable source of funds in time of need.

Equities

Common stock is the most widely owned type of equity. The income from common stock varies and may be zero. Even though there is no promised return, if the directors of a corporation declare a dividend, each stockholder is entitled to his share. If he owns one-fourth of the outstanding stock, he is entitled to one-fourth of the dividends declared. Other types of equities are the ownership of partnerships and proprietorships. The net profit of those enterprises is the difference between their receipts and expenditures, and the amount of this residual is uncertain. A proprietor is the sole owner and receives all of the net income of the business. Partners share the net income of the enterprise in accordance with the terms of the partnership agreement.

Prices of common stock and the sale value of a proprietorship or partnership vary. If the price of a share of common stock rises, the owner receives a capital gain in addition to the dividends. The total annual income earned is equal to the annual dividend plus the annual appreciation in the price of the stock. Professors Fisher and Lorie estimate that for stocks listed on the New York Stock Exchange, the average rates of return on stocks purchased in December 1930 or in any subsequent year and held until December 1965 were between 7 and 20 percent per year. These are after-tax estimates and assume that dividends are not reinvested. Rates of return vary and depend on the period for which estimates are made.[2]

Physical Capital

Physical capital consists solely of the physical assets owned by individuals. It excludes physical capital owned by business enterprises because this is already represented by bonds and equities. The most important nonbusiness physical asset is owner-occupied homes, but also included are land, automobiles, antiques, art, household equipment, and jewelry. These assets usually yield the owner an income in kind rather than a money income. They may also appreciate or depreciate in price. Many persons in the United States have gained from the appreciation in the value of their homes. Wealthy persons may purchase fine pieces of art not solely for their own enjoyment, but also for financial speculation.

Human Capital

The fifth category of wealth is human capital, people themselves. Human beings are not normally conceived of as capital because human beings cannot be sold. Yet human beings are the principal source of income. Most people hire out their services in return for wages. Wages typically amount to over 70 percent of the national income. People also may invest in themselves through education and training. People receive a rate of return from investments in themselves similar to the rate of return typically earned from investments in equities. Professor Becker estimates that the rate of return to higher education (from money spent and forgone earnings) was approximately 14.5 percent for white males graduating from college in 1939, and 13.0 percent for similar persons finishing in 1949.[3] By including human capital in this classification of the different types of wealth, the list includes all possible sources of real and money income, and thus all wealth.

DEMAND FOR REAL CASH BALANCES BY INDIVIDUALS

Once money is conceived of as a type of wealth, the general factors that affect the demand for money are apparent. A person can choose how he wants to hold his wealth. If he wishes to hold more common stock and less money, he can do so. A rational person distributes his total wealth among the various types so that the marginal utility of each type of wealth is the same. As a result, the demand for money changes if the attractiveness of other types of wealth changes. If total wealth increases, one would expect an increase in the demand for each type of wealth—including the demand for money—although possibly not in exactly the same proportion. Also, the demand for money depends on how much people want the particular advantages of convenience in transactions and the security provided by holding money. The analysis of the demand for money is similar to the analysis of the demand for consumer goods and services except that, as a type of wealth, money provides services in the future.

The amount of *real* cash balances (*M/P*) that an individual desires is the quantity of money demanded expressed in terms of the volume of goods and services that the money will buy. The higher the expected price level, the more money people want in order to have the same real command over goods and services. If the expected price level were to double, people would probably want to hold twice as much money in order to have the same convenience in making transactions and the same security against contingencies. What is important to people is the real quantity of money that they hold rather than the nominal quantity.

The factors that affect a person's demand for real cash balances may be summarized in the following equation:[4]

$$(M/P)^d = f(y, w; r_m, r_b, r_e, 1/P \ dP/dt; u) \tag{16.1}$$

where $(M/P)^d$ = the demand for real cash balances, y = expected real income, w = the fraction of wealth in nonhuman form, r_m = the expected rate of return on money, r_b = the expected rate of return on bonds, including expected changes in their prices, r_e = the expected rate of return on equities, including expected changes in their prices, $1/P \ dP/dt$ = the expected rate of change in prices of goods and services, and u = other factors that may affect the usefulness of real cash balances. When the variables in this equation change, they either affect the attractiveness of holding money relative to other assets or reflect an increase in total wealth. Each of the variables affects the individual's demand for real cash balances in a different way.

Expected Real Income

The actual level of real income that persons are receiving may be different from the real income that they expected or that they anticipate for the future. In periods of prosperity, for example, the current level of real income is often larger than the real income people expect in the future, because people realize that periods of prosperity are followed by periods of recession. Also, in recessions, when real income declines, the real income that people expect in the future may be larger than the level of real income that they have received. The principal factor determining expected real income is probably the real income that people have experienced in the past. Statistically, economists usually measure expected real income by a weighted average of past values of annual real income.

If interest rates are given, an increase in expected real income is equivalent to an increase in total wealth because wealth is the source of all income. When an individual's total wealth is increased, he will probably want more of each type of wealth. The following formula shows the relation between total wealth (including the productive capacity of human beings), total expected income, and the rate of interest:

$$W = Y/r \qquad\qquad (16.2)$$

The value of the stock of wealth (W) is equal to the expected annual income (Y) produced by that wealth divided by the rate of interest (r). Or, the total income expected per year is equal to a percentage (the rate of interest) of the value of the total stock of wealth: $Y = rW$. The formula is similar to the capitalization formula used for determining the price of a particular type of wealth.

Experience in many countries indicates that when expected real incomes rise, the demand for real cash balances increases more than in proportion to the increase in real income. In countries that have developed rapidly, it has been noted that the rise in real income has been accompanied by a rise in the amount of real cash balances held by people. The history of the United States provides an example of this relationship. From the Civil War to World War II, real cash balances per capita (based on Money Supply II) rose sharply.[5] The average annual increase in Money Supply II per capita during this long period was 3.7 percent, and the average annual increase in prices was only 0.9 percent. When real income per capita in the United States rose 1.0 percent, the demand for real cash balances per capita rose about 1.7 percent—an income elasticity of demand for real cash balances greater than unity. In 1869, Money Stock II amounted to only 25 percent of the net national product; in 1960, about 58 percent. The demand for Money Stock II appears to be like the demand for luxuries, such as travel and entertainment: as real income rises, people want relatively more of it.

In the expansion phase of business cycles, the actual level of real income rises more rapidly than expected real income; and in the contraction phase, the actual level of real income falls more rapidly than expected real incomes. This is because expectations are based primarily on past experience. The demand for real cash balances declines in the expansion phase of the cycle if it is based on actual levels of real income. As was explained in Chapter 15, the velocity of money—which is affected by the actual level of money and prices—has typically risen during periods of prosperity and fallen during periods of recession. On the other hand, if the demand for real cash balances is related to expected real income, the relationship between them is quite different—the demand for real cash balances rises during periods of expansion and falls during periods of contraction.[6]

Expected Rate of Return on Money

It would seem reasonable that the higher the expected rate of return on money, the larger the demand for real cash balances. Money Stock II includes interest-bearing time deposits in commercial banks. The higher the rate of interest paid on savings deposits (and assuming those higher rates are expected to continue in the future), the larger would be the demand for Money Supply II. In countries where interest is paid on demand deposits as well as on time deposits, changes in the expected rate of return would affect the demand for both types of deposits. When demand deposits are subject to service charges, the rate of return is negative. For deposits of this type, the larger the service fees, the smaller the amount of deposits people would want to hold.

Expected Rate of Return on Bonds and Equities

The expected rate of return on bonds and equities is believed to be an important factor affecting the demand for real cash balances. Money competes with bonds and equities as a type of wealth, and the higher the expected rate of return on bonds and equities, the less attractive the holding of real cash balances. If rates of return expected on bonds and equities were low, people would desire to hold larger real cash balances because the holding of real cash balances would not impose as large a penalty in the form of earnings forgone. Individual and corporation income taxes on interest and dividend income affect the attractiveness of money relative to stocks and bonds. The rate of return on stocks and bonds is less than it appears to be because of these taxes.

Several statistical studies have found a reliable relationship between the demand for real cash balances and interest rates in the United States.[7] Professor Latané concluded that from 1909 to 1959 the ratio of the gross national product to Money Supply I—which is similar to, but not exactly the same as, the inverse of real cash balances—was closely related to corporate bond yields. He believes that the secular decline in this measure of velocity in the United States from 1918 to 1945, which corresponds to the secular rise in real cash balances per unit of output, was the result of the decline in interest rates. Professor Meltzer examined data for the period from 1900 to 1958 and concluded that changes in the level of real cash balances could be explained by changes in both interest rates and the value of nonhuman wealth.

Expected Rate of Change in Prices

When prices rise 10 percent during a year, a dollar—with its fixed nominal value—becomes worth 10 percent less in purchasing power. Other assets, such as corporation stock and physical assets, are well-known hedges against inflation because their prices tend to rise with prices in general. If prices were expected to rise 20 percent a year, holding physical assets or corporation stock would be even more attractive than with a 10 percent increase. The higher the rate of inflation that people expect, the smaller the real cash balances they want to hold. Expected rates of inflation are usually calculated statistically in the same way as expected real income. It is a weighted average of past rates of inflation, and it is based on the assumption that the rate of inflation people expect is derived from the rates of inflation they have experienced.

Statistical studies of countries with high rates of inflation have found that changes in the rate of inflation can be the predominant factor affecting real cash balances.[8] The experience in South Korea from 1953 to 1961 is an example. The rate of inflation fell from 4.5 percent a month in 1953 to less than 1.0 percent a month in 1961, and the ratio of the amount of money people held relative to income more than doubled. As the rate of inflation decelerated, Koreans apparently began to expect less inflation and were willing to hold more money relative to their incomes. The increase in real cash balances was also partly the result of the economic recovery following the Korean War and the rise in real income per capita.

The experience in Brazil from 1948 to 1964 is another example. There the rate of inflation accelerated, and, as one would expect, real cash balances fell. The rate of inflation rose from less than 1 percent a month in 1948 to 5 percent a month in 1964, and the ratio of the amount of money people held to income fell 15 percent for Money Supply I and 33 percent for Money Supply II. The rapid rise in per capita real income in Brazil during this period probably offset, in part, the impact of the accelerated inflation and caused the decline in real cash balances to be smaller than it might have been.

Division of Wealth into Human and Nonhuman Forms

The major asset of most persons is their own earning capacity. Although it is usually quite easy to shift from money to stocks and other types of wealth, it is not as easy to shift quickly from various types of property wealth to human wealth; it is nevertheless possible. An example would be a person who sold his stocks and bonds in order to pay for the cost of a medical education. Shifting in the other direction is more common.

As people approach retirement, they usually use part of their earnings to invest in financial assets. As they accumulate real estate, stocks, and bonds, they gradually hold a larger percentage of their total assets in nonhuman forms.

The demand for real cash balances may be affected by the fraction of a person's total wealth in the form of property. If the fraction in the form of property increases, the marginal utility of property wealth—including real cash balances—would probably decline relative to that of human wealth. The opposite would occur if the fraction of total wealth in the form of property should decrease. The demand for property, including real cash balances, would increase and the demand for human wealth would decrease.

Other Factors That Affect Tastes and Preferences

There are some influences affecting tastes and preferences for holding money that are important even though difficult to measure precisely. The degree of economic instability that people expect to prevail in the future affects how large a reserve persons wish to hold in case of sickness, the loss of a job, or business losses. If people believe conditions are unstable —as they did after the depression in the 1930s—one would expect them to feel secure only if they held larger real cash balances. During the 1930s, the ratio of Money Supply II to income actually did rise sharply. The shortness and mildness of the recessions since World War II probably caused a change in attitude. Because people now have greater confidence in the security of their jobs, they are satisfied with smaller holdings of real cash balances.

Historically the decline in the self-sufficiency of family units has probably caused people to hold larger real cash balances. As countries industrialize, the use of money becomes more widespread. When most people become wage earners, acquiring one's needs by purchasing them from others becomes more common, and a larger portion of the population becomes involved in the market economy.

Another factor affecting the desire for real cash balances is the extent to which people move from one part of the country to another. When geographic mobility increases, as during major wars, persons generally prefer to hold a larger fraction of their wealth in money. Real money balances relative to income rose sharply during World War II probably because of increased travel and more frequent changes of residence. The separation of members of families during the war also resulted in less economy in the holding of real cash balances.

DEMAND FOR REAL CASH BALANCES
BY BUSINESS ENTERPRISES

The demand for real cash balances by business firms is different from that by individuals. The business demand for real cash balances is large. It has been estimated that almost two-thirds of demand deposits are held by business firms, farms, and nonprofit organizations. To the business firm, money is one of the productive resources that it uses to produce its output and is listed as such in its balance sheet. The demand for real cash balances by business firms is significantly related to their size, which may be measured by their total sales, net income, total assets, net worth, or value added. Business firms can expand the total amount of their productive assets by borrowing and by selling stock in capital markets, and they attempt to obtain the amount of resources that will maximize returns. By comparison, individuals typically allocate a given volume of total wealth among the various types of wealth. Although there are some differences between the determinants of the demand for money for individuals and for business firms, rates of return on money and other assets and the rate of inflation are significant for both. Much less empirical work has been done on the business demand for money than on the aggregate demand including both persons and business firms, because of the lack of data on the amount of money held solely by business firms.

AGGREGATE DEMAND FOR
REAL CASH BALANCES

The aggregate demand for real cash balances for the economy as a whole is the sum of the demands of each of the individuals and business firms in the economy. This aggregate demand varies with population and other factors influencing the size of the economy. It is usually assumed that the aggregate demand for real cash balances increases with the growing real income of the economy. It may also vary with the distribution of total real income and with changes in the number of business firms because of mergers. So little is yet known, however, about the effect of the two latter factors that it is not possible to take them into account.

AGGREGATE DEMAND
FOR MONEY

The relationship between the aggregate demand for money and expected national income may be illustrated by the L schedule in Figure 16.1. The symbol L stands for the demand for money. On the vertical axis is ex-

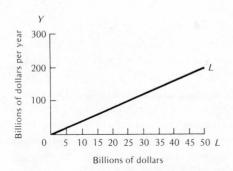

Figure 16.1   Aggregate Demand for Money

pected national income; on the horizontal axis is the quantity of money demanded.

In Figure 16.1, the quantity of money demanded (L) varies directly and in proportion to the expected national income (Y). The ratio of money to income is constant and at every point on the L schedule is equal to one-fourth. The demand for money schedule would rise in this way if, for example, when the national income increases 10 percent, the amount of money people want to hold also increases 10 percent. This increase in the national income may be the result of an increase either in prices or in real income.

The equation for the demand for money schedule shown in Figure 16.1 is as follows:

$$L = g(w, r_m, r_b, r_e, 1/P \ dP/dt; u) \cdot Y \qquad (16.3)$$

This equation is slightly different from the equation for the demand for real cash balances (Equation 16.1). The index of prices (P) is moved from the left-hand side of the equation to the right-hand side and included in national income (Y). The expected real income (y) is removed from the function g and is also included in Y. In Equation 16.3, the demand for money varies directly and in proportion to both prices and real income, but its relationship to the other variables varies with g—the slope of the L schedule with respect to Y. Although the assumption that the demand for money varies directly and in proportion to expected prices is probably realistic, the assumption that it varies directly and in proportion to expected real income is not. Historical experience indicates that increases in per capita real income tend to shift the L schedule in Figure 16.1 downward as shown in Figure 16.3.

CHANGES IN THE DEMAND
FOR MONEY

Figure 16.2 illustrates a decrease in the demand for money. The L schedule shifts to the left from L_1 to L_2. When the demand schedule for money decreases, people wish to hold smaller money balances relative to their income. At a level of income of $100 billion, people had wanted to hold $25 billion of money; after the decrease in demand they want to hold only $20 billion. A decrease in the demand for money may be caused by higher expected rates of return on stocks and bonds, lower expected rates of return on money, a higher expected rate of inflation, a change in preferences such as a feeling of greater security, or an increase in the portion of wealth owned in nonhuman forms.

Figure 16.3 illustrates an increase in the demand for money. The L schedule shifts to the right from L_1 to L_2. When the demand for money increases, people want to hold more money relative to their incomes. At a level of income of $100 billion, people had wanted to hold $25 billion, but after the increase, they wanted to hold $30 billion. The factors causing an increase in the L schedule are the opposite of those causing it to decrease: higher expected rates of return on money, lower expected rates of return on bonds and equities, a low expected rate of inflation, a feeling of insecurity, or a smaller fraction of wealth in nonhuman forms.

PREDICTING CHANGES IN THE
DEMAND FOR MONEY

If the factors affecting the demand for money were perfectly understood, economists would be able to predict changes in the demand for money.[9]

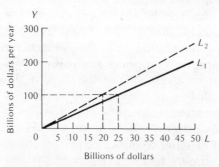

Figure 16.2   Decrease in the Demand for Money

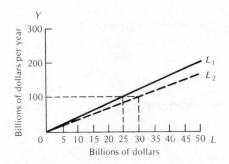

Figure 16.3 Increase in the Demand for Money

An ability to predict such changes combined with control over the money stock would add significantly to the Federal Reserve System's ability to control inflation and fluctuations in the national income. As will be explained in Chapter 17, an increase in the demand for money tends to lower the national income, and a decrease in the demand for money is associated with an increase in the output of the economy. Economists still have a long way to go before they can predict changes in the demand for money, even though in recent years many statistical studies of the demand for money have been made. Statistical data are available for many of the variables affecting the demand for money, and correlation tests of their relationship to the demand for money can be carried out. The statistical studies have shown that such factors as per capita real income, interest rates, and rates of inflation affect the demand for money, although much is still to be learned about the exact relationships. One of the problems in making these studies is that it is necessary to make estimates of expected national income, expected rates of return, and expected inflation from the available data on actual rates. Although statistical techniques have been developed to convert actual series to expected series on the assumption that expectations are based on recent experience, these techniques are not able to take into account all of the possible conditions affecting expectations. Another problem is that the factors affecting tastes and preferences are often difficult to quantify.

The demand for both Money Supply I and II in the United States appears to have decreased sharply between World War II and 1960. From 1960 to 1973, the demand for Money Supply I relative to national income declined, but the demand for Money Supply II relative to national income remained approximately constant. The decrease in the demand for both Money Supply I and II from 1945 to 1960 contributed to the expansionary conditions in the economy during this period.[10] A sharp rise in interest rates—such as that which occurred during this period—would, in fact, tend to cause people to reduce their holdings of money. In addition, because of the sudden inflation during the Korean War and the creeping inflation that occurred during 1955–1959, people may have started to anticipate gradually rising prices. The decrease in the demand for money was particularly sharp at the outbreak of the Korean War in the early 1950s. Remembering shortages of goods during World War II and wartime pressures on prices, people hurriedly purchased physical goods. Since World War II, there has also probably been a significant change in the attitude of people toward the stability of the economy. At the end of World War II, it was widely predicted that the United States would soon experience a serious depression. Secular stagnation was also feared. These predictions turned out to be wrong. The postwar recessions were mild and short. Although changes in attitude are difficult to measure, people probably became more confident about business prospects and less fearful of losing their jobs. This also would have decreased the demand for money.

OTHER CONCEPTS OF THE DEMAND FOR MONEY

The Transactions Demand for Money

Some economists conceive of the demand for money exclusively as a medium of exchange rather than as a type of wealth. In accordance with this point of view, the demand for money is expected to increase in proportion to increases in income as shown in Figure 16.1, and shifts in the demand-for-money schedule are attributed primarily to changes in the frequency, regularity, and coordination of receipts and payments, and to the stage of development of the credit and financial system.[11]

If the demand for money depended primarily on its use in transactions, then the shorter the interval between receipts, the smaller would be the demand for money. For example, consider a person who is paid $600 monthly on the first day of each month and spends his income at a uniform rate of $20 per day for thirty days. The amount of money he needs to hold would decline uniformly over the course of the month, and his average balance would be $300, half his monthly income. However, if this same person were paid every fifteen days, he would receive $300 twice a month, and his average balance would be only $150. Also, a decrease in the frequency of disbursements may increase the average amount of money held because people would hold larger amounts between the times when expenditures are made.

The demand for money may also be influenced by the regularity of income receipts. The time period between paydays and the amount of a person's pay check may vary. The more irregular the receipt of money, the larger the amount of money a person needs to tide him over relatively long periods between paydays or periods when income is relatively low. If the timing and amount of a person's receipts and expenditures correspond, less money is needed. If, for example, because of more widespread use of charge accounts, people customarily pay off their debts on payday rather than spreading their expenditures throughout the income period, the demand for money would decrease.

Another factor affecting the demand for money for transactions is the development of credit institutions. If people can borrow money easily and quickly, it is not necessary for them to hold as much money for contingencies or transactions. Also, owners of excess funds would more likely lend them rather than hold them as money if well developed credit markets were available.

The demand for money as a type of asset is not entirely separate from the demand for money for transactions. For example, an increase in the expected rate of inflation might reduce the demand for money as a type of asset, through its effect on payments practices. This would occur if more rapid inflation caused pay periods to become more frequent so as to avoid longer-term contracts. The principal shortcoming of the transactions conception of the demand for money is that the historical trend toward more frequent payments to workers and toward a larger variety of credit facilities, particularly in the nineteenth century, would lead one to expect that the demand for money in the United States would have decreased. Instead the demand for money rose.

The Transactions Plus Asset Demand for Money

The theory of the demand for money in Keynes' famous work, *The General Theory of Employment, Interest, and Money,* separates the demand for money into two parts: the *transactions* demand and the *asset* demand.[12] In this theory, money includes only the medium of exchange—currency and demand deposits—and would be measured by Money Supply I. The transactions demand is determined primarily by the level of the national income, as shown in Figure 16.4(a). The transactions demand for money is designated as L_I to distinguish it from the asset demand for money which is designated as L_{II}.

People are expected to increase their holdings of money for transactions approximately in proportion to increases in their income so as to have the same convenience in making current expenditures and to have additional security in providing for possible future contingencies. Under-

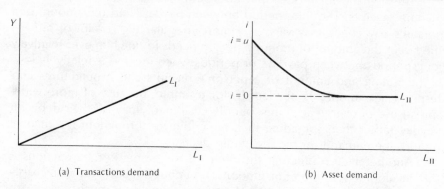

(a) Transactions demand   (b) Asset demand

Figure 16.4   The Demand for Money

lying the transactions demand are both the transactions and precautionary motives for holding money. The demand schedule, L_I, may shift upward or downward if *transactions costs* involved in converting other assets into money change. It is useful to have some money on hand in order to avoid the inconvenience of having to cash a savings deposit or to sell bonds every time one needs money. There may also be fees charged for selling bonds, or lower rates of return received on time deposits cashed before their maturity date. The less inconvenient and costly it becomes to convert interest-earning assets into money, the smaller would be the demand for money for transactions and the larger would be the demand for savings deposits and bonds. This would cause the L_I schedule to shift upward. Or, if it should become more costly and time-consuming to convert interest-earning assets into money, the L_I schedule would shift downward. The demand for money for transactions also varies with the frequency, regularity, and coordination of receipts and payments and with the development of new types of credit.

The asset demand for money depends primarily on interest rates and is illustrated in Figure 16.4(b). It is based on the speculative motive for holding money. This figure shows that if interest rates are as high as $i = u$, there would be no demand for money as an asset. The speculative objective of holding money is to be in a position to purchase stocks, long-term bonds, inventory goods, and other types of real property when their prices are low or are expected to rise. The principal alternative to holding money for this purpose is short-term government securities. If the rate of return on short-term government securities is very high, persons interested in speculating would hold those securities rather than money. There are two reasons: (1) the high rate of return on the short-term securities is attractive; and (2) if their yield were high, the prices of those securities would be low, and the risk of capital loss would be minimal because there would be little chance that their prices would fall further.

Figure 16.4(b) also shows that if interest rates are as low as $i = 0$, the demand for money as an asset would be infinite. For the speculator, there would be two reasons for this preference for holding money rather than short-term government securities: (1) the low yield on the short-term securities would be unattractive; and (2) since the prices of these securities would be very high, the risk of incurring a capital loss if one wished to sell these securities to obtain funds to purchase other assets would be great. In between $i = u$ and $i = 0$, the demand for money as an asset would increase as interest rates fell because holding money for speculative purposes would become more attractive relative to holding short-term bonds.

Because all money holdings may be used either for transactions or asset purposes, the separation of money holdings into balances held for transactions and balances held for speculation has been criticized as unrealistic. The justification for the separation is theoretical and is based on the belief that the demand for money for transactions is primarily determined by income, and the demand for speculation is determined primarily by interest rates. There is a difference of opinion concerning whether the conception of money should be restricted to currency and demand deposits or broadened to include all assets with a fixed nominal value. The transactions plus asset demand for money is based on the narrower definition of money. There is also a difference of opinion concerning the spectrum of assets with which money competes. Should this spectrum include long-term bonds, equities, physical assets, or even human capital, or should it be restricted primarily to short-term securities? In the transactions plus asset demand for money, the holding of money competes primarily with the holding of short-term securities. Another question is whether the demand for money should be related to current income or to expected income. In the conception of money as a type of wealth, the demand for money is related to expected income.

SUMMARY

The demand for money varies with changes in the expected level of prices; expected real income; the expected rate of return on money, bonds, and equities; the expected rate of change in prices; and the division of wealth into human and nonhuman forms.

If the demand for money decreases, individuals want to hold less money relative to their incomes; and if it increases, they want to hold more money relative to their incomes.

If individuals expect a more rapid rate of inflation or if they expect higher rates of interest, the demand for money will decrease. If they expect less inflation or lower rates of interest, the demand for money will increase.

There are several different conceptions of the demand for money. In addition to the demand for money as a type of wealth, there is the transactions demand for money and the transactions plus asset demand for money.

NOTES

1. John R. Hicks, "A Suggestion for Simplifying the Theory of Money," *Economica* 2 (February 1935), pp. 1–19, reprinted in Friedrich A. Lutz and Lloyd W. Mints, eds., *Readings in Monetary Theory* (New York: Blakiston, 1951), pp. 13–32; Milton Friedman, "The Quantity Theory of Money—A Restatement," in *Studies in the Quantity Theory of Money* (Chicago: University of Chicago Press, 1956), pp. 3–21; James Tobin, "Liquidity Preference as Behavior Towards Risk," *Review of Economic Studies* 25 (February 1958), pp. 65–86, and "Money, Capital, and Other Stores of Value," *American Economic Review* 51 (May 1961), pp. 26–37; and David E. W. Laidler, *The Demand for Money: Theories and Evidence* (Scranton, Pa.: International Textbook Company, 1969).

2. Lawrence Fisher and James H. Lorie, "Rates of Return on Investments in Common Stock, The Year-by-Year Record, 1926–1965," Table 2, *Journal of Business* 41 (July 1968).

3. Gary S. Becker, *Human Capital* (New York: Columbia University Press, 1964), pp. 75–78.

4. See Milton Friedman, "Money, Quantity Theory," in *International Encyclopedia of the Social Sciences,* Vol. 10 (New York: Macmillan, 1968), p. 440.

5. Milton Friedman and Anna P. Schwartz, *A Monetary History of the United States, 1867–1960* (Princeton: Princeton University Press, 1963), p. 5; and Milton Friedman, "The Demand for Money," in *Dollars and Deficits* (Englewood Cliffs, N.J.: Prentice-Hall, 1968), p. 199.

6. Milton Friedman, "The Demand for Money," pp. 195–206.

7. Henry A. Latané, "Income Velocity and Interest Rates, A Prag-

matic Approach," *Review of Economics and Statistics* 42 (November 1960), pp. 445–449; and Allan H. Meltzer, "The Demand for Money: The Evidence from the Time Series," *Journal of Political Economy* 71 (June 1963), pp. 219–246.

8. See Phillip Cagan. "The Monetary Dynamics of Hyperinflation," in Milton Friedman, ed., *Studies in the Quantity Theory of Money* (Chicago: University of Chicago Press, 1956), pp. 25–117, for examples of the effect of hyperinflation on real cash balances in seven European countries after World War I and during World War II. See also John V. Deaver, "The Chilean Inflation and the Demand for Money," and Colin D. Campbell, "The Velocity of Money and the Rate of Inflation: Recent Experience in South Korea and Brazil," in David Meiselman, ed., *Varieties of Monetary Experience* (Chicago: University of Chicago Press, 1970), pp. 7–67 and 339–386.

9. Milton Friedman, "The Demand for Money;" and Carl Brunner and Allan H. Meltzer, "Predicting Velocity: Implications for Theory and Policy," *Journal of Finance* 18 (May 1963), pp. 319–354.

10. Richard T. Selden, "Cost-Push versus Demand-Pull Inflation, 1955–57," *Journal of Political Economy* 67 (February 1959), pp. 1–20.

11. Irving Fisher, *The Purchasing Power of Money* (New York: Macmillan, 1926), pp. 79–89; and Lester V. Chandler, *Introduction to Monetary Theory* (New York: Harper & Row, 1940), pp. 34–40.

12. See Robert E. Weintraub, *Introduction to Monetary Economics* (New York: Ronald Press Company, 1970), chapter 13, "Keynesian Money Demand," pp. 249–266.

QUESTIONS

16.1. What is the difference between the supply of money and the demand for money?

16.2. Explain the unique characteristics of each of the following types of wealth: money, bonds, equities, physical capital, human capital.

16.3. Why would you expect the demand for money to vary with the price level?

16.4. Explain the difference between actual real income and expected real income.

16.5. Explain the way in which the demand for real cash balances is affected by
(a) a rise in expected real income,
(b) a fall in expected interest rates,
(c) a rise in the expected rate of inflation,
(d) a rise in the expected rate of return on money,
(e) an increase in human wealth relative to nonhuman wealth.

16.6. Name some factors, other than those listed in Question 16.5, that may affect the demand for real cash balances.

16.7. Draw a schedule on a graph showing the relationship between the aggregate demand for money and income. Explain the meaning of an increase in the demand schedule for money. Explain the meaning of a decrease in the demand schedule for money.

16.8. Explain the decrease in the demand for money in the United States from 1945 to 1960.

16.9. Compare the different concepts of the demand for money:
(a) the demand for money as a type of wealth,
(b) the transactions demand for money,
(c) the transactions plus asset demand for money.

16.10. Know the meaning and significance of the following terms and concepts: demand for money, wealth, equities, human capital, real cash balances, expected income, expected inflation, transactions costs, increase in the demand for money, transactions demand for money, asset demand for money.

Chapter 17
The Relation of Money to Income: The Portfolio Adjustment Explanation

In order to increase the national income, an increase in the money supply must cause persons to spend more relative to their incomes. Monetary policy may stimulate total spending by causing the supply of money to be greater than the demand.

Monetary theory attempts to explain how an increase in the money supply may raise the national income or how a decrease in the money supply may lower it. A higher national income may represent either a larger real income or higher prices, even though the usual objective of monetary policy is to expand real income with as little inflation as possible. A rise in real income resulting from a more expansionary monetary policy would usually mean increased employment, and a decline in real income would mean reduced employment.

There are two principal theories of the way changes in the money supply may cause changes in total spending: one in terms of portfolio adjustments, and the other in terms of the effects on interest rates and investment. The first is the point of view of the *monetary* or *quantity theorists;* the second is that of the *Keynesian theorists.* This chapter is concerned with the first of these, the way that changes in the quantity of money cause portfolio adjustments leading to changes in total spending.

MEASURING NATIONAL INCOME

The statistics on the national income of the United States in 1973—both by type of expenditure and by distributive shares—are shown in Table

17.1. The gross national product (GNP) by type of expenditure is divided into consumption, investment, net exports, and government purchases. *Personal consumption expenditures* include primarily expenditures for food, clothing, housing, transportation, and entertainment. *Gross private domestic investment* consists of purchases of capital goods—machinery, plant and equipment, houses, and the change in inventories. These types of goods are used to produce other goods and services in the future. Gross investment includes expenditures that are necessary to replace capital goods that have depreciated during the year—called capital consumption allowances—as well as net additions to the total stock of capital. *Net exports of goods and services* are the difference between total United States exports of goods and services and total imports. Only net exports are included because consumption, domestic investment, and government purchases include the total amount of imports. It would be double counting to include in the national income both the total value of the goods and services imported and the total value of goods and services exported. *Government purchases of goods and services* consist of the amount spent by all levels of government—federal, state, and local. They do not include welfare payments because these are considered transfer payments rather than payments to people for their contribution to production either from their own labor or from the capital they own.

Table 17.1
National Income of the United States, 1973
(in billions of dollars)

GNP BY TYPE OF EXPENDITURE		NATIONAL INCOME BY DISTRIBUTIVE SHARES	
Personal consumption expenditures	$ 805.0	Compensation of employees	$ 785.3
Gross private domestic investment	201.5	Proprietors' income	84.3
Net exports of goods and services	4.6	Rental income	25.1
Government purchases of goods and services	277.2	Net interest	50.4
		Corporation profits	109.2
Gross National Product	$1,288.2	National income	$1,054.2
Less: Capital consumption allowances	109.6		
Indirect business taxes, etc.	124.3		
National Income	$1,054.2		

Columns do not add to totals because of rounding.
Source: *Economic Report of the President, February 1974* (Washington, D.C.: U.S. Government Printing Office, 1974), pp. 249, 265, and 266.

The statistics on the national income by distributive shares show the amounts of the different types of income paid to people and earned by business firms. By far the largest type of income is the compensation of employees. Proprietors' income is the profit received by persons who run their own businesses, and it includes only the income of unincorporated businesses—proprietorships and partnerships. Rental income consists of both the net rent that people receive from leases on real estate and the implicit rent from home ownership. To obtain the amount of implicit rent, an estimate is made of the amount persons would have to pay to rent the homes they live in if they did not own them. Net interest consists of the interest income that people receive from savings accounts and from corporate, municipal, and U.S. government bonds. Corporation profits include the total amount of the profits of these enterprises and consist of the amount paid in corporation income taxes, the profits retained by the enterprises, and the dividends paid to the stockholders. Dividends distributed to stockholders usually amount to approximately 30 percent of total corporate profits before corporation income taxes are deducted.

The two ways of measuring national income—by type of expenditure and by distributive shares—must be equal. This is because the amount received for the goods and services produced, after deducting the appropriate amounts for capital consumption allowances and indirect business taxes, is distributed to the owners of labor and capital. Although the retained profits of business firms are not paid out to the owners, they are retained in the business to the benefit of the owners. The equality between income and total spending may be illustrated by the flow of income diagram in Figure 17.1. In this diagram, businesses sell the goods and services they produce directly to consumers. These transactions are shown in the upper half of the diagram. To produce the goods and services, they must hire labor and must rent the use of capital from its owners and pay both of these groups in money. These transactions are shown in the lower half of the diagram. As a result of both of these types of transactions, money is continuously being circulated from business firms to persons and then back to business enterprises. The national income can be measured statistically by gathering data on the types of payments made in either the upper or lower half of the circular flow. Data on the different types of expenditures would come from the upper half of the circular flow. Data on income by distributive shares would be obtained from the lower half of the circular flow. Figure 17.1 has been simplified by assuming no production of capital goods, no retained profits, no government spending or taxation, and no exchange among firms such as the purchase of materials by one business enterprise from another.

The rise in GNP from 1960 to 1973, both in current prices and in

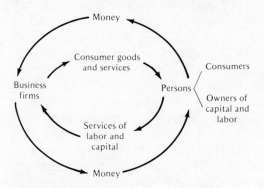

Figure 17.1   The Circular Flow of Income

1958 prices, is shown in Table 17.2. GNP in current prices rose more than in 1958 prices because of inflation. Real GNP declined or increased relatively little in 1960–1961, 1967, and 1969–1970, which were periods of recession or economic slowdown.

The gross national product is larger than the national income for two

Table 17.2
Gross National Product, 1960–1973

YEAR	GNP IN CURRENT PRICES (IN BILLIONS)	CHANGE FROM PREVIOUS YEAR (PERCENT)	GNP IN 1958 PRICES (IN BILLIONS)	CHANGE FROM PREVIOUS YEAR (PERCENT)
1960	$503.7	4.1%	$487.7	2.5%
1961	520.1	3.3	497.2	1.9
1962	560.3	7.7	529.8	6.6
1963	590.5	5.3	551.0	4.0
1964	632.4	7.1	581.1	5.5
1965	684.9	8.3	617.8	6.3
1966	749.9	9.5	658.1	6.5
1967	793.9	5.9	675.2	2.6
1968	864.2	8.9	706.6	4.7
1969	930.3	7.6	725.6	2.7
1970	977.1	5.0	722.5	—0.4
1971	1,052.5	7.7	745.4	3.2
1972	1,155.2	9.8	790.7	6.1
1973	1,288.2	11.5	837.3	5.9

Source: *Economic Report of the President, February 1974*, pp. 249–250.

reasons. Part of gross domestic investment consists of the replacement of plant or machinery that has depreciated during the year. This causes the GNP to be larger than the national income because rental income, corporate profits, and the income of proprietors—types of income shown on the right-hand side of Table 17.1—are estimated net of the costs of depreciation. Official statisticians often put greater reliance on estimates of the gross national product than on the national income, because of the difficulty of estimating the dollar value of depreciation or capital consumption allowances. In the United States the total amount spent to cover depreciation usually comes out to about one-eleventh of GNP. The second reason why GNP is larger than national income is that expenditures for property and sales taxes (called indirect business taxes) are included in the prices of the goods and services included in the GNP; but those expenditures are costs which, like depreciation, are deducted before estimating rental income, corporate profits, and the income of proprietors.

There are several types of transactions that are not included in the GNP. The GNP does not include purchases of securities or of houses that were built in previous years. Neither of these would represent payments for current production. Also, some goods are *intermediate goods* that are sold from one producer to another. The purchase of steel by the automobile manufacturers is an example. It would be double counting to include in the GNP both the value of the steel sold to the automobile companies and the value of the automobiles produced with the steel. The GNP is the sum of the values of only the *final goods* produced. The production of goods and services goes through various stages from one producer to another. The cost of labor and capital at each stage is referred to as the *value added* by each of the producers. As shown in Table 17.3, the value of the total production of final goods (woolen suits at retail stores in this example) is equal to the sum of the values added at each stage of production. Note that the cost of intermediate goods at each stage of production is equal to the value of the goods sold at the previous stage.

The GNP includes the estimated value of a few items that are not purchased from others, such as the value of home-consumed food produced by farmers and the consumption value of owner-occupied housing. It does not include the value of most goods and services people provide for themselves: the work of housewives in child care, cooking, housework, and sewing; home-grown garden crops; lawn mowing; and home improvements. In recent years, approximately 60 percent of married women have been full-time housewives. The total value of their household work which is excluded from the GNP would be very large. The decision of these housewives to refrain from entering the labor force

Table 17.3
The Relationship Between the Value Added
at Each Stage of Production and the Sales
Value of the Final Goods

STAGE OF PRODUCTION	COST OF INTERMEDIATE GOODS	VALUE ADDED (WAGES, INTEREST, RENT, AND PROFIT)	VALUE OF GOODS SOLD
Wool	—	$ 200,000	$ 200,000
Woolen cloth	$ 200,000	300,000	500,000
Woolen suits, at factory	500,000	600,000	1,100,000
Woolen suits, at retail store (final goods)	1,100,000	400,000	1,500,000
Sum of Value Added		$1,500,000	

indicates that the value of their household work and leisure was to them greater than their potential wage rates in employment.[1]

Critics of GNP statistics have pointed out that because the pollution caused by some products is larger than for others, estimates of production that do not take into consideration the costs of pollution distort the estimates of total output. Goods that pollute are said to be over-valued in the GNP compared to goods that do not pollute. According to this point of view, the cash value of the damage done during the year by smoke, noise, spillages, and industrial wastes ought to be deducted from the value of the output of each good and service included in the GNP, in accordance with the amount of the damage done. Another suggestion is to divide the components of GNP into two groups: Type I GNP would include components produced with renewable resources and recyclable wastes; Type II would be the total value of items either that are produced with irreplaceable resources or that end up as indestructible wastes.[2] While it would be desirable for an economy to maximize the output of Type I GNP, efforts should be made to minimize the output of Type II GNP.

Despite these shortcomings of the GNP as a measure of total output, the data on GNP as presently measured provide the best estimates available of a country's economic growth and fluctuations in total spending. We are interested in how monetary policy may influence prices or the total real output of the economy. In Table 17.2, trends in GNP are shown both in current prices and in 1958 prices, in order to differentiate increases in GNP resulting from higher prices from those resulting from the growth in real output. These measures of GNP serve quite well as measures of the goals that monetary policy is attempting to influence.

AGGREGATE DEMAND AND INCOME

Changes in national income are caused by changes in aggregate demand —the total amount that people desire to spend for consumer goods and services, investment goods, and government goods and services. For a change in the money supply to cause changes in the national income, it must affect aggregate demand.

In real terms, disregarding any changes in prices, total desired spending $(C + I + G)$ may differ from the national income because of the large inventories of goods carried over from previous years. If total desired spending is greater than national income, inventories of goods will shrink; and when aggregate demand is less than national income, inventories will expand. Actual total spending is different from desired total spending: actual total spending is equal to desired total spending less the decline in inventories.

On the vertical axis of Figure 17.2 is total desired spending $(C + I + G)$. The symbol I represents investment and combines investment spending with net exports of goods and services. On the horizontal axis is the national income (Y). The two axes have the same scale, and on the 45-degree line, aggregate demand is equal to the national income. The $C + I + G$ schedule in Figure 17.2 slopes upward, indicating that total spending becomes larger as the national income increases. At Y_1, the $C + I + G$ schedule crosses the 45-degree line. Only at Y_1 is aggregate demand equal to the national income. At levels of national income smaller than Y_1, aggregate demand is greater than the national income. To the right of Y_1, total spending is smaller than the national income, and the difference between the two becomes larger as national income increases.

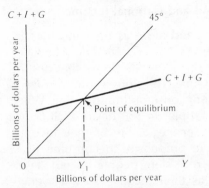

Figure 17.2   The Equilibrium Level of National Income

Equilibrium between Aggregate Demand and National Income

At Y_1, the equilibrium level of national income, there is no tendency for the national income either to increase or decrease. The national income would fall to Y_1 if it were larger than Y_1; and it would rise to Y_1 if it were less. If prices are assumed to be unchanged, a difference between desired spending and the national income affects inventories, and this leads to adjustments by business firms that bring spending and output into balance and cause the level of income to move toward Y_1. It is possible for people to plan to buy more than the economy is producing, by using up inventories. Both merchants' and manufacturers' inventories act like a buffer between desired spending and output. Inventories rise if output is larger than desired spending, and they fall if spending exceeds output. A condition in which inventories are falling, however, cannot last long. Inventories would soon be depleted. Business firms cannot operate effectively without adequate inventories. It is necessary to have goods on hand to avoid delays in delivery to their customers. As a result, if aggregate demand exceeds the annual output of the economy, output will rise, because only in this way can an eventual depletion of inventories be avoided. In addition, when desired spending exceeds the output of the economy, firms are strongly induced to expand output because of high profits and the expansion in the market. When inventories are low, profits tend to be high because of the lower storage costs and the lower credit costs of financing inventories. The opposite conditions prevail if output is larger than desired spending: people desire to buy less than is being produced, and inventories are growing. Firms react quite quickly to larger stockpiles by cutting down their output. The carrying of large inventories is costly. To avoid a drop in their profits, they are forced to reduce output in order to get inventories back to normal levels.

Relationship between Aggregate Demand and National Income

One would expect people to want to spend more as their incomes increase, as shown by the upward sloping $C + I + G$ schedule. However, the gradualness of the upward slope of this schedule shows that desired spending does not increase as fast as income. The slope of the $C + I + G$ schedule is based largely on the behavior of consumption spending. When income rises in periods of prosperity, people do not desire to increase their spending for consumer goods and services as fast as their income, so that as income increases, the average propensity to consume (C/Y) decreases. And when income falls in a recession, people do not desire to reduce their consumption as much as their income, so the average propensity to consume increases. This behavior of consumption is typical of the business cycle—not of longer trends in the economy. It is thought to reflect the feeling by persons that when their incomes rise, not all of the increase will last. Unless the increase in income is expected to last, as would be the case in the long run, consumption spending would increase by a smaller proportion than does income.

An Increase in the $C + I + G$ Schedule

For monetary policy to be expansionary, it must raise the $C + I + G$ schedule. In Figure 17.3, an upward shift in the $C + I + G$ schedule causes desired spending at Y_1 to be larger than the national income. If aggregate demand shifted upward to $(C + I + G)_2$, the level of the national income would rise to Y_2. As income rises, desired spending would increase further, but not as fast as income, and eventually spending would be equal to income.

In order to raise the $C + I + G$ schedule, an increase in the money supply must cause people to spend more even though their incomes are the same. Most increases in spending are closely related to increases in the income people receive. In Figure 17.3, the upward slope of the $C + I + G$ schedule shows that total spending increases as the national income increases. But what is required of monetary policy is more than this. There must be an increase in total desired spending for some other reason than an increase in income. The terms used to describe this type of increase in spending are *autonomous* or *exogenous*.

The strength of monetary policy depends on whether it is able to create sources of desired spending in addition to the normal increase caused by an expansion in income. The evidence that the banking system

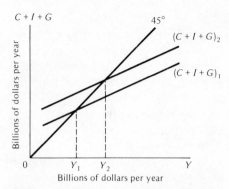

Figure 17.3   Effect on National Income of an Increase in the $C + I + G$ Schedule

can do this either by providing additional supplies of credit or by providing the public with additional amounts of money is the reason for the importance of monetary policy. Changes in investment spending are more apt to be autonomous than changes in consumption. Since it is usually believed that consumption is determined predominantly by the amount of income people have received, one would not expect large enough autonomous changes to occur in consumption to raise the $C + I + G$ schedule. Much investment spending is financed by an expansion in the total amount of bank loans or by money saved in the past. Investment spending financed in either of these ways, since they are not based on income changes, would be autonomous and would shift the $C + I + G$ schedule upward. If government expenditures are financed by new money, total desired spending would probably increase, and the $C + I + G$ schedule would shift upward. If the government finances additional expenditures by taxation, the increase in government spending could be largely offset by a decrease in private spending.

The Multiplier

If monetary policy causes an autonomous increase in spending, the national income would tend to expand by more than that increase. The multiplier expresses this relationship. It is the ratio of an increase in income (Y) to an autonomous increase in spending (I) and may be expressed as $\triangle Y / \triangle I$. The symbol I is used for autonomous increases in spending, because such spending is frequently in the form of purchases of capital goods. The relationship between autonomous increases in spending and income is shown in Figure 17.3. The increase in income—the distance between Y_1 and Y_2—is larger than the vertical distance between the $(C + I + G)_1$ and the $(C + I + G)_2$ schedules. The results of statistical studies indicate that in the United States the multiplier is approximately two: if the increase in autonomous spending were $1 billion, the increase in national income would be $2 billion.

The way in which an autonomous increase in spending may cause an even larger expansion in real output, assuming no change in prices, is illustrated in Table 17.4. In this example, each period is equal to three months, and there is only one increment in investment—in the first period. The first period shows the effect of the autonomous increase in planned spending for capital goods in the first quarter, the second period shows the effects in the second quarter, and so on.

As shown in Table 17.4, in period 1 the increase in planned investment causes an equal increase in national income in the form of wages, rent, interest, and profits, because someone was paid to produce the additional investment goods. In the first period, because people have

Table 17.4
The Multiplier Process for a Single
Increment of Investment

PERIOD	ΔPLANNED INVEST-MENT	ΔCON-SUMER GOODS PRO-DUCTION	ΔNATIONAL INCOME	ΔCON-SUMER SPEND-ING	ΔSAVING	AMOUNT THAT INVEN-TORIES ARE BELOW ORIGINAL LEVEL
1	$1,000	—	$1,000	$ 600	$ 400	$600
2	—	$ 600	600	360	240	360
3	—	360	360	216	144	216
4	—	216	216	130	86	130
5	—	130	130	78	52	78
6	—	78	78	47	31	47
7	—	47	47	28	19	28
All subsequent periods	—	69	69	41	28	—
Total	$1,000	$1,500	$2,500	$1,500	$1,000	0

larger incomes, there would also be an increase in spending for consumer goods. Assuming that people have a *marginal propensity to consume* ($\Delta C/\Delta Y$) of 60 percent, consumption spending would rise by $600, and saving—which is anything that people do with their income other than spending it for consumption—increases by $400. If people have a 60 percent marginal propensity to consume, it means that they would spend for consumption 60 percent of the increase in their income. The increase in consumer spending in period 1 does not affect the production of consumer goods until the second period. The effect of the increase in consumption spending in period 1 is to reduce inventories of consumer goods by the amount of the increase in consumption. It should be noted that in period 1, measured investment (planned investment plus the change in inventories) increased only $400—the same amount as the increase in saving.

If business firms wish to maintain their inventories at the same level as existed prior to the increase in investment, they have to replenish the $600 worth of inventories lost in period 1. This is the reason for the increase in the output of consumer goods in period 2. Additional persons are hired to produce the consumer goods needed to replenish inventories, and the national income rises by $600 in this period. With a 60 percent marginal propensity to consume, these persons would increase consumption spending in period 2 by $360 and save $240. Although merchants had attempted to replace the inventories they had lost because of the increase in investment in period 1, their inventory levels in period 2 would still be $360 below customary levels. As a result, the process continues. Merchants order $360 worth of consumer goods in period 3; the output of consumer goods increases; there is an increase in the national income, consumer spending, and saving—and inventory levels are still below customary levels. The final result, accumulating the effects in all periods, is an increase of $1,500 in consumption, $2,500 in national income, and $1,000 in saving. The multiplier is equal to 2.5. The amount of the increase in national income depends on people's marginal propensity to consume (MPC). The formula is as follows:

$$\triangle Y = \frac{\triangle I}{1 - MPC}$$

where $\triangle Y$ = increase in income, $\triangle I$ = increase in planned investment, and MPC = marginal propensity to consume. Thus,

$$\triangle Y = \frac{\$1,000}{1 - .60} = \$2,500$$

The smaller the MPC, the smaller the multiplier.

In Table 17.4, accumulated saving amounted to $1,000—equal to the increase in planned investment in period 1. In period 1 people had desired to invest more than the increase in saving. This caused inventories to fall. The replacement of those inventories then increased income sufficiently to create a volume of saving equal to the larger amount of planned investment.

In the illustration in Table 17.4, it is assumed that the economy was not operating at full employment. In each period it was possible to hire additional persons to produce the larger output. It is also assumed that there was no change in prices. If merchants had raised prices instead of letting the level of their inventories drop below customary levels, there would not have been secondary effects on the output of consumer goods.

RELATIONSHIP BETWEEN DEMAND FOR AND SUPPLY OF MONEY

The way in which differences between the demand for and supply of money may affect aggregate demand, and thus either real output or prices, is shown in Figure 17.4. In this figure, the supply of money (M) is $4 billion, and the perfectly vertical money supply schedule indicates

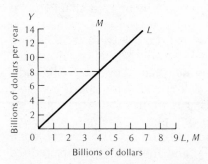

Figure 17.4   Determination of National Income

no change in the money supply when income changes. Actually, the relationship between the money supply and income is more complicated than this. In periods of cyclical expansion an increase in income could affect either the ratio of excess reserves to demand deposits that banks desire to hold or the ratio of currency to demand deposits that the public wishes to hold. Changes in either of those ratios could cause changes in the money supply.

The money demand schedule (L) in Figure 17.4 shows that desired money balances vary directly and in proportion to expected income. At every point on this schedule, the ratio of the total amount of money demanded to expected national income is equal to one-half. The schedule is drawn so that it is a straight line rising from the intersection of the two axes. Expected income may rise because of a rise either in real output or in prices. A change in any of the other factors affecting the demand for money, such as expected interest rates or the expected rate of inflation, would cause the demand-for-money schedule to shift. Although expected national income may temporarily be different from national income as currently measured, when current national income falls, expected income soon falls; and when current levels of national income rise, expected income soon rises. This is because people's expectations lag behind their experience. Differences between expected income and current income are usually the result of unexpected changes in the current levels of national income. At equilibrium, expected income is equal to current income.

The equilibrium level of national income is where the quantity of money demanded is equal to the quantity supplied—at $8 billion in Figure 17.4. At this income, the quantity of money people have is just equal to the amount they want. If the national income were larger, there would be a tendency for it to fall to the equilibrium level, or if it were less, there would be a tendency for the national income to rise to $8 billion. There is no inducement for the national income to change once it is equal to $8 billion.

Consider why the national income would rise if it were at $6 billion. At that level of income, people want to hold only $3 billion in money, half of their income. They have more money than they want. The individual who has excess money balances will spend it for goods and services, lend it, or buy stocks and bonds. His money balance would go down to the level he desires. But when one person attempts to reduce his money balance, he increases the amount of money held by someone else. The public has $4 billion in money, and the public cannot reduce this amount by spending it. In the process of trying to reduce their excess money balances, people spend more, and this spending increases aggregate demand. As soon as the level of expected income rises to $8 billion, the ratio of the money people have to their expected income is one-half, and they no longer have excess money balances. If employment can be expanded, the increase in aggregate demand would increase real output. If employment cannot be expanded, the increased spending would push up prices. In either case, the increase in expected national income, as people experience higher levels of income, increases the quantity of money demanded, and eventually desired money balances are brought into equality with actual money balances.

Consider why the national income would fall if it were at $10 billion. At this level, people desire to hold $5 billion even though they have only $4 billion. Or even though they desire that the ratio of their money holdings to their income be 50 percent, they are actually holding a ratio of only 40 percent. If persons want to hold more money than they have, they can cut down on their spending for goods and services or they can sell stocks, bonds, or physical assets. Both of these would tend to reduce the national income. Consuming less and saving more out of any given level of income directly reduces spending. Selling bonds and stocks causes their prices to fall and raises their yields and interest rates generally. This tends to reduce investment spending and thus the level of income.

Even though an individual can increase his money balances by saving more or by selling other assets, the public as a whole cannot increase the total money balances in the economy in this way. When one person increases his balance, the balance of another person must be reduced. There is a conflict between what the individual can do and what the public as a whole can do. The attempted adjustments by individuals lower the income of the economy and eventually eliminate this conflict. When income falls from $10 billion to $8 billion, the public's ratio of money to income rises from 40 percent to 50 percent, which is the desired ratio.

EFFECT OF CHANGES IN THE SUPPLY OF AND DEMAND FOR MONEY ON INCOME

Shifts in either the money supply or money demand schedules will cause changes in the level of the national income. A change in any of the factors in the money supply function, such as the monetary base and the currency demand deposit ratio, could shift the M schedule. As shown in Figure 17.5(a), an increase in the money supply to $5 billion would raise the level of national income in the economy from $8 billion to $10 billion. At the initial level of income, the supply of money would be larger than the demand, people would have excess money balances, they would increase their spending, and the level of national income would rise to $10 billion, thus increasing money demanded to $5 billion.

If there were no change in the supply schedule, but if instead the demand schedule shifted upward, as in Figure 17.5(b), national income would again increase. The L schedule could shift upward if people expected higher interest rates or a more rapid rate of inflation.

When the M schedule in Figure 17.5(a) shifts, such a change may itself cause the L schedule to shift. For example, an increase in the money supply could result in inflationary expectations which would shift the L schedule upward, thus adding to the stimulating effect on income of an increase in the money supply. Or interest rates may fall temporarily when the money supply is increased. If people expected lower interest rates, the L schedule would shift downward. This would lessen the stimu-

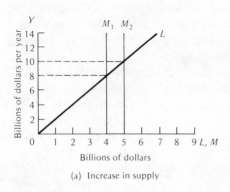

(a) Increase in supply

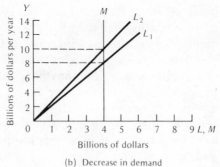

(b) Decrease in demand

Figure 17.5   Effect on National Income of an Increase in the Supply of Money and of a Decrease in the Demand for Money

lating effect on income that an increase in the money supply would be expected to have.

In Figure 17.5(a), when the supply of money increases causing the national income to rise, at the points of equilibrium where $M = L$, there is no change in the income velocity of money, Y/M. The income velocity of money is 2 per year both when Y is equal to $8 billion and when Y is equal to $10 billion. In Figure 17.5(b), however, when the demand for money schedule decreases, causing the national income to rise, at the higher level of income the velocity of money, Y/M, is larger. The velocity of money is 2 when Y is equal to $8 billion, and rises to 2½ when Y is equal to $10 billion. Whether or not statistical data on income velocity represent the points of equilibrium shown in Figure 17.5 depends on how quickly equilibrium conditions are reached in the economy, and on possible differences between expected and current national income. The statistical data measure current national income rather than expected income. If equilibrium conditions are reached quickly and current income is equal to expected income, increases in velocity as measured by the statistical data will reflect an upward shift in the liquidity preference schedule shown in Figure 17.5(b), and decreases in measured velocity will reflect a downward shift in this schedule.

PORTFOLIO ADJUSTMENT
PROCESS

A principal channel through which an increase in the money supply, relative to the demand for money, may cause an increase in aggregate demand is through its impact on the portfolios of banks and the public. When there is an increase in the money supply, persons and banks experience an increase in their money holdings relative to the other assets they own. This change in their portfolios may cause them to make adjustments that result in an increase in spending.

There are many different situations that can start the portfolio adjustment process working—anything that affects the portfolios of banks or the public when the money supply is increased.[3] Most often it is set in motion by open-market purchases—the principal instrument of monetary control. When the Federal Reserve purchases securities in the open market, the action usually affects the portfolios of both the member banks and the public. If the purchase is from a nonbank dealer, the supply of money held by the public will be increased by the amount of the open-market purchase. The public's portfolio has been changed: they now have less in bonds and more in money. In addition, such an open-market purchase affects the portfolios of the member banks. Their reserves have been increased, and there has been no change in their other assets. If the increase in bank reserves results in a multiple expansion of their deposits, this expansion will have further effects on the portfolios of the public. The portfolio adjustment process is concerned with analyzing the reaction of both the banks and the public to this change in their portfolios.

Adjustments of the Commercial Banks

Commercial banks have three principal types of assets: reserves, bonds, and loans. Assume that they have a certain *structure of assets* which they consider the best possible distribution among the different types, as shown below:

TYPE	DESIRED DISTRIBUTION OF BANK ASSETS
Reserves	15%
Bonds	30
Loans	55
Total	100%

This desired structure of bank assets is partly the result of legal reserve requirements and partly the result of the banks' objectives of maximizing profits, avoiding losses, and providing for adequate liquidity. Chapters 6 and 7, which describe the different types of assets of commercial banks, explain the various considerations that affect the management of their portfolios. The desired structure is not rigidly fixed. It changes over time as the banks adjust to changing conditions and changing yields on different types of assets.

Open-market operations cause the actual structure to be different from the desired structure. Suppose the Federal Reserve System, through open-market purchases, increased bank reserves by $1.5 billion and did not purchase the securities from the commercial banks. The banks' bonds and loans would be unaffected. They would now hold a higher proportion of their total assets in reserves than formerly. Will the individual banks attempt to reduce the amount of reserves they hold? If they do, there will be portfolio adjustments that will almost certainly stimulate total spending in the economy. As was pointed out in Chapter 9, when banks have received additional reserves, they have usually reacted by expanding their investments and their loans.

What are some of the conditions under which the disturbance to bank portfolios might not affect national income? Much depends on how strongly banks try to maintain a particular portfolio distribution. When the actual structure is changed, there might be a simultaneous change in the desired structure. Because the increase in reserves created by the Federal Reserve is usually not supplied in response to a desire of the banks for additional reserves, such a possibility would be unusual.

If open-market purchases altered the desired structure of bank assets, it would be through the effects on interest rates. When the Federal Reserve buys securities in the open market, it bids up their prices and lowers yields. If the Federal Reserve banks purchased bills, the bill rate would be slightly lower than it otherwise would be. If the bill rate declined, banks might wish to hold a somewhat larger quantity of excess reserves. But even if there was some impact, it would probably be small. The bulk of the additional reserves received by the banks would be used to make loans and investments for two reasons: (1) the additional reserves earn no interest, and (2) highly liquid Treasury bills are available for purchase that are virtually riskless, yield a rate of return, and are practically as liquid as excess reserves. Or, banks with excess reserves may lend them to other banks through the Federal funds market.

When banks attempt to return to their normal structure of assets, they will probably first invest in Treasury bills or lend Federal funds. This would cause either the bill rate or the Federal funds rate to fall, and this decline would cause those investments to become less attractive than they had been relative to longer-term securities or loans. This would induce banks to move into intermediate- or long-term securities. As a result, their prices would also rise and their interest yields would fall. The decline in interest yields on investments relative to those on loans would then induce banks to expand their loans. The volume of loans would expand and their interest rates would also fall.

If, when banks get an increase in reserves, they eventually expand their loans, there is little doubt that this would increase aggregate demand. The proceeds of the loans are almost always spent. Even when banks buy outstanding securities the effect may be expansionary, because the person who receives payment for the securities now has money which he will probably spend—or lend to someone else who will spend it. The market for bank credit is an important channel through which open-market purchases and other tools of monetary policy affect the level of economic activity.

The portfolio adjustment approach stresses the willingness of the lenders to lend rather than the willingness of borrowers to borrow. In this approach, it is usually assumed that there is an array of borrowers willing to borrow at various interest rates, and if banks are more willing to lend and lower their interest charges, the volume of borrowing will increase. In order to increase their loans, there must be borrowers. Critics who are skeptical of the power of monetary policy have believed that borrowers are insensitive to changes in interest rates, and have doubted whether lending would be increased when interest rates are lowered.

The individual bank gets rid of reserves it does not wish to hold by lending or investing them. The banking system as a whole cannot get rid of reserves by increasing loans and investments although there may be a currency drain as deposits expand. The bulk of the reserves lent by one bank will be deposited in another bank. Banks as a whole return to their original structure of assets by expanding their total loans and investments. In the example above, if reserves are increased by $1.5 billion and remain at that level, investments must be increased by $3.0 billion, and loans by $5.5 billion, in order to retain the same percentage of total assets in reserves. Although interest rates play an important part in this process (through declining interest rates, the impetus is transmitted from an increase in the ownership of one asset to another), this approach emphasizes the expansion in bank portfolios rather than changes in interest rates.

The process by which the increase in reserves is transmitted into an increase in spending takes time. The initial impact is probably on financial markets. Banks can expand their investments immediately, but it takes time to process loans. One reason why some persons may have underestimated the power of monetary policy control measures is probably because they take time to produce their effects. If one looks for immediate results, monetary control measures would not be appropriate.

Adjustments of the Public

Like the banks, the public has a variety of different assets, including money, bonds, stocks, physical assets, and consumer goods, and they probably have a certain structure of assets that they consider to be most desirable. They distribute their total assets among the components in the way they consider best. If there is an unexpected increase in the quantity of any one of the assets in the portfolio or a decrease in interest rates on that particular asset, the attractiveness of other assets will probably increase. If the Federal Reserve increased the money supply, people would probably respond by attempting to reduce their money holdings by spending them. The public as a whole, however, cannot reduce the total amount of money in the economy in this way.

If additional money were injected into the system by open-market purchases, the public's holdings of bonds would decrease at the same time that their holdings of money increased. There would be no increase in total wealth and thus no wealth effect on total spending. There would be a wealth effect only if the increase in the money supply were created by gold mining or money created by the printing press rather than through open-market purchases. The important effect of open-market purchases is to raise security prices and lower interest rates. It is the rise in bond prices that induces people to sell their securities. The high bond prices could cause the public to change the desired structure of their assets, tending to increase the demand for money and reduce the demand for bonds. But more is involved than just the relative attractiveness of money and bonds. The increased supply of money and the lower yields on bonds would increase the relative attractiveness of other assets such as corporation stock, physical capital goods, and consumer goods.

The changes in the relative prices of the different assets are the principal way in which the stimulating effect of an increase in the money supply is transmitted from the financial markets to the real sector of the economy. When the public gets additional money, some persons shift to bonds. This causes bond prices to rise further and interest yields to fall. As a result, bonds become relatively unattractive compared to stocks, and the public is then induced to purchase the latter. This raises prices of stocks, reduces their earnings-to-price ratios, and causes stocks to become relatively unattractive compared to physical assets. Then as people purchase physical assets, prices of those assets rise. As a result, it becomes a better bargain for some persons to purchase the services of capital rather than the capital itself. For example, if the prices of houses rise, some persons would be induced to rent rather than purchase a house.

An increase in the money stock may also increase the demand for consumer goods and services directly rather than by first increasing the demand for financial assets and physical capital assets and causing them to become relatively unattractive. Whether an increase in the money stock initially affects financial markets or the market for goods and services probably depends on who gets the increase in the money stock. If it is primarily in the hands of financial institutions, the initial impact would be on financial assets. But if it is in the hands of consumers (many of whom seldom invest in financial securities), it may have its initial effect on the market for consumer goods and services. Some statistical studies have concluded that retail sales are sensitive to changes in monetary policy, indicating that there are direct effects of increases in the money supply on consumption.

For an increase in the money stock to have no impact on spending, the immediate decline in interest rates because of the open-market purchase must induce the public to want to hold all of the additional money rather than other assets, or to adjust their portfolios in such a way as to affect only financial markets. Those who doubt the power of monetary policy believe that there may be a wide gap between the desire for financial assets and the desire for physical assets and consumer goods and services. Even though the prices of financial assets are raised and their rates of return are reduced, they believe that this does not induce persons to add to their holdings of physical assets.

The extent to which the supply of capital goods and consumer goods responds to the increase in the demand for them determines the impact of monetary policy on income. If an increase in the money supply adds to the demand for existing houses and raises their prices relative to the cost of constructing them, this probably would stimulate the output of new houses. If the prices of bonds and stocks rise, interest rates fall, and it becomes less costly for corporations to finance capital expenditures by issuing bonds. This could stimulate investment in the same way that a lower rate of interest on bank loans would.

REVERSE EFFECT FROM INCOME TO MONEY

The explanation thus far shows how changes in the money supply affect income. Changes in income may also affect the expansion of the money supply. One of the principal variables bringing about changes in the money supply is changes by the public in the proportion of its money balances held in currency. Changes in the level of business activity affect the public's currency-to-deposit ratio and thus the total money supply. The studies by Professor Cagan showed that historically the cyclical behavior of the currency-to-deposit ratio has been quite regular.

A very simple dynamic business cycle model can be based on the propositions that changes in the money supply cause changes in the same direction in income and that the currency-to-deposit ratio of the public varies with the level of income. An increase in the money supply would cause income to rise; the rise in income would cause the currency-to-deposit ratio to rise; this would cause the money supply to decline; the fall in the money supply would cause income to decline; the lower level of income would cause the currency-to-deposit ratio to fall; this would increase the money supply; and so on for another cycle.

Under the gold standard, changes in the level of income also had significant monetary effects. Higher incomes caused a deficit in the balance of payments, a loss of gold, and a decline in the amount of money. A fall in income had the opposite effect. The resulting surplus in the balance of payments led to an inflow of gold and an increase in money.

Variations in income may also affect the money supply through their effect on interest rates. When income rises, interest rates tend to rise, and when income falls, interest rates tend to fall. When interest rates are higher, banks tend to economize on their excess reserves and reduce the ratio of their reserves to their deposits, thus increasing the amount of money. On the other hand, when interest rates are low, banks are likely to hold a larger amount of reserves relative to their deposits, thus causing a monetary contraction. Another possible result of an increase in interest rates resulting from a rise in national income is that it may induce people to hold more time deposits relative to demand deposits. An increase in t, the ratio of time deposits to demand deposits, would tend to increase Money Supply II but to decrease Money Supply I.

Historically, relatively large changes in the amount of money in the United States have usually not been the result of changes in income. Prior to the 1970s, the periods of rapid monetary expansion and inflation in the United States have all occurred during wars, when the money supply was increased by the government to finance military expenditures. The gradually rising quantity of money from 1896 to 1913 was a result of the increase in the gold stock rather than an increase in income. This increase occurred because of the discovery of new mines and improved techniques of extracting gold from low-grade ore. In the 1970s, the Federal Reserve System has continued the rapid expansion in the money supply that it provided during the late 1960s. The principal reason appears to be the reluctance to risk the adverse effects on unemployment that the Federal Reserve expects would occur if the rate of expansion in the money supply were sharply curtailed.

In serious depressions, the relatively large declines in the amount of money have almost always been caused primarily by financial panics—bank failures, runs on the banks, and bank hoarding—rather than by declines in income. In 1920–1921, the decline in the money stock was largely the result of Federal Reserve policy rather than changes in income. The Federal Reserve raised the discount rate sharply. This was followed by a sharp decline in borrowing at the Federal Reserve banks and a decline in bank reserves. In 1937–1938 Federal Reserve policy again had the same effect. At that time the reserve requirements of the member banks were doubled. Although it was thought that unwanted excess reserves would be absorbed, the banks reacted by increasing the ratio of their reserves to deposits. Although there have been important interrelationships between money and income in minor recessions, changes in income in major depressions and periods of inflation have not been a major cause of changes in the money supply.

SUMMARY

The statistical data on the national income measure the dollar value of the total output of the economy. Monetary theory attempts to explain how variations in the money supply may stimulate or restrain the growth of the national income.

In real terms, disregarding any changes in prices, aggregate demand $(C + I + G)$ will be equal to the national income (Y) under conditions of equilibrium. Otherwise levels of inventories will be growing or contracting excessively.

Either real output will get larger or prices will rise if total spending is greater than the national income. An expansionary monetary policy may increase either prices or real output if it has a stimulating effect on total spending.

When national income is in equilibrium, the demand for money must be equal to the supply. If supply and demand are not equal, prices or real output will increase if people want to hold less money than they have, and decrease if they want to hold more money than they have.

People own a variety of different types of assets. An increase in the money supply may cause people to have a larger portion of their total assets in money than they desire. An attempt to shift to other types of assets will raise their prices and have a stimulating effect on the demand for both financial and real assets.

NOTES

1. See Reuben Gronau, "The Intrafamily Allocation of Time: The Value of the Housewife's Time," *American Economic Review* 63 (September 1973), pp. 634–651; and Gary Becker, "A Theory of Marriage, Part I," *Journal of Political Economy* 81 (July–August 1973), pp. 813–846.

2. See Edwin G. Dolan, *Tanstaafl, The Economic Strategy for Environmental Crisis* (New York: Holt, Rinehart, and Winston, 1971), pp. 9–10.

3. Milton Friedman and Anna J. Schwartz, "Money and Business Cycles," *Review of Economics and Statistics* 45, Supplement (February 1963), pp. 32–78; reprinted in *The Optimum Quantity of Money and Other Essays* (Chicago: Aldine, 1969), pp. 189–235. See particularly Section 3, "A Tentative Sketch of the Mechanism Transmitting Monetary Changes."

QUESTIONS

17.1.   Compare the two ways of measuring the national income: by distributive shares and by types of expenditures.

17.2.   What accounts for the difference between gross national product and national income?

17.3.   Draw a graph showing the relationship between the national income and the sum of consumption, investment, and government spending.

17.4.   Why does the average propensity to consume decrease when total income increases?

17.5.   What is the meaning of an increase in autonomous spending? Illustrate by using a graph showing the relationship between aggregate demand and national income.

17.6.   What is the formula for the multiplier? Explain why an increase in autonomous spending results in an increase in national income larger than the increase in autonomous spending.

17.7.   If the quantity of money demanded is less than the supply of money, why will the national income rise? What determines how much the rise in income will be?

17.8.   If the supply of money is less than that demanded, why will national income fall? What determines how much the fall in income will be?

17.9.   Assuming no change in the supply of money, if the demand for money decreases, what would be the effect on the national income?

17.10.   Explain the way an open-market purchase initially may affect the portfolios of both the member banks and the public.

17.11.   If open-market operations increase bank reserves relative to their loans and securities, will the banks respond so as to increase total spending? Why?

17.12.   If open-market operations increase the money holdings of persons relative to their other assets, will the response of persons increase total spending? Why?

17.13.   Explain how changes in income may affect the supply of money.

17.14.   Know the meaning and significance of the following terms and concepts: personal consumption expenditures, gross private domestic investment, net exports of goods and services, income of proprietors, capital consumption allowances, autonomous increase in total spending, desired spending, planned investment, marginal propensity to consume, average propensity to consume, aggregate demand, equilibrium level of national income, multiplier, structure of assets, portfolios of banks.

TIME 315
TEMPERATURE 57
PRIME INTEREST RATE 1175

Chapter 18
The Relation of Money to Income: The Interest Rate-Investment Explanation

An increase in the money supply will have a stimulating effect either on real output or on prices if an increase in the money supply lowers interest rates, if lower interest rates increase investment, and if the larger amount of investment increases total spending.

The interest rate–investment theory of the relationship between the money stock and total spending was developed primarily in the 1930s and 1940s and has been predominant until the recent development of the portfolio adjustment theory.

LIQUIDITY PREFERENCE FUNCTION AND THE SUPPLY OF MONEY

The liquidity preference schedule (L) in Figure 18.1 slopes downward from left to right, indicating that the quantity of money people wish to hold increases as interest rates (i) fall. Persons choose between holding money and securities, and rates of interest affect the attractiveness of the two. When interest rates are high, people wish to hold smaller amounts of money and more securities; when interest rates are low, the demand for money becomes larger.

Changes in factors that affect the demand for money other than interest rates would cause the liquidity preference schedule to shift. An increase in expected real income would cause it to shift to the right. At all possible levels of interest rates, the demand for money would be greater. Or, if people feel that the contingencies of doing business have become hazardous, the schedule would shift to the left. At all possible interest rates, people would want to hold less money.

The money supply schedule (M) in Figure 18.1 slopes upward to the right. When interest rates rise, the quantity of money tends to increase because banks economize on their excess reserves. Excess reserves earn no interest and become less attractive to hold as interest rates on bank loans and investments rise. The ratio of the excess reserves of banks to their deposits is one of the variables in the money supply function; when this ratio gets smaller, the quantity of money expands. Also, when interest rates rise, the amount of Money Supply II would tend to increase because the rise in interest rates would induce persons to hold larger amounts of time deposits relative to demand deposits. In the equation for Money Supply II (Equation 9.7), an increase in t—the ratio of time deposits to demand deposits—would cause an increase in the supply of Money Supply II.

If the money supply schedule were M_1, the equilibrium level of interest rates in Figure 18.1 would be where the M_1 schedule intersects the liquidity preference schedule. At this rate of interest, 6 percent, the supply of money would be equal to the demand. If interest rates were above 6 percent, the quantity of money supplied would be greater than that demanded. Some persons with excess money would use it to purchase securities. This would raise the prices of securities and lower their interest yields. As interest rates declined toward 6 percent, the quantity of money demanded would increase and the supply would decrease until the point of equilibrium was reached. Or if interest rates were below the equilibrium level, the quantity of money demanded would be greater

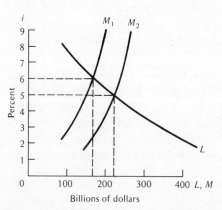

Figure 18.1 Determination of Interest Rates

than that supplied. To get larger cash balances, some persons would sell securities. This would lower the prices of securities and raise interest yields.

When the demand for money is different from the supply, the conditions confronting an individual are not the same as those for the public as a whole. Although an individual can build up his money balances by selling securities, such selling merely reduces the money balances of someone else. If an individual tries to reduce his money holdings by spending them, he adds to the balances of others. The total money supply held by the public is unchanged. Conditions for the economy as a whole return to equilibrium only as interest rates change, causing the quantity of money demanded to equal the supply.

An increase in the money supply resulting from an increase in the monetary base would shift the money supply schedule from M_1 to M_2 (in Figure 18.1) and cause interest rates to fall, because the supply of money would exceed the demand. When the supply of money is increased, equilibrium conditions will not prevail until the quantity of money demanded is also increased. In order to get people to hold a larger quantity of money, interest rates have to go down. At the lower interest rates, people are willing to hold more money relative to their holdings of other financial assets.

The decline in interest rates shown in Figure 18.1 is known as the *liquidity effect* on interest rates of an increase in the money supply.[1] The liquidity effect occurs in the short run and is different from the long-run effects. It has been estimated that the short-run effect is limited to the first three to five months following a more rapid expansion of the stock of money.[2] A basic assumption of this liquidity effect is that when the money stock increases, there is not an equivalent rise in prices or an increase in real income. The fall in interest rates is the result of increasing the real quantity of money. A rise in prices or real income would cause the liquidity preference schedule to shift to the right. Actually, an increase in the money stock does not ordinarily have an immediate impact on prices or real income.

INTEREST RATES AND INVESTMENT

In the second step of the interest rate–investment theory, the fall in interest rates increases the volume of spending for net investment, as shown in Figure 18.2. It is assumed that the economy is operating at less than full employment and that real output can be expanded. In 1973 gross private domestic investment amounted to $201.5 billion and consisted

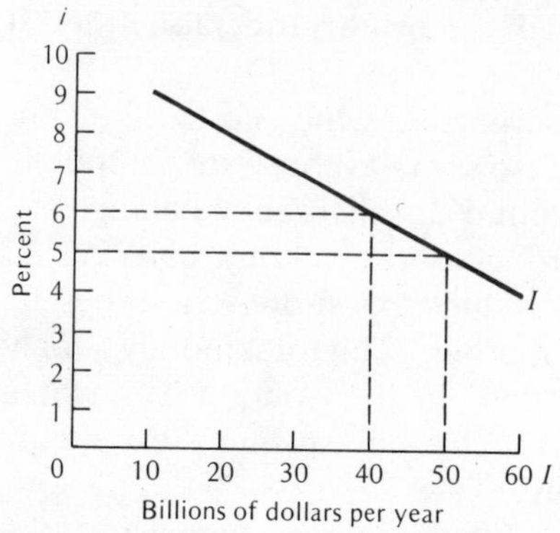

Figure 18.2 Net Investment at Different Interest Rates

of the four major components shown in Table 18.1—nonresidential construction, producers' durable equipment, residential construction, and changes in business inventories. Except for housing, most expenditures for capital goods are made by business firms.

In 1973, depreciation expenditures to replace worn-out equipment and to repair building structures amounted to over 50 percent of gross private domestic investment. The prices at which goods are sold are normally high enough to generate the funds needed to finance depreciation expenditures. The volume of depreciation expenditures in a country depends primarily on the amount of real capital (plants, machinery, and housing) in use, and on the speed with which it depreciates. However, depreciation expenditures vary over the business cycle, because capital

Table 18.1
Private Investment, 1973

TYPE OF INVESTMENT	AMOUNT IN BILLIONS
Nonresidential construction	$ 48.3
Producers' durable equipment	87.7
Residential construction	58.0
Change in business inventories	7.4
Total gross private domestic investment	$201.5
Less: depreciation	109.6
Total net private domestic investment	$ 91.9

Columns do not add to totals because of rounding.
Source: *Economic Report of the President, February 1974* (Washington, D.C.: U.S. Government Printing Office, 1974), pp. 264–265.

equipment need not be replaced as soon as it wears out. In periods of depression, depreciation expenditures may be deferred, and when conditions improve there is likely to be a sharp increase in those expenditures.

Net investment consists of that portion of capital expenditures in excess of depreciation. Table 18.1 shows that in 1973 net private investment—the addition to the total stock of capital in the economy—amounted to $91.9 billion. Net investment must be financed by retaining profits, borrowing, or selling stock. The growth in gross and net investment from 1964 to 1973 is shown in Table 18.2. The amount of investment has varied with business conditions. The declines in both gross and net investment in 1967 and 1970 show the slackening of economic activity in those years.

MARGINAL EFFICIENCY OF INVESTMENT

The attractiveness of net investment to a business enterprise—the purchase of a new machine, for example—depends on the expected rate of profit that can be made on that capital expenditure as compared with the cost of borrowing. The rate of profit, called the *marginal efficiency of investment* (*MEI*), is found thus:

$$\text{Marginal efficiency of investment} = \frac{\textit{Expected annual net return}}{\textit{Cost of machine}}$$

Table 18.2
Investment in the United States 1964–1973
(in billions of dollars)

YEAR	SPENDING FOR DEPRECIATION	NET INVESTMENT	GROSS PRIVATE DOMESTIC INVESTMENT
1964	$ 56.1	$37.9	$ 94.0
1965	59.8	48.3	108.1
1966	63.9	57.5	121.4
1967	68.9	47.6	116.6
1968	74.5	51.5	126.0
1969	81.6	57.4	139.0
1970	87.3	49.0	136.3
1971	93.8	59.4	153.2
1972	102.4	75.9	178.3
1973	109.6	91.9	201.5

Source: *Economic Report of the President, February 1974*, pp. 265 and 272.

If the expected annual net return from a machine were $2,000 and its cost was $20,000, the rate of profit would be 10 percent. Even though estimates of the rate of profit are not easy to make, they must be made implicitly, if not explicitly.The expected annual net return is the amount of income expected per year from the use of the machine. It is a net return after deducting the cost of operating the machine, additional taxes, and the cost of depreciation. By allowing for the cost of depreciation, it is assumed that the machine is maintained indefinitely or replaced through amortization so that this annual return may be expected to continue in the future. The cost of the machine is the purchase price.

If the estimated marginal efficiency of a particular capital investment were 10 percent and the rate of interest were 8 percent, for example, it would be advisable for a business to finance the purchase of this capital equipment by borrowing. Making the investment would add to the profits of the business. On the other hand, if the *MEI* were less than the cost of borrowing, such an investment would not be advisable. Even if a business firm does not have to borrow, the same rule holds. If the *MEI* is less than the rate of interest, the firm should itself lend the money at the higher rate rather than invest it in capital equipment earning a lower rate.

For the economy as a whole, net investment (*I*) is related to the marginal efficiency of investment, as shown in Figure 18.3. In this figure, at an *MEI* of 6 percent, $40 billion of new investment is possible. But $50 billion of new investment could be made, yielding 5 percent. The downward slope of the investment schedule indicates that if net investment in the economy is increased, firms will receive lower rates of profit from additional investments. Among the wide range of investments that firms might make, only a few investments can promise very high rates of return. As a larger total amount is invested, more investments with lower rates of return would have to be included.

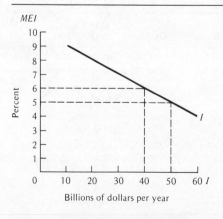

Figure 18.3   The Relationship between Net Investment and the Marginal Efficiency of Investment

   A fundamental reason why the *MEI* tends to get smaller when the total amount invested increases is related to the law of diminishing returns. Larger amounts of investment tend to increase the proportion of capital to labor, and this tends to reduce the marginal productivity of capital. The principle of diminishing returns applies when there are changes in the proportion of one type of resource used with a relatively fixed amount of another. If capital increases relative to labor, the productivity of capital tends to decline and the productivity of labor tends to rise.

   Because business firms tend to spend for new capital up to the point where the *MEI* is equal to the cost of borrowing, the schedule relating investment to the rate of interest in Figure 18.2 is the same as that relating investment to the *MEI* in Figure 18.3. In Figure 18.2, a reduction in interest rates from 6 percent to 5 percent would increase the amount of net investment from $40 billion to $50 billion. The total amount of investment would increase because investments with lower rates of profit now become worthwhile.

   Figure 18.2 shows that at any given rate of interest the volume of investment will be larger if the investment schedule shifts to the right. Factors that would cause the investment schedule to shift to the right are: a more optimistic psychological attitude prevailing in the business community, important scientific and technological innovations, lower corporate income taxes, and lower labor costs. Any of these changes would cause business enterprises to invest more even though interest rates were unchanged. An improvement in psychological expectations, for example, would increase the expected annual net return from capital expenditures and thus the *MEI,* and an increase in the *MEI* relative to the cost of borrowing would increase the total amount of net investment. Also, scientific and engineering improvements increase net investment by reducing the cost of capital equipment. This lowers the denominator of the formula for the *MEI* and thus increases the marginal efficiency of some investments relative to the cost of borrowing. If technological advances come in spurts, this would cause similar irregular changes in the *MEI* and in the volume of investment. In addition, a reduction in any of the costs that are involved in the use of capital also has a stimulating effect on investment. For example, lower labor costs or lower taxes would increase the expected annual net return and thus the marginal efficiency of investment.

INVESTMENT AND INCOME

The third and final step in the interest rate–investment theory is shown in Figure 18.4. Although the vertical axis of this figure measures the amount of saving or investment rather than total spending $(C + I + G)$, it shows the same relationships as shown in Figure 17.2. In both Figure 17.2 and Figure 18.4, the equilibrium level of national income is where saving is equal to investment. In Figure 18.4, a fall in interest rates would shift the investment schedule upward from I_1 to I_2, increasing the equilibrium level of national income from $600 billion to $620 billion. The net investment schedule would shift upward if lower interest rates caused business firms to spend more for additional capital goods. The amount of desired net investment is now $50 billion compared to desired saving of $40 billion. This has a stimulating effect on total spending; and as income increases, desired saving increases more rapidly than desired net investment, until at a level of national income of $620 billion desired saving is equal to desired net investment.

In 1973 total *personal saving* amounted to approximately $53 billion. People received $883 billion of disposable income—income left over after the payment of all taxes but including income from welfare payments. Of the $830 billion spent for consumption during the year, $805 billion went for consumer goods and services—food, clothing, rent, transportation, and so on—and $25 billion mostly for interest on consumer loans and mortgages. The $53 billion saved—the difference between disposable income and consumption—is used for such things as purchases of corporation stocks, U.S. savings bonds, or savings deposits in savings banks. The most important factor determining the amount of personal saving each year is the size of people's incomes. Figure 18.4 shows that when people's incomes increase, saving increases. This is be-

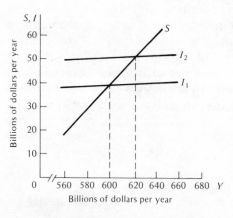

Figure 18.4   Effect on Income of Increase in Net Investment

cause an increase in current income causes people to want to accumulate more assets to provide also for a larger income in the future when they retire. It is reasonable that when incomes rise, people would want to increase both their current consumption and—through saving—their future consumption. At very low levels of national income, the amount of saving may be negative. Such conditions are rare, but, in a severe depression, people may spend for consumption more than their incomes— by using past savings or by borrowing.

In addition to personal saving, a considerable portion of total saving in the economy consists of *business saving* in the form of retained profits. The saving schedule in Figure 18.4 includes personal and business saving, but not the portion of the gross receipts of business firms used to maintain depreciating capital equipment, even though depreciation expenditures are also a type of business saving. Business as well as personal saving would be expected to rise with an increase in income. Business saving usually rises when total profits become larger and declines when total profits are smaller.

An important characteristic of the saving function is that the *average propensity to save (APS)* increases as income increases. The average propensity to save is the ratio of total saving to national income:

$$APS = \frac{Saving}{National\ income} = \frac{S}{Y}$$

In Figure 18.4, when income is \$600 billion, the *APS* is 6.7 percent, and when the level of income rises to \$620 billion, the *APS* rises to 8.1 percent. It was originally thought that in the long run the *APS* would be higher when incomes were larger because people would not need to consume as much: they could afford to save. This "need" theory has gradually been replaced by other theories, such as the *permanent income hypothesis*. Over the years, the *APS* in the United States has not become larger as incomes have risen. People tend to save the same proportion of their incomes today as they did many years ago when average incomes were much lower. Nor have comparisons of different countries supported the hypothesis that the higher the level of income, the larger the *APS*. The *APS* for some countries with relatively low per capita incomes is higher than for other countries with high per capita incomes. In some poor countries, there is considerable saving for various needs such as education, marriage dowries, and ceremonies—and this saving has not all been done by a few wealthy individuals.

Even though the *APS* has not increased over the years, it usually does vary cyclically, rising in periods of prosperity and falling in periods of contraction. The saving function in Figure 18.4 is of this type and is known as a *short-run saving function* to distinguish it from the *long-run saving function* in which the *APS* is constant. According to the permanent income hypothesis, when incomes rise, many of those receiving a higher income view this increase as transient. As a result, they do not increase their consumption as much as their incomes. Since that portion of income not consumed is saved, saving as a proportion of income tends to increase. Only if the higher level of income continues do people view the increase in their incomes as permanent and adjust their consumption and saving to the rise in their incomes. The opposite occurs when incomes fall. People view the decline in their incomes as temporary and do not reduce the level of their consumption as much as the drop in their incomes. As a result, the *APS* falls.

Although income is the most important determinant of the total volume of saving in the economy, other factors that may affect saving are interest rates, wealth, expectations regarding inflation, the stock of consumer goods, and attitudes of optimism and pessimism concerning the future. A change in any of these other factors causes the saving schedule to shift either upward or downward. Higher interest rates, for example, might cause the saving function to shift upward because of the greater attractiveness of saving. Or a more confident attitude toward the stability of the economy might shift the saving function downward.

Table 18.3 shows the changes from 1964 to 1973 in two measures of the average propensity to save—the ratio of personal saving to disposable income and the ratio of personal saving plus retained profits to the *NNP*. The ratio of personal saving to disposable income has varied from 6.0 percent to 8.1 percent, and the ratio of personal saving plus retained profits to the net national product has varied from 6.9 percent to 9.1 percent. During this period, the *APS* did not rise in every year even though income did. In 1968, 1969, and 1972, personal saving declined despite the large increases in disposable income—persons spent roughly the entire increase in their incomes on consumption. Nor did the change in personal saving plus retained profits in these same years parallel the substantial increases in *NNP*. When saving does not increase even though income has increased, the saving schedule has shifted downward, indicating that other factors decreasing saving have offset the usual expansionary effect on saving of an increase in income.

In Figure 18.4, the investment schedule rises slightly, but not nearly as steeply as the saving function. The investment function slopes upward because spending for additional capital equipment is related to the capacity utilization of existing facilities. When income is high, plants tend to operate closer to capacity, stimulating the expansion of facilities. On the other hand, when income is low, plants are probably operating far below capacity, discouraging the expansion of existing facilities. Unless

Table 18.3
Two Measures of the Average Propensity
to Save, 1964–1973

YEAR	PERSONAL SAVING	DISPOS-ABLE INCOME	RATIO OF PERSONAL SAVING TO DISPOSABLE INCOME	RETAINED COR-PORATE PROFITS	PERSONAL SAVING PLUS RETAINED PROFITS	NNP	RATIO OF PERSONAL SAVING PLUS RETAINED PROFITS TO NNP
	(in billions)				(in billions)		
1964	$26.2	$438	6.0%	$20.6	$46.8	$ 576.3	8.1%
1965	28.4	473	6.0	26.7	55.1	625.1	8.8
1966	32.5	512	6.3	29.1	61.6	685.9	9.0
1967	40.4	546	7.4	25.3	65.7	725.0	9.1
1968	39.8	591	6.7	24.2	64.0	789.7	8.1
1969	38.2	634	6.0	20.5	58.7	848.7	6.9
1970	56.2	692	8.1	14.6	70.8	889.8	8.0
1971	60.2	746	8.1	22.5	82.7	961.6	8.6
1972	49.7	797	6.2	29.3	79.0	1,052.8	7.5
1973	53.8	883	6.1	42.4	96.2	1,178.6	8.2

Source: *Economic Report of the President, February 1974,* pp. 265, 268, and 335.

the amount of net investment that business firms desire to make is as large as the amount of saving by persons and by businesses in the form of retained profits, the level of economic activity would decline. On the other hand, if businesses desire to acquire an amount of new capital that exceeds the volume of personal saving plus their retained earnings, business activity will expand.

If the economy is operating at less than full employment, and if it is assumed that prices are unchanged, an increase in investment relative to saving could have a stimulating effect on income by causing inventories to decline. When desired investment increases, aggregate demand increases relative to output, and unless output is increased so as to match the growth of aggregate demand, inventories would eventually be depleted. In Figure 18.4, the increase in investment of $10 billion causes income to rise from $600 to $620 billion. The increase in income is two times the increase in investment and the multiplier is equal to 2.

INTERACTION BETWEEN INTEREST RATES AND INCOME

The theory of the relationship between changes in the money supply and changes in income, as explained thus far, may be summarized briefly. An increase in the money supply tends to lower interest rates, the lower interest rates tend to increase investment, and the increase in investment tends to increase total spending. Assuming no change in prices and the existence of idle capacity in the economy, the increase in total spending causes an increase in real output. This is not a complete explanation because the increase in income has repercussions on the demand for money. As shown in Figure 18.5(a), the rise in income shifts the liquidity preference schedule (L) to the right. This limits the fall in interest rates to i_3. Because of the smaller decline in interest rates, total investment will be only I_3, and the smaller amount of investment limits the increase in income to Y_3. Still, the final result is an increase in the level of income.

The tendency for an expansionary monetary policy eventually to cause interest rates to rise is called the *income effect* on interest rates. The initial liquidity effect of monetary expansion causes interest rates to fall. The income effect is the result of the fact that a fall in interest rates may stimulate investment and thus increase income. The increase in income causes the liquidity preference schedule in Figure 18.5(a) to shift to the right because the higher the income expected, the larger the quantity of money people want to hold for convenience in making transactions and for security against contingencies. It has been estimated that it takes approximately eighteen months for the income effect to have its full impact on interest rates.

Although the income effect tends to reverse the downward movement of interest rates caused by the liquidity effect of an expansionary monetary policy, as shown in Figure 18.5(a), the final level of interest rates (i_3) is below the original level of interest rates (i_1). In this figure, interest rates cannot go back to the original level that existed prior to the expansion in the money supply. This is because interest rates would not

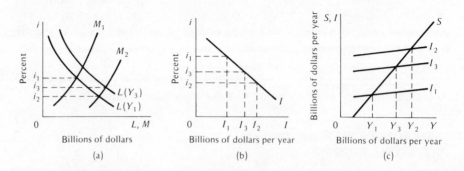

Figure 18.5   Graphic Description of the Sequence of Interest Rate–Investment Effects

rise at all unless there is an increase in income, and there would be no increase in income unless interest rates were below their original level.

THE LM–IS MODEL

In Figure 18.6, the three graphs in Figure 18.5 are consolidated into one graph based on six variables—the demand for money or liquidity preference (L), the supply of money (M), investment (I), saving (S), interest rates (i), and national income (Y). On the vertical axis of Figure 18.6 is interest rates, and on the horizontal axis is the national income. The LM schedule is based on points of equilibrium between the demand and supply of money. The IS schedule is based on points of equilibrium between saving and investment. At the point where the LM schedule crosses the IS schedule, there is a combination of national income and interest rates at which the demand for money is equal to the supply and saving is equal to investment.

The shape of the LM schedule is derived from Figure 18.7. In this figure, an increase in income would cause the liquidity preference schedule (L) to shift to the right from $L(Y_1)$ to $L(Y_2)$. At the original level of interest rates, i_1, the demand for money would be greater than the supply and would cause interest rates to rise from i_1 to i_2. The larger the increase in income, the further the L schedule would shift, and the higher interest rates would be. The upward-sloping LM schedule in Figure 18.6 shows that as Y increases, L will be equal to M only at higher interest rates. This relationship between interest rates and the national income is that found in different phases of the business cycle. In the expansion phase of the cycle when the national income is increasing, interest rates almost always do actually rise, and in the contraction phase, interest rates fall. The IS schedule in Figure 18.6 is derived from Figure 18.4. If interest rates fall, the investment schedule would shift upward, causing investment to be equal to saving at a higher level of income. The further the decline in

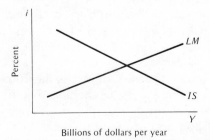

Billions of dollars per year

Figure 18.6   Income and Interest Rate Determination

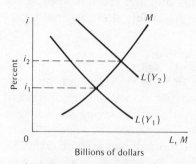

Figure 18.7   Effect on the Interest Rate of an Increase in the Demand for Money

interest rates, the larger the increase in income. The downward-sloping *IS* schedule shows that if interest rates fall, investment would be equal to saving at a higher level of income.

Shifts in either the *LM* or the *IS* schedule affect both income and interest rates. If the *LM* schedule shifts to the right, income rises and interest rates fall. If the *IS* schedule shifts to the right, both income and interest rates rise. The point of equilibrium is where the *LM* schedule intersects the *IS* schedule.

A shift of the *IS* schedule to the right may be caused by anything that increases the marginal efficiency of investment—more optimistic expectations, technological advances reducing the cost of capital, and lower labor costs or operating costs involved with the use of capital. As shown in Figure 18.4, changes of this type would raise the investment schedule and cause income to rise. Note that a fall in interest rates does not shift the *IS* schedule to the right. A shift of the *IS* schedule to the right occurs when investment increases because of changes other than a reduction in interest rates. When income rises because interest rates are lower, investment is equal to saving at a lower point on a *given IS* schedule.

A principal cause of a shift of the *LM* schedule to the right would be an expansionary monetary policy increasing the monetary base and thus the money supply. There are two ways of viewing a shift in the *LM* schedule to the right in Figure 18.6: at a given level of income (Y_1), *L* is now equal to *M* at a lower rate of interest; or at a given rate of interest, *L* is equal to *M* at a higher level of income. As was shown earlier (in Figure 18.1), a shift to the right of the money supply schedule would cause *M* to be equal to *L* at a lower rate of interest, assuming no change in the liquidity preference schedule (*L*) and no change in income. Also, if a shift of the money supply schedule to the right in Figure 18.1 is matched by a shift of the liquidity preference schedule to the right because of an increase in income, M could be equal to L at a higher level of income, but with no change in interest rates.

The LM schedule may also shift to the right if the money supply schedule (M_1 in Figure 18.1) is unchanged, and if the demand-for-money schedule (L) shifts to the left because of some other reason than a fall in income. L would again be equal to M at a lower interest rate. The factors that might cause the L schedule to shift to the left are greater confidence in the stability of the economy, the expectation of more rapid inflation, or an expected fall in interest rates (rise in bond prices).

In Figure 18.8, the effect of an expansionary monetary policy, shifting the LM schedule to the right, is to lower interest rates and increase income. If the IS schedule is unchanged, the initial effect of the increase in the LM schedule is to lower interest rates from i_1 to i_2. But at i_2, LM is not equal to IS. Neither interest rates nor income are at the point of equilibrium. The lower interest rates increase investment, and the increase in investment relative to saving raises the level of income from Y_1 to Y_2. The higher level of income would limit the fall in interest rates by causing the liquidity preference schedule to shift to the right, as shown in Figure 18.5(a). When interest rates are at i_3, income is at equilibrium at Y_2 because IS is then equal to LM.

THE LIQUIDITY TRAP

Under certain circumstances, an expansion in the money supply and a shift of the LM schedule to the right need not have the stimulating effect on income shown in Figure 18.8. It depends on the relationships between the demand for money and interest rates, and between interest rates and investment.

When interest rates are very low, for example, the liquidity preference schedule might become horizontal as shown in Figure 18.9. The

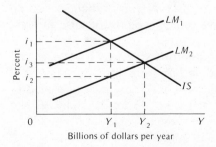

Figure 18.8   Effects on Income and Interest Rates of an Increase in the Money Supply

area in which the liquidity preference schedule is horizontal is called the liquidity trap. In that region a shift in the money supply schedule to the right would not cause a fall in interest rates. At very low rates of interest, it is believed that, because of the speculative motive for holding money, people might not attempt to shift from money to bonds, even though their money holdings are increased. When interest rates are at bottom levels, bond prices are at peak levels. People might expect that eventually bond prices will fall, and under such circumstances they might prefer to hold larger quantities of money rather than buy bonds.

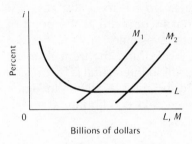

Figure 18.9   The Effect of an Increase in the Money Supply, Assuming a Liquidity Trap

When rates of interest are in the liquidity trap, a shift to the right in the money supply schedule does not shift the *LM* schedule to the right, and it would have no effect on interest rates, investment, or the level of income. In addition, an increase in income—which would shift the *L schedule* to the right, as in Figure 18.10—would not affect interest rates. Because of the trap, the quantity of money demanded would not exceed the supply and there would not be upward pressure on interest rates. Under these circumstances, the *LM* schedule would be perfectly elastic at a very low level of interest rates, as shown in Figure 18.11. A shift of the *IS* schedule to the right would cause income to rise, but it would not raise interest rates.

In recent years, there have been numerous statistical studies of the shape of the liquidity preference schedule.[3] There is little evidence that there ever has, in fact, been a liquidity trap, and most historical studies indicate that the liquidity preference schedule (*L*) has actually sloped downward. One study has estimated an *interest elasticity* of Money Supply I for the United States from 1900 to 1958 of about −0.7.[4] This interest elasticity of the demand for money is measured by the percentage change in the quantity of money divided by the percentage change in interest

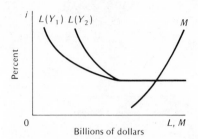

Figure 18.10   Interest Rates Are Unaffected When the Liquidity Preference Schedule Rises, Assuming a Liquidity Trap

rates. This estimated elasticity would mean that if the rate of interest fell 10 percent, the demand for money would rise 7 percent. Since World War II, interest rates have been rising and have become relatively high. The conditions in which one might expect a liquidity trap have not existed. The slope of the L schedule is no longer considered an important reason for doubting the effectiveness of monetary policy in influencing income. There is little doubt that the liquidity preference schedule (L) slopes downward and the LM schedule slopes upward.

WILL INVESTMENT BE LARGER WHEN INTEREST RATES FALL?

Another possible problem concerns whether or not the volume of investment will increase when interest rates fall. Even without a liquidity trap, if investment does not increase when interest rates fall, an increase in the money supply might not affect income. If the investment schedule were perfectly inelastic, as shown in Figure 18.12, the volume of investment

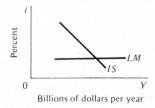

Figure 18.11   The LM Schedule Is Perfectly Elastic When There Is a Liquidity Trap

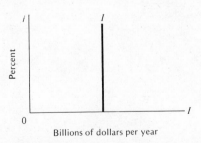

Figure 18.12 Changes in Interest Rates Have No Effect on Investment, Assuming an Inelastic Investment Schedule

would not vary with changes in the cost of borrowing money, investment would not increase relative to saving, and the level of income would be unaffected.

If the investment schedule is perfectly inelastic, the *IS* schedule is also perfectly inelastic as shown in Figure 18.13. Under these conditions, an increase in the *LM* schedule as a result of monetary policy would lower interest rates but would raise the level of income.

The belief that investment is not significantly affected by changes in interest rates has been widely held. For short-term investments, it was felt that interest rate costs were too unimportant to affect the volume of investment. Although interest costs were admitted to be important for long-term investment, many persons have thought that, compared to the other uncertainties, interest rates would not significantly affect decisions to invest. A large portion of capital spending, moreover, is financed with undistributed profits and depreciation reserves. The market rate of interest, it has been claimed, is irrelevant for such investment.

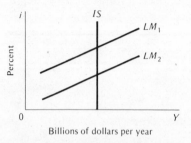

Figure 18.13 An Increase in the LM Schedule Lowers Interest Rates, but Has No Effect on Income, Assuming an Inelastic IS Schedule

There have been numerous statistical studies of the effect of changes in interest rates on investment.[5] The earliest studies tended to support the point of view that investment was not affected by changes in interest rates. Surveys asking businessmen whether their investment plans were affected by the rate of interest concluded that there was little effect. In the early regression studies, which were attempting to discover the determinants of investment, the rate of interest did not turn out to be an important variable. More recent studies have questioned the results of some of the earlier regression studies; and a growing number of studies have found certain types of investment to be affected by interest rates.

THE PIGOU EFFECT

The discussion of monetary policy thus far has assumed no shifting of the IS schedule as a result of monetary policy. In Figure 18.8, the LM schedule shifted to the right while the IS schedule was unchanged. In fact, a rise in real balances, M/P, may shift the IS schedule to the right. Real cash balances may increase if the money supply is held constant and prices fall or if the money supply is increased and prices are unchanged. Shifts in the IS schedule as a result of changes in real balances are known as the Pigou effect.[6]

An increase in real cash balances may stimulate spending by increasing people's wealth. If people's real cash balances are increased, they might spend a larger percentage of their income for consumption and save less, because now that they are wealthier there is less need to save. Or if their wealth is decreased by a decline in real cash balances, they may consume less from their current income and save more because there is a greater need to accumulate additional wealth in order to provide adequately for the future. Wealth will always increase if real cash balances rise because of a fall in prices, the quantity of money being kept constant. However, wealth does not always increase when real cash balances rise because of an increase in the money supply. In the United States, increases in the money supply are usually the result of open-market purchases which take from people an amount of government securities equal to the increase in the money supply. Under such circumstances, wealth held by the public would not be increased. Only if the larger quantity of money were the result of mining gold, or of financing a deficit by printing more currency or creating deposits, would there be an increase in wealth.

In Figure 18.4, an increase in wealth as a result of larger real cash balances would lower the saving schedule, causing investment to be equal to saving at a higher level of income. Because interest rates are unchanged, this would cause the IS schedule to shift to the right. Assuming no change in the *LM* schedule, a shift of the *IS* schedule to the right would cause both income and interest rates to rise.

The Pigou effect is significant because it means that even if the economy were in a liquidity trap and the investment schedule were perfectly inelastic, a rise in real balances would still affect output. By holding the money supply constant while prices are falling, the monetary authorities could stimulate spending. Thus, monetary policy may affect spending either through its effect on interest rates or through changes in real cash balances. Early studies that took into account only the effects of interest rate changes led some economists to underestimate the power of monetary policy. On the other hand, those economists who question the power of monetary policy doubt that there is sufficient downward price flexibility in the economy to cause real cash balances to rise in a recession.

The principal importance of the Pigou effect is that it may play a crucial role in ensuring that there is an automatic tendency for the economy to operate at full employment. This would occur only if the Federal Reserve System avoids sharp fluctuations in the stock of money. In a recession, they must prevent the money stock from falling; and in periods of inflation, they must prevent the money supply from rising. The Pigou effect tends to eliminate persistent excess unemployment—because excess unemployment would tend to cause prices to fall. If the money supply were held constant, falling prices would increase real cash balances, have a stimulating effect on spending, and eventually eliminate the excess unemployment.

COMPARISON WITH THE PORTFOLIO ADJUSTMENT APPROACH

Although there are some similarities between the interest rate–investment and portfolio adjustment approaches to analyzing the relationship between changes in money and income, there are also differences between them:

1. The two theories view interest rates and their role differently. In the interest rate–investment approach, investment increases because interest rates (conceived of as the cost of borrowing money) fall relative to the marginal efficiency of investment. In the portfolio adjustment theory, investment is expected to increase because investments in capital goods become relatively more attractive than investments in other types of assets. When prices of bonds, stocks, and other assets rise, the rate of

return on them declines relative to the rate of return on capital goods. The effect of an expansionary monetary policy is transmitted to the market for capital goods because of a change in the relative prices of financial and real assets. In both approaches, monetary expansion causes interest rates to fall, but the portfolio adjustment theory views the changes in interest rates more broadly than a change in the cost of borrowing money.

2. In the two theories, the relationship between monetary policy and saving is different. In the interest rate–investment approach, it is usually assumed that monetary policy does not shift the saving schedule. In the portfolio adjustment approach, an expansionary monetary policy would shift the saving schedule downward, and a restraining policy would shift it upward. The point of view of the interest rate-investment approach is that even though an expansionary monetary policy lowering interest rates might reduce saving by lowering the rate of return to saving, if rates of interest fall, it takes a larger amount of saving to achieve a given target level of income. Because of these contradictory effects on saving, it was concluded that the effect of interest rate movements on saving was unclear. In the portfolio adjustment approach, it is believed that if the supply of money is increased relative to the demand, people will spend some of it on a variety of things—consumption goods as well as capital goods. The saving schedule would shift downward if an expansionary monetary policy caused people to spend a larger portion of their income for consumer goods.

There is also a difference in the conception of the process by which the increase in the money supply affects consumption and investment.[7] The interest rate–investment model suggests that a more expansionary monetary policy first stimulates investment, which then, through the multiplier, has secondary effects on consumption. In the portfolio adjustment approach, an expansionary monetary policy may first stimulate consumer demand and then have a stimulating effect on investment because an increase in the demand for capital goods is generated by the rising demand for consumer goods.

3. A third difference between the two approaches concerns the evidence of the effect of easier monetary conditions on investment. In connection with the interest rate–investment theory, it has been difficult to show statistically a relationship between interest rates and the volume of investment spending. In connection with the portfolio adjustment approach, however, it has not been difficult to show that a more expansionary monetary policy eventually results in an expansion in total bank loans. In the interest rate–investment theory, little attention is given to the effects of monetary policy on the markets for credit. In the portfolio adjustment approach, the expansion in total bank credit that may occur as a result of

open-market purchases is an important part of the transmission process. Because an expansion of bank loans would appear to be an indication of expanding investment, the effect of monetary policy on investment appears to be stronger when looked at from the perspective of portfolio adjustments.

4. A fourth difference concerns the movement of interest rates. In the interest rate–investment model, a more expansionary monetary policy must permanently lower interest rates. There is some overshooting; but unless interest rates remain lower than they were originally, there is no expansion in total income. In this approach, it is assumed that because of less than full employment, the more expansionary monetary policy causes a rise in real income rather than in prices. In the portfolio adjustment approach, the immediate effect of a more expansionary monetary policy is to lower interest rates; but eventually a more rapid rate of increase in the money supply causes nominal interest rates to rise and fully offset the initial decline in these rates. This is because in the long run an expansionary monetary policy raises interest rates not only because of the income effect, but also because of a *price anticipation effect*. The income effect is the result of the fact that when people have excess money holdings, there will be stimulating effects on spending that will increase the demand for loanable funds, causing interest rates to rise. Also, a rise in income would shift the liquidity preference schedule to the right, causing interest rates to rise.

The price anticipation effect results if people come to anticipate a more rapid rise in prices as a result of the more rapid increase in the money supply. The higher the rate of inflation, the more costly it is for people to hold money. Because people prefer to hold less money relative to their incomes when they anticipate a more rapid rate of inflation, the velocity of money increases, causing prices to rise more rapidly than would be expected solely because of the increase in the money supply. The more rapid rate of inflation causes nominal interest rates to rise, because people will attempt to protect themselves against inflation and will be unwilling to invest in securities unless the rate of return exceeds the rate of inflation that they expect. The long-run tendency for a more rapid increase in the money supply to cause nominal interest rates to rise, and for a slower increase to cause nominal interest rates to fall, is well supported by comparisons of different countries. In Brazil, Argentina, and Chile, where rates of increase in the money supply and rates of inflation are very high, interest rates are also very high. In Switzerland, the United States, and other countries where rates of inflation have been low, interest rates have been relatively low. Also, the results of recent statistical studies of the relationship between money and interest rates in the United States support the point of view of the portfolio adjustment approach that although a more expansionary monetary policy reduces interest rates for a period of several months, eventually the effect is to raise nominal interest rates.[8]

SUMMARY

Changes in the money supply may affect national income through their effects on interest rates and investment. In the interest rate–investment theory, the strength of monetary policy depends on how responsive interest rates are to changes in the quantity of money, how responsive investment is to changes in interest rates, and how large the increase in income is when investment increases.

The immediate effect of an increase in the money supply is to lower interest rates. By causing the supply of money to be greater than the demand for money, an expansionary monetary policy induces persons to purchase bonds and lower their yields.

Lower interest rates may increase the amount of investment spending by lowering the cost of borrowing relative to the rates of profit that business managers estimate they can obtain from capital expenditures.

In real terms, disregarding any changes in prices, saving will be equal to investment under equilibrium conditions. If investment is larger than saving, inventories will fall, and if saving exceeds investment, inventories will rise.

Real cash balances rise when prices fall, and they decline when prices go up. By affecting the amount of wealth that people have, changes in real cash balances have significant effects on total spending—causing spending to rise when real cash balances get larger and to fall when real cash balances get smaller. If prices were flexible, changes in real cash balances would have important effects on total spending.

NOTES

1. See Milton Friedman, "Factors Affecting the Level of Interest Rates," *Savings and Residential Financing, 1968 Conference Proceedings* (Chicago: United States Savings and Loan League, 1968), pp. 10–27.
2. William E. Gibson, "Interest Rates and Monetary Policy," *Journal of Political Economy* 78 (May–June 1970), p. 453.
3. David E. W. Laidler, *The Demand for Money: Theories and Evi-*

dence (Scranton, Pa.: International Textbook Company, 1969), pp. 79–119.

4. *Ibid.*, p. 94. This summarizes the results in Allan Meltzer, "The Demand for Money: The Evidence from the Time Series," *Journal of Political Economy* 71 (June 1963), pp. 219–246.

5. See the summary of these studies in Thomas Mayer, *Monetary Policy in the United States* (New York: Random House, 1968), pp. 120–123.

6. See A. C. Pigou, "The Classical Stationary State," *Economic Journal* 53 (December 1943), pp. 343–351.

7. "Monetary Policy and Corporate Capital Spending," First National City Bank, *Monthly Economic Letter* (New York, April 1970), pp. 42–45.

8. William E. Gibson, "Price-Expectations Effects on Interest Rates," *Journal of Finance* 25 (March 1970), pp. 19–34.

QUESTIONS

18.1. Why does the liquidity preference schedule slope downward?

18.2. What are some factors that can cause the liquidity preference schedule to shift to the right? Explain why.

18.3. Explain the way in which an increase in the money supply may lower interest rates.

18.4. What are the different types of investment spending?

18.5. Define the marginal efficiency of investment.

18.6. Why does investment increase when interest rates fall?

18.7. Draw on a graph and explain the shape of the saving function showing the relationship between saving and income.

18.8. Define the average propensity to save.

18.9. Draw a graph showing the *LM* and *IS* schedules. Why does the *LM* schedule slope upward to the right? Why does the *IS* schedule slope downward to the right?

18.10. What are some factors that may cause the *IS* schedule to shift to the right? Explain why.

18.11. Explain how an increase in the money supply may cause the *LM* schedule to shift to the right.

18.12. If interest rates are in the liquidity trap, explain why monetary policy would be unable to affect income.

18.13. If the investment function is inelastic, explain why monetary policy would be unable to affect the level of income.

18.14. Define the Pigou effect.

18.15.   It is claimed that the Pigou effect would stimulate recovery in a period of depression—if the Federal Reserve System prevents a decline in the money stock. Explain.

18.16.   What are the major differences between the portfolio adjustment and the interest rate–investment explanations of the relationship between the money supply and the national income?

18.17.   Know the meaning and significance of the following terms and concepts: liquidity preference schedule, net private domestic investment, marginal efficiency of investment, personal saving, business saving, short-run saving function, long-run saving function, average propensity to save, permanent income hypothesis, liquidity trap, inelastic investment schedule, Pigou effect, liquidity effect on interest rates, income effect on interest rates, price anticipation effect on interest rates.

Chapter 19
Fiscal Policy

If budget deficits are financed by new money there is an automatic relationship between fiscal and monetary policy—the larger the deficit, the larger the expansion in the money supply. When budget deficits are financed by borrowing, fiscal and monetary policy may move in opposite directions.

Fiscal policy involves primarily the use of the powers of the federal government to tax and spend so as to influence overall economic activity. But fiscal policy may also be significantly related to monetary policy. If expenditures are increased without an equivalent increase in taxes, the funds to pay for the excess expenditures must be obtained in some way. The government might raise the funds needed by borrowing, thus increasing the amount of its debt. If the needed revenue were obtained by creating additional money, fiscal policy would affect the quantity of money. On the other hand, when there is a budget surplus and taxes exceed expenditures, the surplus could be used to retire outstanding government securities; or it could be used to reduce the money supply. There is little disagreement among economists that fiscal deficits financed by new money are expansionary. But there are differences of opinion concerning the effects on aggregate demand of deficits financed by borrowing.

NATURE OF FISCAL POLICY

When the government increases its tax revenues, it takes from individuals and businesses some of the income they would otherwise have received. With lower incomes, they have less money available to spend for consumption and investment. On the other hand, when the government raises its expenditures, there tends to be an increase in total spending. The government spending may be for a variety of things—military equipment, office buildings, the services of teachers, larger social security benefits, or subsidies to farmers that will enhance their purchasing power.

If the reduction in spending because of heavier taxes were just equal to the increase in spending because of larger government expenditures, the government's fiscal policies would not have much effect on total spending. But there is not always such a balance. The government may attempt to control the relationship between its taxes and its spending, sometimes increasing and sometimes decreasing total spending in the economy. A stimulating fiscal policy involves either reducing taxes or increasing government expenditures or both. To restrain the economy, the federal government would do the opposite—increase taxes or reduce government spending.

Over the years, concepts of appropriate fiscal policy have changed.[1] Starting in the 1930s when rates of unemployment were high, full employment gradually became more important as a goal of fiscal policy, and the primary emphasis was on increasing government *expenditures* as a method of stimulating recovery. At that time, income taxes did not cover many persons, and because income taxes were not withheld, a reduction in taxes would not have had the immediate effect it has today. During World War II, budget deficits became more widely accepted as the way to achieve full employment. Changes in *taxes* as well as in expenditures became a central part of fiscal policy. The wartime achievement of full employment added further to the interest in fiscal tools. Near the end of the war, it was widely feared that the war would be followed by a serious depression unless the economy were stimulated by appropriate fiscal policies.[2] This led to the enactment of the Employment Act of 1946—"to promote maximum employment, production, and purchasing power." The Council of Economic Advisers, established by this act, is the principal group in the executive branch of the federal government responsible for the formation of fiscal policy, and its members assist the president in making a required economic report to Congress at the beginning of each year.

A principal difficulty in administering fiscal policy is its inflexibility. Most decisions to make changes in taxes and expenditures must go through Congress. The process is slow, and short-term political considerations may influence the actions taken. By the time action is taken, it is often less appropriate than it was when first proposed. It often takes over a year between the time a change in taxes is first proposed by the president and the time it is enacted.

The way in which tax revenues and government expenditures are affected by changes in business conditions complicates the administration of fiscal policy. When the economy prospers, tax receipts rise automatically, tending to create a budget surplus. When there is a recession, some government expenditures, such as those for relief, rise automatically while tax receipts fall off, creating a budget deficit. For many years, these changes were referred to as *automatic stabilizers*. It was felt that they helped to restrain inflationary pressures and to moderate recessions, and they were believed to be particularly desirable because of the slowness of congressional changes in taxes and government spending. In the 1960s, the attitude toward the automatic stabilizers changed. The tendency of taxes to rise while unemployment was still above 4 percent was referred to as a *fiscal drag*. It was felt that the decline in total spending resulting from the rapid rise in taxes was keeping the economy from operating at its full potential. Even so, the automatic movements of taxes and expenditures have the important characteristic of varying countercyclically.

ALTERNATIVE WAYS OF FINANCING DEFICITS

If a fiscal deficit is financed by borrowing, the sale of government securities provides the funds needed to pay for an excess of expenditures over tax revenues. The total amount of the national debt is increased. The owners of the new securities receive interest, and there is an increase in the government's expenditures for interest.

In countries in which the money supply consists largely of paper money, little more is required than a printing press to finance a deficit by creating money. The government pays for the excess of its expenditures over revenues with new paper bills. The Continental currency issued during the Revolutionary War involved this type of finance.

With modern central banking, many countries finance fiscal deficits by creating money—demand deposits or paper notes—with the assistance of the central bank. The treasury department of the country typically would sell its bonds directly to its central bank in return for either deposits or paper notes. Assume that the treasury department wishes the new money to be half in deposits and half in central bank notes. The effect on the central bank's balance sheet would be as follows:

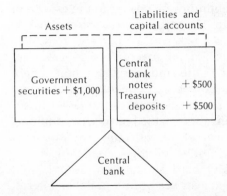

The central bank receives interest on the government securities it has acquired, but this is usually unimportant because modern central banks are almost always public institutions, and the additional income they receive would be returned to the treasury. When the treasury spends the new central bank notes and deposits, the persons acquiring them would in turn spend them again, and the notes and deposits would continue to circulate in the economy.

The way in which the United States Treasury finances a fiscal deficit by new money is slightly different from the process just described. But the result is the same, even though money-creation to finance the deficit appears to be borrowing. Such money-creation occurs in the United States if at the same time that the Treasury is selling new securities to the public the Federal Reserve banks are purchasing them in the open market. When the Federal Reserve banks and the United States Treasury act together in this way, no additional U.S. government securities need be held by the public, and there is no additional borrowing from the public. There is, however, an expansion in the money supply because of the open-market purchases. The increase in bank reserves created by open-market purchases enables the commercial banks to expand their loans and investments, and there would be a multiple expansion in their deposits. The additional reserves that banks receive as a result of open-market purchases may be used to purchase a portion of the additional U.S. government securities issued to finance the deficit.

The expansion of the money supply in the United States during the past two decades has been quite closely related to the size of the Treasury's fiscal deficits.[3] Figure 19.1 shows the similar trends from 1952 to 1973 in (1) the total federal government debt held by private investors and the Federal Reserve banks, (2) the total federal government debt held by the Federal Reserve System alone, and (3) Money Supply I. From 1952 to 1961, the average annual rate of growth in federal government debt was only 1 percent because of small budget deficits in those years. In the 1960s, budget deficits increased because of more rapid rates of expansion in both defense and nondefense expenditures compared to the growth of tax receipts. The federal debt rose to 1.5 percent a year from 1961 to 1966, 2.6 percent a year from 1966 to 1970, and 5.4 percent from 1970 to 1974. The accelerated expansion in federal government debt was accompanied by a more rapid expansion in the amount of government debt purchased by the Federal Reserve banks, and consequently a more rapid expansion in Money Supply I. Larger budget deficits lead to larger open-market purchases because the short-run effect of the issuance of additional government securities is to increase market interest rates. The monetary authorities purchase government securities during periods of deficit financing in order to counteract this upward pressure on interest rates. Over the years, one of their major objectives has been to stabilize interest

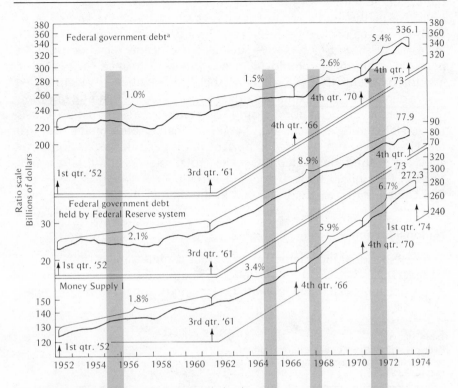

[a]The sum of debt held by the Federal Reserve banks and private investors
Shaded areas represent periods of business recession.   Percentages are annual rates of change.   Latest data plotted: Money supply—1st quarter of 1974: others—4th quarter of 1973.

Figure 19.1   Trends of Federal Government Debt and Monetary Expansion, 1952–1973 (seasonally adjusted data)

Source: Federal Reserve Bank of St. Louis, *Review,* May 1974, p. 3.

rates. A side effect of using open-market purchases to prevent interest rates from rising is to increase the supply of money and bank credit.

MEASURING FISCAL POLICY

The federal government has three types of budgets showing the changes in its expenditures and receipts: the unified budget, the national income accounts budget, and the high-employment budget.[4]

Unified Budget

The unified-budget concept first replaced several other budget concepts in the fiscal year 1969. The amounts of the principal types of receipts and outlays in the budget for the fiscal year 1973 are shown in Table 19.1. The objective of this budget is to show the cash flows of the United States Treasury. A major change from the previous budget concepts was the inclusion of the trust accounts—such as those of the Social Security Administration. Both the employment taxes used to finance social security and the payments to those receiving social security benefits were added. The expenditures in the unified budget also include the lending of various federal credit agencies for housing, agriculture, and international assistance. Net lending is equal to the excess of loan disbursements over loan repayments and has become important because of the expansion in the activities of the federal credit agencies. Total receipts and total expenditures in the unified budget from 1964 to 1973 are shown in Table 19.2. The United States has had a deficit in the unified budget in most years.

National Income Accounts Budget

The new national income accounts budget is quite similar to the unified budget, but is based on a conception of output used in the national income accounts. Like the unified budget, it includes both the regular

Table 19.1
Receipts and Outlays in the Unified Budget
of the United States, Fiscal Year 1973 (in
billions of dollars)

Receipts:		
Individual income taxes	$103.2	
Social insurance taxes	64.5	
Corporation income taxes	36.2	
Excise taxes	16.3	
All other	12.0	
Total		$232.2
Outlays:		
Defense, space, foreign affairs	$ 82.3	
Agriculture, natural resources, transportation, housing	24.0	
Education, health, income security, veterans	113.7	
General government	5.5	
Revenue sharing	6.6	
Interest	22.8	
Intragovernmental transactions	—8.4	
Total		$246.5
Budget deficit		$ 14.3

Source: *Economic Report of the President, February 1974* (Washington, D.C.: U.S. Government Printing Office, 1974), p. 326.

Table 19.2
Unified Budget of the United States, 1964–
1973 (in billions of dollars)

FISCAL YEAR	RECEIPTS	EXPENDITURES AND NET LENDING	SURPLUS (+) OR DEFICIT (−)
1964	$112.7	$118.6	−$5.9
1965	116.8	118.4	− 1.6
1966	130.9	134.7	− 3.8
1967	149.6	158.3	− 8.7
1968	153.7	178.8	−25.2
1969	187.8	184.5	+ 3.2
1970	193.7	196.6	− 2.8
1971	188.4	211.4	−23.0
1972	208.6	231.9	−23.2
1973	232.2	246.5	−14.3

Details do not add to totals because of rounding.
Source: Federal Reserve Bank of St. Louis, *Federal Budget Trends,* various issues.

government transactions and trust fund accounts. The government's contributions to government employee retirement are included as part of compensation. The expenditures also include both income-generating purchases of goods and services and transfer payments that enhance the purchasing power of the private sector. Net lending is not included in expenditures, as it is in the unified budget. The purchase and sale of existing real and financial assets are also excluded because they do not represent current income or production. Expenditures are recorded when delivery is made to the government, and taxes are usually recorded when the tax liability is incurred.

High-Employment Budget

Use of the high-employment budget was developed in the 1960s. If this budget shows a growing deficit, it means that the federal government has altered its tax and expenditure programs so as to make its fiscal policy easier. If it shows a growing surplus, it means that the federal government has adopted a more restraining fiscal policy. In this budget, both the estimated tax revenues and expenditures of the national income accounts budget are adjusted to show what they would be if the economy were operating at a steady and high level of employment. For example, although tax receipts might be relatively low because unemployment was high, this budget would show what the level of tax receipts would be if the level of unemployment were approximately 4 percent. By holding the level of resource use constant, the high-employment budget attempts to measure the effect solely of the changes in fiscal policy made by the governmental authorities. The unified and national income accounts budgets are affected by changes in the level of economic activity. The concept of the high-employment budget was developed to provide a measure of fiscal policy that does not reflect changes in the level of the national income. Such a measure is useful for planning fiscal and monetary policy and for appraising past policy decisions. Although changes in the high-employment budget are a better measure of the direction of fiscal policy than changes in the unified or national income accounts budgets, use of the high-employment budget has several limitations.[5] The impact of government expenditures begins when business firms start producing to fill government contracts rather than when government expenditures are made, as shown by the high-employment budget. On the revenue side, the impact of taxes on private expenditures probably occurs when persons and business firms start to accrue funds to pay taxes rather than when they pay the taxes. The national income accounts treat corporate taxes on an accrual basis, but personal taxes are on a cash basis. There are also problems in measuring high employment expenditures and receipts. It is not certain that 4 percent unemployment is the proper target for high employment. If the correct target were 5 percent unemployment, that should be used to estimate high-employment expenditures and receipts rather than the usual 4 percent.

Table 19.3
High-Employment Budget, United States,
1964–1973 (in billions of dollars)

FISCAL YEAR	RECEIPTS	EXPENDITURES	SURPLUS (+) OR DEFICIT (−)
1964	$125.5	$115.6	+$9.9
1965	124.7	118.4	+ 6.3
1966	131.3	132.3	− 1.0
1967	146.4	154.8	− 8.3
1968	159.5	172.5	−13.0
1969	191.4	186.2	+ 5.1
1970	207.5	195.8	+11.7
1971	213.0	209.1	+ 3.9
1972	226.5	229.2	− 2.7
1973	249.4	252.3	− 3.0

Source: *Federal Reserve Bank of St. Louis, Federal Budget Trends,* various issues.

Measuring Budgetary Effects

The usual way of measuring the economic effect of fiscal policy is by the change in the deficit or surplus from one year to the next. Consider the change from 1972 to 1973 in the unified budget shown in Table 19.2. The deficit fell from $23 billion to $14 billion. Taxes increased almost $24 billion, but expenditures increased less—by $15 billion. The larger increase in taxes than in government expenditures withdrew funds from the spending stream. The net deflationary effect on total spending was $9 billion. The larger the decrease in the deficit, the more deflationary the impact would be. Table 19.2 shows that the effects of fiscal policy became more expansionary each year from 1965 to 1968 and may have contributed to the remarkably long cyclical expansion that occurred in the 1960s and the inflation that developed. Note that having a deficit does not necessarily indicate that fiscal policy is expansionary, and that having a surplus does not necessarily indicate that fiscal policy is restraining. Fiscal policy is expansionary only if the deficit is getting larger or the surplus is getting smaller, and it would be restraining only if the deficit is becoming smaller or the surplus larger.

Another way in which the economic impact of fiscal policy is measured is by changes in government expenditures. The larger the increase in such spending, the larger the expected impact on the national income. The use of this measure of fiscal policy is the result of the development of econometric forecasting models in which it has been found that historically the increase in total government expenditures is more closely related to the national income than changes either in taxes or in the budget deficit. An interesting study by Andersen and Jordan of the Federal Reserve Bank of St. Louis found that an increase in government spending is mildly stimulative in the quarter in which spending is increased and in the following quarter.[6] In the subsequent two quarters, there are offsetting negative influences, and the overall effect is relatively small. This study found no evidence that fiscal actions, as measured by the high-employment budget or changes in tax receipts due to changes in tax rates, have a significant effect on GNP.

FISCAL POLICY AND INCOME

The way changes in fiscal policy may cause changes in total spending may be explained with the same figures as those used in Chapter 18 to show the effects of changes in the money supply. Consider first a partial explanation that does not take into consideration the way the deficit is financed.

Partial Explanation of the Effect of Fiscal Policy on Income

The initial effect of fiscal policy on income may be illustrated by the two graphs in Figure 19.2. The $S + T$ schedule includes taxes and saving. The $I + G$ schedule includes government spending and investment. Taxes are like saving, because they are part of a person's income not spent for consumption. Government purchases of goods and services are like private investment. Both are types of autonomous spending and are determined primarily by factors other than the level of national income. In the example in Figure 19.2(a), increased government spending has shifted the $I + G$ schedule upward, and it is assumed that taxes and the $S + T$ schedule are unchanged. In Figure 19.2(b), lower taxes have shifted the $S + T$ schedule downward, and it is assumed that government spending is unchanged. The $S + T$ schedule falls when taxes are reduced because of the smaller proportion of income withdrawn from consumption.

An increase in government expenditures, assuming no change in taxes, would cause a rise in either real output or prices. At Y_1 in Figure 19.2(a), $(I + G)_2$ would be larger than $S + T$. Income would rise to Y_2. A decrease in taxes, assuming no change in government spending, would also be expansionary. At Y_1 in Figure 19.2(b), $I + G$ would again be larger than $(S + T)_2$. Both increasing government expenditures and lowering taxes would have an expansionary effect because they cause aggregate demand to increase, and either real output or prices would rise in response to the larger demand. Also, both of these fiscal policies have a multiplier effect. The increase in income is greater than the increase in government expenditures or the decrease in tax receipts.

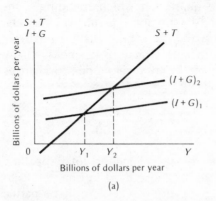

(a)

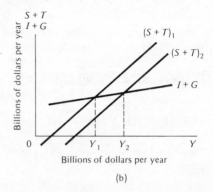

(b)

Figure 19.2   Effects of Fiscal Policy on Expenditures and Income

The Relationship between Fiscal Policy and Income, Taking into Consideration the Way the Deficit Is Financed

An analysis of fiscal policy that includes consideration of the way the deficit is financed is shown in Figure 19.3. Included is the income-expenditure graph shown in Figure 19.2, but added to it is an *LM-IS* graph and a liquidity preference graph. In the *LM-IS* graph, government expenditures are combined with investment, and tax revenues are combined with saving, as they were in Figure 19.2. Assume (1) an increase in government spending, (2) no change in taxes, and (3) a deficit financed by borrowing. The case of a deficit financed by borrowing is of particular interest because there is disagreement among economists as to how expansionary such a fiscal policy may be. Initially the $I + G$ schedule would rise to $(I + G)_2$, and the equilibrium level of income would rise from Y_1 to Y_2. The cause of this shift in the $I + G$ schedule is different from the cause of the shift of the I schedule in Figure 18.4 in the last chapter. It is due to an autonomous increase in government spending, not an increase in investment because of lower interest rates. An increase in government spending shifts to the right the *IS* schedule in the *LM-IS* graph in Figure 19.3(b).

Because the deficit is financed by borrowing, the money supply schedule in Figure 19.3(c) is unchanged. The increase in national income shifts the L schedule to the right by increasing the amount of money people want for transactions and for precautionary needs. This brings about a rise in interest rates to i_2. At the original level of interest rates, i_1, the quantity of money demanded would be larger than the supply. As interest rates rise, the quantity demanded decreases and the supply increases until they are equal at i_2.

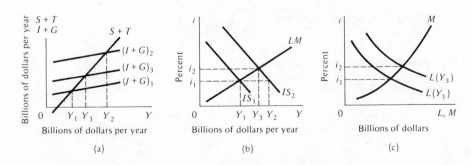

Figure 19.3 **Graphic Description of the Interaction of the Effects of Fiscal Policy on Expenditures and Interest Rates**

The rise in interest rates would then tend to reduce investment somewhat, and in Figure 19.3(a) the $(I + G)_2$ schedule would drop to $(I + G)_3$. This would limit the increase in income to Y_3. Even though the rise in interest rates causes income to be smaller, interest rates would not have risen in the first place unless income were larger. The $I + G$ schedule cannot fall back to its original level. On the LM-IS graph, the final equilibrium between LM and IS is at Y_3 and i_2. Given an upward-sloping LM schedule, a shift of the IS schedule to the right must increase both the national income and interest rates.

The precise effect of fiscal policy on national income depends on the shapes of the IS and LM schedules. To take an extreme case, suppose the LM schedule were horizontal as shown in Figure 19.4(a). If the LM schedule is perfectly elastic, it means that when an increase in income shifts the L schedule to the right as in Figure 19.4(b), interest rates would be unaffected because of the liquidity trap. Compare this with the rise in interest rates resulting from an increase in income shown in Figure 19.3(c). If fiscal policy does not cause interest rates to rise, it would have the maximum effect on income because investment would not decline and would not offset in part the increase in government spending. The LM schedule would not be perfectly horizontal unless interest rates were very low and the economy very depressed. Although such conditions would be extreme, the purpose of this example is to show that the smaller the rise of interest rates, the more expansionary fiscal policy will be.

Consider another possible condition—a vertical IS schedule as in Figure 19.5. The IS schedule would be perfectly inelastic if investment were completely unaffected by interest rates. Even if interest rates rose because of an expansionary fiscal policy, the rise would have no effect on investment. Under these conditions, a shift of the IS schedule to the right because of increased government spending would have the maxi-

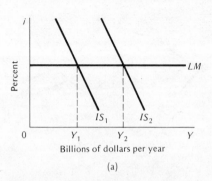

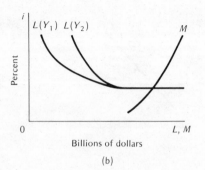

(a)

(b)

Figure 19.4 Effect of Fiscal Policy on Income, Assuming a Liquidity Trap

mum possible effect on income. Although it is unlikely that changes in interest rates would have no effect on investment, the purpose of this illustration is also to show that the less the decline in investment because of the rise in interest rates, the more expansionary the fiscal policy financed by borrowing will be. Note that the examples in Figures 19.4 and 19.5 show that the conditions in which fiscal policy is most expansionary —interest rates at liquidity trap levels and an inelastic investment schedule—are the same as those in which monetary policy is least effective.

Other Effects of an Expansionary Fiscal Policy

In addition to the stimulating effect on aggregate demand of increases in government spending and lower tax receipts, there are other effects of an expansionary fiscal policy financed by borrowing that may both add to the expansionary effect or counteract it. The results of those effects are ambiguous. The additional government securities created to finance a fiscal deficit may have an additional stimulating effect on total spending, by adding to total wealth. An increase in total wealth would reduce saving, lower the $S + T$ schedule in Figure 19.3(a), and cause an increase in total output. Stimulating effects on velocity might also occur as a result of the higher interest rates caused by the additional borrowing. Expected higher interest rates would reduce the demand for money and increase the velocity of money. Given a constant money stock, if velocity rises, there would be a stimulating effect on output. On the other hand, the increase in the supply of bonds might have a restraining effect on spending by causing people to want to hold more money to match the increase in their holdings of bonds. This would cause a leftward shift in the LM schedule and, given the IS schedule, would tend to lower the equilibrium level of income.[7] The LM schedule would shift leftward if the increase in wealth caused the liquidity preference schedule to shift to the right.

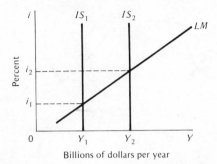

Billions of dollars per year

Figure 19.5 Effect of Fiscal Policy on Income, Assuming an Inelastic Investment Schedule

Given the money supply, the demand for money would be equal to the supply at a higher rate of interest with no change in income. In addition, if interest rates rise as a result of additional borrowing, this would tend to lower the capitalized value of existing wealth. This would tend to offset the expansionary effect on wealth of the increased supply of government securities.

The Effect of Fiscal Deficits Financed by Newly Created Money

A fiscal deficit financed by newly created money is very expansionary. A deficit created by an increase in government spending, holding taxes constant, would raise the $I + G$ schedule in Figure 19.6(a) from $(I + G)_1$ to $(I + G)_2$. In Figure 19.6(b), the increase in government spending would cause the IS schedule to shift to the right.

As shown in Figure 19.6(c), if a deficit is financed by newly created money, a shift to the right of the money supply schedule would keep interest rates from rising. As a result, the $I + G$ schedule in Figure 19.6(a) would rise the maximum amount. The stimulating effects of the increase in government spending would not be offset by a decrease in investment caused by rising interest rates. In the LM-IS graph, an increase in the money supply would shift the LM schedule to the right. The LM schedule and the IS schedule would intersect at a higher level of national income, and there would be no rise in interest rates.

Figure 19.6 illustrates why the role of monetary policy has often been viewed as supplementary to fiscal policy. Fiscal policy has been thought to be the primary means of controlling the output of the econ-

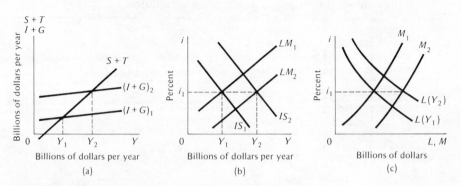

Figure 19.6   Graphic Description of the Effect of Fiscal Policy on Income, Assuming a Deficit Financed by New Money

omy. The unique contribution of monetary policy was to prevent a possible rise in interest rates that might result from an expansionary fiscal policy. The use of monetary policy in this way is one of the reasons for the close relationship between the growth of the national debt and monetary policy, shown in Figure 19.1.

Is a Fiscal Deficit Financed by Borrowing Always Expansionary?

Even though a fiscal deficit financed by borrowing is not as expansionary as one financed by new money, the analysis in Figure 19.3 shows that it would still be expansionary. Some economists have rejected this analysis and believe that the stimulating effect on national income of a deficit financed by borrowing would last only a short time. These critics claim that if there is a deficit, interest rates may rise because of the need to sell additional securities to finance the deficit—not solely because of an increase in income. In Figure 19.3, there would be no rise in interest rates at all unless income rose. However, if interest rates rise because of the financing of the deficit rather than because of an increase in income, the increase in spending because of an expansionary fiscal policy may be completely offset by a decrease in private spending because of the higher interest rates.

The critics also believe that sales of additional Treasury bonds take funds away from private borrowers. This is known as the *crowding-out effect*.[8] Consider the effect of deficit financing when bonds are sold to commercial banks. If the Federal Reserve banks made no open-market purchases during a period in which the Treasury was financing a deficit, bank reserves and the total amount of bank credit would be unchanged. Commercial banks would have to cut down on the volume of loans made to the private sector of the economy if they purchased some of the additional government securities issued by the United States Treasury. This would reduce the private capital expenditures that might have been financed by these loans. Commercial banks usually purchase some of the new securities issued by the Treasury. Commercial banks are a major part of the market for U.S. government securities, and the yield on the new securities issued would probably have to be sufficiently attractive to induce them to purchase some of them.

There may also be crowding-out effects on the spending of other financial institutions and the public. Funds that might have been invested in other ways would now be invested in U.S. government securities. If the deficit financing had been accompanied by an expansionary Federal Reserve policy, the public's holdings of money would have been increased and the demand as well as the supply of bonds would be larger. The increased demand comes about when the total amount of money held by the public is increased and when people desire to increase the amount of other assets that they own. However, if there were no increase in the money supply, rates of return would have to rise in order to induce persons to hold more bonds, stocks, and physical assets relative to their money holdings. The higher rates of return would reduce the supply of these other assets because it is more difficult to earn the higher rates of return. As a result, the issue of additional U.S. government securities would tend to be offset by a decline in the supply of some of those other assets and thus in private investment. Because crowding-out effects probably do not occur immediately, fiscal policy may temporarily stimulate total spending. However, eventually the positive effects of increased government spending could be offset by a decrease in private spending.

A third concern of the critics is the usual assumption that higher interest rates will not affect saving. In the model in Figure 19.3, it is assumed that saving is not affected by the rise in interest rates. It is possible that higher interest rates increase saving—either because of the higher rate of return or by reducing consumption of items purchased on credit—and thus raise the $S + I$ schedule and lower the level of income. Many economists believe that the effect of interest rates on saving is small, but little is known about the exact relationship.

FISCAL POLICY DURING WORLD WAR II

The widespread confidence in the power of fiscal policy is based largely on experience during World War II. Table 19.4 shows that government outlays rose sharply from 1940 to 1945. Tax receipts also rose rapidly, but not by as much. The federal government had very large deficits. During this same period, unemployment dropped sharply. In 1940 the rate of unemployment in the United States had been 14.6 percent. By 1945 it had fallen to only 1.9 percent.

The large increases in the size of the deficit from 1940 to 1943 would be expected to have a stimulating effect on the economy. The experience in World War II still does not provide a test of the possible expansionary effects of a deficit financed by borrowing. A significant portion of the wartime deficits were financed by money-creation. Money Supply I rose from $42.3 billion at the end of 1940 to $102.3 billion five years later—about two and a half times. In the early years of the war, the commercial banks were able to expand their total assets and liabilities by using excess reserves that they had acquired in the latter part of the 1930s. The ratio of their reserves to their deposits fell sharply. As the war progressed, the Federal Reserve banks purchased enough securities in the open market

Table 19.4
Federal Budget, Consolidated Cash Statement,
1940–1948 (in millions of dollars)

YEAR	RECEIPTS	OUTLAYS	SURPLUS (+) OR DEFICIT (−)
1940	$ 6,879	$ 9,589	−$ 2,710
1941	9,202	13,980	− 4,778
1942	15,104	34,500	− 19,396
1943	25,097	78,909	− 53,812
1944	47,818	93,956	− 46,138
1945	50,162	95,184	− 45,022
1946	43,537	61,738	− 18,201
1947	43,531	36,931	+ 6,600
1948	45,357	36,493	+ 8,864

Source: *Economic Report of the President, February 1974,*
p. 324.

and increased bank reserves sufficiently to enable the banks to create the money the United States Treasury needed to finance its deficits.

Experience shortly following World War II raised some doubts concerning the strength of fiscal policy. As shown in Table 19.4, there was a sharp change from a deficit of $45 billion in 1945 to a surplus two years later. The federal government reduced expenditures much more sharply than taxes. Some economists predicted that this restraining fiscal policy would cause a serious depression, but their predictions turned out to be wrong. After World War II, the money supply did not expand rapidly as it had during the war. However, there was no reduction in the money supply, and from 1945 to 1947 Money Supply I rose gradually from $102 billion to $113 billion.

THE MONETARIST–FISCALIST DEBATE

The monetarists and the fiscalists disagree on whether the national income is more affected by changes in the money supply or by fiscal changes.[9] The monetarists believe that more money means more spending, and less money the opposite, although some monetarists doubt that monetary policy can be effectively administered so as to control national income. Fiscalists believe a growing budget deficit would induce more spending and income-creation, while a shift toward a surplus would be restraining.

Ultimately, the test of a theory depends primarily on its predictive ability. In the latter half of the 1960s, greater popular acceptance of the monetarist approach developed because of its apparent superiority as a basis for forecasting.[10] There were three occasions that tested the relative importance of fiscal and monetary policy quite well, and in each test the monetary models seemed to predict best. To test the relative strength of the two policies, there must be occasions when their indicators move in opposite directions.

Experience in 1966–1967

Beginning in the spring of 1966 and extending for seven months, monetary growth dropped to near zero while the high-employment deficit continued to get larger. Monetarist predictions for 1967 ranged from pause to recession. Fiscal policy indicated a continued rapid growth in spending. In fact, the economy slowed abruptly, real GNP declined for one quarter, industrial production dipped moderately, and inflation slowed. The period has been characterized as a mini-recession.

Experience in 1968–1969

A second test occurred in 1968 when Congress passed a 10 percent surtax at about midyear. There resulted an $18 billion shift in the high-employment budget, from a $13 billion deficit in fiscal 1968 to a $5 billion surplus in fiscal 1969. At the same time, monetary growth accelerated as a result of fear by Federal Reserve officials of possible "overkill" resulting from the tax increase. Fiscal policy indicated an abrupt slowing in the economy, a reduced rate of inflation, and lower interest rates, while monetary policy indicated the opposite. In fact, the economy remained strong, inflation became more severe, and interest rates rose.

Experience in 1970

Monetarists uniformly projected a recession for 1970 whereas most fiscalists expected real output to increase at a rate of approximately 2 percent. From June to December of 1969, there had been only a very small increase in Money Supply I, and Money Supply II declined by over $5 billion. The year 1970 turned out to be a year of recession.

A recent econometric study by two economists at the Federal Reserve Bank of St. Louis tested the relative importance of monetary and fiscal actions in stabilizing the United States economy for the entire period from 1952 through early 1968.[11] Using quarter-to-quarter changes in quarterly averages of GNP and similar data on the money stock and various measures of fiscal actions, fiscal policy was not shown to exert a larger influence on economic activity than monetary actions. Nor was it shown to be more predictable or faster in its effect. Fiscal actions, measured by the high-employment surplus, appeared not to have a significant influence on GNP. Changes in tax receipts due to changes in tax rates did not appear to affect economic activity, and the overall effect of a change in government expenditures was not large enough to be significant. The authors concluded that "the money stock is an important indicator of the total thrust of stabilization actions, both monetary and fiscal," because of the dependence of the effectiveness of fiscal policy on monetary policy.

DEBT MANAGEMENT

When the United States Treasury sells new securities, it must decide what kind to issue—short-term, intermediate-term, or long-term. Decisions about the composition of the debt may have economic effects on output and prices. These decisions are referred to as debt management.

To assist in making debt-management decisions, the Treasury has a committee of prominent bankers, insurance company executives, and other persons from financial institutions to advise it on the kind of offerings they believe are readily marketable. This committee meets with Treasury officials shortly before each exchange or cash issue. Even though the Treasury makes use of the committee's advice, final decisions are made solely by the Treasury, and the committee members do not know what the Treasury decision is until it is announced. Between 1946 and 1952, it was the usual policy of the Treasury to replace maturing debt with debt maturing within one year, and no securities of over five years' maturity were offered. Since that time, the Treasury has attempted periodically to lengthen the maturity of new issues.

The Treasury is continuously faced with the problem of replacing maturing securities. Budget surpluses have been infrequent, and these have been more than offset by deficits. A large portion of the total national debt matures each year. The 91-day regular bills have to be "rolled over" four times during the year, the 180-day bills twice, and the 1-year bills once. The substantial amounts of notes and bonds coming due each year must also be replaced. There is no set policy about the maturity of the replacements for notes and bonds.

It is sometimes suggested that the Treasury ought to manage the debt so as to counteract the ups and downs of business activity.[12] Debt management is considered a method of controlling aggregate demand similar to fiscal and monetary policy. To have a countercyclical effect, the

Treasury must issue short-term debt when there is slack in the economy and long-term debt when it wishes to restrain inflation.

The sale of additional long-term bonds tends to lower the prices of long-term bonds and increase interest rates not only for bonds but also for mortgages and other long-term investments that compete with bonds. The higher interest rates tend to discourage private borrowing and investment spending. The fall in bond prices also causes capital losses for bondholders, which may have a further restraining effect. In addition, when maturing issues are replaced by long-term bonds, the total supply of liquid assets tends to be reduced.

The impact is different when short-term securities are offered. If maturing issues (always short-term as they near maturity) were replaced by new short-term securities, the quantity of liquid assets would be unchanged. If, however, short-term securities were sold to finance a deficit, the total supply of liquid assets would be increased. Some economists place great emphasis on the maturity of the debt created to finance a deficit.[13] An increase in the supply of liquid assets probably tends to lower long-term interest rates. When financial institutions are more adequately supplied with liquid assets, they become more willing to purchase long-term bonds. This causes prices of those bonds to rise and their interest yields to fall. If the economic effect of the decline in long-term interest rates more than offsets the effect of the rise in short-term rates, as more short-term securities are created, the net effect is expansionary.

The principal measure of the effect of debt management policy is the average maturity of the marketable interest-bearing debt. The average maturity of the marketable debt tends to fall automatically as outstanding securities gradually approach their maturity dates. When the Treasury issues longer-term debt, the average maturity of the debt tends to rise.

Despite the proposals to manage the debt so as to stabilize aggregate demand, the debt has not been managed in this way. Table 19.5 shows that in the recession years of 1953–1954, 1957–1958, and 1960–1961, the Treasury issued longer-term securities, raising the average maturity of the debt. In the intervening periods of prosperity, the average maturity of the debt typically decreased. From 1961 to 1965, the average maturity of the debt was increased substantially, although this was a period of relatively high unemployment. The average maturity of the debt has decreased from over nine years in 1946–1947 to slightly over three years in 1973.

There are several reasons why the Treasury manages the debt the way it does. The usual explanation is that the Treasury attempts to keep its own interest costs as low as possible and thus is hesitant to create long-term debt when interest rates are high in periods of prosperity. Another explanation is that the statutory ceiling rate of 4¼ percent on

Table 19.5
Average Length of Marketable Interest-
Bearing Public Debt, 1946–1973

END OF FISCAL YEAR	AVERAGE LENGTH		END OF FISCAL YEAR	AVERAGE LENGTH	
	Years	Months		Years	Months
1946	9	1	1960	4	4
1947	9	5	1961	4	6
1948	9	2	1962	4	11
1949	8	9	1963	5	1
			1964	5	0
1950	8	2			
1951	6	7	1965	5	4
1952	5	8	1966	4	11
1953	5	4	1967	4	7
1954	5	6	1968	4	2
			1969	4	0
1955	5	10			
1956	5	4	1970	3	8
1957	4	9	1971	3	6
1958	5	3	1972	3	3
1959	4	7	1973	3	2

Source: *Economic Report of the President, February 1974*, p. 334.

bonds has usually been below market rates during periods of prosperity and has thus impeded efforts to sell longer-term securities. Although these interest ceilings have made it impossible to offer debt maturing in over seven years, it would still be possible to raise the average maturity of the debt by selling intermediate-term securities.

The Treasury usually tries to lengthen the maturity of the debt whenever it seems feasible. One of the traditional views of Treasury officials is that "good government requires lengthening the maturity of the debt." Whenever the average maturity of the debt is lengthened, it is pointed to with pride. If the Treasury never issued long-term debt, eventually the entire marketable debt would be short-term.

If, because of its other objectives, the Treasury must manage the debt in such a way as to be expansionary in periods of prosperity and restraining in periods of recession, the effects of debt management could be offset by appropriate monetary policy. If debt management during a recession tended to raise interest rates or reduce the stock of liquid assets, a more expansionary monetary policy could offset these effects. But the need to counteract the impact of debt management and the difficulty of determining how much of an offset is necessary makes the administration of monetary policy more complicated.

SUMMARY

In recent decades, the rate of expansion of the money supply in the United States has been closely related to the rate of expansion of the national debt. There appears to be an important relationship between fiscal and monetary policy.

A budget deficit financed by new money is more expansionary than a deficit financed by borrowing. A budget deficit financed by borrowing causes interest rates to rise, and lenders are induced to purchase government securities rather than to make loans to private borrowers.

The combination of a tight money policy and an easy fiscal policy occurs when the rate of increase in the money supply declines at the same time that there is an increase in the high-employment budget deficit. The opposite combination occurs when the rate of increase in the money supply rises at the same time that the high-employment budget deficit gets smaller.

For many years, it was generally taken for granted that fiscal policy had a more powerful effect on the national income than monetary policy. Recent experience has resulted in a re-evaluation of the relative power of these two policies—with the viewpoint of the monetarists gaining support.

NOTES

1. Herbert Stein, *The Fiscal Revolution in America* (Chicago: University of Chicago Press, 1969), chapter 9. For a description of the operation of fiscal policy, see Lester C. Thurow, ed., *American Fiscal Policy, Experiment for Prosperity* (Englewood Cliffs, N.J.: Prentice-Hall, 1967), pp. 1–27.
2. See, for example, Henry A. Wallace, *Sixty Million Jobs* (New York: Simon and Schuster, 1945).
3. Kenneth Stewart, "Government Debt, Money, and Economic Activity," Federal Reserve Bank of St. Louis, *Review,* January 1972, pp. 2–9.
4. For an analysis of the federal budget for the fiscal year 1975, see Michael E. Levy, Delos R. Smith, Juan de Torres, and Vincent Massaro, *The Federal Budget, Its Impact on the Economy* (New York: The Conference Board, 1974).
5. For a description of an alternative measure of fiscal policy, the *instant stimulus* measure, see E. Gerald Corrigan, "The Measure-

ment and Importance of Fiscal Policy Changes," Federal Reserve Bank of New York, *Monthly Review,* June 1970, pp. 133–145. The expenditure component of this measure is the quarter-to-quarter change in total federal outlays as recorded in the national income accounts budget. The revenue component measures the initial dollar impact of discretionary changes in the various tax rates and their bases.

6. Leonall C. Andersen and Jerry L. Jordan, "Monetary and Fiscal Actions: A Test of Their Relative Importance in Economic Stabilization," Federal Reserve Bank of St. Louis, *Review,* November 1968, p. 18.

7. William L. Silber, "Fiscal Policy in *IS-LM* Analysis: A Correction," *Journal of Money, Credit, and Banking* 2 (November 1970), pp. 461–472.

8. See John M. Culbertson, *Macroeconomic Theory and Stabilization Policy* (New York: McGraw-Hill, 1968), pp. 462–463; and Roger W. Spencer and William P. Yohe, "The 'Crowding-Out' of Private Expenditures by Fiscal Policy Actions," Federal Reserve Bank of St. Louis, *Review,* October 1970, pp. 12–24.

9. For a debate on this issue, see Milton Friedman and Walter W. Heller, *Monetary vs. Fiscal Policy* (New York: W. W. Norton and Company, 1969). For the monetarist point of view, see Beryl W. Sprinkel, *Money and Markets: A Monetarist View* (Homewood, Ill.: Richard D. Irwin, 1971), pp. 8–16; and A. James Meigs, *Money Matters* (New York: Harper and Row, 1972). For the fiscalist point of view, see Arthur M. Okun, *The Political Economy of Prosperity* (New York: W. W. Norton and Company, 1970).

10. In newspapers and news magazines, interest in the monetarist approach centered on articles about Professor Milton Friedman, the leading theorist responsible for its development. See *Time* (19 December 1969), pp. 66–72; and Milton Viorst, "Friedmanism," *New York Times Magazine* 25, January 1970, pp. 22–23 and 80–84.

11. Leonall C. Andersen and Jerry L. Jordan, "Monetary and Fiscal Actions: A Test of Their Relative Importance in Economic Stabilization," Federal Reserve Bank of St. Louis, *Review* 50 (November 1968), pp. 11–24.

12. John M. Culbertson, *Full Employment or Stagnation?* (New York: McGraw-Hill, 1964), chapter 9.

13. James Tobin, "An Essay on Principles of Debt Management," in Commission on Money and Credit, *Fiscal and Debt Management Policies* (Englewood Cliffs, N.J.: Prentice-Hall, 1963), pp. 143–213.

QUESTIONS

19.1. What is the meaning of an expansionary fiscal policy? A restraining fiscal policy?

19.2. What are some of the difficulties encountered in administering fiscal policy?

19.3. Explain the way a fiscal deficit may be financed in the United States either by borrowing or by an expansion in the supply of money.

19.4. What are the differences between the unified budget, the national income accounts budget, and the high-employment budget.

19.5. What is the special usefulness of the high-employment budget?

19.6. What are some ways of measuring how expansionary fiscal policy is?

19.7. Explain with the use of graphs the way either an increase in government expenditures or a decrease in taxes is expected to increase national income—disregarding the question of how the deficit may be financed.

19.8. Explain with the use of graphs why a fiscal deficit financed by new money has a more expansionary effect on income than a fiscal deficit financed by borrowing.

19.9. Explain some of the factors that determine how expansionary deficit financing through borrowing may be.

19.10. Would it be possible for deficit financing through borrowing to have no effect on income?

19.11. Explain the differences in the point of view of the monetarists and fiscalists toward fiscal and monetary policy.

19.12. What would be the nature of an expansionary debt-management policy?

19.13. What are some of the reasons why the United States Treasury does not follow a countercyclical debt-management policy?

19.14. Know the meaning and significance of the following terms and concepts: budget deficit, budget surplus, unified budget, national income accounts budget, high-employment budget, automatic stabilizers, fiscal drag, crowding-out effect, debt management.

Chapter 20
Basic Types of
Monetary Regulation

The discretionary monetary system in the United States, in which monetary policy is determined by government authorities, contrasts sharply with the monetary systems of many countries, in which monetary policy depends largely on the balance of international payments.

In the United States, the monetary system is regulated by the authorities of the Federal Reserve System. It is a *discretionary* system. The monetary authorities are provided with instruments of control such as open-market operations. They have considerable latitude in determining policy objectives and actions. Many countries have a different type of system in which changes in the money supply are *automatic*. In those countries, the quantity of money usually varies with the balance of payments rather than being controlled by monetary authorities. Some economists advocate a third type of monetary system—one in which monetary policy is *based on a rule*. In a system of this type, the monetary authorities would have at their disposal means of controlling the monetary base and the money supply, but the purposes and targets of monetary policy would be narrowly defined. Congress might prescribe by law that the monetary authorities increase the money supply at a particular rate, or stabilize a price index. This chapter is concerned with the different types of monetary regulation.

AUTOMATIC SYSTEMS

If monetary policy is used to balance a country's imports and exports, the monetary system must to some extent work automatically—with the money supply increasing when there is a surplus in the balance of payments and decreasing when there is a deficit. In such a system there could be little discretion, and establishing a monetary rule would not be possible. A discretionary system or a system based on a rule could be used only when the country's international balances are regulated in other ways than by monetary policy.

Monetary Systems Regulated by the Balance of Payments

In countries in which variations in the money supply are determined primarily by the country's balance of international payments, if there is a surplus and exports exceed imports, their bank reserves increase. This makes possible an increase in the money supply. Or if there is a deficit and imports exceed exports, their bank reserves decrease, resulting in a decline in the money supply. For most countries, imports must eventually be balanced by exports. If a country had continuous deficits, its supply of international reserves would soon be exhausted. To avoid such a contingency, each country must have some technique of adjustment. Countries which have a monetary system based on their balance of payments have a fairly efficient technique for keeping payments in balance. Monetary restraint tends to correct a deficit in the balance of payments, and monetary ease tends to bring an end to a surplus. As explained in Chapters 17 and 18, a policy of monetary restraint eventually reduces income, lowers prices, and in the short run raises interest rates. Monetary ease raises income and prices and in the short run lowers interest rates. These effects tend to change the flows of international trade and bring about a reversal of conditions that started the imbalance.

Suppose a country has a deficit in its balance of payments. The resulting monetary conditions would reduce imports and expand exports in the following ways:

1. A shortage of bank reserves would cause monetary tightness; domestic prices would fall relative to the prices of international goods. This would induce business enterprises to produce for export. The prices of international goods would not fall as a result of the tight domestic monetary policy, because their prices depend on international market conditions. Lower domestic prices would also make the country relatively attractive for foreign tourists and thus stimulate tourism as a type of export. Imports of all types would be discouraged, since they would now have to compete with cheaper local goods; and the lower costs resulting from the tight money policies would make it easier to compete in foreign countries.

2. Tight monetary conditions would tend to correct a deficit in the balance of payments by reducing the national income. Lower incomes

would reduce the consumption of imported goods and goods containing imported materials. There would also be a decline in imports of services such as travel in foreign countries.

3. The rise in interest rates resulting from tight money conditions would increase exports and decrease imports in the capital markets. High United States interest rates would discourage the purchase of foreign securities or investment in foreign enterprises, which are both types of imports. The higher rates of return on investments in the United States would induce foreigners to purchase our securities and result in an expansion in exports of this type.

When a country has a deficit in its balance of payments, monetary tightness as an adjustment technique usually slows down economic activity. Many countries of the world are so in need of development that it might seem unwise ever to allow a restraining policy. Actually, having a monetary system geared primarily to equating a country's balance of payments does not necessarily retard a country's economic development. Mexico, for example, has had the highest average growth rate in Latin America in the three decades since 1940—6 percent annually in real terms—despite letting its bank reserves fluctuate with changes in the balance of payments and having no changes in its exchange rate since 1954.[1] To attempt to avoid the depressing effects when income and price movements are used to balance international payments, some countries have tried direct controls over foreign exchange—attempting to reduce imports by restrictions on the purchase of foreign exchange—but these measures usually are not reliable. Ultimately, most countries either have to use monetary controls to keep payments in balance, or if a crisis develops they may change their exchange rates, devaluing their currency.

Japan's Relatively Automatic System

Japan is an example of a large industrial country in which the balance of payments has been regulated primarily by monetary policy. The monetary authorities have some discretion, but their policies are significantly influenced by the country's international trade position. Figure 20.1 shows the close relationship between the trade balance and the rate of increase in the money supply in Japan from 1956 to 1967. The trade balance does not include capital movements and certain other items found in the balance of payments. However, information is more quickly available on Japan's trade balance than on other items in its balance of payments, and weakness in the trade balance is usually indicative of weakness in the overall balance of payments. When there has been a trade deficit, the principal way the monetary authorities have maintained their interna-

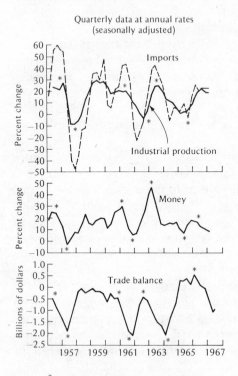

Quarterly data at annual rates
(seasonally adjusted)

*Indicates peaks and troughs which are postulated
to be related to trade balance considerations.

Figure 20.1 The Percent Change in the Money Supply and the Trade Balance in Japan, 1956–1967

Source: Michael W. Keran, "Monetary Policy, Balance of Payments, and Business Cycles: The Foreign Experience," in Federal Reserve Bank of St. Louis, *Review,* November 1967, p. 11.

tional reserves has been by taking restrictive actions. On the other hand, they have responded to a trade surplus with an easier monetary policy because of the desire to promote economic growth.

The three periods of tight monetary policy in Japan between 1956 and 1967 appear to have been related to the three recessions during that period.[2] In Figure 20.1, the cyclical movements in the economy are shown by the rate of change in industrial production. In the late boom phase of each cycle, higher incomes caused imports to rise sharply relative to exports. The monetary authorities then tightened their monetary policy.

As a result, industrial production declined and imports dropped. The decline in imports improved the trade balance and eventually permitted monetary policy to become easier. This caused production and imports to resume their normal growth rate until another deficit in their balance of payments developed, and the cycle had to be repeated. Since World War II, this interrelationship between the trade balance, monetary policy, and output has also occurred in Italy, France, and West Germany.

Guatemala's Balancing Mechanism

Guatemala provides an example of a small developing country that has a monetary system that is controlled primarily by balance of payments trends. In Central American countries, the bulk of their international reserves consist of dollar deposits in United States banks, and the amount of their dollar deposits varies with their balance of payments. In Guatemala, when a local exporter is paid in dollars, he sells them to the Bank of Guatemala for deposits denominated in *quetzals,* the money of his own country. The dollar reserves of the Bank of Guatemala are increased. On the other hand, purchases of dollars by importers reduce the Bank of Guatemala's dollar reserves when those dollars are spent for foreign goods. In Guatemala, a surplus in their balance of payments increases their bank reserves. When there is a deficit, reserves decrease.

As in Japan, basing monetary policy on the balance of payments has the advantage of keeping payments in balance. Guatemalan monetary authorities do not attempt to adjust their balance of payments through variations in exchange rates. The exchange rate between the quetzal and the dollar has been one for one since 1925. In recent years, there have been some official restrictions on the exchange by Guatemalans of quetzals for dollars, but such controls can usually be evaded to some extent.

Pure Commodity Standard

Another type of automatic system for regulating the money supply is the pure commodity standard. There are probably no systems of this type in the world today, although historically the use of commodity money—usually gold and silver coins—was very common. Increasingly, commodity money has been replaced by paper money and deposits. In recent years, a return to commodity money and especially gold has been advocated by those who distrust types of money created by governments. There has been growing distrust of governmental types of money because of the acceleration in the rate of inflation.

In a system based on gold or some other commodity, there would be no need for a central bank, deposit insurance, or bank examinations.

About all the government would have to do is to designate a particular commodity as money and see to it that there was no other type of money in the economy. The production of money would be left to private enterprises operating under competitive conditions. If gold were the commodity money, any enterprise that desired to produce gold would be allowed to do so, and private firms would be expected to produce gold if it were profitable enough. The unit of account might also be gold, and the price of everything would be in ounces of gold. Or the prices could be in dollars or another unit of account defined as equal to a certain quantity of gold.

In a pure commodity standard, the money supply would vary automatically with the profitability of producing the commodity money, and there would be no legal limits to the amount produced. Despite this, there is in this system an effective limit to the amount of money created, since a rapid increase in the production of gold would cause a rise in the prices of all other goods and services in terms of gold. This would cause other goods to become more profitable to produce than gold and bring about a decline in gold production. Although accelerated inflation is impossible with a commodity standard, there may be gradual inflation. This occurred under the gold standard whenever it became cheaper to produce gold because of the discovery of new resources or improvements in technology. Because of the reliability of commodity money as compared to paper money, people in some countries have had a strong preference for it. In Panama when the United States government started construction of the canal in 1904, canal employers were surprised to discover that the native employees expected to be paid in silver coins and would not accept dollar bills even though they were legally convertible into gold.

A pure commodity standard works quite well when there is a recession. Suppose prices fell because of a decline in business activity. The relative profitability of producing gold would increase. A more rapid increase in the money supply would tend to have a stabilizing effect on prices and real output. Employment would be stimulated among the producers of the commodity money, providing jobs for the unemployed. These stabilizing features have attracted the interest of some economists, and attempts have been made to conceive of pure commodity standards that would be an improvement over existing monetary systems.[3]

If the commodity used as money were acceptable in international trade, this type of system would also provide a balancing mechanism for international payments, as under the international gold standard. In a country with a deficit in its balance of payments, the supply of money would decline. This would cause prices to decline, interest rates to rise, and income to fall. These changes would encourage exports and discourage imports, eventually restoring balance to the country's international payments.

Despite its attractive characteristics, a pure commodity standard also has disadvantages. It is costly in terms of the use of real resources. The cost of mining additional quantities of the monetary metal is higher than one would expect. To keep prices stable in the United States, the money supply would probably have to be increased about 4 percent a year to match the growth in real output and a possible decline in velocity. In 1970, a 4 percent increase in Money Supply I would have amounted to over $10 billion—approximately 1 percent of the national income. It is an advantage to have a type of money that requires a much smaller amount of real resources to produce.

A second shortcoming of a pure commodity standard is that it tends to break down and evolve into a mixture of commodity and fiduciary money. Roughly, this is what occurred historically with the development of fractional reserve banking.

Automatic Systems with Fractional Reserves

Because of the convenience of paper money, a commodity standard would probably evolve into a system of paper money backed by the commodity. If the paper money were backed 100 percent by the commodity money (specie), a bank issuing paper money (bank notes) would have a balance sheet of the following type:

Commodity Standard Bank

Assets		Liabilities	
Specie	$100,000	Notes	$100,000

The notes of the bank would be "warehouse receipts." The bank would store the commodity and issue paper money backed 100 percent by the commodity.

A system of paper money backed 100 percent by a commodity would undoubtedly break down soon. Although the notes would legally be convertible into specie, most persons would not attempt to convert them. A bank would discover that it could get along by holding specie reserves equal to only a fraction of its outstanding notes. It would buy investments or acquire loans. With the interest income received from the loans and investments, it would be able to issue paper money at a lower cost and outcompete banks that attempted to operate with 100 percent reserves. The balance sheet of such a bank might be as follows:

Fractional Reserve Bank

Assets		Liabilities	
Specie	$10,000	Notes	$100,000
Loans	90,000		

It would be a fractional reserve bank because its reserves would be equal to only a fraction of its notes. In the United States, the state bank notes prior to the Civil War and the national bank notes that were issued later were fiduciary money of this type.

In the above example, the bank has 10 percent of its notes backed by specie. The public would hold some specie and some bank notes. For example, the public might have $25,000 in specie and $100,000 in bank notes—a ratio of 1 to 4. Given the desire of the public to hold a specie-currency ratio of 1 to 4, there would be an upper limit equal to $100,000 to the quantity of bank notes that could be issued. The formula would be as follows:

$$\text{Notes} = \frac{\text{Specie}}{(r + c)} = \frac{\$35,000}{(.10 + .25)} = \$100,000$$

where r = the bank's reserve ratio, and c = the public's ratio of commodity money to paper money. The amount of this upper limit would vary, depending on changes in the quantity of specie in the system, the bank's reserve ratio, and the public's ratio of specie to paper money.

A fractional reserve bank must keep a certain percentage of its notes in specie reserves because notes are legally convertible into specie on demand. In the above example, if the public should wish to hold $30,000 rather than $25,000 in specie, the bank's holdings of specie would fall by $5,000. The reserve ratio that banks would customarily keep would depend on the expected variations in the public's demand for specie. If the public's ratio never changed, the banks would not have to hold any reserves behind their notes. However, if banks misgauged the size of the variation in the public's ratio of specie to notes and ran out of specie, they would be in difficulty. A reason for the historical instability of fractional reserve banking is that fractional reserve banks make contracts that they may not be able to keep, because their notes are not backed 100 percent by specie. To make matters worse, banks are induced to issue more and more notes and to hold very little specie behind them. The smaller their reserve ratio, the larger the profits. But, the smaller the reserve ratio, the more vulnerable banks are to changes in the amount of specie the public wishes to hold relative to notes. This inherent weakness eventually led to the establishment of central banking and deposit insurance.

In the nineteenth century, the principal measure taken in the United States to strengthen fractional reserve banks in time of crises was to require banks to hold reserves equal to a percentage of their deposits. At that time, the United States was the only major country in the world that had such laws. However, these laws were so widely accepted in the early years of the Federal Reserve System that the authorities viewed legal reserve requirements as a method of providing adequate bank liquidity rather than as an instrument of control. These laws were unfortunately based on a misunderstanding of the problem. In a fractional reserve banking system, banks hold reserves both to meet ordinary demands for cash and to provide for unusual demands for cash whenever they might arise. The legislated reserve requirements prohibited banks from using reserves for the principal purposes they were designed to accomplish.

A fractional reserve banking system does require certain types of government regulation, even though early attempts to regulate such a system by establishing reserve requirements were misguided. In a system with fractional reserves, the quantity of money may vary sharply because of changes in the banks' reserve ratios or in the public's ratio of specie to notes. These ratios typically increase in serious depressions, which makes matters worse. One of the objectives of government regulation through a central bank is to manipulate total bank reserves so as to offset the undesired effect on the money supply of changes in the banks' reserve ratios or the public's ratio of specie to notes. In addition, government regulation through periodic bank examinations is necessary because of the opportunities for fraud in fractional reserve banking. The notes issued may not be backed by bona fide loans. This is difficult to regulate, because some bank loans are inherently risky. Bank examiners attempt to ascertain that the loans and investments behind the liabilities of fractional reserve banks are sound.

DISCRETIONARY SYSTEMS

Monetary Regulation in the United States before 1914

Before 1914, the United States had a monetary system guided primarily by the balance of payments. At that time, gold and gold certificates were held directly by commercial banks, and an outflow of gold caused a decline in their gold reserves. Importers in need of foreign exchange could purchase gold from commercial banks. For every dollar of gold reserves lost to another country, there tended to be a multiple contraction of bank loans and deposits throughout the banking system. On the other hand, if there was a surplus in the balance of payments, the opposite occurred. Gold flowed into the United States, increasing bank reserves and permitting the multiple expansion of bank loans and deposits.

For several decades after the Civil War, increases in the world production of gold did not keep up with increases in the production of other goods. This was one factor causing the world-wide decline in prices during this period because gold was then the principal determinant of bank reserves and the expansion in the supply of money. From 1890 to 1914, the gold stock of the world doubled because of new discoveries and improved processes of extracting gold, which was probably a cause of the world-wide price rise that occurred at that time. Wholesale prices in the United States rose 49 percent from 1897 to 1914. The price rise started later in the United States than in most countries, because of monetary difficulties caused by agitation for unlimited coinage of silver. The political movement to coin more silver money probably had the opposite effect on prices than that expected or intended by its supporters. It threatened inflation and discouraged foreigners from holding dollars. This meant smaller capital inflows, larger outflows of gold, and a deflationary monetary policy. The upturn in prices started in 1897, when the United States acquired gold because of sharply increased exports— owing in part to good harvests in the United States in contrast to crop difficulties elsewhere.

When the Federal Reserve was established in 1914, the founders visualized the continuation of a monetary system based on gold. Open-market operations were not expected to be an instrument of control, and legal reserve ratios of member banks could not be changed. The only types of discretionary control available were changes in the discount rate and variations in the volume of lending to member banks. The system was not purely automatic, but it was expected that changes in the amount of gold would be the predominant factor determining member bank reserves, and that an excess of imports over exports would be paid for primarily with gold. At that time, gold and the British pound were the two important types of international money. The dollar itself had not yet achieved the important position that it has today as an international currency.

In the first three decades of the 1900s, numerous developing countries were anxious to revise their monetary arrangements and hired British or American consultants to help them. Professor Edwin Kemmerer of Princeton, a leading economist of his day, was one of the principal consultants hired. Between 1917 and 1931 he advised Mexico, Guatemala, Colombia, Chile, Ecuador, Bolivia, and Peru. He had started his work as a "money doctor" in the Philippines in 1903–1906 and was later hired to go to Poland, Germany, Turkey, China, and the Union of South Africa. He was paid by the countries that hired him, but otherwise his missions were similar to some of our more recent foreign-aid programs. His blueprint for the monetary system of those countries was a system similar to the original conception of the Federal Reserve System—a central bank based on the gold standard. Many countries set up central banks in this period, and although many of them went off the gold standard in the 1930s, their monetary systems have usually been guided by balance of payments considerations.

The development of a discretionary system in the United States was the result of special circumstances. During the period between World War I and World War II, surpluses in the balance of payments made it possible to use monetary policy for goals other than controlling the balance of payments. In order to stabilize prices, gold inflows were sterilized (that is, their impact on bank reserves was offset by the use of Federal Reserve instruments of control). This was a step away from reliance on an automatic monetary system, because gold flows no longer determined our domestic monetary policies. During this period, many foreign countries went off the gold standard, and their economies also were not automatically regulated by gold flows. The point of view of Governor Strong of the Federal Reserve Bank of New York in the 1920s was that although other countries should go back on the gold standard, the United States should not allow gold inflows to cause domestic inflation.

After World War II, the United States was still able to manage a discretionary monetary system. Even though the balance of payments of the United States shifted to a deficit, the large amount of gold that the Treasury had accumulated during the 1930s and 1940s was available to cover the deficit. Also, the use of U.S. dollars as an international money was becoming more common. This made it possible to cover a large portion of the deficits by expanding the volume of dollars held by foreigners.

In a discretionary system, the monetary authorities have a wide range of choice about what targets and goals to pursue and how to achieve them. It is left up to them to use their powers as they judge best. As problems change, their targets and goals may change.

Over the years the Federal Reserve System's policy goals have been conceived of both broadly and flexibly, allowing much discretion. The authorities are legally independent of the executive departments of the government and relatively free of control by Congress—even though they submit an annual report to Congress and are occasionally called to testify before committees. When the monetary authorities administer open-market operations, they decide whether to buy or to sell, and how much to buy or sell. Their decision is a group decision, based on the information assembled for them by their research staffs. Group decisions have both advantages and disadvantages. Many points of view are represented, and those advocating a particular policy must persuade others of its merits. But the group may also be significantly influenced by a dominant personality whose policies may not be the best. There may also be an unfortunate dispersion of responsibility. It may be easier to do nothing than to risk doing the wrong thing.

The use of targets to carry out a discretionary monetary policy was discussed in Chapter 14. Monetary policy may move toward ease or tightness, and various targets have been used to measure the direction and extent of the actions taken. The principal reason why the monetary authorities must use a target is that the impact of monetary policy takes too long for changes in their goals—changes in prices, income, or the rate of growth—to be useful measures of the impact of the actions taken.

In its purest form, a discretionary monetary system does not have an *explicit* target. This was characteristic of Federal Reserve operations during most of the period since 1951. During that period, financial analysts were usually uncertain about what the direction of monetary policy was and spent considerable effort trying to determine its nature. Without a specified target, it is difficult to evaluate Federal Reserve actions.[4] Unless it is clear what the Reserve is trying to do, success in reaching the target cannot be evaluated and the target cannot be judged for appropriateness in terms of broad goals. Much of the discussion of Federal Reserve policy by the monetary authorities has been in terms of the "tone" or "feel" of the money market. These concepts have been criticized by persons outside the system as indefinite and subjective. Since 1970 the Federal Reserve authorities have had as targets monetary aggregates such as the rate of increase in money and reserves available for private deposits (RPDs). This has reduced the discretion allowed and simplified the evaluation of Federal Reserve policy.

A principal difference between a discretionary policy and a monetary policy based on a rule is whether or not the targets are adjusted as conditions change. In a discretionary system, the target level would be changed continuously. For example, if the monetary base were used as a measure of ease or tightness, in a depression the monetary base might be expanded more rapidly, and in a period of inflation the rate of increase in the monetary base might be reduced. On the other hand, in a system based on a rule, changes in the rate of increase in the monetary base would not be left up to the authorities' evaluation of conditions in the economy. Central banking authorities almost always prefer a discretionary system. They argue that a rule might prevent them from doing what ought to be done to meet certain problems, and that the problems are always changing, complex, and unpredictable. They also argue that it is difficult to formulate a rule that would work well.

Because the Federal Reserve System has several important goals, a major difficulty in administering monetary policy is that the goals may conflict. At times the authorities may have to decide which they prefer, less inflation or less unemployment. An expansionary policy designed to reduce unemployment may also result in balance of payments problems. The broad goals of monetary policy are not easy to define.[5] Some of the issues connected with defining goals are:

1. Economists differ on what rate of unemployment should be the goal. Should it be 3 percent, 4 percent or 5 percent? Some economists believe there should be no set goal for the rate of unemployment.

2. There are several price indexes—consumer prices, wholesale prices, and the GNP deflator. These do not always move in the same direction. If the wholesale price index is steady, but the GNP deflator is rising, should Federal Reserve policy become tighter? There has been considerable discussion among economists of upward biases in the consumer price index that are difficult to measure.

3. For the United States, a reasonable balance of payments is a particularly difficult objective to define. There are now two measures of the deficit in the balance of payments, and they do not always agree. If the dollar is used as a type of international money, a policy of balancing payments would eliminate any growth in dollars as a form of international reserves. If the balance of payments should not be balanced, how large a deficit is desirable?

4. The appropriate rate of economic growth is difficult to define. Growth should be sufficiently rapid to prevent a rise in unemployment; but beyond this how rapidly should per capita income rise? Should the goal be 1, 2, or 3 percent a year? Although rapid economic growth used to be considered a cure-all for many social and economic problems, in recent years some political groups have advocated zero growth.

MONETARY RULES

Fixed Rate of Increase Per Year in the Money Supply

If monetary policy were based on a rule, the present discretion of the monetary authorities would be replaced by a relatively precise rule that would govern the monetary actions taken. The rule that is most often suggested is to increase the money supply at a fixed rate.[6] Based on experience in the 1960s, an annual rate of increase in Money Supply II of 4 percent would be roughly consistent with long-run price stability because it would be equal to the expected rate of increase in real output. During the 1960s, the velocity of Money Supply II changed little.

The suggestion that monetary policy be based on a rule has had some political recognition. In 1968 a report of the Joint Economic Committee recommended that Congress advocate an annual rate of expansion in the money supply of between 2 and 6 percent.[7] If the Federal Reserve exceeded these limits, it was to be required to report to Congress on the reasons. The recommendation grew out of a rising opinion that wide swings in monetary policy have had a destabilizing influence on the economy.

Professor Friedman, the principal advocate of a rule, believes that such a policy is "the best we can do in the light of our present knowledge." He bases his skepticism about discretionary changes on the long and variable lag of changes in income behind changes in the rate of change in the money supply. Six to nine months is the average lag, but his studies of past business cycles show a significant deviation from the average, and the causes of those deviations in lags are not well understood. If the estimated lag is incorrect, monetary policy may be destabilizing rather than stabilizing, even if the forecast is correct. Also, estimating the rate of increase in the money supply necessary to achieve a given increase in income is difficult. In the interest rate–investment model, this would depend on the relationships between the demand for money and interest rates, between interest rates and investment, and between investment and income. Without precise knowledge of each of those relationships, one would not know exactly how much the money supply ought to be increased.

Suggestions that monetary policy be based on a rule usually include a proposal for flexible exchange rates to provide an adjustment technique for balancing imports and exports. The way in which flexible exchange rates may be used to adjust imports to exports is explained in Chapter 24.

Stable Price Level or a Fixed Quantity of Money

Two other rules that have been suggested as guides to monetary policy are to stabilize a price index and to fix the quantity of money at a given level. The first of these was advocated by Irving Fisher, and in the 1920s and early 1930s several bills were introduced in Congress to enact such a rule.[8] The second rule—to fix the quantity of money at a given level—was advocated by Henry C. Simons in the 1930s although he also advocated stabilizing the wholesale price index because it seemed more feasible.[9]

If a rule to stabilize a price index were adopted, when prices fell the monetary authorities would be required to expand the money supply sufficiently to bring the price index back to the prescribed level. If prices rose, the money supply would have to be reduced until prices returned to their original level. The principal argument against this rule is that the time lag between changes in the money supply and changes in prices is so long that it would be difficult to implement. Recent statistical studies indicate that the average time lag is as long as two years.

Professor Simons' rule to fix the quantity of money would be much simpler to administer than attempting to stabilize a price index. The authorities would have to use open-market operations with sufficient skill to offset both the effect of changes in the other items in the bank reserve equation on the monetary base, and the effect of changes in the currency-deposit and reserve-deposit ratios on the money supply. But this could probably be done reasonably well. The disadvantage of this rule is that it would result in gradual deflation. As output rose and the money supply was held constant, prices would gradually fall.

AVOIDING SEVERE BUSINESS FLUCTUATIONS

An argument in favor of a rule is that it would avoid the extreme type of monetary instability that occurred in the Great Depression. Money Supply II declined about 35 percent from 1929 to 1933. Consumer prices fell about 24 percent. If any of the major rules—to increase the quantity of money at a fixed rate, stabilize prices, or fix the quantity of money—had been in effect at the time, the unfortunate monetary policy of that period would not have occurred.

The errors in monetary policy during the Great Depression were the result of a series of policies that changed as the short-run problems facing the monetary authorities changed. For sixteen months prior to the peak of the boom in 1929, there was no increase in the quantity of money. The monetary authorities were attempting to combat stock market specula-tion. From 1921 to 1928, the money supply had gradually expanded. The tight money policy prior to 1929 would be expected to have a restraining effect on the economy and bring on a recession. Income was still rising rapidly, and the ratio of the money balances held by the public to their incomes fell. This caused people to want to hold more money than was available and eventually led to a decline in spending.

From the October 1929 stock market crash to 1933, the quantity of money continuously declined. The standard explanation of this monetary contraction used to be that there were no willing borrowers despite an expansionary policy of the Federal Reserve authorities. The recent studies of Milton Friedman and Anna Schwartz have concluded that the Federal Reserve authorities could have prevented the decline in the money supply if they had wished to do so.[10]

During the first year of the depression, from October 1929 to October 1930, the monetary base—and the money supply—declined because there was less discounting by member banks at the Federal Reserve banks. The monetary authorities had lowered the discount rate, but at the same time other short-term rates fell rapidly. Even though there was less borrowing, the monetary authorities could have prevented the decline in the monetary base by open-market purchases, but they did not make such purchases.

In October 1930 a financial panic started and the reason for the declining money supply changed. Large numbers of banks failed. Runs on banks became common, and banks started to hoard. The quantity of money depends on the public's ratio of currency to deposits and the banks' ratio of reserves to deposits, as well as on the amount of the monetary base. From October 1930 to March 1933, both of those ratios rose sharply, reducing the quantity of money. The authorities might have increased the monetary base sufficiently to offset the effects of runs and hoarding, but they did not.

In September 1931 when Great Britain went off the gold standard, the Federal Reserve authorities shifted from what had been a relatively laissez faire policy to one of restraint. Their objective was to strengthen the balance of payments position. Gold had started to flow out of the country because foreigners expected that the United States would also go off the gold standard and that the price of gold would rise. The discount rate was raised from 2½ percent to 3½ percent. At this time the monetary base did not decline, even though there was a gold outflow, because member banks increased their borrowing despite the increase in the discount rate. The money stock declined because of an intensification of runs on banks and a rise in the public's ratio of currency to deposits. Great Britain's going off the gold standard had a panicky effect on the public. Federal Reserve policy toward the gold outflow in 1931 was a major step toward the even worse crisis in 1933.

Starting in April 1932, the Federal Reserve for several months purchased large amounts of U.S. government securities. This action appeared to have a desirable effect, but it was not continued, and at the beginning of 1933 another wave of bank failures and runs started. Another gold drain followed, and the Federal Reserve authorities again reacted by raising the discount rate. The financial panic became so bad that on March 6, President Roosevelt declared a bank holiday, and all banks in the United States were closed for a period of seven days. Following the holiday, the banks were gradually opened, monetary policy was reversed, and a long period of monetary expansion began.

Monetary policy during the Great Depression might have been different, even if not guided by a rule, if the authorities had taken a less passive attitude and had had a better understanding of the nature of bank panics and the importance of money. But it can still be argued that a rule would be useful, because it would keep the authorities from being misled by short-run problems such as stock market speculation or a gold drain. There were undoubtedly strong pressures on the authorities to do something to meet those problems, and these pressures caused them to neglect their primary objectives.

Some critics have felt that in recent years as well as during the Great Depression a monetary rule would have been superior to the kind of discretionary policy that we have had. Particularly from 1967 to 1973, the Federal Reserve has been criticized for expanding the money supply too rapidly. It is believed that if there had been a rule setting an upper limit to the rate of increase in the money supply, the excessive expansion in the money supply that has occurred, and the subsequent acceleration in the rate of inflation, would have been prevented. In a simulation analysis of the period from 1962 to 1972, Professor Ecstein concluded that much of the instability of the economy was caused by monetary and fiscal policies that were at times too restrictive and at other times too accommodating.[11] Using econometric models that were designed for forecasting and are composed of equations derived from historical experience, he substituted stable monetary and fiscal policies for the actual policy record. The result was substantially less inflation, smoother real growth, and smaller variations, but little change in the rate of unemployment for the entire period.

100 PERCENT RESERVE BANKING

Closely related to the proposal that monetary policy be based on a rule is a basic reform known as *100 percent reserve banking*. This reform was originally proposed by Irving Fisher as a fundamental way of avoiding bank panics.[12] In recent years, proponents of this reform have argued that it would make it possible for the monetary authorities to control the money supply more effectively than under present arrangements.

The way in which this proposal would work may be illustrated by comparing the balance sheet of a 100 percent reserve bank with a fractional reserve bank. In each of the examples, deposits are the same.

100 Percent Reserve Bank

Assets		Liabilities	
Reserves	$100,000	Deposits	$100,000
Loans, etc.	100,000	Capital stock	100,000

Fractional Reserve Bank

Assets		Liabilities	
Reserves	$ 10,000	Deposits	$100,000
Loans, etc.	100,000	Capital stock	10,000

In both types of banks, reserves would consist of cash in vault and balances at the Federal Reserve banks. In the 100 percent reserve bank, deposits are backed 100 percent by reserves, persons would write checks on deposits as at present, and deposits could be cashed on demand. Under the plan as proposed by Professor Friedman, banks would be paid interest (roughly equal to the prevailing Treasury bill rate) on their reserve deposits at the Federal Reserve banks.[13] This expense could be paid for with the interest that the Reserve banks earn on their investments in U.S. government securities. Currently, the bulk of this income is returned to the Treasury.

Paying interest on these deposits appears to be a subsidy to the commercial banks, paid for ultimately by the taxpayers. Although commercial bank profits would increase in the short run, in the long run the subsidy would probably be passed on to the depositors. Because of increased bank profits, banks would compete for additional deposits by offering higher rates of interest on time deposits (assuming no federal ceilings) and lower service fees to owners of demand deposits.

If the Federal Reserve did not pay interest on the deposits of the member banks, the 100 percent reserve system would appear very unattractive to bankers. They would not be permitted to invest part of their depositors' funds in earning assets. To cover the cost of processing checks and keeping deposit records, they would have to charge much higher service fees than at present. This would have the unfortunate effect of discouraging the use of demand deposits as money. Persons and business firms would be induced to spend time and effort keeping their deposit balances at a minimum and investing instead in interest-earning short-term securities.

Every dollar lent by a 100 percent reserve bank would come from the sale of equity shares. Currently, banks obtain only a very small portion of their loanable funds through the sale of bank stock. Banks would have to obtain funds for lending in much the same way as mutual funds now do. It is expected that bank stock would become a very common type of investment. As with other types of stock, there would be a market for bank stocks, and if a person wished to sell his bank stock, he would have to sell it in the market for whatever price it would bring. Bank stock would not be redeemable at the bank for cash.

The advantage of 100 percent reserve banking that was stressed by Irving Fisher was its stability. When he advocated this proposal, bank failures were a major problem. For a 100 percent reserve bank, runs are never a problem because its deposits are fully backed, and a decline in deposits would not cause undesirable repercussions on its lending and investing activities. Also, in 100 percent reserve banking, bad loans would depress the price of the bank's stock; but since the stockholders cannot cash their stock at the bank, the cash reserves of the bank would be unaffected.

It might appear that one of the disadvantages of 100 percent reserve banking is that it would reduce the supply of bank credit and thus the volume of funds for real investment. Actually this need not be a problem. The money supply could be increased sufficiently to induce persons to purchase enough bank stock or other types of securities to provide a sufficient quantity of credit to keep the economy booming. The Federal Reserve banks would increase the money supply in the same way as they currently do—by open-market purchases.

The 100 percent reserve banks would temporarily have more than 100 percent reserves whenever they sold additional stock, a loan was paid off, or they sold securities from their portfolios. These transactions would cause their deposits to decline relative to their reserves. Such banks would not need to hold excess reserves to cover unfavorable clearing balances or to assure that they have sufficient liquidity. It is doubtful whether they would ever want to hold more than 100 percent reserves. However, if holding excess reserves did, for some reason, become a problem, the plan might include a fine on excess amounts held.

In a system of fractional reserve banking, whenever the public desires to hold a larger ratio of currency to demand deposits, whenever banks wish to hold larger excess reserves relative to demand deposits, or whenever time or demand deposits are shifted to banks with higher required reserve ratios, the money supply declines. Or if the public or the banks wish to hold smaller ratios of currency or reserves to deposits, the money supply tends to increase. To control the money supply with a system of fractional reserve banking, changes in these ratios have to be offset by appropriate changes in the total amount of the monetary base.

The principal advantage of 100 percent reserve banking is that the ability of the monetary authorities to control precisely the rate of increase in the money stock would be greater. At present, forecasting changes in the public's currency ratio, the ratio of excess reserves to demand deposits, and the ratios of required reserves to demand and time deposits for the overall banking system is not easy, and adjustments have to be made after the changes become known. As a result, some delay in achieving the intended increase in the money stock is probably unavoidable. With 100 percent reserve banking, the increase in the money stock would always be equal to the increase in high-powered money. Changes in the public's ratio of currency to deposits would not affect the total money supply.

SUMMARY

A principal advantage of an automatic monetary system, in which monetary policy varies with a country's balance of payments, is that it provides an adjustment mechanism for avoiding continuous balance-of-payments deficits or surpluses.

With a pure commodity standard, the only type of money in use would consist of a commodity such as gold, and there could be a minimum of government regulation of the monetary system.

The monetary system of the United States has become discretionary, because the United States has not had to use monetary policy to keep its international payments in balance.

Advocates of basing monetary policy on a rule, such as requiring the Federal Reserve authorities to increase the money supply at a fixed rate, believe that such a policy would result in greater stability of prices and less unemployment than a discretionary policy.

With 100 percent reserve banking, the Federal Reserve System would have greater control of the money supply, because variations in the public's currency-deposit ratio would not affect the supply of money, and the reserve-deposit ratios of banks would no longer vary.

NOTES

1. See Dwight S. Brothers and Leopoldo Solis, *Mexican Financial Development* (Austin: University of Texas Press, 1966), p. 128;

and B. Griffiths, *Mexican Monetary Policy and Economic Development* (New York: Praeger, 1972), pp. 77–83.

2. Michael W. Keran, "Monetary Policy, Balance of Payments, and Business Cycles: The Foreign Experience," Federal Reserve Bank of St. Louis, *Review,* November 1967, pp. 7–20; and "Monetary Policy and the Business Cycle in Postwar Japan," in David Meiselman, ed., *Varieties of Monetary Experience* (Chicago: University of Chicago Press, 1970), pp. 163–248.

3. Frank D. Graham, *Social Goals and Economic Institutions* (Princeton: Princeton University Press, 1942), pp. 94–119; and Milton Friedman, "Commodity-Reserve Currency," *Essays in Positive Economics* (Chicago: University of Chicago Press, 1953), pp. 204–250.

4. For a discussion of the need for measures of fiscal, debt-management, and monetary policy, see John M. Culbertson, *Full Employment or Stagnation?* (New York: McGraw-Hill, 1964), pp. 83–121.

5. Thomas Mayer, *Monetary Policy in the United States* (New York: Random House, 1968), pp. 3–22.

6. Milton Friedman, *A Program for Monetary Stability* (New York: Fordham University Press, 1960), pp. 84–99; and "How Much Monetary Growth?" *Morgan Guaranty Survey,* February 1973, pp. 5–10.

7. U.S., Congress, Joint Economic Committee, *Standards for Guiding Monetary Action,* 90th Cong., 2nd sess., 1968; and George G. Kaufman, "Proposed Experiment in Monetary Policy," *Financial Analysts' Journal* (November–December 1968), pp. 90–93, reprinted in John T. Boorman and Thomas M. Havrilesky, eds., *Money Supply, Money Demand, and Macroeconomic Models* (Boston: Allyn and Bacon, 1972), pp. 82–88.

8. For a discussion of this legislation, see Charles O. Hardy, *Credit Policies of the Federal Reserve System* (Washington, D.C.: The Brookings Institution, 1932), pp. 199–226.

9. Harry C. Simons, "Rules versus Authorities in Monetary Policy," *Journal of Political Economy* 44 (February 1936), pp. 1–30.

10. Milton Friedman and Anna J. Schwartz, *A Monetary History of the United States, 1867–1960* (Princeton: Princeton University Press, 1963), chapter 7.

11. Otto Ecstein, "Instability in the Private and Public Sectors," *Swedish Journal of Economics,* March 1973, pp. 19–26.

12. Irving Fisher, *100 Percent Money* (New York: Adelphi Company, 1935).

13. Milton Friedman, *A Program for Monetary Stability* (New York: Fordham University Press, 1960), pp. 65–76.

QUESTIONS

20.1. Why do many countries have a relatively automatic monetary system based on the balance of payments?

20.2. Explain the way a restraining monetary policy would correct a deficit in the balance of payments.

20.3. Explain the relationship between business fluctuations and the balance of payments in Japan.

20.4. What is the upper limit to the increase in the quantity of money in a pure commodity standard?

20.5. Why does a pure commodity standard tend to break down?

20.6. What are the reasons why fractional reserve banking requires considerable governmental regulation?

20.7. Explain the nature of a discretionary monetary system and how it differs from an automatic system.

20.8. Why has the United States been able to have a discretionary monetary system?

20.9. Explain the difference between a monetary system based on a rule and a discretionary monetary system.

20.10. What are the arguments for and against a monetary system based on a rule?

20.11. Explain the reasons for the sharp decline in the money supply during the Great Depression.

20.12. Explain the differences between a 100 percent reserve bank and a fractional reserve bank.

20.13. What were the objectives of the early proposals for 100 percent reserve banking?

20.14. What are the objectives of current proposals for 100 percent reserve banking?

20.15. Know the meaning and significance of the following terms and concepts: automatic monetary system, discretionary monetary system, pure commodity standard, fractional reserve bank, 100 percent reserve bank, monetary rules.

Chapter 21
Inflation: Causes and Effects

Inflation has become a major economic problem in the United States and in many other countries. The major cause of inflation has probably been the excessively expansionary fiscal and monetary policies of the federal government.

Attitudes toward inflation have changed in the past few decades. When World War II ended, it was thought that deflation rather than continued inflation would be the major threat for the postwar period. After the inflation of World War I, there had been a sharp drop in prices in the depression of 1920–1921. After the Civil War, there had been almost three decades of declining prices. In the 1950s it became widely accepted that 2 to 3 percent inflation was necessary to maintain a high level of employment. It was thought that vigorous government economic policies to keep employment high were desirable even though such policies would occasionally cause inflation by overshooting. It was also believed that if inflation could be kept slow and irregular enough to cause people to think that they were better off than they actually were, it would help solve conflicts over the distribution of income and serve as a "social lubricant." In the 1960s, when the rate of inflation accelerated, interest shifted from the possible beneficial effects of slow inflation to methods of keeping inflation from getting out of hand and to ways of reducing the rate of inflation without causing a rise in the rate of unemployment.

In 1973, the purchasing power of a dollar was worth only 31 per cent as much as it was worth in 1939. We usually measure inflation by changes in the general price level. The more rapidly prices rise, the faster the decline in the purchasing power of a unit of money: the less it will buy in terms of goods and services.

The problem of inflation is worldwide. Table 21.1 shows the annual rates of depreciation of money in 60 countries from 1968 to 1973. In most countries, prices have risen between 4 percent and 8 percent a year. In three South American countries—Argentina, Uruguay, and Chile —they rose at annual rates of 25 percent or higher.

Table 21.1
Annual Rate of Depreciation of Money,
1968–1973

Ethiopia	2.7%	Greece	5.3%	Haiti	6.9%
Honduras	3.0	Paraguay	5.3	New Zealand	6.9
Venezuela	3.0	Switzerland	5.3	United Kingdom	7.0
Morocco	3.2	Italy	5.4	Ecuador	7.5
Guatemala	3.4	China (Taiwan)	5.5	Turkey	7.9
Tunisia	3.4	South Africa	5.5	Zaire	8.1
Panama	3.7	Finland	5.7	Ireland	8.2
Cyprus	4.1	Sweden	5.7	Jamaica	8.6
Zambia	4.3	France	5.8	Korea	9.0
Canada	4.4	Mexico	5.8	Portugal	9.2
West Germany	4.4	Dominican Republic	5.9	Philippines	9.4
Kenya	4.4	Denmark	6.0	Colombia	11.1
Luxembourg	4.4	Sri Lanka	6.0	Yugoslavia	12.2
Iraq	4.5	Trinidad and Tobago	6.0	Indonesia	12.3
Belgium	4.6	India	6.1	Iceland	12.5
Singapore	4.8	Netherlands	6.4	Brazil	15.8
United States	4.8	Norway	6.4	Vietnam	22.3
Austria	4.9	Peru	6.5	Argentina	25.0
Iran	4.9	Japan	6.6	Uruguay	30.3
Australia	5.2	Spain	6.6	Chile	43.1

Source: First National City Bank, New York.

MEASURES OF CHANGES IN THE PRICE LEVEL

There are three price indexes that are widely used in the United States: the consumer price index, the wholesale price index, and the GNP deflator. The first two are published by the Bureau of Labor Statistics, and the third by the Department of Commerce.

The *consumer price index* measures changes in the prices of goods and services purchased by typical urban wage-earners and clerical workers, including families and single persons.[1] It measures the total cost of a "market basket" of about 300 goods and services. The kinds and quantities of the items included are based on the amounts purchased by a fairly small sample of households. Although the use of sampling raises the question of its reliability, over time the sampling errors are probably not major. Retail prices for each item are collected in a large number of cities each month in the kinds of establishments in which wage-earners and clerical workers shop. The Bureau of Labor Statistics is preparing an expanded index based on expenditure patterns of the unemployed, the self-employed, the retired, and rural dwellers, in addition to urban wage-earners, which will be published in the near future.

The wholesale price index is based on prices paid by businesses rather than by consumers.[2] Nearly 2,200 commodities are included, weighted by the sales value of each flowing into markets. There are no prices of services in this index. The prices used are those on organized commodity exchanges and those charged at the first transaction for each commodity. Wholesale prices usually react more quickly to changes in business conditions than consumer prices. When there is an upward trend in the consumer price index because of higher prices for services, the wholesale price index may move differently than the consumer price index. In the first half of the 1960s, when wholesale prices were stable, consumer prices rose between 1 and 2 percent a year. However, the long-run movements of both indexes are usually similar. During the accelerated inflation in 1973, wholesale prices rose much more rapidly than the consumer price index because the rise in prices of agricultural products and international commodities was especially sharp.

The *GNP deflator* is the most comprehensive price index. As its name indicates, it is a by-product of the estimates by the Department of Commerce of the GNP in terms of constant dollars. It is, in effect, an index of the prices of all the goods and services that make up the GNP. One of the major differences between the GNP deflator and the other indexes is that it includes the cost of government services.

A major problem in measuring changes in the general level of prices is taking into account quality changes resulting from improvements in technology. When prices of goods rise, they may reflect either a "true" increase in prices or an improvement in quality. A higher-priced new model automobile would be an example. What portion of the higher price should be attributed to the model changes? Because of the inability adequately to take into account improvements in quality, most economic studies have concluded that the price indexes have a small upward bias that exaggerates inflation.

Another difficulty is that the movements of the major components of the overall indexes vary considerably. Except in 1973, prices of services in the consumer price index have usually increased much more rapidly than prices of commodities. In the wholesale price index, food prices frequently move in the opposite direction from other prices. In the GNP deflator, the prices of new construction, producer durables, and services have risen much more rapidly than prices of consumer goods. When relative prices change, one would expect consumers to change their buying habits and substitute other things for those goods with the most inflated prices. The usual practice is not to change weights often, because when weights are altered, changes in the index reflect both price movements and the different weights. If, however, the kinds of goods and services purchased change because of changes in relative prices, ideally the weights of the index ought to be changed.

THEORIES OF INFLATION

Variations in the money supply appear to be of crucial importance in explaining long-run movements of prices. Historically, it is difficult to find examples of countries where inflation has occurred without an increase in the money supply, or where a substantial increase in the money supply has not been accompanied by a rise in prices. The close relationship from 1952 to 1973 in the trends of Money Supply I and the general price index used in the National Income Accounts is shown in Figure 21.1. The annual percentage rates of increase for each of the series for selected periods are shown above the trend lines. From the first quarter of 1952 to the fourth quarter of 1965, the general price index increased at an average rate of 1.8 percent a year, from late 1965 to the middle of 1969 at 3.8 percent, from mid-1969 to the fourth quarter of 1972 at 4.3 percent, and from the fourth quarter of 1972 to the third quarter of 1973 at 6.8 percent. During this twenty-one-year period, Money Supply I increased at an annual rate of 1.8 percent from early 1952 to the third quarter of 1962, 3.8 percent from late 1962 to early 1967, and 6.2 percent from early 1967 to late 1973.

Figure 21.1 shows that the trend in the rate of inflation has lagged behind the trend in the rate of expansion in the money supply. When the rate of increase in the money supply started to accelerate in the third quarter of 1962, prices did not start to rise more rapidly until almost three years later. Also, the acceleration in the rate of expansion in the money supply in 1967 did not appear to affect prices until two and a half years later—in 1969. When people become accustomed to a certain rate of inflation, the rate of inflation that they anticipate seems to persist even after the rate of increase in the money supply accelerates.

Figure 21.1 also shows that despite the similarity in the long-run movements of money and prices, from 1952 to 1973 prices have not fallen during periods of recession. Also, in the short run, prices may be affected primarily by such things as labor union pressure, weather, boycotts and embargoes, devaluation, and changes in wage and price con-

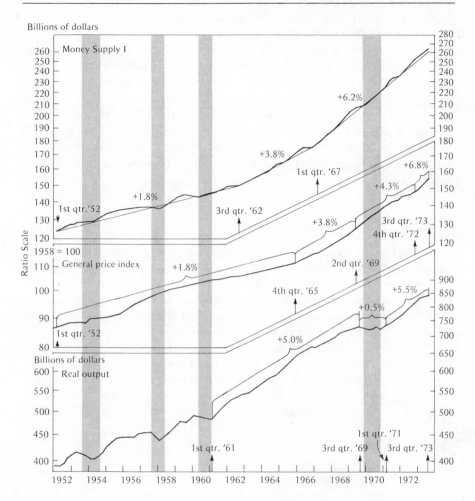

Shaded areas represent periods of business recession, as defined by the National Bureau of Economic Research.
Latest data plotted: 3rd Quarter

**Figure 21.1   Monetary Growth, Prices, and
Output, 1952–1973 (seasonally adjusted)**

Source: Federal Reserve Bank of St. Louis, *Review*, December 1973, p. 3.

trols.[3] The relationship between money and real output is different from
that between money and prices. In each of the four recessions between
1952 and 1973—shown by the shaded areas in Figure 21.1—real output
declined and was preceded by a drop in the rate of increase in the money
supply. On the other hand, long-run economic growth has not acceler-

ated as a result of the accelerated increase in the money supply. Economic growth depends primarily on the growth of the labor force and the accumulation of capital equipment.

The relationship between the money supply per unit of output and price trends in several Latin American countries from 1955 to 1968 is shown in Table 21.2. Although the rates of inflation in those countries were different, in each of them the average annual rate of growth in the money supply per unit of output has been similar to the average annual rate of inflation. The historical experience with inflation in these South American countries, as well as in other countries, is important. The belief that price trends are closely related to the rate of increase in the money supply is based on historical experience.

Portfolio Adjustment Theory of Inflation[4]

In the portfolio adjustment model, there will be inflation if at the full employment level of income, the supply of money is greater than the demand for money. This is illustrated in Figure 21.2. When there is full employment, the labor market is in equilibrium, and at the prevailing level of wages the supply of labor is equal to the demand. As shown in Figure 21.2, if the money supply were increased from M_1 to M_2, the quantity of money supplied at the full employment level of income, Y_F, would exceed the demand. This would cause prices to rise because total spending would increase if people have more money than they want. The rise in prices would cause income to rise to Y_{INFL}. As prices rise, the quantity of money demanded would increase, because people would

Table 21.2
Rates of Change in Money and Inflation in
Seven Latin American Countries, 1955–1968

| | COMPOUND ANNUAL RATE OF CHANGE IN | |
COUNTRY	Money Supply/Real Gross National Production	Consumer Price Index
Brazil	35.3%	37.9%
Chile	29.0	27.6
Argentina	22.6	26.6
Colombia	11.2	10.4
Peru	7.7	9.0
Ecuador	4.4	2.3
Mexico	3.8	3.6

Source: Beryl W. Sprinkel, *Money and Markets: A Monetarist View* (Homewood, Ill.: Richard D. Irwin, 1971), p. 189.

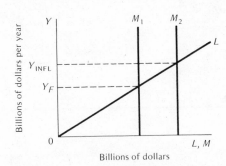

Figure 21.2   Effects on Income and Prices of an Increase in the Supply of Money

want to hold more money in order to have the same real convenience in purchasing goods and services and the same real protection in case of contingencies.

In the portfolio adjustment theory, inflation may also be caused by a decrease in the demand for money, even though historically an increase in the money supply has been the predominant cause. The decreased demand for money would raise the L schedule in Figure 21.2, causing the supply of money to exceed the demand at the full employment level of income. Income and prices must rise so as to increase the quantity of money demanded until it is equal to the supply. The L schedule might shift upward because of greater optimism or expectations of inflation. In countries in which people have begun to anticipate a more rapid rate of inflation, the demand for money has usually decreased and caused prices to rise even faster.

Interest Rate–Investment Theory of Inflation

In the interest rate–investment theory, inflation may also be caused by an increase in the money supply. This explanation of inflation also assumes full employment. An expansion in the money supply would lower interest rates, increase investment, and create an *inflationary gap* as illustrated in Figure 21.3. Prior to the increase in desired investment, $C + I_1 + G$ was equal to Y_F (the level of income at full employment). The increase in desired investment causes the spending schedule to rise to $C + I_2 + G$. At Y_F, people would desire to spend more than the maximum real output of the economy at existing prices. The prices of investment goods would rise because of the increase in the demand for them relative to the supply, and this would cause prices in general to rise. Producers who found themselves unable to get the investment goods they wanted would

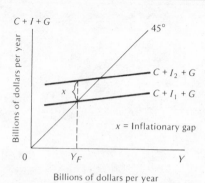

Figure 21.3   The Inflationary Gap Caused by an Increase in the Money Supply, Lower Interest Rates, and an Increase in Desired Investment

offer to pay higher prices, and one would expect sellers to try to get higher prices whenever possible. Price flexibility may be a problem when prices fall but probably not when prices rise. Assuming competition and price flexibility in the market for investment goods, buyers would bid up prices for such goods, reducing demand until it was again equal to the supply.

The inflationary gap shown in Figure 21.3 may be created not only by an increase in the money supply, but also by an increase in autonomous spending caused by such factors as optimistic expectations, new technological developments, lower taxes on business profits, or government fiscal policy. As illustrated by the equation of exchange, $MV = Py$, if there were no increase in the money supply and output could not be increased because of conditions of full employment, a rise in prices would require a higher velocity of money. It is sometimes claimed that this will occur because the rise in prices will increase the demand for money relative to the supply causing interest rates to rise. The higher interest rates will then induce persons to want to hold less money relative to securities, and thus increase velocity. Although inflation may have some impact of this type on velocity, the effect is probably small. Inflations that are based solely on increases in velocity with no increase in the money supply are very rare.

Cost-Push Theory

The cost-push theory explains inflation in terms of factors other than an increase in the money supply or autonomous factors increasing aggregate

demand. Instead of the traditional *demand-pull* forces, the cause of inflation according to this theory is primarily union demands for higher wages
or price increases by large producers. This view of inflation became popular during the 1960s. In 1973, some economists developed a new type
of cost-push theory based on higher commodity prices. The inflation
was referred to as a *commodity inflation.*

In the cost-push theory, the higher union wages and the higher prices
of the products produced by unionized firms must not be offset by lower
wages and prices in the nonunionized sector of the economy. If they
were, large union wage demands could not cause inflation. The higher
union wages would merely lead to a change in relative prices and a
reallocation of resources. The lower wages in the nonunion sector would
induce employers to hire more labor and produce a larger output. The
higher wages in the union sector would induce employers to cut down
on their hiring and to produce less. There need be no increase in overall
unemployment. However, if wages in the nonunion sector do not fall
when union wages are raised, the result of higher union wages would
be both an increase in unemployment and higher prices in general. The
increase in unemployment resulting from higher union wages is not
caused solely by the rise in the cost of union labor. It is also caused by
the overall rise in prices resulting from higher union wages. The higher
prices would increase the demand for money, raise interest rates, and
reduce aggregate demand.

Because of the dominance of full employment as a goal of government economic policy, one would expect monetary and fiscal policy to
become more expansionary if unemployment was increasing—no matter
what the cause. The monetary authorities would tend to react to higher
unemployment by lowering interest rates and increasing the rate of
growth of the money supply. Or fiscal policy might be more stimulating.
The wage pressures may be considered the basic cause of this type of
inflation even though a more stimulating monetary or fiscal policy may
be a supplementary part of the process. The inflationary forces initiated
by unions are said to be validated by monetary and fiscal policy.

Some economists believe that if the monetary authorities did not
attempt to prevent the unemployment attributed to union wage demands, cost-push inflation would be limited to the short run. When
unemployment increases, the supply of labor in labor markets tends to
be greater than the demand, causing wages to fall to equilibrium levels.
As unemployment rose, unions would become more moderate in their
demands because it would be more difficult for them to get higher
wages, and the wages of nonunion labor would be depressed. With less
upward pressure on wages, the rate of inflation would diminish.

Structuralist Theory

The structuralist theory of inflation has been used to explain South American inflations, primarily those in Argentina, Brazil, and Chile.[5] All three of these countries have had rapid inflation for many years. Although temporary reversals in the rate of inflation have occurred, none of these countries has been able to slow down the rate of inflation to that typical of most other countries.

The structuralists believe that inflation is a necessary accompaniment of growth. Although they agree that inflation could be curbed by monetary or fiscal policy, these policies are rejected because an excessive amount of unemployment might result. Initially, rising incomes and the growth of population tend to raise the prices of food or of imports—products with an inelastic supply. A rise in the price of imports does not increase the supply because the total amount of imports depends on the amount of exports. The output of food does not increase when prices rise, it is claimed, because of feudal land-tenure systems or various government controls removing incentives to increase output.

In the structuralist theory, it is assumed that the rise in the prices of imports and of agricultural commodities causes prices in general to rise, because prices in other sectors of the economy are not flexible downward. This inflexibility is partly the result of the fact that wage and price movements in those countries tend to become adjusted to the rate of inflation that people expect, and these expectations are slow to change. Any governmental attempts to force prices down in other sectors of the economy would cause unemployment. Because prices tend to be inflexible in the short run, when aggregate demand is cut back, real output falls. Moreover, to prevent a rise in unemployment, the money supply must be expanded rapidly enough to accommodate the overall rise in prices caused by economic growth. The structuralist theory of inflation does not claim that inflation is possible without rapid increases in the money stock. The basic cause of the inflation is said to be growth combined with supply inelasticities and downward inflexibility of prices. The growth in the money stock is essential, but still supplementary and permissive.

To some extent, the money supply in these South American countries automatically expands when prices rise. Firms need larger loans from banks as prices rise. The total volume of bank loans and that of deposits rise together, assuming that bank reserves are not rigidly controlled. Also, as prices rise, more money may be needed to finance larger government deficits. This will occur if government wages and expenditures rise more rapidly than tax revenues. Such conditions tend to occur when government wages are tied to cost-of-living indexes by wage contracts with escalator clauses and when import and export duties are a major source of revenue. Tax receipts from import and export duties may not be very sensitive to changes in prices.

WEALTH TRANSFER EFFECTS OF INFLATION[6]

When prices in general rise, some persons are hurt and others benefited. The retired person with a fixed pension income is often cited as an example of one who is hurt by inflation. The person with a fixed monthly payment on his mortgage, it is usually believed, is benefited. Identifying the effects of inflation is not as easy as it might seem at first, despite these familiar examples. In order to know who is harmed and who benefited, it is necessary to distinguish between anticipated and unanticipated inflations. When people forsee inflation, the effects are different than when it is unexpected. When prices rose 4 percent, for example, did people *expect* that prices would rise this fast and adjust their actions and decisions in advance accordingly? Or did prices rise 4 percent even though people expected that prices would be stable? Sometimes prices rise 4 percent when people are anticipating a 2 percent increase. Probably only rarely is the anticipated rate of inflation exactly the same as the actual rate of inflation. It is a common error to assume that people usually do not expect any inflation. Even in the many countries in which rates of inflation have ranged as low as between 2 percent and 4 percent a year, people undoubtedly have expected these rates of inflation to continue.

The steadiness of an inflation determines whether or not it becomes anticipated. An inflation need not be perfectly steady, but if the rise in prices remains approximately the same for a long period of time, the public will come to expect prices to rise at that rate, and they will adjust their economic activities to take into account the expected future price rises. The effects of intermittent inflation are quite different. Inflations of this type are unanticipated because people are usually slow to recognize the change that has occurred.

Anticipated Inflation—Effects on the Distribution of Wealth

An important consequence of anticipated inflation is that interest yields on securities tend to discount in part the expected rate of inflation. If, for example, prices rise 3 percent a year, nominal yields must be 7 percent in order to give people a real return of 4 percent. As a result, if people expect to earn a real return of 4 percent and also expect 3 percent inflation, the demand for securities with nominal yields lower than 7 percent would probably decline, and their prices would fall until their yields rose to 7 percent. Also, if borrowers anticipate a rate of inflation of 3 percent, they would expect to be able to afford to pay 7 percent. They could realize a rate of return of 3 percent by holding goods whose prices were rising at that rate, and in addition they might expect to earn a real rate of return of 4 percent.

When inflation is anticipated, *nominal interest rates* are usually higher than the rate of inflation, and the more rapid the expected rise in prices, the higher the nominal interest rates. There are some striking examples of this relationship. In China in 1947, when inflation was 600 percent a year, interest rates on bank deposits were 2 percent a day compounded daily. In South Korea, when inflation ranged from 100 percent a year during the Korean War to 40 percent immediately following the war, interest rates of 5 to 10 percent a month were typical.

The effect of expectations of inflation on interest rates probably explains the long-observed historical relationship between the movement of prices and the movement of interest rates. When prices have risen, interest rates have risen, and when prices have fallen, interest rates have fallen. This relationship was noted by economists in the early nineteenth century and was called the *Gibson paradox* because it contradicted the classical theory in which an increase in the money supply would cause prices to rise and interest rates to fall. At least a partial explanation of the Gibson paradox is that there is a difference between nominal and real interest rates. Nominal interest rates discount the expected rate of inflation and, as a result, rise and fall with the rate of inflation.

During the period of accelerated inflation in the United States from 1965 to 1973, the rate of inflation does not appear to have been fully anticipated. Interest rates on bonds have not risen enough to yield much of any real rate of return, considering the rate of inflation and the income tax on additional interest income. If nominal rates of interest were to rise enough so that they fully discounted the rate of inflation, the wealth transfer effects of inflation would be sharply reduced. The interest received would be large enough to offset completely the loss in real value of the bond because of inflation and still pay the owner enough interest to yield a real rate of return. Also, borrowers would have to pay such high nominal rates of interest that they must forfeit the gain they might have made because of inflation. However, there would still be some transfer of wealth, because holders of two important types of money assets—currency and demand deposits—cannot protect themselves because these assets have no interest rate that can be used to adjust their values.

When inflation is anticipated, even though people know that money is depreciating in value and there is no way of holding money without taking a loss, people continue to use money because it is still more convenient than barter. When holders of money lose through inflation, the creators of money—the banks and the government—gain. If the inflation were fully anticipated, borrowers from banks would not gain since the rate of interest charged would be high enough to discount the rate of inflation. However, bank owners benefit because the monetary assets that earn no interest for the bank (cash in vault, deposits at the Federal Reserve banks, and checks in process of collection) amount to less than its monetary liabilities on which it pays no interest (demand deposits). Although banks are usually considered to be net money creditors, their equity would increase more rapidly than the rate of inflation if inflation were fully anticipated.

The United States Treasury is a major beneficiary of anticipated inflation—through its connection with the Federal Reserve banks. The Federal Reserve banks gain even when interest rates effectively discount the rate of inflation. Their monetary debts on which they do not pay interest (their Federal Reserve notes and their deposits) exceed their monetary assets on which they earn no interest (gold certificates). Although inflation would increase the equity of the Federal Reserve banks, the size of their annual dividend and accumulations of capital surplus are limited by law. As a result, the gains made by the Federal Reserve banks would be passed on to the Treasury. Because the gains received by the Treasury from anticipated inflation would reduce the need for tax revenues, people as taxpayers would ultimately benefit.

A surprising result of anticipated inflation is that creditors may benefit rather than debtors. It depends on whether the inflation is underanticipated or overanticipated. When the rate of inflation declines, if interest rates had risen so as to adjust for a rapid rate of inflation, creditors who had lent money at the high rates would gain if the inflation turned out to be less than expected, and debtors would find paying the high rates of interest very burdensome. The old conception of inflation as the "euthanasia of the rentier"—gradually exterminating creditors—is based on the failure to recognize the importance of anticipations. There is, in fact, little evidence that the number of creditors has significantly diminished in South American countries that have experienced rapid inflation.

Unanticipated Inflation—Effects on the Distribution of Wealth

In an unanticipated inflation, in which interest yields have not risen so as to discount the rate of inflation, wealth is transferred from net money creditors to net money debtors. The person in the following example has some money assets, some real assets, and also some debts. He is a net money debtor because his total money debts are larger than his total money assets. In order to analyze how inflation affects him, it is necessary to calculate his overall net position before and after inflation. This may be done by combining assets and liabilities in the form of a balance sheet. A person's net wealth is the balancing item—the difference between his total assets and his total money debts.

Net Money Debtor

	ASSETS			LIABILITIES AND NET WEALTH	
	Original	After 100% Inflation		Original	After 100% Inflation
Money assets	$ 5,000	$ 5,000	Money debts	$20,000	$20,000
Real assets	30,000	60,000	Net wealth	15,000	45,000
Total	$35,000	$65,000	Total	$35,000	$65,000

Money assets consist mostly of currency, demand deposits, time deposits, bonds, and private pensions. All of these are claims to a fixed amount of money now or in the future, and the amounts claimed would be unaffected by inflation. Real assets include houses, automobiles, and one's own labor. These are not claims to a fixed amount of money. If prices in general rise, their prices usually rise. Money debts consist of the amounts a person has borrowed. These may consist of a mortgage, automobile loan, or a personal debt—all contracts to pay a fixed amount of money. In the above example, we have assumed that the money debtor owns no corporation stock. As we shall see, the classification of corporation stock depends on the financial position of the corporation. Not all companies are net money debtors.

In the above example, prices doubled. The value of the net money debtor's real assets would probably also double, rising from $30,000 to $60,000. The amounts of his money assets and money liabilities would not be affected. His net wealth triples, rising to $45,000. He has benefited because the rise in his net wealth is greater than the rise in prices. The reason is that his money debts are larger than his money assets. He had *borrowed* to buy real assets. Note that owning real assets helps one keep up with inflation, but only those who borrow to buy real assets can expect their net wealth to rise more rapidly than prices.

The way inflation affects monetary creditors—those whose money assets are larger than their money debts—is different:

Net Money Creditor

ASSETS			LIABILITIES AND NET WEALTH		
	Original	After 100% Inflation		Original	After 100% Inflation
Money assets	$13,000	$13,000	Money debts	—	—
Real assets	2,000	4,000	Net wealth	$15,000	$17,000
Total	$15,000	$17,000	Total	$15,000	$17,000

In the example of the balance sheet of a net money creditor, the creditor has no debts, but $13,000 in money assets. His original net wealth is $15,000, the same as that of the net money debtor in the previous example. If prices doubled, his real assets would probably rise from $2,000 to $4,000, and his net wealth would rise to $17,000. His net wealth would not have kept up with the rise in prices.

There are many familiar examples of net money debtors—persons who bought their homes by taking out mortgages. Examples of net money creditors are also familiar—persons who saved cautiously, never borrowed, and preferred to rent rather than buy a home. When inflation is unanticipated, inflation transfers wealth from people who are net money creditors to those who are net money debtors.

It is usually assumed that one way to protect oneself against inflation is to own corporation stock. This is not necessarily true. Corporations, like persons, may be either net money creditors or net money debtors. Only if a corporation is a net money debtor can the stockholder expect to benefit in real terms from unanticipated inflation. The money assets of corporations consist of bank deposits, short-term marketable securities, and accounts receivable. Their real assets consist of plant, equipment, and inventory. Money debts of business firms include their debt to banks, bonds outstanding, commercial paper outstanding, accounts payable, and income taxes payable. If a corporation had financed enough real assets by borrowing, it would be a net money debtor, and during inflation the value of its equity would increase more rapidly than prices. But those corporations that have financed their activities primarily by the sale of stock or by retained earnings are typically net money creditors. They would not benefit from inflation.

An interesting economic study has compared the performance of the stock of corporations that were net money debtors with that of net money creditors.[7] The results were what one would expect. In periods of inflation, on the average the prices of the stocks of the net debtor corporations rose more than the prices of the stocks of the net creditors. In periods of deflation, the net creditors did better than the net debtors. The corporations included in this study were those listed on the major exchanges. About half of them were net money creditors, and half were net money debtors. The period studied was from 1914 to 1952.

The holders of assets and debts may be divided into three groups—households, businesses, and governments. Households on the average are net money creditors, because their money assets exceed their money debts, while governments and businesses are net money debtors.[8] Inflation in the United States has caused a transfer of wealth from households primarily to the federal government, and increasingly in recent years to businesses. The transfer of wealth to businesses benefits their owners. The transfer of wealth to the federal government benefits taxpayers who now have to pay less in taxes to meet the payments of interest and principal on the national debt. The transfer of wealth from households, as owners of U.S. government securities and other monetary assets, to taxpayers and owners of businesses would be substantial even at low rates of inflation if inflation were completely unanticipated and interest rates did not rise to discount the rate of inflation. Since the mid-1960s, interest rates appear to have discounted at least part of the rate of inflation, reducing significantly the transfer of wealth caused by inflation. However, if interest rates had not risen, the 44 percent increase in prices from 1965 to 1973 would have caused a similar reduction in the real value of the national debt.

EFFECTS ON THE DISTRIBUTION
OF INCOME

Inflation may change the distribution of income as well as the distribution of wealth. If, when prices rise 3 percent, all of the different types of income—wages and salaries, dividends, interest, rental income, profits from unincorporated enterprises, and pensions—were to rise by the same percentage, there would be no redistribution. But some types of income, such as interest and rent, tend to be inflexible. Since profits are a residual type of income, dependent upon whatever is left after meeting all other expenses, owners of enterprises would benefit from inflation if some of their costs did not rise. Persons whose income is governed by a contract for a specific period of time are generally hurt by inflation, because these types of income remain unchanged when prices rise. Rent covered by a lease, interest on government bonds, and wages under a union contract are examples.

The analysis of the effects of inflation on the distribution of personal income and on the distribution of wealth overlaps. This is because wealth is the source of income, and the value of each type of wealth is the capitalized value of the expected flow of income from that wealth. If one analyzes the effects of inflation on the distribution of wealth, holders of money assets such as time deposits and bonds are hurt because these assets have a fixed nominal value. If one analyzes the effects of inflation on the distribution of income, the holders of those same assets are hurt because the interest received by the owners of time deposits and bonds remains the same when the rate of inflation becomes more rapid and the costs of the goods and services they buy increases.

The effects of inflation on the distribution of income may be different from those commonly expected. As we have seen, it is not true that owners of business firms as a group benefit from inflation because their income consists of profits. Instead, it depends on whether the firms are creditors or debtors. Also, the idea that wages lag behind prices has been widely accepted. The redistributive effects of inflation were thought to be primarily the result of a lag of wages behind prices. Some recent historical research has questioned this point of view.[9]

THE UNDESIRABLE EFFECTS OF INFLATION

There are several reasons why inflation—especially unanticipated, intermittent inflation—is undesirable. Probably the major objection to conditions of price instability is that government policies to reduce the rate of inflation usually cause a slowdown in the economy and a rise in unemployment. In addition, the wealth transfers when inflation is not fully anticipated may be large and are difficult to justify. In the period from 1965 to 1973, during which rates of inflation rose to 6 percent, it was difficult for many persons to find ways to save that yielded a real rate of return. Real after-tax rates of interest on savings deposits and on most types of bonds were typically near or below zero, and with little appreciation in stock prices during much of this period, real dividend-price ratios were below zero. Also, unanticipated fluctuations in the rate of inflation may hinder the effective operation of credit markets by increasing the risk of borrowing and lending. Interest rates tend to adjust to the rate of inflation, and every time there is a change in the rate of inflation there is confusion and serious loss for some persons. When the rate of inflation rises unexpectedly, debtors gain; when the rate of inflation falls unexpectedly, creditors gain. Under these circumstances, business success depends primarily on the ability to forecast changes in prices and to adjust rapidly to them. This involves a waste of resources because persons must use some time (and often other resources) monitoring the inflation in order to avoid incurring losses or to take advantage of changes in the rate of inflation.

Even a steady, anticipated inflation should be avoided if possible. Cost accounting becomes complicated, and it becomes difficult to keep meaningful records. If prices are rising rapidly, nominal prices do not give an accurate picture of the costs of items purchased at different times. Under extreme circumstances, bookkeeping becomes very complicated and requires adjustments with price indexes.

During inflation, the usefulness of money declines because it becomes more costly to hold in real terms. As people begin to anticipate the rise in prices, they will attempt to hold other real or financial assets instead of money. But real assets are expensive to store and handle and do not serve well as liquid resources because their prices usually do not rise in exactly the same proportion as prices in general. The holding of financial assets, even when interest rates discount inflation, is risky because the market seldom discounts the rate of inflation exactly. Only if inflation is avoided does money maintain its real value and provide the kind of liquidity that people want. There are no fully adequate substitutes.

Inflation also has important, and probably undesirable, effects on the policies of labor unions. If inflation is unanticipated and union wage contracts do not include escalator clauses, workers may more frequently resort to strikes. The resulting harm to the economy may be considerable.

In countries with inflation, particularly serious economic distortions result from the rigidity of certain prices or from governmental programs of price control. Fixed rates of exchange result in growing balance-of-payments deficits. Sources of credit dry up when interest rates on savings deposits are kept from rising. The expansion in the output of goods and services whose prices are controlled tends to become inadequate. Shortages and delays in obtaining necessary resources impede production. A country may attempt to avoid these distortions either by eliminating inflation or by keeping prices as flexible as possible. Brazil is an example of a country which has been unable to avoid continuous inflation but since 1967 has quite successfully avoided many of these distortions through the quick upward adjustment of all prices. Savings banks not only pay depositors interest but periodically credit their accounts with a "monetary correction" equal to the rate of inflation over the period. Loans, mortgages, government securities, and wages are all adjusted upward in a similar way. Under this system the economic growth of Brazil from 1967 to 1974 has been one of the most rapid of any country in the world.[10]

Inflation also has significant effects on fiscal policy. Inflation in the United States automatically, and without any necessary action by Congress, increases the tax revenue received by the federal government. This is because inflation pushes persons into higher tax brackets, because the rates of the federal income tax are progressive. In addition, the fixed amount of the exemption allowed per person shrinks in real value when prices rise. Also, taxes on capital gains are increased, even though the capital gains are "paper gains" from inflation rather than real gains. In the 1960s and early 1970s, social security benefits had to be reviewed and raised more and more often by Congress as inflation progressed—in order to avoid a reduction in the real value of social security benefits. In 1972, the federal old-age and survivors insurance program was revised extensively to allow for automatic adjustments of taxes and benefits as prices rise.

One effect of the accelerated inflation in the United States in the 1960s was to worsen the nation's balance of payments problem. If all nations have similar rates of inflation, these problems should be at a minimum. However, since the mid-1960s, United States prices have increased more rapidly than previously. Prior to the adoption of flexible exchange rates between the dollar and other major currencies, it became increasingly difficult for our exports to compete in world markets. The result was a series of international monetary crises, much speculation, and considerable international tension.

SUMMARY

Price indexes are not perfect measures of the rate of inflation because of quality changes and different variations in the prices of the items included in the index.

In recent decades, the rate of increase in prices in the United States has been similar to the rate of increase in Money Supply I, although the lag of changes in the rate of increase in prices behind changes in the rate of increase in the money supply is very long.

If the economy is operating at full employment, with wages at equilibrium where the demand for labor is equal to the supply, an increase in the money supply would create an inflationary gap by causing desired total spending to be greater than national income at full employment.

In most versions of the cost-push theory of inflation, excessive union wage demands result in an increase in unemployment—which causes the federal government to follow more expansionary fiscal and monetary policies.

When inflation is unanticipated or underanticipated, there is a transfer of wealth from net money creditors to net money debtors.

When inflation is anticipated, interest rates tend to rise so as to discount the expected rate of inflation. The rise in interest rates reduces the wealth transfer from net money creditors to net money debtors.

NOTES

1. U. S. Department of Labor, Bureau of Labor Statistics, *BLS Handbook of Methods for Surveys and Studies,* Bulletin No. 1458 (October 1966), chapter 10.
2. Ibid., chapter 11.
3. William Nordhaus and John Shoven, "Inflation 1973: The Year of Infamy," *Challenge,* May–June 1974, pp. 14–22.
4. Milton Friedman, "Inflation: Causes and Consequences," in *Dollars and Deficits* (Englewood Cliffs, N.J.: Prentice-Hall, 1968), pp. 21–71.
5. Roberto de Oliveira Campos, "Two Views on Inflation in Latin America;" David Felix, "An Alternative View of the 'Monetarist'– 'Structuralist' Controversy;" and Joseph Grunwald, "The 'Structuralist' School on Price Stability and Development: The Chilean Case," in Albert O. Hirschman, ed., *Latin American Issues* (New York: Twentieth Century Fund, 1961), pp. 69–123.
6. See Armen A. Alchian and William R. Allen, *University Economics,* 2d ed. (Belmont, Calif.: Wadsworth Publishing Company, 1967), pp. 646–681.
7. Armen A. Alchian and Reuben A. Kessel, "Redistribution of Wealth through Inflation," *Science* 130 (4 September 1959), pp. 535–539.
8. G. L. Bach, *The New Inflation: Causes, Effects, Cures* (Englewood Cliffs, N.J.: Prentice-Hall, 1972), pp. 23–27.
9. Reuben A. Kessel and Armen A. Alchian, "The Meaning and Validity of the Inflation: Induced Lag of Wages Behind Prices," *American Economic Review* 50 (March 1960), pp. 43–66.
10. Milton Friedman, "Using Escalators to Help Fight Inflation," *Fortune* 90 (July 1974) pp. 94–97 and 174–176.

QUESTIONS

21.1.   Compare the consumer price index, wholesale price index, and GNP deflator.

21.2. What are some of the problems in measuring changes in the price level?

21.3. Discuss the relationship between changes in the rate of increase in the money supply and changes in prices in the United States from 1952 to 1973. Compare this relationship with the relationship between the rate of increase in the money supply and changes in real output during the same period.

21.4. Using a graph, explain the meaning of an *inflationary gap*.

21.5. Explain how an increase in the money supply may cause inflation. Use both the interest rate–investment approach and the portfolio adjustment approach.

21.6. Using the interest rate–investment approach, explain how an increase in aggregate demand not caused by an increase in the money supply may cause inflation.

21.7. How do aggressive union wage demands cause inflation? Could unions cause inflation if at the same time the Federal Reserve System had a tight money policy?

21.8. Explain the structuralist theory of inflation.

21.9. If people expect 5 percent inflation a year, how will this affect interest rates?

21.10. Define and give some examples of money assets, real assets, and money liabilities.

21.11. What is the relationship between a person's net wealth and his money assets, real assets, and money liabilities?

21.12. Using figures, give an example of the balance sheet of both a net money debtor and a net money creditor.

21.13. Explain why an unanticipated inflation of 100 percent would harm net money creditors. Why would an unanticipated inflation of the same amount benefit net money debtors?

21.14. Why is the effect of inflation on the distribution of wealth much less when inflation is anticipated?

21.15. Would it be better to live with inflation or to try to prevent it?

21.16. What harm is done by inflation?

21.17. Know the meaning and significance of the following terms and concepts: price index, GNP deflator, nominal interest rate, inflationary gap, cost-push inflation, demand-pull inflation, wealth transfer effects of inflation, net money debtor, net money creditor, net wealth, anticipated inflation, Gibson paradox.

Chapter 22
Inflation and
Unemployment

*The effect of changes in the rate of increase in the money supply
on real output and unemployment is probably only temporary.
In the long run, the rate of increase in the money supply
determines the rate of increase in prices—the larger the rate of
expansion of the money supply, the more rapid the rate of inflation.*

The economic policy goals of the United States include both stable prices
and a low rate of unemployment. How to achieve each of these goals
is one of the major concerns of economics.

MEASURING UNEMPLOYMENT

The unemployment rate is the ratio of the total number of unemployed
to the total labor force.[1] Rates of unemployment were from 15 percent
to 25 percent during much of the 1930s—as a result of the Great Depression from 1929 to 1933 and then another fairly serious depression in
1937–1938. Since World War II, the annual rate of unemployment has
varied from a low of 2.6 percent in the second quarter of 1953 to a high
of 7.4 percent in the second quarter of 1958, as shown in Figure 22.1.
During the past twenty years, the average rate of unemployment has been
4.9 percent. The rate of unemployment varies inversely with the business
cycle, falling in periods of expansion and rising in periods of contraction.
    The *labor force* consists of those who are working and those who
want to work. Not counted in the labor force are children under sixteen
years of age, students, retired persons, the disabled, and wives who are
not looking for work. The estimates of unemployment are based on
direct interviewing of a scientifically selected sample of the total population. A person is counted as employed if he did any work at all during
the sample week. In addition to those who are fully unemployed, there

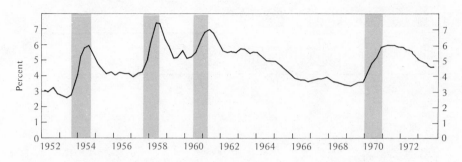

Unemployment rates shown are quarterly averages of monthly figures, seasonally adjusted. Shaded areas represent periods of business recession.

Figure 22.1   Unemployment Rate, 1952–1973

Source: Federal Reserve Bank of St. Louis, *Review,* January 1972, p. 4; and *Employment and Earnings,* February 1973, p. 179.

are persons who would like to work more hours a week. Estimates of unemployment do not include partial unemployment.

The meaning of a particular level of unemployment may be illustrated by examining the rate of unemployment for a given month. In December 1973, for example, the unemployment rate was 4.8 percent. This corresponds to 4,364,000 unemployed. Table 22.1 shows that almost a third of the unemployed were teenagers, many looking for their first job. Approximately one-third were women workers twenty years of age and over, many of whom do not work continuously. The remaining third consisted of men twenty years old and older. The period of unemployment for most of those without jobs was short. Over half had been unemployed less than five weeks, and the average duration of unemployment was slightly less than nine weeks. In December 1973, the total number of hard-core unemployed who had been out of work for six months was estimated to be 331,000 persons, 7.6 percent of the total number of unemployed. The rate of unemployment varies both with the total number of different persons unemployed and the length of time they are unemployed. If persons take a slightly longer time to find new jobs, the rate of unemployment rises.

Although full employment is often stated to be an economic goal, there is no agreed-upon measure of it. People are counted as unemployed while they are negotiating for employment or moving from one position to another. This kind of unemployment is caused by the mobility of labor and is called *frictional unemployment.* Unemployment of this type need not be undesirable, because the economy benefits when people shift

Table 22.1
Total Unemployment, Persons 16 Years of
Age and Over, December 1973

AGE GROUP	THOUSANDS OF PERSONS, (SEASONALLY ADJUSTED)
16 to 19	1,265
20 years and over	
Females	1,573
Males	1,526
Total	4,364

Source: *Economic Report of the President*, January 1974 (Washington, D.C.: U.S. Government Printing Office, 1974), p. 278.

from lower-paying to higher-paying jobs. Also, changes in consumer demand cause much unemployment that is not considered undesirable. When the demand for a particular product declines, workers who had been manufacturing that product will be laid off and will have to look for jobs in other types of firms. In addition, certain types of employment are unavoidably seasonal and require a regular inflow and outflow of labor. To allow for this frictional unemployment, government policymakers have usually assumed that full employment was reached when the unemployment rate was around 4 percent or perhaps a little less. Except during wars, the rate of unemployment has seldom been much below 4 percent, even in periods of prosperity.

Frictional unemployment is much higher for teenagers and women than for men aged twenty and over. This is primarily because they often do not work continuously throughout the year. Teenagers may work only a few months in the summer and spend the rest of the year in school. At least once a year they are looking for a job, and each time they may be counted as unemployed between the time they start looking and the time they start work. In the 1960s, the percentage of the total labor force consisting of women and teenagers increased. This change in the structure of the labor force would raise the overall rate of unemployment for the economy even though the rates of employment for each of the component groups—women and men over twenty, and teenagers—were unchanged. In recent years, there has been increasing concern that a target of 4 percent unemployment or less was too low and that its use as a goal would be inflationary.

A new measure of unemployment—called the *index of unemployment severity*—reflects changes in the length of unemployment as well as changes in the number of unemployed.[2] The index of unemployment severity is the fraction unemployed multiplied by the average number of days the unemployed have been out of work in that year. In 1973, for example, the index would be 2.5 days (the unemployment rate of 4.9 percent, expressed in hundredths, multiplied by the average length of unemployment, fifty days). The index is equal to the average duration of unemployment for the entire labor force. It tends to rise in recession periods and fall in periods of prosperity. It is less affected by structural shifts in the age and sex distribution of the labor force than the unemployment rate alone.

Changes in the rate of unemployment are more significant than a particular *level* of unemployment. Such changes vary with business activity and indicate trends in the use of our most important resource, human labor. Increases in the rate of unemployment are usually caused by declines in economic activity. Following the enactment of the Employment Act of 1946, there was increased use of both fiscal and monetary policy to prevent unemployment caused by insufficient aggregate demand.

In recent years, there has been growing interest in types of unemployment other than that caused by inadequate demand. Whether or not expansionary fiscal and monetary policy can be used effectively to reduce the rate of unemployment below its average long-run level of almost 5 percent has become a major economic issue.[3] There are two divergent points of view toward the problem of unemployment as it has existed in the United States since World War II. The conventional view is that the growth of aggregate demand has not kept up with the expansion of the labor force and the rise in labor productivity. It is believed that an unnecessarily high rate of unemployment results because firms do not hire the expanding labor force rapidly enough. Those who hold this view advocate more aggressive fiscal and monetary policy to increase aggregate demand as fast as the growth of the labor force. The more recent view is that the high rates of unemployment in the postwar period have been the result of the difficulties new entrants into the labor force have in finding out where the jobs are, the low job attachment among those at work, and unnecessary seasonal and cyclical fluctuations in labor demand. This point of view rejects the conception of the labor market as one in which the number of job seekers is typically larger than the number of jobs available. Instead, the labor market is conceived of as operating effectively enough so that in a short time the supply of labor becomes equal to the demand.

Recent statistical studies of unemployment have uncovered information that tends to support the new point of view that high rates of unemployment are not the result of inadequate total spending. It has been found that less than half of the unemployed were laid off by their employers. The bulk of the unemployed either had voluntarily left their jobs, were reentering the labor force, or were looking for their first jobs. Also, even if expansionary government policies reduced the rate of unemployment of men over twenty-four years of age to very low levels, there would still be excessively high rates of unemployment among particular groups of workers such as teenagers and women. Advocates of the new point of view believe that an important way in which the long-run rate of unemployment could be reduced is by the creation of a special Youth Employment Service primarily concerned with the transition of young workers from school to permanent employment. Another proposal is to encourage firms to provide young workers with training on the job and opportunities for significant advancement, in order to reduce labor turnover by making jobs more attractive. Also, it has been suggested that the system of unemployment compensation be reformed so as to remove the present incentive to the unemployed to take as long as possible before locating a new job.

INFLATION OR LARGER OUTPUT?

There is considerable statistical evidence that in the United States a high rate of increase in total spending initially increases the rate of expansion of real output (and lowers the rate of unemployment) and some time later causes prices to rise more rapidly. In addition, there is evidence that the stimulating effect on real output is temporary, while the effect of the higher rate of spending on the rate of inflation lasts. The diagrams in Figures 22.2, 22.3, and 22.4 are used to analyze the way in which total spending affects real output and prices.

The aggregate demand schedule in Figure 22.2 is for a particular level of national income. The level of national income depends on the supply-demand conditions of money and on investment and saving, as explained in Chapters 17 and 18. If the national income increases, this schedule would shift to the right; and if national income decreases, it would shift to the left. The aggregate demand schedule is a rectangular hyperbole. The national income is equal to prices *times* real output, the two axes of the graph. A rectangle drawn under the schedule would be equal to the national income, and all rectangles from different points on the same demand curve would be equal in area. The schedule shows that, given the level of national income, real output varies inversely with prices. The higher the prices, the smaller the quantity of real goods and services that people would be able to purchase and business firms would be able to sell.

The aggregate supply schedule in Figure 22.3 shows the amount of goods and services that firms would be willing to sell at various prices.

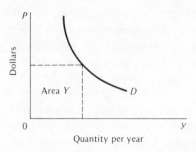

Figure 22.2   Aggregate Demand Schedule

It assumes that the level of money wage rates and technological and resource conditions affecting the productivity of labor are given. If money wage rates rise, the schedule would shift upward. Firms would be willing to sell the same real output only at higher prices because of the increase in their costs per unit of output. On the other hand, if the productivity of labor increased because of better technology, the supply schedule would shift downward. Firms would be willing to sell the same real output at lower prices because of the decrease in their costs per unit of output.

At low levels of real output, the aggregate supply schedule slopes upward very gradually if at all. If there is idle capacity in plants, costs per unit of output do not rise as more labor is hired and output is expanded. Eventually, however, the aggregate supply schedule slopes upward, indicating that as real output increases, costs per unit of output and prices rise. This is because it becomes necessary to use additional labor with a given quantity of other resources. Because of the law of diminishing returns, labor productivity declines when workers have smaller amounts of other resources to work with.

Figure 22.3   Aggregate Supply Schedule

In Figure 22.4(a), the aggregate supply and demand schedules are combined. The point of equilibrium which determines the level of prices and the level of real output is where the two schedules intersect. To be in equilibrium, prices must be at a level where people are able to purchase the entire real output of the economy. If prices were higher than P_1, aggregate demand would be less than aggregate supply. People would not have large enough incomes to purchase the output of the economy, and prices would fall to P_1 as producers lowered their prices so as to sell their entire real output. If prices were below P_1, aggregate demand would be greater than aggregate supply. People would be able to purchase the entire output of the economy and still have some income left to spend. With excess incomes, they would bid up prices until the value of the goods purchased was just equal to the incomes they had to spend.

Figure 22.4(b) illustrates the conditions in which the principal effect of an increase in total spending will be to increase real output. An increase in total spending, possibly because of easier monetary or fiscal policies, would shift the aggregate demand schedule to the right, causing output to increase (from y_1 to y_2) and prices to increase only very slightly (from P_1 to P_2). It is assumed in this figure that the increase in total spending does not shift the aggregate supply schedule upward by causing wages to rise more rapidly. When total spending increases, wages probably do not rise immediately. Instead, persons work overtime and spend less time in between jobs. As a result of the lag of wages behind total spending, the increase in total spending has a stimulating effect on real output and little effect on prices. If the aggregate supply schedule is unchanged, the only reason why prices would rise is that the average productivity of labor might decline if more workers were hired and used with a relatively fixed quantity of other resources. This would cause costs per unit of output to rise and would result in higher prices.

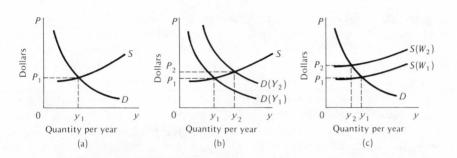

Figure 22.4   Factors Affecting the Equilibrium Level of Prices and Real Output

Figure 22.4(c) shows how an increase in total spending may eventually raise prices if the increase in aggregate demand causes wages to rise more rapidly—and the higher prices would reduce real output. An increase in wages would shift the aggregate supply schedule upward, raising prices from P_1 to P_2 and lowering output from y_1 to y_2. Because higher wages would increase their costs and thus the prices of what they sell, firms would expect that they would not be able to sell as much and would lower their planned output. Prices would rise because the public would bid up prices until their expenditures were equal to the value of the goods produced. A more rapid rate of expansion in total spending would probably cause wages to rise more rapidly eventually. Persons would not want to work overtime permanently, and they would eventually take the customary amount of time between jobs. When wages rise, the stimulating effect of the increase in total spending on real output and the reduced rate of unemployment do not last. Instead, the long-run effect of an increase in aggregate demand is a higher rate of inflation.[4]

Increases in the productivity of labor because of greater amounts of capital used with labor, and improvements in education and technology, cause the supply schedule in Figure 22.4 to fall. Historically the productivity of labor in the United States has increased, on the average, 2 percent a year. Given no change in national income, increases in productivity tend to increase real output and lower prices. In order to sell the larger output of goods that they are now able to produce, firms would have to lower prices. The effect on prices and output of the upward shifting of the supply schedule as a result of wage increases is typically offset in part by the effect of the downward shifting of this schedule as a result of the improvement in the productivity of labor.

DETERMINANTS OF WAGE MOVEMENTS

The graphs in Figure 22.4 show that changes in wages may have an important effect on the movement of prices and real output. The more rapidly wages rise, the larger the rise in prices and the smaller the increase in real output. There are several factors that affect the movement of wages.

The rate of unemployment is a major factor determining how fast wages rise. The relationship between unemployment and the rate of increase in wages is illustrated graphically in Figure 22.5—with the *Phillips curve*, named for Professor A.W. Phillips.[5] In this graph, the higher the rate of unemployment, the less rapid the rise in wages; and if the rate of unemployment is high enough, wages may even fall. One would expect

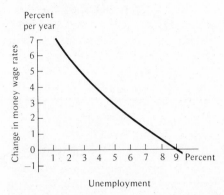

Figure 22.5   The Rate of Increase in Wages and Unemployment

wages to rise more slowly when many people are unemployed. The supply of labor would be large relative to the demand. Some persons would accept lower wages rather than not work at all. On the other hand, when there is little unemployment, there will be strong upward pressure on wages. The demand for labor may be greater than the supply. Rather than not get the labor they want, business firms will bid up wages. Although there is considerable downward inflexibility of wages, there is undoubtedly much less resistance to wage increases.

Not only does a low rate of unemployment speed up the rate of increase in wages, but also rapid increases in wages will lower the rate of unemployment. When wages are rising rapidly, persons will be more inclined to accept job offers quickly and will spend less time looking for them; the shorter the time persons spend looking for jobs, the lower the rate of unemployment. On the other hand, when wages are rising slowly, persons may decide to incur the cost of spending more time looking for jobs. This will cause the rate of unemployment to rise.

In addition to the level of unemployment, whether or not the rate of unemployment is rising or falling is an important factor affecting wage movements. Even when there is still a relatively large amount of unemployment, if business is expanding and the rate of unemployment is falling, wages tend to rise more rapidly because some employers have to bid up wages to get the labor they need. In a statistical study of Great Britain, Professor Lipsey found a good relationship between the rate of change in money wages and the rate of change of unemployment.[6] He found that wage rates tended to rise fastest when unemployment was falling and slowest when unemployment was increasing.

Wage movements may also be affected by the rate of increase in wages that people have become accustomed to. These expectations have an important effect on union bargains, the wage policies of business enterprises, and the attitudes of job-seekers. Expected increases in wages change slowly because it takes some time for persons to assess new conditions. When total spending slows down, workers who lose their jobs may believe that the layoff is temporary and not seek work elsewhere. If they do look for other jobs, they will probably be reluctant to work for lower wages than they were accustomed to. As a result, when aggregate demand declines, wages will not fall immediately despite the poor job market.

An additional factor affecting wage movements is union power. If higher union wages are not offset by lower nonunion wages, average wages rise. Particularly in periods when abnormally large numbers of union contracts must be renegotiated, union wage increases may be large. Although it is probably a common error to underestimate the effect of market conditions on what labor unions demand, they need not be guided solely by such conditions. Union demands may be large even though there is considerable unemployment or even though aggregate demand is declining.

EFFECT OF AN EXPANSIONARY MONETARY POLICY

A major problem for the monetary authorities is that an expansionary policy, designed to increase real output, may instead raise prices.[7] As illustrated by Figure 22.4(b), the immediate impact of a higher rate of increase in total spending is usually the result desired—a more rapid rate of expansion of real output. This is because the expectations of business firms and unions significantly determine their wage and price policies, and those expectations are based primarily on their recent experience. As a result, wages and prices are not immediately adjusted upward to an increase in aggregate demand. Instead, business firms may let their inventories decline temporarily and persons may work longer hours than usual.

Eventually, however, business firms will probably raise their prices in response to the larger demand for their products, and workers will ask for more rapid increases in wages. Business firms will restore their inventories to customary levels, and persons will probably wish to return to their customary hours of work and amount of employment. If prices and wages rise more rapidly, the long-run effect of a more expansionary monetary policy would be on prices rather than on real output.

The rate of unemployment that can be expected to prevail in the long run is probably determined primarily by institutional arrangements rather than by changes in aggregate demand resulting from monetary policy. These arrangements include the efficiency of employment offices, how well organized the system of publicizing job opportunities is, and other factors affecting the speed with which persons can shift from one job to another. An increase in aggregate demand would cause the actual rate of unemployment to fall temporarily. But a relatively low rate of unemployment would not last because it would cause wages to rise more rapidly. This would discourage the hiring of labor and raise the rate of unemployment back toward its customary level. Nor would a relatively high rate of unemployment last—because it would cause wages to rise more slowly. This would encourage persons to hire more labor, and the rate of unemployment would fall back to its customary level.

Attempts by the monetary authorities to keep the rate of unemployment below its normal long-run rate could cause a continuous acceleration in the rate of inflation.[8] Suppose that 4 percent were the long-run rate of unemployment. At first, if the rate of increase in the money supply were raised, for example, from 2 percent to 3 percent a year, output would increase, and unemployment might fall to 3½ percent. But as people became adjusted to the new rate of spending, prices and wages would rise more rapidly, output would fall, and unemployment would rise back to 4 percent. To again reduce the rate of unemployment back to 3½ percent, the rate of increase in the money supply would have to be increased further, for example from 3 percent to 4 percent. This kind of situation appears to have occurred during the late 1960s. Unemployment was kept relatively low, but the rate of increase in the money supply was accelerated and this caused the rise in prices also to accelerate.

EFFECT OF ANTI-INFLATIONARY POLICIES

Recent attempts by the Federal Reserve System to combat inflation have caused output to decline and the rate of unemployment to rise.[9] When the federal government attempted to halt inflation through a restrictive monetary policy in 1959–1960, the rate of unemployment rose from 5.5 percent in 1959 to 6.7 percent in 1961. In 1969–1970, when efforts were taken to combat inflation, the rate of unemployment rose from 3.5 percent in 1969 to 6.0 percent in December 1970.

If wages and prices declined immediately when monetary policy was tightened, output need not decline and unemployment need not rise. However, at the same time that monetary policy is becoming more restrictive, wages and prices are usually rising more rapidly. This is because during an expansion, wage increases typically lag behind increases in aggregate demand, and when monetary policy becomes tighter, wage increases are still trying to catch up. Both the tighter monetary policy restricting aggregate demand and the relatively large wage increases cause the rate of unemployment to rise.

The restrictive monetary policies in 1959–1960 eventually caused wholesale prices to level off, and slowed up the rise in consumer prices and the GNP deflator. Also, after the restrictive policy in 1969–1970, the rate of inflation dropped to approximately 3½ percent in 1971–1972. This slowing down in the rise in prices tended to increase output and decrease unemployment. However, before the slowing down of the rate of inflation, output declined and unemployment rose.

In the South American countries that have rapid rates of inflation, economic activity also appears to be sensitive to changes in monetary policy. While those countries are trying to cut back on the growth of the money supply, prices and wages continue to rise because people have come to expect them to rise. The lags in adjustment to the slower growth in the money supply are so long that it is almost impossible for these governments to hold to a tight money policy. Initially, when strong efforts are made to control inflation, output has declined and unemploment has increased.

TRADE-OFF BETWEEN INFLATION AND UNEMPLOYMENT

Table 22.2 shows that in the early 1960s, when the rate of unemployment was relatively high, the rate of inflation was relatively low. In the mid-1960s, when the rate of unemployment declined, the rate of inflation rose. Experience of this type supports the belief that there is a trade-off between inflation and unemployment. The cost of a low rate of unemployment, it is claimed, must be a higher rate of inflation. From 1961 to 1963 the rate of inflation was fairly steady, even though unemployment generally was falling. Prices may have held steady because unemployment was still relatively high, and there may have been enough slack in the economy for an increase in demand to have little effect on prices. From 1964 to 1966, as the rate of unemployment fell, the rate of inflation became more rapid. Then from 1966 to 1969, despite a more rapid rate of inflation, the rate of unemployment did not fall. When unemployment gets relatively low, it probably cannot be reduced much further. In 1970, when the rate of unemployment rose, the rate of inflation, as measured by the GNP deflator, also rose. When inflation occurs in a period of expansion, prices usually continue to rise even after the peak of the cycle

Table 22.2
The Rate of Unemployment and the Rate of
Change in the GNP Deflator, 1960–1973

YEAR	RATE OF UNEMPLOYMENT	RATE OF INFLATION (GNP DEFLATOR)
1960	5.5%	1.6%
1961	6.7	1.3
1962	5.5	1.1
1963	5.7	1.3
1964	5.2	1.6
1965	4.5	1.8
1966	3.8	2.8
1967	3.8	3.2
1968	3.6	4.0
1969	3.5	4.8
1970	4.9	5.5
1971	5.9	4.7
1972	5.6	3.2
1973	4.9	5.3

Source: *Economic Report of the President, February 1974* (Washington, D.C.: U.S. Government Printing Office, 1974), pp. 254 and 279.

has been passed. Also, during the recovery in 1972 after the recession of 1969–1970, prices continued to fall even though the rate of unemployment was falling. In recent years the rate of unemployment has been high despite high rates of inflation, and there appear to be important exceptions to the idea that there is a trade-off between inflation and unemployment.

FULL EMPLOYMENT DILEMMA

The popularity of full employment as a goal of economic policy has created a dilemma in regard to the wage policies of unions and the price policies of business firms. When business firms raise their prices, their sales tend to decline. When unions raise wages, employment opportunities for the union members will tend to be fewer. These adverse effects could have a restraining effect on price and wage increases. Employers would be more restrained if they thought that their sales would be less whenever they raised their prices. Unions would be more restrained if they thought their policies would mean fewer jobs for their members. If unions and business firms are confident, however, that the monetary authorities will take whatever measures are necessary to maintain output and employment, they need not be concerned about the effects of their wage and price policies on output and employment. They know that the unemployment that might be caused by increasing wages and prices can be avoided by a sufficiently expansionary monetary or fiscal policy.

If business firms increase prices excessively, probably the only way to force them to cut down on their price increases is to allow aggregate demand to fall and thus reduce the demand for their products. Only if they have difficulty selling what they have produced will they be willing to alter their pricing policies. The same applies to the labor market. Probably the only way to induce workers not to seek such large wage increases is to allow unemployment to increase, making it more difficult to get jobs. At times, it may be impossible for the federal government effectively to combat inflation without temporarily causing unemployment, even though the basic cause of the difficulty is the wage policies of unions and the price policies of business firms.

PRICE AND WAGE CONTROLS

An alternative to monetary policy as a method of controlling inflation is government wage and price controls. If wages are controlled, prices must also be controlled because real wages depend on price movements. There are different types of wage and price controls. During World War II, wages and prices were "frozen." In the mid-1960s, the federal government established guidelines for both wages and prices. The guidelines program was much milder than the wartime controls. In August 1971, the federal government initiated a series of programs to control wages and prices—including temporarily freezing both wages and prices, temporarily freezing prices but not wages, and establishing mandatory and then voluntary controls.

Freezing Wages and Prices in World War II

During World War II, the federal government used the most extensive program of wage and price controls that we have ever had. Wartime government expenditures had to be greatly expanded; it was not possible to tax heavily enough to prevent inflation or to drain off enough purchasing power through the sale of savings bonds. To regulate wages, Congress established the National War Labor Board. The Board froze most wages and salaries at the levels of September 1942. In addition, President Roosevelt set up the Defense Mediation Board to keep industry functioning smoothly, and he appointed the War Manpower Commission to mobilize the nation's manpower for the war effort. Management and labor agreed that there would be no strikes and that all disputes would be settled by the National War Labor Board. Congress also passed the Smith-Connally Act authorizing the government to take over private plants in which there were strikes and to maintain the same working conditions as prevailed under private operation.

The problem of keeping retail prices under control was put in the hands of the Office of Price Administration. Ceiling prices were set on retail commodities at levels that prevailed on a certain date, generally in late 1942. To avoid shortages, the Office of Price Administration also instituted a system of rationing. A ration book containing stamps was issued to each individual, and the proper number of stamps had to be given the merchant whenever any of the rationed commodities, such as sugar and meat, were purchased.

One of the problems resulting from rationing and price control was a decline in the quality of certain types of goods. Labor costs rose in spite of the wage freeze because of the upgrading of labor and the use of overtime. Business enterprises were able to continue to operate profitably without price increases often only by reducing quality. Another problem was the development of black markets, where rationed goods were sold at prices above the legal ceilings and without ration stamps. Black markets sprang up in meat, gasoline, radios, and a number of other commodities. In addition, the red tape associated with the controls was annoying and the programs were so unpopular that they were terminated very quickly following the war.

The price and wage controls during World War II were quite effective. From 1941 to 1945, consumer prices rose only 20 percent, although some economists believe that this estimate of the rise in the cost of living is too low. From 1945 to 1948, after price and wage controls were lifted, consumer prices rose 33 percent, even though fiscal and monetary policy were no longer inflationary. A principal effect of the wartime controls was to delay the rise in prices. Average hourly earnings in manufacturing rose almost 40 percent from 1941 to 1945, but then another 30 percent from 1945 to 1948.

The main objection to freezing wages and prices is that such controls do not attack the problem at its roots. Unless the money supply is controlled, inflationary pressures will continue. Monetary expansion is probably unavoidable in major wars, but not under normal circumstances. Wage and price controls merely repress the inflation and eventually create other problems that may be even worse.

The serious problem created by putting ceilings on wages and prices is that such controls simultaneously freeze *relative* prices. If A costs $2 and the price of B is $1, the ratio of the two prices is 2 to 1. Freezing prices not only makes these prices the maximum that can legally be charged, but freezes this ratio. As a result, the pricing system can no longer operate effectively in allocating resources. In a dynamic economy in which consumer demands change and techniques of production are improved more for certain goods than for others, changes in relative prices guide the reallocation of resources from uses that are declining in importance to those that are increasing in importance. If the economy needed more chemical engineers, for example, the salaries of chemical engineers would rise relative to the wages of other types of engineers. This would induce more engineering students to choose chemical engineering as their special field of study, and the supply of chemical engineers would soon be adjusted to the larger demand. Without such changes in relative wages and prices, the economic system would not adjust promptly to changes in demand and to changes in the cost of production. In a free pricing system, changes in relative prices adjust the supply to changes in demand for every occupation and every good and service in the economy. Normally, changes in relative prices and wages work well enough in reallocating resources, so that we take the process for granted. But when relative prices are frozen, the pricing system as a method of reallocating resources can no longer perform this function as effectively as it should.

A dramatic example of the importance of efficient resource allocation occurred in West Germany in 1948.[10] In the six months following the abolition of their system of rationing and price controls, industrial production rose by about 46 percent. Following World War II, similar experiences occurred in Italy and Japan. During the war, wage and price controls did not disrupt the economic organization of countries as much as they did after the war. While at war, the use of the pricing system to allocate resources and guide the economy could be replaced by administrative controls designed to maximize military production. Following the war, when the military objectives were discarded, the controls impeded the transition to a peacetime market-oriented economy.[11]

Wage and Price Guidelines in the 1960s[12]

The United States government initiated a policy of guidelines for prices and wages in 1962. Appeals were made to labor unions to be moderate in their wage demands and to business enterprises not to raise prices. Critics referred to the guidelines as a "policy of exhortation." The guidelines for wages attempted to limit the annual increases in wages to the increase in labor productivity. Wage increases that did not exceed increases in productivity would not be inflationary. Although exceeding the guidelines for wages was not illegal, the federal government used its influence to persuade unions and business enterprises not to exceed them.

Experience with the guidelines indicated that the federal government had quite effective powers over the pricing policies of some large corporations. In 1962, when the steel companies raised prices, President Kennedy was able to force them to retract. Many large corporations are sensitive to adverse publicity and dislike being accused of social irresponsibility. Through its own contracts with business enterprises, the federal government could have exerted much more power than it did. Government contracts are so important to most large corporations that the fear of losing them for failure to comply with the wishes of the federal government would keep them in line. It is doubtful, however, whether controlling the prices charged by some of the large corporations is an effective way to control prices in general. If certain prices are kept down, people are left with more to spend on other products whose prices cannot so easily be controlled. These uncontrolled prices will tend to rise more than they otherwise would have, and the rise may offset the effect of the lower prices in the controlled sector. The most that can be expected from controls of this type is to postpone the wage or price increase. Eventually, union wages or the prices of goods produced by large corporations would be raised as much as other wages and prices.

Unless governmental efforts to control prices of goods and services are successful, the guidelines for wages will not be followed by the labor unions. Unions expect wages to rise enough both to keep up with inflation and to reflect productivity gains. After 1965, both fiscal and monetary policy were so expansionary that it is doubtful that the guidelines could have worked. Because prices rose despite the guidelines, unions would not limit their annual wage increases to productivity gains, and the guideline targets had to be discarded in 1966.

Although guidelines tend to be ineffective as a method of controlling a demand-pull inflation caused by excessive aggregate demand, some economists believe that they would work well under conditions of cost-push inflation. Effective wage controls directly prevent cost-push inflation caused by excessive increases in wages. Although the federal government might attempt to restrain union wage demands and price increases of enterprises by letting unemployment rise, guidelines are viewed as a method of preventing unemployment caused by excessive wage increases from occurring in the first place. But under changing conditions in which demand-pull forces alternate with cost-push forces in raising prices, it is not easy to establish effective guidelines.

Wage and Price Controls in the 1970s

In August 1971, at a time of international crisis, President Nixon introduced the first of several programs to directly control wages and prices. Phase I of these programs consisted of a ninety-day freeze of wages and prices.[13] The purposes of the freeze were to curtail inflation and help solve the balance of payments problem.

In November 1971, the freeze was followed by Phase II, which consisted of a mixture of voluntary and mandatory regulations. Stores were required to post their retail prices, guidelines were set for wages, and firms were permitted to increase prices without approval only if they could show that profit rates were not above those for two of the three previous fiscal years. During 1972 the rate of inflation declined, and it appeared that the wage and price controls had been quite effective. At the beginning of 1973, controls were relaxed somewhat. The new regulations were known as Phase III and were considered to be a step back toward the long-run goal of a free market. Phase III removed rent controls, and smaller firms no longer had to keep records used by the federal government to audit their price and wage decisions.

The initial success of the Nixon administration in combating inflation was short-lived. In 1973, the rate of inflation rose to new peaks. In June 1973, President Nixon announced the beginning of a second price freeze lasting sixty days. In July, the freeze was replaced by Phase IV, which provided that firms could raise their prices only if their costs rose. Larger firms were required to notify the federal government of planned price increases. Smaller firms were required to submit quarterly or annual reports, depending on their size. Only very small firms were exempt from reporting. The policy toward wages was to continue the guidelines that had already been established—a 5.5 percent increase in wages per year plus 0.7 percent for fringe benefits. During 1971–1973, union wage increases were generally within the guidelines that had been set. It was hoped that the tightening of price controls in Phase IV would keep wage demands moderate and reduce the danger of an upward wage-price spiral.

The sharp acceleration in the rate of inflation in 1973, despite the wage and price control programs of the Nixon administration, may have been caused by the relatively rapid increase in the money supply from 1971 through 1973. Also, the devaluation of the dollar, poor agricultural harvests, and the worldwide rise in commodity prices added further to the inflation. The controlled price ceilings, particularly on food items and petroleum, eventually caused shortages and appeared to have the undesirable effect of discouraging an expansion in their supply and thus of leading eventually to even higher prices. Even though Congress had originally urged President Nixon to use wage and price controls to combat inflation, in 1974 Congress permitted the controls to expire.

SUMMARY

Although the rate of unemployment varies with changes in business activity, the high levels of unemployment in the United States are probably related to conditions in the labor market, such as the difficulty new entrants into the labor force have in finding out where the jobs are.

An increase in the expansion of total spending tends to reduce unemployment in the short run, because increases in wages and prices lag behind increases in total spending. Also, in the short run, decreases in total spending increase unemployment, because wages and prices do not fall immediately when total spending declines.

In a period of economic expansion, when wages and prices eventually catch up to an increase in total spending, wages and prices may rise more rapidly than total spending and have an adverse effect on real output.

Governments often attempt to combat inflation by legislating wage and price controls. Such controls have important side effects on the functioning of the free-market system. In a free-market system, unless prices are free to fluctuate, production will not be efficiently adjusted to changes in demand and to changes in the cost of production, and there will be shortages or surpluses of many goods.

NOTES

1. U. S. Department of Labor, Bureau of Labor Statistics, *BLS Handbook of Methods for Surveys and Studies,* Bulletin No. 1458 (October 1966), chapter 1.
2. See Geoffrey H. Moore, *How Full Is Full Employment?* Domestic Affairs Study No. 14 (Washington D.C.: American Enterprise Institute, July 1973), pp. 17–21.
3. Martin S. Feldstein, *Lowering the Permanent Rate of Unemployment,* Joint Committee Print, Joint Economic Committee, 93rd Cong., 1st sess. (Washington, D.C.: U.S. Government Printing Office, 18 September 1973); and "The Economics of the New Unemployment," *Public Interest,* Fall 1973, pp. 3–42.

4. For a comparison of Marshallian and Keynesian theories on the adjustment to disequilibrium, see Axel Leijonhufvud, *On Keynesian Economics and the Economics of Keynes* (New York: Oxford University Press, 1968), pp. 50–54.

5. A. W. Phillips, "The Relation between Unemployment and the Rate of Change in Money Wage Rates in the United Kingdom, 1861–1957," *Economica* 25 (November 1958), pp. 283–299.

6. Richard G. Lipsey, "The Relation between Unemployment and the Rate of Change of Money Wage Rates in the United Kingdom, 1862–1957: A Further Analysis," *Economica* 27 (February 1960), pp. 1–31.

7. See David I. Fand, "Some Observations on Current Stabilization Policy," in Alfred K. Ho, ed., *Economic Policies in the 1970s*, Michigan Business Papers, Number 57 (Ann Arbor, Mich.: The University of Michigan, 1971), pp. 31–47.

8. Milton Friedman, "The Role of Monetary Policy," *American Economic Review* 58 (March 1968), pp. 1–17, reprinted in *The Optimum Quantity of Money and Other Essays* (Chicago: Aldine, 1969), pp. 95–110.

9. For a discussion of anti-inflationary policy for 1974, see James Tobin, "Monetary Policy in 1974 and Beyond," and William Poole, "Reflections on U.S. Macroeconomic Policy," *Brookings Papers on Economic Activity*, 1 (1974), pp. 219–246.

10. Egon Sohmen, "Competition and Growth: The Lesson of West Germany," *American Economic Review* 49 (December 1959), pp. 986–1003.

11. See Walter Eucken, "On the Theory of the Centrally Administered Economy: An Analysis of the German Experiment; Part I," *Economica*, May 1948, pp. 79–100.

12. For a description and evaluation of this program, see George P. Shultz and Robert Z. Aliber, eds., *Guidelines, Informal Controls, and the Marketplace* (Chicago: University of Chicago Press, 1966).

13. Marten Estey, "Wage Stabilization Policy and the Nixon Administration," in *A New Look at Inflation* (Washington, D.C.: American Enterprise Institute, 1973), pp. 107–133.

QUESTIONS

22.1. How is the rate of unemployment measured?

22.2. Discuss some of the factors affecting the long-run rate of unemployment.

22.3. Draw an aggregate demand schedule on a graph and explain its shape.

22.4. Graph an aggregate supply schedule and explain its shape.

22.5. The equilibrium level of prices and real output is where the aggregate demand schedule intersects the aggregate supply schedule. If prices are above the equilibrium level, explain why they will fall to that level. If prices are below the equilibrium level, explain why they will rise to that level.

22.6. Given the aggregate supply schedule, explain why an increase in total spending, shifting the aggregate demand schedule to the right, will cause primarily an increase in output and little increase in prices.

22.7. Given the aggregate demand schedule, explain why an increase in wages may cause prices to rise and real output to fall.

22.8. Given the aggregate demand schedule, explain why an increase in the productivity of labor may cause real output to increase and prices to fall.

22.9. "A more expansionary monetary policy may reduce the rate of unemployment in the short run, but not in the long run." Explain and discuss.

22.10. Explain why a tight money policy, designed to reduce the rate of inflation, causes an increase in the rate of unemployment.

22.11. Discuss the factors affecting how rapidly wages rise.

22.12. Explain why a policy of freezing wages and prices is an impediment to the use of the market system for allocating resources.

22.13. What were some of the problems associated with the freezing of wages and prices during World War II?

22.14. Discuss and evaluate the use of wage and price guidelines as a method of preventing inflation.

22.15. Know the meaning and significance of the following terms and concepts: rate of unemployment, labor force, frictional unemployment, full employment, Phillips curve, wage and price guidelines, wage and price freeze, trade-off between inflation and unemployment.

Chapter 23
International Finance

Most countries need to hold some international reserves—gold, dollars,
pounds, or SDRs—in case they are short of foreign currencies because of
a deficit in their balance of payments. Borrowing from the International
Monetary Fund is also a means of temporarily obtaining foreign exchange
to cover an excess of imports.

The governments of most countries typically hold a supply of international reserves (gold, dollar deposits, pound deposits, or special drawing rights). This enables them to obtain foreign exchange for business
firms engaged in international trade, in case there occurs a temporary
excess of imports over exports in the balance of payments for the country
as a whole. In addition, the governments of most countries must set up
some type of technique for avoiding continuous deficits. Otherwise their
international reserves sooner or later become exhausted. Because the
money of the United States and Great Britain, the dollar and the pound,
have themselves been types of international money, conditions for the
United States and Great Britain have been different from those for other
countries. These two nations have been able, over an extended period,
to have continuous deficits.

   This chapter is concerned primarily with the exchange transactions
involved in settling international payments. It includes a description of
the ways in which international payments are transacted, of the operations
of the International Monetary Fund, and the statistical statement of the
balance of payments.

FOREIGN EXCHANGE MARKETS

Transactions in international trade involve exchanging the money of
different countries. In the New York foreign exchange market, American
importers who need foreign money of any kind can get it. And American
exporters who have received payment in foreign money can exchange it

for dollars. The exchange of money may take place either in the importing or the exporting country. It is not usually necessary for an American importer to acquire foreign money to purchase foreign goods. He may pay for the goods he has imported with dollars. But then the foreign exporter from whom the goods were purchased will usually exchange the dollars he has received for his own money.

The two large foreign exchange markets in the world are located in London and New York, but there are a dozen or so others of lesser importance. The New York market is somewhat different from the others, but it illustrates the basic operations involved. It has no centralized meeting place, no fixed opening or closing time, and no formal requirements for participation. There are three relatively distinct parts of the overall market: (1) the transactions between commercial banks and their customers who desire to exchange money, (2) the transactions between the foreign exchange brokers located in New York and the trading banks—the small number of commercial banks that have departments operating foreign exchange markets—and (3) the dealings of the trading banks with banks in other countires.[1]

Importers and exporters buy and sell foreign exchange at commercial banks rather than from each other. Exchanging foreign money is one of the services of most commercial banks. The banks without relationships with foreign banks can accommodate their own customers through one of the trading banks. An importer in New Hampshire, for example, can exchange dollars for pounds at his local bank. His local bank would purchase the pounds for this customer from a trading bank (probably one of its correspondent banks). The trading bank has deposits in pounds in a foreign correspondent bank, or in one of its own foreign branches in Great Britain, and arranges for the payment of pounds to the firm to which the New Hampshire importer owes money. Correspondent or branch banking provides the base in each country for the foreign exchange system.

Currently, eight foreign exchange brokers in New York serve as middlemen for the trading banks. They handle the leading types of foreign money in which most trade is transacted—especially the pound sterling, the Canadian dollar, and the Swiss franc. On some days, a trading bank's purchases of a particular type of foreign money will exceed its sales of that money, and on other days sales will be higher than purchases. When it accumulates more foreign money than its customers are demanding, it will have funds tied up not providing an immediate source of income. On the other hand, when the demands for a type of foreign money are greater than the supply coming from its clients, the bank runs the risk of losing business by being unable to satisfy its customers. The brokers provide a wholesale, interbank market where these banks may buy and sell foreign exchange. The trading banks do not trade with each other directly. For their services, the brokers receive a commission paid by the selling bank. The banks seek the best terms available, and the brokers are able to match bids and offers from various banks.

The third part of the foreign exchange market consists of the transactions of the trading banks with their branches or correspondent banks in foreign countries. Several dozen United States banks operate as traders in foreign exchange, but only a small number of these carry out most of the transactions. Branches and representative offices of foreign banks and a few dealers that are not banks also operate in this field. To engage in this type of trading a bank must have balances in accounts in banks in foreign countries. When a New York bank sells a type of foreign money, it sells deposits that it owns in a foreign bank; and when it buys a type of foreign money, it acquires additional deposits in a foreign bank. These international transactions are carried on primarily by telephone, but also by telegraph, cable, and by mail.

Consider the impact on the balance sheet of a New York bank when it sells $1,000-worth of British pounds to an American importer. As shown in the following T-account, the New York bank's deposit in the British bank would decline by $1,000 when it sold this amount to the importer. If the importer were also a depositor of the New York bank, his own deposit would be reduced by the amount he paid for the pounds.

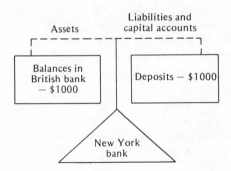

When the bank purchases pounds from an exporter in the United States, the impact on its balance sheet is the opposite. The T-account below shows that the New York bank's deposit at the British bank increases. If the exporter has a deposit at the New York bank, the bank would pay the exporter for the pounds by increasing his deposit by $1,000.

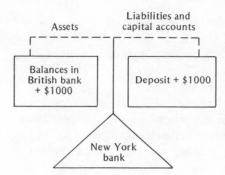

The trading banks in the United States do not have to own balances in correspondent banks in all foreign countries. To obtain the money of many of the smaller countries, the procedure is different. Important foreign banks have dollar balances in banks in New York. To obtain the money of Colombia, for example, the New York bank would probably make a payment to the dollar account of a Colombian bank in this country in exchange for a peso account in the Colombian bank.

Cable Transfers

The principal way in which money is exchanged is by the cable (telegraphic) transfer. When an American exporter wishes to exchange pounds that he has received for dollars, he would cable his bank in London to transfer the pounds to the account of a New York bank in London. Or if the exporter does not have a deposit in a London bank, he would cable the importer from whom payment is due to transfer pounds to the account of the New York bank in London. He would then receive a dollar deposit in the New York bank equivalent to the pounds sold. When an American importer purchases pounds from a New York bank, this bank would cable its branch or correspondent in London to transfer pounds from its account to the British exporter's account. The New York bank then collects the equivalent amount of dollars from the importer. The transfer of funds by cable is usually completed on the first or second day following the purchase or sale, and same-day transfers may in some cases be arranged.

Bills of Exchange

A type of document that has been used in the foreign exchange market for many years is the *bill of exchange,* though the speed and ease of cable transfers has reduced their use. An American exporter may draw a bill of exchange (or draft) on a foreign buyer. The bill of exchange is an order (similar to a bank check) on the foreign buyer to pay a certain amount of money to the exporter on a certain date. The American exporter has the right to draw up such a bill of exchange because he has sold goods to the foreign firm. A bill of exchange is similar to the usual type of bill that is sent to persons who owe money. In foreign transactions, the bill of exchange is for payment in a foreign money. The date on the bill may give the foreign importer some time to pay it, as is typical of many business transactions. Bills that are payable 30, 60, 90, or 180 days after a specified date are known as *time drafts*. Those that must be paid immediately are called *sight drafts*.

For greater security, many bills of exchange are written on the importer's bank rather than on the importer himself and are known as *bankers' bills of exchange*. In order to write a bill of exchange on the importer's bank, the exporter must have received a *letter of credit* from the importer. The latter would obtain this from his bank. It is the bank's assurance to the exporter that the bank will accept his bill of exchange. The exporter has greater assurance of payment because of the superior credit of a bank.

The exporter often attaches to a bill of exchange the shipping documents. Bills of exchange are then exchanged for dollar deposits at a trading bank. The New York bank that buys the bill has legal title to the products sold, until he is assured of payment by the importer. To get possession of the goods, the importer in the foreign country must have made certain arrangements in connection with the payment for them. The New York bank sends the bill of exchange to its foreign branch or correspondent bank, and the latter will collect the amount due on the appropriate date.

If a bank purchases a bill of exchange that is payable thirty days or so in the future, it will purchase the bill at a discount. The bank is in effect lending the exporter money, and the bank would expect to receive interest on the money lent. It is a loan because the exporter receives payment for the bill of exchange immediately, while the bank must wait thirty days or more before it can demand payment from the importer or his bank on which the bill of exchange was drawn. If the bank that purchased the bill of exchange would like to be reimbursed immediately, it may ask the bank on which it is drawn to accept it. After an officer of the bank acknowledges that it has been accepted and "Accepted" is written on the face of it, the bill of exchange becomes a *bankers' acceptance* and may be sold on the open market at a discount. From the point of view of investors, bankers' acceptances are a type of short-term paper similar to United States Treasury bills and commercial paper.

Bills of exchange may also be used by importers as a method of paying for goods that they have purchased. An American importer would purchase a bill of exchange designated in foreign money from one of the trading banks that has deposits in a foreign bank. The bill of exchange would be written by the trading bank in this country on its correspondent bank in the foreign country. The importer would then mail the bill of exchange to the foreign exporter. The foreign exporter gets paid when he presents the bill of exchange to his bank.

Foreign Bank Notes

In addition to the exchange of deposits, part of the international market for foreign exchange consists of the purchase and sale of foreign bank notes and coins. The foreign exchange dealers that are not banks typically trade in this type of exchange. The demand for foreign bank notes comes mainly from American tourists, and the supply comes from foreign tourists visiting the United States. A fairly large volume of Canadian bank notes is acquired by United States merchants in the border areas.

Travelers Checks

The use of travelers checks by tourists is another way of exchanging money. An American may purchase travelers checks in dollars from the American Express Company, Cook's, or one of the large banks that issue these checks. When cashing them in a foreign country, the tourist receives foreign currency for the dollar travelers checks at the going exchange rate. The foreign person or bank that accepts the check may return it to New York for dollars. Such checks are obligations of the American Express Company or the other issuers. The financial standing of the issuers of travelers checks is beyond question so that any foreign person or bank cashing them can be sure of receiving payment. An American may purchase travelers checks in pounds, francs, or other foreign currencies rather than in dollars. By purchasing travelers checks in a foreign currency, a person may protect himself from any adverse change in the exchange rate between the time the checks are purchased and the time he uses them.

EXCHANGE RATES

Each type of foreign money has its price in terms of the dollar. In May 1974, the exchange rate between the dollar and the pound was $2.40 per pound; a French franc was exchanged for approximately 21 cents, and the Mexican peso for approximately 8 cents, and so on for every type of money.

For each type of foreign exchange, the buying price (market bid) is different from the selling price (market offer). This is because the New York trading banks operate on the basis of a small spread between their buying and selling rates, rather than charging a commission for each transaction. There are also *spot* and *forward* exchange rates. Spot exchange is delivered within one or two business days and applies mostly to cable transfers. In a forward exchange transaction, the buyer purchases a foreign currency for delivery in the future. Forward exchange rates depend on the exchange rate that is expected in the future. They are quoted either at a discount or premium from the spot rate. Forward exchange rates are useful guides to various types of transactions. A New York bank that purchased a bill of exchange payable in thirty days, for example, would use the forward exchange rate in calculating the price to be paid for the bill of exchange.

There are several ways in which the exchange rates between currencies may be determined. They may be quite rigidly fixed, as under the gold standard that existed up to the 1930s; they may be fixed in a somewhat less rigid way, according to the arrangements established by the International Monetary Fund in 1944; and they may be flexible, as some of the major currencies of the world have been, particularly since February–March 1973.

Fixed Exchange Rates under the International Gold Standard

With the gold standard, the dollar was defined in terms of a physical quantity of gold. From 1832 to 1934, the official price of an ounce of fine gold was $20.66. When the dollar was devalued in 1934, the price of an ounce of fine gold was raised to $35. The value of the dollar was reduced from approximately $\frac{1}{21}$ to $\frac{1}{35}$ of an ounce of fine gold. Other major countries also specified that their money was equal to a certain physical quantity of gold. As a result of fixing the value of each type of money in terms of gold, the values of different types of money were fixed in relation to each other. From 1819 to 1931 the weight of the British pound in gold was 4.76 times that of the U.S. dollar, and for most of this period up to 1931 the exchange rate between the dollar and the pound was $4.76 to the pound.

Exchange rates between currencies under the gold standard were determined by the declared gold value of different currencies and were kept close to those rates by the willingness of the governments of countries to buy and sell gold at their official gold prices. An American importer, for example, could get pounds by buying gold from the United States Treasury at the official U.S. price. shipping the gold to Great Britain, and selling it to the Bank of England for pounds at their official price. Although the bulk of the pounds needed by American importers came from the receipts of American exporters, the fact that pounds could be obtained in exchange for a certain quantity of gold established an upper limit to the price that importers would pay exporters for pounds. Because there were costs involved in shipping gold, the price of foreign exchange varied within what was known as the *gold points*. These were the upper and lower limits for the price of a foreign currency set by the cost of shipping gold. From 1819 to 1914, the gold export point for the pound was approximately $4.78 and the gold import point was approximately $4.74. Because of the cost of shipping gold, American importers desiring pounds were willing to pay a little more than the fixed rates; and American exporters who had pounds to be exchanged for dollars were willing to receive a little less than the fixed rate.

The IMF System of Fixed, but Adjustable, Exchange Rates

The International Monetary Fund was established at an international conference in Bretton Woods, New Hampshire, in 1944. One of its major functions is to supervise a system of fixed exchange rates.

Under the IMF system, as under the gold standard, the currencies of all member nations were set in terms of gold. However, under the IMF system, the way exchange rates are kept at their official level usually does not involve shipments of gold. Instead, a country's monetary authorities must buy or sell foreign currencies in the foreign exchange market, whenever it is necessary to do so in order to keep their country's exchange rate within one percent of the official rate. In 1972, for example, there was a tendency for the price of a dollar in terms of deutsche marks to fall below the fixed rate of 3.2 DM. At this exchange rate, receipts of dollars by West Germany were greater than their payments of dollars to other countries, and the supply of dollars in West Germany exceeded the demand. To keep the price of a dollar from falling below 3.2 DM, the West German Bundesbank had to buy billions of dollars. The opposite problem has arisen in many other countries. Measures have been needed to prevent the value of their currency from falling. To avoid this, the government of a country must use its holdings of foreign currencies to bid up the price of its own currency.

When a country desires to change its official exchange rate, the International Monetary Fund provides arrangements by which mutual agreement may be reached by the countries involved. Although the International Monetary Fund has usually discouraged countries from changing their exchange rates, their initial objective was to avoid the excessively rigid system of fixed exchange rates that existed under the gold standard.

The reason for the frequent changes in exchange rates that occurred prior to the float in 1973 was the tendency for countries to follow their own independent monetary, fiscal, and wage policies. When countries experience different rates of inflation and different rates of industrial development, their exchange rates must be changed so as to avoid disequilibrium in their balance of payments.

For many years following World War II, the United States did not have to use domestic monetary policy to control its balance of payments because foreigners were willing to hold increasing amounts of dollars. The United States was able to settle continuous international deficits with dollars (usually in the form of checking accounts, time deposits, and short-term U.S. government securities). This combination of an independent domestic policy together with fixed exchange rates lasted up to 1971, and was possible only because the dollar was used as an international type of money. In the early 1970s, when a major adjustment appeared necessary to bring American imports and exports into closer balance, the United States chose to devalue the dollar twice—in 1971 and 1973—rather than attempting to correct the deficit by pursuing a tight money policy.

Floating Exchange Rates

Under a system of floating or flexible exchange rates, countries no longer attempt to keep their exchange rates within certain agreed limits. After the dollar-mark-yen crisis of February–March 1973, many of the major countries of the world announced that they would let their exchange rates float. Great Britain had started to float the pound in mid-1972. In 1971 and in 1973, the adjustments in the exchange rates between the dollar and several currencies were preceded by currency crises. At first the central banks of the surplus countries—West Germany and Japan primarily—bought dollars to prevent the price of the dollar in terms of their currencies from falling. However, they had to purchase so many dollars that they soon gave up the attempt and suddenly announced that they would let the value of the dollar fall. A major difficulty was that when a currency such as the mark became undervalued and it appeared that an upward revaluation would be necessary, speculators shifted from holding other types of currency to holding marks. There was almost no chance that the price of the undervalued mark would decline; it could either stay fixed or rise. If the price were raised, the holder of marks would make a large profit. If it stayed fixed, he could lose only a little—the transactions costs and the interest forgone. A principal objective of allowing exchange rates to be flexible is to discourage speculation. Whenever exchange rates rise sharply under a system of floating rates, speculation is discouraged by the fear that a decline may follow. The floating of major exchange rates has also provided for smooth rather than abrupt changes in exchange rates. In addition, the governments of the surplus countries are no longer embarrassed when, after they have purchased large amounts of foreign currencies, they upvalue their own currency relative to the foreign currency and incur large losses on the foreign currency they purchased.

BORROWING FROM THE INTERNATIONAL MONETARY FUND

In addition to its objective of fixing exchange rates and promoting orderly changes in them, the International Monetary Fund provides a stock of currencies that member countries may borrow in case of need. To cover a deficit or to keep its exchange rate at a fixed level, a country normally has a reserve of international money. But if the amount of its international reserves is not adequate, a country may borrow from the IMF. The offices of the Fund are located in Washington, D.C. In 1973, 125 countries were members. The staff of the Fund provides advice to countries having balance of payments difficulties. The IMF's monthly publication, *International Financial Statistics,* has become a major source of economic statistics on the member countries. Since its founding in 1944, the Fund has promoted multilateral trade among nations and the ending of direct restrictions on trade and discriminatory practices, many of which had developed during the depressed years of the 1930s.[2]

Table 23.1 shows the major items in the IMF balance sheet in 1973. Each member country is required to contribute gold and some of its own currency to the Fund. There is a quota system setting the amount to be contributed by each country. Periodically, the quotas have been increased so as to provide for the expanding needs of the member countries as world trade has grown. The assets of the IMF consist mostly of the gold and currencies received, and on the liabilities side of the balance sheet, the amounts received are accounted for as member subscriptions. As shown in Table 23.1, the unit of account now used by the IMF is the special drawing right (SDR). One SDR is equal to 0.0888671 grams of fine gold, and after the change in the U.S. price of gold in 1973, one SDR was equal to $1.20. If a country needs to obtain foreign money, it may obtain the currency it needs by drawing upon the Fund's stock of gold and currencies. The country would pay for the currency received by replacing it with its own currency. There would be no change in the total assets of the IMF, and member subscriptions would be unchanged. A country is ordinarily limited to borrowing or drawing an amount equal to its own quota; however, additional amounts may be obtained, under certain circumstances. There are different types of regular drawing rights. The *ordinary gold tranche right* is equal to 25 percent of the country's total quota and is virtually available on demand. The *credit tranche rights* are those for the remaining 75 percent of a country's quota. These rights become less available as the amount drawn increases. The amount drawn by a country is a type of credit and is expected to be paid back by the borrowing country as soon as its balance of payments position improves.

Table 23.1
International Monetary Fund: Major Balance Sheet Items, April 30, 1973 (in millions of SDRs)

ASSETS		CAPITAL AND LIABILITIES	
Gold	SDR[a] 5,370	Member subscriptions	SDR 29,169
Currencies and securities	23,742	Reserves and other	789
Unpaid member subscriptions	219	Total	SDR 29,958
Other assets	627		
Total	SDR 29,958		

[a] One SDR = $1.20.
Source: International Monetary Fund, *1973 Annual Report,* pp. 112–113.

SWAP ARRANGEMENTS

The major trading countries also have made swap arrangements with central banks in other countries to obtain foreign currency on call. These swap arrangements are handled through the Bank for International Settlements (BIS) located in Basle, Switzerland. The functions of this bank have changed several times since it was organized in 1930. During the 1960s, it had an important role in programs to stabilize foreign exchange markets and in providing a forum where the central bankers of the world could maintain continuing contact with each other. National governments may use the swap arrangements of the BIS to assist them in preventing the exchange value of their own currency from falling below the limit they had set. They would use the foreign currency obtained from the BIS to purchase their own currency and bid up its price in the foreign exchange market.

SPECIAL DRAWING RIGHTS

In 1970, the IMF made its first allocation of SDRs to aid national governments in need of reserves.[3] The SDRs increased the international reserves of governments and thus provided more adequately for temporary imbalances between exports and imports. SDRs are an alternative to gold as a type of international reserve and have been called "paper gold." They consist of accounts kept by the IMF and are separate from the balance sheet shown in Table 23.1. When the IMF makes an allocation, the recorded amount of the SDRs owned by each national government is increased; when a government uses its SDRs, the amount of SDRs owned by it declines and the amount owned by the national government receiving them is increased. Once issued, it is not possible for member governments to reduce the total amount of SDRs in existence. They are the first deliberately created international monetary reserves. The amount of SDRs issued amounted to $3.4 billion in 1970, $2.9 billion in 1971, and $2.95 billion in 1972. None was issued in 1973 or in 1974. It is expected that there will be further issues in the future as determined by the managers of the IMF, the amount depending largely on the expansion occurring in other types of international reserves.

The government of a country wishing to use its SDRs and in need of pounds, for example, would notify the IMF, and they would arrange for an exchange with the government of a surplus country such as West Germany that had accumulated large holdings of pounds. The government of the country receiving the pounds would then sell them to its importers in need of foreign exchange.

The government of a country receiving additional SDRs earns interest at a rate of 1½ percent on the amount that it owns in excess of its allocation. The governments of countries that have used their SDRs pay interest at the same rate on the difference between their allocations of SDRs and the amount still held by them. The government of a surplus country is not required to accept unlimited SDRs; it may refuse to take them when its holdings are equal to two times its own allocation. The government of a country can use only 70 percent of its total SDR allotment to settle its accounts for the first three years, and must hold the remainder in reserve. The allocations of SDRs to national governments are based on their present quotas in the fund. The quota for the United States is 24 percent of the total. The policy of allocating the bulk of the SDRs to the governments of the more highly developed countries has been criticized.

BALANCE OF PAYMENTS

Table 23.2 presents estimates made by the United States Department of Commerce of items entering into our balance of payments for 1973. These estimates are based on records kept of all types of international financial transactions of persons, business firms, and the federal government. The items are listed in double-entry form and the resulting totals for receipts and payments must be equal. Since World War II, the volume of international trade has increased rapidly. Table 23.2 shows that in 1973 the total value of the transactions between the United States and foreign countries amounted to $115.9 billion.

The balance of payments includes five major categories: (1) the current account, including both the volume of goods and services bought and sold and transfer payments; (2) the capital account, including payments and receipts for private capital transactions and government loans; (3) miscellaneous items; (4) changes in U.S. reserve assets; and (5) changes in U.S. liquid liabilities. In the receipts column is the value of exports and all items that give business firms in the United States, persons, and the federal government either foreign currency or dollars used in international trade. In the payments column is the value of everything purchased by the United States or causing the United States to pay dollars or foreign currencies held by this country to foreigners.

The most important category in Table 23.2 is the *current account*. By far the largest type of transaction in the balance of payments is for *merchandise trade* (goods), which is the first type of transaction under the current account. In 1973, exports of goods amounted to $70.3 billion and imports of goods amounted to $69.6 billion. The dollars that foreigners typically receive when we purchase their goods are used in general to purchase goods from us. Underlying most foreign exchange transactions is real trade.

The second category under the current account is *services*. In 1973, payments for *military services* amounted to $4.5 billion, and receipts for such services amounted to $2.4 billion. An important part of these payments includes the cost of hiring foreigners for the operation of United States military installations in foreign countries. It also includes military aid given to foreign governments.

Investment income arises from interest and dividend payments. American citizens own stocks and bonds of foreign corporations, and large American corporations own the stock of foreign subsidiaries. Also, foreigners own the stocks and bonds of American corporations. Receipts by American owners and by creditors of foreign corporations amounted to $18.6 billion. Payments to foreign owners and to creditors by American corporations amounted to $8.8 billion.

Table 23.2
United States Balance of Payments, 1973
(in billions of dollars)

TRANSACTIONS	BALANCE OF PAYMENTS ACCOUNTS		
	Receipts	Payments	Balance
Current Account	$101.0	$ 97.8	+$3.0
Merchandise Trade (goods)	70.3	69.6	+ .7
Services	30.7	24.3	+ 6.2
Military	2.4	4.5	− 2.1
Investment Income	18.6	8.8	+ 9.8
Travel and Transportation	8.7	11.0	− 2.3
Other	1.0	—	+ 1.0
Transfer Payments	—	3.9	− 3.9
Private	—	1.2	− 1.2
Government	—	2.6	− 2.6
Capital Account	6.7	12.8	− 6.0
Private Long-Term	6.2	6.6	− .4
Direct Investment	2.1	4.9	− 2.8
Portfolio Investment	4.1	.8	+ 3.3
Bank and Other Loans (net)	—	.9	− .9
Private Short-Term Claims and Liabilities	.5	4.7	− 4.2
Government Loans (net)	—	1.5	− 1.5
Miscellaneous	—	4.8	− 4.8
Allocation of Special Drawing Rights	—	—	—
Errors and Omissions	—	4.8	− 4.8
Changes in U. S. Reserve Assets (Increase is payment, decrease is receipt)	.2	—	+ .2
Gold	—	—	—
Special Drawing Rights	—	—	—
Convertible Currencies	.2	—	+ .2
I M F Gold Tranche	—	—	—
Changes in U. S. Liquid Liabilities[a]	8.0	.5	+ 7.6
Foreign Official Holders	5.5	.5	+ 5.1
Liquid Liabilities	4.4	—	+ 4.4
Readily Marketable Liabilities	1.1	—	+ 1.1
Special Liabilities	—	.5	− .5
Foreign Private Holders	2.5	—	+ 2.5
Total	$115.9	$115.9	.0

[a] Includes some liabilities with original maturities of more than one year which can be quickly liquidated, under specified circumstances, with little or no capital loss.
Note: Figures may not add because of rounding.
Source of data: Federal Reserve Bank of St. Louis, *Review*, May 1974, p. 19; *Federal Reserve Bulletin*, May 1974, pp. A64–A65.

When Americans travel in other countries, they exchange dollars for the foreign currencies needed to pay for hotel accommodations, transportation, and other expenses involved in foreign travel. When foreigners travel in the United States or use American carriers, dollars are received back by the United States. In 1973, payments by Americans for *travel* in foreign countries and *shipping charges* on foreign carriers amounted to $11.0 billion. Receipts from foreign travellers in the United States and for shipping charges on American carriers amounted to $8.7 billion.

In 1973, there were receipts of $1.0 billion for *other services*. An example of such services would be the advice of an engineering consultant hired by a foreign firm or government.

Private transfer payments consist of private gifts of money to persons or organizations in foreign countries. Money sent to relatives or to foreign missions is included in this category, which in 1973 amounted to payments of $1.2 billion. *Government transfer payments* measure the dollar aid given to foreign governments under the federal government's foreign aid program. When aid is given to a foreign government, it represents a payment of dollars to them from tax revenues. In 1973, the total amount of foreign aid was $2.6 billion. This aid is usually used to pay for goods purchased from the United States.

The second major category in the balance of payments is the *capital accounts. Direct investment,* a type of long-term private transaction, is done primarily by the large multinational corporations. During the past twenty-five years, the rapid growth of these corporations has resulted in a growing volume of direct investment.[4] When an American corporation constructs a new plant in a foreign country, it involves a payment to persons in that country. If a foreign corporation invests in a new plant in the United States, this would result in receipts by the United States.[5] Over the years, payments by the United States for real capital expenditures in foreign countries have tended to exceed receipts, and in 1973 payments amounted to $4.9 billion and receipts to $2.1 billion.

The second major type of private long-term capital transaction *portfolio investment,* consists of net sales of stocks and bonds to foreigners by persons in the United States, and net purchases of foreign stocks and bonds by United States citizens from persons in foreign countries, for the year as a whole. Because of the interest equalization tax that was levied from 1963 to 1974 on most purchases by United States citizens of foreign securities, such purchases have been restricted, and they amounted to only $0.8 billion in 1973. Sales of United States securities to foreigners amounted to $4.1 billion.

The third type of private long-term capital transaction consists of *bank and other loans.* A loan by a bank in the United States to a business in a foreign country represents a payment of dollars to them. When such loans mature and are paid off, they are recorded as a receipt. In 1973, the net balance on bank and other loans amounted to a payment of $0.9 billion.

Private short-term capital transactions are nonliquid claims and liabilities reported by American banks and nonbanking concerns that represent largely trade financing. Nonliquid claims increase when the amounts owed to American banks and firms by foreigners increase, and nonliquid liabilities increase when the amount owed to foreigners by American firms increases. The nonliquid claims in 1973 amounted to a payment by the United States of $4.7 billion, and the nonliquid liabilities amounted to a receipt of $0.5 billion.

Government loans consist of loans to foreigners under the various lending programs financed by the federal government. Government loans are similar to bank loans—when made to foreigners, they represent a payment of dollars to them, and when paid off at maturity, a receipt. Receipts also include purchases of government securities by foreign official institutions. In 1973 the net balance on those items amounted to a $1.5 billion payment.

The *miscellaneous* category includes errors and omissions, and would have included the annual allocation of SDRs to the United States from the International Monetary Fund if there had been any. *Errors and omissions* is the statistical discrepancy between all specifically identifiable receipts and payments.

DEFICIT IN THE BALANCE OF PAYMENTS

If a country purchases foreign goods and services with funds obtained from its own exports, such payments are sustainable. But if a country buys goods and services and has to pay for them by using its balance of dollars or other international reserves held for covering temporary imbalances in international payments, such payments are not sustainable. Deficits or surpluses in the balance of payments attempt to measure the extent to which the international reserves of a country have weakened or improved.

In each of the years immediately following World War II, the United States had surpluses in its balance of payments. Our exports of food, machinery, and capital equipment were much larger than our imports. It was only through Marshall Plan aid and government grants that foreigners were able to obtain the funds necessary to purchase our exports. The aid tended to reduce our surpluses, but did not eliminate them entirely.

In 1950 the surplus in our balance of payments shifted to a deficit, and since then the United States has had a deficit in its balance of payments in every year except 1957 and 1968, if measured on a net liquidity basis. In 1971 the United States had the first balance of merchandise trade deficit since 1873, although Table 23.2 shows that in 1973 we again had a small merchandise trade surplus. This shift to deficits came as a surprise to most students of international trade. It had been thought in the late 1940s that certain structural changes had occurred in the international economy that would cause the United States to have a continuous surplus in its balance of payments. The United States, it was said, would import little because the country was well stocked with goods and because of tariff protection. On the other hand, American exports were expected to be large because Europe needed the primary commodities produced in the United States and because of the rapid development of American exports of manufactured goods. These conditions were expected to create a "dollar shortage" because our imports, which supply others with dollars, would be less than our exports.[6]

The change to a deficit has been attributed to many factors. These include the economic recovery of Europe and the consequent decline in their need for our exports of machinery and capital equipment, the increase in American purchases of foreign goods as they became available, the devaluation of the pound from $4.00 per pound to $2.80 per pound in 1949, the continuation of relatively heavy military expenditures by the United States in foreign countries, the replacement of the Marshall Plan by aid programs to less developed nations, the large capital expenditures by American enterprises in foreign countries, the desire of foreigners to accumulate dollar balances as a type of international reserves, and the more rapid rate of inflation in the United States starting in 1965.

Because the dollar is an international type of money, the significance of a deficit in the balance of payments of the United States is different from that of other countries. When other countries have deficits, their international reserves get smaller. When the United States has a deficit, the principal effect is not that our reserve assets get smaller, but that other countries build up larger amounts of international reserves in the form of dollars. The principal significance of the size of the U.S. deficit in the balance of payments is that it affects the growth of international reserves in the form of dollars. For other countries, the significance of a deficit is that it shows that its balance of international payments is in need of adjustment so as to avoid a continuous deficit that would deplete its reserves.

The fourth category in Table 23.2 shows the *changes in the reserve assets* of the United States in 1973. These reserve assets consist of gold, SDRs, convertible currencies, and the IMF gold tranche. A deficit in the

U.S. balance of payments would tend to cause a decline in the total amount of those reserve assets. In 1973 there was a decline of only $0.2 billion in the amount of convertible currencies owned by the United States government, and no change in any of the other types of reserve assets. The IMF gold tranche represents the drawing rights of the United States government at the IMF. A decline in the IMF gold tranche would indicate a contraction in the amount the United States Treasury is entitled to borrow automatically from the IMF. It decreases when other member governments of the IMF repay dollars to the Fund for their own currencies.

The fifth category in Table 23.2 shows the *changes in U.S. liquid liabilities* during 1973. These liabilities may be held either by foreign official institutions or by foreign private owners. The sub-category of liquid liabilities consists of foreign holdings of demand or time deposits in American banks. The readily marketable liabilities listed under U.S. liquid liabilities consist primarily of short-term U.S. government securities. The special liabilities consist of types of nonmarketable U.S. government securities sold to foreign governments. Central banks of foreign countries often prefer to hold their international reserves in the form of interest-bearing deposits or securities rather than in demand deposits.

In recent years a deficit in the U.S. balance of payments has resulted primarily in an increase in the total amount of U.S. liquid liabilities to foreigners rather than a decline in reserve assets. Table 23.2 shows that the total amount of those liquid liabilities increased by $7.6 billion in 1973 and was a much more significant indicator of the balance of payments condition of the United States than the change in U.S. reserve assets. This situation of the United States is unique. It is because the dollar is an international money that the United States is able to settle its balance-of-payments deficits by expanding the dollar holdings of foreigners. Foreigners would not accumulate balances of most other currencies. They are willing to accumulate balances of dollars because they are used in payment for international transactions and because they are used by governments of countries as international reserves.

TWO MEASURES OF THE U.S. DEFICIT

The U.S. deficit in the balance of payments is measured in two ways—by the *net liquidity balance* and by the *official settlements balance*. In 1973, the deficit on the net liquidity basis was equal to $7.8 billion. The increase in total U.S. liquid liabilities amounted to $7.6 billion, and the decrease in U.S. reserve assets amounted to $0.2 billion. In the same year, the deficit on the official settlements basis amounted to $5.3 billion. The increase in U.S. liquid liabilities to foreign official holders alone was $5.1 billion. Adding to this the decrease in U.S. reserve assets of $0.2 billion gives a deficit of $5.3 billion. The official settlements balance is equal to the net liquidity balance less changes in foreign private holdings of U.S. liquid liabilities.

The significance of the measures of the U.S. balance of payments has usually been explained in vague terms. It has been said, for example, that the size of the deficit indicates the "net exchange market pressure on the dollar" or "underlying developments" in the balance of payments.[7] It has also been claimed that increases in foreign holdings of dollars are significant because they are a claim on United States reserve assets. However, since 1971 no United States liquid liabilities to foreigners—private or official—have been convertible into U.S. reserve assets. Because of the international role of the dollar, it is probably realistic to view U.S. deficits as a method of providing dollars for foreigners desiring them for international transactions, rather than as a claim on reserve assets.

EURODOLLARS

Eurodollar banks are foreign commercial banks and foreign branches of American commercial banks that have deposits denominated in dollars.[8] Table 23.3 shows that Eurodollar deposits grew rapidly from 1964 to 1973. These deposits may be created when persons transfer deposits from banks in the United States to the Eurodollar banks. Although the deposits are in banks outside the United States (not necessarily in Europe), they are obligations to pay dollars, usually by a check on a deposit in a bank in the United States. They must be backed by some reserves in the form of demand deposits in banks in the United States. Statistical studies indicate that the expansion in Eurodollar deposits is closely related to the expansion of the monetary base in the United States.[9] This may be because American banks tend to expand their domestic and foreign operations in a balanced way and thus increase their foreign operations along with the domestic expansion. The principal reason for the expansion in Eurodollar deposits is that Eurodollar banks have to keep reserves equal to only a fraction of their deposits. On the basis of each dollar of reserves, there may be a multiple expansion of Eurodollar loans and Eurodollar deposits.

Table 23.3
Total Eurodollar Deposits in Banks in
Eight European Countries

END OF DECEMBER	TOTAL AMOUNT (IN MILLIONS)
1964	$ 9,650
1965	11,390
1966	14,770
1967	18,120
1968	26,870
1969	46,200
1970	58,700
1971	70,750
1972	96,730
1973	130,470

Source: Bank for International Settlements,
Annual Report, various years.

The growth of Eurodollar deposits has occurred primarily because rates of interest in these banks are above those on time deposits in banks in the United States. This expansion has been stimulated by the lower reserve requirements for these deposits than for deposits in the United States. In addition, prior to 1974 when the foreign credit restraint program was discontinued, the Eurodollar market made it possible for American banks to finance the activities of large American firms in foreign countries without violating United States government regulations.

The bulk of the deposits received by the Eurodollar banks are invested or used to make Eurodollar loans. In addition, funds acquired by foreign branches of American banks may be lent to their head offices in the United States. Figure 23.1(a) shows the trend in Eurodollar borrowings by United States banks from 1965 to 1973. The exceptionally large increase in those borrowings in 1968–1969 was the result of a rise in Eurodollar interest rates above those allowed on certificates of deposit in the United States by Regulation Q. Figure 23.1(b) shows that Eurodollar rates for ninety-day time deposits rose to over 10 percent in 1969—much higher than the ceiling rates of from 5½ to 6 percent that were set at that time in the United States on the shorter-term CDs. This caused a sharp decline in CDs in American banks and an increase in deposits in the Eurodollar banks. However, the Eurodollar banks then lent a large portion of the funds thus acquired back to banks in the United States. The increase in Eurodollar borrowings largely offset the sharp decline in the CDs of the United States banks. Because of the development of Euro-

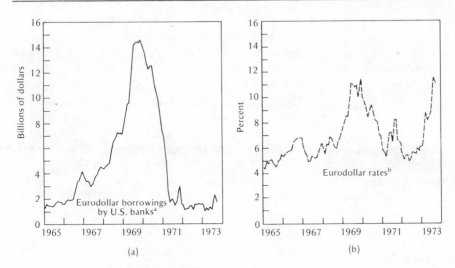

[a]Monthly averages of Wednesday figures. Eurodollar borrowings represent gross liabilities of United States banks to their foreign branches.

[b]Monthly averages of Friday figures for ninety-day Eurodollar rates.

Latest data plotted: September 1973

Figure 23.1 Eurodollar Borrowings by United States Banks and Eurodollar Rates, 1965–1973 (in billions of dollars)

Source: Federal Reserve Bank of St. Louis, *U. S. Balance of Payments Trends,* 24 October 1973, p. 7.

dollar banks, the principal effect of Regulation Q was to reroute the flow of funds to American banks rather than to prevent a rise in interest rates on their sources of funds.

In June 1970, the Federal Reserve suspended Regulation Q interest ceilings of thirty-day through eight-nine-day certificates of deposit issued by banks in the United States in denominations of $100,000 or more. In May 1973, all interest rate ceilings for large-denomination CDs due in ninety days or longer were suspended. It was expected that those changes would enable United States banks to compete more effectively for CDs. Figure 23.1(a) shows that after those changes Eurodollar borrowings by American banks did not increase in 1973 when interest rates rose.

SUMMARY

International transactions require foreign exchange markets in which the money of each country may be exchanged for the money of other countries. Traditionally, most countries have had exchange rates that were not permitted to vary much above or below a fixed rate. In 1973, several of the major countries of the world let their exchange rates float.

Member countries of the International Monetary Fund may borrow foreign currencies from the Fund if they have a deficit in their balance of payments and are in need of foreign currency. They borrow from the IMF by exchanging their own currency for the kind of currency they need.

When the United States has a deficit in its balance of payments, either international reserve assets owned by the United States government decrease or the amount of dollar liquid liabilities owned by foreigners increases. An increase in dollar liquid liabilities owned by foreigners is significant, because those dollars are used to make international payments, and they are held by foreign governments as international reserves.

NOTES

1. See Alan R. Holmes and Francis H. Schott, *The New York Foreign Exchange Market* (New York: Federal Reserve Bank of New York, 1965).

2. For a history of the International Monetary Fund and its policies, see W. M. Scammell, *International Monetary Policy,* 2d ed. (New York: St. Martin's Press, 1961), chapters 5–7.

3. For a history of the development of SDRs, see Fritz Machlup, *Remaking the International Monetary System* (Baltimore: The Johns Hopkins Press, 1968).

4. See Raymond Vernon, *Sovereignty at Bay* (New York: Basic Books, 1971).

5. Receipts of this type have grown rapidly in recent years. Brookings Institution, *Conference on Foreign Direct Investment in the United States* (Washington, D.C.: Georgetown University, Institute for International and Foreign Trade Law, 1970), p. 11.

6. Charles P. Kindleberger, *The Dollar Shortage* (New York, John Wiley and Sons, 1950).

7. David T. Devlin, "The U.S. Balance of Payments: Revised Presentation," *Survey of Current Business* (June 1971), pp. 24–29.

8. For detailed accounts of the operations of the Eurodollar banks, see Milton Friedman, "The Eurodollar Market: Some First Principles," *The Morgan Guaranty Survey,* October 1969, pp. 4–14; Fred H. Klopstock, "The Eurodollar Market, Some Unresolved Issues," *Essays in International Finance,* No. 65 (Princeton, March 1968); Joseph G. Kvasnicka, "Eurodollars—An Important Source

of Funds for American Banks," *Business Conditions* (Federal Reserve Bank of Chicago, June 1969), pp. 9–20; and Fred H. Klopstock, "Money Creation in the Eurodollar Market—A Note on Professor Friedman's Views," Federal Reserve Bank of New York, *Monthly Review* (January 1970), pp. 12–15.

9. "The Eurodollar Market's Big Test," *First National City Bank Monthly Economic Letter,* July 1974, pp. 9–15.

QUESTIONS

23.1. Describe the role in the foreign exchange market of trading banks and foreign exchange brokers.

23.2. Explain the way in which imports and exports affect the foreign exchange balances of the trading banks.

23.3. How are bills of exchange used by exporters in foreign exchange transactions?

23.4. What is a bankers' acceptance, and why are they used in foreign exchange transactions?

23.5. What are the objectives of the International Monetary Fund?

23.6. Explain how member countries may obtain foreign exchange from the IMF.

23.7. Explain what a country has to do to prevent the exchange rate between its money and the money of other countries from rising above its fixed level.

23.8. What are the limits to the amount of foreign exchange that a country may obtain from the IMF?

23.9. Explain the nature of special drawing rights. What is the objective of the IMF's allocations of SDRs?

23.10. Explain why the following types of transactions are payments in the balance of payments: imports of goods, travel in a foreign country, dividends on U. S. corporation stock owned by foreigners, purchases of stock in a foreign corporation, a loan by a United States government credit agency to a foreign government, and a grant of aid by the United States government to a foreign government.

23.11. Explain why the following types of transactions are receipts in the balance of payments: exports of goods, travel by foreigners in the United States, dividends on foreign corporation stock owned by American citizens, and sales of U.S. corporation stock to foreigners.

23.12. What is the meaning of a deficit in the balance of payments?

23.13. What is the difference between a deficit as measured by the liquidity balance and a deficit as measured by the official settlements balance?

23.14. What is a Eurodollar bank, and why have these banks grown in recent years?

23.15. How is the balance of payments affected when persons transfer deposits to a Eurodollar bank and when a Eurodollar bank lends money to a bank in the United States?

23.16. Know the meaning and significance of the following terms and concepts: foreign exchange market, bill of exchange, deficit or surplus in the balance of payments, trading bank, foreign exchange brokers, exchange rate, international gold standard, International Monetary Fund, floating exchange rates, fixed exchange rates, swap arrangements, Eurodollar banks, Eurodollar rates, special drawing rights (SDRs).

"*Then it's agreed. Until the dollar firms up, we let the clamshell float.*"

Chapter 24
Alternative Methods of Balancing International Payments

There are three major methods that a country may use to balance its international payments: monetary policy, changes in exchange rates, and the use of direct controls over imports and exports of goods and capital flows. In 1973, the floating of the exchange rates for several major world currencies resulted in much wider use of changes in exchange rates as an adjustment mechanism.

This chapter is concerned with the use of adjustments in exchange rates to correct deficits or surpluses in a country's balance of payments, and with the use of direct controls over imports or exports. The use of monetary policy to balance international payments was discussed in Chapter 20. In the late 1960s and early 1970s, there were several international financial crises consisting primarily of massive shifts from holding dollars to holding deutsche marks. During this period the use of periodic changes in exchange rates and of floating exchange rates became more common. Such policies avoid balance-of-payments deficits created by the setting of fixed exchange rates above equilibrium levels, and they probably give a country greater control over its domestic economic policies. Direct controls over imports and exports have been widely used by countries, but they have seldom been sufficient to manage a country's balance of payments. It is difficult to devise direct controls that persons are not able eventually to circumvent. Controls usually have to be supplemented to some extent by the use of monetary and fiscal policy or by changes in a country's exchange rate.

CHANGES IN EXCHANGE RATES

Changes in the exchange rate between the dollar and other currencies would be expected to affect the quantity of dollars supplied and demanded in the foreign exchange market. If, for example, the exchange rate between the dollar and the deutsche mark fell from 3 DM to 2.5 DM to the dollar, one would expect an increase in the demand for dollars because to a West German, a dollar would cost only 2.5 DM instead of 3 DM. In addition, there would be a decrease in the supply of dollars to be traded for deutsche marks because deutsche marks would now be more expensive. An American could get only 2.5 DM for a dollar instead of 3 DM.

Figure 24.1 shows the way in which the supply and demand for U.S. dollars vary in the market for foreign exchange. The exchange rate between the dollar and the deutsche mark is on the vertical axis. Although there are different exchange rates for each foreign currency, the price of dollars in this figure is, for convenience, stated in terms of only one currency. The quantity of dollars demanded and supplied is measured on the horizontal axis. In foreign exchange markets, the amount of dollars demanded and supplied is the amount desired per year to make payments for international transactions.

In Figure 24.1, the demand for dollars is based on the demand for the exports of the United States. Foreigners need to acquire dollars to purchase our exports. As the exchange rate falls from 3 DM per dollar to 2.5 DM per dollar, for example, the demand for U.S. exports would

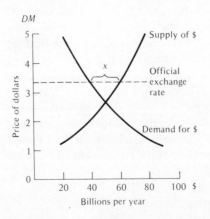

Figure 24.1   Market for Dollars

increase. To foreigners, American goods would be cheaper. Foreigners would almost certainly want to purchase more American exports. With a given price of American exports, the lower exchange rate would increase the total amount of exports purchased and thus the quantity of dollars needed for those purchases.

Underlying the supply of dollars in Figure 24.1 is the demand for imports by Americans. When Americans buy foreign goods, they pay for those imports by exchanging dollars for foreign currency, thus supplying dollars in the foreign exchange market. When the exchange rate rises from 3 DM per dollar to 4 DM per dollar, American imports tend to increase because one dollar can now buy 4 DM worth of goods instead of 3 DM worth, and each item imported is cheaper. For instance, if the price of a good in West Germany is 3 DM and the exchange rate is $1 for 3 DM, the item costs us $1. But if the exchange rate rises to $1 for 4 DM, the item priced at 3 DM would now cost an American 75 cents. The upward-sloping supply schedule for dollars assumes that the demand for imports is elastic. This means that when the price of dollars rises and imports become cheaper for Americans to buy, the quantity of imports demanded increases enough so that, despite the lower price, the total amount spent for them is larger.

If the demand schedule for dollars slopes downward and the supply slopes upward, there is an equilibrium exchange rate where the demand for dollars is equal to the supply. If the United States had a policy of setting a fixed exchange rate rather than letting the exchange rate be determined by market conditions, it would be an unusual coincidence if the official rate set were the same as the equilibrium rate, since the latter varies as conditions of supply and demand change. If the fixed exchange rate were above the equilibrium rate, as it is in Figure 24.1, American imports would be larger than exports, the quantity of dollars supplied would be larger than that demanded, and the United States would have a deficit in its balance of payments. The surplus of dollars, x, would represent primarily the increase in dollar balances accumulated by foreigners plus, prior to 1971, the increase in their holdings of gold acquired from the United States.

If a fixed exchange rate were below the equilibrium rate, exports would be larger than imports, the quantity of dollars demanded would be greater than the supply, and the United States would have a surplus in its balance of payments. Under these circumstances, the dollar balances owned by foreigners would diminish or, prior to 1971, the United States might have acquired larger international reserves in the form of gold.

One way a country may attempt to bring its exports and imports into balance is to change its official exchange rate so that it is close to the equilibrium rate. A country having a deficit might lower its official exchange rate. Such a change would be a *devaluation,* because the country's money would now be cheaper in terms of other currencies. If a country had a surplus, it might raise its official exchange rate, or *upvalue* its money. The upvalued money would now be more expensive in terms of other currencies. There are several different ways in which a country may change its exchange rate. It may (1) alter its fixed rate of exchange immediately; (2) permit its exchange rate to float temporarily, and eventually set a new fixed rate of exchange; (3) let its exchange rate float permanently; or (4) have an announced policy of adjusting its exchange rate to a new fixed level periodically, such as every month or half-year.

Immediate Revaluation

Great Britain devalued the pound in 1949 by declaring an immediate reduction in the rate of exchange from $4.00 to $2.80 a pound. In 1967, the pound was again devalued immediately to $2.40 a pound. Also, West Germany in 1961 upvalued the mark with a surprise announcement that the rate would be reduced from 4.2 DM to 4 DM to the dollar. Members of the International Monetary Fund may unilaterally vary their exchange rates in either direction by 5 percent. Countries typically postpone needed changes in their exchange rates for so long that a 5 percent change would not be sufficient. For larger devaluations, a country is expected to discuss the change with the IMF, and the various countries primarily involved are expected to concur with the action taken and not start a chain of competitive devaluations. Countries have not always adhered to these procedures because of the fear that any discussions concerning a possible devaluation would become known to the public and lead to adverse speculation.

Figure 24.1 shows that a devaluation would reduce the deficit in the U.S. balance of payments provided that the demand and supply schedules did not shift in such a way as to offset the devaluation. There would be no improvement in the balance between exports and imports if, at the same time as a currency was devalued, the demand schedule shifted to the left or the supply schedule shifted to the right because of, for example, more rapid inflation.

A Temporary Float

In 1969, when West Germany upvalued the deutsche mark, its exchange rate was permitted to float for almost a month before setting a new official rate of approximately 3.7 DM to the dollar. In 1971, West Germany again permitted the exchange rate to float for several months before setting a new official rate—of approximately 3.2 DM to the dollar—and other European countries did likewise. Much earlier, in 1948 and 1949, Mexico's exchange rate was also allowed to float before it was reset. Statistical demand and supply schedules for a country's money are difficult to estimate and they vary over time with changing conditions. Rather than attempt to estimate the equilibrium rate, it may be better to let the market determine the rate by permitting exchange rates to float.

The temporary float has the advantage of making it unnecessary to overdo the devaluation. When countries have announced an immediate devaluation of their exchange rates, they usually have devalued substantially so as to be on the safe side and avoid speculation over the need for any further devaluation. Although a substantial immediate devaluation was often successful from the point of view of the deficit country, by replacing the deficit with a surplus, it often shifted the problem to other countries that were now in a deficit position. This has been the history of devaluations in France and England over several decades. France has followed the more aggressive policy, tending to undervalue the franc first and putting Great Britain in a deficit position.

A Permanent Float

The principal country that has floated its currency for a long period of time is Canada. The exchange rate between the United States and Canada floated from 1951 to 1962. It was then fixed at 92.5 American cents for one Canadian dollar; in June 1970, it was again allowed to float. In June 1972, Great Britain floated the pound. Then in February–March 1973, the exchange rate between the dollar and several other major currencies—the deutsche mark, the French franc, yen, the Swiss franc, and several other important European currencies—was allowed to float. The exchange rate system in the world became a mixture, with some exchange rates floating and others fixed. The exchange rates of eight countries in Europe were fixed in relation to each other, but they floated relative to the dollar. Table 24.1 shows the fluctuations in the exchange rates between the dollar and the deutsche mark, the pound, and the yen under floating exchange rates from March 1973 to March 1974.

The way in which countries float their exchange rates is for their central banks to cease buying and selling foreign currencies for the purpose of keeping exchange rates within their prescribed limits. When exchange rates are not controlled, they tend to be where the quantity demanded is equal to the quantity supplied. If, for example, the supply of deutsche marks were larger than the demand, some American holders of deutsche marks would be unable to exchange them at the current

Table 24.1
Foreign Exchange Rates, March 1973–
March 1974 (in cents per unit of
foreign currency)

MONTH AND YEAR		WEST GERMANY Deutsche mark	UNITED KINGDOM Pound	JAPAN Yen
1973	Mar.	35.5	247.2	0.38
	Apr.	35.3	248.4	0.38
	May	35.8	253.0	0.38
	June	38.8	257.6	0.38
	July	42.8	253.7	0.38
	Aug.	41.2	247.6	0.38
	Sept.	41.2	241.8	0.38
	Oct.	41.4	242.9	0.38
	Nov.	38.8	238.7	0.36
	Dec.	37.6	231.7	0.36
1974	Jan.	35.5	222.4	0.34
	Feb.	36.8	227.5	0.34
	Mar.	38.2	234.1	0.35

Source: *Federal Reserve Bulletin*, April 1974, p. A83.

exchange rate. Rather than hold deutsche marks, they would probably be willing to sell them for fewer dollars, and (for example) the exchange rate might fall from 37 cents per DM to 36 cents per DM. On the other hand, if the demand for deutsche marks exceeded the supply, some American importers who wanted deutsche marks and were unable to obtain them would bid up the price, offering more dollars per DM, and the exchange rate might rise (for example) from 37 cents per DM to 38 cents per DM. Only when the quantity of deutsche marks demanded was equal to the supply would there be no tendency for the rate to change. Changes in free exchange rates occur when either the demand schedule or the supply schedule shifts.

A floating exchange rate that is managed to some extent, in order to keep it from rising or falling too much, is referred to as a *dirty float*. The purpose of a dirty float is usually to keep the price of one's own currency relatively low so as to encourage exports. However, a country using this system would not enjoy all the benefits of a clean float. In order to keep the price of its currency low, a country might have to purchase excessively large amounts of dollars.

Periodic Adjustments

A policy of adjusting exchange rates periodically can be similar to a permanently floating exchange rate if the adjustments are made often enough. For several years prior to 1968, Brazil changed its official exchange rate for the cruzeiro every six or seven months. This system did not work well because the adjustments were not frequent enough in view of Brazil's rate of inflation of 30 percent a year. During the intervals between adjustments, severe shortages of foreign exchange developed, and black markets for foreign exchange flourished. In 1968, Brazil adopted a policy known as the *trotting peg*.[1] Under this system, the cruzeiro has usually been devalued by 1½ or 2 percent every five or six weeks. These more frequent adjustments in their exchange rate appear to have worked well. The necessary changes in the exchange rate are so small that speculation is discouraged. In countries with continuous rapid inflation, frequent changes in exchange rates have the advantage of preventing the harmful effects on international trade resulting from a combination of inflation and fixed exchange rates.

PURCHASING-POWER PARITY

If countries do not peg their exchange rates, different rates of inflation from one country to another are a major cause of changes in exchange rates. Suppose prices were stable in the United States but doubled in Argentina. Unless controlled, the exchange rate between the dollar and the Argentine peso would tend to reflect the different price movements in the two countries. The price of a dollar in terms of Argentine pesos would tend to double. Instead of an exchange rate of, for example, 3.5 pesos to the dollar, the price of a dollar would rise to 7 pesos. This is known as the principle of purchasing-power parity. When exchange rates are free to fluctuate, people will exchange one type of money for another at rates that roughly express their relative purchasing powers.[2]

The reason why free exchange rates reflect the purchasing power of different types of money is that the demand for a currency depends on what it will buy in real goods and services. The worth of dollars to a person in Argentina depends on the things he can buy with them. So does the worth of his own pesos. Therefore, the number of pesos that he will give for a dollar must depend on the quantity of goods and services that he can get for the pesos and for a dollar. If the exchange rate did not reflect accurately the purchasing power of each currency in the two countries, persons engaged in foreign trade would profit by taking advantage of the discrepancy. For example, if the exchange rate were 3.5 pesos per dollar and traders could (allowing for transportation costs and tariffs) purchase more petroleum in the United States for a dollar than in Argentina for 3.5 pesos, they would be induced to purchase petroleum in the United States and sell it in Argentina. The demand for dollars to purchase goods in the United States would increase, causing the exchange rate to rise above 3.5 pesos per dollar to a point where this type of trade was no longer profitable.

Although many goods and services that are produced and sold in a country are not traded internationally and consequently would have little effect on exchange rates, enough are traded so that exchange rates roughly reflect varying price movements in different countries. A free exchange rate would not be expected to vary exactly with variations in the official price indexes of the two countries because the prices that affect exchange rates are not exactly the same as those included in official price indexes.

PRICE MOVEMENTS IN
COUNTRIES WITH FIXED
EXCHANGE RATES

Latin American countries that have fixed exchange rates with the dollar and do the bulk of their trading with the United States constitute what may be called a *dollar bloc*. Small countries that have fixed exchange rates with the pound and trade extensively with Great Britain are known as the *sterling bloc*. Price movements in the countries in the dollar bloc have roughly paralleled price movements in the United States. When prices in the United States rose sharply in the 1940s because of the financing of World War II, countries such as Mexico, Costa Rica, El Salvador, and Honduras experienced a somewhat similar rise in prices, as shown in Table 24.2. In none of those countries could inflation be attributed to war finance. Instead, given their fixed exchange rates with the dollar, U.S. wartime inflation was transmitted to them. When prices rose in the United States, those countries were able to sell more to the United States because their prices had not yet risen and their exchange rates were fixed. They tended to have a surplus in their balance of payments. As a result, their international reserves increased, their money supply expanded, and eventually their prices also rose. Although the exchange rates between the currencies of Costa Rica, El Salvador, and Honduras were not changed substantially from 1940 to 1950, Mexico devalued its peso in 1948 and 1949. This accounts for the relatively large rise in prices in Mexico compared to the inflation in the other countries shown in Table 24.1. If Mexico had not devalued, its price trends would probably have been closer to those of the United States and of the other countries listed in Table 24.2. The deflation in the United States during the Great Depression was transmitted to other countries in the same way as the World War II inflation.

Although the exchange rates for many of the major currencies of

Table 24.2
Cost of Living Indexes: United States,
Mexico, and Three Central American
Republics, 1940–1950
(1940 = 100)

YEAR	UNITED STATES	MEXICO	COSTA RICA	EL SALVADOR	HONDURAS
1940	100	100	100	100	100
1941	106	105	105	112	104
1942	117	123	127	115	109
1943	125	159	162	126	125
1944	127	200	170	165	135
1945	129	214	181	185	144
1946	140	268	189	182	145
1947	160	305	216	194	149
1948	173	323	222	197	151
1949	171	336	238	206	158
1950	173	359	262	241	165

Source: United Nations, *Statistical Yearbook, 1955*, pp. 446–447. Reproduced by permission. Copyright, United Nations (1955).

the world are now floating, most small countries still have fixed exchange rates between their currency and other major currencies. It is useful for small countries to have rigid convertibility at a fixed price between their currency and the currency of a major country with which the small country trades extensively or on which it depends for capital for investment. An advantage of dependence on the currency of a large country is that, in contrast to the currency of a small country, it can be used directly to purchase a great diversity of goods and assets. By having a fixed exchange rate with the currency of a larger country, the smaller country will not risk a change in the value of its currency because of fluctuating exchange rates, and its currency will be more acceptable.[3] Another possible advantage of fixed exchange rates for a small country is that its monetary policy may be more stable when guided by its balance of payments than if left to the discretion of its central bankers.[4] When monetary policy is controlled by government officials, there is always the temptation to inflate, because inflation provides additional sources of revenue for the government. A disadvantage of dependence on a major currency is that with fixed exchange rates, inflation or deflation in the major country will be transmitted to the smaller country. However, if prices are stable in the major country, prices will also be stable in the smaller country—and monetary policy is likely to be less inflationary in the larger countries than in smaller countries that are attempting to follow an independent domestic economic policy.

FIXED OR FLOATING EXCHANGE RATES? [5]

The principal argument in support of fixing exchange rates among the major trading countries of the world is that it facilitates international trade. If floating exchange rates caused a slower growth of international trade, they would stifle this important source of economic development throughout the world. Fixing exchange rates eliminates uncertainties that exist when exchange rates are permitted to vary. If the exchange rate should fall between the time a contract was made between an exporter and an importer and the time when the exporter was paid, he would receive less in payment than he had expected. Protection against adverse movements of a free exchange rate would be possible through hedging on the *forward exchange markets* that exist among the major currencies. But such markets are not available for all currencies, and the need to use markets of this type would make trading with foreign countries more complicated.

Hedging can be used to protect oneself against losses resulting from changes in prices of foreign exchange, in the same way as *future markets* are used for commodities.[6] With a forward exchange market, an American exporter to West Germany, for example, could protect himself against loss by simultaneously *selling* deutsche marks in the forward market. If the value of the goods sold was 100,000 DM, and payment was to be made on a date three months later, he would contract to sell 100,000 DM in the futures market on that date. Then, if the deutsche mark, for example, became worth 5 percent less (if the exchange rate fell from 27.3 cents to 26.0 cents to the deutsche mark), the American exporter will probably gain 5 percent in the forward market and lose 5 percent on the amount received for his exports. The payment of 100,000 DM received by the American exporter would be worth 5 percent less because of the fall in the price of the deutsche mark. But in the forward market he would gain because of the decline in the price of deutsche marks in terms of dollars. On the date of payment, he would be able to purchase deutsche marks for a lower price than the price at which he had contracted to sell them.

The argument that floating rates may impede the growth of international trade would be stronger if countries had been able to keep their exchange rates fixed without periodically changing them. The frequent changes in fixed exchange rates in the early 1970s were probably more disruptive than free exchange rates are likely to be because they were large, unexpected, and accompanied by financial crises.

A principal argument against fixed exchange rates is that if the rate is fixed above the equilibrium level at which the supply of a country's currency is equal to the demand, the fixing of the exchange rate would itself be a cause of a country's deficit in its balance of payments. Disequilibrium between supply and demand is the inevitable result of price fixing, for currencies as well as for commodities.

A major advantage of floating exchange rates is that with them monetary policy need not be used to keep international payments in balance. When exchange rates are fixed, it is almost always necessary that a country correct a deficit by a tighter monetary policy. This would probably have the effect of temporarily increasing unemployment. And if a country with a payments surplus follows an easier monetary policy, it may cause inflation. In recent decades, many countries have pursued their own domestic goals apart from international conditions. If countries with fixed exchange rates have different trends in prices and rates of growth, these differences usually result in imbalances in their exports and imports. The system of fixed exchange rates requires a certain degree of harmony in the domestic policies of different countries in order to work satisfactorily. Floating exchange rates give countries greater freedom to pursue the kind of domestic economic policies they desire. The exchange rates of countries with very rapid inflation, such as Argentina, Brazil, and Chile, have had to be changed quite often. Inflation has reduced their exports and increased their imports, creating deficits in their balance of payments. To correct the deficits, they have reduced the value of their own money in relation to the money of other countries, instead of bringing a halt to the inflation.

Another argument against a system of fixed exchange rates is that it leads to the adoption of numerous types of direct controls. Countries attempt to correct the imbalances that arise by enacting restrictions over imports and exports. This hampers free trade and capital flows. A system with fixed exchange rates plus an elaborate system of direct controls may actually impede the development of international trade more than a system of flexible rates.

Before floating their currencies in 1973, Germany, Japan, and some other countries were reluctant to revalue their currency upward even though they were accumulating large surpluses in their balance of payments. They feared that to revalue would harm their prospering export industries.[7] Their exchange rate policies have had the same objectives as the mercantilist policies of former times. A country can just as effectively stimulate exports, discourage imports, and create an inflow of international money through setting a favorable exchange rate as through raising tariffs or subsidizing export industries. This type of international policy had a stimulating effect on the economies of those countries and is one of the reasons for their economic success during the past twenty-five years. The inflow of international money increased their monetary base and resulted in a continuous and rapid increase in the supply of credit and money.

The principal reason for the shift to floating exchange rates in 1973 is that this appeared to be the only way to avoid the speculative disturbances that occurred periodically in the late 1960s and early 1970s.[8] The problem of speculation arises when there is a possibility that a particular fixed exchange rate may have to be changed. When persons expect a currency to be revalued upward, they shift to that currency. Starting in 1969, whenever certain foreign countries—especially West Germany and Japan—began to accumulate large dollar balances because of the large surpluses in their balance of payments, another wave of speculation became imminent. People would speculate that the value of the deutsche mark or the yen would soon have to be upvalued relative to the dollar. In West Germany, this caused people to exchange their dollars for deutsche marks at the West German Bundesbank. In 1969, 1971, and 1973, the Bundesbank tried to avoid upvaluing the deutsche mark, but did not succeed. The shifts from dollars to deutsche marks reached panic proportions. After accumulating billions of dollars, the Bundesbank gave in. The speculators who had shifted from dollars to marks made large gains, and the Bundesbank suffered large losses. The objective of the Bundesbank in floating the deutsche mark in 1973 was to avoid taking further losses of this type and to avoid a repetition of this type of international monetary panic. Under the system of floating exchange rates, it would no longer be necessary for the Bundesbank to purchase dollars in order to prevent the price of dollars from falling.

Although the international panics in 1969–1973 affected primarily those countries that were attempting to avoid upvaluing their currency, panics may also affect countries that are having deficits and are attempting to avoid devaluing their currency. Central banks have typically cooperated with one another to enable the financially weakened country to maintain its exchange rate. As long as the financially weak country can borrow a sufficient volume of foreign currency that it may use to bolster the demand for its own currency, it can prevent a devaluation from occurring at that time. Countries have used foreign exchange borrowed from the International Monetary Fund and swaps of currency through the Bank for International Settlements for this purpose.

Several proposals have been made to provide for greater flexibility of exchange rates without going so far as to let exchange rates float. Some economists have advocated that one of the original provisions in the IMF agreement—for unilateral changes of 5 percent in a country's exchange rate—be used more frequently. Others believe that "widening the band" to allow for greater movements of exchange rates would be useful.[9] The Smithsonian Agreement of December 1971 widened the band from one percent to 2¼ percent up or down for many countries. Another proposal that is a compromise between fixed and freely fluctuating exchange rates is to have a system of *gliding bands*. Such a system would allow both the official exchange rates and the bands which limit their fluctuations to move up or down annually by a given percentage. For example, if the exchange rate that prevailed during the year was near the top of the band, the official rate of exchange and the band would be shifted upward. Or if the exchange rate had been near the bottom of the band, they would be shifted downward for the next year. Such changes would make possible a gradual drift in the bands to accommodate diverse trends in inflation and productivity in different countries.

DIRECT CONTROLS

An alternative way in which countries have attempted to keep their payments in balance is through the use of direct controls. This type of control has been used extensively by the United States. Decreasing the international deficit has been an objective of federal government policy, even though the use of the dollar as an international money has lessened the urgency of this problem in the United States as compared to other countries.

The use of direct controls was the principal adjustment technique available to the United States when the exchange rates between the dollar and other major currencies were fixed. The federal government used monetary policy and fiscal policy primarily to influence unemployment, and it was unwilling to deemphasize this objective in order to use these instruments of control to balance international payments. Direct controls were adopted reluctantly because the United States has also attempted to promote free international trade. Direct controls include tariffs, quotas, voluntary guidelines, and limitations on investments—all types of restrictions that make the economic system less flexible, reduce competition, and prevent gains that countries might achieve through specialization and trade.

The three goals of free trade, fixed exchange rates, and stabilization of the national income cannot all be achieved simultaneously. If a country with fixed exchange rates wishes to maintain stable domestic conditions, it must use direct controls to balance its payments. Or if a country with fixed exchange rates has free trade, it must use monetary policy to balance its payments. But if a country has free trade and uses its techniques of control to stabilize domestic economic conditions, it must adjust its balance of payments through variations in exchange rates.

Government Control of the Purchase and Sale of Foreign Exchange

In its most extreme form, the government of a country may directly control sales and purchases of foreign exchange. All exporters would be required to sell their foreign exchange to the government, and all purchases of foreign exchange would have to be from the government. Even though the demand for foreign exchange at the official exchange rate might be much larger than the supply, the government could limit the amount sold to the amount that it had available—by rationing it for those imports that were considered most important. This type of regulation was characteristic of some European economies following World War II, although by 1958 most currencies had become freely exchangeable in a foreign exchange market. The dollar has always had *market convertibility* —foreigners have been able to use dollars as they wish, to buy American goods, to invest in American securities, and also to convert dollars into other currencies at the prevailing rate. This convertibility of the dollar contributed to the growth of world trade in the period since World War II.

Direct Controls in the United States

The most important type of direct controls used by the United States has been restraint on foreign investment. In March 1965 the Federal Reserve initiated a "voluntary restraint" program in which banks and other financial institutions were asked to increase their lending to foreigners in that year by only 5 percent over the amount at the end of 1964. The Department of Commerce asked over 600 large industrial and commercial corporations engaged in international trade and investment to repatriate their liquid funds and whatever earnings they could. These companies were also asked, in 1965 and in 1966, to limit dollar outflows from the United States plus reinvested earnings to 35 percent more than in the 1962–1964 base period for twenty-two developed countries. Investment financed by borrowing abroad was exempt, since it would not harm our balance of payments and eventually might improve it when earnings flowed back to the United States. The program was initially made voluntary, in order to make it possible to act quickly to stop the abnormally large outflow of long-term capital loans and funds for direct foreign investment, which had shown a 20 percent increase in 1964.

For 1966 the targets for banks were set at 109 percent of the 1964 base; revised guidelines for direct investment by industrial and commercial corporations were also established. In 1968 participation was made mandatory, and permissible increases above the end-of-1964 base were reduced to 3 percent for most banks. Banks were requested not to make any new loans of more than one-year maturity in Western European countries, and not to renew loans when paid off. In 1968 industrial and commercial corporations operating overseas were required to observe annual limits on the transfer of new capital, repatriate a specified share of total annual earnings, and reduce short-term financial assets held abroad to their 1965–1966 level.

From 1963 to 1974, another important type of direct control over capital imports was the *interest equalization tax*. The rate of the tax was initially 15 percent of the purchase price of foreign stocks, and from about 1 percent on notes and bonds maturing in one year to 15 percent on those maturing in twenty-eight and a half years or more. The tax also applied to bank loans. Excluded from the tax were the securities of Canada and many underdeveloped countries.

As a result of the improvement in the U.S. balance-of-payments position in 1973, the interest equalization tax and restraints on foreign investment were dropped completely in early 1974. Both the Commerce Department's program of controls over the amount of money American companies could send abroad for new plants and equipment, and the Federal Reserve Board's program of guidelines limiting lending and investments overseas by American banks, were terminated.

There has been a variety of other programs to encourage American exports and discourage imports. The United States Department of Commerce has given awards to manufacturers who have expanded their exports by a sizable amount. Tourist offices have been set up in important European capitals, in order to stimulate foreign travel to the United States. The duty-free limit on foreign purchases by American tourists was reduced from $500 to $100 per person in the 1960s, explicitly for the purpose of cutting down on imports. Both the leveling off of the foreign aid program and some reductions in our armed forces stationed in foreign countries have had balance-of-payments considerations as one of their objectives. One of the justifications given in recent years for smaller quotas for imports of many basic commodities is that it would benefit our balance of payments. In addition, to induce Americans to travel in the United States rather than in foreign countries, and thus to reduce this type of import, the Department of the Interior initiated a "See America" program. The way direct controls may eliminate a deficit may be illustrated by referring again to Figure 24.1. Direct controls that were designed to expand exports would reduce the gap between the supply and demand for dollars by shifting the demand schedule to the right. Direct controls designed to reduce imports would achieve the same objective by shifting the supply schedule to the left.

THE CONTINUOUS U.S. DEFICIT

A major reason for the continuous deficits in our balance of payments is that foreigners have desired larger dollar balances for use as international money alongside gold, the pound, and, since 1970, SDRs. The dollar has become the most important type of international reserve; it has been used for private international transactions and by foreign governments for intervening in foreign exchange markets for the purpose of controlling exchange rates. During the past twenty-five years, world trade has expanded rapidly. Countries need reserves to cover temporary deficits, and the larger the normal volume of a country's international trade, the larger the occasional deficits a country can expect to have. Also, the larger the number of enterprises engaged in international trade, the larger the number of firms needing dollar balances or some other type of foreign exchange to cover their regular needs for this type of money. In order to accumulate larger international reserves, foreign countries have had to have surpluses in their balance of payments and the United States has had to have deficits.

Although the need for increased world liquidity might have been met by an increased quantity of gold, the quantity of gold in the world has increased at a much slower rate than total international trade. In addition, world liquidity might have expanded by letting the price of gold rise, and with a higher price more gold would probably have been produced. However, until 1968 measures were taken by the major trading countries of the world to prevent the free-market price of gold from rising.

The view that the deficits in our balance of payments are a needed source of international liquidity is different from the traditional explanation of deficits. It has usually been assumed that when a country had a continuous deficit, it was the result of having a high rate of inflation relative to other countries, or of having relatively small improvements in productivity. The traditional solution was either a tighter monetary policy to slow down the rate of inflation or a devaluation in the exchange rate. The difference between the two explanations of the U.S. deficit has been a source of confusion, and the policy that the United States government ought to pursue depends on which explanation is correct. If the continuous deficits have been the result of the desire of foreign countries for additional international reserves, it would have been unwise for the government to pursue a tight monetary policy for the purpose of balancing our payments. Such a policy would both curtail the growth of international reserves and cause economic hardships in the domestic economy of the United States.

With the introduction of SDRs in 1970, the need for growth in dollar balances as a type of international exchange may diminish. If the SDRs allocated to countries provide them with sufficient international reserves, the amount of dollars that they want to accumulate may decline, and the deficit in the U.S. balance of payments needed for this purpose may be much smaller. During the first year after SDRs were issued, the expansion in dollar holdings of foreigners was larger than expected, and it was feared that the expansion in the world's stock of international reserves—SDRs, gold, and the dollar—was excessive and might be inflationary. In 1973 and 1974, the expansion in the volume of dollars owned by foreigners was so large that no additional SDRs were issued.

Despite the important role of the deficits in the U.S. balance of payments in providing for an expanding supply of international money, the continuous deficits in our balance of payments eventually led to important changes in the international monetary system. The continuous deficit has had two effects that have attracted attention: our gold reserves have declined, and the dollar balances owned by foreigners have increased. Figure 24.2 shows the trend of both of these from 1951 to 1973. The excess dollars that foreigners have received from us because of our deficits have been used to accumulate dollar balances and, prior to 1971, to purchase gold from the United States.

The decline in the U.S. gold stock relative to foreign liquid dollar holdings because of the continuous deficit in our balance of payments eventually led to the *inconvertibility* of dollars into gold. Figure 24.2 shows that after 1959 foreign liquid dollar holdings exceeded the gold stock; the United States did not hold enough gold to satisfy all the claims that might be made against it. Under these circumstances, whenever foreigners believed that the official price of gold might have to be raised, they might want to hold gold rather than dollars, and there could be a scramble for it. Intense speculation in gold and widespread hoarding did in fact occur in 1967 and in 1970–1971. This speculation made it necessary for the United States Treasury to change its policy of buying and selling gold. In 1968, the Treasury discontinued all sales of gold to domestic industrial users and all purchases of gold from domestic producers. Cutting off domestic sales of gold helped to conserve gold for use as international reserves. At the same time, the United States Treasury announced that in the foreign market, it would sell gold only to foreign governments, and then only for "monetary purposes." Conversion of dollars into gold became a matter of governmental negotiation rather than a demand obligation. European governments still claimed that the United States had

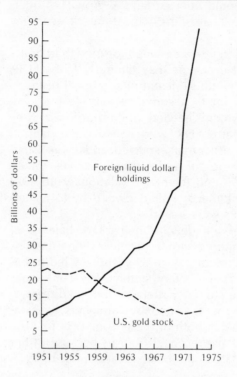

Figure 24.2   U. S. Gold Stock and Foreign Liquid Dollar Holdings, 1951–1973

Source: *Federal Reserve Bulletin,* various issues, tables A67 and A68.

an obligation to convert the dollars they owned into gold whenever they wished to convert them. In 1970, our gold stock decreased as a result of sales to foreign governments, and in 1971, a financial crisis developed in which foreign governments wished to convert large amounts of dollars into gold. This crisis was ended in August 1971 when the United States government declared the dollar inconvertible into gold. Although it is still popular in Europe to demand that steps be taken to make the dollar again convertible into gold or some other type of international reserve, to do so would undoubtedly require a major restructuring of the international monetary system and the development of an alternative to gold.

The second important consequence of the deficits in our balance of payments is that they led eventually to the adoption of floating exchange rates among the major currencies. The continuous deficits led to periodic speculation that the currencies of countries that had large surpluses in their balances of payments would have to upvalue their exchange rates. Under the fixed exchange rate system, countries whose currencies were in demand by the speculators had to purchase excessively large amounts of dollars. The major trading countries shifted to floating exchange rates in order to avoid the need to purchase dollars for the purpose of maintaining their fixed rates of exchange.

The dollar ought to work reasonably well as a type of international money if countries are willing to maintain some flexibility in their exchange rates.[10] Countries with persistent deficits in their balance of payments should depreciate their currencies or let them float rather than deplete their international reserves or attempt to cover their deficits by excessive borrowing. Countries with a persistent surplus should appreciate their currencies or let them float up if they do not want to add to their international reserves, or if they want to prevent inflation resulting from an increase in their international reserves. Between June 1970 and December 1973, the United States devalued the dollar twice, many other countries upvalued their currency, and, starting in February 1973, many exchange rates were permitted to float. As a result of the decline in the value of the dollar, in 1973 American merchandise exports increased 44 percent, there was a net inflow of long-term private capital into the United States for the second time in the last fifteen years, and the United States had a surplus in its balance of trade. The period of excessively large deficits in the U.S. balance of payments may be over.

An alternative to the present *dollar standard* would be to replace the dollar with SDRs as the predominant type of international money. In some foreign countries, particularly in those with strong nationalistic feelings, the dollar standard is regarded as an unjustified special privilege of the United States. In the United States also, the dollar standard is often looked upon as a burden and a source of international embarrassment. However, even with an SDR standard, greater flexibility toward exchange rates would probably be needed for the same reasons as under the dollar standard—to avoid running out of international reserves or accumulating more than desired.

The principal contribution that the United States can make to improving the world's financial system is to keep prices in the United States relatively stable. The lower rate of inflation in the United States in the period following World War II than in most major European countries and in Japan is one reason for the wide use of the dollar as a type of international money. The acceleration in the rate of inflation in the United States that started in the 1960s was undoubtedly a cause of the international financial crises that occurred in the late 1960s and early 1970s. By keeping prices relatively stable in this country, the United States would contribute to world-wide price stability. The dollar could still have an important role as a world currency. It will fulfill this role well only if the United States prevents its purchasing power from eroding.

SUMMARY

A high price of the dollar in terms of other currencies could cause the United States to have deficits in its balance of payments, by encouraging imports by Americans and discouraging exports.

The problem of international financial panics ended with the floating of the exchange rates of some of the major currencies in 1973. With floating exchange rates, the price of the currency of a country with a surplus in its balance of payments will rise immediately, and there is no longer speculation over official changes in an exchange rate.

The principal direct controls used by the United States government to reduce balance-of-payments deficits—restraints on foreign investment and the interest equalization tax—were terminated in 1974.

After 1959, foreign liquid dollar holdings exceeded the value of the United States gold stock. This led to the inconvertibility of the dollar into gold.

In 1970, special drawing rights were created by the International Monetary Fund to serve as a new type of international reserves. They could eventually replace the use of the dollar and other types of international reserves.

NOTES

1. Juergen B. Donges, *Brazil's Trotting Peg, A New Approach to Greater Exchange Rate Flexibility in Less Developed Countries* (Washington, D.C.: American Enterprise Institute, 1971).
2. See Leland B. Yeager, "A Rehabilitation of Purchasing-Power Parity," *Journal of Political Economy* 66 (December 1958), pp. 516–530.
3. Harry G. Johnson, "The Case for Flexible Exchange Rates, 1969," Federal Reserve Bank of St. Louis, *Review*, June 1969, p. 16.
4. Milton Friedman, *Money and Economic Development, The Horowitz Lectures of 1972* (New York: Praeger, 1973), pp. 44–48.
5. For further discussion of the issues, see Meredith O. Clement, Richard L. Pfister, and Kenneth J. Rothwell, *Theoretical Issues in*

International Economics (Boston: Houghton Mifflin Company, 1967), chapter 6; and Fritz Machlup, Gottfried Haberler, Henry C. Wallich, Peter B. Kenen, and Milton Friedman, "Round Table on Exchange Rate Policy," *American Economic Review, Papers and Proceedings* 59 (May 1969), pp. 357–369.

6. Egon Sohmen, *Flexible Exchange Rates, Theory and Controversy* (Chicago: University of Chicago Press, 1961), chapter 4.

7. Harry G. Johnson, "The International Monetary System and the Rule of Law," *Journal of Law and Economics* 15 (October 1972), pp. 289–290.

8. Harry G. Johnson, "The World Monetary Crisis," *Encounter,* August 1970, pp. 43–52; and Gottfried Haberler, *The Dollar-Mark-Yen Crisis, 1973,* Reprint Number 16 (Washington, D.C.: American Enterprise Institute, 1973).

9. George N. Halm, "Toward Limited Exchange-Rate Flexibility," *Essays in International Finance,* No. 73 (Princeton: Department of Economics, Princeton University, March 1969), pp. 9–15.

10. Gottfried Haberler, "Prospects for the Dollar Standard," *Lloyds Bank Review,* July 1972, pp. 1–17; reprinted by American Enterprise Institute, Reprint Number 3, August 1972.

QUESTIONS

24.1. Draw a supply schedule for dollars in the foreign exchange market. Explain its shape.

24.2. Draw a demand schedule for dollars in the foreign exchange market. Explain its shape.

24.3. If exchange rates are free to fluctuate, why will exchange rates in the exchange market for dollars be where the demand for dollars is equal to the supply of dollars?

24.4. Why may a country have a deficit in its balance of payments if its fixed exchange rate is relatively high? Why a surplus if its fixed exchange rate is relatively low?

24.5. Explain why the demand for dollars in the foreign exchange markets would increase if the exchange rate is lowered. Why would the supply of dollars decrease?

24.6. What is meant by the devaluation of a country's money?

24.7. Explain the different methods of changing exchange rates: immediate revaluation, temporary float, permanent float, and trotting peg.

24.8. What are the arguments for a fixed exchange rate?

24.9.   What are the principal reasons why many of the major countries of the world let their exchange rates float starting in 1973?

24.10. What is the principle of purchasing-power parity? Why are the exchange rates between the currency of one country and another affected by this principle?

24.11. Explain why prices in countries with fixed exchange rates move in the same direction.

24.12. Give some examples of direct controls.

24.13. Explain, with the use of a supply and demand graph, the way in which direct controls attempt to influence a country's balance of payments.

24.14. Explain the gold problem created by the continuous deficit in the balance of payments of the United States and the various policies adopted to solve it.

24.15. Would it be desirable to replace the dollar as an international money with the SDR?

24.16. Explain the possible effects of rapid inflation in the United States on the use of the dollar as an international money.

24.17. Know the meaning and significance of the following terms and concepts: devaluation, upvaluation, trotting peg, purchasing-power parity, interest equalization tax, foreign credit restraint program, dollar bloc, market convertibility, dollar standard, inconvertibility of the dollar.

Glossary *

aggregate demand   Total spending for consumption, investment, and government goods and services. It increases as the national income increases. (17)

appreciation bonds   Bonds such as Series E savings bonds which are purchased for less than their maturity value. The interest received consists of the difference between the purchase price and the redemption value of the bond. (4)

asked price   The price at which dealers are willing to sell marketable United States government securities. It is slightly higher than the dealer's bid price. (4)

attrition   The amount of securities not exchanged when new securities are offered to owners of maturing issues in an exchange or refunding by the United States Treasury. Attrition is the amount of cash taken by such owners. (4)

automatic stabilizers   Types of taxes which automatically increase more rapidly than increases in national income—thus tending to reduce total spending. Also, some types of federal expenditures may automatically decrease when national income rises. (19)

autonomous increase in spending   An increase in total spending that is not the result of an increase in income. Examples of autonomous spending are increases in spending financed from savings, increases in government spending, and increases in investment resulting from lower interest rates. (17)

average propensity to save (APS)   Ratio of total saving to the national income—S/Y. (18)

bank-holding company   A separate corporation that owns enough of the stock of one or more banks to exert control. Such companies are subject to special government regulations. (5)

Bank Holiday of 1933   A period of seven days during which all banks in the United States were ordered closed by President Franklin D. Roosevelt. Just before the holiday there were runs on banks and many bank failures. (12)

Bank for International Settlements   Located in Basle, Switzerland. Its principal purposes are to aid governments of countries in their efforts to stabilize their exchange rates and to provide a forum for discussing international financial problems. (23)

bank reserve equation   Shows factors determining the amount of member bank reserve deposits at the Federal Reserve banks. (12)

---

* Numbers in parentheses after each item indicate the chapter in which the concept is discussed.

bankers' acceptance   A negotiable bill of exchange on which a foreign importer's bank has written "accepted." (13)

barter   Trading a good or service for another without the use of money. (2)

bill of exchange   A bill written by a creditor on the person or enterprise owing him money. The bill may be payable on demand or after a specified period of time. (23)

bill rate   The rate of return, adjusted to an annual basis, received by investors in United States Treasury bills. (4)

bills-only policy   Limiting open market operations of the Federal Reserve System to United States Treasury bills or other short-term securities. (13)

bimetallic standard   Existed in the United States when the dollar was defined in terms of both a certain weight of gold and a certain weight of silver. The United States had such a standard until the Coinage Act of 1873 demonetized silver. Under the bimetallic standard, the United States Treasury would purchase gold and silver at their official prices. (3)

bond-support program   The Federal Reserve's policy of keeping bond prices up and interest rates low. A bond-support program existed during and following World War II—from 1941 to 1951. (14)

book value of a share of corporate stock   Based on the value of the capital accounts on the balance sheet of the corporation. It is equal to the total value of the following items listed on the balance sheet divided by the number of shares of stock outstanding: capital stock, .surplus, undivided profits, and various types of reserves for contingencies. (8)

branch banking   A type of banking organization in which a bank has more than one banking outlet. (5)

budget deficit   Federal government expenditures in excess of tax receipts. (19)

business saving   Retained profits of business enterprises. It may be defined to include expenditures to maintain depreciating capital equipment. (18)

capital accounts   The items on the liabilities side of the balance sheet of a company showing the claims of the owners on the assets. These items include the par value of the stock issued, surplus, undivided profits, and reserves for various contingencies. (6)

capital consumption allowances   The part of gross private domestic investment representing expenditures to cover depreciation. (17)

capital stock   The amount of a corporation's stock outstanding. It is listed under capital accounts on the liabilities side of the balance sheet. (8)

central reserve cities New York and Chicago. Member banks in central reserve cities used to be required to hold higher reserve requirements than member banks in reserve cities or elsewhere. This classification was dropped in 1960. (13)

certificates of deposit (CDs) A type of time deposit which matures at an agreed-upon date and which is typically issued to business enterprises. They often have denominations of $100,000 or more and their interest rates depend upon money market conditions at time of issue. (8)

check loan A type of personal loan available to a bank depositor who has arranged with the bank to be able to borrow a limited amount of funds immediately by overdrawing his checking account. (7)

closed-end investment company Similar to a mutual fund, but the number of shares is fixed. Shares can be sold to other investors, but are not redeemed by the company. (10)

collateral Security given by a borrower to a lender as a pledge for repayment of a loan. It usually consists of real estate, an automobile, equipment, securities, or a passbook. (7)

commercial bank A bank offering checking accounts. It may also offer time and savings deposits and engage in other types of banking activities. (5)

commercial loans Short-term loans to businesses, usually for the financing of inventory. (7)

commercial loan theory of bank liquidity A theory of banking that was based on the belief that only short-term, self-liquidating loans were appropriate for banks. (7)

commercial paper Short-term securities issued by industrial corporations, finance companies, and bank-holding companies. They usually have a maturity of less than 9 months and are sold at a discount. (6)

common stocks A financial security issued by corporations to raise capital. The owners of common stock share in the profits and the control of the corporation. (16)

Comptroller of the Currency The head of the Office of the Comptroller of the Currency in the United States Treasury Department. He is appointed by the President and supervises the regulation and examination of national banks. (5)

constant dollars Dollars adjusted for changes in buying power. (21)

correspondent banks Banks connected through interbank deposits. The bank holding the deposit usually provides advice and special services for the bank making the deposit. (5)

cost-push theory of inflation Attributes inflation to excessive wage demands by unions or price demands by large producers. (21)

country banks All member banks of the Federal Reserve System except those classified as central reserve city or reserve city banks. (13)

creation of deposits The ability of the commercial banking system to expand its deposits by several times the amount of an increase in its reserves. The process of creating deposits is called the multiple expansion process. (9)

credit Loans made by lenders to borrowers. Examples are bank loans; corporate, municipal, and United States government bonds; doctors' bills; and charge accounts. (1)

credit risk The risk that the borrower may default. (4)

crowding-out effect The effect on other lending and investing when newly created federal securities are purchased. (19)

currency Coins and paper money. (3)

currency in circulation Currency outstanding, excluding the amount held by the United States Treasury and the Federal Reserve banks. (3)

currency outstanding All United States coins and paper money whether held by the United States Treasury, the Federal Reserve banks, or the public. It includes money held by persons and banks in foreign countries and some that has been lost or destroyed after issuance. (3)

debt management Policies of the United States Treasury designed to influence economic activity by altering the maturity of the United States government debt. (19)

defensive operations Federal Reserve open market operations to prevent changes in items in the bank reserve equation, such as float and gold flows, from causing undesired changes in member bank reserve deposits. (13)

deferred availability cash items A liability account on a Federal Reserve bank's balance sheet. When member banks deposit checks on banks in other Federal Reserve districts in a Federal Reserve bank, this item is temporarily credited for a period of up to two days. (12)

demand deposits Deposits in a commercial bank that usually pay no interest and may be transferred by check or converted into currency at any time. (8)

demand-pull theory of inflation Attributes inflation to excessive aggregate demand. (21)

depositary intermediary A financial institution that creates deposits for savers and lends the money so acquired out at interest to business firms and investors. (10)

deposits at a Federal Reserve bank Checking accounts convertible into Federal Reserve notes. These accounts pay no interest. Ownership is limited to member banks, some nonmember banks, foreign governments or their central banks, the United States Treasury, and a few federal government agencies. (6)

depreciation   The wearing out of plant and equipment, machinery, and housing. (17)

desired investment   The amount of expenditures for capital goods that enterprises desire to make. This may be different from the actual amount of investment because of unintended declines in inventories. (21)

devaluation   A rise in exchange rates, usually as a result of government action. In 1971, for example, the dollar was devalued when the dollar price of deutsche marks rose from 27.5¢ to 30.0¢. (24)

dirty float   A flexible exchange rate that is being manipulated by government intervention in the foreign exchange markets. (24)

discount rate   Rate charged by the Federal Reserve banks for member bank loans. (13)

discounted loan   A type of loan in which the amount received by the borrower is less than the principal amount of the loan. The interest paid consists of the difference between those two amounts. (7)

disintermediation   A reduction in the amount of deposits in mutual savings banks and savings and loan associations, in the value of insurance policies owned by persons, or in the activity of other financial institutions outside the commercial banking system. (10)

disposable income   Personal income less the amount paid in personal taxes. (18)

dollar bloc   Countries that have fixed exchange rates with the dollar and do a large portion of their foreign trading with the United States. (24)

elastic currency   An expansible supply of currency. An objective of establishing the Federal Reserve System was to create a central banking system that could provide additional currency whenever the banks and the public desired it. (12)

eligibility requirements   Federal Reserve regulations determining the types of commercial bank loans or securities that can be used as collateral for loans made by Federal Reserve banks to member banks. (13)

equation of exchange   An identity stating that the total amount of money multiplied by the velocity of money (the number of times money is spent per year) is equal to the annual output of goods and services sold multiplied by their prices. In symbols the equation is expressed either as $MV = PT$ or as $MV = Py$, depending on whether the annual output of goods and services sold consists of all items transacted or only of those items included in the national income. (15)

equilibrium level of national income   Exists when total spending is equal to the economy's total output, or when desired saving equals desired investment. (17)

equities   A type of asset providing a variable amount of income and with a variable sale price. The principal examples of equities are corporation stock and the ownership of unincorporated enterprises. (16)

Eurodollar deposits   Deposits denominated in dollars, held in banks outside the United States—usually in overseas branches of American banks. (23)

even keel policy   Actions of the Federal Reserve banks to keep interest rates from rising during periods of exchanges or refundings of United States Treasury securities. (14)

excess reserves   Bank reserves above the amount legally required. (9)

exchange rate   The price of a foreign currency in terms of a country's own money. (23)

exchange-rate band   The limits below and above its official fixed exchange rate that a government permits its exchange rate to vary. (24)

Exchange Stabilization Fund   An office of the United States Treasury that holds gold and SDRs for international currency stabilization operations. (12)

Federal funds sold   A member bank's deposits at the Federal Reserve bank that have been lent to another bank. (6)

Federal Open Market Committee   An important policy-making unit of the Federal Reserve System. Its membership includes the seven members of the Board of Governors of the Federal Reserve System plus the presidents of five of the Federal Reserve banks. (11)

Federal Reserve notes   The most common type of paper currency in use in the United States today. They are issued by the Federal Reserve banks and are liabilities of these banks. (3)

finance company   Makes personal loans and loans to purchasers of automobiles and other consumer durables. It may also buy installment loans negotiated by automobile dealers and other retailers. (10)

financial assets   Stocks, bonds, commercial paper, *CDs,* or similar claims to physical assets or money. (17)

financial intermediaries   Financial institutions including commercial banks that create deposits or other types of liquid debt to obtain funds which are invested in less liquid types of loans and securities. (10)

flexible exchange rates   Also called floating exchange rates. They are determined in a free market by demand and supply rather than fixed by the government. (23)

float   The difference between cash items in process of collection (on the asset side of the Federal Reserve banks' combined statement) and deferred availability cash items. (12)

foreign credit restraint program   Restrictions established by the United States between 1965 and 1974 on bank lending to foreigners, foreign investment, and the holding of liquid funds and earnings overseas by large American corporations. (24)

fractional coins   Coins with denominations less than one dollar—pennies, nickels, dimes, quarters, and fifty-cent pieces. (3)

fractional reserve bank   Holds reserves equal to only a portion of its deposits. (20)

free banking acts   Laws of the early 1800s that made it easy for entrepreneurs to obtain charters from state government authorities to form banks. (5)

"free" gold   Gold owned by the United States Treasury on which no gold certificates have been issued. (12)

free reserves   Excess reserves of member banks less their borrowings from the Federal Reserve banks. They have been used as a target of Federal Reserve actions. (14)

free trade   International transactions unrestricted by quotas, tariffs, and direct controls. (24)

frictional unemployment   Short-term unemployment caused by the shifting of persons between jobs. (22)

full employment   Usually considered to exist when the rate of unemployment allows for frictional unemployment of about 4 percent. (22)

general obligation bonds   Bonds whose interest and principal will be paid primarily by future taxes collected by the state or local unit of government issuing the bond. (6)

Gibson paradox   Evidence that interest rates are higher at higher rates of inflation, contradicting the theoretical expectation that a more expansionary monetary policy would lower interest rates. (21)

gliding bands   A proposal to allow both the fixed exchange rate and the bands set by a government to vary periodically with the average levels of exchange rates within the bands. (24)

GNP deflator   An index of the prices of the goods and services that make up the *GNP*. (21)

gold certificate   A type of paper money which has not been in circulation in the United States since 1933 and is currently issued by the United States Treasury only to the Federal Reserve banks. It is backed by gold bullion owned by the United States Treasury. (3)

gold certificate account   An asset on the combined balance sheet of the Federal Reserve banks representing the amount of gold certificates owned by the Federal Reserve banks. (12)

gold pool   Operated in London from 1961 to 1968 by the major trading countries of the world. The pool sold gold whenever necessary to keep the price of gold from rising above $35 an ounce. (3)

gold standard   Exists when a national government defines its currency in terms of a given weight of gold and will convert its currency into gold at that rate on demand. From 1879 to 1933 when the United States was on the gold standard, the United States defined the dollar as equal to approximately 1/21 of an ounce of gold. (3)

Gresham's law   A very old principle stating that any type of money that becomes more valuable in some other use than as money will cease to be used as money. (3)

gross national product (GNP)   The value of all the final goods and services produced in a country during the year. (17)

gross private domestic investment   Purchases of newly created capital goods—machinery, plant, and houses—and changes in inventories. Includes purchases to replace depreciated capital goods as well as additions to the total amount of capital goods. (17)

hard-core unemployed   Persons who have been out of work for at least six months. (22)

hedging   Done by exporters and importers to protect themselves from possible losses from unanticipated variations in exchange rates. This is done through forward exchange markets. (24)

high-employment budget   Federal revenues and expenditures estimated at the level they would have reached if there were full employment. This budget is used as a measure of the ease or tightness of fiscal policy. (19)

high-powered money   The monetary base. (9)

human capital   The capitalized value of the earning capacity of individuals. It is increased by education and training. (16)

income velocity   The ratio of the national income during a year to the amount of money in the economy. It is equal to Y/M. (15)

index of unemployment severity   Product of the unemployment rate in decimal terms and the average number of days the unemployed have been out of work in that year. (22)

indirect business taxes   Sales, excise, and property taxes. (17)

inflation   A decrease in the real value of a unit of money. It is usually measured by a rise in the price indexes covering a wide variety of goods. (21)

inflationary gap   The amount by which aggregate demand exceeds the output of the economy at full employment. (21)

insolvent bank   A bank whose deposit liabilities plus borrowings are larger than its assets. (8)

interbank deposit   A deposit of a bank in another bank. (8)

interest equalization tax   Tax imposed by the United States from 1963 to 1974 on the purchase price of foreign stocks, notes, and bonds. (24)

interest rate   The annual rate of return received for lending or investing money, expressed as a percentage of the amount lent or invested. (1)

interest risk   The risk that the price of a security will fall because of a rise in interest rates. (4)

interlocking directors   Directors of one company who are directors of one or more other companies in the same or a similar line of business. (5)

International Monetary Fund (IMF)   An international organization whose principal purpose is to assist the governments of countries experiencing balance-of-payments difficulties. (23)

IMF credit tranche   A type of borrowing rights at the International Monetary Fund. It is less available than the gold tranche right and is equal to three-fourths of a country's quota of its own currency and gold paid in to the *IMF*. (23)

IMF gold tranche   A type of borrowing rights at the International Monetary Fund. It is equal to one-fourth of a country's quota of its own currency and gold paid to the *IMF* and is available almost on call. (23)

international money   The types of money used in international trade—gold, dollars, pounds, and special drawing rights. (23)

labor force   Persons working plus those seeking work. (22)

law of diminishing returns   A basic principle stating that when larger amounts of one resource are used in combination with a fixed amount of another resource, eventually both the marginal productivity and the average productivity of the variable resource will get smaller. (18)

leakages   Uses of the monetary base that lower the size of the money multiplier. The principal leakages result from expansions of currency in circulation, time deposits, and excess reserves. (9)

legal tender   Legally-approved types of money which may be used to pay debts. (2)

line of credit   An agreement by a bank to lend up to a given limit to a business borrower without detailed negotiations over a period of time in the future. (7)

liquid assets   Assets that may be converted into money quickly and without loss in nominal value. (2)

liquidity preference   The demand for money at different interest rates. The demand for money tends to be larger at lower rates of interest. (18)

liquidity trap   May exist when interest rates are so low that persons will not invest additional money holdings in securities because of the expectation that security prices will fall as interest rates rise. (18)

margin requirement　The difference between the amount of a loan and the value of the security or other property purchased with the loan. (7)

marginal efficiency of investment (MEI)　The expected annual net return from an investment in capital goods—allowing for taxes, operating costs, and depreciation—divided by the cost of the capital goods. (18)

marginal propensity to consume (MPC)　The percentage of additional income that persons spend for consumption—$\Delta C/\Delta Y$. (17)

marketability　Exists when a security can be sold quickly with relatively low transactions costs and at a price regularly determined in active markets. (6)

marketable United States government security　One that can be transferred from one owner to another by sale. (4)

maturity date　The date on which the principal value of a bond, loan, savings certificate, or similar debt instrument will be repaid to the lender. (4)

medium of exchange　Money used to purchase goods and services and to pay debts. (2)

mercantilist policies　Governmental policies aimed at maintaining an excess of exports over imports. (24)

mint ratio　The ratio of the official value of one unit of gold (usually one ounce) to the same weight of silver when a country is on a bimetallic standard. (3)

monetary aggregates　A type of target or indicator used to guide Federal Reserve policy. The principal monetary aggregates used are reserves behind private deposits (*RPDs*), total member bank reserves, the monetary base, Money Supply I, and Money Supply II. (14)

monetary base (B)　Total member bank reserve deposits with the Federal Reserve banks plus currency in circulation. The monetary base is also called high-powered money. (9)

monetary reform　A conversion from one unit of account to another, involving a reduction in the quantity of money. (2)

monetary system　The institutional arrangements for supplying the economy with money. (1)

monetary theory of inflation　Attributes inflation to excessive increases in the money supply per unit of output. (21)

money multiplier (m)　The ratio of the amount of money in the economy to the monetary base. The money multiplier is also called the expansion ratio. In symbols it is M/B, and it may be computed for Money Supply I or for Money Supply II. (9)

Money Supply I   Demand deposits plus currency in circulation, excluding currency in the vaults of commercial banks. (1)

Money Supply II   Money Supply I plus time and savings deposits in commercial banks, excluding certificates of deposit in denominations of $100,000 or more. (1)

Money Supply III   Money Supply II plus time and savings deposits in mutual savings banks and savings capital in savings and loan associations. (1)

municipal bonds   Bonds issued by states and by units of local government. Interest from municipal bonds is exempt from federal income taxes. (6)

mutual fund   An open-end investment company that offers to sell an unlimited amount of its shares to obtain funds to invest—usually in corporation stock. The company redeems its shares on demand at a price that reflects the value of its asset holdings. (10)

national bank   One that has received its charter from the United States Comptroller of the Currency. National banks have been required to be members of the Federal Reserve System since 1914 and to be insured by the *FDIC* since 1933. (5)

national bank notes   A major type of paper currency used in the United States from 1863 until 1914. They were issued by national banks in accordance with the terms of the national bank acts of 1863 and 1864, and were liabilities of the banks that issued them. (3)

national debt   The total amount of United States government securities outstanding. The federal government issues securities as a means of borrowing to meet its expenditures when the federal budget is in deficit. (4)

national income (NI)   The total amount of wages, proprietors' incomes, rental income, net interest, and corporation profits received per year. It is equal to gross national product less the cost of depreciation and less the total amount of indirect business taxes. (17)

national income accounts budget   A record of the expenditures and receipts of the federal government, adjusted in accordance with the concept of expenditures for goods and services used in the national income accounts. (19)

near money   Liquid assets other than money. (2)

net borrowed reserves   A negative level of free reserves. (14)

net investment   Gross private domestic investment minus capital expenditures to cover depreciation. (18)

net liquidity balance in the balance of payments   The amount of the annual change in all foreign holdings of United States liquid liabilities. It is a measure of the deficit or surplus in the United States balance of payments. (23)

net money creditor   A person whose money assets exceed his money debts. Also applicable to business enterprises. (21)

net money debtor   A person whose money debts exceed his money assets. Also applicable to business enterprises. (21)

net national product   Gross national product less the cost of depreciation. (15)

net wealth   The value of a person's total assets minus his debts. (21)

noncompetitive bidders   Investors who do not submit a bid price, but offer to pay the average price of accepted competitive bids in an auction of United States Treasury bills. The amount sold to a noncompetitive bidder is limited to $200,000. (4)

NOW accounts   Interest-earning deposits using negotiable orders of withdrawal that are similar to checks. These deposits are permitted in commercial banks and thrift institutions only in Massachusetts and New Hampshire. (8)

official settlements balance in the balance of payments   Equal to the net liquidity balance less changes in foreign private holdings of United States liquid liabilities. It is a measure of the deficit or surplus in the United States balance of payments. (23)

100% reserve bank   Holds an amount of reserves equal to its deposits. (20)

operation twist   Federal Reserve open market operations attempting to change the relative yields of short-term and long-term United States government securities. These operations were important in the early 1960s. (13)

overdraft   A negative balance in a checking account. Overdrafts may be treated like loans, the depositor being charged interest on the amount overdrawn. (7)

permanent income   The level of income expected by a person. When incomes are rising, permanent income tends to be less than the income actually received. (18)

personal consumption expenditures   Spending for food, clothing, housing, transportation, and entertainment. (17)

Phillips curve   A curve showing lower annual percentage increases in wage rates at higher rates of unemployment. (22)

Pigou effect   The effect on total spending of a change in real cash balances, M/P. (18)

portfolio   The real and financial assets owned by a person or financial institution. (17)

price index   A measure of changes in prices in general. (21)

prime rate   The lowest interest rate charged by banks on short-term business loans. Announcements of changes in the prime rate by large banks are widely publicized. (7)

purchasing-power parity   The principle that if exchange rates are free to fluctuate, they will vary so that the currencies of different countries have roughly similar purchasing power. (24)

pure commodity standard   A monetary system in which the only type of money consists of a commodity that circulates. (20)

rationing   A system of distributing goods and services in which there is a maximum limit to the quantity of a good or service that each consuming unit can purchase or obtain. (2)

real cash balances   The quantity of money relative to the level of prices. Real cash balances rise when prices fall. In symbols it is M/P. (16)

real interest rates   Nominal interest rates less the rate of inflation. (14)

real value of money   What a given quantity of money will purchase. It varies inversely with prices. (1)

refunding   An exchange in which new United States goverment securities are offered to owners of maturing United States government securities. (4)

Regulation Q   A Federal Reserve regulation prohibiting the payment of interest on checking accounts and setting interest rate ceilings for savings and time deposits. (13)

remit at par   Required of member banks of the Federal Reserve System. Banks that remit at par do not deduct an exchange charge on checks written by their depositors and returned for payment by the recipient of the check through clearing channels. (11)

required reserves   Regulations requiring banks to hold a percentage of their deposits in certain types of liquid assets or reserves. For member banks, required reserves consist of either cash in vault or deposits at the Federal Reserve banks. (9)

reserve cities   Certain large cities designated by the Federal Reserve System as areas in which member banks were required to hold higher reserve requirements than banks in communities that were less important as financial centers. After 1972 when a new policy for reserve requirements based on bank size rather than geographical location was adopted, this classification ceased to be important. (13)

reserves against private deposits (RPDs)   Total member bank reserves less reserves required behind United States government demand deposits and net interbank deposits. (14)

revenue bonds   The interest and principal of these bonds are paid from earnings of the state or local government project financed. They are secured by the property of the enterprise. (6)

savings bonds   A type of United States government security. They are nonmarketable and available in both appreciation or current-income forms. (4)

savings certificate   A type of time deposit. The owner receives a certificate showing the amount deposited, interest rate, maturity date, and other terms. They are sold only to individuals, nonprofit organizations, and fiduciaries. (8)

savings deposits   Interest-bearing bank deposits with no set maturity date. The principal type is called passbook deposits. They cannot legally be withdrawn without written notice 30 days or more in advance, but they are usually convertible into currency or demand deposits on demand. (8)

seigniorage   The profit that the Treasury of a country makes on its coinage. It varies with the difference between the nominal value of the coin and its cost of production. (3)

selective instruments of control   Federal Reserve controls that affect the use of a particular type of credit. The principal examples are margin requirements on loans for the purpose of purchasing corporate stock and the regulation of interest rates on time and savings deposits. (13)

silver certificates   Treasury-issued paper currency in process of retirement since 1968 and formerly backed by silver. (3)

token coins   Coins whose metal content is worth less than their face value. (3)

special drawing rights (SDRs)   A new type of international money usable as international reserves. (23)

special issues   A type of government security owned only by United States government agencies—mainly retirement funds. (4)

standard silver dollars   Dollar coins that contain three-quarters of an ounce of silver. Following the rise in the price of silver above $1.29 an ounce in the 1960s, they became collectors items and were no longer used as a medium of exchange. (3)

state bank   One that has received its charter from the state government. (5)

state bank notes   A major type of paper currency used in the United States prior to 1865. They were issued by state-chartered banks and were liabilities of the banks. The issuance of state bank notes was discontinued after 1865 as a result of the levying of a federal tax on them. (3)

sterilization of gold flows   A central bank policy of taking actions to offset the effect of gold flows on the quantity of bank reserves. (21)

sterling bloc   Countries that have fixed exchange rates with the pound and do a large portion of their trading with Great Britain. (24)

structuralist theory of inflation   Attributes inflation to economic growth combined with supply inelasticities usually of food and imports. (21)

subscription   An offering of new issues of United States Treasury notes or bonds at announced coupon rates. (4)

surplus   A type of capital account on a company's balance sheet. Together with undivided profits, it shows the amount that the total assets of a company exceed its total liabilities, capital stock, and various reserves for contingencies. When surplus is increased by the directors of a company, the undivided profits are reduced by the same amount. (8)

swap arrangements   Used between governments of countries to obtain foreign currencies on call through the Bank for International Settlements. (23)

tax and loan account   A deposit of the United States Treasury in a commercial bank. (8)

tax-anticipation bills   United States Treasury bills that mature one week after federal tax-payment dates and are accepted in payment for federal taxes a week before their maturity date at their maturity value. (4)

tax-exempt securities   Municipal bonds. Under federal income tax laws their interest payments are not taxable. (6)

ten-percent rule   A rule used by bank examiners that banks ought to keep capital accounts equal to approximately 10 percent of their deposit liabilities. (8)

time deposits   Interest-bearing bank deposits that have a maturity date. The principal types are savings certificates and certificates of deposit. They usually cannot be withdrawn before maturity without penalty. (8)

transactions costs   The costs of shifting from one type of asset to another or to money. It includes the fees paid to brokers or dealers handling the transaction as well as the value of any time and effort required of the owner. (16)

transactions velocity   The number of times per year that money changes hands and is used for all types of monetary transactions. (15)

transfer payments   Personal gifts and government welfare payments. They are payments of money that are not made in return for any services or for the use of real property. (17)

transfer payments between countries   Private gifts of money to persons and organizations in foreign countries plus government aid given under the foreign aid program. (23)

Treasury bill   A short-term, marketable United States government security sold at a discount. They are typically issued in maturities of 3 months, 6 months, 9 months, and 1 year. They are always sold by auction when issued. (4)

Treasury cash holdings   Coins, paper money, and free gold held by the United States Treasury. There tends to be an inverse relationship between Treasury cash holdings and member bank reserve deposits at the Federal Reserve banks. (12)

Treasury-Federal Reserve Accord   An agreement reached in 1951 to drop the Federal Reserve's bond-support program that had been initiated during World War II. (14)

Treasury notes   A type of marketable United States government security having an initial maturity of one to seven years. There is no legal ceiling to the coupon rates on these notes. (4)

trotting peg   Fixed exchange rates that are frequently changed—as used by Brazil. (24)

turnover of demand deposits   Total value of checks written during the year divided by the average quantity of demand deposits—used as a rough measure of transactions velocity. (15)

undivided profits   A type of capital account on the balance sheet of a company. It is similar to surplus. Undivided profits increase when the total assets of the company expand relative to the sum of: its liabilities, the par value of its capital stock outstanding, surplus, and the amount of the various reserves for contingencies. (8)

unemployment rate   The percentage of the labor force that is not working. (22)

unified budget   The record of all the expenditures and receipts of the federal government, including the trust accounts. (19)

unit of account   Used to measure the value of goods or services. Prices are expressed in the unit of account. (2)

unit bank   A bank without branches. (5)

United States liquid liabilities to foreigners   Foreign holdings primarily of demand and time deposits in American banks plus their non-marketable and short-term marketable United States government securities. (23)

U.S. notes   A type of paper money initially issued by the United States Treasury during the Civil War. They are popularly called green-backs. (3)

unsecured loan   A loan not backed by collateral. (7)

value added   The amount spent by a business enterprise for labor and the use of capital. (16)

wage-price guidelines   Goals set by the federal government to limit increases in wages and prices. (22)

working reserves   Liquid assets held by banks in excess of their legally required reserves. These usually consist of short-term United States government securities, commercial paper, or federal funds sold. (6)

world liquidity   Total amount of international money available for international trade and for settling accounts between nations. (24)

yield curve   A curve showing the comparative yields on United States Treasury securities of different maturities. (4)

Name Index

Subject Index